THE LEGISLATIVE BRANCH OF FEDERAL GOVERNMENT

People, Process, and Politics

Gary P. Gershman

A B C   C L I O

Santa Barbara, California   Denver, Colorado   Oxford, England

Library of Congress Cataloging-in-Publication Data
Gershman, Gary P.
   The legislative branch of federal government : people, process, and politics / Gary P. Gershman.
      p. cm. — (ABC-CLIO's about federal government set)
   Includes bibliographical references and index.
   ISBN 978-1-85109-712-8 (alk. paper)
   1. United States. Congress. 2. United States—Politics and government. I. Title.
JK1021.G47 2008
328.73--dc22
                           2008019137

12   11   10   09   08   1   2   3   4   5   6   7   8   9   10

ISBN: 978-1-85109-712-8   E-ISBN: 1-85109-717-1

Senior Production Editor: Vicki Moran
Production Manager: Don Schmidt
Media Editor: Jason Kniser
Media Resources Manager: Caroline Price
File Management Coordinator: Paula Gerard

ABC-CLIO, Inc.
130 Cremona Drive, P.O. Box 1911
Santa Barbara, California 93116–1911
This book is also available on the World Wide Web as an eBook. Visit abc-clio.com for details.

This book is printed on acid-free paper ∞ .
Manufactured in the United States of America

CONTENTS

FOREWORD

Most of us know something about the federal government. At the very least, we can name its three branches—executive, legislative, and judicial—and discuss the differences between them. At an early age, we are taught in school about the president of the United States and his official roles and responsibilities; we learn about Congress and the courts and their place in our government. In civics classes, we often get a skeletal picture of how the nation's government works; we are told that Congress writes the laws, the president executes them, and the Supreme Court acts as the interpreter of the U.S. Constitution. News reports, blogs, and editorials we read as adults add to this knowledge. Many of us can go further and explain some of the basic interactions among the branches. We know that the laws Congress passes are subject to the president's veto power and the Supreme Court's powers of judicial review; we understand that the president names the members of his Cabinet and nominates justices to the Supreme Court, but that the Senate has to confirm these nominations; and we can discuss how the Supreme Court, as the "caretaker" of the Constitution, can declare laws unconstitutional, but that it is up to the legislative and executive branches to enforce these rulings. We bandy around such terms as *checks and balances* and *separation of powers*. We talk about majority votes and filibusters in the Senate.

For most of us, however, this is about as far as our knowledge goes. According to newspaper accounts spanning decades, most Americans have trouble naming members of the Supreme Court, or key figures in the congressional leadership, or the members of the president's Cabinet. Still fewer of us can explain in detail how a bill becomes a law, or the president's authority in foreign affairs, or how the Supreme Court decides a case. If we ask about the historical development of these institutions and officials and their powers, the numbers of those who understand how our federal government works drop even further.

It is not surprising that most of us do not know a lot about the workings of our government. Government is a large and complex enterprise. It includes thousands of people working on subjects ranging from tax reform to national security, from voting rights to defining and enforcing environmental standards. Much of the work of government, although technically open to the public, is done out of sight and hence out of mind. We may know about those parts of the government that affect us directly—the Social Security Administration for the elderly, the Defense Department for those with family members in the military, or the Supreme Court when the news is filled with such controversial topics as abortion or the right to die or prayer in schools—but our understandings are generally limited to only those parts that directly affect us. Although this state of affairs is understandable, it is also dangerous. Our form of government is a democratic republic. This means that, although elected or appointed officials carry out the duties of government, "We the People of the United States" are the ultimate authority, and not just because we choose those who run the government (or those who appoint the men and women who run the day-to-day business of government). In the end, it is our choices that shape (or, at least, should shape) the scope and function of the federal government. As Abraham Lincoln gracefully put it, ours is a government "of the people, by the people, for the people."

Yet what sort of choices can we make if we do not understand the structures, workings, and powers of the federal government? Choices made in ignorance are dangerous choices. When a president goes on TV and claims a power not granted by the Constitution, we need to know that this claim is something new. It might be that what the president is asking for is a reasonable and necessary extension of the powers already held by the executive branch—but it might, on the other hand, be a radical expansion of his powers based on nothing more than his say-so. If we do not understand what is normal, how can we judge whether abnormal and exceptional proposals are necessary or proper? The same is true when pundits and politicians rant on about the dangers of "activist judges." How can we know what an "activist judge" is if we do not even understand a "normal" judge's job? What one person calls dangerous activism could be courageous defense of constitutional rights in other people's eyes—or what one person praises as a creative reading of the Constitution, another person might denounce as an irresponsible and unwise judicial experiment.

This is the point: without knowledge of the way things are supposed to be, how can we judge when the powers of government are being underused, misused, or even abused? The need for this knowledge is the root from which the three volumes of the About Federal Government series have grown. Our goal is to present the federal government as a living, working system made up of real people doing jobs of real importance—not just in the abstract, but for all of us in our daily lives. Knowledge is power, and this is as true today as when Lord Francis Bacon wrote it about four hundred years ago. Understanding how our government works, and how each of its institutions works, and how they interact with one another and with "We the People" is not just something we might need to pass a civics test or a citizenship exam—it is a source of power for us as citizens. Knowing how a bill becomes a law and the many ways that a good idea can be derailed by the process of lawmaking is a source of power—for some day, there may be a bill that you want to see enacted into law, or that you want to prevent being made a law. Knowing the stress points at which a bill is most vulnerable to defeat can give you the opportunity to put pressure where it would do the most good. We can find similar examples for the other two branches as well.

One way of showing the living and evolving nature of the federal government is to place it into its historical context. Our government did not just come into being fully formed. The government we have today is the result of over two hundred years of growth and change, of choices made and laws passed. Much of what we hold to be gospel today, when it comes to the goals and methods and powers of the national government, resulted from our experiences—good and bad—in the past. How can one understand today's civil rights laws, for example, without first understanding the impact of slavery, the Civil War, and Reconstruction on the structure of our government? Forgetting the past leaves us powerless to deal with the present and the future. A second way to bring our government to life is to focus on the interactions among the three branches of the federal government, as well as between these three branches and the states. Most of the controversy shaping our governing structures grew out of conflicts among the various branches of the federal government, or between the federal government and the states. When Congress fights with the president over budgets or the Supreme Court overturns a popular law passed by Congress and signed by the president, or when a state defies a mandate issued by the U.S. Supreme Court and the president must put that state's National Guard under his authority to enforce the Court's decision, those crises clarify the actual working structures of our government. Like flexing a muscle to make it strong, these interactions define the actual impact of our government—not only today, but in the future as well. Finally, we can understand the living nature of the federal government by examining the people who make up that government. Government is not an abstract idea: it is people doing their jobs as best they can. If government can be said to have a personality, it is the direct reflection of the collective personalities of those who work in our government. Hence, when we talk about Congress, we are talking about the people who are elected to the House of Representatives and the Senate and whose values, views, beliefs, and prejudices shape the output of the national legislature. The About Federal Government series integrates all three of these approaches as it sets out the workings and structures of our national government. Written by historians with a keen understanding of the workings of government past and present, these volumes stress the ways in which each of the branches helps form part of a whole system—and the ways that each branch is unique as an institution. Finally, we have given special stress to bringing the people and the history of these branches to life, in the process making clear just how open to our own intervention our government really is. This is our government, and the more we understand how it works, the more real our "ownership" of it will be.

Charles L. Zelden, Set Editor
Nova Southeastern University

HISTORY OF THE LEGISLATIVE BRANCH

1787   The Constitution is drafted, establishing a bicameral legislature with a Senate and a House of Representatives.

1789   The House of Representatives holds its first full meeting in New York City.

       The Senate meets for the first time.

       The U.S. Congress adopts the Bill of Rights (the first ten constitutional amendments) and sends it to the states.

1790   Congress meets in Philadelphia and remains there until completion of Capitol in Washington, D.C.

1794   In the first contested election in Senate history, Albert Gallatin of Pennsylvania is refused his seat because it was alleged that he did not satisfy the citizenship requirement mandated by the Constitution.

1795   The Senate opens hearings to the public.

1798   The Senate convenes its first impeachment trial, trying William Blount.

       Congress authorizes the Quasi-War with France.

1800   Congress takes up residence in Washington, D.C.

1801   The presidential election goes to the House of Representatives, where Thomas Jefferson is eventually elected. The need to amend the Constitution produces the Twelfth Amendment.

1803   In *Marbury v. Madison*, the Supreme Court declares an act of Congress unconstitutional.

1804   In the first conviction following an impeachment trial, federal judge John Pickering is removed from office.

1812   Congress declares war on England.

1814   The Capitol is burned by the British during the War of 1812.

1818   Congress designates the American flag with thirteen stripes and one star for each state.

1820   The Missouri Compromise is passed.

1824   The U.S. Supreme Court asserts the Supremacy Clause in *Gibbons v. Ogden*, confirming that the federal government has authority over the states in interstate commerce.

1825   When no candidate receives a majority of electoral votes in the election of 1824, the selection goes to the House of Representatives, which chooses John Quincy Adams as president.

1830   The Nullification Crisis begins, and the Senate debates states' rights.

1834   The Senate censures President Andrew Jackson, the only time in the history of the United States a president has been censured.

1836   The gag rule is put in place, automatically tabling all petitions to Congress concerning slavery.

1837   The Senate expunges the censure of Andrew Jackson.

1841   The first continuous and extended filibusters take place in the Senate, concerning the dismissal of printers of the Senate and the establishment of a national bank. Each one lasts fourteen days.

1845   Circumventing the two-thirds majority required to bring Texas into the Union by treaty, Congress annexes Texas by means of a joint resolution and a simple majority.

1846   Members begin to sit together in the Senate chamber according to party affiliation.

The Senate begins to make committee assignments based on recommendations of its political party caucuses rather than separate balloting of the full Senate.

Congress declares war with Mexico.

The Wilmot Proviso, banning slavery in territories acquired through the war with Mexico, is introduced but not passed in the House.

1850   Sen. Daniel Webster gives one of the most famous speeches in congressional history, defending both the Union and slavery. It is his last great speech in his illustrious career in the Senate and helps pave the way for a new generation of senators and representatives.

Congress adopts the Compromise of 1850, beginning a decade of attempts to resolve the problems surrounding slavery and sectional strife. It signaled the emergence of Stephen Douglas as a new power in Congress and the end of the dominance of Henry Clay, Daniel Webster, and John C. Calhoun.

1856   In the wake of a speech on Kansas, Sen. Charles Sumner is viciously assaulted by Rep. Preston Brooks.

1857   The House of Representatives moves into its current home in the south wing of the Capitol.

1859   The Senate moves into its current home in the enlarged north wing of the Capitol.

1861   The Crittenden Compromise, a final attempt to avert the Civil War by amending the Constitution, is defeated in the House and Senate, making war inevitable. The Confederate States of America is formed as the exodus of southern states, which begins in 1860, from the Union is completed. Southern states secede. Reacting to Lincoln's suggestions for reconstruction following the war, Congress passes the Wade-Davis Bill, a far more stringent plan for readmitting southern states into the Union. Although Lincoln killed the bill with a pocket veto, its provisions were adopted following his assassination.

1866   Congress passes the Civil Rights Act of 1866.

1867   Congress challenges President Andrew Johnson with the Tenure of Office Act, passing it over his veto. The ensuing controversy will lead to impeachment proceedings.

Congress passes the Reconstruction Acts.

1868   The impeachment trial of Andrew Johnson ends in acquittal by one vote.

1870   Hiram Revels of Mississippi is sworn in as first African American senator.

Joseph Rainey of South Carolina is first black member of the House.

1873   The first *Congressional Record is* published.

1898   Congress declares war on Spain.

1907   Charles Curtis of Kansas becomes the first Native American member of the Senate.

1910   The seniority system emerges with a revolt against the Speaker, "Uncle Joe" Cannon.

1913   The Seventeenth Amendment for direct election of senators is ratified.

1916   Jeannette Rankin of Montana is the first woman elected to Congress.

1917   The Senate limits filibusters with adoption of the cloture rule.

Congress declares war and the U.S. enters World War I.

1918   Rep. Jeannette Rankin becomes the first woman of a major party to run (unsuccessfully) for a Senate seat.

1925   Senate Republicans officially designate their floor leader for the first time, choosing Charles Curtis.

1927   In *McGrain v. Daugherty,* the U.S. Supreme Court firmly establishes the general power of congressional committees to compel testimony from witnesses.

1928   Oscar De Priest, Republican from Illinois, is the first black to be elected to Congress in the modern era. He is also the last black Republican elected to the House until J. C. Watts (R-OK) is elected in 1995.

1932   Arkansas's Hattie Wyatt Caraway is the first woman popularly elected to the Senate.

1941   Congress declares war on Japan and the U.S. enters World War II.

1946   President Harry S. Truman signs the Legislative Reorganization Act, which transforms the committee system, eliminating those that were obsolete, eradicating redundancy in committee work, and establishing an effective congressional staff system.

1947   Implementing aspects of the Reorganization Act, each member of Congress and each committee hire professional staff for the first time.

1954   On April 22, the Senate begins a fifty-five-day series of hearings, pitting Joseph McCarthy against the U.S. Army. The televised hearings become a national spectacle.

Five Congressmen are shot on the floor of the House of Representatives by Puerto Rican nationalists.

1957   On August 28–29, Sen. Strom Thurmond (R-SC) delivers the longest speech in Senate history (twenty-four hours and eighteen minutes) in a filibuster against the 1957 Civil Rights Act.

1964   On June 10, cloture is invoked to end a lengthy filibuster, allowing for passage of the historic Civil Rights Act of 1964.

The Gulf of Tonkin Resolution, authorizing American intervention in Vietnam, is passed by Congress.

1967   Edward Brooke III is sworn in as the first black senator since Reconstruction.

1969   Shirley Chisholm is sworn in as the first black female to be elected to Congress. She serves from 1969 to 1983.

1973   The Senate Select Committee on Presidential Campaign Activities (also known as the Watergate Committee) begins public hearings.

In an attempt to restrain the President's powers to deploy American armed forces overseas, Congress passes the War Powers Act. It is passed over President Nixon's veto and has been considered by all presidents since, as unconstitutional.

1975   The Senate revises the cloture rule to allow three-fifths of the senators voting to end debate, rather than two-thirds.

1990   Congress authorizes Operation Desert Storm, or Gulf War I.

1994   The Republican Party wins control of both houses of Congress for the first time since 1955.

1998   The House of Representatives votes to impeach President Bill Clinton on charges of perjury and obstruction of justice in the Monica Lewinsky scandal.

1999   The impeachment trial of President Bill Clinton begins on January 14, and the Senate votes on articles of impeachment on February 12, ending the trial with acquittal.

2001   Following the 2000 election, the Senate is divided evenly between the two parties, Republican and Democrat. From January 3 to January 20, the Democrats hold the majority, because of the tie-breaking vote of Vice President Al Gore. When Dick Cheney becomes vice president on January 20, 2001, the Republicans regain majority status and hold it until June 6, 2001, when Sen. James Jeffords's switch from Republican to independent status returns the majority to the Democrats.

Congress authorizes Operation Enduring Freedom in the wake of the Septermber 11, 2001, attacks, giving its approval to the war in Afghanistan.

2002   Congress authorizes Operation Iraqi Freedom, or Gulf War II.

2007   The first female Speaker of the House in history, Nancy Pelosi, is selected.

1

U.S. CONSTITUTION AND THE FEDERAL LEGISLATURE

To understand the United States Congress, one must start with the Constitution of the United States, which is the document that organizes the legislature. The Constitution established the parameters of congressional power and delineated not only how the other branches would relate to it but how the two houses would interact with each other and American society.

EARLY ANTECEDENTS

To understand the modern Congress and how it grew from a small organization meeting in Philadelphia to the current sprawl of buildings and bureaucracy in Washington, D.C., it is important to identify and comprehend its historical roots and antecedents. First, one must understand why its predecessor failed. If the Confederation Congress had functioned successfully and not proved incapable of running the government and dealing with the problems of the new nation, there would have been no need for calling a Constitutional Convention in Philadelphia. Those failures helped the Convention to determine that the Articles of Confederation were not sufficiently amendable to change and to de-

U.S. Constitution. (Library of Congress)

_____

cide to throw out the old system of government and institute a new one. It was the failures of government under the Articles of Confederation, that is , the national legislature, which precipitated a change and the creation of what is the modern Congress. In making that change, the Framers radically altered the

1

nature and power of the federal government as a whole, and specifically the legislature, by creating a body that was able to govern effectively and not be held hostage by the state governments.

The Framers did not operate in a vacuum. Many of the men at Philadelphia had government experience at both the local and national levels. In addition, aside from the practical examples that sat before them, they were well schooled in the philosophy of the day and were able to blend it with practical realities. Political ideas of Locke, Hume, and Montesquieu, among others, both tempered and seasoned their debate.

By the time the Declaration of Independence was written in 1776, colonists had governed themselves, often with little or no interference from the mother country, for approximately 150 years. The Virginia legislature, the House of Burgesses, had first met in 1619. The Mayflower Compact, which established a rudimentary form of government for the settlers in Plymouth, was signed a year later. From those early years on, colonial history was one characterized by gradualism, an evolution of ideas and institutions that saw changes in attitudes toward the function of government, as well as in the practical operation of the various legislative bodies and government institutions that marked the colonial political landscape. With the Revolution, nearly all the states rewrote their constitutions, at times redesigning their legislatures, often making them the focus of power. And during the period preceding the Revolution, various national congresses had met to protest British actions, establishing that a central government was not outside the pale of colonial thought.

ARTICLES OF CONFEDERATION

The Articles of Confederation, the document that governed the states during the Revolutionary period and beyond, was the first national government. Adopted by Congress and sent to the states in the fall of 1777, the document was not ratified for four years, when the last of the thirteen states signed the document. However, the country effectively operated under the Articles during that time period, when it served as the de facto plan for government.The Articles placed virtually all national power, what little there was of it, in Congress; in fact, almost the entire national government *was* Congress. There was no national court system, no president, and heads of executive departments were either members of Congress or chosen by it. The way the national government was designed reflected fear of a strong central government, state jealousies, and the role of the British parliamentary system.

When dissatisfaction with the national government began to appear and shortcomings in the government became increasingly apparent, criticisms focused on the Congress, the central and the only real agency of the national government. Congress's ability or inability to function was the key to a properly operating government in the eyes of those men in Philadelphia. They were very conscious of the fact that the very shortcomings they sought to change often reflected what the design of the Articles had intended.

The Articles of Confederation specified that delegates, elected by state legislatures, would meet annually. Despite the establishment of such a national government, the second section of the Articles noted that each state preserved "its sovereignty, freedom and independence." This meant that states, not the national government, were supreme, and far too often the national government was at the mercy of state government. This was evident when Congress attempted to procure money and men for the Continental Army, often to be rebuffed by state government. In such a system, Congress tended to operate like a meetinghouse, where locals discussed local problems, rather than as a stage for national debate over national issues.

Congressional delegates had close ties to the state legislatures that elected them. In contrast to the modern Congress, where members are elected by the people and theoretically represent those people, members of the Confederation Congress served at the whim of the states they represented. It was almost impossible for them to act independently.

There was no definitive stipulation in the Articles as to exactly how many representatives should be sent from each state. States could send as few as two delegates and as many as seven to Congress each year, and regardless of the number, each state had one vote. Terms were for one year. Delegates could serve only three years out of any six. State legislatures were allowed to recall delegates at any time, for any reason. Pay came from the state legislature, making the delegates that much more beholden to state interests than to national ones. Such a focus on state control assured that Congress would not be a seat of national power.

Weaknesses in the Articles were apparent in the day-to-day operation of Congress. Since the delegates were elected by the state legislatures, they had no real relationship to the people. No laws passed by Congress were binding on the states. Thus, attempts by Congress to raise money to fight the war and raise troops to create an army were at times rejected by the states. A law passed by Congress was really a request, not a mandate. Taxes, levies for troops, and so on were often ignored as states focused on local concerns rather than national ones. In this atmosphere it is amazing that Congress that met and attempted to govern the country was able to prosecute a war, which involved raising an army, paying the soldiers (at times), borrowing money, and negotiating agreements with foreign countries.

What little power Congress did have was compromised by its structure, which made it almost impossible for Congress to exercise that power. For example, while the Confederation Congress had a committee system, it was really one in name only. In contrast to many modern legislatures, where committees form the backbone of the work that is done, Confederation committees were weak, having almost no independence. Committees were ad hoc rather than standing and so did not permit the development of any system of expertise, seniority, or power. (While this system temporarily prevailed in Congress in the new government, standing committees quickly expanded and grew.) Thus, whether it was one of the Continental Congresses or Congress under the Articles of Confederation, between 1774 and 1788, over 3,200 committees existed at various times.

The problems associated with this inadequate committee system were compounded by the lack of coherent or sensible rules, which made it difficult to carry on business. Members were limited in the number of times they could speak on any question, but at the same time, once a delegate began speaking, there was no limit on the time they could speak. These rules made members reluctant to relinquish the floor once they had it. Any motion had to be dealt with immediately. Any item, no matter its topic or where it originated, could demand immediate consideration. For example, there was no way to guarantee that a bill dealing with a loan from France would be considered before a petition from a citizens' group moving to secure a captured cannon for display in the town square.

An incident in 1783 highlighted the confusion that permeated Congress during the period of the Articles. In June of that year, troops upset over not being paid mutinied in Philadelphia, demanding their money. Congress immediately retreated up the river to Princeton, New Jersey, to decide what to do. One of the important, although seemingly trivial and easy, issues Congress had to consider was where should they convene. It could not decide. Hoping that a simple major-

ity could make the decision where to meet, putting each state up for a vote, no state garnered enough votes. Highlighting the locally oriented nature of Congress and the delegates' inability to work together on simple as well as complex matters, only New York and Maryland garnered as many as four votes. There being no location that seemed amenable to enough delegates, a motion was made to limit the choice to two locations: one was near Trenton on the Delaware River, and the other was Georgetown on the Potomac. This motion led to an amendment from a delegate who wanted the capital moved close to Wilmington, Delaware, also on the Delaware River. Then it got more complicated.

The rules specified that in a case of amending a motion, a simple majority (seven votes) was needed. The motion received five votes, with three states voting no, and three divided. (Since congressional delegations had one vote no matter how many of its members were in attendance, an evenly divided delegation would fail to register a yea or nay vote.) The failure to get enough votes meant the problem of where to meet was still not solved and because no other sites received even as much support as the original two, no new location for the capital was secured.

A motion was made to adjourn, move to Philadelphia, and then move to Trenton. This produced an amendment to eliminate Philadelphia from the original motion. This motion failed, but a motion for Trenton, then Philadelphia, also failed. A motion to temporarily move to Annapolis also failed to garner enough votes. After letting the matter rest, a compromise was reached to build two capitals! One was to be near Trenton, and one near Georgetown. Congress would be able to alternate between the two, placating the opposite sides of the argument. When the idea was called to a vote, one delegate delayed the balloting for a day. In the end, Congress alternated between Trenton and Annapolis before moving to New York .

This debate over a capital highlights the inability of Congress to move discussions about anything through in a meaningful and efficient manner. Almost all debates produced endless rounds of gridlock on almost any issue. Not only did popular sentiment eventually turn against Congress, but the delegates themselves became fed up with the body. Absenteeism was a serious problem. At any given time, 10 to 20 percent of the delegates were absent, with sometimes over half of the representatives missing.

THE CONSTITUTIONAL CONVENTION

With all of these problems, it was obvious to some that change was needed, and so the Philadelphia Convention was

The U.S. Constitution is signed on September 17, 1787, at the Constitutional Convention in Philadelphia. The Constitution was drafted by legislators in Philadelphia between July and September 1787. (Library of Congress)

called, despite continuing controversy over its necessity and legality. However, as indicated by the above debate and problems such as Shays' Rebellion in Massachusetts, a change in governance was needed.

If one accepts the notion that one of the guiding principles of the Convention was, as James Madison believed, to provide a republican remedy for problems that had plagued government under the Articles of Confederation, then the structure and form of the new U.S. Congress made perfect sense. It was created to resolve conflicts that had arisen under the old form of government and were expected to arise under the new form. It was at the Constitutional Convention in Philadelphia in 1787 that the essential blueprint was laid out. But the blueprint did not appear out of nowhere, and the Convention and the Constitution generally, and Congress specifically, had their genesis in the preceding years.

In many ways, the seeds of the Convention were sown two years earlier during a dispute between Virginia and Maryland. Arguing over boundaries and commercial traffic on the Potomac River, the two states signed an agreement to resolve their problems. In the wake of that agreement, the Maryland legislature proposed that Pennsylvania and Delaware join them in a conference to solve growing commercial problems between the four mid-Atlantic states. Squabbling between the states over commercial borders, territorial boundaries, and western lands, among other issues, made the fate of the United States seem very precarious, and these disputes highlighted the need for the states to come together to try to resolve their differences. Maryland's call was followed by that of Virginia, which asked that all the states meet to try to settle commercial issues that were plaguing the new nation.

Although nine states agreed to meet, only five states showed up in Annapolis in the fall of 1786. Five state delegations were hardly enough to resolve the growing number of problems. However, instead of resigning themselves to the fact that not enough states were represented and just adjourn, the delegations present called for another meeting in May 1787 in Philadelphia. They recognized the need for the states to come together to attempt to solve their problems in an amicable fashion by forging political solutions before the nation disintegrated, with each state going its own way. While the focus of the Annapolis Convention had been narrow, the new invitation called for a far broader discussion, including a possible revision of the Articles of Confederation and an attempt to grapple with the obvious problems that were arising under it.

These problems stretched from basic matters of commerce to the more immediate and pressing problems raised by events such as Shays' Rebellion. This uprising in western Massachusetts, which invoked the principles of the Revolution in challenging high taxes, combined with a depressed economy to expose the weaknesses in the government under the Articles. Armed bands roamed the countryside, shutting down local government and even interrupting the state supreme court in Springfield. There was no way for the central government to respond effectively. These issues combined to push the country toward a new structure of government.

In February, the Confederation Congress endorsed the idea of a conference, conceding the near impossibility of amending the Articles as they existed and the need to do something. Despite a lack of enthusiasm and some resignation, Congress called for a convention in Philadelphia that summer.

The Constitutional Convention that was to meet in Philadelphia in 1787 was originally composed of delegates from only seven states. Other states were apprehensive about gathering without official approval by Congress. In February, Congress officially endorsed the meeting of the Grand Convention. By May, however, the only state missing was Rhode Island. One of the first items on the agenda, once it was agreed that the Articles of Confederation must be scrapped and a new constitutional structure developed, was how to design a legislature. There was no question that under the Articles, Congress, being seriously limited in its power and often not able to use what power it had, failed to act decisively. Various events showed the need for a stronger central government. Given this need, it seemed obvious that a focus, if not *the* focus, of national power under a new constitution would be in the legislature.

However, the men in Philadelphia were not quick to forget lessons learned under British rule. It had been laws of the British Parliament (Townsend Duties, In-

Shays' Rebellion (1786–1787) brawl between Massachusetts government supporters and rebels. (Bettmann/Corbis)

tolerable Acts, and so on) that enraged colonial leaders. British parliamentary excesses and Parliament's failure to respect local wishes helped ignite the Revolution. The delegates at the Convention saw no reason to repeat this problem by re-creating a legislature with excessive power that would mirror the British Parliament. On the other hand, as noted above, it was obvious that a much stronger government generally, and a legislature specifically, were necessary. Thus, an important threshold problem, if not the key issue, was how to design a legislature that appeased the sectional and demographic interests of the thirteen states so that no one section dominated or felt dominated, and at the same time create a structure that could govern all. Small states feared being subservient to the interests of the larger, more populous states, and the larger states resented the notion that smaller states could manipulate the system to conform to their interests, to the detriment of the larger units.

The Virginia Plan

With this debate brewing, Virginia delegate Edmund Randolph introduced the first proposal. His Virginia Plan provided for a bicameral legislature with a lower and upper house. The lower house was to be elected by the people of the states for three-year terms. The upper house was to then be chosen by the lower house from candidates selected by the state legislatures and elected for seven-year terms. The plan based representation in both houses on population. Authored by James Madison, the plan created a government with three branches, and most

notably a strong legislature that chose the executive.

Virginia's plan reflected a vision of federalism that saw both the federal and state governments as having absolute jurisdiction within their respective spheres. Any conflict within this structure would be resolved by the legislature, which could also resolve conflicts between the states, even by, if necessary, negating state legislation. Congress was empowered to "negative all laws passed by the several States, contravening in the opinion of the National Legislature the articles of the Union." Unlike the Confederation Congress, the new legislative body was not weak. Its authority was not ambiguous nor dependent upon state concessions, but rather was based on a strong structure aimed at making for an effective, working national government.

The other major increase in Congress's power was the right to "legislate

James Madison represented Virginia in the Second Continental Congress and is often called the "Father of the Constitution." (National Archives)

in all cases to which the separate States are incompetent, or in which the harmony of the United States may be interrupted by the exercise of individual Legislation." What exactly that meant was not clear, except that it suggested some type of supremacy, which later manifested itself in the Article VI Supremacy Clause of the Constitution. Under the Virginia Plan it was obvious that Congress had the benefit of the doubt and a great leeway and freedom in defining its own power while limiting the power of the states.

Madison supported language in the Virginia Plan, originally submitted by Edmund Randolph of Virginia, that went on to authorize Congress "to call forth the force of the Union against any member of the Union failing to fulfill its duties under the articles therof." The negative over state legislation was reminiscent of power the Board of Trade had exercised over colonial assemblies prior to the Revolution. The Board of Trade was an English agency that examined colonial legislation to make sure it fit into British trading practices. However, in contrast to the reactive power of the Board of Trade, Madison's suggestion was proactive. Congressional power was triggered prior to the state legislation's taking effect or in the absence of state action. Its purpose was to make the national legislature in effect a supervisor of the state legislatures, or a super-state legislature.

Originally in the Virginia Plan, the only check on congressional power was to be the Council of Revision, composed of members of the executive and judicial branches. The Council was to examine every act of Congress before it became law and had veto power. The Council could reject any law that it considered outside the scope of congressional authority. This included any act by Congress that nullified state actions. In the end the Convention rejected this proposal. Among their worries was giving too much power to the judiciary, and the historical examples before them (the Privy Council in England and the New York State version of a Council of Revision) that had impaired legislative effectiveness and hurt public confidence in the judiciary. In the end, such a concept would have compromised their vision of government and the concept of separation of powers.

With the Virginia Plan up for debate, Edmund Randolph suggested that the Convention needed to create something more than just an agreement, like a treaty, among the states. Rather, he said, it was necessary "that a national government ought to be established consisting of a supreme Legislature, Executive and Judiciary." This meant they needed to do more than simply empower a federal government with some additional power. Rather, Governor Morris argued, there had to be a supreme power, and there could only be one, and that supreme power must be in the central or federal government. While some delegates objected that this would destroy state sovereignty, the Convention adopted a resolution to this effect with only Connecticut voting against it.

The acceptance of Randolph's point of view seemed to assure that a new government would be organized. The

Virginia governor Edmund Randolph, a delegate to the Constitutional Convention, initially refused to sign the U.S. Constitution, fearing that it gave the executive too much power. However, he pressed for ratification when he realized that Virginia needed the stability and resources that accompanied membership in the burgeoning nation. Randolph joined the administration of George Washington, where he served as the nation's first attorney general and later succeeded Thomas Jefferson as secretary of state. (Library of Congress)

Convention had been called merely to modify the Articles of Confederation, but it was obvious by the time the Virginia Plan was debated, and with the ensuing counterproposals, that the Convention had discarded the idea of modification and was focused on creating a whole new structure and concept of government. It was also apparent that

Congress was to be the centerpiece of this new concept of government. Those who advocated retaining the Articles as well as the supporters of maintaining strong state sovereignty were on the defensive, and those who argued for a strong central government had the early upper hand.

The Issue of Representation

Many delegates expressed grave concerns. The Virginia Plan's shifting of power to a legislature dominated by the large states caused serious consternation, especially among the delegates from the smaller states. In addition, the proposed legislature's structure raised anxiety levels. This trepidation involved a fundamental question that plagued the nation until the conclusion of the Civil War: where did the basis for the new government's authority reside, in the people or the states? Until that question was answered, the problem of representation in the legislature could not be solved.

If the states were the basis of the federal government's authority, then each state should be represented equally by delegates chosen by the state legislatures, as the representatives of small states desired. But if, on the contrary—as the large state delegates noted—the people were the basis of authority, then both houses needed to be chosen by direct elections and, more importantly, with representation in both chambers apportioned according to population. A government and legislature based on representation of states would maintain the essence of the Articles of Confederation. It would not degrade state power and would guarantee state sovereignty. To the chagrin of the small state delegates, the Virginia Plan rejected such an approach and rooted the power of the central government in the people as a whole, compromising the sovereignty of the states.

Objecting to Randolph's plan, the smaller states quickly counterattacked. Despite wide agreement with the idea of direct popular election of the lower house, very few members agreed that another idea, election of the upper house by the lower, should move forward. This would have reinforced the very thing the small states protested: the concentration of power in the hands of the large, populous states. In its place, John Dickinson proposed that a senate, or upper house, be elected by the state legislatures.

In the debate that followed, one can see the different philosophical approaches to not only the question of how a government should work, but also to the issue of what gave government its validity. Madison argued that a national government's authority must emanate directly from the people. Because power flowed from the people, a proportional system was necessary in which the people, not the states, were represented, and in which a state's population determined the number of representatives it would have.

In contrast, delegates such as Roger Sherman, speaking for the smaller states, argued that using the Confederation as

the model for representation would maintain a proper balance between state and national government and secure state sovereignty. And while it was clear at this point that the smaller states might accede to the direct election of the lower house, reflecting state population, they were unwilling to completely abandon the system used under the Articles in at least one house. Therefore, Dickinson's resolution was adopted unanimously. The Convention then moved on to how representation should be apportioned: according to population or by state.

One can only imagine the discomfort of the delegates, walled away at Independence Hall in Philadelphia, windows shut, uncomfortable in their heavy clothes, trying to maintain decorum as debates, which often became rancorous, raged on concerning the fate of the new nation. Madison and James Wilson focused on the idea that government must flow from the people, not the states. Only a system based on proportional representation was proper. In a proportional system, they argued, the *people* of Delaware, a small state, would be just as represented as the *people* of Virginia, a large state. Despite their reassurances, they could not quell the apprehensions of the smaller states that in such a system the interests of the large states and their people would swallow up and dominate the smaller states.

William Paterson of New Jersey protested that his state would "never confederate on the plan before the Committee. She would be swallowed up." According to Madison's notes, he would "rather submit to a monarch, to a despot, than to such a fate. He would not only oppose the plan here but on his return home do every thing in his power to defeat it there." Wilson countered that Paterson's fears were baseless. In fact, he noted, it was Paterson's argument that promoted imbalance. Because all citizens, be they from Pennsylvania or New Jersey, were equal, they should be equally represented. For Wilson, population was the key to representation. Therefore, anything else was imbalanced. He criticized the smaller states for their unwillingness to make sacrifices to the Union and stated that their failure to concede some aspect of their sovereignty meant the government would fail. States were like people, and as each individual gave up something of his freedom when he entered the social contract, so must each state part with some part of its sovereignty to make a union work: "We have been told that each State being sovereign, all are equal. So each man is naturally a sovereign over himself, and all men are therefore naturally equal. Can he retain this equality when he becomes a member of Civil Government? He can not. As little can a Sovereign State, when it becomes a member of a federal Governt. If N.J. will not part with her Sovereignty it is in vain to talk of Govt."

A faction among the small states appeared willing to compromise, but delegates favoring a strong central government controlled the Convention and refused to compromise. A proposal by Roger Sherman that would have satisfied the moderates from the small states was rejected as counter to a national government rooted in the people. Other suggestions were also rejected.

The New Jersey Plan

As the Committee of the Whole prepared to present its revised draft of the Virginia Plan to the floor of the Convention, the small states found their voice and stopped the Convention dead in its tracks. New delegates arrived from Maryland, Delaware, and New York (which sided with the small states) and realized it was time to stop the apparent flow of power to the large states and the consequent overly strong central government. Paterson introduced an alternate plan that was claimed to be "purely federal" in principle, as opposed to the Virginia Plan.

The New Jersey Plan was really a modification of the Articles of Confederation (in line with the original purpose of the Convention) that expanded the powers of Congress by giving it the power to tax and regulate commerce. This was in stark contrast to the Virginia Plan, which in addition to concentrating power in the central government, failed to delineate what the exact powers of the new government would be. One could argue that either Randolph assumed those powers would gravitate toward the federal government in his Virginia Plan or that, as some historians argue, the key issue in the Convention debates was not whether there would be a strong central government, but who would control it. Sectional rivalries and philosophical notions of the nature of the Union, which would begin to tear the country apart four decades later, were already evident here, compounded by issues of population and economics. Unquestionably, the centralizers' concern was with a plan that would give the central government enough power, not with local or state matters. Paterson and his supporters were obviously concerned not only with the need to curb any type of government that allowed the large states to squash them, but also with the importance of retaining state sovereignty and a state voice even at the federal level.

Small states and states' righters fell in line to support the New Jersey Plan. They feared the diminution of state authority and the emergence of a strong central government dominated by a legislature. To check attrition of state authority, Paterson's plan called for state equality in the legislature. While the plan did not eliminate a supremacy clause elevating the federal government, it did appear to check congressional power in favor of the states.

The New Jersey Plan clarified the lines of demarcation in the Convention. At one extreme were men like Alexander Hamilton, who argued for a Congress along with a life-tenure executive and for a national government so strong that the states would become mere shadows of their former selves. On the other side were those who focused on preserving the power of the individual states and had little willingness to compromise state sovereignty.

Despite these developments, the small states were still in the minority, and the New Jersey plan went down to defeat,

Alexander Hamilton helped frame the U.S. Constitution and was a founding father of the new nation. (Library of Congress)

7–3. However, the small states realized they were an important minority and despite their lack of control, they realized that their votes were needed.

Resolving Differences on the Framework

The modified Virginia Plan that had been on the floor before being derailed by the New Jersey Plan now came to a vote. Most of the Convention agreed on a lower house, popularly elected, and an upper house, elected by the state legislatures. While the issue of proportional representation seemed to create a stumbling block, the ensuing vote of 6–4 in favor of proportional representation in the lower house showed compromise was possible. It was obvious the less populous states could accept a lower house as contemplated by the Virginia Plan as long as the upper house did not mirror it. When the idea of proportional representation in the upper house was put to a vote, the smaller states flexed their muscles and deadlock ensued.

At this point, a new committee was appointed with one representative from each state to try to resolve the problem. The committee created a solution known to history as the Great Compromise that solved it by recommending a lower house based on population and an upper house in which each state would have an equal vote.

Despite the sectional differences that had occasionally flared previously, the differences in the Convention had been mainly along size lines (large state versus small state) or philosophical lines (centralizers versus states' righters). With this compromise, the Convention's politics transformed itself into a competition of sectional interests in addition to conflicts between large and small states.

Some of this sectional anxiety was evident as the supporters of the New Jersey Plan recoiled at everything being proportionate to population. New Jersey, New Hampshire, Maryland, Delaware, Connecticut, and even New York foresaw and feared any attempt by the large states of Virginia, Pennsylvania, and

Massachusetts to take away equal suffrage. And while at the time many southern states were not that populous, the anti–Virginia Plan faction were filled with concern that those states would soon grow in population, overwhelming the others.

Conversely, southern states had great concerns related to resolving western land disputes and how to deal with slaves in counting population. The Northwest Ordinance, perhaps the most significant piece of legislation passed by the government under the Articles of Confederation, solved the problem of what to do with the western territories. It created a political structure for the territories, established a mechanism for them to attain statehood, and reflected sectional needs and interests.

The sectional concerns included northern worries about slavery expanding into the new territory, and both regions' concerns about too many new states dominated by the other region, being created out of the territory. Southern states agreed to abandon Jefferson's Ordinance of 1784, which called for the creation of ten new states, in exchange for a concession that made statehood possible with a smaller population in a shorter time period. In the end, the Northwest Ordinance exposed concerns and possible conflicts over slavery, and the ability of southern states to compromise when necessary, as the Ordinance forbid slavery in the new states that would arise out of the territory.

Some historians have suggested it was the ability of the South and North to compromise on the Northwest Ordinance that laid the groundwork for the Great Compromise. The Great Compromise was palatable because, like the Northwest Ordinance, it met the needs of both the North and the South. It is important to remember that both regions were looking to the future, so that although the North was more populous at present, it was expected that the South would eventually outnumber the North. For the North this meant that it would require protection from the South in the future, which would be provided by equal representation in the Senate. For the southern states, conceding this point meant it was important to guarantee through proportional representation that they could protect their interests in the House of Representatives. An irony of the Great Compromise is that the reverse happened. The Senate would become the platform for the South to protect its agricultural interests and slave society, while the House would become the body of Congress where northern and especially antislavery interests found their voice.

In addition, the Great Compromise paved the way for other compromises based on sectional lines and negotiated by the mid-Atlantic states. For example, southerners had originally demanded that all commerce and navigation laws require a two-thirds majority. Such a provision would have prevented the northern states from instituting unfair economic legislation, most notably tariffs that would unfairly impact southern agricultural interests. Eventually, they accepted a plan for simple majority approval of commerce bills in exchange for

a constitutional provision that barred taxes on exports, thus protecting southern crops like cotton and tobacco.

A clearer reflection of the sectional compromises built into the Constitution in the wake of the Great Compromise were the three provisions dealing with slavery. The most important impact on the new Congress of these three was the three-fifths clause, which counted slaves as three-fifth of persons in calculating population for the determination of representation. In essence, the three-fifths clause was part of the Great Compromise. The southern states wanted slaves counted for apportioning representation in the House but excluded from direct tax assessments. Not surprisingly, northern states wanted the opposite. The Great Compromise solved the problem by provided that free residents would be counted fully, to which number three-fifths "of all other persons," excluding Indians not taxed, would be added. Thus, the slave states gained additional political representation, which in the end did not give them any marked increase of power in the House, while northern states received assurances that the owners of nonvoting slaves would have to bear part of the cost of any direct taxes.

Issues Surrounding the Powers of Congress

The Great Compromise ended the first phase of the Convention, which focused on the general framework of a stronger national government. With the basic structure of Congress decided, it was then necessary to determine what powers the legislature, and in essence the federal government, had. As Article I evolved, the framework of Congress was expanded and explained, and its powers delineated.

Article I is probably the most specific of the three articles that lay out the three branches of government. While Articles II and III provide the basic dimensions of the executive and the judiciary, Article I is far more specific in what Congress can and cannot do and the structure under which it will operate. Since 1787, Congress has expanded beyond the original parameters laid out in the Constitution as society has become more complex. However, despite this expansion over more than two centuries, there is no question that when the first government came into operation in 1789, the members of Congress had a far clearer picture of what they could do and would do, and what was expected of them, than the executive or judiciary.

In spite of the fact that the debates in the Convention and the apparently explicit nature of Article I seemed to limit federal power generally, and congressional power specifically, questions still abounded. As the Constitution moved to the states for ratification, the Federalists' argument in favor of the new government focused much of the debate on the legislature. Many numbers of the *Federalist Papers* discussed Congress. Madison, Hamilton, and John Jay devoted a great deal of energy to convincing various constituencies that they had nothing to fear from the new government, and especially from the legislature with its

new, expanded powers which was far more powerful than the legislature under the Articles of Confederation. They strove to reassure the state conventions, called to ratify the Constitution, that Congress would not become oppressive and tyrannical.

With the ratification of the Constitution, problems continued to arise that either were not anticipated by the Founders or that arose as the passage of time raised issues that were not significant or apparent in the late eighteenth century. Other problems resulted from the convoluted way the Senate had come into being and the questions concerning its role and what exactly it represented.

The concept of senators as agents of state sovereignty led to repeated but largely unsuccessful efforts by state legislatures to make senators accountable to them. Despite the fact the legislatures elected them, there seemed to be very little quid pro quo in their election. Once they reached the Senate, senators felt no obligation toward the state legislatures and tended to act as independent agents. Some members of Congress, though, representatives as well as senators, felt a duty to make occasional reports to the state legislatures.

As a result, a continuing controversy ensued over the right of state legislatures to instruct their senators. Instruction was more common in the South than in the North, but there was no unanimity of opinion on the question. In 1812 Virginia debated the right of the legislature to instruct its senators, with the general assembly asserting that it was the "indubitable right of the state legislatures to instruct their Senators in Congress, on all points." "All points" meant it was the duty of the senators to obey any such instructions. Resolutions in the North Carolina legislature in 1843 asserted the right of the legislature to instruct its senators. And forty-five years later, the governor of Oregon repeated this admonition in his inaugural address, stating that senators were nothing more than agents of the state. Not only did the state legislature have a duty to instruct its senators, but that duty went both ways, with senators duty bound to obey the local legislature. They were bound by "any and every matter of public interest, and it is the duty of the agents to obey the behests of the principal." No honorable senator would refuse such an order. If he could not follow such dictates, then it was the duty of the senator to resign, so the voice of the state could be heard.

Over time, with the emergence of political parties, party loyalty gradually took the place of the expected state allegiance. Any continuing efforts by state legislatures to control and issue mandates to their senators disappeared with the ratification in 1913 of the Seventeenth Amendment, which mandated the direct election of senators.

While the two chambers of Congress were seen to be equal, early commentators suggested that the House, because it was popularly elected and therefore more directly connected to the people, would be the dominant force in Congress. The Senate, it was projected, would act more as a reactive body, working to revise the actions of the House, rather than as a proactive one, initiating legislation and policy.

At first the House did overshadow the Senate, both in power and prestige, but within a few decades the Senate—endowed with powers that the House did not share, including a more active role in executive functions like the approval of presidential appointments and of treaties, and containing a smaller and more stable membership—achieved primacy over the House. And while the balance of power shifted from time to time, the Senate was always an equal body at the least.

As Madison noted in *Federalist* No. 52, the federal legislative power was not unitary. Two houses divided the power, making the people safer. In addition, the two houses were restrained not only by their dependence on each other, but by the people, and finally were "controlled and watched by the several collateral [state] legislatures, which other legislative bodies are not." Because the Constitution was ambiguous in defining the relationship between the House and the Senate, the results of the Great Compromise left a branch of government within which there was competition for power. This competition meant that both houses spent a great deal of energy attempting to define their place and duties within the government, thereby helping to shape their individual histories and that of Congress as a whole.

In the end, the creation of a House and Senate left much room for evolution. The way the two houses manipulated power within themselves, against each other, and within the national government created a functioning government. With the blueprint in place, Congress would be shaped by how the blueprint's provisions were interpreted, who interpreted them, and how various individuals wielded power that would shape the Congress.

FURTHER READING

Banning, Lance. *The Sacred Fire of Liberty: James Madison and the Founding of the Federal Republic.* Ithaca, NY: Cornell University Press, 1995.

Collier, Christopher, and James Lincoln Collier. *Decision in Philadelphia: The Constitutional Convention of 1787.* New York: Ballantine Books, 1986.

Levy, Leonard W., and Dennis J. Mahoney, eds. *The Framing and Ratification of the Constitution.* Birmingham, AL: Palladium Press, 2003.

McCaughey, Elizabeth. *Government by Choice: Inventing the United States Constitution.* New York: New-York Historical Society, in association with Basic Books, 1987.

Rakove, Jack. *Original Meanings: Politics and Ideas in the Making of the Constitution.* New York: Knopf, 1996.

Urofsky, Melvin I., and Paul Finkleman. *A March of Liberty: A Constitutional History of the United States.* 2nd ed. New York: Oxford University Press, 2002.

Wills, Garry. *Explaining America: The Federalist.* New York: Penguin Books, 2001.

Wood, Gordon. *The Creation of the American Republic.* New York: Norton, 1993.

2

ROLES, FUNCTIONS, AND POWERS

When the Founders designed Congress, they envisioned a government of limited powers. The Antifederalists feared that federal power, the power being most explicitly spelled out in the powers of Congress, would destroy the nation. They saw the legislature as being given the power to suppress liberty and destroy the states, through both powers that were too broad, such as the power to legislate for the general welfare, and more specific powers as well. The limited powers given to Congress soon took on a shape and scope of their own, in some cases fulfilling the fears of the early detractors, in other cases assuming a proportion never anticipated. Since Congress's primary function and most important power is creating laws, to understand that power, and the people who wield it, it is important to reflect on the power generally. One must look at not only the nature and scope of the authority granted to Congress as a whole, but the specific powers granted to each house of Congress.

In designing Congress, the Framers relied upon the examples of both the British Parliament and the numerous state assemblies formed in the wake of the Revolution. From the beginning of the Constitutional Convention, in the Virginia Plan, a bicameral legislature was proposed. As noted in chapter 1, the Great Compromise was one of the key moments in the Convention, establishing a bicameral legislature in which the House of Representatives, apportioned on population, represented the people, and Senate represented the states equally. The Great Compromise enabled the delegates to go forward and work out the specifics of the new government they were designing.

The two houses helped enshrine the important principles of separation of powers and checks and balances in the Constitution. As James Madison noted in *Federalist* No. 51, the legislative power was not only an important part of the checks and balances in the system, but the splitting of the power between the two houses created an intralegislative check to quell the fears of the people. Thus, the Constitution required that before any bill became a law, it had to be debated in *both* houses, which allowed for real debate and real difference—and therefore checks—since the members of each house were obliged to different constituencies. In addition, each chamber was given some powers not possessed by the other.

EXCLUSIVE POWERS OF THE HOUSE OF REPRESENTATIVES

The Constitution granted the House of Representatives exclusive authority in three areas. Perhaps the most important of these powers was that of initiating tax legislation. This seems to have been forgotten in modern times, as in the twenty-first century multiple branches of government, including the Senate, the president, and various agencies, suggest taxation programs and appropriation bills and propose a budget; however, the initiating power still lies in the House. While the responsibility for creating and shaping the budget has always been shared with the Senate, according to Article 1, Section 7 of the Constitution, all revenue bills must originate in the House. This provision arose in response to the taxation issues that surrounded the debate over revolution in the 1770s. The Framers firmly believed that the power to originate tax bills must be entrenched in the lower house, which was directly elected by the people. (While there was a

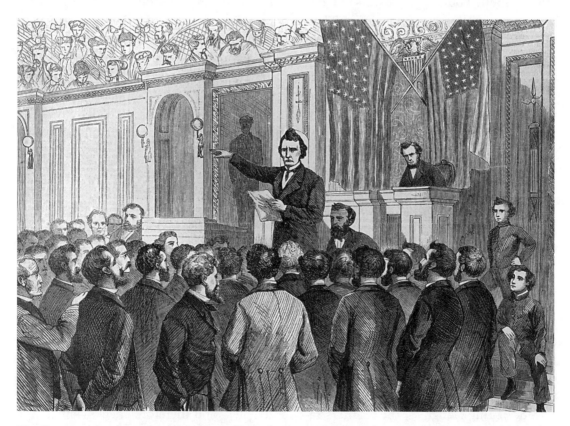

Thaddeus Stevens closes the debate on Andrew Johnson's impeachment in 1868. (Library of Congress)

growing movement in the early twentieth century to give voters more effective control over their senators, until passage of the Seventeenth Amendment in 1913, not all senators were generally elected by the states.) This linked the House more directly to the electorate. Also, because House members stood for election every two years, their sense of accountability was reinforced. Very rapidly the House assumed the power to originate all spending and appropriation bills as well as tax legislation.

The second special power the House holds is the right to recommend removal of federal officials through the impeachment process (Article I, Section 2). Impeachment by the House is similar to the process that produces an indictment in the common law criminal justice system (see chapter 6). If the House finds enough evidence, the process moves to the Senate, where a trial is held. While the early 1800s saw several impeachments and attempted impeachments of federal judges, only twice in American history has Congress used this power against the presidency. The first time was during Reconstruction after the Civil War, as Radical Republicans exercised their power to challenge President Andrew Johnson. The second time was during Bill Clinton's presidency in the late 1990s. In both cases, the Senate failed to convict, although in Johnson's case, by only one vote. A third president, President Richard Nixon, would have been impeached, historians suggest, had he not resigned in August 1974, denying Congress the opportunity to throw him out.

The impeachment power is an important part of the checks and balances system built into the Constitution. It is a procedure that is not just a congressional check on the president, but also a mechanism to keep the judiciary in line. However, often the effort dies in the House. In fewer than one-quarter of the proposed impeachments has a trial taken place in the Senate. Only seven times were individuals (federal judges in all the cases) removed from office. Despite many objections to the impeachment of Clinton as a frivolous exercise of partisan power because Clinton's offenses, it was argued, were not impeachable ones, the rare use of the power makes it an effective check. Many critics argue it was the threat of impeachment and the actual commencement of the formal proceedings (although they did not advance far) that prompted Nixon to resign.

The third and final special power of the House of Representatives is to elect the president of the United States when electors fail to do so because of a tie or a failure of anyone to gain a majority of votes in the Electoral College. This has happened two times in U.S. history. First, in 1800 a glitch in the Electoral College system sent the election of the president into the House. Under the original system, electors did not vote for president and vice president, but voted for two candidates for president. In 1800 Thomas Jefferson and Aaron Burr tied for most votes. This threw the election into the House of Representatives, which eventually chose Jefferson. (The result of the confusion was the Twelfth

Democratic presidential candidate Al Gore (left) and Republican candidate George W. Bush shake hands before the first presidential debate on October 3, 2000, at the University of Massachusetts in Boston. (AP/Wide World Photos)

Amendment, under which electors were to cast one vote for president and one for vice president.)

The second time was in 1824, when no candidate received a majority of electoral votes. Under the Twelfth Amendment, the House chose among the top four electoral vote getters. Although Andrew Jackson had won a plurality of electoral votes, the House elected John Quincy Adams after Henry Clay threw his support to Adams.

In 1876 Democrat Samuel Tilden, running against Republican Rutherford B. Hayes, won the majority of the popular vote nationally. However, a dispute arose over the local counts in three states, and the electoral vote counts in South Carolina, Florida, and Louisiana all came into question. Congress, split between a

Republican Senate and Democratic House, solved the problem by establishing a special, fifteen-member electoral commission consisting of senators, representatives, and Supreme Court justices. In the Compromise of 1876, the commission assigned the disputed electoral votes so that Hayes was elected president without the House having to make the decision. In 2000 it seemed that the House might have to decide the election, but it was resolved by the Supreme Court in the case of *Bush v. Gore* (2000), which allowed Florida's electoral votes to go to George W. Bush, making him president.

EXCLUSIVE POWERS OF THE SENATE

Like the House, the Senate—besides having a special role in disputed elections (choosing the vice president)—has a specific job during impeachment proceedings, based in Article I, Section 3, which gives the Senate "the sole power to try all impeachments." In essence, the Senate sits as the trial court, making the decision as to whether or not the the president is guilty of the House's articles of impeachment. The Senate has performed this function seventeen times, responding with a guilty verdict seven times, but never in the case of an official from the executive branch.

In addition to its responsibilities during impeachment proceedings, the Senate has two other constitutional powers exclusive to that body. It has the power to approve treaties and the right to confirm the president's nominations to executive branch posts and all federal judgeships. Under Article II, Section 2, the Senate is authorized to give "advice and consent" by a two-thirds vote on the adoption of treaties. This means the Senate has a stronger voice in foreign policy and international affairs than the House. Treaties are referred to the Committee on Foreign Relations. Nominations are referred to one of the various committees of the Senate before going to the Senate floor; usually the committee that reviews the nomination is the one that handles the legislation on subjects under the jurisidiction of the position. For example, judicial positions all go to the Judiciary Committee.

The Senate has rejected relatively few of the numerous treaties that the president has sent to it. More often, treaties that the Senate does not favor die in committee or are withdrawn by the president rather than face defeat. Only twenty-one treaties have been defeated by the full Senate. As noted below, presidents may sometimes include key members of the Senate in negotiations, and failure to do so can hurt the treaty's chances. For example, President Woodrow Wilson's exclusion of Sen. Henry Cabot Lodge, the chairman of the Senate Committee on Foreign Relations, from the negotiations over the Treaty of Versailles tolled the death knell for that treaty. A mechanism for the president to avoid the treaty approval process is executive agreements. While these circumvent the need for Senate ratification, however, they die with the end of the president's term.

The Senate's right to provide advice and consent on treaties is a major, if not the single, essential key, to congressional checks on the president in foreign affairs. In fact, this power of the Senate raised serious concerns on the part of the Framers. By resting the power in the Senate, as John Jay noted in *Federalist* No. 64, all states would be equally represented, checking the "fears and apprehensions of some, that the President and Senate may make treaties without an equal eye to the interests of all the States."

While the Constitution lays out the procedure to ratify treaties, it is silent on their termination. During the Carter Administration, two treaties were abrogated. In 1978 President Jimmy Carter, acting unilaterally, terminated the United States' defense treaty with Taiwan. That same year, acting in concert with Congress, he negotiated a new Panama Canal Treaty to replace the previous ones. It is not clear who is responsible for terminating treaties. Some argue it is the sole right of the executive, because that branch is the one with regular, open channels to foreign governments. But as Sen. Russ Feingold argued on the floor of the Senate in June 2002 during debate over the ABM (Anti-Ballistic Missile) Treaty, a treaty was equal to a law, and citing Jefferson, he continued, "A law cannot be declared to be repealed by the President alone. Only an act of Congress can repeal a law. Action by the Senate or Congress should be required to terminate a treaty." This problem has never been completely resolved.

In contrast to the two-thirds vote required for treaty approval, the advice and consent role in nominations for office is by a simple majority vote. From the beginning of the new government, the provision on nominations has created tension between the two branches, and while some of that conflict will be discussed in chapter 6, it is important to understand the general power here.

The scope of the Senate's authority to confirm presidential nominations is vast because of the wide range of appointments a president needs to make. After a nomination is received and referred to the appropriate committee, hearings may be held, and after the committee votes, the nomination may be reported to the full Senate. If the nomination is confirmed, a Resolution of Confirmation is transmitted to the White House and the appointment is then signed by the president.

The list of presidential nominees is extensive. As the government has grown bigger, and despite the fact that a large civil service has supplanted the numerous patronage appointments that early presidents made, it is still an expansive list. The president nominates all federal judges; U.S. attorneys; U.S. marshals; and some, but not all, officers in Cabinet-level departments, independent agencies, the military services, the Foreign Service, and uniformed civilian services. The Constitution specifically gives him this authority in Article II noting the power to appoint "Officers of the United States." Congress is authorized by the appointments clause to vest the appointment of "inferior offices" at its discretion, "in the President alone, in the Courts of Law, or in the Heads of Departments." Thus, for many positions, the power is designated to a subordinate authority, but it still leaves room for controversy as to exactly what an "inferior office" is. Approximately 4,000 civilian and 65,000 military nominations are submitted to the Senate during each two-year session of Congress. Most of these nominations move through the Senate fairly quickly and are rapidly confirmed. Even many of the more controversial appointees, who are subjected to grueling interrogatories, get confirmed. The vast majority are routinely confirmed, while a very small but sometimes highly visible number fail to receive action.

The importance of the post to be filled often affects the tenor of the hearings. The individual's record, the political climate, whether there is divided government between the political parties, and the nature of the Senate's leadership all influence the character of the debate. There is disagreement over the exact role of the senators in these hearings. Some view the Senate's role as almost perfunctory, with the Senate's role being to confirm unless the nominee is extremely lacking in character or competence. Others suggest the Senate has broad latitude and can refuse to confirm a nominee for any reason it chooses. Just as the president is not required to explain why he selected a particular nominee, neither is the Senate obligated to give reasons for rejecting a nominee. In practice, the Senate has explicitly rejected fewer than 2 percent of all Cabinet nominees since 1789, while nearly one-quarter of all Supreme Court nominations have failed to be confirmed, with the nominations rejected, withdrawn, or declined.

In contrast to Supreme Court nomination hearings, appointments to judicial posts below the Supreme Court have generated little controversy throughout the nation's history. A major factor is the large number of such appointments, and another is a tradition of "senatorial courtesy," which is the practice of consulting with home-state senators on a nominee. The Senate rarely confirms a nomination if the nominee's own senators do not approve. However, in the last decade of the twentieth century, a Democratic president and Republican Senate began to battle more vociferously over lower court appointments, and while most federal judgeships have still made their way through the Senate rather quickly, during both Bill Clinton's and George W. Bush's administrations, senators strove to block various lower court judges.

With the exception of appointments to Cabinet departments and the Supreme Court, most rejections in modern times have taken place at the committee level, through either inaction or by a vote not to send the nomination to the Senate floor. This is especially evident in the blocking of judges noted above after 1992. During Clinton's presidency a Republican majority in the Senate stymied many appointments, and President George W. Bush's administration experienced similar problems, especially when the Republicans failed to garner 60 seats in the chamber, enabling the Democrats in holding up appointments.

Before the 1860s, the Senate considered most nominations without referring them to the committee holding jurisdiction over the vacant post. The Senate rules of 1868 provided for the first time that nominations be sent to "appropriate committees." Not until the middle of the twentieth century, however, did those committees routinely require nominees for major positions to appear in person.

At the Constitutional Convention in Philadelphia, no consensus could be reached regarding how judges and executive officials should be selected. Most of the state constitutions provided for the legislature to make appointments or for appointments to be made by some mechanism provided for by the legislature. Because there had been no executive under the Articles of Confederation, Congress made all appointments.

Originally, it was proposed that appointment power be divided, with Congress controlling the filling of judicial offices and the president selecting executive officers. The advice and consent role was eventually confined to the Senate, as it was thought that the smaller size of that body would make it possible for the process to be kept secret—which at that time was deemed important—and would also make it more efficient.

More important was the question of who was best able to recognize suitable nominees. In the end, the system was set up as part of the checks and balances that permeate the Constitution, often focusing on denying any one branch, especially the executive, too much power. The Convention delegates had feared that a president with exclusive appointment power was a danger. The framework of the Senate, and its role as a representative of the states, protected the small states, who feared that House control of the process would mean that appointees sympathetic to the large states would predominate. Even Hamilton, the great Federalist and centralizer, supported the dual responsibility, believing the president would still control the process because the Senate could not initiate it, but only accept or reject the nominee.

The First Congress addressed many issues left unsettled at the Constitutional Convention. Among those related to appointments was the power of removal. Did the president have the power of removal or did he share it with the Senate? Or was the impeachment process the proper removal method? It was Congress's obligation to resolve this problem, since the Constitution was mute. Madison argued this was an executive prerogative, once the Senate had confirmed.

From the start, there was a problem with the meaning of "advice" and "consent." President George Washington and the Senate struggled over this. Washington saw Congress's "advice and consent" function as almost automatic: he would visit the Senate and, for example, in the case of a treaty, read it out loud, get the senators' advice and then their vote of consent. However, some senators objected to this perfunctory role.

In its very first session, the Senate rejected Washington's interpretation. In 1789 he hoped to get quick approval of a treaty. He counted on an immediate response, only to see the Senate refer the matter to committee for further discussion. Washington, irate at what he considered the impudence of the Senate, never sought the advice of the Senate in person again.

When it comes to appointments, traditionally the Senate usually has allowed a president wide latitude to select his executive branch appointees, who after all will be carrying out the policies of the administration. Judicial appointments that are for life, and thus carry on far beyond the end of a particular administration, received closer Senate scrutiny, especially Supreme Court nominations. In the last two decades of the twentieth century and carrying into the next century, this close scrutiny was far more acrimonious, turning into bitter political battles.

The power to confirm meant the power to reject, and the Senate wasted little time before rejecting a nomination. On August 5, 1789, the Senate, for the first time, rejected a nomination. President Washington submitted 102 names for the posts of collectors, naval officers, and surveyors to seaports. The Senate confirmed all but one—Benjamin Fishbourn of Georgia. Washington, although then submitting an alternative name, sent a letter of protest along with it. His protest was not against the Senate action per se, but rather because senators had not talked to the president first so they could consult and come to a common agreement about appointments. This request would evolve into what is known as "senatorial courtesy." In rejecting Fishbourn, a motion was introduced that suggested the Senate should give its "advice and consent" with the president present. Washington, ever conscious of the prestige of his office and the precedental value of any action he took, felt such a procedure would demean the office of the president and possibly embarrass the Senate by forcing presidents to say nothing or argue. Washington concluded that he could nominate whomever he wanted for whatever reasons and did not have to spell them out. Conversely, the Senate countered that it could reject his nomination without giving reasons. The Senate then reversed its earlier agreement to vote in secret on nominations and treaties. The nomination process, expected to be civil and courteous, quickly became contentious as partisan politics were injected. Washington was unabashed about his desire to appoint men politically loyal to him. Subsequent presidents found themselves at odds with the Senate, which insisted on an active role in the process. John Adams was more amenable than Washington to working with Congress and consulted with the Senate, and the House as well, giving more consideration to the legislators' recommendations than had Washington. However, despite consultation, both Adams and Jefferson, his successor, maintained control over the process, especially the latter, setting the stage for executive-legislative battles over the nomination process.

The first Senate rejection of a Supreme Court nomination came in 1795, and the first rejection of a Cabinet-level nomination occurred in 1834. In the latter half of the twentieth century, senior executive appointments began receiving more exacting review, noting in particular the confirmation hearing of attorneys general under both President Bill Clinton, with the eventual installation of Janet

Reno, and the partisan wrangling under President George W. Bush over the appointment of John Ashcroft. Other heated fights arose over the hearings on Robert Bork, Clarence Thomas, and (in the early twenty-first century) Samuel Alito for the Supreme Court.

Events since 1787 have undermined the reasons for bicameralism rooted in separation of powers and federalism. In particular, the adoption of the Seventeenth Amendment for the popular election of senators reduced the differences between the two chambers.

POWERS OF THE ENTIRE CONGRESS

In designing the federal government, especially Congress, the Founders designed a government of enumerated powers. In other words, all three branches could exercise only those powers specifically granted to them. The powers of the executive and judicial branches were described much less definitively than those of the legislative. Yet even as he read the Constitution in an expansive manner to widen congressional power, Chief Justice John Marshall noted in *McCulloch v. Maryland* (1819):

> This government is acknowledged by all, to be one of enumerated powers. The principle, that it can exercise only the powers granted to it, would seem too apparent, to have required to be enforced by all those arguments, which its enlightened friends, while it was depending before the people, found it

necessary to urge; that principle is now universally admitted.

Necessary and Proper Clause

The Constitution lists congressional powers in several places. The key location is Article I, Section 8. The eighteen paragraphs of that section define what Congress can do. However, it is perhaps the last paragraph of Section 8 which may be the most important. In that section, the Constitution opened the door to the expansion of lawmaking authority when it noted that Congress had the power "to make all laws which shall be necessary and proper for carrying into execution the foregoing powers"—the "Necessary and Proper Clause," also called the "elastic clause." The extent of congressional power was put to the test early, when Alexander Hamilton and Thomas Jefferson debated the efficacy of a national bank and whether or not Congress had the power to create such an institution, although no such power was explicitly given. Hamilton argued that the Necessary and Proper Clause should be read broadly to authorize the exercise of many implied powers, while Thomas Jefferson reasoned that "necessary" really meant *necessary*.

Jefferson argued that to interpret the Constitution in a way that allows Congress to expand its power under the Necessary and Proper Clause would do damage to the ideal of a government of enumerated or limited powers. He noted that "all powers not delegated to the United States, by the Constitution, nor

prohibited by it to the States, are reserved to the States or to the people." To
move beyond this limitation would destroy the boundaries drawn by Article 8
around congressional power and would
"take possession of a boundless field of
power, no longer susceptible of any definition." He argued it would destroy the
essence of the Constitution and reduce it
to a single phrase, which opened the door
for Congress to do whatever it wanted
"for the good of the United States"; the
only restraint would be members of Congress themselves, allowing them to do
whatever good or evil they wanted.

While acknowledging the need of implied powers, he believed these should
exist only in the context of explicit specified powers and noted that this was recognized by the use of the word *necessary*
in the phrase *necessary and proper.* Jefferson chose a narrow definition of that
phrase. He noted that while a bank may
be convenient and had a natural connection to the power to collect taxes, an explicit power given to Congress, *convenient* did not equal *necessary.*

> If such a latitude of construction
> be allowed to this phrase as to give
> any non-enumerated power, it will
> go to everyone, for there is not one
> which ingenuity may not torture
> into a *convenience* in some in-
> stance *or other,* to *some one* of so
> long a list of enumerated powers.
> It would swallow up all the dele-
> gated powers, and reduce the
> whole to one power, as before ob-
> served. Therefore it was that the
> Constitution restrained them to

the *necessary* means, that is to
say, to those means without
which the grant of power would be
nugatory.

Jefferson was a strict constructionist
and a states' righter in the early days of
the Republic while sitting in Washington's Cabinet. He feared an overreaching
central government, especially a legislature that would dominate the states and
shatter their sovereignty.

In contrast, Hamilton, always a backer
of strong central government, argued for
a broad or loose interpretation of the
Necessary and Proper Clause that would
gather power to Congress. He argued that
to define narrowly or strictly this "elastic" clause would be the death knell of
the new government. He said *necessary*
had a more generous definition than Jefferson's and could be interpreted to mean
"needful, requisite, incidental, useful or
conducive to." To read the word narrowly would put too much uncertainty
into what government could do and how
it could do it. He did not reject the idea
of a government of limited powers, but
how much power was actually delegated
could only be determined by looking at
the Necessary and Proper Clause in light
of the general principles of government
and the ends that government was created to achieve.

In looking at that elastic clause,
Hamilton argued that implied powers
were delegated by the Constitution just
like expressed ones. Thus, in the case of
the bank, a government-created corporation, to establish whether Congress had
the power to create such an institution,

one had to look at both the specific power granted combined with the implied powers of the Necessary and Proper Clause. The question, then, was not whether Congress could create a corporation but, rather, whether the power exercised in creating one was implicitly granted by the expressed power. Did the created corporation, in this case the national bank, have a natural relation to an explicit power granted. Thus, Hamilton argued, Congress could not create an entity that would oversee the Philadelphia police force, because it was not authorized to regulate the police at all. In contrast, a corporation could be created to deal with powers explicitly granted, such as power over trade between the states, the Indian tribes, trade with foreign countries, or the collection of taxes. This made absolute sense "because it is the province of the federal government to regulate those objects, and because it is incident to a general sovereign or legislative power to regulate a thing, to employ all the means which relate to its regulation to the best and greatest advantage."

Hamilton contended it was obvious that the Convention had intended the Constitution to be read liberally when the specified powers were exercised. Any power explicitly vested in the government had to be "construed liberally in advancement of the public good." Hamilton said that was the essence of government, implicit in its very nature.

President Washington embraced Hamilton's argument, the bank was created, and the door was opened for a more expansive view of congressional, and thus federal, authority. The Hamiltonian view was reinforced and enshrined almost three decades later in Chief Justice Marshall's decision in *McCulloch v. Maryland.*

Taxing Power

Since the first debates, the elastic clause has been used to enhance and expand the three main powers that Congress has: the power to tax, the power to spend, and the power to regulate commerce. Section 8, which lays out congressional authority, begins by giving Congress the power to "lay and collect Taxes, Duties, Imposts and Excises, to pay the Debts and provide for the common Defence and general Welfare of the United States; but all Duties, Imposts and Excises shall be uniform throughout the United States." This is not an unlimited power, but one subject to certain qualifications.

The main qualification was the concept of federalism and the tenth amendment. While Congress had broad powers to act under its taxing authority, that power was not unlimited. Originally, critics of federal power attempted to limit taxing authority, and were supported by the Supreme Court that noted all taxes' primary purpose needed to be to raise revenue, not regulation, and all direct taxes must be assessed by the rule of apportionment and indirect taxes by the rule of uniformity.

However, in both these circumstances, over time, the Supreme Court emphasized the massive power this represented. The Court granted that for the most part, Congress could use its taxing authority in almost any circumstance, and that almost no method of taxation was implausible. This does not mean the Court has not at times restricted the use of congressional taxing power by looking at what was being taxed, how the taxes were imposed, or why the taxes were being assessed. Just because Congress had the authority to tax does not mean that the purposes for which it used that authority were always justified.

A key limitation on the taxing power was that any tax which impaired a state's sovereignty was not valid. However, what is viewed as a limitation on state sovereignty has changed over time. The Court ruled in *Collector v. Day* (1871) that Congress did not have the authority to tax the salary of a state official. However, the Court overruled that decision in 1939 and granted Congress the right to do so, and since the New Deal, the Court has for the most part seemed fairly reluctant to impose restrictions on congressional taxing power, and in fact restored powers previously denied.

Congress has gravitated to a Hamiltonian view of taxing, which regards taxing as a power in and of itself, so that Congress can tax (or spend) in any way that it deems will benefit society as whole. This is in contrast to the more narrow view, as espoused by Madison, that the taxing authority must be tied to another specifically enumerated power. The latter view took hold for a period of time at the beginning of the twentieth century.

For about the first three decades of that century, the Court narrowly interpreted the federal taxing power to at some points inhibit Congress's ability to regulate a variety of items, and other times to allow it to act. At that time the Court tended to view the taxing authority as a revenue function and argued that Congress could not get through the back door what it could not bring through the front. The result was in *U.S. v. Doremus* (1919); the Harrison Narcotic Drug Act, a law that effectively controlled drugs such as cocaine through a tax, was found as within the scope of congressional taxing power. However, three years later, the more narrow interpretation appeared in *Bailey v. Drexel Furniture Company* (1922), which denied Congress the right to tax child labor as an impermissible extension of congressional taxing authority. The tax was meant to regulate products made by child labor by placing a 10 percent levy on the profits of employers who used child labor, but the Court rejected the congressional attempt to use its taxing authority in this manner. This ban on taxes that served a primarily regulatory purpose was later rejected by the Court in *Steward Machine v. Davis* (1937), which validated unemployment compensation schemes under the New Deal. Another example in which Congress was allowed to use the taxing authority as a regulatory mechanism was in 1953, when the Court, in *U.S. v. Kahriger,* allowed Congress to tax bookies, which effectively drove them out of business. Over Tenth Amendment objections, the Court conceded that the "power of Congress to tax was extensive and sometimes falls with crushing effect on businesses deemed unessential or inimical to the public welfare." Despite dissents by Justices Felix Frankfurter, Hugo Black, and William O. Douglas that objected to opening the door to congressional use of the taxing power to regulate conduct, Congress was given wide latitude in its taxing authority, being allowed to tax not only things, but conduct, for regulatory purposes.

Congressional authority to tax took a decided shift in 1913 with the ratification of the Sixteenth Amendment. The amendment was a direct consequence of the Court's 1895 decision, *Pollock v. Farmers' Loan & Trust Co.* In that case the Court had struck down an attempt by Congress to tax income uniformly. The Court had argued such a tax was really a tax on property, and therefore a direct tax, which according to Article I, Sections 2 and 9, Congress could impose only by the rule of apportionment according to population.

In the years following the *Pollock* decision, concern grew over national solvency. Despite generous interpretations of what qualified as a direct tax by the Court, the problem grew, with a confusing bit of constitutional interpretation to go with it. It appeared that *Pollock* was headed to being overturned as the Court, bit by bit, chipped away at the ruling. The Sixteenth Amendment, however, ended the need for judicial gymnastics by the Court and reversed the case, opening the door for a national income tax.

Spending Power

Another major piece of power Congress exercises rests in its spending power. The Constitution grants Congress the power to "provide . . . for the general welfare,"

a simple phrase that raises two basic problems: how may Congress provide for "the general welfare" and what is "the general welfare" for which it is authorized to provide? Thomas Jefferson, in his opinion on the Bank, noted this power was narrow. He saw it not as a power in its own right but one that is plenary to other congressional powers.

The stickier question was what "the general welfare" itself meant. Even the authors of the *Federalist Papers* disagreed about its meaning and scope. Not surprisingly, Alexander Hamilton, as he reiterated in his opinion on the Bank, viewed the clause literally, giving it a broad meaning. Madison approached it in a more Jeffersonian manner, limiting its scope. Early on, Congress approached the power in a Hamiltonian way as it appropriated monies for more and more internal improvements. By the second decade of the twentieth century, it has become the norm that federal monies are distributed to the states for specific uses (for example, highway funds) with stipulations attached. On several occasions the scope of congressional spending power has been challenged. It was not until *United States v. Butler* in 1936, when the Supreme Court acknowledged the Hamiltonian view of the taxing authority, that it also adopted a broader view of the spending authority. The two were viewed as separate authorities not dependent on each other or necessarily connected to subsequent powers explicitly stated in Article I. Justice Owen Roberts acknowledged limits on federal taxing authority while simultaneously noting that congressional spending authority, the power to authorize expenditures of public money for public purposes, was not constrained "by the direct grants of legislative power found in the Constitution." Some limitations were placed on congressional spending in *Butler*, to the effect that Congress could not do what was called "purchase compliance" with federal regulations via the spending power, forcing state and local governments to act in a certain way using the power of the checkbook. That limit was removed a year later in *Steward Machine v. Davis* when, as noted above, the Court reiterated a broad view of the spending authority. The Court noted that relief of unemployment was a legitimate goal of Congress and that the expenditure involved could be justified under the "general welfare" clause, making the Social Security Act a reasonable method to try to fix the problem through cooperation between the state and federal governments.

The limitation—that the money spent, or that authority used to spend that money, must be used in furtherance of the "general welfare"—seems to be a paper barrier. As with the taxing authority, *South Dakota v. Dole* (1987) also opened the door to congressional spending, conceding that Congress had the right to establish a national drinking age via the spending authority. In that law, Congress conditioned highway funding grants on the individual state raising its drinking age to twenty-one.

This power was extended in *Sabri v. United States* (2004), in which the Court rebuffed Tenth Amendment challenges as it acknowledged Congress's power under the Spending Clause to impose criminal penalties rather than conditions for federal funding. In the *Sabri* case, the federal law in question stated that when an organization or local government accepted federal funds, it and any third party that might bribe it were criminally liable for bribery at the federal level, although in any other case prosecution would have been at the state level. A unanimous Supreme Court ruled the Spending Clause empowered Congress to spend money for the general welfare, and the elastic clause authorized the Legislature to take any reasonable steps to prevent the allocated funds from being misspent. Thus, while the congressional statute did impact local government, the impact was seen as incidental in light of the broad policy objectives accomplished by the act. The apparent boundaries placed on congressional spending power, as noted in *Dole*, were superfluous, and concerns related to federalism that could restrict congressional power in other cases did not seem to apply when it came to the spending power.

Regulation of Commerce

In addition to the taxing and spending authority, the other major authority by which Congress legislates is the commerce power. Article I gives Congress the right "to regulate Commerce with foreign Nations, and among the several States, and with the Indian Tribes." What these words have been interpreted to mean has served often as the focus for determining the constitutional legitimacy of congressional power in legislating. In addition, those words serve as a limitation upon state governments, which opens the door to probably the greatest assertion of congressional power and authority under any clause in the Constitution.

The restrictive character of the clause dominated its impact for a long period. Of the approximately 1,400 cases that reached the Supreme Court under the clause prior to 1900, the majority emanated from questions about state laws. Because the original emphasis was on using the Commerce Clause to curb power rather than as a means to exercise it, the early focus of the clause was on the word *commerce,* not the other key word, *regulate.* This ended with the New Deal and a reassessment of what the clause meant.

As with many powers of Congress, the core question is, how does one define the word *commerce*? Early on, Chief Justice John Marshall, in *Gibbons v. Ogden* (1824), rejected a narrow interpretation of commerce. The case arose because New York had granted Ogden a monopoly to operate steamships in its waters. Gibbons, who ran a line that took passengers from New York to New Jersey, challenged the law. Marshall, in his ruling, tried to define commerce and what the power over it meant.

He broadly interpreted the idea of commerce. In true Federalist form, he defined commerce in a way that would see power accrue to the federal government and give Congress a wide range of power.

He defined commerce as intercourse but then qualified that interpretation by saying it meant commercial intercourse. However, today commerce tends to be interpreted as not just the movement of people or things, but all those things involved in the general flow of business whether directly or indirectly affecting interstate commerce. The use of that definition, and the broad extension of power to Congress that it allowed, peaked during the latter half of the twentieth century. It is also toward the end of that century that a shift can be seen that seems to reject the "anything is commerce" view noted above that developed in the wake of the New Deal, and in its place the Court began to rein in congressional power and place some limits on Congress's ability to legislate under its commerce authority. This late-twentieth-century development is reminiscent of, although it did not go as far as, the early-twentieth-century trend in which the Court went to great pains to try to limit the regulatory powers of the federal government and ruled that various activities were not covered by the Commerce Clause and therefore could not be regulated by Congress. Distinctions were made between direct and indirect impact on commerce, manufacturing versus commerce, and so on. In these cases, the Court failed to recognize the changing nature of the economy and how important it was to enable Congress to participate in its regulation. Thus, until the justices acknowledged the vertical nature of industrial enterprises as well as the impossibility of drawing a fine line between the movement of goods and when they were stopped, Congress was left with an awkward patchwork quilt of power.

These late-twentieth-century attempts to contain the power reflected in part Marshall's unwillingness to grant Congress a blank check in *Gibbons*. Marshall focused on the phrase "among the several States." He said that meant interstate, not intrastate traffic. It was obvious, he stated, that the Founders made a distinction between them. It must mean that traffic which resides exclusively in one state is outside the reach of the Congress. This did not mean that commerce within a state was off limits per se, for as Marshall noted, "commerce among the states, cannot stop at the exterior boundary line of each state, but may be introduced into the interior." The chief justice then announced the rule that has basically guided interpretation of the clause:

> The genius and character of the whole government seem to be, that its action is to be applied to all the external concerns of the nation, and to those internal concerns which affect the states generally; but not to those which are completely within a particular state, which do not affect other states, and with which it is not necessary to interfere, for the purpose of executing some of the general powers of the government.

Chief Justice Marshall continued by asking, what exactly, then, was the power of "commerce"? He defined it as the power to regulate, or to determine the rules by which commerce was to be controlled. He saw this power, like all powers vested in Congress, as a power "complete in itself," which needed to be exercised and did not have any limitations except those explicitly noted in the Constitution. As a Federalist, Marshall perceived that Congress needed power for the nation to function properly, and considering that it was to a great degree problems with interstate commerce that led to the convention in Philadelphia, he was not about to hamstring congressional power. The power to regulate that commerce was complete in itself. In *United States v. Darby Lumber Company* (1941), the Court reinforced this wide notion of commerce when it not only accepted the authority of the federal government to regulate goods made by child labor, but noted that concerns about federalism were really nonconcerns. Justice Harlan Stone stated in the decision that the Tenth Amendment is but a truism. The Court argued Congress's commerce power was as wide and all encompassing as states' police power and should be given similar courtesy.

As with taxing and spending authority, commerce power became contingent upon its connection to the elastic clause, and it is the linking of these two clauses that seems to grant Congress its widest range of power. Numerous cases permit Congress to reach what can be perceived as purely intrastate activities, because those activities are seen as having a real or potential impact on interstate activity. So to effectively regulate truckers on the highways and make sure the flow of interstate commerce proceeds unimpeded, Congress needs to be able to regulate them as they move within any single state and obstruct states' ability to regulate them within their respective borders. Anything less would, the argument goes, destroy commerce and emasculate the congressional commerce power.

This broad view of congressional commerce power had earlier been blocked by emphasis on federalism concerns. After the Court overlooked the Tenth Amendment in *United States v. Darby* and its progeny, however, those concerns faded. In the latter part of the twentieth century, the Rehnquist Court refocused on the importance of the Tenth Amendment, so that federalism again reared its head to trump the commerce power.

The question of whether Congress's power to regulate commerce "among the several States" embraced the power to prohibit it provided for an ongoing argument that began in 1841 and seemed to culminate with the Fair Labor Standards Act in 1941 and the Court ruling in *United States v. Darby.* The year 1941 represented a watershed that saw the end to a clash between two different views of commerce authority that had crippled Congress at times, especially during the Great Depression.

Prior to then, two apparently divergent views had emerged regarding the power of Congress to legislate about commerce. The stronger, more dominant school tended to view the congressional power restrictively, making distinctions between direct and indirect effects on commerce and looking at business practices from the perspective of which dealt with commerce and which with manufacturing, with only the former coming under Congress's commerce power.

In 1890 Congress passed the Sherman Antitrust Act in an attempt to control the growing power of monopolies and the problems they created. In its first test, in *United States v. E. C. Knight* (1896), the Court denied Congress the power to regulate a monopoly in the manufacturing of refined sugar. In essence, until the product went into motion, Congress could not regulate it. This very formalistic approach to the Commerce Clause limited congressional power by focusing on questions like: Was the thing being regulated in the "stream of commerce"? Was the activity local or interstate? Was the effect on commerce direct or indirect? Questions such as these served to limit authority and made it impossible for Congress to create the sweeping changes demanded by reformers at the turn of the century during the Progressive Era. It also meant an inconsistent and haphazard approach to the application of congressional power.

Thus, Congress could not regulate the sugar trust, and other monopolies managed to wiggle away from congressional reach. In contrast, at the other end of the workplace, labor and working conditions were not viewed as commerce. Congressional attempts to help workers by establishing minimum wage or maximum hour laws, or even conditions in the workplace, oftentimes were struck down as outside the scope of congressional commerce authority. At the same time that Congress was unable to regulate certain aspects of commerce, the door was thrown wide open in others. The issue was whether the Commerce Clause bestowed on the federal government a police power akin to what the states had and thereby the right to prohibit certain items from interstate traffic. While the Court was loathe to acknowledge such a power directly, it often seemed as if one existed. *Champion v. Ames* (1903) confronted this issue early in the twentieth century. That case dealt with a law that forbade the transportation of lottery tickets in interstate commerce. In *Champion,* the Court in a 5–4 decision held that lottery tickets were indeed "subjects of traffic" and that independent carriers may be regulated under the Commerce Clause. The Court emphasized the broad discretion Congress enjoys in regulating commerce, noting that this power "is plenary, is complete in itself, and is subject to no limitations except such as may be found in the Constitution." The Court argued that Congress was merely assisting those states that wished to protect public morals by prohibiting lotteries within their borders.

In the wake of *Champion,* Congress repeatedly acted to repress a variety of activities offensive to public morality. Thus, for example, Congress passed the Mann Act, or the White Slave Traffic Act, in 1910 to help prohibit prostitution. In acknowledging this power, the Court noted in *Hoke v. United States* (1913) that

> Our dual form of government has its perplexities, State and Nation having different spheres of jurisdiction . . . but it must be kept in mind that we are one people; and the powers reserved to the States and those conferred on the Nation are adapted to be exercised, whether independently or concurrently, to promote the general welfare, material, and moral.

The Court made it plain that in prohibiting commerce among the states, Congress was equally free either to support state legislative policy or to devise a policy of its own. Congress could act independently of the states. State laws could not limit congressional commerce authority.

In *Brooks v. United States* (1925), the Court sustained the National Motor Vehicle Theft Act to protect automobile owners. The statute was designed to curtail car theft, even though the robberies preceded any interstate transportation of the stolen car. The Court clearly stated that Congress was allowed to regulate interstate commerce to help prevent "the use of such commerce as an agency to promote immorality, dishonesty, or the spread of any evil or harm to the people of other States from the State of origin." The Court went on to discuss how the invention of the automobile had changed the nature of commerce and crime and therefore, in this instance, Congress was authorized by the Constitution to curtail any activity that had such negative impacts on interstate commerce as in this case. In contrast to *Champion,* where the lottery tickets were deemed harmful in themselves, in this case the Court ruled it did not matter that the stolen cars were harmless.

Despite these instances of Congress flexing its commerce power, simultaneously that power was reined in so that Congress was unable to guard against the exploitation of child labor. In *Hammer v. Dagenhart* (1918), any thought that the congressional commerce power might be unrestricted was decimated as the Court declared unconstitutional a congressional statute that banned items produced by child labor from interstate commerce. The Court resurrected the local versus national, direct versus indirect distinctions that had prevailed previously in its rulings. In this decision the Court regarded the congressional law as an attempt to regulate a purely local activity. The harm of child labor had nothing to do with interstate commerce and therefore could not be controlled by the Congress under the guise of its commerce authority.

Direct and indirect distinctions were also used by the Court to limit Congress's ability to effect change under the Commerce Clause. Pressure to open the door for Congress began to build during the Depression as various New Deal programs were declared unconstitutional because of their supposed unconstitutional expansion of congressional power. Attempts to regulate wages and hours in 1936 in the coal mines were struck down as being local and not having a direct effect on interstate commerce.

Pressure continued to build, and in *United States v. Darby* (1941) the Court, in sustaining the Fair Labor Standards Act, expressly overruled *Hammer v. Dagenhart*. It rejected the distinctions of that case, stating that the drawing of lines that did not make sense—especially in light of modern industrial, economic, and social needs—needed to be stopped. Earlier delineations by the Court were seen as novel and unsupported by any provision of the Constitution and needed to be abandoned permanently.

It was in this environment that the Court several times, both expressly and more subtly, noted that Congress's exercise of power under the Commerce Clause is akin to the police power exercised by the states. It should follow, therefore, that Congress may achieve results unrelated to purely commercial aspects of commerce, and such results in fact have often been accomplished. Paralleling and contributing to this movement was the virtual disappearance of the distinction between interstate and intrastate commerce. Thus, any action by Congress was a legitimate extension of commerce authority as long as the activity, or thing, regulated had a "substantial effect" on interstate commerce. This broad power was extended even more the next year, when in *Wickard v. Filburn* (1942), the Court asserted that Congress could regulate any activity, even if it affected interstate commerce in an apparently trivial manner, if the cumulative effect of that activity, combined with others, had substantial interstate impact.

This opened the door for Congress to legislate, under its commerce authority, in two other important areas of law: civil rights and criminal law. Previous attempts by Congress to regulate civil rights had been repeatedly rebuffed, and it was not until 1964 that the Court unanimously and unequivocally granted that Congress had the right to control discrimination under its commerce authority. The Civil Rights Act of 1964 was a wide, comprehensive law that outlawed all discrimination on the basis of race, color, religion, sex, or national origin. The Court sustained the law and dismissed objections which argued that the discriminating businesses in question were local in character. It obliterated the local versus interstate distinction, asserting that "the power of Congress to promote interstate commerce also includes the power to regulate the local incidents thereof, including local activities in both the States of origin and destination, which might have a substantial and harmful effect upon that commerce." It did not matter that the act was tinged with moral concerns. The bottom line was that racial discrimination, whether local or national, had a negative impact on interstate commerce and therefore could be regulated by Congress.

However, by anchoring its power to fight discrimination in the Commerce Clause, Congress was faced with some limitations, most notably those raised by the Fourteenth Amendment, which limited the manner in which Congress may attack discriminatory conduct. Foremost among them was the principle that the amendment prohibited only state action, not private conduct. Thus, while the reach of Congress to stop discrimination under the Commerce Clause was wide and unparalleled, it was not boundless and limitless.

In the area of crime, as with civil rights, Congress's authority was enhanced by its ability to bootstrap the Commerce Clause to other powers and create a mechanism whereby Congress could fight crime generally. Often, what Congress has done is to look at those acts that are traditionally state crimes, and by way of their connection, no matter how tangential, to an activity that may be regulated by the federal government, such as the postal power, make it subject to federal regulation and a federal crime. Examples of federal criminal statutes based on this foundation included the Mann Act, noted above; the National Motor Vehicle Theft Act, noted in *Brooks*; and the Lindbergh law, punishing interstate transportation of kidnapped persons. The connection of congressional power to the Commerce Clause seemed to leave little beyond Congress's control. A good illustration would be the Consumer Credit Protection Act of 1968. This law, passed under the Commerce Clause, went after loan sharks, arguing that prohibitive interest rates on credit affected interstate commerce because loan sharks were integral aspects of organized crime and organized crime had an extremely negative impact on interstate commerce. While there was no doubt that individual creditors' actions might be totally intrastate in nature, looking at the "cumulative effects" doctrine of four decades earlier, the Court determined that these types of activities did in fact affect interstate commerce, and therefore that Congress could regulate the individuals and the class as a whole.

However, in the latter part of the twentieth century, the Court reversed this trend in two notable cases, *United*

States v. Lopez (1995) and *United States v. Morrison* (2000). Striking down the Gun-Free School Zones Act in *Lopez*, the Supreme Court ruled that the act exceeded Congress's Commerce Clause authority. The Court seemed to draw a new dividing line between economic and noneconomic activity for understanding congressional commerce authority. In the eyes of the Court, the law neither regulated "a commercial activity nor contains a requirement that the possession [of guns] be connected in any way to interstate commerce." Gun control on a high school campus, while an admirable goal, was not an acceptable one for Congress. The possession of a gun in a local school zone was not economic activity. And while it might in a very tangential, indirect manner have an effect on interstate commerce, to interpret the commerce authority that broadly would eviscerate the meaning of the Tenth Amendment and the concept of federalism. This law, the Court held, was a purely criminal statute with no connection to commerce, with nothing but its very tangential grasp on the commerce power to authorize it. Too many inferences were necessary to connect it to commerce, and therefore to connect congressional commerce authority to the subject matter in this case.

This restrictive view of congressional power under the Commerce Clause was reiterated five years later in *United States v. Morrison*, when the Court ruled that the Violence against Women Act was an unconstitutional extension of congressional authority. To extend congressional power in the manner of this act would open the door to federal police powers, something not contemplated by the Constitution, either explicitly or implicitly. This would mean Congress could legislate regarding not just violence, but marriage, divorce, child rearing, and so on. Actions by Congress in these areas under its commerce authority would blur if not eradicate the distinction between what is national and what is local. Federalism would die. "In recognizing this fact," the Court ruled, "we preserve one of the few principles that has been consistent since the [Commerce] Clause was adopted. The regulation and punishment of intrastate violence that is not directed at the instrumentalities, channels, or goods involved in interstate commerce has always been the province of the States." Although some narrowing of the commerce authority did thereby occur, Congress's commerce power is nevertheless still wide. Commerce power was extended to congressional attempts to interact with Native Americans. At one point in history, Congress's power to regulate commerce "with the Indian tribes" was almost obliterated. In 1871 Congress forbade the making of any further treaties with Indian tribes. Nevertheless, the clause authorizing Congress to "regulate Commerce with foreign Nations, and among the several States, and with the Indian Tribes," provides the nexus for federal authority over Native Americans. This, coupled with federal treaty-making power, on which the Senate must advise and consent, rests power in Congress. Since *Worcester v. Georgia* (1832), Indian tribes have been recognized as unique. They are sovereign, and in theory they control both tribal members and their territory. The reality is they were never really outside the scope of the United States government completely, and they no longer were fully sovereign after their absorption into the United States, which compromised many of their rights. As the Court noted in 1978, in *United States v. Wheeler*, "The sovereignty that the Indian tribes retain is of a unique and limited character. It exists only at the sufferance of Congress and is subject to complete defeasance." While the power of Congress over Indian affairs is broad, it is not limitless. Congress is conceded power coupled with what the Supreme Court has called a special obligation toward the Indians, developed over time and through the history of their relationship with each other, and the merging of two clauses in Article I that give Congress authority over commerce and treaties.

Additional Powers

Other powers possessed by Congress are simple and to the point. And while some seem to have become less important over time, they all provide important anchors for congressional authority. Many of these powers were granted precisely because they were absent under the Articles of Confederation and were seen as necessary for the centralization of power.

Naturalizaion and Monetary Authority

Congress has the exclusive power to naturalize citizens. Historically, Congress has placed various limitations on who can become a citizen, including limitations based on race and ethnicity. While these two qualifications were eliminated over time, Congress can still create barriers. For example, persons may be denied naturalization on the basis of bad moral character. Such persons have included "habitual drunkards," adulterers, polygamists or advocates of polygamy, gamblers, convicted felons, and even homosexuals (under the term "psychopathic personality" in the Immigration and Nationality Act of 1952).

Another power of Congress revolves around money. Congress is given the authority "to coin Money, regulate the Value thereof, and of foreign Coin." The disorderly state of the money system in the late eighteenth century caused the Founders to attempt to bring some order to it. While order did not necessarily emerge under Congress, it accrued to itself a great deal of power through its authority over money. Going back to *McCulloch v. Maryland*, the words granting this authority have been broadly construed to permit any congressional action that deals with the subject of currency. This includes chartering banks, restraining the right to issue notes, forcing the population to turn in gold and silver coins as well as the power to coin money and block other entities, like the states, from doing likewise.

Postal Authority

The postal authority has provided a window to power. It has often been coupled with other powers to give Congress wider authority. As with many constitutional provisions, in the early years of the Republic power hinged on a single word. In the case of the postal authority, the word was *establish,* in "to establish Post Offices and post Roads." How broad was that power? Some saw it is a means for Congress to build post offices and post roads. Others felt it meant Congress had the power only to designate certain places and pathways already in existence as postal centers or routes. Its meaning was unclear. So when Congress wanted to negotiate a contract with Pennsylvania for the use of a road, its power to do so was part of the authority that came with what the Supreme Court called in *Searight v. Stokes* (1845) being "charged . . . with the transportation of the mails," and under the postal authority, Congress could enter into a compact for use and maintenance of part of a road within the state. But when Congress in 1855 sought to build a bridge under its postal power combined with the commerce power, courts declared it could not. Further debate over this power was precluded by Congress's appropriation of a parcel of land in Cincinnati for the site of a post office, making it federal land, and avoiding the question of whether the federal government could build something on state land, under the postal authority. The real power of the post office seemed to emerge in regulating the use of the mail to prevent the sending of harmful items. This power appears to have been somewhat circumscribed prior to the Civil War. President Andrew Jackson attempted to prevent the use of the mail to send antislavery materials, but this was resisted by Sen. John C. Calhoun of South Carolina, a proslavery and strong states

rights advocate, as giving Congress too much power regarding what could and could not be sent through the mail. It was the states who determined their own security and what could and could not be distributed within the state's borders. He feared that if Congress were allowed to limit what was sent through the mail, it would then be able to decide what had to be circulated, destroying state sovereignty. However, by the late nineteenth century, Jackson's view had begun to prevail.

In 1876 Congress used its authority under the postal clause to exclude from the mail any publication that might "defraud the public or corrupt its morals." A broad view of congressional power in this area was embraced by the Supreme Court, which stated in *Ex Parte Jackson* (1878) that congressional power to establish "postoffices and post-roads embrace[d] the regulation of the entire postal system of the country. Under it, Congress may designate what shall be carried in the mail and what excluded." This meant Congress had the right to make distinctions about what could and could not move through the mail and what could be inspected. While later cases limited this authority through other constitutional provisions such as the First Amendment's free speech right and the Fourth Amendment's right against unreasonable search and seizure, it remained broad and extensive.

Often the postal authority was used in conjunction with war powers. While congressional military authority will be discussed in the next section in connection with how that power is used in light of similar powers held by the president, it is important to first discuss its scope outside the context of its possible conflict with presidential power.

War Power

The focus of congressional military authority seemed to revolve around the power "to declare War." Hamilton declined to focus on this specific constitutional phrase in *Federalist* No. 23 and saw Congress's war authority as the natural extension of all the other powers in Article I, Section 8 combined. Others argued that the power to declare war was one of the enumerated powers from which other authority flowed or that the war power was an inherent attribute of national sovereignty. The Civil War and court cases surrounding the prosecution of that war seemed to suggest that it was a fairly extensive power that extended to "all legislation essential to the prosecution of war with vigor and success, except such as interferes with the command of the forces and conduct of campaigns." However, the Civil War also raised the problem of declaring war and what it meant.

Early drafts of the Constitution provided the power "to make war" instead of giving Congress the power to "declare war." Many delegates, while remembering the difficulty of running the Revolutionary War under the Articles and realizing that a single individual could run a war more efficiently than many, nevertheless feared that an executive could prosecute a war in an unrestricted manner. Considering the importance of establishing checks and balances in the new government, it was essential that some kind of check be instituted here; thus, it was pivotal that the president and the legislature agree before the nation went to war. Congress therefore was given the power to "declare war," which was to balance the need for a president who could act quickly in case of times of emergency but would not to be able to drag the nation into an unwanted conflict. The changing of the word from *make* to *declare* meant the conduct of the war was vested exclusively in the president. The question of who, then, had the power to "make war," despite the change in wording, would be tested on various occasions. During Thomas Jefferson's term as president, the question arose of what happens when hostilities were initiated against the United States, rather than vice versa. To counterattack, was it necessary for Congress to declare war, thereby authorizing presidential action? Jefferson authorized action, but only in a defensive posture. Hamilton argued that once the United States was attacked, it was unnecessary to declare war, as the nation was already *at* war. While Congress passed legislation authorizing presidential actions, war was never declared.

Six decades later similar questions arose as the country erupted into Civil War. As hostilities escalated, and without Congress in session, President Abraham Lincoln acted to counter Confederate hostilities. In addition to Congress's subsequent authorization of Lincoln's actions, as it had done for Jefferson, the Court also weighed in, and in a sharply divided decision in *The Prize Cases*

President Franklin D. Roosevelt signs a declaration of war against Japan on December 8, 1941. (Library of Congress)

(1863), it conceded that the president had acted properly and did not need congressional approval. However, the sharply worded dissent argued that Congress's authorization, declaring the insurrection a war, had been needed to trigger the presidential power for Lincoln to act as he did.

Two military actions seemed to resolve the question of whether a state of war could officially exist without a formal declaration by Congress. The deeper question, which manifested itself in the wake of World War II and the ensuing cold war and military involvement in Vietnam and Iraq, was whether a president could initiate military confrontation without congressional approval.

Another important aspect of Congress's war-making authority was the right to raise and support armies. Considering the historical antecedents of that power, there did not seem to be much question that they could exercise this authority. It was an obvious problem during the Revolutionary War, and the Constitution sought to resolve it. The real issue in the Constitution was not whether the federal government had the authority, but rather whether Congress was the specific branch to exercise that authority.

If an army is to be raised, how is it to be done? The last half of the twentieth century has seen both an all-volunteer army after Vietnam and an army based on a draft before it. Despite some protest, it was not until World War I that legal challenges against conscription manifested themselves. Challenges during the War of 1812 died when the war ended, and anticonscription attitudes during the Civil War manifested themselves in draft riots rather than formal challenges in court.

In 1917 Congress passed the Selective Service Act. The Supreme Court rejected all challenges to it. In essence, the Court argued that it would make no sense for the Constitution to give Congress the power to raise an army and not allow the means necessary, a draft, to exercise that power. While the *Selective Service Cases* (1918) conceded Congress the power to raise an army in wartime, the right to raise such an army without a formal declaration of war or in peacetime has never been resolved.

Arguably, the power to declare war means the power to prepare for war and the power to deal with the inevitable problems that arise at the end of a war. Justice Joseph Story noted this problem when he stated that

> it is important also to consider, that the surest means of avoiding war is to be prepared for it in peace. . . . How could a readiness for war in time of peace be safely prohibited, unless we could in like manner prohibit the preparations and establishments of every hostile nation? . . . It will be in vain to oppose constitutional barriers to the impulse of self-preservation.

The Court seemed to recognize this when, in *Ashwander v. Tennessee Valley Authority* (1936), it conceded Congress had the authority to build and operate a dam and power plant under the National Defense Act of 1916. The Court noted the benefits accrued by the construction performed by the TVA, which constituted what the justices called "national defense assets." Another example of the peacetime use of war powers would be the Atomic Energy Act of 1946, which created a body to oversee research for military and civil purposes. Other instances include the construction of an interstate highway system, as important for the transportation of military hardware as it was for citizens on which to drive their cars, and the National Defense Education Act. In the post–World War II period, the omnipresence of the cold war meant that—although the United States was often not in a shooting war—Congress had the opportunity to pass a great deal of legislation under its war powers and military necessity. Importantly, the Court has validated congressional military power after the cessation of hostilities. Thus, the War Time Prohibition Act, passed after the armistice of 1918 ended World War I, was seen by the Court as an acceptable effort to promote war efficiency since the war emergency was not seen as being over just because the war had officially stopped. After World War II, Congress continued to regulate rents through its war power. In approving the Housing and Rent Control Act, passed two years after World War II had ended, but under the auspices of the war power, in *Woods v. Miller* (1948), Justice Douglas stated that the war power does not necessarily end with the cessation of hostilities and was wide enough "to cope with a current condition of which the war was a direct and immediate cause."

This postwar power, however, was not endless. Six years after the end of World War I a rent control law, previously upheld, was declared no longer valid because the war which validated the law had ended. And even in *Woods*, while Justice Robert Jackson's concurring opinion agreed that the war power was a valid reason for many laws, he was not "willing to hold that war powers may be indefinitely prolonged merely by keeping legally alive a state of war that had in fact ended. I cannot accept the argument that war powers last as long as the effects and consequences of war, for if so they are permanent."

Another problem that arises in wartime but is not necessarily exclusive to a time of war is the delegation of legislative powers. War provides an opening for Congress to delegate authority. While the Court has always been insistent on the importance of separation of powers, it has noted that delegation is sometimes permissible, and that this delegation is more apt to happen during times of emergency. In striking down the National Industrial Recovery Act during the Depression, a unanimous Supreme Court in *Schechter v. United States* (1935) ruled that "Congress is not permitted by the Constitution to abdicate, or to transfer to others, the essential legislative functions with which it is vested." Because the NIRA gave the president the power to make codes and rules, a definitively legislative function, the law was declared unconstitutional. However, in wartime the situation is different because the source of power being tapped into is different than in peacetime.

The Court has never resolved the problem of delegation but has hinted at two different theories. The first theory is based on the fact that the war power is shared in the Constitution, as opposed to the situation in *Schechter*, in which the power used to pass the NIRA was the Congress's Commerce Clause authority. Some jurists argue that therefore Congress, in contrast to the circumstances in *Schechter*, does not really delegate war power. Because war power is a different power, it is exercised differently. However, the second theory challenges that argument on the grounds that it overlooks the fact that the Constitution expressly vests the war power as a legislative power in Congress. Regarding the latter theory, it has been suggested that Congress's power to delegate in wartime is limited as in other situations but that the existence of a state of war is a factor weighing in favor of the validity of the delegation.

Both of these ideas came into play in *Hirabayashi v. United States* (1943), the decision upholding a curfew against Japanese Americans in the wake of the bombing of Pearl Harbor. Chief Justice Harlan Stone's opinion alluded to both theories of wartime delegation. Thus, it is still not clear exactly what Congress can concede to the president during war. Because the president and Congress often work together in wartime, it is hard to determine if any delegation is really happening. It is not until Congress formally challenges presidential actions, or refuses to accede to presidential wishes, that real problems occur.

Investigatory Power

When problems do occur between Congress and the president, or between any other part of government and society, one of Congress's most important powers is triggered. No provision of the Constitution expressly authorizes the Congress to make investigations and hold hearings. But the Framers understood that if a system of checks and balances was to function and the legislature was to hold the executive accountable, then Congress needed a mechanism by which it could do that.

James Wilson, one of the Framers and a future Supreme Court justice, talked about the need for the House and Senate to be able to investigate. They must be able, he said, to "diligently inquire into grievances, arising both from men and things." George Mason spoke of legislators not only as lawmakers but as men with "inquisitorial powers." Despite these and other allusions to congressional power to investigate, force people to appear before the legislature, and punish them for nonresponsiveness, the Constitution does not explicitly provide for power to investigate, issue subpoenas, and punish for contempt. The gap created by the lack of explicit power was filled by implicit recognition of such power and practice.

In the First Congress, the House wasted no time in debating a request to investigate Robert Morris's conduct as superintendent of finance in the Confederation Congress. The Senate also took up the matter. The House authorized a select committee to investigate, but the Senate authorized the president to conduct a probe on the matter. The House investigation was significant because it established that if needed, a congressional investigation could be conducted to acquire information so that, in the words of James Madison, Congress could "do justice to the country and to public officers."

An important part of investigation is the ability to access documents that another branch may not wish to give up. In 1790 Alexander Hamilton, the secretary of the Treasury, asked Congress for financial compensation for Baron von Steuben, who had fought in the Revolution. The Congress demanded documents from Hamilton, some of which were withheld. Congress passed the compensation bill because it felt it had enough information, but it was apparent that if the administration did not cooperate, Congress could refuse to pass the bill, giving the investigatory procedure new power.

Two years later a major investigation began regarding a defeat of Maj. Gen. Arthur St. Clair by Indian tribes in the Northwest Territory and the heavy casualties that accompanied that loss. The investigating committee was authorized to "call for such persons, papers, and records, as may be necessary to assist their inquiries." The Cabinet seemed to understand that the panel might ask for certain papers and it would be proper for the executive to concede to such demands, within reason. In this case the Cabinet concluded that all papers requested could be produced.

The House committee examined papers, interviewed department heads and other witnesses, and received written comments from General St. Clair. Importantly, the principle of executive privilege was established because the Cabinet had acted under the principle that it had the right to refuse papers that would be injurious to the public. Because in this case the Cabinet did not consider the papers harmful, it produced them.

In the following decade, the House engaged in an investigation and exercised its contempt power. Robert Randall and Charles Whitney were accused of trying to bribe members of the House. The

House decided there was enough evidence of an attempt to "corrupt its proceedings" and passed a resolution ordering the sergeant at arms to arrest Randall and Whitney, and hold them until the House could act. Randall was brought to the House, publicly reprimanded, and held in custody for one week.

In the late 1790s, the Senate opened an investigation surrounding an article in a newspaper. William Duane, the editor of the newspaper in question, was ordered to appear in the Senate. After appearing he demanded counsel, which was granted. Duane then refused to return and was held in contempt by the Senate. A warrant was issued for his arrest, but the sergeant at arms was unable to capture him. After the Senate asked the president to pursue prosecution of Duane via the judicial system, he was indicted but never convicted.

With the investigatory authority apparently in place, within two decades the Supreme Court moved to place some limitations on this implied power. In 1821 Col. John Anderson, accused of attempting to bribe a member of the House, was held in contempt and in violation of the privileges of the House. He was reprimanded by the Speaker and released from custody. Anderson sued the sergeant at arms for assault and battery and false imprisonment, citing the lack of authority for the House to issue a warrant.

The Supreme Court held that the House action was valid. The power to punish for contempt of the chamber, it ruled, was necessary for purposes of self-preservation. The Court also stated that the basis of the House's power "must be either in virtue of the Constitution of the United States, of usage and precedent, or as inherent in, and incidental to, legislative bodies," affirming the existence of such a power, and that it could be expanded by statute. Also, the Court cited the Necessary and Proper Clause as allowing this action, but stated that the power to punish was limited, not endless, especially the power of imprisonment, which ended when the congressional session ended.

This limitation on the ability to punish was very severe when it was applied at or near the end of a session. To resolve this problem, Congress in 1857 passed legislation which mandated that witnesses had to appear when summoned by either chamber. Failure to appear, or a refusal to answer a question, was a criminal offense against the United States with prescribed penalties. The Supreme Court has rejected any challenges to this act, noting it supplements power already retained by the Congress. When it had the chance, the Court narrowly defined the legislative power to investigate. In *Kilbourn v. Thompson* (1881), the Court noted that Congress, in this case the House of Representatives, did not have investigatory power unless the investigation could "result in . . . valid legislation on the subject to which the inquiry referred." The Court was concerned that if the investigation was not focused, it would be "fruitless" and open the door to frivolous investigation into people's personal lives.

Kilbourn, however, did not begin a trend toward limiting Congress's investigatory power. In 1927 congressional activities again came under Court purview during an investigation into executive actions concerning the Justice Department. Importantly, the Court recognized a congressional "power of inquiry." It saw the investigation as an "essential and appropriate auxiliary of the legislative function." In contrast to *Kilbourn*, the 1927 decision in *McGrain v. Daugherty* widened the investigative power so that it was not confined to investigations focused on possible legislation. Daugherty challenged his citation for contempt, saying he did not need to appear at the hearing he had skipped since the purpose of the investigation had nothing to do with the committee's legislative purpose. In rejecting his argument, the Court talked in terms of "legislative purposes," which broadened the scope of Congress's power, establishing a presumption the congressional investigations have a legislative purpose and are therefore legitimate. Legislation was not a necessary outcome to validate the investigation. Rather, the ability to have hearings, and the process to enforce it, is a necessary element of the legislative function. For the Congress to be able to function properly, it needs information, and how else is it to acquire such information? The Court stated this was part of the historical duties of a legislature, and the Constitution implicitly included this power by creating the Congress. In addition, the Court stated that since one of the Congress's jobs was oversight, in

line with the checks and balances system of government, such an investigation as took place in this case was legitimate. Later cases reiterated this point by noting that the investigatory power is so essential to the legislative function as to be implied from the general vesting of legislative power in Congress. In the late 1950s in *Watkins v. United States* (1957), the Court reiterated that congressional power to investigate is very broad. Being an inherent part of the basic legislative process, it includes a broad right to inquire into current laws and laws that might be needed. Congress has the right to explore general problems in society, be they social, economic, or political, as part of an attempt to remedy them. This meant that in pursuing these ends, Congress could investigate all aspects of the federal government "to expose corruption, inefficiency or waste." In *Barenblatt v. United States* (1959), the Court noted that the power of inquiry was a historic power that Congress had used throughout its existence to investigate a multitude of subjects. As Justice John Harlan wrote in *Barenblatt*, the "scope of the power of inquiry, in short, is as penetrating and far-reaching as the potential power to enact and appropriate under the Constitution."

Wherever the behavior of individuals is subject to congressional regulation, then Congress's power of inquiry exists, so that in practice the areas of any individual's life immune from inquiry are probably fairly limited. This was very obvious during the cold war, especially in the period immediately following World

War II, when both the Senate and the House assumed new investigatory roles. In the late 1940s and the 1950s the House Un-American Activities Committee and its Senate counterpart under Sen. Joseph McCarthy focused its probes on possible subversion directed at the U.S. government. This signaled a new and larger intrusion into the private lives of citizens. No one has questioned Congress's right to pass laws that protect the country and its citizens against danger from abroad, including espionage and sedition. Going back to 1798 and the passage of the Alien and Sedition Acts, Congress was active in trying to protect the nation from enemies abroad, and from within as well. However, it seemed that congressional power in this regard expanded in the postwar period as Congress investigated almost any every of personal life, in every area from labor to Hollywood films to education. But in those years it was not so much what Congress investigated that angered people, but rather how Congress did it. In the end, despite admonitions against such broad authority, it appears there is little Congress cannot investigate. But occasionally, limits do emerge.

For example, *Watkins v. United States* (1957) (noted before) dealt with a challenge to a HUAC investigation in which witnesses were asked to inform on others. Chief Justice Earl Warren noted that while the congressional power to investigate was broad, it was not unlimited. Congress did not have the authority to expose individuals' private affairs with no justification, and the justification had

to be in terms of the functions of Congress. An inquiry could not be an end in itself; there had to be some relation between the investigation and a legitimate task of Congress. Also, Warren noted in strong words that neither the First Amendment nor any part of the Bill of Rights could not be run over roughshod in Congress's pursuit of information. Most justices have conceded this broad power but agreed with both Harlan's comment from *Barenblatt*, noted above, and Warrren in *Watkins*, who did not question the basic power, and noted its broad reach.

POWERS DENIED CONGRESS

As important as the powers of Congress are, what Congress cannot do is also important. One of the key powers that seems to be denied Congress is the ability to suspend the writ of habeus corpus. Article I, Section 9, clause 2 notes that "the Privilege of the Writ of Habeas Corpus shall not be suspended, unless when in Cases of Rebellion or Invasion the public Safety may require it." At the Constitutional Convention, initial proposals spoke of vesting authority to suspend the writ in the Congress. This language did not survive, and the language quoted above, a more general proscription, was adopted.

Nevertheless, early commentators such as Joseph Story seemed to assume that Congress had this power and noted so in *Ex Parte Bollman* (1807). President Lincoln ignored these opinions when he suspended the writ of habeus corpus during the Civil War, arguing that because Congress was not in session, he could act. However, the political fallout was heavy, and he rapidly sought and received congressional approval of his actions in a law of March 1863. Suspension of the writ was authorized three other times, on apparent order of Congress. During Reconstruction, the privilege of the writ was suspended in nine counties of South Carolina to help deal with the rising power of the Ku Klux Klan. In the early 1900s Congress suspended it in the Philippines, an American territory at that time. Finally, it was suspended in Hawaii during World War II.

The question is, what is actually suspended when suspension operates? In *Ex parte Milligan* (1866), the Court sidestepped the issue. First, it said suspension of privilege of writ of habeas corpus does not suspend the writ itself. The Court still needs to make a decision. The writ issues as a matter of course, and then the Court moves forward on whether to deny the writ. Second, it stated that military rule, under which Milligan had been arrested, could not supersede civilian courts in areas where the civil courts remained open and operational, and thus Milligan could apply for and receive a writ of habeas corpus. The ability to suspend the writ seems, therefore, to be a qualified privilege.

The Constitution is more specific regarding bills of attainder and ex post facto laws. Article 1, Section 9, clause 3 provides that "no Bill of Attainder or ex post facto Law shall be passed." It was adopted unanimously at the Philadelphia Convention with no debate. Dealing with bills of attainder first, they are statutes that single out an individual or a specific group to be punished without a trial. Historically, it was—prior to the nineteenth century—a parliamentary act that carried with it capital punishment for those who attempted to overthrow the government in England. The use of bills of attainder was not limited to England. During the American Revolution, all thirteen state legislatures passed statutes directed against the Tories, among them a large number of bills of attainder.

Historically, the Supreme Court's aversion to bills of attainder is evidenced in three cases. In *Ex parte Garland* (1867), the Court struck down a statute that required attorneys to swear they had not participated in the Confederacy and the rebellion against the United States before they could practice in federal courts. The statute was struck down as a legislative act inflicting punishment on a specific group for the actions its members had taken. The next use of the clause barring bills of attainder to declare a congressional act unconstitutional was in *United States v. Lovett* (1946). Here the Court struck down a rider to an appropriations bill that denied the use of the appropriated money to pay the salaries of people whom the House wanted fired because they had been classified as subversive.

Subsequently, a sharply divided Court in *United States v. Brown* (1965) declared a law unconstitutional for making it a crime for a member of the Communist Party to serve as an officer or as an employee of a labor union. Chief Justice Warren's majority opinion acknowledged congressional authority under the Commerce Clause to protect the economy from harm, as this statute purported to do. However, it could not, under this guise, make it a crime to choose a class of persons—members of the Communist Party—as being forbidden to hold union office. Warren argued that the bill of attainder clause was not supposed to be a narrow, technical prohibition, but was passed in part to strengthen the principle of separation of powers. It reflected the Framers' belief that the legislative branch would not be able to function properly as politically independent judges and juries in trying to discern the blameworthiness of people and fixing punishment on them.

As James Madison commented in *Federalist* No. 44, it was not just bills of attainder, but also ex post facto laws too that were contrary "to the first principles of the social compact, and to every principle of sound legislation." When the Constitution was adopted, most people understood the term *ex post facto laws* to mean laws that were retroactive, in other words, statutes governing past actions. *Calder v. Bull* (1798), one of the Supreme Court's earliest decisions, limited the term to penal and criminal statutes. Any statute that makes what was an innocent action at the time a criminal act after the fact, or increases the punishment for violating a law after the crime has been committed, is considered an ex post facto law and forbidden by the Constitution. As with bills of attainder, ex post facto laws seem to breach the separation of powers gap by handing the legislature too much power and opening the door to tyranny.

Despite guarantees articulated in the *Federalist Papers*, many Americans feared the new powers given to the federal government generally and the Congress specifically. These fears were evident in the demand for a Bill of Rights to protect individual liberty from federal encroachment and a guarantee of federalism in the Tenth Amendment.

While on paper it may seem that the government was one of limited powers, it would be how the Congress used those new-found powers and how the other branches checked each others' powers that would prove whether Madison and his supporters' reassurances were real or hollow. All of these powers were meaningless unless Congress used them to create law and policy, and it is the process of lawmaking that gave meaning to the various provisions of Article I and allowed them to come to life

FURTHER READING

Arnold, R. Douglas. *The Logic of Congressional Action.* New Haven, CT: Yale University Press, 1990.

Asbell, Bernard. *The Senate Nobody Knows.* New York: Doubleday, 1978.

Baker, Richard A. *The Senate of the United States: A Bicentennial History.* Malabar, FL: Krieger Publishing, 1988.

Costello, George. *CRS Report for Congress: Legislative Powers of Congress: A Brief Reference Guide.*

Damascus, MD: Penny Hill Press, May 13, 1998.

Halstead, T. J. *CRS Report for Congress: Overview of the Impeachment Process,* Damascus, MD: Penny Hill Press, April 20, 2005.

Peterson, R. Eric. *CRS Report for Congress: Roles and Duties of a Member of Congress.* Damascus, MD: Penny Hill Press, October 10, 2006.

Remini. Robert. *The House: The History of the House of Representatives.* New York: Harper Collins, 2006.

Sharp, James Roger. *American Politics in the Early Republic.* New Haven, CT: Yale University Press, 1993.

Thomas, Kenneth R., and Todd B. Tatelman. *CRS Report for Congress: Power to Regulate Commerce: Limits in Congressional Power.* Damascus, MD: Penny Hill Press, July 17, 2005.

Zelizer, Julian E., ed. *The American Congress.* New York: Houghton Mifflin, 2004.

3

STRUCTURE AND PROCESS

The focus of this chapter is upon how a bill becomes a law. Making law is the essence of Congress. When Congress is in session and doing its job, it legislates—it creates and passes laws. The chapter will discuss the various intricacies of the legislative process, including the committee system, how legislation makes its way to the floor, and the differences in the workings of each house.

Article I (as noted in the chapter 2) vests the power to legislate, to make law, in the Congress of the United States. Since that is its primary purpose, Congress is often measured by how often it meets and how much legislation it passes, which is then used to determine how effective a body it is. Thus, various Congresses are labeled as "do-nothing" because of their sparse meeting schedules or meager legislative records. While on its face Congress's job of passing laws may seem simple, it will become obvious that the path from proposal to law can be complicated and filled with potholes.

Perhaps the first major roadblock is that Congress is not a single body, but rather two independent and—in contrast to the British House of Lords and House of Commons—equal chambers. In essence, Congress is two legislative assemblies that must both agree for a proposal to become law. However, such agreement often is difficult, since each chamber has different charges, varying rules of procedure, and distinct traditions.

Because of these differences and the structure and procedures of Congress, it often does not act as an efficient, homogenous unit. Rather, it is two bodies in conflict with one another, creating a cumbersome and difficult path to legislation. One commentator has noted that the U.S. legislative process is a form of Social Darwinism, where only a few survive the meat-grinder process that takes legislation from inception to law.

THE DIFFERENT PERSPECTIVES OF REPRESENTATIVES AND SENATORS

Part of the difficulty in passing laws stems from the very design of the Congress itself—not only how Congress was meant to function, but how each house

The Capitol building in Washington, D.C., is where Congress holds its sessions. Built on a site chosen by George Washington and begun in 1793, the building was not completed until 1829 and has had many additions since then. (Becky Snyder)

fulfilled that function. In designing Congress, the Framers viewed each house as serving a different role. They saw the House of Representatives as the body most closely connected to the population. Because the House was directly elected every two years (more frequently than any other part of the federal government), it was expected to be more accountable and therefore more responsive to the American people. It was assumed that representatives would have a close contact with the people they represented and thereby be able to reflect their constituents' needs. Therefore, as attitudes and society changed, the House would reflect those shifts.

In contrast, senators face reelection only once every six years. Whereas the entire House turned over every two years, the Senate was seen as an institution with greater continuity, since there was a maximum turnover of only one-third of its members every other year. This greater continuity would theoretically place the Senate above the vagaries of public opinion unlike the House and make it possible for senators to avoid regularly placating the voters. In addition, because in the beginning senators were not directly elected by the people, their mission would, the Founders believed, encompass more general and national concerns than that of House members, and thus senators would be able to look beyond the boundaries of the districts from which they came. The Framers theorized that this would enable the Senate to balance the House and provide a more stable leadership, with one chamber reflecting the concerns of the voters and the other focusing on broader concerns. These differences between the chambers have resulted in two different approaches to the lawmaking process on both a theoretical and practical level.

In theory, the House is meant to reflect the wishes of the majority of the American people in the lawmaking process. House rules allow the majority to dominate so that the people's views can be acted upon, unblocked by the minority. This majoritarian domination is reflected in the leadership which is often drawn from those states with the greatest number of representatives, whereas in the Senate, leadership often comes from less populous states, and its rules are designed to reflect a certain independent, and at times antimajoritarian, view. The minority party in the Senate can wield far more power and have greater success than the minority in the House in directing debate and agenda. Senate rules and traditions such as unlimited debate help make this possible.

EVOLUTION OF PROCEDURE

The parliamentary procedures in both houses start with the standing rules. There are fifty-one standing rules in the House (in the *House Rules and Manual*) and forty-two in the Senate (in the *Senate Manual*). Precedents fill the gaps in those rules. Past rulings by presiding officers, often made to answer anomalies in the standing rules or explain discrepancies, create precedent. These precedents, which are regularly catalogued and combined with past rulings, have the force of standing rules when determining proper procedure. At times this system is very complicated, and even more so when actions on the floor proceed according to standards established in a piece of legislation (for example, the Congressional Budget Act of 1974) rather than the normal procedural rules.

In specifying that Congress would "make" the law, Article I failed to designate how. The Constitution is silent on the procedure to be used. The bulk of Article I deals with what the Congress can legislate about. It was left to the two houses to design and create a system by which they made the law.

Any diagram of "how a bill becomes a law" explains that a piece of legislation, once introduced, moves through subcommittee and committee, then to the House and Senate floors, then to a House-Senate conference, and finally to the president for his signature or veto.

In a technical sense, of course, the diagram is accurate. But it paints an incomplete picture of how complicated and, at times, chaotic the legislative process can be. The fate of any legislative proposal lies in not only marshalling support in one of the houses of Congress, but in then convincing the other house that it is necessary legislation and persuading the executive branch, too. The senators and representatives must work hard to get a bill passed, keeping a constant eye on their colleagues in the other chamber and the White House.

Despite the fact the legislative process sometimes appears to be a confusing and complicated muddle, there is a structure to the proceedings; and the structure, while not as simple or smooth as a textbook diagram suggests, is a set framework. It is the complexity of the process and the politics of it that create the path by which law is made.

The rules in both houses developed to reflect the needs of each house, demonstrating how the two houses are very different institutions. House rules demonstrate the majoritarian influences noted above, so that simple majorities can dominate action in the House. The rules are both a product of and enable this behavior. The rules of the House run nearly seven hundred pages. The Senate rules are brief (approximately a hundred pages) and complement the chamber's desire for a more freewheeling open debate and enhance the ability of minorities to at times dominate business. In the Senate, in contrast to the House where simple majorities rule the day, only supermajorities can limit debate or amendments. It is easier to make rule changes in the House than in the Senate.

House rules make it more difficult to circumvent committees; more strictly limit participation on the floor; and give the majority a greater ability to act, when confronted with an obstructionist minority.

In the end, the legislative process is a product of over two centuries of rule making and precedents. It is the evolution of the process that makes it difficult, at times, to understand. From time to time both houses have adjusted rules and procedures to deal with problems and issues of the day. But because past decisions have become incorporated into the rules at large, confusion can result. Over time, both houses have revised the rules by which they operate. Those rules, in essence, have become how a bill becomes a law. The rules and procedures that governed the House and the Senate became disorganized and created problems in understanding how the system worked. Archaic forms and modern inventions often mixed, leading to confusion and misunderstanding.

SOURCES OF LEGISLATION

As noted above, the chief function of Congress is to make law. Because an important component in designing the government was creating a system of separation of powers and checks and balances, Congress was seen as the sole legislative body. However, while it is Congress's responsibility to *make* the law, it is not the sole *initiator* of legislation. There are multiple sources of origin. At the grassroots level, both the people themselves and their local representatives in state legislatures can suggest laws. Indeed, the Constitution guarantees American citizens the right of petition. Congress regularly receives individual petitions as well as memorials from state legislatures. While a member of either chamber may introduce the proposals in these petitions, they have no obligation to do so.

Another important source of legislation, especially in the past century, has been the White House. More and more, the president is the source and inspiration for a great deal of legislation, including even budgetary legislation, which by the terms of the Constitution would appear to be the sole province of the House. The chief executive communicates his ideas to Congress in messages that often contain drafts of a proposed bill. While some critics challenge this procedure as counter to the notion of separation of powers built into the Constitution, Article II, Section 3 does obligate the president to report to Congress from time to time on the "State of the Union."

In recent times, the president has fulfilled this constitutional obligation by personally addressing a joint session of Congress. Otherwise, and especially in the nineteenth century, the president often communicated with the legislature by sending written messages to the other end of Pennsylvania Avenue. Especially in the latter part of the twentieth century, the State of the Union message has become a preview of the upcoming agenda of the president, to be proposed in a series of bills.

FORMS OF LEGISLATION

While the system allows for outside input, only members of Congress can formally introduce a piece of legislation, which they can do in one of four ways: the bill (the most common form), the joint resolution, the concurrent resolution, and the simple resolution.

A bill is a legislative proposal that, if passed, becomes a law. A bill's subject matter can be private or public. (Private bills differ from public because the scope is narrower, usually providing a specified benefit for specific individuals.) The vast majority of congressional legislation takes the form of a bill. (Both houses number their bills sequentially, using the designation of "S." and "H.R.") When passed by both chambers in identical form and signed by the president (or repassed by Congress over a presidential veto), they become laws. Bills pertain to a wide range of subjects. They usually authorize or reauthorize federal policies and programs. Sometimes a bill may amend an existing law (although this can also be done by joint resolution). Bills are used to create federal departments or agencies or alter the structure of ones already in place. All revenue legislation begins as bills from the House of Representatives. Annual general appropriations and supplemental appropriations take the form of bills, although the latter can also be done by joint resolution. A reconciliation bill alters the spending authority pursuant to the directives in a congressional budget resolution.

Joint resolutions can have the same effect as bills and become law. As with bills, joint resolutions need the assent of both houses and presidential action. In practical impact, there is no real difference between a joint resolution and a bill. As the *House Rules and Manual* (section 397) says, joint resolutions refer to "incidental, inferior or unusual purposes of legislation." The most obvious example is a declaration of war. A continuing resolution extends appropriations for specified purposes until regular appropriations are enacted. Wartime again provides a good example, as armies may need more money than originally thought as a conflict continues. Joint resolutions are used to transfer appropriations and adjust debt limits.

Some of the things accomplished by joint resolution, because they do not act like a bill which becomes a law, do not need the assent of the president. For example, Congress decides through joint resolution when it will meet. Finally, constitutional amendments may be initiated via the joint resolution with a two-thirds majority vote in both houses. Presidential signature is not needed in this case, and the proposed amendment becomes law when it is ratified by three-quarters of the states.

Concurrent resolutions (designated H.Con.Res. and S.Con.Res.) are usually employed to articulate what is called the "sense of the Congress" on a given issue. This expresses "facts, principles, opinions or purposes of the two houses." Other uses for concurrent resolutions include creating a joint committee or correcting the language of measures already passed by one or both houses. Like a bill or joint resolution, a concurrent resolution must pass both chambers in identical language. However, in contrast to the previous forms of legislation, a concurrent resolution is not sent to the White House for a presidential signature nor is it signed by the leaders of either body. Concurrent resolutions, while not attaining the status of law, are not frivolous acts and can have a major impact on governmental business, such as the concurrent resolution that is passed to establish the annual spending and revenue levels. Other uses for the concurrent resolution involve the recessing of either house for more than three days, correcting conference reports, and providing for a joint session of Congress.

The fourth form of congressional action is simple resolutions, which do not constitute laws. They represent the views of only one house and are not submitted to the other chamber. Often, these resolutions are used to take care of simple housekeeping matters, such as creating a new committee or expressing the opinion of one of the chambers on an important issue. In the House of Representatives, simple resolutions are used for special rules for considering a measure, known as "order of business" resolutions. Principally, the House uses the simple resolution to do what is known as securing a "chamber's rights, safety, dignity or integrity of proceedings." Something called a "blue slip resolution" returns a Senate tax measure as in violation of the House privilege to originate such measures. When requesting information from the executive branch in a "resolution of inquiry," the House predominantly does so by simple resolution.

The Senate usually uses simple resolutions to establish a standing order and commemorate certain events. The latter used to be done by joint resolution. The Senate also, when ratifying a treaty, does so by a simple resolution, since no action by the House is needed.

Both Senate and House use the vehicle of simple resolutions for a variety of actions. Thus, adopting and amending the chamber's rules and electing committee members or chamber officers, fall under their umbrella. A simple resolution is required when expelling (a two-thirds vote being needed), censuring, or disciplining a member and deciding a disputed contest over a seat in one of the chambers. Other actions carried out with simple resolutions are creating a special or select committee, spending money from a chamber's contingent fund, providing notification to the other house or another branch of the federal government, issuing citations for contempt of Congress, and authorizing a response to a subpoena by members or employees.

INTRODUCING A BILL OR RESOLUTION

Whether as a bill or joint resolution, a piece of legislation must be introduced. In the House of Representatives, any member (including representatives from the fifty states, delegates (the District of Columbia, American Samoa, Guam, and the U.S. Virgin Islands are represented by one delegate each), or the resident commissioner from Puerto Rico) can do so. The process is simple and requires merely that the introducing member place the proposed legislation in the hopper, traditionally a simple wooden box situated either next to the rostrum in the House chamber or on the clerk's desk.

In the Senate, a member has two options. He or she can simply present the proposed legislation to one of the clerks at the presiding officer's desk or, more formally, introduce the proposed bill or resolution on the floor of the Senate. When the latter method is used, usually the senator makes some remarks introducing the proposed legislation.

Both House and Senate rules require that all bills be read three times before passage. This is a traditional parliamentary procedure. In the House the official introduction of the bill and its printing by number and title into the *Congressional Record* qualifies as the first reading. The second reading occurs when debate on the floor begins. The third reading takes place just before the vote on final passage. Senate rules require that bills and resolutions be read twice, on different legislative days, before they are referred to committee. The third reading occurs following debate on the floor and voting on amendments.

COMMITTEES

After a House bill receives an official number, the rules demand that the bill be assigned to a committee by the Speaker. It is with the referral to the committee that the most important part of any bill's life begins.

The committee system is the mechanism by which investigation of the merits of the bill takes place. This is done in a forum, usually public, that includes an opportunity for witnesses to be subpoenaed and heard and for background investigation by committee members and their staff. Twenty standing committees in the House and sixteen in the Senate (plus numerous subcommittees, joint committees, and ad hoc committees, numbering almost 250) perform the bulk of this work.

Each committee has a specific jurisdiction. This is not as simple as it sounds, because House and Senate rules allow bills to be classified in over two hundred different ways. These classifications far outnumber the number of committees, creating overlap and, at times, conflict. Until 1975 the Speaker of the House, who is charged with referring a bill to a committee, had to single out one committee. Since then, House rules permit a bill to be referred to more than one committee. Each committee can consider those parts of the proposed legislation that fall under its jurisdiction. This change in procedure means more overlap may occur and, consequently, more conflict between committees.

Members and Chairpersons

In the House, committee membership is determined by party. The number of members of each party on each committee is determined by the majority party. One exception to this rule is the Committee on Standards of Official Conduct, which is split fifty-fifty. The party caucuses of each party nominate members for each standing committee at the be-

ginning of each Congress. The general rule (with some exceptions) is that House members may serve on only two committees and four subcommittees. In addition, members are limited regarding the number of committee chairs they may hold. In the Senate, the chair of each committee and a majority of its members represent the majority party. The duty of the chair is to control the committee's business. Each party assigns its own members to committees, and each committee distributes its members among its subcommittees. The Senate places limits on the number and types of panels any one senator may serve on and chair. The limits in the Senate on number of committees are more complicated, with committees and panels broken down in classifications of A, B, and C. Senators may serve on two Class A committees, on one Class B panel, and on an unlimited number of Class C panels.

In the House, the committee chair was historically selected on a seniority basis. Over time that system broke down, and from 1975 to 1995, party caucuses determined who became committee chairs. In 1995 Republicans established term limits on committee chairs in the House. The rules of the House require that committee chairpersons be elected from nominations submitted by the majority party caucus at the commencement of each Congress.

With the beginning of each Congress, a resolution appoints Senate committees with the power to continue their work until successors are appointed. As in the House, the committee chair is a member of the majority party. He or she is chosen by order of the Senate and is usually, but not always, the senior member in point of service among the committee's majority members. In addition to the committees in their respective houses, both senators and representatives serve on joint committees.

Schedules, Referrals, and Jurisdictions

Generally, each committee adopts its own rules. While there is some variance, they must not be inconsistent with the standing rules in their respective houses. These rules govern the procedure of the committee. The rules of each committee are published in the *Congressional Record* each year.

Committees tend to meet on a regular basis. It is not, however, uncommon for them to meet irregularly at the behest of their chair, especially when special issues arise that call their attention. When a committee meets, there are scheduled issues to address, but any matter within the committee's jurisdiction may be considered. Often, investigative functions will overlap due to both jurisdictional conflicts and political considerations. For example, when the president's authorization of warrantless wiretaps by the National Security Agency was revealed late in 2005, it became an issue for both the Committee on Foreign Affairs and the Judiciary Committee. Both had jurisdiction, and politics helped determine decisions about the investigation and its scope.

Once a bill has been introduced in Congress and has been referred to com-

mittee, it is officially entered on the committee's Calendar of Business. Since most committees have standing subcommittees, pending bills are often referred to those smaller panels for further study. When the bill involves a new or novel subject, a committee will create an ad hoc subcommittee to study the topic.

The jurisdictions of the standing committees are spelled out in House Rule 10 and Senate Rule 25, and referrals are fairly routine. For example, banking bills go to the banking committees in both houses, and so on. However, many issues that come before Congress touch on the jurisdictions of multiple committees. Sometimes the authors of a bill try to take advantage of overlapping jurisdiction by attempting to get their bill referred to the committee that they feel will be most sympathetic to it.

When multiple subjects are involved, as is often the case, the Senate committee receiving the bill is the one that normally deals with the bulk of the material covered by it. That is despite the fact that the bill may involve issues outside that committee's purview. However, in the House, the Speaker may designate one committee as the primary committee and the other as secondary. When this is done, the designated committees can deal only with those sections of the legislation over which each has jurisdiction. The House also permits what are called sequential and split referrals. In the first case, the bill moves from one committee to the next as each one completes its consideration of the proposal and then passes it on, although nothing forces one committee to move it on to

Newly elected Speaker of the House Nancy Pelosi holds up a gavel at the U.S. Capitol on January 4, 2007. (AP/Wide World Photos)

———————

the next. The final committee can then report the bill to the floor of the House. A split referral breaks down the bill so each committee receives only those titles of the bill that coincide with the committee's jurisdiction. All of the titles must be reported to the floor for the bill to be considered. If any part is held up in committee, the bill dies.

The Speaker of the House makes the final decision on how to refer a bill. This decision is usually determined by her or his personal and her or his party's political agenda and any advice she or he may receive from the parliamentarian. A bill not favored by the Speaker may go to

more than one committee, as the more committees consider a bill, the harder it is to move it onto the floor for a general vote.

Committees are not obligated to move on a bill. Once a bill has been referred to a committee, it remains there until the committee either reports it out (which requires a majority vote of the committee membership) or has it "discharged from further consideration," ending its life in the committee. In the ordinary course of a congressional session, committees cannot act on all the large numbers of bills they receive. How and when a bill gets acted upon by a committee is up to the chair, who for political and strategic reasons will schedule some bills and disregard others. An important part of the political games that are played in Congress revolve around the ability of members to convince their committee chairs to consider various bills. The decision to bury a bill is its death knell, since there is very little recourse for opposing members on the committee.

Hearings and Markup

One of the major functions of committees and subcommittees is to conduct hearings regarding legislation that they are considering. These hearings help to hone the final draft of the proposal before it is reported to the full Senate or House. There is no set length for these hearings, and the number of witnesses as well as the days committed to the hearings are at the discretion of the chair.

All committee and subcommittee hearings, with very few exceptions, must be open to the public. Hearings must be publicly announced, giving at least one week's notice of the date, place, and subject matter. "Open to the public" usually means televised, which grants access to great numbers of people. The exception to this requirement is when the committee (or subcommittee), in open session and with a majority present, determines that national security or sensitive law enforcement information would be compromised because of the evidence to be presented.

After hearings have been completed, a committee engages in what is called the "markup session" if it is going to move forward on the legislation under consideration. In this session, the committee members have the opportunity to make changes in the proposal. The term *markup* refers to the fact that members actually write their changes on the bill. Amendments to bills at this stage keep the essence of the original but shape it to meet the needs and concerns of the committee members. Sometimes they may feel a bill is necessary but that the proposal in its existing form is unacceptable and not fixable, so they create a brand new bill. This new product is introduced by the committee's chairman and referred to as a clean bill, with the committee then voting on whether or not to refer it to the floor.

Disposition of a Bill

With the markup session completed, the full committee must choose what to do with the bill or resolution: report it favorably with or without amendments; submit an adverse report; report the bill

without recommendation; or vote not to make a report of any kind. Any changes made in the bill (such as insertions, deletions, substitute sections, and so on) are indicated in the reprinted bill that is reported with italics for any additions and a line drawn through the portions that have been stricken. The original text is printed in roman type. This enables members outside the committee to understand the alteration process the bill has gone through.

In the end, nothing compels a committee to act on a bill. While there are mechanisms to extract a piece of legislation from a committee to send it to another committee for reconsideration, many proposals simply die in the committee to which they first go.

Whether the committee makes changes because of subcommittee recommendations, member input, or new information, committee amendments are still subject to approval by the House as a whole. It has the right to accept or reject these changes.

If the committee decides to report the bill favorably, it can do so in various ways. First, it can send the bill to the floor without amendments. Second, the committee can introduce and report a clean bill. Committees may authorize the chair to postpone votes in certain circumstances. If the committee has approved extensive amendments, it may decide to report the original bill with one "amendment in the nature of a substitute," consisting of all the amendments previously adopted, or it may report a new bill incorporating those amendments, presenting it as a clean bill. The new bill is introduced and, after referral back to the committee, is reported favorably to the house by the committee.

A committee may table a bill, or not take action on it, thereby preventing further progress on a bill. Because of this, adverse reports or reports without recommendation to the floor of the chamber by a committee are unusual.

If the committee votes to report the bill to the house, the committee staff writes a committee report. The report covers a lot of ground. It explains the purpose and scope of the bill and any amendments made by the committee to the original bill. The report spells out what changes to existing law may occur. It projects any additional costs that may be incurred by the government because of the law and, finally, it includes all official communications. If there is objection in the committee to the bill or to specific sections, a minority report is solicited. In addition, current rules demand that all votes taken on any amendments must be included in the published reports, as well as the final vote to report the bill.

The report describes the purpose and scope of the bill and the reasons for the committee's favorable recommendation. Generally, a section-by-section analysis is set forth explaining precisely what each one is intended to accomplish. All changes in existing law must be indicated in the report and the text of laws being repealed must be set out. In the House of Representatives, this requirement is known as the Ramseyer rule. A similar rule in the Senate is known as the Cordon rule. Committee amend-

ments also must be set out at the beginning of the report, and explanations of them are included. Executive communications regarding the bill may be referenced in the report.

The language of the report can be as important as the bill itself. It is a common practice for committees to include in their reports instructions and guidelines to government agencies regarding interpretation and enforcement of the law. This can be crucial down the line should the judiciary become involved in interpreting the law. A committee report is perhaps the most valuable single guide to the legislative history of a law, used by other branches and the public at large to help discern the purpose and meaning of the law.

ON THE HOUSE AND SENATE FLOORS

Being reported is not a guarantee that a bill will be considered on the floor. Often a political decision determines when and if the bill will reach the floor for consideration. Scheduling involves a myriad of issues. One thing that may determine if or when a bill is to be scheduled for debate can be who is present in the chamber. Certain members' presence or absence may help determine a favorable or unfavorable vote for the proposed legislation. As a result, there is often a considerable gap between the day a committee reports out a bill and the day it is taken up on the floor for consideration by the entire chamber.

In the House, bills are placed on one of two calendars: the Union or House Calendar. They then sit on the calendar until a scheduling decision is made. The only difference between the two calendars is that the first one is restricted legislation that spends money or raises revenue. All other bills are placed on the latter calendar. In the Senate, measures await consideration on the Legislative Calendar, known formally as the Calendar of General Orders.

In both houses, the majority party's leaders are responsible for calling a bill for consideration by the whole chamber. In the House, the decision is usually preceded by conferencing with various leaders, such as the Speaker, majority leader, majority whip and party conference chairman. Once a decision is made, individual members of the chamber cannot change it. The legislative agenda is the sole prerogative of the leadership, and the rank-and-file members are at their leaders' mercy unless they can garner 218 votes, a simple majority. That majority can pass a discharge motion, which compels a committee to bring the bill to the floor, despite opposition from the House leadership. While a possible procedural tool for those rebuffed by leadership, it has not been used often, although in the late twentieth century it was employed more frequently. Historically, the procedure has rarely been attempted because it is rarely successful. Between 1931 and 2003, 563 discharge petitions were filed in the House, with only 26 of them actually pushing legislation to the floor; in those cases, only two bills became law. (Two others changed House rules.) Occasionally members may lose the battle and win the war, as the peti-

tion will lead to indirect success, by bringing attention to the bill, generating popular support, or some other influence that may result in the bill moving forward perhaps in a different form.

Once a matter is called up, the leadership determines how the bill will be considered. In the House, normal procedure limits debate to one hour for each party. Each amendment is allocated five minutes of debate per party. If there is objection to this procedure, the leadership can adjust the debate procedure and provide for "special order of consideration" via special rules. Special rules emanate from the House Rules Committee.

In the Senate the majority leader reserves the right to call up a bill. While the leader, like his or her counterpart in the House, will consult with fellow members of the leadership as well as individual senators who have been involved in the legislation, he or she also consults with the minority leader in establishing the agenda. The Senate majority leadership, with less power than the House leadership, must be more conciliatory to individual senators and must grant them more input and power in the agenda-setting process.

A bill is moved forward upon unanimous consent of all senators or a motion to proceed to the consideration of a bill. A single senator can inhibit the bill if the unanimous consent route is chosen. Each and every concern of individual senators must be mollified. The alternative mechanism is a motion to proceed. This avenue also has its pitfalls, because it is a debatable motion and therefore can be blocked through filibuster.

The House as the Committee of the Whole

To make debate more manageable among its 435 members, the House of Representatives often uses a parliamentary procedure which converts that body into the Committee of the Whole. This allows for more open discussion and less formal debate. Also, under this procedure the quorum for conducting business is only 100, not the normal 218.

It is these rules, whether members are sitting as the House or as the Committee of the Whole, that make debate possible. Although at times they seem quite formalistic and even archaic, without them order would break down and chaos ensue. Once a piece of legislation has made its way to the floor, the Committee on Rules acts by reporting a rule allowing for immediate consideration of a measure by the Committee of the Whole and sets the amount of time the Committee of the Whole may debate the proposed legislation. The length of debate usually depends on the importance of the bill.

Even after the general time has been announced, other issues remain to be resolved. While a general amount of time is given to each party, the chairman and the ranking minority member of the committee that introduced the bill control how that time is divided among the members. In many cases, that allotment is predetermined by members who make prior arrangements for their time of debate. Overall, the structure is not that rigid; it allows representatives to interrupt for questions and yield to other members who want to make a brief statement. Also, even when a member's time has expired, he or she is often permitted to place additional remarks into the official *Congressional Record.* However, they are noted in the *Record* as additions, and can only expand upon what was already said. Add-ons from outside the scope of allotted time cannot change the gist of what was previously said on the floor.

Once the rule is adopted, the Speaker declares that the House is now the Committee of the Whole. At that point the Speaker is not in charge, since the House is no longer officially meeting as the House of Representatives. She or he leaves the Speaker's chair and appoints a chair, who presides over the meeting of the House as the Committee of the Whole. Then discussion begins.

The rules of the House determine the rules of debate. The House adopts its rules at the beginning of each session of Congress. The rules have come to be what they are through time and precedent. By House tradition, the presiding officer's rulings on points of order are rarely challenged. (At times members have challenged certain aspects of the rules to break what is seen as a manipulation of the rules by the Speaker, or party leaders, to create an unacceptable concentration of power in their hands. These challenges usually do not pertain to the basic rules of debate.) One of the major authorities for governing debate is the *Manual of Parliamentary Practice,* prepared by Thomas Jefferson while he was president of the Senate from 1797 to 1801. The House has a long-standing rule that the provisions of Jefferson's *Manual* should govern the House in all applicable cases, unless they are inconsistent with other accepted rules of the House.

After general debate, the second reading of the bill begins. The second reading is a section-by-section reading of the proposed legislation. It is during the second reading that members propose amendments to the bill. Proposed amendments must pertain to the section being read. They must be "germane," or to the point. The germaneness rule applies to the proceedings in the House, the Committee of the Whole, and the standing committees. (The germaneness rule, for example, would not permit a bill dealing with a bridge in California to be amended to include a provision about a lighthouse in Maine.)

In the House, on most occasions a member has five minutes to explain and justify a proposed amendment. After that, the first member to be recognized has five minutes to challenge the proposed amendment. There is technically no further debate on that amendment; thus, a filibuster is not acceptable in the House. The five-minute rule, however, is not ironclad, and members often get around the limitation by offering amendments to the amendment, giving them five more minutes, and so on. The most common way this is done, without changing the substance of the amendment or the ensuing debate, is by offering an amendment "to strike out the last word." This means the amendment remains the same, but debate is extended. Each substantive amendment must be adopted by the Committee of the Whole.

With debate at an end, the Committee of the Whole officially reports the bill to the House and ceases to be a committee, reverting back to its status as the House of Representatives. This action is noted as the Committee of the Whole "rising." It is possible for the Committee of the Whole to rise prior to finishing all of its business on the debated bill by not considering all the proposed amendments. Such an action means the bill cannot be considered by the House and must be returned to the Committee of the Whole. This is an important mechanism that enables members to halt consideration of a particular bill.

VOTING ON A BILL

A vote on a bill only takes place after a third reading of the bill. Article I, Section 5 of the Constitution requires that a quorum—a simple majority—of 218 in the House and 51 in the Senate—be present for either chamber to conduct any business. The House often meets as the Committee of the Whole to get around that provision.

The House

The rules of the House limit when a member can try to prevent a vote by making a point of order that a quorum is not present. In the absence of a quorum, fifteen members may initiate a call of the House to compel the attendance of absent members. For such a motion to succeed, a majority of those present must agree to it. A call of the House is then ordered and the call is taken by electronic device or by response to the alphabetical call of the roll of members. Absent members have a minimum of fifteen minutes from the ordering of the call of the House by electronic device to have their presence recorded. In modern times, however, attendance has rarely been compelled, nor have orders gone out for the arrest of members not in attendance. The normal quorum call takes about fifteen to seventeen minutes, and roll call votes are considered key moments for members of Congress. Roll call establishes a member's attendance record, and a good attendance record is a necessity in a member's reelection campaign. Otherwise, opponents can make political hay of the incumbent's absences.

There are three methods of voting: voice, division, and record. The most popular method is a voice vote. For a voice vote, which is the way most questions are first tested, the chair asks those in favor to say "Aye" and those opposed to say "No." The chair then declares which side has won. Before a winner is pronounced, a member may ask for a division or record vote.

For division votes, sometimes called standing votes, those in favor, and then against, literally stand up and are counted by the chair. The chair then announces the results. (Division votes are rare in the Senate. If they take place, it is often by show of hands, and the number voting on each side is not announced.)

The two chambers differ in how they proceed on record votes. After a voice or division vote has taken place in the House, but before the final result has been announced, members of the House can demand a recorded vote, a yea and nay vote. This must be supported by at least one-fifth of a quorum of the House (44 members). The vote may be ordered automatically if a member protests a pending vote on the grounds that a quorum is not present.

Recorded votes in the House are for the most part done electronically. Members vote with electronic voting cards, which display their votes on an electronic board. While a vote is taking place, all can see who voted and how. Normally, fifteen minutes are required.

In the Senate, there is no electronic system. The clerk calls the names of all senators (this is referred to as "calling the roll") in alphabetical order. The senators come to the floor, or the "well," of the Senate to vote, with each vote being announced by the clerk. Senators can and usually do call for a roll-call vote any time a question is pending before the Senate, and they do not have to wait for a voice or division vote. In both houses, a member cannot cast another representative's vote.

While the committee work in one house of Congress and the subsequent passage of the piece of legislation by that house constitutes a major piece of the work in passing a bill, it is by no means the end of the process. Because the Congress is a bicameral system, in essence two equal houses, both houses must consider almost all pieces of legislation and agree on the exact wording.

Preparing copies of bills that pass the House of Representatives can often be a convoluted process. Complications arise because of the numerous and diverse amendments that are often attached to a bill throughout the process, especially in its final stages on the floor. To make matters more complicated, often in the House, amendments are proposed and attached with a minimal amount of debate. It is not uncommon for more than one hundred amendments to be attached to a bill.

No matter how many amendments are adopted, it is imperative that the house to which the bill is sent receive a copy that is identical to the bill passed by the house that is sending it. The enrolling clerk is responsible for preparing the copy. Once this clerk has the official copy of the bill as reported out of committee complete with amendments, he prepares what is called the engrossed copy of the bill. Once the clerk has made this copy, the measure officially becomes an "Act." The engrossed bill is printed on blue paper and is signed by the clerk of the House.

The Senate

In the Senate, the majority and minority leaders direct all scheduling and the legislative program as well. To control the Senate, they try to manipulate legislation and rules when possible. Because most measures are passed either on the call of the Legislative Calendar or by unanimous consent procedure, no debate ensues. As noted above, when more important and contentious issues arise, the leaders try to push the Senate to unanimous consent agreements. This limits debate. When unanimous consent is not achieved, debate is unlimited. A measure

that has been on the calendar for one day can be brought to the floor on a motion by a simple majority. Usually, the majority leader makes this motion, and it is usually debatable. This procedural move usually occurs only when a senator objects to a unanimous consent request to proceed to its consideration. On highly controversial matters, the Senate frequently has to resort to cloture (see below). Cloture is the only procedure by which the Senate can limit the amount of time a bill can be considered and it is a way to terminate a filibuster.

The filibuster marks key differences between debate and procedure in the Senate and the House. Filibustering means the use of any "dilatory or obstructive tactics to block a measure by preventing it from coming to a vote." Filibusters exist in the Senate, rather than the House, because of the smaller size of the Senate and the fact that, due in part to its smaller size, the Senate rules place few limits on senators. The most important of those rules is unlimited debate. The size of the House dictates that members are tightly controlled as to how long they may hold the floor, making a filibuster impossible.

Any senator who seeks recognition usually has a right to the floor if no colleague is speaking and then may speak for as long as he or she wishes. Also, there is no motion by which a simple majority of the Senate can stop a debate and allow the Senate to vote.

The cloture rule, however, does enable senators to end a filibuster or any debatable matter the Senate is considering. Sixteen senators initiate the cloture process by presenting a motion to end the debate. The Senate does not vote on this cloture motion until two days after the motion is presented. (For example, if the motion is presented on Wednesday, the Senate will act on it on Friday.) One hour after the cloture motion has matured on the third day, it is put to a vote and an automatic roll call vote is mandated. A three-fifths vote (sixty votes) is necessary to invoke cloture, except on all matters pertaining to rule changes (including the rule of cloture) when a two-thirds majority is required.

The primary effect of invoking cloture on a question is to impose a maximum of thirty additional hours for considering the question. During this thirty-hour period, no senator may speak for more than one hour (although senators can yield some of their time to a colleague). Under cloture, the only amendments that senators can offer are those that are germane and that were submitted in writing before the cloture vote took place.

The ability of senators to engage in filibusters has a profound and pervasive effect on how the Senate conducts its business on the floor. In the case of a threatened filibuster, for example, the majority leader may decide not to call a bill up for floor consideration or to defer calling it up if there are equally important bills that the Senate can consider and pass without undue delay. Similarly, the prospect of a filibuster can persuade a bill's proponents to accept changes in the bill that they do not support but that are necessary to prevent an actual filibuster. The use of it, or threat to use it, gives the minority an influ-

ence unheard of in the House. Battles over judicial nominees in the 1990s and early twenty-first century often resulted in the failure of the Senate to bring judicial nominees' names to the floor of the Senate because of the filibuster threat. Indeed, the continued threat of a filibuster by Democrats during the administration of George W. Bush, especially concerning Supreme Court appointments, almost created a showdown and radical change in the rules that would have forbade use of filibusters in certain circumstances.

Once a bill or resolution is before the Senate, it can be amended. Amendments can be attached both in the committee and by individual senators on the Senate floor. Committee amendments are considered first, then floor amendments. Once the committee amendments have been disposed of, any senator may propose amendments to any part of the bill not already amended, and while an amendment is pending, a senator may propose an amendment to the amendment.

There are certain special procedures in the Senate that limit the amendment process. For example, germaneness applies to all general appropriations bills. This includes any amendment that is not only nongermane, but increases the appropriation in conflict with previously allocated funds. Germaneness applies to almost all amendments, including those introduced once cloture has been invoked. And in the case of cloture, for an amendment to be considered it must have been submitted prior to the cloture vote.

Senate committees, while reviewing a bill sent over from the House, have a choice as to whether or not to make changes. As in the House, all Senate committee meetings, including those to conduct hearings, must be open to the public. (This is in contrast to practice in the early Senate, when debate was closed to the public.) However, a majority on any committee may close a meeting. The grounds for shutting out the public include fear that the subject of the hearings, if made public, could breach national security. A variety of other issues may be grounds for closing a meeting. If the issues at hand pertain solely to internal committee staff management or procedure, the committee will often vote to close. A risk that an individual may be charged with a crime or misconduct as a result of the hearings, or that the hearings, if made public, may destroy an individual's professional life and hold him or her in public contempt or disgrace are also causes for denying public access. Hearings related to law enforcement might be closed if the probe might compromise an investigation by revealing confidential information. Also, a hearing that may reveal information regarding trade secrets might have to be closed.

The Constitution mandates that for the Senate to conduct business, a majority of its members must be present. If a senator asserts that there is no quorum, a roll call is conducted. If a majority of the members do not respond to their names, the Senate has three options: adjourn, recess, or attempt to find the necessary members to reach quorum and continue business. Quorum calls, however, are usually strategic maneuvers to suspend activity on the floor temporarily rather than attempts to sandbag senators and bring them to the floor. These temporary stoppages serve several purposes. They may, for example, be to accommodate senators by giving them time to discuss problems that may have arisen concerning anything from procedure to policy or even time to arrange meetings. Thus, most quorum calls are ended by unanimous consent prior to the completion of a roll call.

Article I, Section 5, paragraph 3 of the Constitution provides that one-fifth of those present (eleven senators, if no more than a quorum is present) can order a roll-call vote or recorded vote. If a senator asks for the yeas and nays on a pending question and the Senate orders them, this does not mean that a vote will occur immediately. It does mean that whenever the vote does occur, it will be by roll call; otherwise, votes usually are taken by voice vote.

RESOLVING DISPARITIES

A bill cannot become a law until it has been approved in identical form by both houses of Congress. Once the Senate amends and agrees to a bill that the House already has passed—or the House amends and passes a Senate bill—the two houses can begin to work toward resolving their differences. This is done by convening a conference committee, composed of members of both houses, or through an exchange of amendments between the houses.

Conference committees arise when both chambers have passed similar bills. Usually, comparable bills are introduced at about the same time in the House and Senate. The bills' sponsors try to get both houses to consider the legislation simultaneously, although this does not usually happen, and rarely do the two chambers reach a synchronized decision. As a result, the chamber which finishes first (almost always the House of Representatives) sends its completed measure to the second. The second chamber takes up its own bill, but passes it in the form of a grand substitute amendment to the first chamber's version. This creates a fiction that both houses have passed the same bill, albeit differing versions, and the next stage of the legislative process is reached.

An alternative to the above scenario occurs when a bill does not have a sponsor in each chamber. In that case, the House, for example, would pass a piece of legislation that would then move to the Senate. The Senate would consider the bill, make amendments, and pass it. The House and Senate have now both passed a bill on the same subject, but with substantive differences.

At this point it is necessary for the two houses to resolve the disparities between their versions before the legislation can be sent to the president. Differences between House and Senate versions of a bill may be resolved most easily when one chamber simply adopts the other's version without change. Because it is rare that both houses so readily agree, differences are more regularly settled either by amendments sent back and forth between the houses or by conference committee negotiations.

As each house proposes amendments, the bill is like a ping-pong ball, bounding back and forth between both chambers. This continues until one house adopts the other's amendments without changes. Normally, each side is only permitted to return the bill twice. In special situations, when it seems that agreement is close, the House Rules Committee can extend the process and allow an extra volley. In the Senate, unanimous consent accomplishes the same thing. Rarely are exceptions to the two-volley rule not granted. Such a denial would defeat the purpose of trying to create law and would scuttle the momentum which often builds toward moving a bill toward becoming law.

Conference Committees

The more common method to resolve differences between the two chambers is a conference committee. In the House, the Speaker—at the recommendation of the committee chairs involved—appoints conferees, also known as the House managers. The Speaker has the sole power to make these appointments, a power that cannot be challenged.

House rules govern how the Speaker selects conference committee members. Stipulations for the Speaker are that, first, a majority of the conferees must generally support the House version of the bill. A second requirement is that committee members must have been integrally involved with the legislation during its journey through the House.

The third condition requires that they had to have been proponents of any provisions that were added to the bill on the House floor. Although by tradition the Speaker considers majority and minority viewpoints, it is not a mandatory requirement. The conferees can reflect the makeup of the House or be drawn exclusively from the Speaker's party. The Speaker alone determines whether or not a majority of the members selected meet the stipulated criteria.

In the Senate, committee chairs choose conferees. Seniority is a major factor in who gets to participate on the conference committee, and like the House, those on the conference committee must be a member of one of the standing committees that originally considered the bill.

The popular name for the conference committee is the "Third House of Congress." Although the managers or conferees for both houses meet together as one committee, they are in effect two separate committees, each of which votes separately and acts by a majority vote. For this reason, the number of managers from each chamber is largely immaterial.

Once appointed, conference committees are bound by only a few rules. The emphasis is on negotiating a compromise, and it is recognized that too many rules make this work cumbersome and difficult. The goal, to create a consensus bill that a majority in each chamber can vote to support, is not an easy task. One major constraint does exist on members from both houses: conference committee members cannot radically change the character of the bill. Rather, they are limited to considering those items upon which the Senate and House disagree. They are also forbidden to delete provisions that are identical in both bills, and they cannot insert new material not in the original bills.

Nevertheless, a committee can and often does make wide changes. General appropriation bills have more stringent requirements, and the committee is mandated to stay within the original boundaries defined by both bills. If cloture has been invoked, germaneness again applies. As noted above, an amendment proposing substantive legislation to an appropriation bill is prohibited. However, a two-thirds vote suspends this bar. Debate must be germane during the first three hours after business is laid down, but again, the committee can waive this provision, through a procedural motion which needs to be adopted by unanimous consent.

Despite these apparently stringent guidelines, in reality they are often violated in the interest of creating a piece of legislation palatable to both chambers. History shows that successful negotiations require flexibility and freedom. If consensus can be reached and votes garnered by adding new programs, they will be added. When violations of the rules of procedure produce a bill that carries with it political support in both houses, the rules are not a roadblock: procedure surrenders to politics.

When the conference committee finishes its review and revisions, the bill is engrossed, the third reading (by title only) takes place, and voting occurs. For example, if the bill originated in the Senate, it would come to the floor with a simple majority necessary for passage. Some procedural hurdles remain in the Senate before a bill is cleared for its return to the House. Any member of the Senate who voted with the victorious side (or abstained) still has an opportunity to make a motion for the Senate to reconsider his or her vote.

At this point, the original engrossed bills, from both the House and Senate, together with any Senate amendments, are returned to the House. The House is officially notified of the Senate action, with the notification including a request, if the Senate has made any amendments, that the House agree to them.

Upon the bill's return to the House, the official papers are placed on the Speaker's table to await House action on the Senate amendments. While the Speaker rarely does so, she or he may send the Senate amendments to the appropriate committee or committees. There is no time limit to this move, and the Speaker can use this option to bury a bill. Usually, for minor amendments that are not divisive, any member, but usually the chairman of a committee that reported the bill, asks the House for unanimous consent to take the bill with the amendments from the Speaker's table and agree to the Senate amendments. If the conference committee has done its job properly, most amendments quickly pass; it is usually only the most contentious bills that stumble at this point.

At this point in the process, the clerk reads the title of the bill and the Senate amendments. If there is no objection, the amendments are then declared agreed to, readying the bill for enrollment.

Engrossed bills are transmitted, or "messaged," to the House of Representatives by one of the clerks in the Senate's office of the secretary, who is announced by a House official. Once the Speaker recognizes him or her, the clerk officially announces that the Senate has passed a bill (giving its number and title), in which the concurrence of the House is requested.

Once the Senate officially notifies the House, the Speaker refers the measures contained in the message to the appropriate committees. If, however, a substantially similar House bill has already been favorably reported by a committee, the Senate bill, unless it deals with a monetary issue, can be substituted for the House bill, and the latter would remain on the Speaker's table instead of being referred to committee. Later on the House may take it up or substitute the text for the House version.

Upon the formation of a conference committee, House conferees do not have great latitude. They are limited to only those items in the bill on which the House and Senate disagree. The House cannot change anything untouched by the Senate. Germaneness is adhered to and no new matters may be inserted that go beyond the variations between the two versions. In an appropriations bill, if the Senate has revised a monetary figure in the bill, conferees must remain between the boundaries set by Senate and House amounts. Finally, no changes can be made to any part of the bill that both chambers have already agreed to separately.

In contrast to the Senate, House managers are under specific guidelines when in conference on general appropriation bills. An amendment by the Senate to a general appropriation bill that would be in violation of the rules of the House, had the amendment originated in the House, cannot be approved by House managers. Such amendments include those providing appropriations not authorized by law, providing reappropriations of unspent surplus, or appropriating money in other than a general appropriation bill. The door is not shut permanently, however, and the House may grant specific authority to agree to such an amendment by a separate vote on a "motion to instruct" on each specific amendment.

The rules of the House require that one conference meeting regarding the legislation be open. This rule can only be negated if the House, in open session, by a vote of the yeas and nays, decides that a meeting will be closed to the public. Otherwise, failure to abide by this rule can have serious consequences. When the report of the conference committee is read in the House, a point of order may be made charging that the committee violated House rules by failing to have an open meeting. If the point of order is sustained, the conference report is considered rejected by the House and a new conference is considered to have been requested.

The conferees can make four different recommendations to their respective houses: (1) the Senate may recede from all (or certain of) its amendments; (2) the House may recede from its disagreement to all (or certain of) the Senate amendments and agree thereto; (3) the House may recede from its disagreement to all (or certain of) the Senate amendments and agree thereto with amendments, and (4) the House may recede from all (or certain of) its amendments to the Senate amendments or its amendments to Senate bill.

Final Action by Congress

In most instances, the result of the conference is a compromise that is the product of the first or third type of recommendation. That is because one chamber has originally substituted its own bill to be considered as a single amendment. Any one of these recommendations can be inserted in the final report concerning the various amendments.

A positive report is not always forthcoming, with conferees unable to reach an agreement. When such an impasse occurs, committee members notify their respective chambers, which can then dispose of any amendments by motion. In the case of such a result, new conferees may be appointed in either or both houses. In addition, with the appointment of new conferees, each chamber may provide a nonbinding instruction to them with regard to what position they should take regarding the controversial provision.

Like a regular committee, a conference committee must make recommendations. In the case of a conference committee, recommendations must be integrated into a written report with a joint statement issued by the managers. If

there are amendments upon which conferees were unable to agree, a statement
to this effect is included in the report.
These are referred to as "amendments in
disagreement." The conferees must report total agreement or disagreement on
the amendments. Partial agreement is
not permitted. Two copies of the report
are then made.

One report is taken by the House conferees and presented to the House. Included in the presentation is an explana-
tory statement. The report must sit for
three days in the House before it may be
considered. (If Congress is in the last
three days of a session, an exception is
made.) Senate conferees take the other
copy, which is presented for printing (as
required by the Legislative Reorganization Act, as amended in 1970). To save
time and expense, this requirement is
frequently waived in the Senate by unanimous consent.

Normally, the chamber initiating a
conference on a bill acts first on a conference report, but either house can act first
if it has the official papers. Reports that
are submitted by the conference committee are privileged communications. Neither house can alter them prior to voting
and must consider the bill as a whole. If
the report contains amendments in disagreement, the amendments are not
acted upon until after the conference report is adopted. After adoption by the
first chamber, the conference report
moves with the official papers to the
other chamber with a message announc-
ing the previous body's action.

The Senate and House of Representatives differ in when they must consider

the report. If, for example, the House of
Representatives passed the first version
of the bill, Senate conferees could then
present their report and ask for its immediate consideration. In contrast to the
mandatory three-day waiting period in
the House, there is no lying-over period
in the Senate. Also, in the Senate the motion to proceed to consideration of the report is not debatable, enabling that body
to act immediately. No matter where the
process begins, a motion to recommit a
conference report may not be made in
the chamber acting second on the report.
This inability to recommit results from
the fact that once the first house's body
agrees to the report, the conferees of that
house are discharged.

At this point, several things can happen. If the conference committee reached
complete agreement on, for example, all
House amendments to a Senate bill and
the House adopts that report, then once
the Senate adopts the report, legislative
action on the bill is complete. However,
when following the adoption of the report there are still amendments that conferees had not agreed upon, the report is,
in essence, in parliamentary limbo. It is
as if no conference had been held.

There are several options at this point.
In the situation where it is House
amendments that are at issue and the
House acts first on the report, the House
can eliminate the amendments by doing
what is called "recede from its amendments." If following such an action the
Senate adopts the report, the legislation
moves to the White House for presidential action. On the other hand, if at issue
are Senate amendments that the House

acted on first, the House could simply concur with the Senate amendments. Such acquiescence by the House clears any amendments in disagreement, and when the Senate agrees to the conference report, the bill is ready for presidential action. Finally, the House can concur in the Senate amendments, which were reported in disagreement with its own House amendments. Under that scenario, after the Senate assents to the report, the House can agree with the House amendments to the Senate amendments, clearing the bill for the president's signature.

In some cases, even when at these late stages the Senate and House cannot agree and amendments reported in disagreement are not discarded, an additional conference on these amendments can be called. If both houses agree to such a conference, the same conferees are usually appointed. This final stage is important, because until all the amendments in disagreement are reconciled by the two chambers, the bill cannot move down Pennsylvania Avenue for executive decision.

The bill may also die if a conference report is rejected by one of the houses. The rejecting body notifies the other chamber. Often another conference is requested, but not always. When an additional conference is not called for, the bill either dies or further action is initiated by either chamber to keep it alive. All of this history is noted on the engrossed bill.

Finally, when the two houses reach complete agreement on all the amendments, the papers are delivered to the enrolling clerk of the house where the bill originated. The enrolling clerk prepares a copy of the bill in its final form as agreed to by both houses and sends it to the Government Printing Office for "enrollment." (Historically, enrollment meant the bill was written on parchment for official presentation.) The original papers pertaining to the bill are retained in the files of the originating house until the end of a Congress, when they are sent to the National Archives.

When the originating chamber receives an enrolled bill from the Government Printing Office, either the secretary of the Senate or the clerk of the House, as the case may be, endorses it, certifying where the bill originated. If, after examination by the enrolling clerk of the receiving chamber, the bill is found to be in the form agreed upon by both houses, a slip is attached to the bill noting that it, identified by number and title, has been examined and found truly enrolled. Usually, enrolled bills are signed first by the Speaker of the House and then—after being sent to the Senate by messenger—by the vice president. The bill is now ready to make its way to the president for consideration.

PRESIDENTIAL ACTION

The house where the bill originated is responsible for officially presenting the bill to the president. Under the rules of the House of Representatives, the responsibility lies with the Committee on House Oversight to present the bill for the president's signature "and report the fact and date of such presentation to the House."

If it is a Senate bill, this responsibility of presenting the bill to the president falls on the secretary of the Senate.

If, as sometimes happens, an error is discovered in a bill, a simple concurrent resolution can resolve the problem and fix the mistake. This solution is available only if the president has not acted on the bill. If the president has already signed or vetoed the bill, the only way to correct the error is pass a new bill.

Even with presentation to the president, Congress's job is not quite finished. According to the Constitution, the president has ten days (Sundays excepted) to make a decision. If the president approves the piece of legislation, he signs the bill, giving the date, and communicates having done this by messenger to the Senate or the House, as the case may be. In the case of revenue and tariff bills, the hour of approval is usually indicated. The enrolled bill is delivered to the archivist of the United States, who designates it as a public or private law, depending upon its purpose, and gives it a number. Public and private laws are numbered separately and serially. An official copy is sent to the Government Printing Office to be used in making the so-called slip law print.

Signing Statements

Some presidents attach signing statements to bills. In the early twenty-first century, the validity of these statements has been questioned. President George W. Bush used them extensively to try to adjust the meaning of a bill by saying he signed it with the understanding it meant a certain thing. Critics have charged this alters the essence of the bill and that the president cannot speak for Congress. In addition, critics assert that it violates the separation of powers. Supporters argue that a signing statement simply explains what the president understands to be the likely effects of the bill. Also, the proponents of signing statements argue it is a way to guide and direct executive officials in interpreting or administering a statute. President Bush, however, has used them in a new and unique way. During a presidency that as of 2007 has been marked by just a single veto (with eight more vetoes as of May 2008), Bush has used signing statements extensively to seemingly alter the meaning and dilute the efficacy of the bill. This has created, some commentators have said, a new kind of veto in which the president signs the bill but in so doing emasculates the measure to the point at which it is effectively vetoed. The Supreme Court has yet to rule on such signings.

Sometimes the president does not want to veto the bill but neither does he choose to act on it. By not returning it to Congress within the ten-day period, it becomes law without his signature and official approval. When this happens, the archivist makes an endorsement on the bill which states that, "having been presented to the President of the United States for his approval and not having been returned to the House of Congress in which it originated within the time prescribed by the Constitution, it has become a law without his approval."

Sometimes, toward the end of a session, the ten-day period can extend beyond the date when Congress is in session. In these situations, the president still has the option of signing the bill into law. However, if the president does not approve and sign the bill before the expiration of the ten-day period, it fails to become a law. This is what is known as a pocket veto, established by the Supreme Court as a valid exercise of presidential power in *The Pocket Veto Case* (1929). A pocket veto can only be used when the Congress is in adjournment.

Questions about what constitutes a viable adjournment were addressed in two more recent appellate cases: *Kennedy v. Sampson* (1974) and *Barnes v. Kline* (1985). In those cases the courts made it clear that a return of the bill is not prevented by an intrasession adjournment of any length by one or both houses of Congress, so long as the originating house arranged for receipt of veto messages. This negated the use of the pocket veto in these cases. In *Kennedy*, the court stressed that the absence of the problems noted in the *The Pocket Veto Case*—long delay and public uncertainty—were not present. *Barnes* made a similar determination regarding intersession adjournment.

If the president does not favor a bill and vetoes it, he returns it to the house of origin without his approval, together with a veto message that outlines his objections to the bill. If, upon reconsideration by either chamber, the house of origin acting first, the bill does not receive a two-thirds vote, the president's veto is sustained and the bill fails to become a law. The other chamber does not get the opportunity to act. If the first house does pass the bill by a two-thirds vote, it is officially endorsed on the back. The endorsed bill, together with a message from the house that has voted on it, is sent to the second chamber for action. If the other house also, by a two-thirds vote, assents to the bill, it is enacted into law. In the case of an override of a veto, the bill is not returned to the White House for presentation to the president. Instead, it is delivered to the administrator of the General Services Administration for deposit in the archives and is printed, together with declarations by the secretary of the Senate and the clerk of the House of Representatives of its passage over the president's veto.

When a bill becomes a law, Congress has performed its primary function. However, Congress is more than just the process by which it moves an idea to a piece of legislation that helps govern the nation. Congress is the individual members and how they not only interact with each other, but exert their power and influence in shaping the laws of the nation.

FURTHER READING

Bach, Stanley. *CRS Report for Congress: A Brief Overview of Floor Procedure in the House of Representatives.* Damascus, MD: Penny Hill Press, January 22, 1989.

Bach, Stanley. *CRS Report for Congress: Cloture: Its Effect on Senate Proceedings.* Damascus, MD: Penny Hill Press, January 24, 2001.

Beth, Richard. *CRS Report for Congress: Bills and Resolutions: Examples of*

How Each Kind Is Used. Damascus, MD: Penny Hill Press, December 8, 2006.

Beth, Richard. *CRS Report for Congress: Bills, Resolutions, Nominations, and Treaties: Origins, Deadlines, Requirements, and Uses.* Damascus, MD: Penny Hill Press, December 28, 2006.

Beth, Richard S. *CRS Report for Congress: "Entrenchment" of Senate Procedure and the "Nuclear Option" for Change: Possible Proceedings and Their Implications.* Damascus, MD: Penny Hill Press, March 28, 2005.

Beth, Richard S. and Stanley Bach. *CRS Report for Congress: Filibusters and Cloture in the Senate.* Damascus, MD: Penny Hill Press, March 28, 2003.

Binder, Sarah A., and Steven S. Smith. *Politics or Principle?: Filibustering in the United States Senate.* Washington, DC: Brookings Institution, 1997.

Davis, Christopher. *CRS Report for Congress: Flow of Business: Typical Day on the Senate Floor.* Damascus, MD: Penny Hill Press, March 8, 2007.

Davis, Christopher M. *CRS Report for Congress: Invoking Cloture in the Senate.* Damascus, MD: Penny Hill Press, June 4, 2007.

Davis, Christopher M. *CRS Report for Congress: Senate Legislative Procedures: Published Sources of Information.* Damascus, MD: Penny Hill Press, June 8, 2007.

Davis, Christopher M. *CRS Report for Congress: The Legislative Process on the House Floor: An Introduction.* Damascus, MD: Penny Hill Press, December 9, 2006.

Deering, Christopher J., and Steven S. Smith. *Committees in Congress.* 3rd ed. Washington, DC: CQ Press, 1997.

Frey, Lou. *Inside the House: Former Members Reveal How Congress Really Works.* Lanham, MD: University Press of America, 2001.

Hamilton, Lee. *How Congress Works and Why You Should Care.* Bloomington: Indiana University Press, 2004.

Heitshusen, Valerie. *CRS Report for Congress: Committee Types and Roles.* Damascus, MD: Penny Hill Press, March 13, 2007.

Heitshusen, Valerie. *CRS Report for Congress: The Legislative Process on the Senate Floor: An Introduction.* Damascus, MD: Penny Hill Press, December 8, 2006.

Library of Congress. *How Our Laws Are Made.* http://thomas.loc.gov /home/lawsmade.toc.html.

Oleszk, Walter J. *CRS Report for Congress: Proposal to Reform "Holds" in the Senate.* Washington, DC: Congressional Research Service. Damascus, MD: Penny Hill Press, December 21, 2006.

Palmer, Betsy, *CRS Report for Congress: Changing Senate Rules: The "Constitutional" or "Nuclear" Option.* Damascus, MD: Penny Hill Press, November 1, 2005.

Palmer, Betsy. *CRS Report for Congress: Introducing A House Bill Or Resolution."* Damascus, MD: Penny Hill Press, July 18, 2006.

Palmer, Betsy. *CRS Report for Congress: Introducing a Senate Bill or Resolution.* Damascus, MD: Penny Hill Press, October 26, 2005.

Rybicki, Elizabeth and Stanley Bach. *CRS Report for Congress: Floor Procedure in the House of Representatives: A Brief Overview.* Damascus, MD: Penny Hill Press, March 15, 2005.

Saturno, James V. *CRS Report for Congress: Amendments between the Houses.* Damascus, MD: Penny Hill Press, December 6, 2006.

Saturno, James V. *CRS Report for Congress: Amendments in Disagreement .* Damascus, MD: Penny Hill Press, November 3, 2004.

Saturno, James V. *CRS Report for Congress: Amendments in the House: Types and Forms.* Damascus, MD: Penny Hill Press, November 18, 2004.

Saturno, James V. *CRS Report for Congress: Amendments in the Senate: Types and Forms.* Damascus, MD: Penny Hill Press. November 2, 2004.

Saturno, James V. *CRS Report for Congress: House Floor Activity: The Daily Flow of Business.* Damascus, MD: Penny Hill Press, December 8, 2006.

Saturno, James V. *CRS Report for Congress: How Measures Are Brought to the House Floor: A Brief*

Introduction. Damascus, MD: Penny Hill Press, December 6, 2006.

Saturno, James V. *CRS Report for Congress: How Measures Are Brought to the Senate Floor: A Brief Introduction.* Damascus, MD: Penny Hill Press, July 18, 2003.

Saturno, James V. *CRS Report for Congress: Procedural Distinctions between the House and the Committee of the Whole.* Damascus, MD: Penny Hill Press, November 9, 2004.

Schneider, Judith. *CRS Report for Congress: Congress: Sources of Legislative Proposals.* Damascus, MD: Penny Hill Press, August 2, 1996.

Schneider, Judy. *CRS Report for Congress: Amendments on the House Floor: Summary of Major Restrictions.* Damascus, MD: Penny Hill Press, March 21, 2007.

Schneider, Judy. *CRS Report for Congress: House Committee Markup: Amendment Procedure.* Damascus, MD: Penny Hill Press, March 13, 2007.

Schneider, Judy. *CRS Report for Congress: House Committee Markup: Preparation.* Damascus, MD: Penny Hill Press, March 13, 2007.

Schneider, Judy. *CRS Report for Congress: House Committee Markup: Reporting.* Damascus, MD: Penny Hill Press, January 18, 2005.

Schneider, Judy. *CRS Report for Congress: House Committee Markup: Vehicle For Consideration and Amendment.* Damascus, MD: Penny Hill Press, June 1, 2006.

Schneider, Judy. *CRS Report for Congress: House Committee Markups: Commonly Used Motions and Requests.* Damascus, MD: Penny Hill Press, December 8, 2006.

Schneider, Judy. *CRS Report for Congress: House Committee Organization and Process: A Brief Overview.* Damascus, MD: Penny Hill Press, February 25, 2005.

Sinclair, Barbara. *Unorthodox Lawmaking: The New Legislative Process in the U.S. Congress.* 3rd ed. Washington, DC: CQ Press, 2007.

Tiefer, Charles. *Congressional Practice and Procedure: A Reference, Research, and Legislative Guide.* New York: Greenwood Press, 1989.

Tong, Lorraine H. *CRS Report for Congress: Senate Manual: A Guide to Its Contents.* Damascus, MD: Penny Hill Press, April 4, 2007.

Vincent, Carol Hardy. *CRS Report for Congress: Conference Committee and Related Procedures: An Introduction.* Damascus, MD: Penny Hill Press, April 3, 1997.

4

THE PEOPLE WHO SERVE

While we tend to view Congress as a single body, the power that Congress as an entity exerts rests in the individual members. The individuals who make up the legislature often act as a barometer of the issues confronting society. The concerns those issues raise then play out in struggles between members in disputes over policy that often emphasize party differences. Senators and congressmen enter the political fray in Congress by wielding power in various ways. Some rise to leadership positions, and through those positions exercise great power and control the legislative process. Others, through their deft political skills and force of personality, become important power brokers and influence the leaders. In the end it is the combination of various individuals, parts of a larger whole, that become the driving force behind Congressional action and the ensuing government policy.

As the makeup and the rules of Congress have changed, so has the power of the people who wield that power. Thus, in the early days, the absence of any clear power structure in the Senate left dynamic individuals such as Henry Clay and Daniel Webster to exert influence in the House. They became leaders because

of who they were and their personal characteristics, not because of the positions they held. As time passed, the growth of bureaucracy, the consolidation of power to certain positions, and the emergence of established leadership positions helped to shape who had power. The passage of the Voting Rights Act in 1965, the growing importance of the African American vote, and the growing number of black members of Congress also changed the dynamic of Congress and have given great importance to the Black Caucus and to those individuals who lead it.

The Constitution placed few limits on who could become a member of Congress. To be a member of the House, one must be at least twenty-five years old. Senators must be at least thirty. However, few members, especially in the House, are near those minimums. Rather, the average age in the early twenty-first century was in the fifties, although the percentage of younger members has slowly increased. Unlike the president, members of Congress do not have to be native-born citizens. In addition, while there is no constitutional requirement that House members live in their districts, they must be inhabitants of their states. Over time, an unwritten rule has developed that they should be residents of the district they represent. Failure to reside in one's district forecasts a likely defeat. One of the main arguments used against incumbents, in the increasingly difficult battles to unseat them, is not just residence in a district, but familiarity with the district. Their ability or inability to exhibit knowledge about the district they represent can often be the difference between winning and losing.

CHANGES IN MEMBERSHIP

With the coming of the new millennium, the traditional description of Congress as a bastion of old white men, Protestant and Anglo-Saxon, is less and less true. While white males still dominate the halls of Congress, major inroads have been made into that monopoly. Since 2000, there has been a growing number of women and minorities, including African Americans and Hispanics, as well as a broadening of the religious makeup of Congress. This is especially true in the House, which tends to have a less elitist tone than the Senate and is more open and available to women, blacks, and Hispanics. The Senate, while also open to change, has been less reflective of demographic shifts.

Congress's makeup, whether representative or not, elitist or common, seems to have always attracted public criticism. At times, attitudes toward the House have differed from those toward the Senate. For example, in the 1830s Alexis de

Tocqueville criticized the House for its "vulgar demeanor" and said he could not detect "even one distinguished man." In contrast, he described the Senate as "composed of eloquent advocates, distinguished generals, wise magistrates and statesmen of note, whose arguments would do honor to the most remarkable parliamentary debates of Europe."

Gallup polls during the twentieth century ascertained the amount of confidence Americans had in various national institutions, and the results indicated that Congress was one of those institutions that ranked very low. In the 1980s only one-third of people questioned said "yes" to the statement that they had "a great deal or quite a lot of confidence in Congress." However, in a seeming contradiction of that assessment, incumbents were returned at a high rate. Poll numbers suggest that in the latter part of the twentieth century, Americans tended to distrust Congress as a whole but support their local representative. Thus, in 1994, when Republicans wrestled control of the House from the Democrats, 91 percent of incumbents were reelected. And moving into the 2006 midterm elections, 65 percent of Americans felt incumbents should lose their job, but over half of those polled felt their representatives and senators should retain their positions.

Party Makeup

During the twentieth century in particular, Congress saw dramatic changes, most notably a shattering of the political norm of Congress, namely, Democratic

Party rule, which had endured for six decades. With a few exceptions in the postwar period (1947–1949 and 1953–1955), Democrats controlled both houses of Congress. From 1981 to 1987, the Republicans controlled the Senate, but not until after the 1994 election and Newt Gingrich's Contract with America did Democratic control really begin to crumble. The result is that except for a brief period in the first years of the twenty-first century, the Republicans gained control of both houses, and even with Democratic control of Congress after the 2006 election (by very slim margins, especially in the Senate) history has yet to reveal whether this is a lasting change or one more brief aberration in the historic Democratic control. Party shifts did not occur in isolation, and other demographics shifted along with them in Congress.

Age

The age of those serving has also changed. The average age of members of Congress went up substantially between the end of the Civil War and the 1950s. It then remained constant until the 1970s. The average age of members in the 41st Congress (1869–1871) was 44.6. By the 85th Congress (1957–1958), the average had jumped to 53.8; it then declined a bit in the next two decades to 50.9. These changes were sharper in the House.

Geographical Shifts

Shifts in age are only one of the changes in membership. For example, American

migration to the South and the West has shifted the balance of power, especially in the House. In 1910 California had only eleven representatives, constituting 2 percent of Congress. As of 2000, California had fifty-two representatives, or 12 percent of the membership. Other states have lost power in the twentieth century because their populations grew more slowly than those of other states: the states in New England, the mid-Atlantic region, Midwest, and the Great Plains states lost between one-half and one-third of their representation in Congress. The resulting geographical power shift was striking. In 1940 the four largest House delegations were New York first, followed by Pennsylvania, Illinois, and Ohio, with California placing fifth. Sixty years later the order was California first, followed by New York, Texas, and Florida. No longer was Congress dominated by the North and East, but rather by the South and West.

These shifts mirrored changes in party dominance. In the 1920s the South was a monolithic Democratic stronghold—almost all members of the House and the Senate from the southern states were Democratic. Nixon's southern strategy during the election of 1968 broke the Democratic stranglehold and the Republicans began to make inroads to the point where by 2004 the Republicans carried all of the southern states in the presidential election.

Democrats in the last quarter of the twentieth century become a bicoastal party rather than a party of the central part of the country. Democratic members of Congress came largely from the

West Coast and the New England and mid-Atlantic states.

Length of Tenure

The postwar period was also marked by a relatively slow turnover of membership. The result was that Congress became a body which contained two extremes, both long- and short-tenured members in both houses. The peak of the seniority trend probably came in the early 1970s; in 1971, 20 percent of House members had been there twenty years or more, and 34 percent had six years or less experience. By the middle of the Reagan Administration in the 1980s, junior House members made up approximately half of the chamber while only 10 percent were considered career politicians. The Senate followed a slightly different path, which in part reflected the longer terms of senators that made longevity more likely, but overall the trending was the same. In the 106th Congress (1999–2000) there were forty-three freshman members, and in 2004 a number of senior members, including Tom Daschle, the former Senate Democratic leader, lost their seats to freshman challengers.

Occupations

Senators traditionally were mostly lawyers, businessmen, and bankers. Over time, as with the overall makeup of Congress, the occupations have become more diverse, reflecting an increasingly complex American society. From 1953 to 2000, the number of lawyers in the House has declined from 247 to 163. The changes in occupations reflected changes in the American economy and other facets of American society. For example, in the 1950s, 12 percent of House members were farmers or from a farming background, while the figure for senators was 20 percent. By 2000, those numbers had dropped dramatically, with only 5 percent of the House and 8 percent of the Senate coming from that occupation, which reflected the shrinking number of farmers and other agriculture-related persons in the United States. In contrast, the number of educators represented in Congress has risen dramatically.

Whereas in the past, a representative's or senator's job was important because of the income it provided, ethics rules and other changes have limited the amount of income that can be earned outside Congress. Thus, those who serve, whether for several terms or just one, tend to make their jobs full-time ones. Since the 1970s, the positions of representative and senator have, more and more, attracted people who would be classified as full-time politicians whose primary earnings have come from service in government.

There is a distinct party difference with respect to occupation that reflects the traditional bases of the two parties, especially in the last half of the twentieth century. Thus, by the twenty-first century more Republicans than Democrats in the House came from the world of business and banking, with that gap widening more and more, with 47 percent of Republicans in those professions compared to 25 percent of Democrats.

Religious Diversity

The religious affiliations of members of Congress reflect the growing religious diversity within the country as well as the entrance of various religious groups into the sphere of political activism. The Christian Right has grown since 1980 and both parites have catered to that constituency in the 2000, 2002, 2004, and 2006 elections. But it is yet to be seen whether the religious affiliations of representatives and senators will reflect these political developments. It would appear, however, that one's religion is less important than one's political agenda, so that while often the two merge, religion is not an absolute. Overall, since the 1960s there has been a steady rise in the number of Catholics and Jews, and since the 1980s a growing number of Baptists are found in Congress.

John Menard was the first African American to be elected to Congress, only to be denied his seat by a fraudulent election investigation in 1868. (CORBIS)

Minorities

Race plays an important role in politics, as in all aspects of American life and history, and the presence or lack of African Americans in Congress serves somewhat as a barometer of race relations in America. In 1990 J. C. Watts became the first African American Republican elected to the House in over fifty years. The 91st Congress (1969–1970) saw a large jump in the number of blacks in the halls of power. In the 90th Congress (1967–1968), there were only five African American representatives, all Democrats, and just one, a Republican, in the Senate. By 1973 the number had tripled in the House. The second great surge in black representation occurred in the 1990s, largely due to the 1990 Census and the ensuing redistricting that created "majority minority" districts. Thus, in 1991 there were twenty-five black Democrats in the House, in addition to Watts on the Republican side of the aisle. Two years later that number jumped to thirty-eight, including one Democratic senator.

In 1868 John W. Menard of Louisiana became the first black elected to Congress, but the election that sent him to Washington was disputed, and the House of Representatives denied him his seat.

Hiram Revels of Mississippi, the first black to sit in either chamber, served in the Senate from February 1870 to March 1871, completing a Senate term. Joseph H. Rainey was the first African American to serve in the House, representing a South Carolina district from December 1870 to March 1879.

Menard, Revels, and Rainey were all elected during the Reconstruction Era, when blacks were enfranchised, many whites were disenfranchised, and Confederate veterans were barred from holding office. During this period fourteen African Americans represented southern districts in the House of Representatives from Alabama, Georgia, Florida, Louisiana, Mississippi, North Carolina, and South Carolina, and two black senators represented the state of Mississippi. Between the end of Reconstruction and 1900 these numbers declined and representation from the Deep South for the most part became just a memory, as only seven black representatives were in Congress, from Virginia and the Carolinas. As federal controls were lifted, the troops were removed from the South following the presidential election of 1876 and Jim Crow took over in the form of literacy tests, poll taxes, and violence. All of these together virtually eliminated black political participation, whether as voters or as officeholders. After Blanche K. Bruce from Mississippi left the Senate in 1871, no black sat in that body until Edward Brooke of Massachusetts took his seat in 1967. And while the number of minority representatives has increased in the House, the Senate has only one black senator as of 2008.

U.S. Representative Jeannette Pickering Rankin of Montana, December 1941. (Hulton-Deutsch Collection/CORBIS)

The last black elected to the House in the nineteenth century was George Henry of North Carolina, chosen in 1896 and 1898. He decided not to run again, and subsequently there were no African Americans in the House until Oscar De Priest, a Republican from Illinois, was elected in 1928 and served three terms. For the next twenty-five years, only three more blacks served, and all of those were from big cities, representing inner-city constituencies: Arthur W. Mitchell (1934) and William L. Dawson (1942) from Chicago and Adam Clayton Powell (1944) from New York. In addition to representing big city constituencies rather than southern districts, they were also all Democrats, whereas Reconstruction-era black members of Congress were all Republicans. The election of Mitchell in 1934 marked the beginning of a fifty-six-year absence of black Republicans in Congress, ending with the election of J. C. Watts.

In contrast, Hispanic gains in both Houses have been slow and do not even closely reflect the growing Hispanic population in America. If either House re-flected this population trend, one in seven members of Congress would have been Hispanic in 2004. As of 2000 there were just sixteen Hispanics in the House and three in the Senate.

Women

After they gained the right to vote in the early twentieth century, the number of women in Congress grew slowly at first and then in sudden jumps. In contrast to

Speaker of the House Nancy Pelosi, surrounded by House Democratic leaders, speaks after the Iraq Accountability Act passed in March 2007. (Office of the Speaker)

blacks, there was at first no partisan tilt to their allegiance: they were Democrats or Republicans in roughly equal proportions. However, this changed slowly, and by the 1970s women Democrats outnumbered women Republicans by two to one. As a result of the 1992 election, the number of women jumped from thirty to fifty-four. While in 1990 women made up 6.4 percent of the House, in 2000 the proportion of women was 13 percent. Similar gains were made in the Senate.

The first woman member of Congress was Jeannette Pickering Rankin, a Republican from Montana, elected in 1916. Until 1992 a high proportion of women in Congress were widows of members. At first, they were elected on the strength of their husband's name but then paved their own way. As women became more and more active in politics, however, this spousal connection diminished and women carved out their own political career path. The culmination of this trend was the election in 2007 of Nancy Pelosi, Democrat of California, to the position of Speaker of the House, making her the highest-ranking woman in American history to that point and second in the line of presidential succession. Pelosi's ascension to the role of Speaker was made possible by the turnover of power to the Democrats that followed the 2006 election.

Turnover

Turnover is part of the life of Congress, and new people rise to power and senior members fall from power during times of conflict and crisis. Congress experienced a high turnover rate in the late nineteenth and early twentieth centuries, principally in the House. This turnover reflected, in part, growing corruption in Congress and the consequent disenchantment of voters, along with the Progressive Era that attempted to bring change and reform. The end of the nineteenth century saw attempts to break party machines in the big cities, and these attempts resulted in turnover in the House.

These efforts to shatter the hold of the political machines took longer to impact the Senate, which experienced far less turnover because senators had longer terms than representatives and were not directly elected. Most were appointed by state legislatures, who tended to send the same men to the Senate time after time. The turnover rate began to increase as the Progressive penchant for reform of the political system manifested itself in the Senate with the ratification in 1913 of the Seventeenth Amendment, which mandated the direct election of senators.

By the middle of the twentieth century, turnover was relatively low in both houses. The highest turnover occurred in the 1970s and 1980s. The elections of 1972 and 1974 were seriously influenced by redistricting in accord with the 1970 Census. Especially since 1960, the election immediately following the Census has resulted in greater turnover than in other elections, particularly when shifts in party control at the state level give the newly dominant party the power to redistrict to their advantage. In 1972, many House veterans in the wake of redistricting retired rather than face what would be stronger challengers than usual. In 1974 Watergate wrecked the Republican Party, with Democrats gaining forty-three seats in the House; of the ninety-two freshmen, seventy-five were Democrats.

Two years later, the upheaval caused by Watergate reverberated through the Senate with eighteen new senators taking seats. In 1978 an even larger turnover occurred, as twenty new members entered the Senate: ten incumbents retired; three incumbents were beaten in primaries, and seven incumbents lost their reelection bids. The House also saw an infusion of new blood as seventy-seven freshmen took their seats.

The year 1980 witnessed the election of Ronald Reagan as president. He had long coattails, and the Republicans gained control of the Senate for the first time in over two decades, ending the longest stretch of a single party's dominance in history, and picked up thirty-three seats in the House. However, two years later the Democrats made a comeback in midterm elections and retook the Senate in 1986.

Similar changes happened in the 1990s as incumbents faced strong challenges. Especially since 1992, both parties have targeted incumbents who they feel are weak and given the challengers strong backing from the party machinery. Thus, while incumbents still have an advantage in getting reelected—they usually have more money and almost always more exposure—even seniority or power in either house is no guarantee of victory, as proven by the defeat of Democratic

Senate minority leader Tom Daschle in the 2004 election.

Turn-of–the-Millennium Membership: New Levels of Diversity

In the later part of the twentieth century, the Congressional Black Caucus boosted its representation in the House by three to 43, all Democrats. The African American representatives included such veterans as Charles Rangel (D-NY), top Democrat on the Ways and Means Committee, and John Conyers (D-MI), senior Democrat on the Judiciary Committee. After the Democratic takeover resulting from midterm election of 2006, Rangel became one of the most powerful men in the House as the chair of Ways and Means. As of 2000, blacks in Congress were still below their 13.3 percent share of the population but now made up 20 percent of House Democrats. Elected in 2004, Barack Obama, son of a black man from Kenya and a white woman from Kansas, was the first African American in the Senate since Carol Moseley Braun (D-IL) left in 1999 and was the first black man in the Senate since Edward Brooke, a Massachusetts Republican who served from 1967 to 1979.

At the beginning of the twenty-first century, Hispanic representation did not reflect that national population but was growing. Nationally, Hispanics make up almost 14 percent of the population but in 2004 there were only twenty-three Hispanic members of Congress, nineteen Democrats and four Republicans. In

Charles B. Rangel represents the 15th Congressional District of New York in the U.S. House of Representatives. A Democrat, he has served in Congress since 1971. Rangel is a veteran of the Korean War. (U.S. House of Representatives)

2004 Hispanics returned to the Senate for the first time since Joseph Montoya (D-NM) was defeated in 1976. Parlaying his role in the Bush Administration as the Cuba-born secretary of housing and urban development, Mel Martinez successfully ran for a Senate seat from Florida in 2004, while Ken Salazar (D-CO) replaced the retiring Colorado Republican Ben Nighthorse Campbell, the only Native American in the Senate.

With Campbell's departure and the defeat of Rep. Brad Carson (D-OK) in a Senate bid, the only American Indian in Congress as of 2004 was Tom Cole (R-OK), a member of the Chickasaw Nation. There were also five Asians in Congress: Hawaii's Democratic senators Daniel Akaka and Daniel Inouye and three Democratic representatives, Michael Honda and Bob Matsui of California and David Wu of Oregon. According to a Congressional Quarterly survey, Congress as of 2004 was more reflective than any previous Congress of the national population, but still not completely representative. Both houses were still dominated by lawyers, with 58 attorneys sitting in the Senate and 160 in the House. In both the Senate and the House, business and public service were the two other most dominant occupations.

Perhaps one of the most telling statistics regarding the degree to which Congress reflects the American population concerns religion. As of 2004, the most common religion in either body was Catholicism, with 28.8 percent of the members belonging to the Catholic Church. This dovetailed nicely with the American population at-large, which was between 24 and 25 percent Catholic. Similarly, the degree to which Baptists, Lutherans, Mormons, and Congregationalists were represented in Congress was close to their proportions of the population. On the other hand, substantial discrepancies existed for groups like Methodists, Presbyterians, Episcopalian, and Jews. For example, 11.4 percent of Congress was Methodist, while only 6.8 percent of Americans cite themselves as members of that church. Jews were also disproportionately represented, with almost 7 percent of Congress (and 10 percent of the Senate) being Jewish, while less than 2 percent of the American population was. However, as Congress shifts, these numbers seem to decline in importance, suggesting that religion, while an important variable in some parts of the country, overall is less important than the individual's political agenda.

CONGRESSIONAL LEADERSHIP POSITIONS

The demographic makeup of Congress is important. However, it is not primarily such demographic variables as the sex, ethnic background, and religion of members that are most important; rather, it is the various positions they hold that are most important in determining which individuals dominate Congressional life.

The Constitution makes a provision for presiding officers in Congress but does not say anything about parties or leaders. This is not surprising, since the Founders hoped to avoid political parties because they were believed to represent narrow self-interest rather than the general good. Much of the Constitution reflects the Founders' belief that parties could be avoided.

However, a two-party system emerged quickly in the 1790s, and party leaders emerged as well. In the House the constitutionally established presiding officer, the Speaker, is powerful. But that power is connected to his or her standing as leader of the majority party. Furthermore, the majority leader, not a constitutionally established officer, can be a powerful force in the House, as proven by such late-twentieth-century and early-twenty-first-century majority leaders as

Richard Gephardt (D-MO), Dick Armey (R-TX), and Tom DeLay (R-TX), all of whom had great authority. In the Senate, the vice president is seldom present, so since the 1940s the majority party has named its most senior member president pro tempore. The president pro tempore is usually busy as a committee chair and assigns the duty of presiding over the Senate to junior senators of his or her party.

The real leadership is exercised by leaders elected by party caucuses. All four parties (two in each chamber) choose a floor leader (the majority or minority leader), assistant floor leader (the whip), conference chair, and various other leaders. The majority party in the House effectively chooses the Speaker. In only rare exceptions, as in the toppling of Joe Cannon at the beginning of the twentieth century, has the Speaker's power been truly challenged, and although the power of the Speaker is not what it used to be, the speakership is still a powerful position.

Nowhere are party leaders' jobs specifically described in the rules. Rather, their jobs, and the responsibilities and duties that accompany them, have developed in response to the needs and expectations of Congress as a whole as well as the individual members. Party leadership helps promote the policy interests of the party at-large and individual members, and aids members during their bids for election. Depending upon the character and temperament of the leaders, the responsibilities assumed by them are often divided among the other high-ranking officials. Majority leaders like Lyndon

Johnson in the Senate helped to consolidate power to himself and made previously unimportant positions important. Johnson's rise to power in the Senate reflected the ebb and flow of authority and how different people exert their power in different manners.

The daily business of the Senate is conducted by that body's secretary. Although the vice president or president pro tempore is technically in charge of day-to-day supervision of legislative and administrative services, it is often the secretary who runs the process.

The Sergeant at Arms

The sergeant at arms enforces the Senate rules. (There is an identical position in the House with almost identical duties.) Originally known as the doorkeeper, this officer maintains decorum on both the floor of the Senate and in the galleries. Elected by the Senate, the sergeant at arms is the chief law enforcement officer, and in addition enforces protocol and is the main administrative manager for most support services in the Senate. The original function of this office, as doorkeeper, was to control access to the Senate sessions, which were originally private. As the sessions opened to the public, it was necessary to have someone to maintain order, and the title of sergeant at arms was added in 1798 to take into account the added administrative duties that were part of the job.

The sergeant at arms is the largest part of the Senate in terms of staff and budget. It provides wide-ranging administrative services and also works in conjunction with the U.S. Capitol Police, the Capitol Guide Service, the Senate Page Program, the Senate Office of Education and Training, and the Capitol Switchboard.

A key responsibility of the sergeant at arms is Senate protocol. The sergeant at arms is responsible for official guests of the Senate, including foreign leaders attending official functions. Other duties include making funeral arrangements for senators who die while still serving and planning the pomp and circumstance that surrounds presidential inaugurations. Newly elected members of the Senate fall under the sergeant at arms's charge as he takes care of orienting them to their new job and the swearing-in ceremony. Finally, when senators leave the Senate as a group, the sergeant at arms is responsible for escorting them. This occurs most often in connection with joint sessions of Congress, which take place in the House, and presidential inaugurations.

The sergeant at arms is the chief law enforcement officer in the Senate and therefore has the grave responsibility of security for the Senate as a whole and for the individual members. Any individual, including the president, who violates Senate rules falls under the authority of the sergeant at arms, who can detain and arrest them. For example, in 1988 the Senate majority leader, Robert Byrd (D-WV), made a motion to have absent members arrested and brought to the floor of the Senate. The reason was delay tactics on the part of some senators to prevent a quorum and delay consideration of campaign finance legislation. The Senate voted that the sergeant at arms issue arrest warrants and he was told to find and bring the absentees to the chamber. The sergeant at arms and his staff detained Robert Packwood (R-OR), forcibly bringing him to the Senate floor. His presence created a quorum, so none of the other warrants were carried out.

The Parliamentarian

While the sergeant at arms guarantees the security of the Senate, the parliamentarian, in essence, guarantees the process of each chamber. This office is not elective but appointive. In the House, the Speaker appoints the parliamentarian, and in the Senate, the parliamentarian serves at the pleasure of the senate majority leader. The parliamentarian's responsibility is to give advice on parliamentary procedure to whoever is presiding over the Senate or House session. Such procedure is very complex, relying in part on rules adopted by the Senate or House and additional basic guidelines such as Robert's Rules of Order. The persons filling this position play a pivotal role in making sure sessions of the Senate or House move smoothly and according to established protocols. Advice is often given not only to the presiding officer but to individual members who desire to participate actively in the business of the chamber. A good knowledge of the rules can enable a member to move his or her proposed legislation faster or help a member to block proposed legislation to which he or she may be opposed.

The Senate: Secretary for the Majority

In the Senate, the secretary for the majority, an elected position, is a support mechanism for the party with duties related to floor activities. One duty is to supervise the cloakroom. The cloakrooms are chambers, next to the Senate chamber, where party members can meet in privacy and in a more informal atmosphere to discuss pressing business. Under the guidance of the majority leader, the secretary helps manage the daily business life of senators by briefing them on upcoming issues and polling members about impending votes. The secretary's role is not limited to the floor of the Senate, but also extends to committees. He or she keeps track of committee requests and staffing needs and makes recommendations to the leadership of majority party candidates for appointment to boards, commissions, and international conferences. While there are certain things the secretary always does, the post's responsibilities have a certain flexibility, depending upon the demands of the majority leader. The minority party has a similar position, whose occupant performs similar tasks for the minority leader.

The Senate: Majority and Minority Leaders

Neither leadership positions are mentioned in the Constitution. The only leadership posts established for the Senate by the Constitution are the president of the Senate (the vice president of the United States) and the president pro tempore. All other leadership positions developed over time. The small size of the Senate in the early days made defined leadership less important than in the House. During the nineteenth century, what leadership did emerge shifted on a regular basis. Usually, floor leadership was assumed by senators on the basis of their individual capabilities. Such persons might be chair of an important committee or the party conference, but there was no designated leadership position. The early twentieth century saw a shift when the Democratic Caucus chairman, John Worth Kern (D-IN), tried to push President Woodrow Wilson's domestic agenda through the Senate, starting in 1913. In doing so he began to act like a majority leader, and so revealed the need for such a position. When the Republicans regained power six years later, in 1919, the Republican Conference leader, Henry Cabot Lodge, acted in a similar fashion. The following year, in an attempt to consolidate their power, even though they were in the minority, the Democrats specifically named Oscar Underwood (D-AL) as the minority leader. In 1925, still in control of the Senate, the Republicans followed the Democratic example, electing Charles Curtis (R-KS) as the majority leader, distinguishing this position from that of party conference chair.

Floor leaders in the Senate are elected by the members of their respective parties at the start of each Congress. The floor leader of whichever party is in power serves as majority leader, and the other floor leader as minority leader. The floor leaders serve as the mouthpiece of their respective parties and often help orchestrate the parties' positions. The position of majority leader carries greater power, including the authority to direct the daily agenda, drive the party's legislative program, and shape unanimous consent agreements. (Unanimous consent agreements help expedite legislation in the Senate. They often act like the rules issued by the House Rules Committee and, most importantly, can specify the amount of time to be designated for debate, rules for amendments, and so on.)

Senate leaders operate on and around the floor of the Senate. They are needed to move legislation, make sure members are there for roll-call votes, and help enforce party discipline. In addition, they are the key defenders of the rights and interests of their party and its members.

One of the key advantages to being party leader comes from the fact that they are called upon first when several members are clamoring to be heard. By preempting other members, the party leaders can put forth amendments or motions before any other senator. The majority leader precedes the minority leader when both wish recognition. Robert C. Byrd, a longtime member of the Senate from West Virginia and an authority on Senate procedure, has called the first recognition right of the leaders "the most potent weapon in the Majority Leader's arsenal."

While the position of floor leader carries great power, it is a power that is not specifically delegated; the extent of the floor leader's power depends in large part upon the individual holding the position. Some are more skilled than others, and the force (or lack thereof) of their personality can turn them into either effective or unproductive leaders. Majority leaders in particular often must balance the need of senators to debate a bill and speak to its merits with the need to move legislation through the Senate at a reasonable pace. Thus, a good majority leader is good at the art of compromise and can often accommodate the needs of the opposition while still moving his or her party's agenda forward.

To accomplish this balance, majority leaders need to work closely with the minority leader. As Sen. Bob Dole (R-KS) has noted, neither should ever surprise the other on the floor. Both majority and minority leader should be fully informed as to what direction debate on the floor will take.

While this accommodationist approach and civil discourse is often apparent in the Senate, in the late twentieth and early twenty-first centuries, this civility has crumbled somewhat as increasing polarization between the two parties resulted in the Democratic and Republican leaders attacking each other rather than accommodating one another. Bill Frist (R-TN), majority leader from 2003 to 2007, was often confronted with unexpected maneuvering by his Democratic counterpart. After the 2006 elections gave Democrats a slim edge, the new majority leader Harry Reid (D-NV) often could not muster the necessary votes to challenge the Republican minority or the Republican White House.

The Senate: Whips

In addition to party leaders, both parties elect whips, who are responsible for keeping members of their parties united on key votes, counting heads, and rounding up members for votes and quorum calls. Not surprisingly, the position of the whip in the Senate developed simultaneously with the development and formalization of the party leadership. James Hamilton Lewis (D-IL) was the first whip for the Democrats, beginning in 1913. Two years later the Republicans created the position for their party when James Wadsworth (R-NY) assumed the position.

While this post is important and can be extremely useful as key votes come to the floor of the Senate, the task of rounding up votes is very difficult. In contrast to many other countries, party loyalty in the U.S. Congress is not strong, and the existence of differing perspectives within a party often means that members do not vote along party lines. In addition, whips are hard pressed to enforce party discipline as the mechanisms for keeping party members in line are not strong. When political debate is particularly polarized, as it was at times in the nineteenth, late twentieth, and early twenty-first centuries, the job becomes somewhat easier, as the middle ground is far smaller and members are far less willing to defect to the other side. This holds true in both chambers.

The House Leaderships Posts

House leadership, while at times as tenuously grounded as in the Senate, has some moorings in the Constitution. The position of Speaker is established in the Constitution, and the person holding it is the most senior officer of the House of Representatives. (He or she is also the third most senior official in the entire federal government. By the terms of the Presidential Succession Act of 1947, the Speaker is second in line for the presidency, following the vice president.) Institutionally, the Speaker holds broad-ranging powers, presiding over debate in the House, making rulings on points of order, holding priority right of recognition on the floor, and setting the agenda by deciding what legislation comes before the House. In addition, the Speaker appoints task forces and commissions and oversees the management of support functions for the House. Finally, by modern practice, the Speaker serves as the primary spokesperson for her or his party in the House. The powers of the Speaker have ebbed and flowed over time as different Speakers have both used and abused their powers to get their agendas across.

The majority leader is the second most senior official in the House. From 1995 to 2007, when the Republicans were in control, he became the day-to-day manager of business on the House floor. In collaboration with other elected leaders, the majority leader has also assumed responsibilities for building and managing consensus on legislation. In the latter part of the twentieth century this proved to be an extremely important position, as men like Tom DeLay used the power and prestige of his position to control tightly the Republican Party.

As in the Senate, the responsibilities of the majority whip in the House include persuading party members to vote with the party. The majority whip is assisted by a network of members assigned to count votes and "whip" or convince their colleagues into supporting their party's legislative position.

The hierarchy of the Republican Party, after the whip, moved down to the House Republican Conference chair, vice chair, and secretary. The House Republican Conference is the organizational vehicle for all Republican members of the House and their staff. The Conference hosts periodic meetings of House Republicans and is the primary vehicle that leaders use for communicating the party's message to members.

The chair of the House Republican Policy Committee assists all House leaders and committee chairs in designing, developing, and executing policy proposals within the House and is assisted by the vice chair and secretary. The chair of the National Republican Congressional Committee (NRCC) oversees a separate political committee of House Republicans. While the Republican political committee and its chair play an important function, neither are funded through tax dollars, nor were they located within the federal buildings that house Congress and its staff.

There is a parallel set of officers and organizations for the minority party, which in the earliest years of the twenty-first century was the Democratic Party. When the House was controlled by Republicans, the most powerful Democrat on the floor of the House was the House minority leader, the senior official for House Democrats. The minority leader worked with his or her party's caucus to set the party's agenda for the congressional session. Other duties included appointing members to task forces and filling positions on commissions.

The minority whip, like the majority whip, was responsible for keeping track of how Democrats intended to vote and using his or her powers of persuasion to convince them to vote in line with the preferred position of the Democratic Caucus. The House Democratic Caucus served all Democratic members of the House and their staff. At all times, whether Democrats are in the majority or minority, their caucus is the main conduit for communicating the party's message to its members. The leaders of the House Democratic Caucus are elected by the members. The two key positions are the chair, who directs day-to-day operations of the caucus, and a vice chair.

SIGNIFICANT MEMBERS IN CONGRESS

As noted above, Congress, like many organizations, is only as strong as the members in general and those members in particular who fill the various leadership roles in the parties. In the early years, the individuals who dominated were men who had helped shape Congress in its original form.

James Madison

James Madison, as much as any early member, had a lasting influence on the institution. Because he helped design Congress at the Constitutional Convention, get the Constitution ratified through publication of the *Federalist Papers*, and eventually served as president of the United States, his time in Congress is often forgotten. Yet it was his early actions and words in the first decade of the new Congress that helped set the course for the ensuing years. There, he was a forceful and influential leader. Perhaps the single greatest achievement of Madison as a U.S. representative was his authorship of nineteen amendments to the Constitution, which when whittled down to ten, became the Bill of Rights.

Antebellum Leaders: The Triumvirate

It was in the antebellum period that an array of major leaders began to emerge. These senators and representatives became instrumental players, inserting Congress into the development of national policy. They also personified the growing clash of opinions over states' rights and slavery that culminated in the Civil War. From the War of 1812 to 1860, various senators and congressmen emerged to play important and sometimes infamous roles during the time of the country's growing divide. These years were marked most importantly, especially prior to 1850, by the potent leadership of three great men.

Henry Clay

Henry Clay was one of them and the first of the major power brokers of this period, first as a representative, than as a senator. Although Clay's great dream was to be president of the United States, running several times, he lost each time. However, Clay probably left a far more lasting influence on America through his roles in Congress than he would have in the White House. Clay was first elected to the House of Representatives in 1810 and served as Speaker from 1811 to 1814. Clay greatly enhanced the power and prestige of the post of Speaker. In addition to presiding over the House, as his predecessors had, he took over leadership of the majority party. This made him the leader of the House in fact as well as name.

Clay, from Kentucky, spoke for expansionist and other western interests. He was a major proponent of war with England in 1812 and led the War Hawks in Congress, who helped drive the United States into hostilities. After resigning from Congress to help negotiate the

Henry Clay addresses the U.S. Senate in 1850. (Library of Congress)

peace treaty to end the war in 1814, he returned to the House, where he began to push his American System. Clay's program tried to secure federal support for internal improvements and protective tariffs. His advocacy of internal improvements brought him into sharp disagreement with others, especially President Andrew Jackson, who vetoed the Maysville Road Bill, an important component of Clay's plan. It was in his second House go-round that Clay also demonstrated his adroit leadership, including the abilities that would win for him the name "Great Compromiser" for brokering the Missouri Compromise of 1820.

Despite a desire to leave the political scene, especially after very contentious elections in 1824 and 1828, Clay moved on to take a place in the Senate and helped form, as the head of what would later be called the Whig Party, the opposition to Andrew Jackson. Clay's Senate tenure in the 1830s, during which he ran for president in 1836, was marked by his constant battles with Jackson over the tariff, the ensuing nullification of tariff legislation by South Carolina, and Jackson's opposition to the Bank of the United States. Hoping to use the bank as a means to topple Jackson, he failed to get the bank rechartered but did succeed, in the wake of Jackson's questionable use of presidential power to remove federal deposits from the bank, in getting the Senate to pass the only resolution in Senate history (later expunged) censuring the president.

Clay ran for president in 1840, 1844, and 1848; only in 1844 did he get the Whig nomination, and then he lost the election. Despite his disappointment at never being president, he reemerged as an important but not key voice during the growing sectional antagonism after the Mexican War. In the latter days of Clay's career, he played a part in shaping the Compromise of 1850, which helped postpone the conflict that eventually erupted ten years later, but he was not the central figure in its passage.

Daniel Webster

The second member of the triumvirate was Daniel Webster. A senator from Massachusetts, during his almost fifteen-year tenure in the Senate he became a major political figure in the United States. Webster's career was marked by serious policy shifts that saw him move from supporting free trade to backing protective tariffs, a reflection of the changing economy of New England. In the states' rights controversies of the antebellum period that focused on slavery and tariff issues, he took a strong pro-Union stand. His Unionist sentiments were immortalized during a historic debate with Robert Y. Hayne of South Carolina in 1830.

The debate focused on the nature of the Union in light of the Nullification Crisis and John C. Calhoun's attempt to move South Carolina and other states into a position where they could annul federal legislation. The debate was carried in many of the national newspapers. It cemented Webster's place in history as a great defender of the Constitution and the Union. He argued vociferously against the idea of nullification, and one of the great, lasting moments of the debates was his declamation, "Liberty and Union, now and forever, one and in-separable!"

Like Clay, Webster was a leader of the Whig Party who aspired to the presidency. However, he fell far shorter than Clay, and his experience in the executive branch was limited to being secretary of state under William Henry Harrison and then John Tyler after Harrison's premature death. While he did not finish out Tyler's presidency, he stayed long enough to negotiate the Webster-Ashburton Treaty before resigning his post and returning to Congress.

Webster's career, especially in his later years, was marked by his staunch antislavery stance, slavery being an institution that he saw as inherently evil, and his rabid pro-Union position. However, his willingness to abide slavery for the sake of the Union began to alienate him from his party and his constituency. This separation culminated with his support for the Compromise of 1850. From the moment he entered public life, Webster was known as a great orator, and on this matter he gave an impassioned three-and-one-half hour speech defending the Compromise, opening with the words, "Mr. President, I wish to speak today, not as a Massachusetts man, nor as a Northern man, but as an American, and a member of the Senate of the United States. . . . I speak for the preservation of the Union. Hear me for my cause." Despite its pro-Union tone, his support of the Compromise, and thus indirectly, of slavery, crippled any political future for him in Congress. He subsequently resigned from the Senate and finished his career in government as secretary of state.

John C. Calhoun

The final member of the Great Triumvirate that dominated antebellum politics was John C. Calhoun, a South Carolina Democrat. Early in his career he allied with Clay in the House as a War Hawk and sought battle with Britain. Upon leaving Congress in the 1820s, he joined the executive branch as President James Monroe's secretary of war. He was elected vice president in 1824 and 1828, serving under John Quincy Adams and then Andrew Jackson.

Jackson's support for the Tariff of 1828 alienated Calhoun from Jackson and the Democratic Party. He resigned from the vice presidency and reengaged in politics as a senator from South Carolina. Calhoun then led the states' rights charge that tried to negate the tariff, and he helped precipitate the Nullification Crisis of 1832.

Calhoun became the leading spokesman for southerners. Alarmed by the growing strength of abolitionism, he was a fierce defender of slavery. Calhoun insisted he was a Unionist and was always concerned to preserve the Union, but never at the price of the supposed sovereignty of the states. Despite his advocacy of states' rights and his support of the right of nullification, he tried to maintain the balance between free and slave states in the Senate. He left the Senate briefly to serve as secretary of state under John Tyler (upon Webster's resignation) in the 1840s and was responsible for the negotiations that saw Texas enter the Union as a slave state.

Portrait of John C. Calhoun, a politician from South Carolina who is best known as part of the "Great Triumvirate" with Daniel Webster and Henry Clay. (Library of Congress)

Upon returning to the Senate in 1845, he tried to broker a compromise regarding the Oregon Territory. He voted against the Wilmot Proviso, and his last year in the Senate was focused on the unsuccessful attempt to deny California's admission as a free state during the debates over the Compromise of 1850.

These three men dominated congressional politics in the antebellum period until 1850. Any major controversy or debate involved their names. It was through them that leadership roles began to develop, especially in the Senate. They set the stage for the continued evolution toward the more structured, hierarchical Congress that we know today. In addition, their prestige and power helped shape American policy and drove the development of the second party system and the structure of the U.S. Congress.

Other Antebellum Leaders

But they were not alone. While not as powerful as these three figures were, another important player in this period was John Quincy Adams. Adams began his political career as a Federalist senator. However, he did not strictly toe the Federalist line, supporting Jefferson in both the Louisiana Purchase of 1803 and the Embargo Act of 1807. The Embargo Act in particular infuriated the Federalists, which resulted in Adams's resignation from the Senate and exit from the party. He then entered the executive branch, serving in a variety of roles. The culmination of his executive branch service occurred when he managed to garner the presidency in 1824 in a disputed election that went to the House of Representatives.

With his defeat by Andrew Jackson in 1828, Adams assumed that his public life was over. However, in an act unthinkable in the twenty-first century, he returned to Congress in 1831 as a member of the House. Adams took an antislavery line, helped eliminate the gag rule against antislavery petitions, and opposed the forced removal of the Indians by Jackson. He provided a calming force in a tempestuous period of congressional history.

David Wilmot

As America expanded westward and engaged in war with Mexico, sectionalism and slavery took center stage. Some members of Congress, like Davy Crockett of Tennessee, are remembered far more for their exploits outside Congress, rather than within it. Other names are attached to specific incidents emblematic of the period. One of these men was David Wilmot. He was a Democratic representative from Pennsylvania whose fame rests with a failed piece of legislation, the Wilmot Proviso, an amendment attached to an appropriations bill during the Mexican War. It stipulated that any new territory acquired as a result of the war would be a free territory, with slav-

This 1848 lithograph chastises President Zachary Taylor's ambiguous stance on the Wilmot Proviso, legislation intended to ban slavery in all U.S. territories newly acquired as a result of the Mexican War. (Library of Congress)

ery forbidden. While passing the House in 1846, it failed in the Senate. The debate over the amendment contributed heavily to growing sectional strife in the decade and a half prior to the Civil War. The two major presidential candidates from the Whig and Democratic Parties ignored the Proviso in the election of 1848, although the issue of slavery was a key element in the contest. However, its provisions were adopted by the Free Soil Party, of which Wilmot became a leader. He later helped to found the Republican Party and served as a Republican senator for two years.

Stephen A. Douglas

In the period immediately prior to the Civil War, the member of Congress who most stood out was Sen. Stephen A. Douglas. Known as the "Little Giant," the Illinois senator, like the older master of conciliation, Henry Clay, fought for passage of the Compromise of 1850 to preserve the Union and calm sectional tensions. Douglas, however, then undid his own handiwork by promoting the Kansas-Nebraska Act of 1854. This legislation was viewed by many not as a compromise, but as a political machination to further Douglas's presidential ambitions. To his dismay, the act exacerbated national division over the issue of slavery, gave rise to a bloody civil war in Kansas, and helped spur the creation of the Republican Party and the rise of Abraham Lincoln.

Douglas first entered national politics as a congressman in 1843, and from 1847 until his death he was a U.S. senator. In the Senate, Douglas was made chairman of the Committee on Territories, an all-important post in the next decade because of the growing battle over slavery in the territories. While Clay created the Compromise of 1850, it was Douglas's crafty submission of the components of the Compromise as four separate bills that guaranteed its passage. It was this political maneuvering that represented the passing of the torch from Clay to Douglas. Douglas, like Clay, strove to be president. Given this desire, and with America expanding westward, Douglas sought to resolve sectional conflict in a way that would help build a transcontinental railroad, aid his home state of Illinois, and resolve growing questions about slavery in the territories. Douglas proposed a bill in which all questions of slavery were left to the residents of the new territory. A conference of leaders changed the bill to provide for two territories, Kansas and Nebraska, rather than one, and with this change the Kansas-Nebraska Act became law in 1854. Douglas believed that popular sovereignty would unite the northern and southern wings of the Democratic Party and at the same time settle the slavery issue peacefully. But he had not foreseen the bitter contest that would develop between proslavery and free-state settlers in Kansas. In his report on the Kansas situation, he blamed the organized interference of interests outside the territory for the failure of popular sovereignty.

Despite his obvious abilities in the Senate, Douglas is most often remembered for his role in the Lincoln-Douglas debates, part of the race for U.S. senator from Illinois. The race was nationally

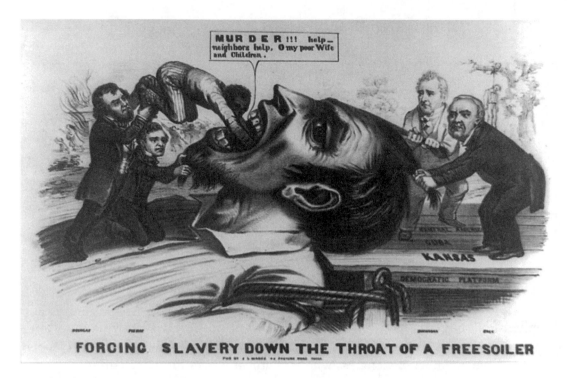

FORCING SLAVERY DOWN THE THROAT OF A FREESOILER

President Franklin Pierce, presidential nominee James Buchanan, Sen. Lewis Cass, and Sen. Stephen A. Douglas force a man down the throat of a giant in an 1856 political cartoon satirizing the Kansas-Nebraska Act of 1854, which allowed popular sovereignty in regard to slavery in the two territories. The act nullified the Missouri Compromise of 1820. (Library of Congress)

watched as a preview of the upcoming national election in 1860. Of the seven debates, the second, held at Freeport on August 27, 1858, had the most important consequences. There, Lincoln shrewdly put to Douglas a question exposing the inconsistency between Douglas's doctrine of popular sovereignty and the Supreme Court's decision in the Dred Scott case the previous year: "Can the people of a United States Territory, in any lawful way . . . exclude slavery from its limits prior to the formation of a State constitution?" Had Douglas answered no, in line with the Dred Scott decision,

he would have offended many of his constituents and doubtless lost his seat in the Senate. As it was, he replied that people of a territory could exclude slavery, since that institution could not exist for a day without local police regulations, which could be legislated only with the people's approval. The Republicans won a popular majority in the ensuing election, but because the Democrats controlled the state legislature which determined who would be Senator because senators were not popularly elected, Douglas was returned to the Senate. However, his Freeport Doctrine made him anathema to southern Democrats. Since they controlled the Senate, he was relieved of the chairmanship of the Committee on Territories. Conversely, the Democratic National Convention at Charleston, South Carolina, adopted in 1860 Douglas's recommendations in a platform advocating federal nonintervention regarding slavery in the territories. Demands of southern delegates that the federal government protect the institution were rebuffed, splitting the party and resulting in the withdrawal of fifty southern delegates (the entire delegations from Alabama, Florida, Mississippi, and Texas, most of the delegates from Georgia, South Carolina, and Virginia, and part of the delegations from Arkansas and Delaware). Although Douglas led on all fifty-seven ballots taken there for the presidential nomination, he was unable to muster the necessary two-thirds of the vote, and the convention adjourned. Reconvening in Baltimore, the Democrats finally chose him only after many of the remaining southern delegates withdrew to nominate their own candidate, John C. Breckinridge. Douglas won only twelve electoral votes in the election of 1860, although he placed second in the popular vote.

In the following months Douglas worked hard to effect a compromise and avoid war. When that failed and the Civil War broke out, he was a War Democrat who vigorously supported Lincoln. One of the greatest orators of his day, he made a speaking tour to rally the people of the Northwest in the crisis, but after an eloquent speech at Springfield, he was stricken with typhoid fever and died.

Douglas's reputation suffered with the growth of the Lincoln legend. However, he was an important force in his own right. His failures were more a product of the times than his own shortcomings. With the outbreak of war, Douglas receded from center stage.

Members in Violent Confrontations

The Wilmot Proviso helped stir distrust and suspicion. But probably no event better exemplified the highly charged nature of the antebellum period and the combustible nature of the slavery issue in Congress then the caning of Charles Sumner by Preston Brooks.

Charles Sumner and Preston Brooks

In a speech in the Senate, Sumner, an ardent antislavery Republican from Massachusetts, discussed the question of whether Kansas should be admitted as a slave state or a free state. His "Crime against Kansas" speech focused on two Democratic senators who were responsible for slowing up Kansas's admission as a free state: Stephen Douglas of Illinois and Andrew Butler of South Carolina. With Douglas sitting in front of him, he depicted the Illinois senator as a "noisesome, squat, and nameless animal . . . not a proper model for an American senator." He continued his harangue by attacking Andrew Butler, who was not in the Senate chamber. He ridiculed southern notions of chivalry, an important symbol of southern life, attacking Butler's assertions that he was a gentleman.

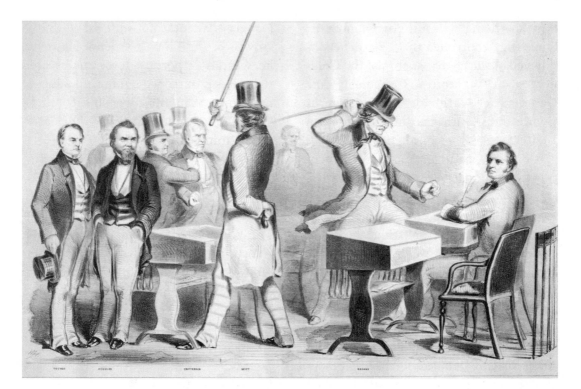

The Brooks-Sumner Affair was a brutal attack that occurred on May 22, 1856, on the U.S. Senate floor against Massachusetts Senator Charles Sumner by South Carolina representative Preston Brooks. The assault was one incident in a series of events in the 1850s connected with the debate on slavery. (Library of Congress)

Sumner accused Butler of consorting with "a mistress . . . who, though ugly to others, is always lovely to him; though polluted in the sight of the world, is chaste in his sight—I mean, the harlot, Slavery."

Rep. Preston Brooks was related to Butler and felt it was his duty to defend his cousin's honor. Because Sumner was not a southerner, and not a gentleman, the South Carolinian declined to challenge him to a duel, a staple in southern society for those whose honor had been

offended. Instead, he chose to treat Sumner in a manner which he felt reflected the same disrespectful way the senator had treated Brooks. Shortly after the Senate had adjourned for the day, Brooks entered the Senate chamber and walked up behind Sumner. Without hesitation, Brooks coldcocked Sumner, crashing his cane against Sumner's head. In a symbolic statement, the cane Brooks used was the same type of cane used to discipline unruly dogs. He repeatedly pounded Sumner and left him bleeding profusely. After the beating, Sumner could not walk and had to be carried away. In contrast, Brooks strode calmly out of the chamber past horrified witnesses. The result was that each man became a hero to his party and region.

The House tried to censure Brooks, but failed; he resigned anyway. Although reelected, he died very shortly after, at the young age of thirty-seven. It took Sumner more than three years to recover from the attack, but Massachusetts reelected him, and he resumed his seat in December 1859, where he became a cause célèbre for the antislavery forces and the Republican Party and a symbol of the evils of slavery.

Sumner's fame is not based just on being the recipient of Brooks's vicious attack. He was an important figure in creating and organizing the new Republican Party and in 1861 was made chairman of the Senate Foreign Relations Committee. Sumner highly approved of Lincoln's Emancipation Proclamation, arguing it should have been issued far sooner.

After the Civil War, Sumner was a leader of the Radical Republicans and helped promote their Reconstruction plans for the postwar South. His views on Reconstruction, which favored a harsh approach toward the former Confederate states, were at odds with President Andrew Johnson's plan. He considered Reconstruction a congressional function and fought Johnson's attempts to run his much more lenient plan through the White House. Sumner was an important player in the attempt to convict President Andrew Johnson of impeachment charges.

Other Violent Incidents

While the assault on Sumner is the most fabled example of violence in Congress, it is by no means the only case of physical confrontation; members have engaged in violence both inside and outside the Capitol. Another casualty of the emotions stoked by the sectional controversy of the 1850s was California senator David Broderick, the only sitting senator to die in a duel. An antislavery Democrat, he moved to California during the gold rush of the 1840s. Moving up quickly in California politics through his control of the California Democratic Party, he was able to parlay his patronage power into a seat in the U.S. Senate in 1857. His fellow California senator, William Gwin, was a member of the proslavery faction of the Democratic Party. The antagonism that peppered their relationship in the battle for Senate seats deepened during California's state elections in 1859. During the election, California chief justice David Terry, a Gwin supporter, blasted Broderick as unfaithful to the Democratic Party, and Broderick responded by insulting Terry's integrity and calling him a "miserable wretch." His honor besmirched, Terry challenged Broderick to a duel. Terry shot Broderick dead.

The Civil War was not the only cause of violence. Sixty years earlier, members of the House first engaged in blows when Roger Griswold (F-CT) attacked Matthew Lyon (D-VT). Lyon, following a heated debate and then a vote on the impeachment of Sen. William Blount, began attacking the Federalists over the merits of a foreign intercourse bill. Tempers already

Portrait of U.S. Sen. David Colbreth Broderick, who was killed in a duel with Chief Justice David Terry in 1859. (Library of Congress)

table, where Griswold approached him. Lyon attacked again, with the two finally being separated.

Violence, especially in the Senate, seemed ironic, since upper chamber rules called for decorum and civil exchange between its members. Half of the first twenty rules in the Senate focused on defining and establishing proper behavior. However, rules seemed at times ineffective as members regularly pushed the limits of acceptable behavior, even among members of the same party.

In 1902 John McLaurin (D-SC) verbally attacked his fellow senator from South Carolina, Benjamin Tillman (D-SC). He called Tillman a "willful, malicious and deliberate" liar, language far beyond the boundaries of decorum in the Senate. Tillman's response was physical: he turned and punched McLaurin in the face. They were both censured, and a new rule was adopted that stated, "No senator in debate shall, directly or indirectly, by any form of words impute to another Senator or to other Senators any conduct or motive unworthy or unbecoming a Senator."

The Reconstruction Era

One of the figures who helped bridge the period from antebellum America to the time of Reconstruction was Thaddeus Stevens. As the power of the presidency waned in the post–Civil War period, Congress strove to the forefront. Many of those who peopled the legislature in these years were products of or were manipulated by the political machines and big business interests of the Gilded Age

high, he accused them of hypocrisy and corruption, among other things. Griswold countered Lyon by bringing up the latter's dishonorable discharge from the Continental Army and then repeated the insult. Lyon, insulted and embarrassed, spit in Griswold's face. Griswold wiped the spittle off, and walked out of the chamber. Two weeks later, Griswold attacked Lyon with a stick, and Lyon countered with a pair of fire tongs. The two were separated, and Lyon retreated to a

Left to right, Benjamin Butler, James F. Wilson, Thaddeus Stevens, G. S. Boutwell, Thomas Williams, John A. Logan, and John Bingham, ca. 1860–1865. These House Republicans pressed charges against Andrew Johnson that ultimately led to the first presidential impeachment in 1868. (National Archives)

and were as important for their failures, or what they did not do, as much as anything, which made people like Stevens that much more important.

Stevens, a representative from Pennsylvania, served in Congress before and after the Civil War, and together with Charles Sumner, he was a Radical Republican leader in Congress. He began political life as an Anti-Mason in Pennsylvania poli-

tics and entered Congress as a Whig and abolitionist. Eventually, he quit the Whig Party over its failure to strongly oppose slavery and helped organize the upstart Republican Party. He returned to Congress just prior to the outbreak of the Civil War as a Republican.

As chairman of the House Committee on Ways and Means, Stevens was a powerful figure throughout the Civil War. It was during the war that Stevens took his place as one of the most radical of the Republicans. Because of Stevens's chairmanship, his support for the war was important as he secured major appropriations for Union forces. Also, during the war Stevens urged the administration to not only emancipate but also arm the slaves.

In the postwar period, Stevens opposed moderate plans for Reconstruction. He saw the southern states as vanquished territories that deserved to be severely punished. He opposed as too lenient President Abraham Lincoln's Ten Percent Plan for readmitting Confederate states to the Union during Reconstruction, and by the end of the war he was advocating black suffrage in the South and the disfranchisement of former Confederates. In addition, he helped defeat President Johnson's plans for Reconstruction, was instrumental in securing the occupation of former Confederate states by federal troops, and helped African Americans gain the vote. In his efforts to guarantee freed slaves equal rights, Stevens proposed the Fourteenth Amendment and helped shepherd the Civil Rights Act of 1866 and the Reconstruction Act of 1867 through Congress. He was one of Johnson's fiercest critics and a major figure in the president's impeachment, chairing the committee that drew up the impeachment charges and serving as one of the House managers in the subsequent trial before the Senate.

When he died in 1868, Stevens, true to his beliefs, was buried in an integrated Pennsylvania cemetery. His epitaph, written by himself, was "I have chosen this that I might illustrate in my death

the principles which I advocated through a long life, Equality of Man before his Creator."

Along with Stevens and Sumner, another figure who played prominently in the impeachment of Andrew Johnson was John Bingham. He gained recognition during the "log cabin" presidential campaign of William Henry Harrison in 1840. Bingham was a moderate Republican, served as a U.S. representative from Ohio from 1855 to 1863 and again from 1865 to 1873. During the Civil War he was an early advocate of emancipation. In January 1864 he was appointed judge-advocate and later helped present the government's case in the conspiracy trial of those responsible for President Abraham Lincoln's assassination.

After returning to Congress, Bingham played a leading role in the impeachment of Johnson. He opposed the first two attempts to impeach the president but changed his position when Johnson violated the Tenure of Office Act by removing Edwin Stanton as secretary of war. Bingham chaired the House committee that argued the articles of impeachment during Johnson's trial in the Senate and gave the closing, three-day summation. During Reconstruction, he was responsible for drafting part of the Fourteenth Amendment, which extended the constitutional protections of due process and privileges and immunities to African Americans and secured them from state government interference.

African Americans

One of the gains made, if only for a brief moment, in the post–Civil War period was the extension of the vote to African Americans and the emergence of black political leaders in the reconstituted southern governments. This radical change became apparent when Blanche K. Bruce, a black senator from Mississippi, became the first African American to preside over a session of the Senate in February 1879.

Bruce was a former slave who escaped during the Civil War. He attended Oberlin College for two years and then moved to Mississippi, where he purchased an abandoned cotton plantation and amassed a real estate fortune. In 1874, while Mississippi remained under postwar military control, the state legislature elected Bruce to the U.S. Senate. While Mississippi had previously sent a black, Hiram Revels, to serve the remainder of a Senate term, Bruce was elected for a full term.

Withdrawal of troops from Mississippi ended Republican control of that state's political institutions and any chance that Bruce might serve more than a single term. That term, however, proved to be an active one as he supported civil rights for blacks, Native Americans, Chinese immigrants, and even former Confederates. It was during a heated debate on a bill to exclude Chinese immigrants that Bruce made history by presiding over the Senate.

Bruce faced tremendous opposition in the Senate, especially from Mississippi's other senator, James Alcorn, who refused to escort him to take his oath of office. As Bruce started down the aisle alone, New York Republican Roscoe Conkling moved to his side and completed the journey to the rostrum. Bruce later named his only son after Conkling.

Gilded Age Politicians

The man who escorted Bruce down the aisle was one of the members of Congress who dominated government in the Gilded Age. As the executive power and the office of the presidency took a back seat because of lackluster presidents, and as the power of the political machines and corruption in government grew, Congress, for better or for worse, took center stage.

Roscoe Conkling

Roscoe Conkling was the undisputed leader of the Republican Party in New York. Conkling's machine was built upon federal patronage, which was entirely under his sway during the Grant Administration. An ardent follower of President Ulysses S. Grant, he reached the Senate in 1867, a quintessential Gilded Age politician. As an important player in his party, he was twice offered a seat on the Supreme Court, by Grant in 1873 and Chester A. Arthur in 1883, refusing both times.

Conkling had running battles with the White House when he did not see eye-to-eye with the president. In 1878 President Rutherford B. Hayes, an advocate of civil service reform, removed two Conkling lieutenants, Chester A. Arthur (later to become president) and Alonzo B. Cornell, from the management of the New York customhouse. Conkling balked, claiming a senator had the right to control federal patronage in his state.

The battle over patronage and civil service reform continued during the election of 1880. Conkling headed a third-term movement for Grant that year and placed him in nomination at the Republican National Convention. Although his Old Guard, or "Stalwart" faction, was unsuccessful, he stymied the move by his political enemy, James G. Blaine, for the nomination. The deadlocked convention chose James A. Garfield as a compromise candidate, while Arthur was named for vice president as a concession to the Stalwarts.

Conkling, ever pressing for control of patronage, gave Garfield tepid support in the presidential campaign. Afterward, he still demanded patronage positions that he said Garfield had promised him. Garfield, aware of Conking's reluctant support, denied this claim and further estranged Conkling by making Blaine secretary of state. When an anti-Conkling man was appointed collector of the port of New York, Conkling resigned from the Senate in protest, expecting to be re-elected. But after Garfield's assassination, Conkling found that his power over the New York legislature was not as supreme as he had thought, and that body did not choose him.

Conkling was always a strong supporter of civil rights for blacks, long after it had receded to the background with the end of Reconstruction. He is better remembered, however, for the political battles he waged with the White House and his fellow representatives and senators.

James G. Blaine

Conkling's bitter foe, James G. Blaine, also a Republican, was one of the most popular, influential, and controversial political leaders of the late nineteenth century. Not a Radical Republican like Conkling during Reconstruction, he had to deal with inner-party rivalry and charges of corruption throughout his career. He began his political career in Kentucky as a follower of Henry Clay. He moved to Maine during the 1850s, entered the newspaper business, and joined the Republican Party. Elected four times to the state legislature, he served as speaker of the house before moving on to the U.S. House of Representatives in 1862.

James G. Blaine was frequently proposed as a Republican presidential candidate, but his main influence was as Speaker of the House and as secretary of state under President Benjamin Harrison. (Library of Congress)

Blaine spent the next thirteen years in the House, including six years as Speaker between 1869 and 1875. Blaine tried to push the Republican Party away from its association with the Civil War through an economic-oriented agenda and by building up the Republicans into a national party with clout below the Mason-Dixon line.

Blaine was elected to the Senate in 1876 and became a leading candidate for the Republican presidential nomination. However, scandal plagued his dreams of becoming president. Controversy over an Arkansas railroad that he had allegedly aided as Speaker and the disclosure of related documents known as the Mulligan Letters tarnished his reputation. He lost the nomination in the wake of the controversy and supported James A. Garfield in 1880. In thanks, Garfield named him secretary of state. Blaine's career in Congress ended in 1881 with that appointment. Blaine and Conkling were two examples of Gilded Age politics and the tempestuous inner-party battles that consumed national politics in the late nineteenth century.

Thomas Brackett Reed is remembered for his firm control of the flow of legislation through the House of Representatives during his two terms as Speaker in the 1890s. (Library of Congress)

Two Powerful Speakers: Joe Cannon and Thomas Reed

Any discussion of Congress in the late nineteenth century must include two towering figures, Joe Cannon and Thomas Reed. Thomas Reed was elected to Congress in 1876 as a Republican. Reed quickly took his place among the leaders of his party. He served as Speaker from 1889 to 1891 and again from 1895 to 1899 and was the most powerful individual in that post since Henry Clay. Reed manipulated and changed the rules to garner authority as he concentrated and centralized power in the House. These changes enabled Reed, as Speaker, to suppress the minority party. As Speaker of the House, he inaugurated what came to be known as the Reed Rules, which enabled the majority to carry out its agenda with little opposition.

Reed did this by eliminating the phenomenon of the "disappearing quorum." Prior to Reed, only voting members were counted toward quorum. Thus, a minority of members, by not answering a roll call, even when present in the chamber, could prevent a quorum and thereby prevent bills from moving forward. One day in 1890, Reed demanded the clerk to count all members who were in the chamber as present without calling their name, but merely by counting heads. Bedlam broke out on the House floor. Some members tried to hide under their desks or run out of the chamber to avoid being counted, but Reed prevailed.

Reed also used the Speaker's power of recognition to push his agenda through. Without being recognized by the Speaker, one could not speak. Through the arbitrary use of this power, Reed prevented the minority from blocking his program. Reed advocated for high tariffs and strongly opposed the war with Spain, the annexation of Hawaii, and the ensuing imperialist bent that enveloped America. Although reelected in 1898, he retired from Congress in 1899 and then practiced law in New York City. While Reed established the rules, it took another figure to take those rules and exploit them to their fullest.

"Uncle" Joe Cannon served as a Republican in Congress from 1873 to 1923, except for the years 1891–1893 and 1913–1915, when first the Populists and then the Progressives were able to defeat him. Reed's rules allowed for more efficiency but were also easy to abuse, and abuse them Cannon did. He took Reed's Rules to new extremes. As Speaker, he acted like a dictator, using the traditional powers of his office to appoint all legislative committees in order to accomplish arbitrary ends. He ruled in the interest of the Old Guard Republicans and suppressed minority groups. Cannon ruled

the House as a tyrant from 1903 to 1911. During his time as Speaker, he regularly blocked not only Democratic legislation, but much of the legislation coming out of the Progressive wing of the Republican Party, including President Theodore Roosevelt's agenda.

On several occasions, Progressive Republicans tried to challenge Cannon's authority but were repulsed because they lacked support from the party's conservative wing. Finally, in 1910 insurgent Republicans, led by George W. Norris and supported by all the Democrats, passed a resolution which provided that the House itself should appoint the important Committee on Rules, with the Speaker ineligible for membership. This broke Cannon's power. But his dictatorial rule of the House and failure to concede anything to the Progressive wing of the party contributed to the split among Republicans that paved the way for the election of Woodrow Wilson to the presidency in 1912.

Early Twentieth-Century Figures

As noted, one of the people who helped break Cannon's power was George Norris, who served in the House from 1903 to 1913 and in 1912 was elected to the U.S. Senate. A liberal Republican, he opposed President Wilson's foreign policy, especially the push to help the Allies after war broke out in Europe during 1914. He voted against American entrance into World War I and sided with other Republicans in opposing the Treaty of Versailles, negotiated by Wilson in the wake of the war. His opposition to White House policy did not end with the election of a Republican president in 1920: he tangled regularly with President Calvin Coolidge and backed the Democratic candidate for president, Alfred E. Smith, in 1928. His disenchantment with the Republican Party continued into the 1930s, when he supported President Franklin Delano Roosevelt. Norris became in an independent in 1936.

Norris played an important role in American politics throughout the 1930s. He was involved in passing important pieces of legislation and a constitutional amendment. Norris wrote the Twentieth Amendment to the Constitution, ratified in 1933, which abolished the lame duck session of Congress and changed the date of the presidential inauguration so that the gap between election and assumption of power was severely narrowed. He supported the attempts by labor to organize and obtain better working conditions by sponsoring the Norris–La Guardia Act (1932), which forbade the use of injunctions in labor disputes to prevent strikes, boycotts, or picketing. Norris also believed in the New Deal approach to an active and involved government and fathered the bills that created the Tennessee Valley Authority and supported farm relief measures. He finally left the Senate after thirty years when his bid for reelection in 1942 failed.

Henry Cabot Lodge: A Foreign-Policy Powerhouse

Another powerful force during this period was Henry Cabot Lodge. Lodge served three terms in the House of Rep-

resentatives before 1893, when the Massachusetts legislature elected him to the Senate. Three years later he was appointed to the Foreign Relations Committee, where he remained throughout his Senate career, rejecting the Progressive wing of the party and becoming a powerful voice for conservative Republican forces in Congress.

Lodge's main focus was foreign policy. He spent little time on domestic issues, and in an era when America was growing into a military power and gathering colonial possessions around the world, Lodge played an important role in promoting American imperialism and overseas ventures.

Lodge welcomed war with Spain in 1898 and favored the acquisition of the Philippines and the development of a strong army and navy. Lodge bitterly opposed Wilson's peace policy following World War I and was incensed when Wilson did not take him to Paris to help negotiate the peace. His confrontation with Wilson resulted in one of the most turbulent relationships between the Senate and the White House in U.S. history, and Lodge's animosity toward Wilson's program killed what could have been the president's greatest achievement, U.S. participation in the League of Nations. It also demonstrated Lodge's power. Through his enormous influence and parliamentary skill, he was able to frustrate the president.

Lodge was, in fact if not in name, the Senate's first majority leader. Commanding party loyalty, he had real power, even if he did not have a corresponding title. Lodge took Wilson's attempt to sidestep the Senate or make it a mere rubber stamp in foreign policy as both a personal and institutional affront. Whether Wilson liked it or not, he needed Lodge's active support to ensure Senate approval of the Treaty of Versailles and its provision for a League of Nations on which he had staked so much of his political prestige. Yet Wilson chose to ignore Lodge, and the president offended the Senate in general by refusing to include senators among the negotiators accompanying him to the Paris Peace Conference and by making conference results public before discussing them with members of the Foreign Relations Committee. In an example of the personal animosity that dominated the relations between the two, Wilson in a fit of anger denounced Lodge and his allies.

After Lodge's committee added numerous "reservations" and amendments to the treaty, the frustrated president took his campaign to the nation. During a cross-country tour in October 1919, he suffered a physical collapse that further clouded his political judgment. In November, Lodge sent to the Senate floor a treaty with fourteen reservations but no amendments. In the face of Wilson's continued unwillingness to negotiate, the Senate for the first time in its history rejected a peace treaty on November 19, 1919.

Lodge then used his powerful position as chairman of the Senate Committee on Foreign Relations to oppose U.S. entry into the League of Nations unless specified and highly limiting reservations were made to protect U.S. interests. He later opposed U.S. entry into the World Court. In 1920 he was one of a group of senators who secured Warren G. Harding's nomination for president, bringing Lodge seemingly to the zenith of his influence and power.

In reality it was the end of his powerful control. In the wake of the war, domestic issues took front stage and isolationism prevailed in foreign policy. Power shifted from the Foreign Relations Committee to the Finance Committee. Lodge held onto his leadership positions and even assumed the chair of the policy-setting Republican Steering Committee in 1921. However, with foreign policy moving to the background, he was no longer able to command the party. Moreover, new factions within the party made inroads into the loyalty to himself that Lodge had fostered on his way to power. He died in office in 1924.

Women Enter Congress

In 1916 Jeannette Rankin was elected to the House from Montana, the first woman to be elected a member of Congress. A year later she joined forty-nine others in the House and voted against U.S. entry into World War I. That vote destroyed her prospects for winning a Senate bid in 1918.

Over the next twenty years, Rankin tirelessly campaigned for world peace. In 1940, riding a tide of isolationism, she won her second term in the House. The December 1941 Japanese attack on Pearl Harbor put an end to isolationism, but Rankin remained true to her antiwar beliefs, becoming the only member of Congress to vote against declaring war with Japan.

Although unsuccessful in her 1918 race, Rankin helped change attitudes about women as members of Congress. During her second House term starting in 1941, she served with six other women members, including Maine's Margaret Chase Smith. Those members carefully avoided making an issue of their gender. Rankin agreed with a colleague's famous comment, "I'm no lady. I'm a member of Congress."

Rankin and Margaret Smith followed separate paths: one promoting pacifism, the other advocating military preparedness. Rankin respected Smith as the first woman to serve in both houses of Congress. Active in Republican Party politics, Smith was elected after the death of her husband in 1940 to finish his unexpired term, becoming Maine's first woman representative. She was reelected to the House four times. Noted for her integrity and independence, Smith was elected U.S. senator in 1948 and reelected in 1954, 1960, and 1966. She was unexpectedly defeated in the 1972 election by her Democratic opponent.

The first woman in the Senate took her seat in 1922. In an attempt to appeal to the newly enfranchised women (the Nineteenth Amendment, giving women the right to vote, was ratified in 1920), but not wanting to create a possible rival for a position he wanted, Georgia's Democratic governor Thomas Hardwick chose eighty-seven-year-old Rebecca Felton to fill a vacant seat. Well known for her advocacy of women's rights, including the right to vote, she also appealed to southern conservatives with her pro-temperance views and her outspoken support of white supremacy and racial segregation.

At the time of her appointment, the Senate was out of session and was not expected to reconvene until after the election. At that time Felton would have to step aside for the person who had been elected. Hoping to see a woman in the Senate, if only briefly, Felton's supporters inundated President Warren Harding with requests to call a special session of Congress before the election. By doing this he would enable Felton to take her seat in the Senate and then step aside after the election. Harding refused to bow to the pressure, and it looked as if she would never actually sit in the Senate. On Election Day, Hardwick—to his chagrin—lost the election to Democrat Walter George. When the Senate convened on November 21, 1922, after the election, George stepped aside so that Felton could claim the honor of being the first female senator—if only for a day.

Democrat Hattie Wyatt Caraway became the first woman elected to the U.S. Senate. In 1932 she was appointed to fill the unexpired Senate term from Arkansas of her late husband, Thaddeus H. Caraway. Later that year she won a full term on her own merits, becoming the first woman to be elected to the U.S. Senate. In addition, Caraway was the first woman to chair a Senate committee and in 1943 became the first woman to take up the gavel on the Senate floor as the Senate's presiding officer. She concluded her career in 1945 after losing to Rep. J. William Fulbright in the primary and was honored for her service with a standing ovation on the Senate floor.

"The Kingfish": Huey Long

One of the major proponents of Caraway was Huey Long. "The Kingfish," as he was called, was elected to the U.S. Senate as a Democrat in 1930, but he did not take his seat until January 1932. Long was a powerful political force at both the national and local levels. Despite going to Washington, he continued to direct the Louisiana government, where he had been governor prior to his move to the Senate. In 1934 he began a reorganization of the state that virtually abolished local

government and gave Long, through a compliant governor, the power to appoint all state employees. As senator, Long initially supported the New Deal. As his power grew and he began to challenge for the presidency, he rapidly became one of Roosevelt's most vociferous critics.

A presidential aspirant, Long gained a steadily increasing national following. Early in 1934 he introduced his plan for national social and economic reform, the "Share-the-Wealth" program. While fiscally unsound and unrealistic once one got passed the rhetoric, it proposed a guaranteed annual family income and a homestead allowance for every family. The plan had wide appeal.

Long was famous for his filibusters. On June 12, 1935, he began what would become his longest and most dramatic filibuster. His goal was to force the Sen-

Louisiana senator Huey Long (1932–1935) was a flamboyant orator and referred to himself as the "Kingfish." (Library of Congress)

ate's Democratic leadership to retain a provision called the Gore Amendment, opposed by President Roosevelt, requiring Senate confirmation for the senior employees of the National Recovery Administration (NRA). It was a typical attempt by Long to use his national office to exert power at both the local and national levels and consolidate his power. The Senate leaders wanted to remove the Gore Amendment, but Long threatened to talk them to death if they tried.

Huey Long took the floor at 12:17 on the afternoon of June 12 and spoke for fifteen hours and thirty minutes, the second-longest Senate filibuster to that time. At first he attacked the NRA ("What is the NRA? Nuts Running America! NRA—Never Roosevelt Again!") and talked about his own programs and life in Louisiana. He then delved into the Constitution, reading and analyzing each section. He claimed that Roosevelt's New Deal programs had trampled on the document, transforming it into a piece of "ancient and forgotten lore."

Long continued, reading from Victor Hugo's *By Order of the King,* and then offered a deal to the leadership. He would agree to stop the filibuster if they would vote on the Gore Amendment the next day. His opponents rejected the proposal and the motion died.

In another attempt to gain adjournment and pass the Gore Amendment, Long teased his fellow senators by appealing to their appetites as dinnertime approached. He began to recite recipes, including one on how to make oysters:

"You fry those oysters in boiling grease until they turn a gold-copper color and rise to the top. . . . There is no telling how many lives have been lost by not knowing how to fry oysters. . . . Many times we hear of some man who was supposed to have had an acute attack of indigestion or cerebral hemorrhage or heart failure, and the chances are the only thing that was the matter with him was that he had swallowed some improperly cooked oysters."

This tactic failing, and following a quorum call (during quorum call, a senator can leave the floor for ten minutes and not surrender the floor) that gave him a brief respite, Long returned to his discussion of the Constitution and his criticism of FDR. He noted that if Roosevelt did not improve upon the job he was doing as president, Long would be forced to run. "If the President we've got doesn't do any better, I may have to take it. If he doesn't improve and some candidate doesn't rise up from the other party, I'll be chosen practically unanimously by both. It's the stumbles and the blunders and the mistakes of my enemies that have made the man Huey Long."

Long continued to look for new ways to pass the time and keep control of the Senate floor. He proposed to teach his colleagues and "give them advice on any subject on which they are in doubt." He sent out for chocolate and sandwiches—eating and talking at the same time, Long returned to the world of recipes.

Opponents would not let him use any procedural mechanisms to gain rest.

They swore they would outlast him and forced him to remain at the podium. *Newsweek* described the event: "At two a.m. Huey Pierce Long's eyelids drooped. He clung to his desk for support. With difficulty he kept on his feet. . . . From his exhausted throat the words came rasping and hollow." Long finally surrendered the floor at about 4:00 in the morning. At that point, having not been to the bathroom since 8:00 the previous evening, he could no longer hold out: he had to exit the chamber to answer the call of nature. The remaining senators quickly voted to extend the NRA without the Gore Amendment, defeating Long's attempt to thwart Roosevelt.

Long's historic filibuster filled eighty-nine pages in the Congressional Record. It is not the longest filibuster on record, but is perhaps the most famous. It was Long's last great appearance on the Senate stage as two months later, in September 1935 on a trip to Louisiana, Long was gunned down by Carl A. Weiss, a physician, who was then slain by Long's bodyguards.

Arthur Vandenberg

Other congressional power brokers during Roosevelt's presidency showed that while the FDR White House was dominant, Congress was not dead. Arthur Vandenberg was an influential Republican leader in the Senate. Before World War II he was generally considered an isolationist, but by 1945 his views on foreign affairs had changed, and he became one of the chief proponents of a biparti-

san foreign policy. He served as U.S. delegate to the San Francisco United Nations Conference in 1945 and as a delegate to the General Assembly of the United Nations (1946). In contrast to Lodge following World War I, Vandenberg—as chairman of the Senate Committee on Foreign Affairs (1947–1949)—was the leading proponent of bipartisan support for President Harry Truman's foreign policy. He was instrumental in securing Senate approval of the Marshall Plan and the North Atlantic Treaty Organization. He is one of those honored with his portrait hanging in the Senate Reception Room.

Robert Wagner

Robert Wagner was a product of the Tammany Hall political machine in New York. A leading advocate for labor, he served in the U.S. Senate from 1927 to 1949, where he was one of the chief leaders in directing New Deal legislation. He was instrumental in guiding one of the first New Deal programs, the National Industrial Recovery Act, in 1933. Even more importantly, the legislation that opened the door for labor to organize and that established the National Labor Relations Board bears his name as the Wagner Act (1935). He also helped draft the legislation that established the Federal Emergency Relief Administration in 1933 and the Social Security system two years later.

One of Wagner's great failures was his attempt, along with Edward P. Costigan (D-CO), to get a federal antilynching bill

Robert F. Wagner guided so many key New Deal bills through the U.S. Senate that he was dubbed the "legislative pilot of the New Deal." (Library of Congress)

passed. It died for lack of support from Roosevelt, who feared alienating southern voters and southern members of Congress.

Robert Taft

While members of Congress like Vandenburg, Wagner, and Long helped drive Congress during the New Deal, the postwar period saw the maturation of several players who entered Congress during the New Deal or came to office in the years just following World War II. One of those men was Robert Taft, a Republican from Ohio who was first elected to the Senate in 1938. Serving for fourteen years, he quickly became the acknowledged leader of conservative Republicans. He was a staunch opponent of Roosevelt and the

New Deal. He balked at the wide range of programs instituted under FDR and called for far more fiscally conservative approaches to government.

Taft is perhaps best remembered for the Taft-Hartley Act (1947). This bill became the new cornerstone for labor relations in America, qualifying much of the Wagner Act, passed ten years earlier, to make it more favorable to employers. It was passed over President Truman's veto and into the twenty-first century remains the key piece of legislation dealing with organized labor.

Taft was a strong isolationist prior to World War II. While he backed American entry into the war and supported the United Nations, he quickly returned to his isolationist views after the conflict. He condemned NATO and reversed his position on the UN. He criticized Truman's efforts in Korea and strongly supported Gen. Douglas MacArthur. Taft became the Senate majority leader after the 1952 elections, but his tenure in that position was cut short by his sudden death in 1953.

Joseph McCarthy

In contrast to the steady statesmanship of Taft in the postwar period, perhaps no member of Congress rose to fame and then disappeared as quickly as Joseph McCarthy. That fame, or infamy, persists, and the era in which he flourished is still known by his name. Raised in rural Wisconsin, he became a circuit judge before joining the Marine Corps during World War II. Upon returning from the war, he quit the Democratic Party and defeated Robert La Follette Jr. in the Republican senatorial primary in 1946. He captured his Senate seat in part

Wisconsin senator Joseph McCarthy speaks in front of a television camera in 1953. (Library of Congress)

by exaggerating his military record and with the use of the moniker "tailgunner Joe."

McCarthy maintained a somewhat conservative voting record, and his first few years were spent fighting for housing legislation and easing sugar rationing. He skyrocketed to fame with a speech in Wheeling, West Virginia, in early 1950, when he accused the government of being littered with hidden Communists. McCarthy announced that he had in his hand a list of 205 Communists in the State Department and that Secretary of State Dean Acheson also knew who they were. The number of Communists changed regularly, from as few as 57 in some instances and then back to 205. Few seemed to question the shift, but focused instead on the charges, and with the specters of China, Korea, the Rosenbergs, and Alger Hiss as a backdrop, McCarthy assumed center stage in domestic politics.

In 1950 a subcommittee under the direction of Maryland Democrat Millard Tydings was established to investigate the allegations. The committee found no grounds for McCarthy's charges, but the Wisconsin senator countered with further accusations. These additional charges received national attention, making McCarthy an important national political figure.

Throughout the early 1950s, McCarthy continued to make accusations of Communist infiltration of the U.S. government, though he failed to provide evidence. He was reelected in 1952, and with the Republicans regaining control of the Senate in 1953, McCarthy became chairman of the Committee on Government Operations and its permanent Subcommittee on Investigations. Especially in his position of the chair of the subcommittee, McCarthy's actions angered and alienated Democrats on the committee, all of whom resigned, and President Eisenhower as well, although he refused publicly to reprimand McCarthy.

The beginning of the end for McCarthy occurred when he investigated a purported espionage ring in the army. Nationally televised hearings in the spring of 1954, known as the Army-McCarthy hearings, opened him up to ridicule for the way he ran the hearings, and his poll numbers began to drop. The climax of the hearings came on June 9, when the senator attacked a young lawyer who worked for the law firm of Joseph Welch, the army's chief counsel. Welch's reply to McCarthy became famous: "Have you no sense of decency,

sir, at long last? Have you no sense of decency?" In the wake of the hearings, public opinion turned as did his Senate colleagues, culminating in his censure by the Senate in December 1954. He faded quickly and died a broken man in 1957.

Richard M. Nixon

Some members of Congress rode McCarthy's coattails and then assumed their own importance, like Richard M. Nixon. Nixon was elected to Congress as a Republican in 1946. In the House of Representatives he became nationally known for his work on the House Committee on Un-American Activities (HUAC), where he was credited with forcing the famous confrontation between Alger Hiss, the accused Soviet spy, and Whittaker Chambers, his accuser, thus precipitating the perjury case against Hiss. In 1950 Nixon was elected to the Senate after a particularly bitter electoral campaign. In the Senate, Nixon denounced President Truman's policy in Asia, supported Gen. Douglas MacArthur's proposal to expand the Korean War, and attacked the Democratic administration as favorable to socialism.

Nixon left the Senate when he was selected as Dwight Eisenhower's vice presidential running mate in 1952 and was eventually elected president in 1968. Nixon, in his role on HUAC, and other members of Congress, like John Parnell Thomas in the House and McCarthy in the Senate, illustrated the ability of congresspersons to manipulate and bully not only the legislature, but even the executive, and drive policy.

Richard Russell

In the postwar period, there were important men on both sides of the aisle whose agendas went beyond just hunting for Communists. Richard Russell, for whom the Senate office building is named, was Democratic senator from Georgia from 1932 to 1971. He served as a father figure to many young senators, most importantly, Lyndon Johnson. He strongly supported the New Deal, was a chairman of the Armed Services Committee, and was

one of the most powerful members of the Senate and in Washington, D.C., generally. Russell was known as the senator's senator and dean of the Senate. He was an adviser to six presidents, from FDR to Richard Nixon.

Russell attained that position of power through his committee assignments. Most importantly, he served as the chair of the Armed Services Committee and had a career-long seat on the Appropriations Committee, where he was chair during his final two years in the Senate. He set the agenda for all agricultural and defense legislation during much of his tenure, as well as for general issues af-

Sen. Richard B. Russell of Georgia, October 14, 1968. (Yoichi Okamoto/Lyndon B. Johnson Library)

fecting the federal budget. Russell was one of the foremost twentieth-century experts on military and defense policy.

Russell could have been the official leader of his party on the floor of the Senate, but preferring to take a back seat in public, he exerted his authority and leadership in committees. While functioning as an important voice in the Senate, he broke with his protégé, Lyndon Johnson, and many other members of Congress over civil rights.

Russell contested civil rights legislation as far back as 1935, fighting the antilynching bill of that year. He was the leader of the southern bloc in obstructing all federal civil rights legislation, arguing such laws were infringements on states' rights. Using Senate rules, Russell regularly blocked passage of cloture motions in the Senate, preserving unlimited debate as a means to halt or weaken any civil rights legislation. Using the filibuster and his ability to manipulate parliamentary rules, Russell managed to block any meaningful civil rights legislation until 1964.

Russell's stand on civil rights cost him. It probably prevented him from garnering a nomination for the presidency, sidetracked him from other duties, and contaminated his historical record. Russell ended his career as president pro tempore of the Senate, making him third in the line of presidential succession.

Sam Rayburn

Sam Rayburn was another major figure of the postwar era. A middle-of-the road Democrat, he rose to the top of his party's political pyramid in the House. He held the office of Speaker from 1940 to 1947, 1949 to 1953, and 1955 to 1961. He was directly responsible for the passage of much New Deal legislation in the House and served twice as long as any of his predecessors in the role of Speaker. Overall, he served forty-eight years in the House from 1913 to 1961.

Rayburn's move up to the speakership really began when he allied himself with the powerful Texas representative John Nance Garner. He served as campaign chairman for Garner's run at the presidency in 1932 and played an important role in getting Garner to be FDR's running mate. Rayburn subsequently became a leading supporter of the New Deal. As the majority leader from 1937 to 1940 and then as Speaker, Rayburn was instrumental in getting much New Deal legislation through the House.

In the postwar years, Rayburn was a strong supporter of President Truman's domestic and foreign policy. He worked very closely with his fellow Texan, Lyndon Johnson, during the Eisenhower years to challenge the Republicans. Rayburn and Johnson formed a powerful pair in the House and Senate, and Rayburn was an important factor in Johnson's decision to run as vice president on John F. Kennedy's ticket in 1960.

Throughout his career, Rayburn was a strong party man supporting the Democratic nominee for president. This meant that he did not march in step with the conservative wing of the party, especially in his home state's politics. This was ev-

Sam Rayburn served in the House of Representatives for almost fifty years, from 1913 to 1961, longer than anyone else in U.S. history. Rayburn was also the longest-serving Speaker of the House, holding that position for seventeen nonconsecutive years. (National Archives)

ident in both the 1952 and 1956 elections, when Rayburn supported Adlai Stevenson for president although most Texas Democratic officials threw their weight behind Eisenhower. Despite this support for the national Democratic leadership and his being a good party man, it would be hard to categorize Rayburn as a New Deal liberal, and often his politics were far more moderate. He acted, at times, in a very independent manner. Rayburn was a man of integrity who prided himself on the fact he accepted no money from lobbyists in forty-eight years and went on only one congressional junket, for which he paid. His reputation, combined with his knowledge of parliamentary procedures and rules, helped him to work his way through the times when he stepped outside the party's bounds. He was known as both a formidable adversary and as someone who was fair and honest. These qualities brought him respect from both sides of the aisle.

Lyndon B. Johnson

The other great Texan in Congress was Lyndon B. Johnson. His exploits in the Senate rivaled in historical importance his years as president. Johnson emerged onto the political scene during the Depression in Texas and made his first mark from 1935 to 1937 as the director of the National Youth Administration in Texas. He learned his early politics as secretary to U.S. Representative Richard M. Kleberg (D-TX). In his work for Kleberg, Johnson set the stage for future political endeavors by taking what seemed to be a meaningless and thankless position and manipulating it into one of great power and strength. Once he got to Washington, Johnson quickly aligned himself with Sam Rayburn and the New Deal. When the representative from Texas's Tenth Congressional District died in 1937, Johnson entered the race to succeed him, running as an ardent New Dealer and supporter of Roosevelt. Johnson served eleven years in the House, honing his skills as a parliamentarian and legislator. He was the chairman of the Democratic Congressional Campaign Committee in 1940 and helped the Democrats retain control of the House. In 1941 he ran for the Senate from Texas but was narrowly defeated in a special election.

Johnson was the first member of Congress to enlist in the wake of America's entry into World War II. He resigned his commission (lieutenant commander in the navy) when given a choice by the president between Capitol Hill and the armed forces. His failure to win a Senate seat did not dim his enthusiasm. He continued as a representative and in 1948 he won election to the Senate. That victory, while an easy win over his Republican opponent, was marked by a hotly contested primary that was marked by charges of ballot-box stuffing and other types of fraud. He became the Democratic nominee by the narrow margin of 87 votes after a protracted legal battle.

As he had in the House, Johnson allied himself with the major power broker in the Senate, who at the time was Richard Russell, a powerful leader in the Senate, as noted above, and the head of the Southern Caucus. The failure of Russell to promote himself meant weak leadership in the Senate, which allowed Johnson to cultivate his relationship with Russell to obtain great power for himself. With Russell's support, Johnson won election as Democratic whip in 1951, and while still a freshman senator he became Democratic minority leader during a two-year period of Republican control. When the Democrats regained majority status in 1955, Johnson became majority leader. In his role as majority leader, Johnson worked the Senate hard and managed to curry bipartisan support for many programs, especially those dealing with foreign policy. In fact, President Eisenhower often found Johnson easier to work with than the Senate Republican leader, William F. Knowland of California. Because his majority was very thin, Johnson was forced to rely on his formidable powers of persuasion, as well as his knowledge of the system and rules, which he knew how to manipulate, to keep control in the Senate.

Following *Brown v. Board of Education*, the 1954 Supreme Court ruling that outlawed school segregation, southern senators circulated a Southern Manifesto that pushed for massive resistance to integration. In a bold and risky move, Johnson refused to sign it. He did recognize the intransigent southern opposition against civil rights, led in large part by his mentor Richard Russell, and the possibility that a Senate filibuster would split his party. Therefore, he helped shepherd the Civil Rights Act of 1957 through Congress by removing key enforcement provisions of the law. As president, however, he would use all of his power to steer the strong Civil Rights Act of 1964 through Congress.

The Democrats enlarged their majority as a consequence of the 1958 election, which created a political environment that was harder for Johnson to control. Furthermore, the election brought young liberals into the Senate who challenged his leadership. Johnson now began to focus more on his aspiration to be president. He was an unsuccessful candidate for the Democratic presidential nomination in 1960, but in a surprise move, John F. Kennedy chose him as his running mate, and the two won the election. As vice president, Johnson still had a role to play in the Senate, which suited him. For as one colleague noted, Johnson really was most at home in the Senate and did not really want to leave. He kept the same office he had as majority leader and thought he could reassert his old authority when his successor, Mike Mansfield (D-MT), proposed that the vice president chair the Democratic Conference. The ensuing protest over what was seen as a violation of the separation of powers ended Johnson's active tenure in the Senate. While president, he often acted as what was called "super majority leader," using his political savvy and powers of persuasion, magnified by his seat in the Oval Office, to push through the Civil Rights Act of 1964, the Voting Rights Act of 1965, and his Great Society programs.

Mike Mansfield

Mike Mansfield served as Senate majority leader from 1961 to 1977, longer than anyone else. His style of leadership was one that helped bridge gaps by sharing power widely among senators. He helped pass much of Johnson's Great Society legislation and was an important figure in breaking the filibuster that blocked the Civil Rights Act of 1964 and getting the legislation enacted. He strongly opposed the Vietnam War and regularly criticized it.

Barbara Jordan

Barbara Jordan was elected to the Texas state senate in 1966, the first black to enter that body since 1883. Elected to the U.S. House of Representatives in 1972, she was the first African American woman from a southern state to serve in Congress. She and Andrew Young of Georgia were the first two blacks elected to Congress in the twentieth century.

Jordan gained national attention as a member of the House Judiciary Committee, which oversaw President Nixon's impeachment hearings. Already known for being an outstanding speaker, she delivered what many consider the finest speech of the hearings. In that address she said, "My faith in the Constitution is whole, it is complete, it is total. I am not going to sit here and be an idle spectator to the diminution, the subversion, the destruction of the Constitution."

In 1975 Jordan worked to expand the Voting Rights Act to include protection for language minorities, and her great oratorical abilities made her the keynote speaker at the 1976 Democratic National Convention in New York City, becoming the first African American and the first woman to earn that distinction. Many considered her speech the highlight of the convention. In 1979, after three terms in the House, Jordan retired from politics. A relentless supporter of civil rights legislation, Jordan received the Presidential Medal of Freedom in 1994.

Adam Clayton Powell

Adam Clayton Powell was first elected to the U.S. Congress in 1945. Although a Democrat, he was often independent minded, and in 1956 he campaigned for President Eisenhower. As chairman of the House Committee on Education and Labor after 1960, he acquired a reputation for flamboyance and disregard of convention. In March 1967 Powell was excluded by the House of Representatives, which had accused him of misuse of House funds, contempt of New York court orders concerning a 1963 libel judgment against him, and conduct unbecoming a member. He was overwhelmingly reelected in a special election in 1967 and again in 1968. He was seated in 1969 but fined $25,000 and deprived of his seniority.

Powell's confrontation with the House membership over his exclusion resulted in a major Supreme Court case in June 1969, *Powell v. McCormack*, in which the Court ruled that the exclusion had been unconstitutional. It challenged core notions of separation of powers as well as delineating both the breadth and limits of congressional powers over its own members. Powell was defeated for reelection in 1970.

Bella Abzug

Another flamboyant figure from this period was Bella Abzug. She was a feminist, lawyer, and politician, born in New York City. She studied at Hunter College and Columbia University and practiced as a lawyer in New York City. Abzug was a prominent peace campaigner and took controversial positions, not hesitating to support and defend those accused of Communist sympathies during the McCarthy era. She cofounded Women Strike for Peace in 1961 and the National Women's Political Caucus in 1971.

Abzug first became a participant in the national political scene in 1970, when she was urged to run, at the age of fifty, for a House seat. Known for her hats and homilies, she became a symbol for the lower part of Manhattan that she represented. She was elected on a women's rights and peace platform and was the first Jewish woman in Congress, pushing an aggressive liberal agenda.

Described as a "creative powerhouse for good," Abzug was an adept politician who represented women, justice, and peace. She worked hard for equal rights for women, voting for the Equal Rights Amendment and bringing large sums of money to New York State, including funding to help people with disabilities and the elderly.

As the chair of the Subcommittee on Governmental Information and Individual Rights, Abzug helped coauthor three major pieces of legislation: the Freedom of Information Act; the Government in the Sunshine Act; and the Right to Privacy Act. All of these bills helped open the window to many secret government activities and for the first time allowed public scrutiny of them. A consequence of this legislation was that Congress could now pursue inquiries into the activities of the CIA, FBI, and other agencies, many of which were covert, illegal, and until then free of any government oversight. In line with her work in uncovering government's dirty little secrets, Abzug was the first member of Congress to call for President Nixon's impeachment.

Abzug's best-known legacy was that of helping to create an equal playing field for women. She initiated the congressional caucus on women's issues, helped organize the National Women's Political Caucus, and served as chief strategist for the Democratic Women's Committee, which achieved equal representation for women in all elective and appointive posts within the party, including as delegates at presidential conventions. Abzug wrote the first law banning discrimination against women in the granting of credit, credit cards, loans, and mortgages and introduced pioneering bills on comprehensive child care, Social Security for homemakers, family planning, and abortion rights. In 1975 she introduced an amendment to the Civil Rights Act of 1964 to include gay and lesbian rights.

Reelected for three terms, Abzug served from 1971 to 1977 and was acknowledged by a *U.S. News & World Report* survey of House members as the "third most influential" House member. In a 1977 Gallup poll, she was named one of the twenty most influential women in the world. Abzug finally left Congress after losing by less than one percent in a four-way Democratic senatorial primary in 1976.

Thomas "Tip" O'Neill

In the 1970s, congressional leaders strove to bring stability to Congress back into the mainstream after the fractious warfare and upheaval of the 1960s. Tip O'Neill was Speaker of the House of Representatives from 1977 to 1987. An old-style politician, he provided a good bridge between the Sixties and the Eighties. O'Neill, from Massachusetts, was an unabashed Democrat and unwavering New Deal liberal. He entered the House of Representatives in 1953, filling the seat previously held by John F. Kennedy, and was an early opponent of the Vietnam War. He became majority whip in 1971, majority leader in 1973, and then Speaker of the House. O'Neill was instrumental in bringing about the resignation of President Richard Nixon following investigations into the Watergate affair, and he instituted many reforms within the House of Representatives.

Sam Ervin

Another key player in Watergate was Sam Ervin. A senator from North Carolina, he began his tenure through an appointment in 1954, at the height of the McCarthy era. Elected for a full term in 1956, Ervin joined the coalition of southern Democrats and conservative Republicans who supported a large defense establishment while opposing civil rights and social welfare legislation. He became chairman of the Subcommittee on Constitutional Rights of the Senate Judiciary Committee in 1961 and won a reputation as a civil libertarian. Ervin attained national fame as chairman of the Senate Select Committee to Investigate Presi-

Tip O'Neill started his political career in 1949 when he was elected speaker of the Massachusetts House of Representatives. He was elected to the U.S. House of Representatives in 1952, serving until 1986. O'Neill served as Speaker of the House from 1977 to 1986 and was the highest-ranking Democrat during the Reagan administration. (Library of Congress)

dential Campaign Practices, which held televised hearings on Watergate.

Ervin's role on the Watergate Committee was not surprising, considering his earlier role in helping to topple McCarthy. Shortly after he arrived in Washington in 1954, then–vice president Nixon appointed Ervin to a committee to study whether McCarthy should be censured, an assignment few were eager to take, because fear of McCarthy was widespread. The freshman senator helped shatter that power, showing his fellow senators McCarthy's true face. Ervin helped strip away the dread that McCarthy inspired in many of his colleagues, thereby playing a role in toppling the Wisconsin senator.

Almost twenty years later, Ervin was selected to head the committee to investigate President Nixon. His strict constructionist view of the Constitution and his unwavering approach to integrity in government made him a perfect chairman, just as they had made him an excellent choice for the McCarthy censure committee. In addition, he was one of the few figures in the Senate that both sides would respect.

Robert Byrd

One of the remarkable aspects of the postwar period was the long tenure of some members of Congress. Robert Byrd began serving as a senator from West Virginia in 1959 after spending six years in the House. In 1971 he defeated Sen. Edward Kennedy for the position of Senate majority whip and was later Senate majority leader (1977–1981, 1987–1988) and Senate minority leader (1981–1987). From 1989 to 1995 and 2001 to 2003, he chaired the Senate Appropriations Committee. Byrd is noted for his oratory and his skill in parliamentary maneuvering.

Strom Thurmond

Strom Thurmond was a longtime senator from South Carolina (1954–2003). He read law while teaching in South Carolina schools (1923–1929) and was admitted to the bar in 1930. Thurmond was elected a state senator in 1933 and became a circuit court judge in 1938. After serving in World War II, he was elected governor of South Carolina in 1946. In 1948 Thurmond was nominated for president by the States' Rights Democrats, known as Dixiecrats, southerners who bolted the Democratic Party in opposition to President Truman's civil rights program. He won thirty-nine electoral votes, helped divide loyalties in the Democratic Party, and thereafter became a divisive figure and a reminder of the ugly past of southern Democrats during the civil rights movement in the 1950s and 1960s.

In 1954 Thurmond was a successful write-in candidate for U.S. Senate. In 1957 he staged the longest filibuster in Senate history, speaking for over twenty-four hours against a civil rights bill. It eventually passed, but in a weakened form, not really accomplishing much and forcing additional showdowns in Congress and the nation at-large. Thurmond switched from the Democratic to the Republican Party in 1964 and later chaired the Senate Judiciary Committee

South Carolina senator Strom Thurmond filibusters against proposed civil rights legislation in February 1957. Thurmond set the record for longest individual filibuster, arguing against civil rights advancement for 24 hours and 18 minutes. (AP/Wide World Photos)

and Armed Services Committee. In 1996 Thurmond became the oldest sitting senator, and in 1997 he became the longest-serving U.S. senator in history.

Thurmond's career ended in controversy with the posthumous revelation in 2003 that he had an illegitimate child in 1925 with an African American maid and that he and his daughter had had a long-standing, warm relationship. In addition, his one-hundredth-birthday party

in 2002 cost Sen. Trent Lott of Mississippi his job as majority leader in the Senate when remarks made by Lott, highlighting Thurmond's racist past with a positive spin, reignited southern racial controversy.

J. William Fulbright

In 1942 J. William Fulbright was elected as a Democrat to the U.S. House of Representatives from Arkansas, and in 1944 he was elected to the Senate, where he served until 1975. He gained international recognition for the Fulbright Act (1946), which provided for the exchange of students and teachers between the United States and many other countries. He was one of the first to criticize Senator McCarthy and was instrumental in bringing about McCarthy's downfall.

Fulbright served as chairman of the Senate Banking and Currency Committee (1955–1959). Subsequently, as chairman of the Senate Foreign Relations Committee (1959–1974), he conducted frequent open hearings to educate the public and reassert the Senate's influence in long-range policy formulation. An outspoken critic of U.S. military intervention abroad, Fulbright opposed the Bay of Pigs invasion of 1961, the landing of marines in the Dominican Republic in 1965, and the escalation of the war in Vietnam. However, Fulbright could be conservative as well, especially on racial issues: he voted against civil rights legislation in the 1960s and 1970s. In the 1974 Democratic senatorial primary in Arkansas, he was defeated by Dale Bumpers.

Turn of the Twenty-first-Century Leaders

Since Watergate, fewer giants have risen in Congress. Since 2000, growing concerns about influence peddling and campaign contributions, battles over term limits, and the resignations and losses of some longtime serving members suggest that the long-tenured men and women who dominated Congress in the twentieth century will not be as common in the twenty-first century. Thus, the 110th Congress (2007–2009) is controlled not just by people with long tenure in the Congress, but also by those who are new to the halls of Congress. Seventy-two have at least twenty years of experience (27 senators and 55 representatives), and 27 have more than thirty years. On the other hand, there are 65 members of Congress serving their first term (10 in the Senate, 55 in the House), some of them already extremely active and powerful. As the twentieth century drew to a close, one could see a growing rate of turnover in leadership positions, due both to electoral upsets and to departures stemming from corruption scandals. Although some rising stars have left Congress earlier in their careers than in previous eras, they still have made noticeable impacts.

One of the major players after the Reagan Revolution of the 1980s was Newt Gingrich. A representative from Georgia, he served as Speaker of the House from 1995 to 1998 and challenged traditional norms through his "Contract with America." A history professor, he was first elected as a Republican from Georgia in 1978 and became the leader of those House conservatives who favored using confrontational tactics to challenge the Democrats' longtime control of the House. He helped force Speaker Jim Wright's resignation in 1989 by question-

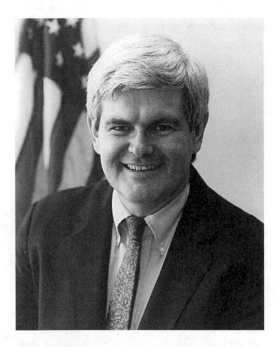

Republican Newt Gingrich was one of the most powerful politicians in America when he served as Speaker of the House from 1994 until his resignation in 1998. Originally elected to the 96th Congress in 1980, he served Georgia's Sixth Congressional District. (Library of Congress)

ing Wright's financial dealings. That same year, Gingrich became House minority whip.

In 1995, after large Republican gains in the 1994 election—during which, touting his "Contract with America," Gingrich championed a balanced-budget amendment, limitations on welfare benefits, and term limits for members of Congress—he became the first Republican Speaker in forty years. Gingrich led Republicans in attempts to pass conservative legislation. This often put him in direct confrontation with President Bill Clinton, especially regarding the budget in 1995 and 1996.

The Republicans' program did not completely succeed, and Clinton's confrontations with Gingrich and the House helped to restore some of the reputation the president had lost after the 1994 elections. While the Republicans retained their majority and Gingrich his speakership, in the 1996 elections he began to lose favor with the conservative bloc, who saw him as backing away from its principles. In early 1997 the House, following an investigation that began in 1995, reprimanded Gingrich for campaign funding violations. In the 1998 congressional elections, Democrats made substantial gains despite being in the midst of the Clinton impeachment process, and Gingrich resigned his speakership and House seat.

Since Gingrich, leadership has shifted back and forth between the parties in both the House and the Senate, and shifting majorities have inhibited any long-term party control. One of the more powerful men in Washington, Tom DeLay, had to resign his post as House majority leader because of the implication of scandal due to his ties with indicted lobbyist Jack Abramoff. Other dominant figures have recently lost their positions of power. Senate Republican minority leader Trent Lott lost his post after making favorable remarks about segregationist Strom Thurmond's 1948 run for president. House Democratic minority leader Dick Gephardt left Congress after an unsuccessful bid for the Democratic presidential nomination in

2004. Senate Democratic minority leader Tom Daschle failed to hold his seat in the 2004 election.

What is apparent, though, is that a succession of Speakers and Senate leaders has often provided strong if not always consistent leadership. The power exerted by men such as Jim Wright and Newt Gingrich in the House and Bill Frist in the Senate has shown that the institution survives and prospers as strong leaders step up to take the reins.

FURTHER READING

Amer, Mildred L. *CRS Report for Congress: Black Members of the United States Congress: 1789–1997.* Damascus, MD: Penny Hill Press, August 13, 1997.

Amer, Mildred L. *CRS Report for Congress: Black Members of the United States Congress: 1870–2007.* Damascus, MD: Penny Hill Press, September 27, 2007.

Amer, Mildred. *CRS Report for Congress: Women in the United States Congress: 1917–2007.* Damascus, MD: Penny Hill Press, May 25, 2007.

Biographical Directory of the United States Congress, 1774–2005. Washington, DC: U.S. Government Printing Office, 2006.

Canon, David T. *Actors, Athletes, and Astronauts: Political Amateurs in the United States Congress.* Chicago, IL: University of Chicago Press, 1990.

Caro, Robert A. *Lyndon Johnson: Master of the Senate.* New York: Knopf, 2002.

Davidson, Roger H., Susan Webb Hammond, and Raymond W. Smock, eds., *Masters of the House.* Boulder, CO: Westview Press, 1998.

Heitshusen, Valerie. *CRS Report for Congress: Party Leaders in the House: Election, Duties, and Responsibilities.* Damascus, MD: Penny Hill Press, December 8, 2006.

Heitshusen, Valerie. *CRS Report for Congress: Party Leaders in the United States Congress, 1789–2007.* Damascus, MD: Penny Hill Press, February 27, 2007.

Peters, Ronald M., Jr. *The American Speakership: The Office in Historical Perspective.* 2nd ed. Baltimore: Johns Hopkins University Press, 1997.

Peterson, Merrill D. *The Great Triumvirate: Webster, Clay, and Calhoun.* New York: Oxford University Press, 1988.

Remini, Robert V. *Daniel Webster: The Man and His Time.* New York: W. W. Norton, 1997.

Remini, Robert V. *Henry Clay: Statesman for the Union.* New York: W. W. Norton, 1991.

Sachs, Richard C. *CRS Report for Congress: Leadership in the U.S. House of Representatives.* Damascus, MD: Penny Hill Press, June 17, 1997.

Sachs, Richard C., Carol Hardy-Vincent, Paul S. Rundquist, and Faye M. Bullock. *CRS Report for Congress: Party Leaders in Congress, 1789–1997: Vital Statistics.* Damascus, MD: Penny Hill Press, January 7, 1997.

Schneider, Judy. *CRS Report for Congress: Senate Leadership Structure: Overview of Party Organization.* Damascus, MD: Penny Hill Press, December 7, 2006.

Schneider, Judy. *CRS Report for Congress: Senate Leadership: Whip Organization.* Damascus, MD: Penny Hill Press, December 7, 2006.

Williams, T. Harry. *Huey Long.* New York: Knopf, 1969.

5

THE POLITICS OF THE FEDERAL LEGISLATURE

The First Congress met in New York City on April 1, 1789, and chose Frederick Muhlenberg of Pennsylvania as its Speaker. The next day it appointed a committee of eleven to draw up the rules of procedure of the House, which were adopted six days later. The first standing committee of the House—the Committee on Elections—made its report, which accepted the credentials of forty-nine members and was approved on April 18. By then the House was already debating its first tariff bill.

In contrast to the speed in which the original House organized and began business, two hundred years later it took five years of study and negotiation to produce an agreement on a limited revision of the House rules. The House of Representatives of the twenty-first century had evolved into a highly structured, to some convoluted, institution governed by an intricate set of rules, precedents, and customs. Changes in those rules and customs often reflected societal changes and changes necessary so the House could respond to the needs of society.

From the beginning, politics and personalities have played their part in influencing the timing and direction of changes in House procedures and organization. Two major developments effected many of the changes. First, as the country expanded, the House saw a rapid increase in the size of its membership in

Frederick Augustus Conrad Muhlenberg was a well-known Lutheran pastor before entering politics as a delegate to the Second Continental Congress in 1779. Muhlenberg was elected U.S. representative from Pennsylvania in 1783, and he became the first Speaker of the House of Representatives in 1789. (Library of Congress)

the nineteenth century. Second, the House saw a marked increase in workload in the twentieth century. Both of these developments were important factors in the development of a legislative body that, among other things, involved strict limitation on floor debate, a heavy reliance on the committee system, and complex methods for organizing and maintaining the flow of House business.

The early Congresses benefited from the fact that many of the representatives elected had served in the Continental Congress or in their state legislatures. Often the procedures followed in those bodies, which were derived in large part from English parliamentary practice, were appropriated to form the basis for the House rules.

Because the Constitution demanded a Speaker, the House elected one. His early duties were to preside over the House, "preserve decorum and order," put questions, and decide all points of order. If any member transgressed a rule, the Speaker, or any other member, was allowed to call the offender "to order." The offending member then had to sit down immediately, unless he was allowed to explain. The early rules also stipulated that the Speaker was to announce the results of votes and all votes were conducted by ballot.

Early rules limited members' ability to act, and the substantial freedom of individual members to act that would characterize the House in later years was not apparent at the start.

The first rules also set forth legislative procedure. As in the Continental Congress, the primary forum for consid-

ering and perfecting legislation was to be the Committee of the Whole House. This was the House itself sitting under another name to provide a more fluid forum for debate and discussion. (Hence, the Constitutional Convention often formed itself into the Committee of the Whole for the purpose of debate in order to allow for a more robust exchange of ideas.) When the House was sitting as the Committee of the Whole, a member other than the Speaker occupied the chair and certain motions permitted in the House, such as the previous question and the motion to adjourn, were not in order, nor were roll-call votes taken. Amendments rejected in the committee could not be offered again in the House except as part of a motion to recommit. As in the House, a majority of the members was needed to make a quorum in the Committee of the Whole (thirty out of fifty-nine in the First Congress).

In the early years of the House, discussion of all major legislative proposals began in the Committee of the Whole. Since there were few if any standing committees, the small size of the early Congress made this a very manageable mechanism for considering legislation. After broad agreement had been reached on the principles involved, the Committee of the Whole named a select committee to draft a bill. When this select committee reported back to the House, the bill was referred to the Committee of the Whole for section-by-section debate and approval and amendment. The committee's work completed, the Speaker resumed the chair, and the House either accepted or rejected the amendments agreed to by the committee.

At first, unlike today, there were no time limits in the House on the right of members to speak. However, even given the small membership of the first two Congresses, this proved to be an unwieldy process. In 1790 the House, in an attempt to curtail the length of time spent on each bill, amended its rules to permit the Speaker to appoint all committees unless otherwise specially directed by the House. Four years later, the Speaker was empowered to name the chair of the Committee of the Whole, who had previously been elected. But these were small deviations from the basic procedure. The fundamental process of fashioning the broad terms of the legislation in the Committee of the Whole before the naming of a select committee to draft the bill (there were 350 such select committees in the Third Congress) continued into the 1800s.

By consigning each proposal to a special committee that ceased to exist when a bill was reported, the House as a body kept effective control over the legislation. But as its business expanded and its membership increased (to 106 after 1790 and 142 after 1800), the House began to delegate increasing responsibility for initiating legislation to standing permanent committees. Four were established in 1795 and six more between 1802 and 1809. Among the most important of the early committees were the Interstate and Foreign Commerce (1795), Ways and Means (made permanent 1802), and Public Lands (made permanent with the Louisiana Purchase in 1803).

EXECUTIVE DOMINATION

One of the shortcomings of Article I specifically and the Constitution generally was the failure of the Founders to take into account the development of political parties. The first rules of the House also reflected the idealistic and somewhat unrealistic view that government could operate in a nonpartisan fashion. This shortcoming was not readily recognized. The Federalist victory in winning ratification of the Constitution, the unanimous and nonpartisan choice of George Washington as president and the great preponderance of Federalists in the First Congress tended to obscure the underlying economic, sectional, and philosophical differences of the times that would soon be encapsulated in an emerging party system.

It is not surprising then, that the domination of the House by Secretary of the Treasury Alexander Hamilton, a member of the executive branch, did not bother members, since most of those in the First Congress shared his outlook, and some even stood to profit from the plans he proposed. James Madison was the first to take issue with the substance of Hamilton's program as well as the dominance of the executive branch in guiding the decisions of the House. He was joined in the challenge to Hamilton by Secretary of State Thomas Jefferson, who strongly opposed Hamilton from within the Cabinet. In a formal complaint, Jefferson wrote to President Washington, criticizing what he saw as Hamilton's attempt to exert undue influence upon Congress, shattering the carefully designed system of separation of powers and checks and balances. The gap between Hamiltonian ideas on government and Jefferson and Madison's views was reinforced by growing U.S. antagonism toward some of the European powers in the 1790s.

By 1792 Madison and Jefferson were the recognized leaders of a nascent Democratic-Republican Party of opposition. The party gave a voice to southern fears about federalism, that is, Hamiltonian, economic policies, which appeared to be unfair to southern agrarian interests. The party also reflected a general dissatisfaction with Hamilton's aristocratic views, which favored a very strong executive branch. Following the election of 1792, the House was closely divided between Democratic-Republicans and Federalists. In 1800 Jefferson's party emerged with a clear majority, and during Jefferson's two terms as president, his party outnumbered the Federalists in the House by a margin of at least two to one.

With the early emergence of political parties, the choice of Speaker soon fell to the party with a majority in the House. Thus, in 1799 Federalist Theodore Sedgwick of Massachusetts was elected Speaker over Democratic-Republican Nathaniel Macon of North Carolina by a vote of 44 to 38, a margin that approximated that of Federalists over Democratic-Republicans in the Sixth Congress (1799–1801). Two years later, the large Democratic-Republican majority of the Seventh Congress elected Macon as Speaker.

The early Speakers were often willing to use their powers in support of party policies. In 1796, when House Democratic-Republicans mounted an attack on Jay's Treaty with Britain, Speaker Jonathan Dayton, a Federalist, twice maneuvered to produce ties that resulted in the defeat of anti-treaty motions. Democratic-Republicans in the Sixth Congress found the rulings of Sedgwick so partisan that they refused to join in the by-then customary vote of thanks to the Speaker at adjournments.

But as noted above, those early Speakers were not the actual political or legislative leaders of the House. Until he left the Treasury in 1795, Hamilton—operating through various members of Congress—dominated the Federalist majority and was a powerful leader. Madison, the leader of the Democratic-Republicans in the House, was also powerful.

As Democratic-Republicans, or Jeffersonian Democrats, Jefferson and Madison were opposed in principle to the concept of executive supremacy embraced by Hamilton (although in practice they often accepted that perspective). When he became president in 1801, one of Jefferson's first actions was to eliminate the personal appearance of the president before a joint session of Congress to read his annual State of the Union Address. Instead, he established the practice (continued until the presidency of Woodrow Wilson) of sending up the message to be read by a clerk. However, despite his displeasure with Hamilton's iron hand, by no means did this mean that Jefferson abandoned Hamilton's practice of trying to lead the House.

Jefferson's secretary of the Treasury, Albert Gallatin, soon became as adept as

Few U.S. politicians have garnered more notoriety than the controversial John Randolph of Roanoke, Virginia. Randolph spent most of his political career in the U.S. House of Representatives as the leader of the Republican opposition to Thomas Jefferson. Randolph's outspoken criticism of the War of 1812 eventually led to his loss in the election of 1813. (Library of Congress)

Hamilton had been in guiding administration measures through the party caucus and the House. Moreover, Jefferson picked his own House floor leader, who was named chair of the Committee on Ways and Means at the same time. The men who held the posts of floor leader and Ways and Means chair during Jefferson's tenure were known as the president's spokesperson. Jefferson's complete control was evident when one of these leaders, John Randolph, broke with the president over policy. In the wake of the defection, Jefferson had him unseated as the Ways and Means chairman.

However, Randolph's removal was not a strong-arm tactic forced upon a recalcitrant House. Many representatives welcomed his removal because he had seriously offended them. Members complained that he tied up committee business by traveling, hid appropriations estimates, and rushed out important bills at the end of the session, after many members had left, so he could ram them through. Jefferson's methods did not handcuff House members. Early representatives had opportunities to act, especially after it was decided that all standing committees be elected by ballot and that the committees would choose their own chairs. However, at the beginning of the Eleventh Congress in 1809, the committees decided to revert to the original system whereby the Speaker chose the committee chairs.

In sum, the first twenty years of the House saw the beginnings of the standing committee system and the emergence of a floor leader and committee chairmen as key men in the legislative process. But despite that development, the legislative process was still dominated, by and large, by the executive branch, and many decisions on legislative issues were reached behind the scenes in closed caucuses of the majority party.

STRONG CONGRESSIONAL LEADERSHIP AND STANDING COMMITTEES

The era of executive supremacy over Congress ended with the presidency of James Madison. Although Democratic-Republican majorities nominally backed him during his two terms, he soon lost control of his party to a group of young War Hawks, first elected to the Twelfth Congress in 1810, who pushed for war against England. Dominated in the House by John Calhoun of South Carolina and Henry Clay of Kentucky, the War Hawks capitalized on Madison's reluctance to use the executive branch to control Congress. They helped effect a shift of power to Congress that was not reversed until Andrew Jackson became president almost two decades later.

It was Henry Clay's election as Speaker that thrust the House, and thereby individuals in that body, into a leading role. Clay came to national attention while serving briefly as a senator from Kentucky in 1810 and 1811. Clay then entered the House in 1811 and, although only thirty-four years old and a newcomer, was promptly elected Speaker. Clay quickly took advantage of

his position and used his power to appoint committees and their chairs, putting his fellow War Hawks in all of the key positions. Together, they took control of the House.

It was the job of the Speaker, said Clay in an 1823 speech, to be prompt and impartial in deciding questions of order, to display "patience, good temper and courtesy" to every member, and to make "the best arrangement and distribution of the talent of the House . . . for the dispatch of the public business." Above all, he said the Speaker must "remain cool and unshaken amidst all the storms of debate, carefully guarding the preservation of the permanent laws and rules of the House from being sacrificed to temporary passions, prejudices or interests."

This was not an easy job in Clay's time due to the prevalence of strong political passions, a growing membership, and the belief that the right to debate was essentially unlimited. And despite his admonitions to the contrary, Clay—an ardent debater with strong policy beliefs—often objected to the very rules he pronounced as so essential. While the rules in place allowed the majority party to limit and shut down debate, they were not often invoked, and skilled representatives (like John Randolph) were able to manipulate and tie up House proceedings. Often the floor of the House became a battleground for struggles between Randolph and Clay, as evident during the jockeying over the Compromise of 1820, in which Clay outmaneuvered Randolph and obtained the bill's passage.

The sometimes chaotic House proceedings ignited efforts to refine the chamber's procedures between 1809 and 1829. The first rule for establishing a daily order of business was adopted in 1811. The following year, the Committee of Enrolled Bills was the first committee given the right to report at any time, a right later granted to other committees. The reason for these modifications was to speed up the process of considering important bills. In the next decade, rules were adopted that enabled the House to protect itself against business it did not wish to consider, created a calendar of the Committee of the Whole, and established that no rule could be suspended without a two-thirds vote.

The chief development in House procedures during this period, however, was the proliferation of standing committees and their emergence as principal forums for the initial consideration of proposed legislation. As the number of select committees created to draft bills continued to drop (from 350 in 1795 to 70 in 1815), standing committees increased (from 10 in 1809 to 28 in 1825).

Among the standing committees were the Judiciary Committee (created in 1813) and the Committees on Military Affairs, on Naval Affairs, and on Foreign Affairs (created in 1822). Clay created a committee on expenditures to check on the economy and efficiency with which monies disbursed by Congress were administered. Between 1816 and 1826, these and other House committees conducted at least twenty major investigations. Inquiries were held on such matters as the conduct of Gen. Andrew Jackson in the Seminole War, charges against Secretary of the Treasury William Crawford, and the conduct of John Calhoun as secretary of war.

PARTY UNITY, CONGRESSIONAL CAUCUSES, AND POPULAR VOTING FOR PRESIDENT

During Clay's speakership the party caucus still afforded the House's Democratic-Republicans an important means of reaching legislative decisions. This system worked because of strict party discipline. By the mid-1820s, however, the disintegration of the party into various factions was manifest, and the party fragmented as personal differences and sectional interests gave rise to new alliances.

The rise and fall of party unity were connected to the rise and fall of the congressional caucus as the agency for selecting party nominees for president and vice president. The choice of the presidential nominee by the caucus began in 1800, when both Federalist and Democratic-Republican members of the House and Senate met secretly to pick running mates for Jefferson and John Adams. In 1804 Jefferson was renominated unanimously and openly by the caucus. Four years later Madison was nominated by the caucus, but not unanimously, and in 1812, only 83 of the 133 Democratic-Republicans in Congress attended the caucus that renominated Madison.

This apathy grew and by 1820, with no real opposition in either party, fewer than fifty members showed up for the caucus. James Monroe—who was credited with the "era of good feelings" and had managed to keep clear of the controversy over the Missouri Compromise—was easily elected to a second term.

The race to succeed Monroe began almost at once. It included three members of the Cabinet—Crawford, Calhoun, and John Quincy Adams—plus Henry Clay and Andrew Jackson. When it appeared that Crawford was going to win in the caucus, supporters of other candidates began to denounce the caucus system. As a result, only 66 of the 261 senators and representatives then in Congress attended the caucus that gave the nomination to Crawford in 1824. This lack of unanimity and growing disaffection with party was evident in the election that year. Despite not being the winner of the caucus, Andrew Jackson won a plurality of the popular vote, but not a majority of electoral votes. When the election then went to the House, neither Crawford (the caucus winner) nor Jackson (the popular winner) won; instead, the House elected Adams.

The 1824 election marked the end of the old party system. Changing voting procedures and an expansion of the suffrage hastened the demise of the caucus system of nomination. Between 1800 and 1824, the number of states in which the electors were chosen by popular vote rather than by the legislature increased from five out of sixteen to eighteen out of twenty-four. When Jackson was elected in 1828, only two states did not rely on the popular vote, which overall had almost tripled since the previous election. With the emergence of a mass electorate,

aspirants for the presidency were forced to seek a much broader base of support than the congressional caucus.

THE ANTEBELLUM ERA

The election of Andrew Jackson as president added to the erosion of congressional power and leadership by increasing the power and prestige of the presidency. He made unprecedented use of the veto and manipulated the patronage powers of his office to establish primacy over Congress. Two new parties emerged during his presidency, the Democrats and the Whigs. True to their name, the Whigs extolled the doctrine of legislative supremacy, and after Jackson's term in office, they tried to weaken the presidency to the benefit of the Congress.

Another reason the power and influence of the House began to decline under Jackson was the increase of its membership to 242, making it more unwieldy and harder to coordinate and drive forward in pursuit of policy initiatives. In addition, those men who had led the House—Clay, Calhoun, Webster—all moved on to the Senate, which now became the major arena of debate on national policy. The party in control of the presidency, the House, and the Senate shifted considerably after Jackson. Increasingly, however, both Democrats and Whigs found themselves divided by the issue of slavery and its extension to the new territories and states west of the Mississippi. The issue was reflected in bitter battles for the speakership that occurred in 1839, 1849, 1855, and 1859.

Intraparty contests for Speaker were not new in the House. For example, in 1805, when Democratic-Republicans outnumbered Federalists almost four to one, it took four ballots to reelect Nathaniel Macon, a southerner from North Carolina, over Joseph B. Varnum, the northern candidate. Two years later, when there were five candidates, Varnum won on the second ballot after Macon withdrew. By 1820, the year of the Missouri Compromise, the issue of slavery was an explicit part of the sectional contest for Speaker. To replace Clay, who had resigned, the House cast twenty-two ballots before electing John Taylor of New York, the antislavery candidate, over William Lowndes of South Carolina, a middle-of-the-road compromise candidate.

The next two decades were littered with multiballot contests that pitted party members against each other, in some cases representatives from the same state. The culmination of this squabbling seemed to occur in 1839. Although Martin Van Buren, Jackson's handpicked successor was elected president in 1836, his coattails were short; Democrats barely won control of the House, which was composed of 120 Democrats and 118 Whigs, with five contested seats in New Jersey. Debate over who would be the next Speaker was marked by days of acrimonious deliberations and multiple ballots, ending with the election of a Democratic Speaker, Robert Hunter from Virginia, who secured the position on the eleventh ballot by uniting Whig votes rather than Democratic ones.

The following period saw control of the House pass back and forth between Whigs and Democrats. And by the time Zachary Taylor, a Whig, was elected president in 1848, neither party had a majority in Congress, because a number of free soil Whigs and Democrats refused to support the leading candidates for Speaker. The pending issue was what to do about slavery in the territory won in the war against Mexico, and the free soilers were determined to prevent the election of a Speaker who would appoint

Howell Cobb was elected Speaker of the U.S. House of Representatives in 1849 and held that position during the hotly debated Compromise of 1850. (Library of Congress)

proslavery majorities to the Committees on Territories and the District of Columbia. It took sixty-three ballots to elect, with a two-vote margin, Howell Cobb, a Democrat from Georgia.

In the first part of the decade leading up to the Civil War, proslavery Democrats held firm control of the House. But their attempt to extend slavery into the Kansas and Nebraska Territories produced a large turnout of antislavery forces in the election of 1854, the first in which the new Republican Party, successor to the Whigs, participated. When the Twenty-fourth Congress convened on December 3, 1855, the House membership was divided among 108 Republicans and Whigs, 83 Democrats, and 43 members of minor parties that sprang up in the 1850s, each catering to different regional and demographic concerns. The disarray resulting from this assortment of parties and concerns meant that a Speaker was not easily elected. Two months passed and 133 ballots were taken before the House membership finally selected Nathaniel Banks of Massachusetts, a member of the Know Nothing Party, by a plurality. These conflicts in the House helped contribute to a lack of strong leadership, which in turn, compromised the chamber's ability to govern effectively.

Some of those fractures seemed to heal with Democrat James Buchanan's election to the presidency in 1856. His coattails helped give control of the House to his party. But the midterm elections reversed their fortunes, and when the Thirty-sixth Congress met for

the first time in December 1859, no party had majority control of the House, which was composed of 116 Republicans, 83 Democrats, and 39 members from other parties. Proslavery and antislavery blocs were again deadlocked over the choice of a Speaker. Rationality being in short supply, passion consumed the debate. The presiding clerk added to the chaos by refusing to decide on points of order. The turmoil that marked the struggle over who would be the next Speaker continued for two months, into 1860. William Pennington of New Jersey, who barely won the contest, lasted only one term.

Slavery was the great issue marking the antebellum House. While its most visible manifestation may have been in the battles over who would be Speaker, it also surfaced in other areas, creating ongoing problems for the Congress. In 1836 John Quincy Adams challenged a House practice of refusing to receive petitions and memorials from citizens about the abolition of slavery. At this time, the first 30 days of each session were dedicated to reading constituents' petitions, and then every other Monday, after that. After each petition was read aloud, it was printed and then given to a committee. Once in committee, the members could address the issue of the petition, or ignore it, and let it die. As the petitions arriving concerning slavery grew in number, the House stopped considering them.

These petitions angered southern representatives who felt, because there was no way slavery was going to be abolished, why hear them. In December 1835, southerners, together with northern Democrats, succeeded in winning a vote to table a petition that called for the abolition of slavery in the District of Columbia. This action induced a strong reaction from northerners, who saw the right of the citizens to petition the government as a basic constitutional right. Adams led the charge to stop what became known as the "gag rule," which stated that no petitions dealing with slavery could be printed or referred to committee, and any petitions submitted would lie untouched with no action taken on them.

Adams, who considered the gag rule a violation of the Constitution and the rules of the House, reopened the issue in 1837 by asking the Speaker how to dispose of a petition he had received concerning slavery. Before the Speaker could act, southerners, deeply offended, moved at once to censure Adams. Adams was able to avoid the censure move, but he continued to push for the House to hear the petitions. Further agitation led the House in 1840 to adopt a rule that no papers "parading the abolition of slavery . . . shall be received by this House or entertained in any way whatever." A series of raucous debates kept the gag rule in force through 1844, when it was finally retracted.

Rule Changes

Rules adopted in this period were significant to the long-range development of House procedures. In 1837, for example, precedence was given to floor considera-tion of revenue and appropriation bills and the inclusion of other legislation in an appropriation bill (which led the Senate to kill a number of bills) was barred.

In 1841 the House finally agreed to limit debate. Each member was limited to one hour. (Proposals like this were not new; similar limitations were first proposed during debates over the Missouri Compromise, when Randolph argued for a four-hour limit.) However, this new rule only fixed the problem of debate on the floor of the House, and constraints were still needed to limit debate in the Committee of the Whole. To resolve this problem, a rule was adopted providing that the House, by majority vote, could discharge the committee from consideration of a bill, disposing of all pending amendments without any debate on them.

Objection to the latter provision led in 1847 to adoption of the five-minute rule, giving members that much time to explain their amendment. Members quickly adapted this rule into a practice of offering and then withdrawing numerous amendments in an effort to delay action on controversial bills. In an effort to stymie this manipulation, the rule was amended in 1850 to prohibit the withdrawal of any amendment without unanimous consent. While this helped, it did not resolve the major difficulties that plagued the House when leadership was weak and a determined minority was bent on controlling proceedings. For example, during discussion of the Kansas-Nebraska Act in 1854, opponents stretched out debate for days with multiple amendments, calls for adjournment, and reconsideration of votes culminating in 109 roll calls.

In 1858 the House agreed to establish a select committee for revising the growing number of rules, which by that time numbered over 150. The committee included the Speaker, this being the first time the Speaker served on any committee of the House. As finally approved by the House in March 1860, this first general revision of the rules was largely of a theoretical nature. While it did make some important, practical changes affecting some of the basic rules of order (like those pertaining to the use of the previous question and motions to strike the enacting clause), the revised rules of 1860 did not fix the problems that had plagued the House in the preceding years. A determined minority was still able to hold the House hostage.

Thus, there was little significant change in House procedures during the antebellum period. The system of standing committees, established in 1825 with twenty-eight committees, had, by 1861, expanded to thirty-six. The Committee on Ways and Means continued to handle both appropriations and revenue bills, and while its chair was not always the designated floor leader of the majority party, he was always among the most influential members. The Speaker continued to appoint members to committees and to designate their chairs. But none of the Speakers who followed Clay achieved his stature or influence. The growing sectional conflict inhibited the institution even more.

THE CIVIL WAR AND RECONSTRUCTION

The Civil War all but eliminated the Confederate South from national politics. The eleven seceding states were largely unrepresented in Congress for eight years; most of the sixty-six House seats held by those states sat vacant from 1861 to 1869. The war emasculated the Democratic Party. Many Democrats from outside the South were linked to that region and presumed to be sympathetic to the Confederate cause. The party suffered as a result. The Republicans maintained control in the House until 1875 (and in the Senate until 1879).

At the same time, the war and its aftermath gave rise to bitter conflict between Congress and President Andrew Johnson, leading to his impeachment in 1868, followed by a prolonged period of legislative dominance. The three decades starting with the Civil War saw the expansion of House membership, an intensification of House efforts to control government spending, an increase in the number and power of House committees, and an ongoing struggle to adapt the rules of the House to its legislative purposes.

During the war, President Abraham Lincoln assumed unprecedented powers at a time when Republican majorities ruled both Houses. The Republican Party, dominated by radicals who were committed to the Whig doctrine of legislative supremacy, often opposed Lincoln's desire for a strong executive to prosecute the war. Disagreement between Lincoln and Congress was sharpest over the issue of reconstructing the Confederate states. Lincoln argued that they had never really left the Union and wanted to reinstate their political rights as quickly as possible. In contrast, the Radical Republicans were determined to punish the Confederate states. They also wanted to secure their own authority by remaking the power structure that existed prior to the war, when northern Republican interests had been counterbalanced by a strong southern and Democratic wing. No matter which view of Reconstruction prevailed, the Radicals insisted that the readmission of the Confederate states and their Reconstruction were legislative responsibilities.

When Lincoln set up new governments in Louisiana and Arkansas, Radical Republicans in the House passed a bill to place all Reconstruction authority under the direct control of Congress. Lincoln pocket-vetoed the bill after Congress had adjourned in 1864. In response, Republican leadership in the House issued the Wade-Davis Manifesto, which asserted the paramount authority of Congress. It mandated that the president "must contain himself to his executive duties—to obey and execute, not make the laws—to suppress by arms armed rebellion, and leave political reorganization to Congress."

The assassination of Lincoln gave new life to the Radical leadership. In the wake of his death and Andrew Johnson's weak leadership upon assuming the presidency, congressional Republicans moved to control all aspects of Reconstruction and to suppress any attempt by the White House

to direct it. Openly sympathetic to the South, Johnson vetoed numerous bills and thereby alienated any support he might have had in Congress, which facilitated the Radical Republican agenda and, in essence, gave Congress full control over Reconstruction.

One of the key pieces of legislation that facilitated this shift of power was the Tenure of Office Act of 1867, passed to prevent Johnson from firing Secretary of War Edwin Stanton. The law made it a high misdemeanor to remove without the Senate's approval any official whose nomination had been confirmed by the Senate. Johnson viewed the law as unconstitutional and proceeded to suspend Stanton from office. In response, the House voted 126 to 47 to impeach him. The Senate then tried him, with supporters of convicting Johnson falling one short of the two-thirds vote required. (The Tenure of Office Act was amended during the Grant Administration and repealed in 1887. The U.S. Supreme Court in 1926 ruled the law unconstitutional.) Significantly, the impeachment process in the House did not generate new leadership in that body.

The Civil War led to renewed efforts by the House to control federal expenditures (up from $63 million 1860 to $1.3 billion in 1865) by a more careful exercise of its power over appropriations. Until the Civil War, the Committee on Ways and Means had handled all supply as well as revenue bills, in addition to bills on monetary matters. But in 1865 the House transferred some of these responsibilities to two new standing committees: the Committee on Appropriations and the Committee on Banking and Currency.

Anticipating massive expenditures during Reconstruction, Congress began to tighten controls on spending. Although Congress continued to make lump sum appropriations to the army and navy, it specified in greater detail the amounts and purposes for which the civilian departments could spend money, limited their ability to transfer funds, and demanded the return of unspent monies. These efforts helped to keep federal expenditures below $300 million in every year except one in the period from 1871 to 1890.

THE GILDED AGE

With the end of Reconstruction, the Democratic Party reemerged as a power in Congress. This power was not uncontested and strife between the White House and Congress helped shape both leadership roles in the House, as well as define the roles of both Congress and the president. Democrats controlled the House during the Forty-fifth Congress (1877–1879) and won control of both chambers in the Forty-sixth, but by margins too small to override a veto. In an attempt to force Hayes' hand, members attached riders to legislation aimed at protecting the civil and voting rights of blacks in the South and preventing fraud in northern cities. The Democrats sought to use those riders to destroy the veto power of the President. Because Hayes favored the legislation, Democ-

rats figured he would not veto the laws. By working their own agenda into these laws, Democrats hoped to consolidate their power, culminating in a Democratic victory in the presidential election in 1880.

Outraged by this tactic, Hayes labeled it "unconstitutional and revolutionary." Congressmen had used riders regularly since the late 1820s, and the Jackson administration, but they rarely were used to derail proposed laws concerning important issues. Hayes saw this as a direct challenge to his power as president. In April, May, and June, Congress passed appropriations bills with riders attached, which Hayes promptly vetoed because, among other reasons, the riders were an unconstitutional attempt to force legislation on the president. Because the Democrats did not have enough votes to override his veto, their attempt to bypass the veto and push their agenda through backfired on them, uniting Republicans, who won the White House in 1880.

Failure to challenge Hayes showed the need to get work done more efficiently and effectively. While power in the House was dispersed among standing committees and their chairs, it was also the case that whoever controlled the appointment of those committees exercised tremendous control over the House. While Speakers had held that authority since the earliest days of the House, its exercise assumed new importance with the widening needs of the country in an era of expanding population and growing economic inter-

Portrait of James Blaine, Speaker of the U.S. House of Representatives, U.S. senator from Maine, and two-time U.S. secretary of state. (Library of Congress)

ests, and the rising importance of the committees.

The Speakers during the post-Reconstruction years had varying degrees of success in using that authority to the advantage of their party. Schuyler Colfax, a Republican Speaker from 1863 to 1869 enjoyed as much personal popularity as had Henry Clay, but he was not forceful. For the most part he was a figurehead, manipulated by Thaddeus Stevens, who while never Speaker, used the Speaker's power and his own position as chair of the House Ways and Means Committee and the Appropriations Committee to run the House.

James G. Blaine, a Maine Republican, succeeded Colfax. Blaine, the Speaker for six years, used the power of the office to further his Republican agenda by manipulating committee assignments to produce majorities favorable to legislation he desired.

When Democrats won control of the House at the end of Reconstruction, the Speaker, Samuel J. Randall from Pennsylvania, prompted a change in House rules in 1880. The revisions made it easier for floor leaders and committee chairs to bring legislation to the floor. The Committee on Rules, which had been a select committee since 1789 and chaired by the Speaker since 1858, was transformed into a standing committee. As a permanent committee, it—and more importantly, its chair—was able to control debate in the House. Special orders and rules adopted by the House and controlled by the committee governed both the length of debate on major bills and the extent to which amendments could be offered on those bills.

From 1881 to 1883 the Democrats lost control of the House. Upon resuming control, this time under John G. Carlisle of Kentucky, the Democrats ruled with a stronger hand than before. Carlisle, who was in the top position for six years, manipulated the rules, such as the Speaker's "power of recognition," to delay if not quash motions he opposed, thereby controlling the floor of the House. He would regularly ask a

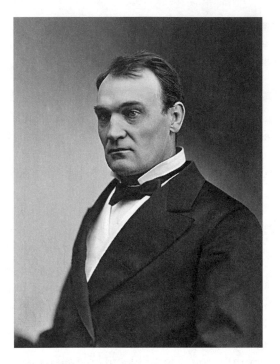

John Carlisle rose through the Kentucky legislature to enter both houses of the U.S. Congress and serve as President Grover Cleveland's secretary of the treasury. (Library of Congress)

under Carlisle's rule, the House fell prey to various delaying tactics. Often, minorities would employ a device known as the "disappearing quorum" or "silent filibuster" to hold up legislation. In this maneuver, quorums would appear and disappear, creating the need for endless roll calls, which made it impossible to conduct proper business. As a result, the House could not legislate meaningfully, which fueled unrest on the part of the public, which demanded that the House do something to allow business to move forward. But without a modification of the rules, not an easy task, the problem could not be solved.

member, "For what purpose does the gentleman rise?" Anytime he disagreed with the "purpose," he denied recognition of that member. In spite of his growing power Carlisle, like his two predecessors, failed to unite the party and was not able to maintain rigid control over House proceedings.

All three Speakers—Blaine, Randall, and Carlisle—played important roles in developing precedents by which Speakers were guided under the House rules. Still, determined minorities were able to obstruct House business. Especially

Samuel Jackson Randall was an important figure in the Democratic Party of Pennsylvania during the nineteenth century, serving as Speaker of the House of Representatives from 1876 to 1881. (Library of Congress)

Portrait of Thomas B. Reed, U.S. representative from Maine, and Speaker of the House (1889–1891 and 1895–1899). (Ridpath, John Clark, Ridpath's History of the World, *1901)*

Speaker Thomas B. Reed

With the return of Republican control in 1889, the door for reform was opened. Thomas B. Reed of Maine was chosen Speaker. Having been in the House since 1876, he had for the most part been a member of the minority. As such, he had grown adept at using the rules to frustrate the Democratic majority and was fully aware of how badly the House needed to fix them. As he noted, "The only way to do business inside the rules is to suspend the rules."

When the Fifty-first Congress convened on December 2, 1889, the House was composed of 330 members, with Republicans in a small majority. Reed was elected Speaker over Carlisle on a strict party-line vote. After the Speaker's election, the rules of the previous Congress were referred to the five-member Rules Committee (of which the Speaker was chair) according to custom, while the House proceeded under general parliamentary procedure. As the committee met, several election contests were still pending. Most expected these races would be settled in favor of the Republicans, increasing their majority and enabling them to adopt new rules.

On January 29, 1890, the Republicans called up a disputed election in West Virginia. Charles F. Crisp of Georgia, the Democratic leader, immediately tried to bring the issue to the floor for a vote. As the roll call was taken, there were 161 yeas, 2 nays, and 165 not voting, mostly Democrats. Democrats, now in the minority, were resorting to the customary device of the "disappearing quorum." By not voting, they created a situation in which no quorum existed, and thus business could not be conducted. (House rules demanded that at least one-half of the members be present to conduct business. Because less than one-half of the members had voted at roll call, there was no quorum, and thus business could not proceed on that issue.) It was expected that, as in previous years, the absence of a quorum would mean that the issue would not be voted on. However, in contrast to previous years, Speaker Reed ignored custom and ordered the clerk to count everyone there, whether they voted or not, as present. With everyone counted, he ruled that a quorum was present and that business could proceed.

All hell broke loose. Members of Congress denounced Reed. Richard Bland of Missouri, a Democrat, decried, "I denounce you as the worst tyrant that ever ruled over a deliberative body." Despite Democratic protest, the rule stood. The next day, in order to make a quorum, he again counted nonvoting Democrats who were present and refused to allow another appeal on the grounds that the House had already decided the question. The Reed Rules were summed up as meaning that the Speaker would never entertain a dilatory motion.

Reed argued that the goal of a parliamentary body was action, not inaction. Therefore, if members took steps to oppose action, even if by using proper parliamentary procedure, it was the right of the majority to refuse to recognize those steps. He remained adamant despite the ensuing commotion and angry debate. He continued to count nonvoting legislators for quorum purposes. Reed even ordered the doors of the chamber locked when Democrats tried to exit. Finally, after five days, the contested election case was taken up and the Republican, Smith, won by a vote of 166 yeas, 0 nays, and 162 not voting.

After four days of debate, Reed's rulings on dilatory motions and the counting of a quorum were incorporated into the revised rules reported by the Rules Committee. In addition to these changes in the rules, the rule revisions of 1890 reduced the size of the quorum required in the Committee of the Whole from one-half of the membership of the House to 100 members. With the size of the House continuing to grow, this change facilitated floor action. The revised rules also incorporated what had, by the end of the nineteenth century, become a custom. Original procedure had required that members obtain leave to introduce bills. For decades, however, that procedure had been abandoned, with members introducing bills simply by filing them with the clerk. This practice was now made a rule.

Under the Reed Rules of 1890, the Speaker had effective command of the House. Because he had the authority to name the members and chairs of all committees, he had the power to reward or punish his fellow members. As chairman of the Rules Committee—which now shared with Ways and Means and Appropriations the right to report at any time and thereby get immediate access to the floor—he could control the timing and content of bills to be brought before the House. Finally, with unlimited power of recognition, he could determine in large measure what was to be taken up on the floor.

Despite their protests, Democrats soon saw the efficacy of the Reed Rules. The breaking of the silent filibuster helped shaped future debate and procedure in the House. When the Democrats briefly retook control of Congress in 1891, they immediately threw out the Reed Rules, opening the door for the use of the disappearing quorum once again. Reed promptly turned it against them. He succeeded in so thoroughly tying up the House that in frustration, the Democrats were compelled to bring back the Reed Rules. Since that time, the House of Representatives has been more responsive to its leadership than has been the case in the Senate. Few bills that are strongly supported by the Speaker's party fail to reach a vote and pass.

Through his forceful leadership of House Republicans, Reed helped reinstitute the concept of party responsibility within the House. To assure party loyalty and responsibility, in the 1890s the Republicans named the first whip in the party's history, James Tawney of Minnesota. He was charged with keeping party members on the floor for important votes and making sure they voted in line with the leadership. Working with the whip, the House Republicans attained remarkable party unity under Reed during the 1890s, occasionally voting solidly for measures on which they had been sharply divided in caucus.

The centralization of power in the House during this period coincided with another important shift. Until the late nineteenth century, few members made a career in the House. In 1880 more than half of the House members were serving for the first time, and the mean length of service among them was only two years. With constant turnover, seniority ceased to be important. Therefore, appointments to committees and chairmanships rarely reflected length of service in the House.

By 1899 only 30 percent of the House was made up of first-time members. As a growing number of representatives aspired to serve in the House longer, they wanted that extended service to be meaningful. "Meaningful" meant having power, and power was exercised through the committees. Thus, members demanded that their seniority be reflected in their committee assignments. This growing reliance on seniority and hence power within the committee structure resulted in growing disenchantment with and resistance to the centralization of leadership. Reed resigned from the House in 1899 because of differences with President William McKinley over American intervention in Cuba and the annexation of Hawaii. His sudden departure left a leadership vacuum. His successor, David B. Henderson, an Iowa Republican, failed to exert the same level of influence and power as Reed had. Highly ineffective, he retired after two terms. In 1903, when Joseph G. Cannon was elected Speaker of the House by the Republicans, he was the oldest representative in age (sixty-seven years) and service (twenty-eight years) ever to have headed the House. But despite his age, Cannon quickly asserted his authority.

Speaker Joseph G. Cannon

Like Reed, Cannon set out to rule the House and its Republican majority through his control of the Rules Committee and the key chairs. He turned over the committee assignments of Democrats to their leader, John Sharp Williams of Mississippi, subject to his veto. Williams, however, used his authority to build party unity among the Democrats, and so Cannon revoked the privilege in 1908.

Joseph G. Cannon, Republican U.S. representative from Illinois, became Speaker of the House in 1903. He was best known for an arbitrary and partisan style of rule that was dubbed "Cannonism." (Library of Congress)

Cannon's politics were very conservative. He invoked nineteenth-century ideas rooted in laissez-faire notions of government's role. This contrasted sharply with Theodore Roosevelt's more progressive agenda, supported by liberal Republicans and Democrats. To combat the growing influence of the Progressive movement and maintain control of the House and the agenda, he made increasing use of his powers as Speaker to block legislation that he opposed and to thwart and punish members who opposed him. In the Progressive Era, there was a growing public interest in political reform. Joe Cannon's use of his position to block measures reflecting that sentiment and the will not only of the majority party but of the majority of the House came to be known as Cannonism. The movement to curb Cannon's unbridled use of power began during the last session of the Sixtieth Congress. Just before the House adjourned on March 3, 1909, the House adopted a rule that set aside Wednesday of each week for calling the roll of committees. The chair or other authorized members of those committees could then call up bills that their committees had reported without getting clearance from the Rules Committee. At the time, Progressives considered this a major reform because it seemed to guarantee the House a chance to act on measures favored in committee but opposed by the leadership. However, the procedure failed to produce the desired results, and the House dispensed with it in later years.

When the Sixty-first Congress first met, in special session, on March 15, 1909, the House was composed of 219 Republicans and 172 Democrats. Among the Republicans were about thirty Progressive insurgents led by George W. Norris of Nebraska and John M. Nelson of Wisconsin. After helping to elect Cannon to a fourth term as Speaker, the Republican insurgents joined with the Democrats to defeat the usual motion to adopt the rules of the preceding Congress. The Democratic leader then offered a resolution to restrict the Speaker's existing authority to appoint committee members and chairs to only five committees (of which the only important one would be Ways and Means), to remove the Speaker from the Rules Committee, and to enlarge that body from five to fifteen members.

Although twenty-eight Republicans joined the resolution, twenty-two Democrats, led by John J. Fitzgerald of New York, voted with the Republican majority to defeat it. Fitzgerald then offered a compromise resolution considerably weaker than the original. The House adopted this watered-down version, which only slightly reduced the Speaker's authority. It established a Consent Calendar for minor bills of particular interest to individual members. On two days each month, bills on this calendar could be called up without the prior approval of the Speaker. While the rule did succeed in getting minor bills processed, it failed to check significantly the power of the Speaker.

The revolt did not die, however, and attempts to break the power of the Speaker and terminate Cannonism continued. The end came in 1910, when the coalition of Democrats and Progressive Republicans finally triumphed. On March 16, Norris demanded immediate consideration of another reform resolution, similar to the prior one. This one had been stuck in committee, and Norris used a parliamentary opening to submit it. Cannon stood his ground and held the motion out of order. This time the House overruled him. Debate then began on the Norris resolution, which stripped the Speaker of all authority to appoint com-

mittees and their chairs, removed him from the Rules Committee, and expanded that committee to ten members who would choose their own chair.

The House adopted the Norris resolution after a continuous session of twenty-nine hours, during which Cannon fought tooth and nail, trying to round up supporters. Realizing his power had been compromised, Cannon invited a motion to declare the chair vacant so that the House might elect a new Speaker. However, since the Progressive Republicans wished only to challenge Cannon's despotic authority and neither to unseat "Uncle Joe" nor elect a Democrat Speaker, the motion was tabled. Cannon remained Speaker until the end of the Sixty-first Congress in 1911 and a member of the House (except in the Sixty-third Congress) until 1923, by which time he had completed forty-six years of service.

DEMOCRATIC PARTY RULE, 1911–1921

The revolt against Cannonism was completed in 1911, when the Democrats took control of the House, elected Champ Clark as Speaker, and adopted a revised body of rules that incorporated most of the changes agreed to in 1909 and 1910. The new rules provided that all members of the standing committees, including their chairs, would be elected at the beginning of each Congress. The new rules of 1911 included previous changes such as Calendar Wednesday and Consent Calendar. They also added a discharge rule, which allowed for a majority of members to free a bill stalled in committee by use of a petition.

In conjunction with the rule changes, and possibly as important, the Democrats adopted new procedures for organizing their control of the House. First, they selected a Speaker, Clark, and a majority leader, Oscar W. Underwood of Alabama, the latter serving also as the chair of the Ways and Means Committee. With those two positions in place, it was decided that the Democratic members of Ways and Means would constitute the party's Committee on Committees. The latter panel designated all committee assignments for Democrats, leaving to the Republicans (who established a similar committee in 1917) the selection of their own committee members. This made the formal election of committee members and their chair merely a token vote that ratified appointments already formally approved by the party caucuses.

The real power in the House was now exercised by Underwood, who as majority leader, chaired the Ways and Means Committee, merging the two positions. He also became the head of the Committee on Committees. In contrast to the past, when Cannon had chosen the Republican majority leader, Clark as Speaker did not select Underwood. Instead, Underwood was chosen majority leader by the party caucus and Underwood himself used rank-and-file support to assert his authority as the Democrats' true leader in the House. This transfer of power fit nicely with Clark's view of House government. As Speaker, Clark

preferred to leave the business of party management to the floor leader and reinforced his emphasis on the party. He noted he was happy to sacrifice power of the speaker and change rules to enhance the power of his party. The Speaker still had power, but could now only influence, and not control, the process of committee assignment.

During this period, changes in leadership and in how that leadership was used became important, as President Woodrow Wilson tried to assert greater authority over the legislative process. Wilson gave his presidency some of the attributes of a prime ministership. Rather than viewing his position as one of purely executive function, he regularly injected himself into congressional life. Wilson worked closely with the Democratic leaders in both chambers and conferred frequently with committees and individual members to solicit support for his legislative program. With Wilson's help, Underwood and the Democrats were able to pass four major pieces of legislation in the House—the Underwood Tariff Act (1913), the Federal Reserve Act (1913), the Clayton Antitrust Act (1914), and the Federal Trade Commission Act (1914).

In contrast to the domestic arena, the Democrats were not so united on foreign policy. Both Clark and Underwood disagreed with Wilson over issues dealing with the Panama Canal, and Clark's successor as Speaker, Claude Kitchin, a Democrat from North Carolina, challenged the president on several issues, including Wilson's appeal to Congress for a declaration of war against Germany in 1917.

As a result of these disagreements, the strong party unity displayed by House Democrats during Wilson's first term began to fracture in his second. Lack of solidarity contributed to loss of the House in the 1918 midterm elections. With no majority and no party unity, the binding party caucus, used so effectively by Clark and his successor, ceased to be valuable in shepherding through legislation. By 1919 the House, in the face of changing majorities and tension with the White House, was no longer willing to accept the centralization of power that had developed since Reed. Congressional leaders now needed new mechanisms to collect the required support for legislative programs.

Accompanying this change—and helping to account for it—was a hardening of the unwritten rule of seniority that virtually guaranteed succession to committee chair by the next-ranking majority member on the committee. Knowing they would ascend to the position, and then hold it, gave the chairs and other ranking members independence. No longer did they see themselves as mere pawns of the Speaker and party leaders, but rather as equal players in the legislative process.

But ranking members were still only a part of the process and did not completely control it. The Committee on Committees, and thus party leaders, still played an important role in filling committee vacancies and deciding who could switch committees. Who made it to which committee was an important determinant of power.

RETURN OF REPUBLICAN RULE, 1921–1933

In conjunction with the overhaul of the House and changes in how the leadership exerted itself, the end of World War I witnessed the Republican return to power. After 1920, Republicans controlled both houses of Congress and, with the election of Warren G. Harding, the presidency.

Presidential leadership and strong party government were not hallmarks of the 1920s. The Harding Administration was rife with corruption. The Coolidge Administration focused on business, with the president saying that "the business of America is business." He pushed only minimal legislative programs through Congress. President Herbert Hoover proved unable to deal with the Great Depression. Republican control of the Senate was occasionally nominal, with a minority of the party often holding the balance of power. Party conservatives were more successful in keeping control of the House during the 1920s, and legislative conflicts between the Senate and the House were common.

Despite reformers' failure to assert themselves as they had in the previous decade, some important changes in House organization and procedure took place during the 1920s. In 1920, full authority over money bills was given to the Appropriations Committee, and in 1927 some minor committees were abolished. Republican leaders introduced, and then abandoned, the use of a party Steering

Committee to guide their legislative program. Under pressure from Progressives, House rules were modified slightly in 1924, but the Rules Committee continued to exercise tight control. Perhaps the most important changes revolved around the budget process.

Until 1920 there was no organized scheme for designing and considering the federal budget. Rather than presenting a formal budget, the secretary of the Treasury merely estimated budgets for various departments. These estimates were then referred to eight different committees in the House. Each committee reported an appropriation bill for its specific area with no concern about the larger context of a complete budget, expenditures, or revenues. Making it more complicated, some department requests were considered, and then appropriated, by multiple committees and bills, and other committees might report bills that included appropriations.

To improve control over expenditures within the executive branch, Wilson proposed a new system in 1919 that eventually became the Budget and Accounting Act of 1921 under Harding. Under this law, the president prepared a formal budget each year, which he then presented to Congress. The budget included projected revenues and expenditures for the ensuing year and noted the prior year's expenses. To help construct the budget, the law created a bureau of the budget (reorganized as the Office of Management and Budget in 1970) and a Congressional watchdog organization, the General Accounting Office, with a comp-troller appointed by the President, but with the advice and consent of the Senate to assist Congress.

Anticipating passage of this bill, the House voted to restore to the Committee on Appropriations the jurisdiction over all supply bills granted to it originally in 1865, and it also increased the size of the committee from twenty-one to thirty-five. The committee was broken down into ten subcommittees of five members who reviewed requests of different agencies. This more organized approach reflected a general concern for greater economy in government, fueled by perceived waste and a debt of $25 billion following World War I, when deficit spending was not seen as an acceptable device for running the government.

These changes took place under a weak Republican leadership. Upon the Republicans gaining control in the House in 1919, the leading contender for Speaker was James R. Mann of Illinois. The minority leader since 1911, Mann was powerful but not well liked. Many party members viewed him as abusing his power. Mann repeatedly blocked passage of private bills, which made representatives fear that his ascension to the position of Speaker would bring back Cannonism. Rejecting Mann, the Republican conference looked for someone who could run the office of Speaker without trying to aggrandize his power or use it excessively. They chose Frederick H. Gillett of Massachusetts. Mann refused the title of majority leader, which went to Frank W. Mondell of Wyoming. For the first time, the majority leader failed to hold the chair of the Ways and Means Committee

Lack of effective leadership and a growing dissatisfaction with what leadership there was helped further the decentralizing trend. Despite a Republican majority of 300 in the Sixty-seventh Congress (1921–1923), party leaders regularly blocked measures that had wide support. However, Republicans suffered heavy losses in the 1922 elections, and when the Sixty-eighth Congress convened in December 1923, the Republican majority was only twenty-two votes. This thin majority enabled about twenty Republican Progressives, intent on reform, to delay electing a Speaker in an effort to loosen the rules. For two days and eight ballots the House battled over three candidates. Nicholas Longworth of Ohio, the Republican majority leader, broke the impasse by promising the dissenters that if they accepted the reelection of Gillett as Speaker, a full debate on revisions of the rules would take place. The promised debate lasted five days and led to some changes in the rules, but nothing that radically altered the workings of the House.

In 1924 Calvin Coolidge was easily elected president. His coattails brought in a twenty-seat increase of Republicans in the House, destroying any leverage that Progressives had previously enjoyed. This enabled party leaders to discipline the dissident members of the party who had caused problems in the previous Congress. Most notably, when new committee assignments were drawn up, many Progressives who had supported

Robert La Follette of Wisconsin for president in the election of 1924 were moved to the bottom of their committees, ensuring party discipline.

House Reapportionment, Direct Election of Senators, and the Lame Duck Amendment

Up to 1920, no state had lost a seat in the House through reapportionment since Maine and New Hampshire were deprived of one each after the Census of 1880. The reason was that the House had regularly agreed to increase its total membership by a sufficient number to prevent such a loss. The 1920 Census showed that unless the size of the House was increased again, eleven states would lose seats through reapportionment while eight would gain. This was due in large part to internal shifts of population that involved not only the migration of blacks from the rural South to the urban centers of the North, but the general shift of the population from the countryside to the city.

Members strongly wished to limit the size of the House. However, they also wanted to avoid reducing the representation of any state. Early in 1921 the House Census Committee reported a bill that would have increased the membership to 483, with additional seats going to twenty-five states whose populations had grown the most. But the House rejected the proposal and voted to keep its membership at 435. Proponents of the limit argued that as membership grew, the right to debate—already limited—would become more so. As the House grew, they feared, power would be concentrated even more than it already was. Finally, they were concerned that increased membership would mean increased cost. No changes were made as the Senate failed to act on a proposal that would have taken twelve seats from eleven states; a subsequent bill, which would have increased the size of the House to 460, died in committee.

By 1925 it was clear that the shift of population from rural to urban areas was permanent. Highlighting that change was the fact that during the 1920s, the population of urban areas was for the first time greater than in rural areas. Rapidly growing cities like Los Angeles and Detroit began to demand increased representation in the House. Yet the House Census Committee still refused to report a new bill. In 1927 Coolidge came out in favor of reapportionment, which gave it impetus. When the House Census Committee refused to act, its chairman, E. Hart Fenn of Connecticut, moved on March 2, the day before adjournment, to suspend the rules and pass his bill to authorize a reapportionment of the House by the secretary of commerce on the basis of the 1930 Census. As a filibuster monopolized the floor of the Senate, the House narrowly rejected Fenn's motion. Continued attempts at creating a reapportionment structure failed. Finally, in April 1929, when President Hoover called the Congress into special session, he pushed through reapportionment legislation on the basis of the upcoming 1930 Census. The measure also

established a permanent system for reapportioning the 435 seats in the House every ten years, following each Census.

The reapportionment based on the 1930 Census resulted in a major reshuffling of House seats in the Seventy-third Congress, elected in 1932. Twenty-one states lost a total of twenty-seven seats. Missouri lost three; Georgia, Iowa, Kentucky, and Pennsylvania lost two each. California gained nine, increasing its delegation from eleven to twenty. Other states to win more than one seat were Michigan (4), Texas (3), New Jersey (2), New York (2), and Ohio (2).

Two other institutional changes occurred during this time period through constitutional amendment. The Seventeenth and Twentieth Amendments both signaled changing needs of the country. The Seventeenth Amendment, which turned the election of U.S. senators from state legislators to the people, reflected progressive agitation to break what was seen as a corrupt state political system. The reform had first been advocated as early as the 1850s. By the 1870s amendments were regularly proposed to shift the selection of senators to popular election. The sentiment for election by the people was spurred in the 1890s as the Senate gained a reputation in the press and among reformers for being unrepresentative, unresponsive, elitist, and lacking in integrity. Senators were often perceived, and rightly so, as beholden to the people who put them in the Senate. They gained their seats as the result of financial influence at the local level and often held their power by acceding to the wishes of state legislators and corporations rather than the desires of the people. In addition, politics at the local level often delayed the filling of seats, with as many as fourteen seats sitting empty for an entire congressional session.

The Populist Party's platform of 1892 and the Democratic platform of 1900 demanded the direct election of senators. Not surprisingly, the biggest roadblock to such a change was the Senate itself, because senators were very happy with their situation. However, growing local movements for passage of a direct election amendment, along with agitation at the national level, exerted considerable pressure.

Ten of the senators who voted against direct election met defeat in the 1910 elections. The replacements, for the most part Progressives, were encouragement for advocates to try again in the next Congress. The House acted first, adopting an amendment in April 1911. The Senate passed an amendment but in different form. A conference committee took up the problem but was not able to reconcile the two proposals. The sticking point became the issue of federal control of elections, demanded by northern members of Congress but shunned by southern representatives and senators. Finally, the House deferred to the Senate version, with its tougher provisions for federal control. For the most part, the opposition came from southern Democrats, who were fearful that popular election of senators, coupled with federal controls, would undercut white power in the South.

By 1909 thirty-three states had demanded such an amendment and only thirty-six were needed for ratification. In addition, by that time, 29 states elected their senators in a general election as nominees of their party's primary. The House of Representatives passed numerous resolutions calling for the Senate to subject its members to direct election, but the Senate rebuffed these efforts. The Senate relented only after the states threatened to call a constitutional convention. With heavy support from many senators in their first term who had been directly elected, the Senate voted for the Seventeenth Amendment in 1912. The amendment, which transferred senatorial selection from the legislatures of each state to "the people thereof," passed the House, and approval by the states came quickly. In 1913, eleven months after congressional passage, the Seventeenth Amendment became part of the Constitution.

The other constitutional change was more of a procedural one that affected both chambers of Congress. As the Senate was reshaped, it championed the effort to make Congress more responsive to the will of the people. While many of them resisted direct election, senators readily championed the lame duck amendment.

This amendment bore more heavily on the House of Representatives because of the need for all its members to face election every two years. The need for such an amendment was precipitated by the long lag between the election of Congress and its first meeting. The original justifications for a lengthy transition of government were no longer relevant. Improved communication and transportation drew attention to the flaws in the congressional calendar, including the huge gap between election and first meeting. The Seventeenth Amendment had the same impact. Since it was passed to make the Senate more responsive to the people, it seemed that the newly elected Congress should meet as soon as possible after the election.

Presidents, starting with Washington, avoided the long gap by calling Congress into special sessions. This moved up the time when the new Congress met, and sometimes the old, expiring Congresses arranged for their successors to convene early, as had been done after the Civil War to prevent Andrew Johnson from acting unilaterally regarding Reconstruction. This enabled Congress to establish for themselves when they wanted to meet, rather than be subject to the whim of the president.

Exacerbating these problems was the fact that the second constitutionally mandated session of each Congress did not begin until after its successor had been elected. Known as the short session, it began on the first Monday in December, after the election, and ended by noon on March 4. The short, or lame duck, session gave both leaders and minorities powerful tactical weapons that could push forward or inhibit legislation. Republican leadership in the 1920s balked at surrendering such effective weapons.

For many, these lame duck sessions were essentially undemocratic in nature. During the short session, members of Congress who had just lost at the polls in November continued to exercise power and drive the national agenda for four months. This problem became very apparent after the 1922 election, which featured the defeat of many Republican incumbents. Hoping to curry favor with the Harding Administration and thus receive appointments in his administration, lame duck members voted for a proposal favored by the administration but with little support in the Senate or the public at-large. Angered by this maneuver, Sen. Thaddeus Caraway of Arkansas, a Democrat, introduced a Senate resolution stating that members of Congress who had been defeated in the past election should refrain from voting on all but routine, nonpolicy matters during the short session. The resolution was shuttled off to the Committee on Agriculture and Forestry with hope of a quick and quiet death.

However, one member of that committee was Nebraska Republican and Progressive George W. Norris. He took the matter seriously, and because he felt the Caraway resolution would unconstitutionally restrict members of Congress, he proposed a constitutional amendment to resolve the problem. Despite the lack of any valid objection to the amendment, it failed to muster enough support. While the Senate approved four different lame duck amendments, the House defeated them all.

With the election of 1930, the Democrats returned to a majority in the House. The inability of the Hoover Administration and Republican House to rectify the problems of the Great Depression showed the need of a new government to be able to take action quicker when coming to power during a time of crisis. In the context of the nation's needs during the Great Depression, the resolution quickly moved through the House under the stewardship of Speaker John Nance Garner of Texas. As finally approved by Congress in March 1932, the Twentieth Amendment provided that congressional terms would begin on January 3 following an election. The new presidential term was designated to begin on January 20. Ratification was completed in the midst of a lame duck session that included eighty-one members of Congress, mostly Republicans, who had been defeated for reelection. The states ratified the amendment in January 1933, too late to change the dates of the inauguration of the new Congress and new president that year. Since, therefore, they could not begin serving until March, a discredited Hoover Administration remained in office, doing little during the worst winter of the Depression. Meanwhile, lame duck votes in the House and a Huey Long filibuster in the Senate brought Congress, and government, to a standstill.

THE FDR YEARS

The Great Depression signaled the end of Republican rule. The former Republican majority of 267 disappeared in 1930 to two and was whittled away by deaths and special elections to become a four-seat majority for the Democrats. That majority was increased significantly in 1932 with the election of Franklin Delano Roosevelt as president.

Roosevelt's years in office, from 1933 to 1945, were marked by strong presidential leadership, and while executive-legislative relations were strong, they began to deteriorate during the war. By the time of FDR's death, Congress was openly protesting Roosevelt's postwar plans.

The 1930s also marked the beginning of a long period of power for southern Democrats that lasted until Republicans took control of the House in 1947. Twenty-eight of forty-seven committees had southern chairs. While Democrats had been in the minority during the 1920s, southerners had constituted more than one-half of their ranks, and since the party was out of power, there was little occasion for complaint about an unwarranted southern influence in party councils. But when the party won control of the House in 1931, northern and western Democrats pressed for a larger voice in committee assignments. They proposed entrusting the assignments to a new committee on committees to consist of one member for each state having Democratic representation in the House. This committee would also choose a nine-member steering committee to be in charge of the legislative program.

The steering committee only functioned for a short time in the early 1930s. Instead, the Rules Committee became the major tool of House Democratic leaders during the Seventy-third Congress, called into special session by Roosevelt on March 9, 1933. FDR asked Congress to pass a series of emergency recovery measures almost sight unseen.

Ten of the measures were brought to the House floor under special closed rules—drafted by the Rules Committee and adopted by majority vote—that barred all except committee amendments, waived points of order, and sharply limited debate. Among the laws enacted at this session of 100 days with the help of these gag rules were the Emergency Banking Act, the Economy Act, the Emergency Relief Act, the first Agricultural Adjustment Act, the Tennessee Valley Authority Act, and the National Industrial Recovery Act.

The hallmark of the Depression years was a leadership that functioned more as facilitators rather than innovators. Leadership shepherded the New Deal legislation through Congress. It scheduled the debates, engineered the compromises, and mustered the votes for passage. The House Rules Committee, the most powerful committee in either house of Congress, and its pro–New Deal chairman, Edward W. Pou of North Carolina, adopted rules limiting the members' ability to amend bills reaching the floor of the House. As a result, once a bill made it out of committee, there was little opposition. Fast-track rules enhanced the power of already powerful committees like Ways and Means, Appropriations, and Interstate and Foreign Commerce, where the real work of the House was done.

During the 1930s not only were Congressional Republicans few in number, but they also made an ideological shift to the left. This shift meant support for many New Deal proposals, rather than constituting a meaningful opposition.

Future seeds of division were sown during this period as southern Democrats consolidated their power, and while for the most part they followed the New Deal agenda in the 1930s, during the post–World War II period they would become a serious problem for Democratic leadership, especially in the Senate.

The other group was the Progressives, nicknamed the "Sons of the Wilde Jackass." More prominent in the Senate than in the House, this group was originally formed in the 1920s to battle conservative Republican leadership. Mostly, they represented the Midwest and West. They provided a counterbalance to the conservative southerners. Pushing for reform, they made major contributions to the New Deal.

Democratic Party unity was badly shaken in 1937 when FDR introduced his plan to reorganize the Supreme Court. The Court had regularly struck down various New Deal legislative plans, and the Depression was persisting. In an attempt to "bring the Court into line," FDR proposed the appointment of additional justices in order to get a majority that "could be counted on" to uphold the constitutionality of New Deal measures. In reaction to what was seen as a brazen attempt to co-opt the Court and upend constitutional checks and balances, a new coalition of conservative Democrats aligned with Republicans in both houses of Congress, but especially in the House.

In reality, the conservative coalition saw its birth before the Court reorganization plan. During the summer of 1937, the Rules Committee voted ten to four against granting a special rule for floor consideration of the bill that eventually became the Fair Labor Standards Act. The committee, chaired by a Democrat from New York, consisted of five northern Democrats, five southern Democrats, and four Republicans. Eventually, House leaders obtained enough signatures on a discharge petition to bring it to the floor, but it was then recommitted to the Labor Committee. When the Rules Committee in 1938 again refused to clear the bill, House leaders once more resorted to a discharge rule to bring the bill to the floor. The resulting Fair Labor Standards Act of 1938 became the first measure to become a law through this mechanism.

John O'Connor, the chairman of the Rules Committee, was a casualty of the fight. Because of his intransigence in originally reporting the bill to the House, he was targeted by FDR as an anti–New Deal Democrat and defeated in the 1938 election. This did not solve the problem. The new chairman, Adolph J. Sabath of Illinois, an ardent New Dealer, fell prey to the strengthening conservative power and was regularly outvoted by a coalition of Republicans and southern Democrats. The committee began the practice of demanding, as the price of sending administration bills to the floor, substantive changes in these bills to accord with the views of conservatives. The coalition used its power to block or water down various administration measures, clear measures opposed by the administration, and authorize investigations of various executive agencies.

THE POSTWAR YEARS, 1945–1970

Talk of need for congressional reform mounted during World War II, when the powers of the executive branch expanded exponentially. Members saw Congress as antiquated and noted the need to modernize congressional machinery to deal with the enlarged and more powerful executive branch. Therefore, the House and Senate agreed early in 1945 to establish a Joint Committee on the Organization of Congress. The committee was composed of six members from each house, divided equally among Democrats and Republicans. For three months, from March 13 through June 29, 1945, they held hearings.

The joint committee's report included a broad range of proposals designed to streamline the committee structure, strengthen congressional control over the budget, reduce the workload of Congress, and improve staff assistance. Most of these reforms were incorporated into the Legislative Reorganization Act of 1946, signed by President Harry Truman in August. Major provisions of the act dealt with committees, the legislative budget, the congressional workload, staff, and salaries.

The law reduced the number of standing committees in the House from thirty-three to fifteen and in the Senate from forty-eight to nineteen. All standing committees (except Appropriations) were directed to fix regular days for meeting, keep complete records, and open all hearings except executive sessions to the public. The act made it the duty of all committee chairs to report or cause to be reported promptly to the House any measure approved by their committee and to take or cause to be taken necessary steps to bring the matter to a vote. But no measure was to be reported from any committee unless a majority of the members were actually present when it was approved.

At the time, the 1946 act was regarded as a major achievement, despite some of its shortcomings, which in retrospect are probably inherent in the way the Constitution structured Congress. It failed to resolve issues of the distribution of power within Congress and did not resolve the question of the balance of power between Congress and the executive. These remained topics of concern throughout the postwar years and into the twenty-first century.

The fifteen years following the act were marked by divided government in which different parties controlled the House and White House and in which there was a strong block of southern Democrats in both the House and Senate that challenged the Democratic Party. These years were marked by fractured parties that often hamstrung congressional and presidential leadership.

None of the post–World War II presidents was in full command of his own party in Congress, whether it was in the majority or minority, so that all were forced at times to seek bipartisan support to get their programs enacted. House Democrats always included sixty or more southern conservatives who were opposed to many of their party's economic and social programs, while a score of moderate-to-liberal Republicans were frequently at odds with the party's conservative leadership.

Leadership in the House was relatively stable in this period. As after the Civil War, control of federal expenditures became a central issue after World War II. Attempts by Congress as a whole, and the House Appropriations Committee in particular, to regain control of financial matters sparked regular controversy. In addition, there were battles within the House surrounding the Rules Committee, which was still able to frustrate the will of the majority by blocking or transforming legislation. These problems spurred talk of the need for broad-scale congressional reform through the 1960s. In 1970 the House finally agreed to a reorganization that had cleared the Senate in 1967.

Prior to that reorganization, the House and the Senate often engaged in what could be viewed as turf wars. The year after the Legislative Reorganization Act of 1946, the Republicans, who controlled both houses of Congress, formed a Joint Committee on the Legislative Budget. The joint committee quickly agreed on a ceiling for appropriations and expenditures, thus curbing the outlays projected in President Truman's budget. The House approved the ceilings, but the Senate increased them and insisted that any budget surplus be used to reduce the public debt rather than to provide the tax cut desired by House leaders. Therefore, the resolution died in conference.

This back and forth generated resentment by the House over the Senate's claim to coequal statutes in the appropriations process, in which the House had always asserted it primacy because of constitutional mandates in Article I, Section 7, of the Constitution, which stated, "All Bills for raising Revenue shall originate in the House of Representatives; but the Senate may propose or concur with Amendments as on other Bills." The issue boiled over in 1962, when the House Appropriations Committee demanded that conference meetings (traditionally held on the Senate side) be rotated between the Senate and the House sides of the Capitol. The Senate Appropriations Committee countered by proposing that it initiate one-half of all appropriation bills. The ensuing deadlock froze action on pending bills for months.

The bickering continued as the House criticized the Senate for dominating the process. For example, in late 1962, the Senate adopted a continuing resolution to let federal agencies keep on spending at the old rate until appropriations for the new fiscal year had been approved. In a rare moment of bipartisanship, the House, with only one dissenting vote, went on record noting that the Senate action infringed on House privileges and authority. The Senate resolved, in turn, that while the Senate may concede that the House could consider appropriation bills first, such action did not compromise the Senate's "coequal power to originate any bill not expressly raising revenue," and the Senate had the power to "originate bills appropriating money for the support of the Government."

The feud died without resolution. While it was true the Senate had consistently voted for larger expenditures than the House, it was also true that Congress had managed to authorize less spending than was proposed by the postwar presidents. Yet the amounts authorized grew more or less steadily after 1947, and it became increasingly apparent that the capacity of Congress to control expenditures through its power of the purse was quite limited. Congress did not pass legislation to reform its budget procedures until 1974.

Reforming the House Rules Committee

Meantime, the dominance of the House Rules Committee and its ability to block or alter legislation was evident during efforts to enact a major housing bill in the Eightieth Congress (1947–1948). The Rules Committee insisted that the Banking and Currency Committee delete provisions for public housing and slum clearance before it would agree to release the bill. The Rules panel also refused to allow the House to vote on a universal military training bill reported by the Armed Services Committee, and it was only under strong pressure from the Speaker that the committee cleared a bill to revive the lapsed Selective Service System.

Although liberals dominated the 263 Democrats who formed a majority of the House elected in 1948, they were still confronted with a Rules Committee dominated by conservatives: four Republicans and three southern Democrats. So with the backing of Speaker Sam Rayburn, the party caucus voted 176 to 48 for a "twenty-one-day rule." This rule authorized the chair of any legislative committee that had reported a bill favorably, and had requested a special rule from the Rules Committee, to bring the matter to the House floor if the Rules Committee failed to act within twenty-one calendar days of the request. This rule was used eight times during the Eighty-first Congress (1949–1951) to obtain House passage of bills blocked in the Rules Committee, including an anti–poll tax bill (stalled by southern Democrats) and statehood measures for Alaska and Hawaii. An effort to repeal the rule in 1950 was rejected, but it was repealed in the following Congress.

Control of the Rules Committee by a conservative coalition was virtually unchallenged for the next decade. The chair made the most of his power to block the legislative program of the House. Because the committee had no regular meeting day and could be called together only by the chair, it was sometimes unable to clear any bills during the final days of a session, when the chair might disappear from Washington.

In 1958, the number of Democrats elected to the House was 283, giving them their largest majority since 1936. Party liberals, frustrated by the fact that they still were unable to get meaningful civil rights legislation passed, again talked of curbing the Rules Committee. Among other things, they suggested altering the relation of Democrats to Republicans on the committee from eight to four to nine to three and reinstituting the twenty-one-day rule. The Speaker, Sam Rayburn, blocked these changes.

However, to placate the liberal wing of the party, he guaranteed them that major parts of their agenda—housing, civil rights, labor, and other social welfare legislation—would not be stalled in committee.

Rayburn, however, was unable to fulfill his pledge during the Eighty-sixth Congress (1959–1961). When John F. Kennedy was elected president in 1960 (along with a reduced Democratic majority in the House), it was clear that many of the proposed social and civil rights programs would die in committee unless liberal, pro-administration Democrats gained control of the Rules Committee. Reversing his earlier stand, Rayburn now decided to try to enlarge the committee from twelve to fifteen members to make room for the addition of two loyal Democrats and create a majority that would act favorably on administration bills. The chair of the Rules Committee and the Republican minority leader blocked his plan, forcing Rayburn into a month of maneuvering to round up enough votes to win.

At the start of the Eighty-seventh Congress on January 31, 1961, the House finally adopted the rule to increase the size of the committee from twelve to fifteen. The new balance, however, was precarious at best, and the Kennedy Administration still struggled to get its agenda passed. The fate of various bills showed that the fractured nature of the Democratic Party, the weaknesses of party leadership, and a powerful Rules Committee could still combine to block legislation. For example, the committee effectively killed a major school aid bill in 1961, when James J. Delaney, a Democrat from New York and a Catholic from a heavily Catholic district, joined the conservative coalition in voting against the measure because no provision was made for aid to parochial schools. The parochial school provision had been excluded in an effort to placate southern Democrats, who opposed parochial school aid. In 1962, two pro-administration southern Democrats on the committee helped to kill a bill to create a department of urban affairs because an African American was expected to be the new secretary.

Although the enlargement of the Rules Committee was made permanent in the Eighty-eighth Congress (1963–1965), Democratic leaders continued to have problems with the panel. But the election of President Lyndon Johnson in 1964, together with a contingent of 295 Democrats in the House, paved the way for three further changes in the House rules at the beginning of the Eighty-ninth Congress in 1965.

The first new rule was the twenty-one-day provision. In the past, the Speaker was required to recognize a member seeking to bring to the floor a bill that had been buried by the Rules Committee. Now, the Speaker was given the option of recognition, thus moving power from the Rules Committee to the Speaker and guaranteeing that legislation opposed by House leadership would not make it to the floor.

The second new rule made it easier for individual members to submit bills to a conference committee with the Senate. The Speaker could now recognize a member to offer a motion that would permit the House to send a bill to conference with the Senate by majority vote, provided the House committee with jurisdiction over the bill approved the measure. This ended the Rules Committee's control over the process, and the reduction to a simple majority from two-thirds made for a quicker passage to the Senate.

The third change agreed to in 1965 repealed a rule dating from 1789 that had permitted any member to demand the reading in full of the final copy of a House bill. Members opposed to legislation frequently used this privilege to delay final passage of a bill.

The twenty-one-day rule was employed successfully eight times during the Eighty-ninth Congress (1965–1967) and the threat of its use persuaded the Rules Committee to send several controversial measures to the floor. As in 1952, however, Republican gains in the 1966 elections opened the way to repeal of the rule at the beginning of the Ninetieth Congress (1967–1969). A coalition of Republicans and sixty-nine southern Democrats struck it down but retained the other two rules.

Repeal of the twenty-one-day rule in 1967 proved to be of little consequence during the Ninetieth Congress, largely because vacancies on the committee were filled with administration supporters. As a consequence, the chairman, William Colmer, a conservative Democrat from Mississippi, was regularly outvoted. The result was that in early 1967 the committee, for the first time in its history, adopted a set of rules to govern its procedures. These rules took from the chair the exclusive power to set meeting dates, required the consent of a committee majority to table a bill, and set limits on proxy voting by members. As a result, the committee's power was broken to a degree, the constant fight over its revision lost its intensity, and committee members were forced to work with the opposition leadership.

NEW REFORMS, 1970–1976

Efforts to modify the organization and procedures of the House after 1946 were not confined to the protracted struggle for control of the Rules Committee. Both the Senate and the House came under pressure to curb the freewheeling activities of their investigating committees in the early 1950s. The questionable conduct of some senators and representatives raised new doubts about congressional ethics in the 1960s, to which both chambers were forced to respond. Mounting criticism of the methods and operation of Congress as a whole led both chambers to begin a reexamination in 1965 that finally produced a second reorganization act in 1970, which initiated a series of changes.

Over a six-year period from 1970 to 1976, Congress ended or revised long-established practices that critics claimed made it the most inflexible of the nation's governmental institutions. The changes were made in the rules and procedures of the Senate and the House under pressure from the rank and file. The result was a much-changed Congress by the middle of the decade.

The changes, which reached a peak in 1975, produced a basic upheaval in the manner in which power was held and exercised in Congress. Theretofore, the rarely challenged seniority system had been the almost absolute determinant of authority. The 1970–1975 revisions, however, drastically changed things. By the end of the first session of the Ninety-fourth Congress (1975–1977) in December 1975, the rigid seniority system was no longer the sole means of moving up the ladder of power. Seniority did not disappear—it still helped determine pecking order on committees—but it ceased to be the governing force. Both chambers created methods by which committee chairs had to stand for election by their colleagues, and in the House, three chairs were removed at the beginning of 1975.

By instituting internal changes, Congress gave itself new tools that reformers deemed necessary for improved operations. This meant stricter accountability of members and the reestablishment of Congress as an equal with the president under the Constitution.

The Legislative Reorganization Act of 1970, the first such law passed since 1946, did not deal with the seniority system, the power of the House Rules Committee, and the two-thirds rule for cutting off Senate debate. But it did include a number of important provisions designed to give both chambers more information on government finances, to guarantee minority party rights, and to maintain a continuing review of legislative needs through a Joint Committee on Congressional Operations.

One of the act's most important provisions regarding the House required that teller votes on the floor be recorded. Previously, teller votes had only been tabulated in total without recording individual members' votes. Members had often employed the teller method to elude accountability. The reform put voting in the House on a par with the Senate, where teller votes did not exist and where all important floor votes were usually recorded by name.

The 1970 law required committees to have written rules, a check on the arbitrary use of power by committee chairs, and to make public the roll-call votes taken in closed committee sessions, a step toward holding members accountable for their actions in committee as well as on the floor. Other features were designed to give members more information and expedite congressional business. For example, committee reports had to be available at least three days before floor consideration and House quorum calls.

A major instrument of reform during the 1970s was a rejuvenated House Democratic Caucus. A powerful instrument in the early twentieth century in implementing Woodrow Wilson's domestic program, the caucus had fallen into disuse, meeting only at the beginning of a new Congress for the pro forma election of the House Democratic leader.

The move to revitalize the caucus was led by the House Democratic Study Group (DSG), an organization of moderate and liberal Democrats forming the largest reform bloc in the House. The opening came in 1969 when, to appease the reformers, Speaker John McCormack agreed to monthly meetings of the caucus. In 1970 the caucus created the Committee on Study, Organization, and Review to study the seniority system. Its report was a prelude to change. Directed by the 150-member DSG, with outside help from Common Cause, the public interest lobby, and the liberal Americans for Democratic Action, the reform forces pushed through three reforms at the beginning of the Ninety-third Congress in 1973.

In a move toward more open government, the House adopted a caucus-inspired reform to curb committee secrecy. Although most hearings had previously been open, until this point mark-up sessions were usually closed. Now, the first reform of 1973 required all committees and subcommittees to open to the public most bill-drafting sessions and other business meetings unless a majority voted at an open session to bar the public. The reform allowed reporters and the public to witness the performance of committee members in shaping bills.

Two years later, first the House and then the Senate adopted rules opening conference committees to the press and public. Conferences, called to iron out differences between the two chambers' versions of a bill, were one of the last and most traditional vestiges of secrecy in Congress. Conferences had become the quiet preserve of senior members, who exercised great powers over the final form of bills as compromises were worked out behind closed doors.

The second major reform in 1973 was aimed at the Ways and Means Committee, which held jurisdiction over key legislative areas: taxes, foreign trade, Social Security, Medicare, and others. Chairman Wilbur D. Mills, an Arkansas Democrat, had long been successful in bringing Ways and Means legislation to the House floor under a closed rule, making amendments impossible. Mills, a skilled parliamentarian and an authoritarian chairman, argued that his legislation was so complex that amendments by individual members would twist the bills out of shape so that the broader goals would be lost.

The caucus struck a compromise between the Mills position and unlimited floor amendments: a minimum of fifty Democrats could propose an amendment to the caucus, and if a majority of the caucus approved it, the Democratic members of the Rules Committee would be instructed to write a rule allowing the amendment to be taken up on the House floor.

The wrangling in the House over the Legislative Reorganization Act of 1970, among other struggles in that body, reflected the evolving nature of the House and the Senate. Neither body was static. The changing character of each, in the way legislation moved through them and the way power was exercised, indicated the ambiguous and fluid nature of Congress as designed by the Founders. As the nation changed and grew, Congress as a whole and the two chambers needed to adjust also.

EVOLUTION OF THE SENATE

Under the Great Compromise of 1787, the House was to represent the "national Principle" while the Senate was to be an expression of the "federal principle." Early commentators suggested that by allowing state legislatures to pick U.S senators, states would be included in the federal process, which hopefully would help to allay Antifederalist fears. Although each state had two senators, they voted as individuals, not as state representatives; they were paid by the federal government, not the states; and the legislature that elected them had no power to recall them. Thus, most senators refused to act as pawns of state governments.

Courtesy, dignity, and informality marked the proceedings of the early Senate. It did not feel compelled to meet in the formal Senate chamber. Size (the early Senate was about the size of a modern-day committee) allowed the members to meet just as easily for dinner or around a fireplace, and formal rules seemed to be anathema to a body with such an approach. At the first session in 1789, the Senate adopted only twenty short rules. Even by 1806, when the number of rules rose to forty, they dealt mostly with nominations and treaties.

In the beginning, the rules left wide discretion to the Senate president, particularly Rule 16, which gave that officer sole authority to decide points of order. Vice President John Adams presided over the Senate with no specific guides on procedure, but Thomas Jefferson, who followed, felt the need of referring to a system of rules. The result was Jefferson's *Manual of Parliamentary Procedure*, which was also adopted by the House in 1837.

Following the practice of the Confederation Congress, the Senate originally met in private. This did not mean that the proceedings were really kept secret, as once the formal meeting ended, senators freely discussed their activities outside the chamber. In addition, the Senate journal occasionally appeared in print. However, the chamber's quasi-secrecy deflected public interest from the Senate to the House while at times raising suspicions as to whether the Senate was a latter-day aristocracy and an antirepublican institution.

Responding to this negative perception, the senators voted to open their sessions in 1794 after voting it down four times. Because there were no public galleries, two more years passed until the meetings were open in fact as well as theory. Ironically, despite the clamor to open the Senate, few people attended, in large part because House sessions were far more entertaining than the sedate, civilized meetings of the Senate.

Early on, senators did not have a heavy workload and met for just a few hours, if at all, in the middle of the day. On many occasions they suspended their own business so they could watch debates in the House. Until 1798, absenteeism was a major issue, leading to the adoption of a rule that prohibited senators from leaving a session without permission.

Because in the early days of the Republic most legislation originated in the House, the Senate had little to do early in the congressional session. Also, since all bills died at the end of each session of Congress, the Senate did not have House-passed bills from previous sessions on which to work. The House, jealous of its power, rejected Senate proposals that the two chambers jointly prepare a legislative program for an entire session. Much of the legislative output of each session was pushed through in the closing days. For example, in the second session of the Sixth Congress (1799–1801), the bulk of the Senate's thirty-five bills were passed on the last day.

Delaying tactics were occasionally used in the early Senate, but they apparently did not present a serious problem. Only three of the rules adopted in 1789 had any direct bearing on limiting debate. Although individual members, with the permission of the majority, could introduce bills after one day's notice, the more common practice was to move the appointment of a committee to report a bill. Thus, only a limited number of bills were introduced, and most of these were passed.

Standing committees did not exist in the early Senate. Legislation was handled by ad hoc committees that were appointed to consider a particular issue and disbanded once their work was finished. Membership on these committees was flexible, with no set numbers or rules.

Political Parties

As in the House, political parties did not exist in the early Senate. However, with the presentation of Hamilton's financial program, parties in the Senate, as in the House, began to emerge. The Federalists held the Senate until 1801, but in 1794 Democratic-Republicans came close to ending that control. The Federalists maintained power by unseating Albert Gallatin, claiming that he did not fulfill the citizenship requirement. He was unseated by a 14–12 vote along party lines. Federalist control was tenuous, however, and on six occasions the Federalists needed the vote of Vice President Adams to break ties and pass legislation.

Approval of the Jay Treaty in 1795 united the Federalists and firmly identified the Senate in the public mind as the focus of the Federalist Party. From that time on both Federalists and Republicans voted with a degree of party regularity. During the Fourth, Fifth, and Sixth Congresses (1795–1801), Federalists had a 2–1 edge over Democratic-Republicans in the Senate, while the House was closely divided between the two parties. But resolution of the undeclared war with France by President Adams deprived Federalists of their principal issue, and this development, combined with the expansion of the chamber to include members from newly admitted southern and western states, broke the power of the Federalists in the Senate. Starting with the election of 1800, Federalist strength in the Senate steadily declined.

The Presiding Officer

The Constitution solved the problem of giving a job to the vice president by making him president of the Senate, and it di-

rected the Senate to choose a president pro tempore to act for him in his absence. But neither of these positions, due to the way they were defined by the Constitution, and not necessarily the caliber of the men who filled them, provided effective legislative leadership.

Vice presidents were not chosen by the Senate but imposed upon it from outside. Being outsiders, there was no compulsion for them to be sympathetic to the Senate's aims, and often they were not. John Adams, the first vice president, was a perfect example. As a member of the majority party, he agreed with the majority of the Senate during his two terms as vice president. Adams was a somewhat active participant in Senate affairs, but overall he perceived his role as simply that of presiding officer and made little effort to guide or direct the Senate. In fact, Adams felt that this would be outside the scope of his position. His successor, Thomas Jefferson, not only took little interest in influencing the Senate, but because of the Federalist majority, had no opportunity to do so even had he wanted to. Some 150 years later, when Vice President Lyndon Johnson proposed that his office be maintained in the Senate, senators rebelled.

The second in command, the president pro tempore, was elected by the Senate. However, because his terms were random and temporary, it was impossible for him to be an effective leader. By custom he was elected only for the current absence of the vice president. His term ended with the reappearance of the vice president, meaning he was never sure how long he would be "in charge." As a result, the Senate saw fifteen different presidents pro tempore in the first six Congresses.

Rise of the Senate

Thus, it was up to individual senators and the executive branch to provide leadership for the chamber. While both Washington and Adams were loathe to show real leadership, Hamilton had no problem doing so, and during Washington's term he exerted great control, giving direction to the Senate, and to the House as well.

By the end of the Jefferson Administration, the Senate had established formal procedures and begun to exercise greater power by performing its various functions. It began to initiate and revise proposed legislation. In line with its constitutional authority to give advice and consent to the president concerning treaties and nominations, the Senate conducted it first investigations and held two impeachment trials, removing a sitting federal judge in the first one and acquitting Supreme Court Justice Samuel Chase in the second. The scope of its powers, however, was not yet clear.

With the election of James Madison to the presidency in 1808, Congress generally, and the Senate specifically, emerged from the shadow of the executive branch and began exercising twenty years of legislative supremacy over the presidency, ending only with the Jackson Administration in 1829. As noted above, neither James Madison nor James Monroe exerted any type of leadership over Congress. In both cases, their obligation to

the congressional caucus that nominated them compromised their ability to exercise control. John Quincy Adams was even less able to deal with Congress, and especially the House, to whom he owed his presidency in the election of 1824 which was decided in that chamber. Further assuring legislative supremacy was the emergence of strong leaders in Congress.

While there was no question the House dominated the legislature, especially under the leadership of Henry Clay, the era also signaled the rising influence of the Senate. That chamber began to exert influence over executive appointments late in Jefferson's administration and more so under Madison. For example, when Madison sought to make Albert Gallatin secretary of state, a group of senators objected, and Madison backed down, nominating Robert Smith instead, who was approved by the Senate. Madison also saw one of his nominees to the Supreme Court, Alexander Wolcott, rejected decisively by a vote of 24 to 9.

The Senate was inhibited during its earliest years by the lack of a formal committee structure like the one in the House. In the first quarter of the nineteenth century, it created only four standing committees, all chiefly administrative in nature. Instead, most of the legislative committee work fell to ad hoc select committees, usually consisting of three members, appointed as the occasion demanded. Eventually, the need to appoint so many committees (100 in 1816) exhausted the patience of the Senate, and eleven standing committees were added in December of 1816. Most of the new committees were parallel in function to those previously created in the House, and the usual membership was five (by 1900 it would be nine).

Senate committees were elected by Senate members until 1823, when the chamber adopted an amendment to its rules giving the presiding officer authority to name committees, unless otherwise ordered by the Senate. At first the power was exercised by the president pro tempore, but early in 1825 Vice President John Calhoun assumed the appointment power and used it to place Jackson supporters in key committee posts. Calhoun's appointments were rife with anti–Adams Administration overtones, and the Senate quickly returned to election by the senators. For the next decade, the Senate flip-flopped back and forth between the two rules on committee selection.

During this period the Senate's legislative importance gradually increased, beginning with the leading role it took in the struggle over the Missouri Compromise in 1820. The Senate forced the House to accept the amendment to the bill that barred slavery north of longitude 36°30' north. The Missouri Compromise signaled the Senate's increased future role. The arrival in the Senate of men capable of leadership at the same time as the issue of states' rights and slavery was growing in importance enabled the chamber to become the chief forum for the discussion of national policy on the preeminent issue of slavery.

During this period sectional interests were more important than party inter-

ests and often blurred party divisions. Three men dominated the Senate between 1830 and 1850: Daniel Webster of Massachusetts, Henry Clay of Kentucky, and John C. Calhoun of South Carolina. With these men in the lead, the Senate became a more stable body. That and the greater stability of its membership contributed to the Senate's preeminence over the House, where the Jacksonian concept of rotation in office led to a great deal of turnover. More significant, perhaps, was the introduction of the spoils system and the Senate's increasing domination of the appointment process. Finally, national growth strengthened the Senate by turning it from a small, intimate body into one large enough for speech making to be appropriate and numerous enough so that parliamentary skills became important.

Early Filibusters

But the courtesy and decorum of the early Senate gradually began to crumble under the mounting pressure of the time. Although debates were for the most part still closed and brief, passions sometimes ran high and legislative obstruction became increasingly common. Filibusters were now often threatened and occasionally undertaken, but they were not yet fully exploited as a means of paralyzing the Senate, and senators seldom admitted that they were employing delaying tactics.

Few major filibusters took place prior to the Civil War. In part, the light workload of senators made filibusters a meaningless tactic except at the end of congressional sessions, when deadlines lurked. The first notable Senate filibuster occurred in 1841, when dissident senators held the floor for seven days in opposition to a bill in regard to hiring the Senate printers.   Later in the same year a Whig move to reestablish the Bank of the United States was subject to an unsuccessful two-week filibuster. Reacting negatively to what he saw as superfluous debate, Henry Clay threatened to introduce a rule to limit filibusters. However, he was unable to get enough support to get a rule passed to accomplish this.

In 1846 a bill providing for joint U.S.-British occupancy of Oregon was filibustered for two months. The measure was finally brought to a vote through use, for the first time, of the unanimous consent agreement—a device still employed to speed action in the Senate. Later in 1846 the Wilmot Proviso to exclude slavery from territories won in the Mexican War was talked to death in the closing hours of the session. Slavery was also the issue in extended debates over the Compromise of 1850. Webster, Clay, and Calhoun made their last joint appearance in the Senate, the dying Calhoun dragging himself into the chamber to hear his final speech read by James Mason of Virginia.

SCENE IN UNCLE SAM'S SENATE.
17th APRIL 1850.

The assassination attempt on Thomas Hart Benton by Henry S. Foote in the Senate chamber in 1850. This incident illustrates the controversy of the admission of California into the Union, and depicts the tension over the Compromise of 1850, which eventually led to the Civil War. (Library of Congress)

During this period, violence intruded into the Senate, inhibiting its ability to function as a legislative body. The Senate was disrupted in 1850 when Senator Henry S. Foote of Mississippi brandished a pistol at Missouri senator Thomas Benton. Only the intervention of other senators prevented bloodshed. The most infamous example of violence in the well of the Senate was the brutal caning of Charles Sumner by Preston Brooks in 1856. In response to a slight of his cousin's character, Brooks snuck up behind Sumner and beat him bloody with a walking stick.

The acts of violence and debates in the Senate reflected the rancor of the antebellum period. Oratory had little place in a chamber where all members were said to carry arms, and by the time the Senate moved into its present quarters in 1859, the great era of Senate debate was at an end.

Appointing Committee Members in the Antebellum Years

The most important procedural development of the antebellum period occurred in 1846, when the Senate transferred responsibility for making committee assignments to the party. Previously, committee assignments had been determined by ballot. Therefore, majority party control of the committees could not be assured, and although by 1829 the majority party usually controlled the working committees, the opposition party still held important chairs.

When the second session of the Twenty-ninth Congress met in December 1846, an unsuccessful attempt was made to let the vice president name the committees, and the Senate returned to the usual system of balloting. Midway through the process, however, the balloting rule was suspended. The Senate proceeded to elect on one ballot a list of candidates for all of the remaining committee vacancies that had been agreed upon by the majority and minority parties. From that time on, the choice of committees has usually amounted to a routine acceptance by the full Senate of lists agreed upon by representatives of the caucus or conference of the two major parties.

The failure until 1846 of parties and their organizations to select committees reflected the lack of party discipline in the early years of the Senate. During this period, party authority limited itself to organizational questions and did not move into substantive issues. Most often, senators voted as individuals rather than as Democrats or Whigs.

Party influence in the Senate was enhanced by the new method of committee selection and the growing importance of seniority, which determined rank in the committees. Prior to 1846, experience had always played a major role in making committee assignments, and as long as committees were elected by ballot, rigid adherence to seniority was impossible. However with the introduction of party lists in 1846, strict compliance with seniority began to be enforced.

There were always some exceptions. For example, the Democratic Caucus removed Stephen Douglas from the chairmanship of the Committee on Territories because he refused to go along with President James Buchanan and the southern wing of the party on the question of slavery in the territories.

By the time of the Civil War, the committee structure of the Senate had radically changed. From being a loose aggregation of ad hoc committees appointed for the occasion, it was transformed into a formal system of standing committees whose members owed their appointments to the party organization and their advancement within committees to the seniority system.

Deterioration of Senate Power

During the Civil War and Reconstruction, Republicans controlled the presidency, the House, and the Senate through seven consecutive Congresses ending in 1875. Not only did Democrats lose southern seats in Congress, most of which were vacant from 1861 to 1869, but many northern Democrats defected to the Republicans rather than remain in a party so closely tied to the southern cause and that effectively had no power, or any chance of power, in a Republican Senate.

The period of Republican control during the Civil War was marked by a power struggle between the White House and Congress, which saw the deterioration of Senate power. Things did not improve during Reconstruction, when the House overshadowed the Senate. But following the failure of the effort to impeach Andrew Johnson and the death of Thaddeus Stevens, the radical Republican leader in the House, House prestige declined and the Senate rapidly became the primary body in the national legislature. During the remainder of the nineteenth century, while control of the House shifted back and forth between the two parties, the Republicans managed to maintain control of the Senate in all except two Congresses, accentuating the development of what can be termed modern party government in the upper chamber.

The Career Senator, Lobbyists, and the Senate's Loss of Respect

The character of the Senate underwent a marked change in the post–Civil War era. Its membership grew from seventy-four in 1881 to ninety in 1901, and as state politics came under more centralized control, a new type of senator appeared. Party bosses and party machines, like the famed Tammany Hall in New York, dominated politics. Professional politicians made their way to Washington only after they had risen through the ranks of their state party organization and consolidated their power over the state party structure. As long as they maintained their control of state politics, they were immune from external political reprisal, but their dedication to party and their acceptance of the need for discipline made them good party senators, willing to compromise their differences in order to maintain harmony within the party. To these men the Senate was a career, and a conspicuous increase in the average length of Senate service occurred during this period.

Lobbying by business groups became a vital element in government during the last part of the nineteenth century. Some of the lobbying practices of the period reinforced the impression, which was often true, of Senate corruption.

Thus, while the power of the Senate apparently grew, at the same time it lost respect in the public eye. By the close of the nineteenth century, the Senate was widely described in derogatory terms, and it was without question the most unpopular branch of the national government. Dissatisfaction with the Senate led to the movement for direct election of senators, through which reformers hoped to curtail both the power of political parties and the political influence of the corporations.

Modern Party Discipline

Political parties assumed responsibility for organizational matters in the pre–Civil War Senate and extended their influence during the war to substantive questions. However, both parties, especially the Republican, were viewed as being products of the issues that had ignited the Civil War. Many expected them to dissolve and new parties to arise, as had happened in the past. Although the demise of the two parties did not occur, party influence in the upper chamber did decline. During Grant's ad-

ministration, the only time party unity seemed to be essential was on organizational questions. Disputes over committee assignments were settled in the party caucus and pressing issues were discussed there, but a lack of strong leadership meant it was almost impossible to enforce party discipline, meaning that caucus decisions were not really binding.

The potential for strong party leadership became apparent in the Senate career of Roscoe Conkling of New York in the 1870s. Conkling gathered around him a loyal following, and after 1873 his faction usually controlled the Committee on Committees, which made it possible for him to reward his supporters with valuable committee posts. But the Conkling forces stood together only on organizational questions; their influence on substantive legislation was not great. When Conkling resigned his Senate seat in 1881, following an altercation with President James Garfield over appointments, the Senate reverted to its old, independent ways.

Republican leadership and modern party discipline made their appearance in the Senate in the 1890s under the leadership of Republicans William B. Allison of Iowa, Nelson W. Aldrich of Rhode Island, and their fellow members of the School of Philosophy Club, an informal group that met regularly for poker at the home of Sen. James S. McMillan of Michigan. When Allison, because he had served in the Senate longer than any other member of his party, was elected chairman of the Republican Caucus in March 1897, this group assumed control of the Senate. Previous caucus chairs had not viewed the office as a vehicle for concentrating party authority, but Allison quickly recognized the position's potential and took advantage of its appointment powers.

Since the mid-1880s a Republican Steering Committee had been appointed biennially to help schedule legislative business. Unlike previous caucus leaders, Allison determined to chair this committee himself, and he filled it with other members of his group. Under Allison the Steering Committee arranged the order of business in minute detail and also managed floor proceedings.

Allison likewise dominated the Committee on Committees, which had responsibility for assignments to the working committees. The caucus chair had great leeway in making appointments to this group and Allison was able to staff it with a majority receptive to his wishes. Committee chairmanships were by this time invariably filled through seniority, and Allison and Aldrich made no attempt to overturn the seniority rule, to which they owed their own committee chairmanships, Allison in Appropriations and Aldrich in Finance. But seniority did not apply to the filling of committee vacancies, and here the party leaders found an opportunity to reward their supporters and punish dissidents. Access to positions of influence soon depended on the favor and support of the party leaders.

Caucus approval of the committee slates and order of business became a mere formality, but the caucus still met to consider important issues. Through the caucus mechanism, divisive questions were compromised in private so that the party could speak with a united voice on the floor. Caucus decisions were not formally binding, but once the party leadership was capable of enforcing discipline on those who broke ranks, party solidarity became the norm.

Under the leadership of Arthur P. Gorman of Maryland, Senate Democrats developed a power structure similar to that devised by the Republicans. As chairman of the Democratic Caucus in the 1890s, Gorman chaired not only the Steering Committee but the Committee on Committees as well, and in some ways his control over his party was greater than that of Allison and Aldrich over the Republicans. At the same time, however, that power was compromised because the Democrats were in the minority most of the time. They often split on substantive issues, and Gorman never attained the power that his Republican counterparts achieved. The lack of harmony within Democratic ranks led, in 1903, to the adoption of a rule making the decisions of the Democratic Caucus binding. Allison had considered such a rule unnecessary for the Republicans, but Gorman enthusiastically supported it for his party.

Not all were in favor of the growth of party government. Many Americans were suspicious of it, and even within the Senate itself, many members had serious qualms. As early as 1872 the Liberal Republicans (opposed to Grant) were protesting efforts by some senators to use the party organization to control the party and thereby the Senate. Similar complaints came from the Mugwumps faction in the 1880s and the Populist

Party in the 1890s. In 1899 the Senate attempted to diffuse authority by distributing the responsibility for major appropriations bills from the Appropriations Committee to various legislative committees. The change emerged not from the caucus, but from the floor, where dissidents within both parties were able to carry this change over the combined opposition of the Republican and Democratic leaders.

By the end of the nineteenth century, political parties had assumed a decisive role in the legislative process. The parties named the committees that made the first tentative decisions on proposed legislation, and also determined what bills would be considered on the floor. Controversial issues were resolved in the caucuses. After differences were settled there, party members exhibited great discipline on the floor of the Senate, often foregoing debate or the formality of a roll-call vote.

The Power of Committee Chairs

Thus, as the twentieth century progressed, the committees were still central in determining congressional career paths. This committee system, coupled with a strong seniority system, helped structure power. The two fed each other and prospered in a symbiotic relationship. The committee system became the center of Senate politics due in part to a fairly stable membership, with well over 50 percent of the House and Senate membership being reelected on a regular

basis. Because seniority led to a committee chair, the more senior members who could have effected change saw no reason to do so, as it would cripple their power.

Since the senior leaders were often free from interference or sanction from within the Senate, they were able to employ almost total control over their committees and agendas and staffs and had a degree of autonomy in how they pursued legislative goals in either proposing bills or blocking legislation. Mutual deference among committees protected most legislation from any serious challenge on the floor of the respective chambers. All chairs had the power to dictate subcommittee structure, membership, staff, and agenda, which enabled them to control the committees' decision making. The result was that a few independent committees headed by very powerful chairs controlled the legislature. Thus, two highly influential southerners largely set congressional defense policy during the 1950s and 1960s: Carl Vinson of Georgia, who chaired the House Armed Services Committee from 1949 through 1952 and from 1955 to 1965, and his fellow Georgian, Richard Russell, who chaired the Senate Armed Services Committee during much of the same time.

Under this system the role of the majority party and its leadership was restricted. The party leaders' limited institutional resources and, especially in the case of the Democrats, party factionalism (the Democratic Party was deeply split between the conservative southern wing and the rest of the party) reduced the scope of the party leadership's influence. It was the predominance of southern influence and control that opened the door to readjustment in the Senate, both formally and informally, as new issues took center stage, forcing shifts in how leadership worked.

Among the reasons for the shifting of power was that as society became more complicated, the need grew for expertise on various subjects. As a consequence, by the late 1950s, the number of subcommittees had begun to mushroom. The members on each subcommittee developed expertise on the panel's subject area, forcing them to rely on each other for knowledge and direction on votes. (The proliferation of subcommittees also helped to break, in part, the control of committees in the Senate by southerners. In 1968, there was an increase of subcommittees from 87 to 103, while simultaneously the proportion of subcommittees with southern chairs decreased from 45 percent to 31 percent.)

Strong committees handicapped general party leadership, and its role in the policy process was largely limited to facilitating the passage on the House and Senate floors of legislation written in committee. Leaders seldom interceded in committees to shape legislation. With no mechanism to hold committees and chairs responsible, the leaders played little policy role. Thus, some leaders, like Sam Rayburn, Speaker of the House for all but four years between 1940 and 1961, relied more on personal persuasion than on actual power to get what they wanted.

The Power of Individual Members

Perhaps the greatest difference that played out between the two chambers, despite apparent similarities, was the difference in formal rules and the attention paid to those rules. Although the actual distribution of influence among committees, the party leadership, and rank-and-file members was similar in the House and Senate in the 1950s, the chambers' formal rules were very different. Beginning in the late nineteenth century, House rules tightly restricted rank-and-file members' debate time and their right to offer amendments. In contrast, at least on their face, Senate rules gave individuals enormous power. In most cases, any senator could offer unlimited numbers of amendments to a piece of legislation on the floor. A senator could hold the floor indefinitely through a filibuster unless cloture was invoked. In the 1950s, however, custom tended to limit these formal rules. Rather than immediately exercise power on the floor of the Senate, first-term senators were expected to pay their dues. It was anticipated that senators would serve what was in essence an apprenticeship. They would spend their early years specializing in the work of their committees; helping other senators, especially on constituency-related matters; and using their privileges under the rules with great restraint. Therefore, although technically individuals had more power in the Senate than in the House, most senators acted in a restrained manner, especially in their first term.

In the 1950s southern Democrats dominated Congress. They disproportionately held committee chairs and positions on the most desirable committees in both chambers. That was because the South was basically a one-party region, so southern Democrats accumulated seniority, and therefore control, disproportionately compared to senators from outside the region.

Through the 1950s, liberal Democrats in both houses felt frustration at this lopsided distribution of influence. They argued that committee chairs and memberships on the most important committees were unrepresentatively held by conservatives. Often, the Rules Committee, which included many conservative members, blocked or watered down liberal legislation. Liberals, many of whom were junior members, were also unhappy with their limited opportunities to participate meaningfully in the legislative process. In the House the liberals complained about autocratic committee chairs. In the Senate they chafed under norms that restricted their full participation and objected to the cloture rule, which made it possible for southerners, a determinative minority in the upper chamber, to filibuster and kill civil rights legislation.

Until 1959 the liberal Democrats lacked the numbers to do much more than complain. The 1958 elections, however, placed sixty-three new Democrats in the House and fifteen in the Senate, chipping away at the alliance of southern Democrats and Republicans in committees and on the floor.

In the Senate the sheer size of the freshman class made unworkable the normal apprenticeship that had previously been a factor in limiting participation by junior members. The Senate was dependent on customs to regulate behavior. That dependence, however, was torpedoed by a large incoming membership that refused to abide by the existing unwritten rules of behavior. The member that best understood this shift of power toward newer members was Lyndon Johnson, then the majority leader, who played to these new members. He gave them good committee assignments and committee chairs who were amenable to requests from junior senators for the establishment of new subcommittees. Due to this pressure from the incoming senators, the distribution of influence began to change.

The Waning Power of Southern Democrats

The incoming classes of 1958 and subsequent elections spelled the end of dominance by southern Democrats, although that change was slow to arrive, and it was not for another decade, or even until the year 2000, that the defection of many southern states to the Republican Party really broke the southern Democrats' hold on the Democratic agenda. In the early 1960s both the change and the lingering influence of conservative Democrats were apparent. Thus, as President John F. Kennedy tried to push certain liberal bills through Congress, conservative strength and southern power in the Senate was evident as some elements of Kennedy's agenda languished in committee, partly because of pressure from southern Democrats.

These developments mirrored earlier developments in the House. The elections of 1958 bolstered the ranks of the Democratic Study Group, an organization aimed at rallying liberal members of Congress to press for progressive legislation and reform of the House. As in the Senate, conservative southerners blocked liberal legislation, leaving it to die in committee. Attempts were made to advance liberal measures by pressuring the Speaker of the House to expand the Rules Committee, the major instrument for stymieing liberal causes. In early 1961 the House voted 217 to 212 to add two more seats to the Rules Committee, which meant two more Democratic seats. However, change was slow, and the Senate needed to move forward as well if any gains were to be realized.

This was most evident regarding civil rights legislation. President Kennedy needed the white southern vote to win reelection in 1964 and the support of southern senators for his foreign policy agenda. As a result, he adopted a cautious and restrained approach to civil rights, often emphasizing enforcement of existing laws rather than pushing for new ones. Kennedy took a similar approach in his efforts to cut taxes and increase funding for education, both of which endeavors died in Congress, at the hands of southern Democrats. Not until Kennedy was pressured by public opinion—namely, the public reaction to

police violence directed at civil rights demonstrators in Birmingham, Alabama, in 1963—did he attempt to buck southern Senate pressure, and finally sent a civil rights bill to Congress, in June of that year.

The Senate changed significantly before the House did, despite the fact that opponents could filibuster proposed changes in Senate rules, whereas in the House a simple majority could pass reforms. During the 1950s and 1960s, Senate liberals made frequent attempts to change the cloture rule so that it would be easier to end filibusters, but these efforts always failed, thwarted by the very rule they were trying to alter.

Media Politics, Personal Agendas, and Rules Changes

However, emergence in the 1960s of new issues meant the senators had to alter their behavior, which in turn changed how the chamber operated. New issues in addition to the omnipresent civil rights matters arose, including environmental protection, women's rights, consumer protection, and Vietnam. The number of interest groups active in Washington grew enormously. The media's role in politics became more and more prominent. In this new environment, senators were highly sought after as champions of causes and as spokespeople by the media. The ability to associate oneself with a positive policy message and to spin that message using good sound bytes brought a politician a reputation in Washington as a "player" and secured him or her favorable media attention. All of that translated itself into continued election and a place of power. Thus, the Senate became a body composed of politicians advocating personal agendas that could best be advanced by utilizing and taking advantage of the prerogatives a senator had rather than sedately moving through an apprenticeship that disparaged such behavior. This change in focus resulted in the expansion of the number of seats on good committees, an increase in the number of subcommittees chairmanships, and the distribution of both much more broadly. The by-product of these actions was an increase in the total number of staff and therefore the amount of staff available to junior as well as senior senators.

This transformation was abetted by rules changes. The Legislative Reorganization Act of 1970 authorized a committee majority to call a meeting if the chair refused to do so. The act limited the number of committee positions, and specifically the number of positions on the most desirable committees, that a senior senator could hold. Importantly, it assured minority members of staff. Additionally, in the mid-1970s both parties subjected committee chairs and ranking minority members to ratification votes in the party conference. Finally, rules changes in the middle of the 1970s mandated that committee meetings be open to the public.

In 1975 the Senate finally succeeded in changing the cloture rule. The threshold for closing debate on legislation was re-

duced from two-thirds of the senators present and voting to three-fifths of the total membership (usually sixty), though stopping debates on a proposal to change Senate rules still required a two-thirds vote. The door remained open for a determined minority, and a simple majority in the Senate is still seen as meaning only tenuous control—for any issue. Sixty is seen as the key number to maintain control and push through desired legislation.

Decentralization of Power

Behavioral as well as structural factors were responsible for change in the Senate. For example, committee chairs became less dominant, in part because of the rules, but more importantly because junior members were less subservient and more inclined to challenge their leadership. Also, as junior members gained access to the more desirable committees—those which had the greatest power to shape the legislative agenda—the subcommittees spawned by them and the ensuing chairmanships were gained not by formal rule changes, but by pressure put on senior colleagues, a pressure that had been unthinkable in previous decades.

Senators now had the incentive and the resources to involve themselves in a broader range of issues—which they did. They became much more active on the Senate floor, offering more amendments. Whereas in the past many limited themselves to offering amendments to bills from the committees on which they sat, now they stepped forward and attempted to interject themselves into legislation that was outside their committee expertise. They exploited extended debate to a much greater extent and the frequency of filibusters increased. These averaged less than two per Congress from 1955 though 1964, but this figure more than doubled to five per Congress between 1965 and 1970, and doubled again to 11.4 in the 1970s. By the twenty-first century, the frequency of filibusters and threatened filibusters, and the tenuous majorities that prevailed in the Senate after 2000, led to threats of major rule changes that would radically alter the filibuster rule and the ability of senators to use it to block legislation. This opening of the door to all members, regardless of seniority, coupled with growing media access for all members, destroyed the hold that a leadership cabal had maintained over the Senate in the previous century.

Responding to the new political environment, the Senate transformed itself from a body that was rooted in government by committee and dominated by seniority. In that Senate, influence and resources had been unequally distributed to a select group of individuals, based on position and longevity, that was not necessarily responsive to outside pressures. The new Senate seemed to be a more outward-looking institution in which there was a more equal distribution of resources. Importantly, at no time did party affiliation really play a major role in these changes. Policy concerns had motivated the liberal reformers, but these did not lead them to strengthen party organs or the powers of the party leadership.

In the immediate wake of the reforms of the 1970s, the decentralizing trend evident in the Senate, in which power accrued to junior members and subcommittees, also prevailed in the House. As in the Senate, by the mid-1970s participation by the House rank and file at the committee and the floor stages had increased enormously. This meant that far more members than earlier participated in the legislative process on any particular bill. This created a bit more instability in the House than it did in the Senate because of the greater turnover in the House, especially in midterm elections. Coupled with the sheer size of the lower chamber, the result was that the proliferation of inexperienced subcommittee chairs and the high degree of participation radically increased the level of uncertainty in the House. This meant that it became much harder to foresee who would be engaged in what legislation; which amendments would be attached to a piece of legislation; and, most importantly, how members would vote.

By the end of the 1970s, many Democrats had become concerned about some unexpected consequences of the reforms. Floor sessions regularly stretched late into the night; legislation crafted by more representative committees was picked apart on the floor; and the Democrats were repeatedly forced to go on record regarding controversial amendments, such as busing and abortion. Democrats were also having great difficulty passing legislation that they and their supporters badly wanted. For example, despite a Democratic president, Jimmy Carter, and big margins in both chambers, in the late 1970s the Democrats failed to enact labor law reform or to establish a consumer protection agency, both high priorities. The House Democrats began to look to their party leadership for assistance. With the election of the Republican Ronald Reagan as president in 1980, that need became greater.

In an attempt to restore some of their lost control, the House Democratic leaders began making more aggressive use of the powers and resources that the reforms had bestowed on them, and by the mid-1980s a centralized House began to take shape. Party leaders such as Jim Wright, a Texas Democrat and Speaker of the House from 1987 to 1989, were more involved in shaping the party's policy direction. This required more assertiveness in constraining members on the floor, especially when it came to the various and numerous amendments that would often be offered there. The whip's role became more important, and the party caucus or conference was more active, demanding party discipline from both chairs of committees and the rank and file. The result was a system that allowed participation by the rank-and-file members, but within the party structure to a greater degree, which restored some order to procedure and raised the importance of the party.

The Senate, in contrast, remained a chamber that indulged the individual. To be sure, as the parties became more polarized ideologically, senators chose to work through their parties more frequently. Yet they refused to give their leaders the sort of powers the House leaders had, because doing so would require severely limiting their own prerogatives under Senate rules. Since the political environment continued to reward with visibility and influence those senators who exploited the chamber's permissive rules, senators were unwilling to curb their prerogatives.

The last part of the twentieth century and the first years of the twenty-first saw polarized politics combined with greater individuality contributing to growing uncertainty and sustained deadlock in the Congress.

FURTHER READING

Binder, Sarah. *Minority Rights, Majority Rule: Partisanship and the Development of Congress.* Cambridge: Cambridge University Press, 1997.

Bowling, Kenneth R., and Donald R. Kennon, eds. *Inventing Congress: Origins and Establishment of the First Federal Congress.* Athens: Ohio University Press, 1999.

Caro, Robert A. *Lyndon Johnson: Master of the Senate.* New York: Knopf, 2002.

Cox, Gary, and Matthew McCubbins. *Legislative Leviathan: Party Government in the House.* 2nd ed. Cambridge, NY: Cambridge University Press, 2007.

Currie, David P. *The Constitution in Congress: Democrats and Whigs, 1829–1861.* Chicago: University of Chicago Press, 2006.

Currie, David P. *The Constitution in Congress: Descent into the Maelstrom, 1829–1861.* Chicago: University of Chicago Press, 1999.

Currie, David P. *The Constitution in Congress: The Jeffersonians, 1801–1829.* Chicago: University of Chicago Press, 2001.

Currie, James T. *The United States House of Representatives.* Malabar, FL: Krieger Publishing, 1988.

Daschle, Tom. *Like No Other Time: The 107th Congress and the Two Years That Changed America Forever.* New York: Crown, 2003.

Dodd, Lawrence, and Bruce Oppenheimer. *Congress Reconsidered.* 8th ed. Washington, DC: CQ Press, 2004.

Gould, Lewis L. *The Most Exclusive Club: A History of the Modern United States Senate.* Cambridge, MA: Basic Books, 2006.

Harris, Fred R. *Deadlock or Decision: The U.S. Senate and the Rise of National Politics: A Twentieth Century Fund Book.* New York: Oxford University Press, 1993.

Harris, Fred R. *In Defense of Congress.* New York: St. Martin's Press, 1995.

Oleszek, Walter J. *CRS Report for Congress: The Role of the House Majority Leader: An Overview.* Damascus, MD: Penny Hill Press, April 4, 2006.

Oleszek, Walter J. *CRS Report for Congress: The Role of the House Minority Leader: An Overview.* Damascus, MD: Penny Hill Press, December 12, 2006.

Polsby, Nelson W. *How Congress Evolves.* New York: Oxford University Press, 2004.

Remini, Robert. *The House: The History of the House of Representatives.* New York: Harper Collins, 2006.

Schneider, Judy. *CRS Report for Congress: House Leadership Structure: Overview of Party Organization.* Damascus, MD: Penny Hill Press, July 10, 2003.

Schneider, Judy. *CRS Report for Congress: House Leadership: Whip Organization.* Damascus, MD: Penny Hill Press, February 12, 2002.

Sinclair, Barbara. *The Transformation of the U.S. Senate.* Baltimore: Johns Hopkins University Press, 1989.

Smith, Norma, and Kathy Anderson. *Jeannette Rankin: America's Conscience.* Helena: Montana Historical Society Press, 2002.

Swift, Elaine K. *The Making of an American Senate: Reconstitutive Change in Congress, 1787–1841.* Ann Arbor: University of Michigan Press, 1996.

Saturno, James. V. *CRS Report for Congress: The Speaker of the House: House Officer, Party Leader, and Representative.* Damascus, MD: Penny Hill Press, January 29, 2007.

6

INTERACTIONS WITH OTHER GOVERNMENT BRANCHES

To understand Congress as a political entity, one integrally involved in making policy and often in determining the battle lines over important social issues, it is particularly important to grasp how Congress and the presidency interact and have been able to wrestle power from one another throughout U.S. history. This constant back-and-forth battle has resulted in a flow of authority between the legislature and the executive, and to a lesser extent the legislature and the judiciary, the latter branch more often serving as referee rather than as a fulcrum of power. In the last half of the twentieth century, that flow seemed to be mostly toward the executive branch, but Congress has not remained dormant and at various times has attempted to reclaim power through actions like the War Powers Resolution of 1973. Then, however, Congress has seemed to have conceded it again, as with the Iraq War Resolution in 2002. It was in such contexts that battles took place on the floor of the House and Senate over policy, forcing members of both houses to fight for power with the other branches of the government.

THE FLOW OF POWER

The congressional role in government from the outset seemed limited. The fact that the Constitution included an executive branch, when the Articles of Confederation had not, suggested that the president and the executive branch in general constituted the focal point of government and the center of leadership, which they in fact became. In addition, the relatively ambiguous nature of Article II and its description of executive authority was in sharp contrast to the explicit nature of Article I in defining what Congress could do.

Hamilton's and Jefferson's Influence

George Washington as president was not always the most dominant of leaders. Some historians have likened his leadership style to that of the chair of a corporate board. Rather, it was the members of the Cabinet, especially Alexander Hamilton, who dominated the first years of the new government. He was the person who communicated with Congress and assumed the role of legislative leadership in many ways. Hamilton did everything short of appearing on the floor of the House and Senate. Ironically, there did not seem to be any objection to his activities, despite the presence of over a dozen members of the Constitutional Convention in the First Congress. While such boldness on the part of a Cabinet member today would meet with serious objections, as when Mike Mansfield suggested that Lyndon Johnson, in his role as vice president, should take an active part in Senate politics, no early members protested, and this acceptance seemed to reflect an early view of the executive branch's primacy.

However, Hamilton undermined his own influence. His vast economic program and proposed financial measures helped polarize Congress and speeded up the rise of the first two-party system. Congressional members then began proposing resolutions condemning Hamilton (although none passed) and began to engage in investigations of the Treasury secretary and his minions. All of these actions reflected a congressional desire to challenge Hamilton personally, escape executive domination, and establish itself as an independent and equal branch.

Despite Hamilton's apparently cozy relationship with Congress at first, early fractures had appeared over the application of the "advice and consent" clause in the relations between Washington and the Senate. In August 1789 he went to the Senate to get its advice and consent to a treaty he was negotiating with the Creek Indians. Each section was read, then the senators were asked "How do you advise and consent?" The Senate responded with silence. They then began to debate each section. In the meantime, Washington grew impatient expecting them to quickly concede each point, so he could leave the chamber with their approval. As debate lengthened, one senator moved that the treaty be submitted to a committee for study. Washington, frustrated, exclaimed, "This defeats every purpose of my coming here." He eventually left the Senate, extremely perturbed and never returned again.

The result helped to usher in the development of committees as a way to deal with the process of shepherding legislation through Congress. Committees such as the House Ways and Means Committee and the Committee on Commerce and Manufactures, unnecessary as long as Hamilton was leading the way, began to appear toward the end of Washington's second term. As congressional needs grew, so did the number of committees, and by the mid-1820s, both houses had a wide variety of committees in place. The result was that rather than working together as had been the case during the early days of Washington's administration, by the middle of the antebellum period, members of Congress in both houses wanted nothing to do with the White House and did not want it to appear that any impropriety was occurring through collusion with the executive.

It was not until Andrew Jackson's presidency, though, that real confrontation ensued and the balance of power between the branches was tested. John Adams did not necessarily get along with Congress, but the system worked, despite the rising vitriol between the two parties. The fact that the same party controlled both the presidency and Congress helped. Thomas Jefferson expanded the powers of the presidency, but he did so in a subtle manner and did not necessarily challenge congressional authority. Jefferson occasionally did some end runs around Congress, though, such as the Louisiana Purchase and the fighting against the Tripoli pirates. In neither case did Congress reject his extension of authority, and so he moved in what could be considered an extraconstitutional manner. At any rate, those were the exceptions, and for the most part Jefferson worked with Congress as a partner, respecting its authority and not using the veto.

However, with the same party controlling both the White House and the Hill, Jefferson was able to direct legislation and policy in a manner somewhat different than his two predecessors. (Washington had preferred to let Hamilton engage in the day-to-day dealings with Congress and Adams had to fight the Hamiltonian insurgency within his own party.) Jefferson was able to hold sway over Congress and his personal relationship with the legislature was reminiscent of the Hamiltonian model, with legislation drafted in one branch and passed in the other.

Madison, Monroe, and Adams

The presidents that followed Jefferson failed to exercise the same type of authority, either by choice or inability. As a result, power began to aggrandize to Congress, culminating with the War of 1812. The war was a product of Henry Clay's leadership rather than James Madison's, and Madison was dragged into the war, as he noted in his special message to Congress.

James Monroe, although remembered for the Monroe Doctrine, which could be seen as an act of executive assertiveness, although well within the executive power, for the most part allowed Congress to take command. He failed to express any view on the Missouri Compromise and signed it despite his opposition. He did not participate in any way in debates over tariffs and gave the nod to Congress when it came to recognizing new republics in Latin America.

John Quincy Adams's administration was marked by failures and accusations of corrupt bargains. Once again, therefore, power shifted to Congress as initiatives by Adams failed to gain legislative support.

Jackson's Presidency

Andrew Jackson's election to the presidency, and the rise to power of equally strong figures in the House and the Senate, disrupted and changed the pattern by which power had shifted back and forth between the executive and legislative branches. Jackson was the product of an expanding electorate. He regularly noted that he was the only individual who represented all the people (whereas the House was elected by districts, and the Senate was not even directly elected) and claimed that this gave him a mandate to

A nineteenth-century political cartoon brands President Andrew Jackson as a king. The Whig Party, composed primarily of opponents of Jackson who viewed him as a tyrannical despot, adopted the name "Whigs" in reference to the political party in England that had opposed King George III in the eighteenth century. (UPI-Bettmann/Corbis)

pursue his program. Fights with Congress resulted in a Senate censure of Jackson. Enmity reached a high point not to be matched until after the Civil War.

The result was not only the executive-legislative split in Washington, but a divide in the country, too. Jackson, labeled with the moniker "King Andrew," helped inspire the formation of a new opposition party, the Whigs. The Whigs took their name from the traditional English idea that a weak executive coupled with a strong legislature was the preferable form of government.

In many of the conflicts during Andrew Jackson's administration, such as the Nullification Crisis and the removal of Indians from the South, both political and personal issues were involved. In the fight over the Second Bank of the United States, the personalities of Henry Clay, Daniel Webster, and Nicholas Biddle all came into play, but in the end it was the relationship between the executive and the legislature that made the biggest imprint of the controversy.

Battle over the Bank

Jackson was a strict constructionist who believed it was beyond Congress's power under the Commerce Clause to create the Bank. Despite the apparent resolution of this issue a decade earlier in the Supreme Court case of *McCullouh v. Maryland* (1819), Jackson asserted his own right to interpret the Constitution and challenged congressional power.

With the Bank's charter close to expiring and the issue of rechartering looming, Congress examined the institution and issued various reports that upheld the Bank's value. They declared that the currency was the soundest ever known in American history and due to the earlier Supreme Court decision the constitutional question seemed to have been settled forever.

Jackson did not care. He repeated his criticisms of the Bank and found a champion in Sen. Thomas Hart Benton of Missouri. Benton went on the attack for Jackson and delivered speeches painting the Bank as an "illicit and alien force that stole Americans' prosperity and contaminated their politics with concentrated financial power." Some of these charges were not completely unfounded, as it was not uncommon to find men like Daniel Webster, a senator of formidable power, also on the Bank's board of directors.

The dispute over rechartering forced partisan politics onto the Bank. The result was that Biddle, president of the Bank, realizing he could never convince Jackson of its efficacy, sought, together with Clay and Webster, to secure the rechartering of the Bank before the election of 1832. The timing of the rechartering bid was a purely political move. The three saw it as an important issue for the 1832 campaign, a means to upend Jackson's attempt at reelection and put Clay in the White House.

Both Clay and Webster were ardent nationalists and champions of broad federal power. Both were also attorneys for the Bank itself. They were also convinced that most Americans understood the value of the Bank and supported it. These subjective views made them believe that Jackson would not dare veto a Bank bill before the election. If he did, they could raise the issue to bring about what they thought would be his downfall.

In January 1832 the Bank formally requested rechartering. Jacksonians controlled the House, but Jackson had not yet drawn a party line against the Bank. In a delaying strategy, Senator Benton convinced Rep. Augustus Clayton of Georgia to investigate the Bank's affairs through a select committee of the House. Speaker Andrew Stevenson appointed an anti-Bank majority to the committee, headed by Clayton. The report from the panel charged it with malfeasance and corruption.

Despite these attempts by Jackson through his spokespersons in the Congress, Bank supporters, who included some Jacksonians, were in a majority. Both houses of Congress passed the rechartering bill in the summer of 1832. Jackson promptly vetoed it.

The president's veto message savaged the Bank and the rechartering bill, attacking it on every front. He denied its constitutionality, resurrecting Jefferson's arguments from four decades before. He claimed the right to judge issues of constitutionality independently of the Congress or the Supreme Court. He appealed to the fact he was the sole representative elected by all of the people. He also appealed to states' rights.

Jackson's veto challenged a tradition, going back to the Revolution, of circumscribing executive authority and regarding the legislative branch as the true embodiment of the public will. Abandoning his predecessors' deference to Congress,

Jackson cast himself as the whole people's sole defender against the "mere jumble of special interests represented by congressmen."

To his critics, and especially his enemies in Congress, this seemed an affirmation of unbridled executive power, and because the Bank issue reflected demographic and class divisions, a reckless invitation to class war. Henry Clay claimed Jackson undermined the very foundations of the American Republic and that the president's ideas were at "odds with the genius of representative government." The congressional session ended with Benton and Clay shouting at each other.

With Clay unable to muster enough support, the vote to override the veto failed in the Senate. To add insult to injury, the hopes of Webster and Clay that the veto would spell defeat for Jackson in the general election backfired, and Jackson soundly defeated Clay in the November presidential contest.

Congress having failed to override Jackson's veto of the Bank recharter, the president took the win as a mandate to continue the fight against it. In what can be construed as an unabashed power grab and end run around Congress, Jackson stripped the Bank of its power and ordered that all of its deposits be withdrawn, even though the existing charter had three years left to run. The House challenged Jackson's decision and voted overwhelmingly that the deposits were safe and should stay.

The next day Congress adjourned. With no one to check him, Jackson once again tried to demolish the Bank. Its charter permitted the secretary of the Treasury to remove federal deposits provided the secretary reported these withdrawals to the Congress immediately. In granting the secretary these rights, the charter noted that he was a separate agent responsible to the Congress and not to the president.

But Jackson, as the people's representative, regarded Cabinet members as his instruments. Most of the Cabinet was opposed to removing the funds, including the secretary of the Treasury, Louis McLane. However, Jackson's confidant, Roger Taney, urged Jackson to have the funds removed. So Jackson removed McLane from his position (making him secretary of state) and replaced him with William John Duane, a foe of the Bank. Jackson was convinced that Duane would remove the funds when ordered to do so, but Duane refused. Jackson then dismissed him and put in his place Taney, who quickly ordered that all federal revenues be placed in state banks, that money be drawn to pay bills, and that all deposits be liquidated.

Congress was dismayed. Many members of the House and Senate, even those who were enemies of the bank, believed Jackson's high-handed action defied not only sound financial policy, but the separation of powers and the letter of the law. It was suggested that his actions smacked of royal prerogative, being the actions of a king, not a president. He had no proper authority to remove government money from a congressionally sanctioned Bank of the United States. In the Senate, Clay, seconded by Webster and John C. Calhoun, denounced Jackson's actions as "open, palpable and daring usurpation as pointing toward a total change of the pure republican character of the government and to the concentration of all power in the hands of one man."

Jackson's relations with the Senate throughout his tenure were stormy, even when he had a majority there. Party ties were not strong during his presidency. Senators had a strong sense of independence that was reinforced by their long terms in office and indirect means of election, and as a result, they often acted independently. Prior to the Bank controversy, the Senate had rejected numerous Jackson appointees to government posts, some by huge margins, with Jackson stalwarts such as Benton joining the majority.

By the end of 1833, Jackson held a shaky majority in the House. After a heated debate, a resolution sustaining the deposit removal passed. In the Senate, Clay, Calhoun, Webster, and others carried the day. The Senate began by demanding a copy of the memorandum Jackson had read to the Cabinet declaring his intentions to withdraw federal deposits from the Bank of the United States. Jackson declined, claiming executive privilege despite the fact the memo had already been published. The Senate then rejected four Jackson appointees to the Bank. He resubmitted their names, and the Senate rejected them again; it then rejected Taney as secretary of the Treasury, making him the first Cabinet-level nominee ever rejected.

Censure

On March 28, 1834, the Senate, for the first and only time in its history, censured the president of the United States. The resolution, sponsored by Clay, stated that Jackson, "in the late executive proceedings and in relations to the public revenue has assumed upon himself authority and power not conferred by the Constitution and laws, but in derogation of both." It passed, 26–20.

Jackson protested angrily. Noting that the Senate was not elected by the people (although technically, because of the Electoral College, neither was he), he said they had no right to pass judgment on the single representative of all the people. Jackson said censure aspired to the moral weight of an impeachment without all of its procedures, but in fact was far inferior because there were no specific charges, no vote by the House, and no chance of a defense. In 1836 Martin Van Buren, Jackson's vice president and heir apparent, easily won the presidential election, and the Senate, now in Democratic hands, expunged the resolution from its records.

The result of the Bank War and ensuing censure was that the presidency was energized and its stature enhanced. In contrast, despite still being a formidable force, the reputation of Congress, and especially the Senate, was diminished. Congress lost a preeminence it would never totally regain and the presidency gained power and authority it would never fully lose.

William Henry Harrison, the first Whig elected to the presidency in 1840, espoused the Whig theory of government in his inaugural address. He emphasized a growing concern about the power of the executive branch. He declared he would work to strip some of that power, saying he would serve only one term, would use the veto sparingly, would not use patronage as a means to expand his power, and would not interfere with the power of Congress to legislate as it saw fit.

EXECUTIVE PREEMINENCE IN THE ANTEBELLUM YEARS

As the United States expanded westward with an economy that at times suffered the vagaries attendant upon the absence of a national bank and a lack of any real controls, it was slavery and war with Mexico that loomed largest in the political sphere, especially as a flash point between the executive and the legislature. The Compromise of 1850, an attempt to resolve the problem posed by the lands gained in the Mexican War and the growing issue of slavery, was the product of Senate initiative, worked out in committee. But it was President Zachary Taylor's interference and Millard Fillmore's help that finally got it through.

To counter the Whigs, the Democrats advocated a strong presidency, an idea expressed by Jackson and his successors. This was exemplified by the use of the veto by Jackson and John Tyler and by Polk as he pushed the United States into war with Mexico against strong congressional objection. Tyler also manipulated Congress into annexing Texas by joint resolution, which required just

a simple majority, rather than through the more formal means of a treaty that demanded a two-thirds majority. These incidents showed that Congress's ability to challenge effectively the executive in this era was limited, despite strong congressional leaders like Henry Clay, Daniel Webster, and John Calhoun. Despite the apparent weakness of Presidents Franklin Pierce and James Buchanan, they did use the veto, but to less advantage. By 1860 legislative initiative seemed to have moved down the street to Congress. The Kansas-Nebraska Act of 1854 was a product of congressional leadership under Stephen Douglas and a president, Franklin Pierce, who was bullied into signing it by southern senators who threatened to withdraw southern support, should he refuse to sign the legislation.

The bottom line, however, was that the presidency was linked to power and perceived as the branch of government with the real power. Thus, the election of Abraham Lincoln resulted in secession; the South did not wait to see what Congress would do or appeal to congressional leaders.

CIVIL WAR AND RECONSTRUCTION

It was under Lincoln that the executive branch would step front and center, so it is not surprising that with the death of Lincoln and the assumption of the presidency by Andrew Johnson, Congress quickly moved to reassert itself and gain supremacy. From the end of the Civil War to the turn of the twentieth century,

Congress took advantage of weak executives and assumed a primary role in American government.

Congress, however, was no shining star, either, during this period. This was not a period of great achievement. While the executive branch did not distinguish itself with a defined program for the country, neither did members of Congress. Congress was manipulated by the political machines of the day and was devoted to laissez-faire ideas in dealing with the economy. To the extent that Republicans and Democrats did respond to pressure for legislation, it was in Congress that the legislation originated. The Whig philosophy of government found a foothold in the Republican presidencies of the period from Ulysses Grant to William McKinley. The one Democratic president of the era, Grover Cleveland, entered office with a similar view, though he distinguished himself by exercising the veto more than any other president in history, mostly on private pension bills.

Confronted with the rebellion of the southern states and a civil war, Lincoln rejected his commitment to a Whig philosophy, which he had espoused as a U.S. representative. From the beginning of his presidency he asserted executive power in a way never seen before. Lincoln's extension of presidential power exceeded even the authority assumed by Jackson. Lincoln pushed the Constitution to its limits, if not challenging the constitutional power of Congress.

However, Congress was also transformed by the Civil War. The lack of an effective opposition party meant that as a one-party body, Congress achieved an extraordinary degree of unity and under very able leaders battled a strong president, often on equal terms. The acrimonious battles fought with Johnson over Reconstruction originated in the latter days of Lincoln's administration, when it was obvious the war would be won and the first plans for dealing with the South began to be floated. This battle was so intense that some historians even argue that by the time of Lincoln's assassination, Congress had pushed back executive encroachments upon its authority and was ready to resume its place as the primary branch of government.

Congress's Limited Civil War Role

Overall, the legislative branch played a small but important role in the Civil War. Most action during the war revolved around military action and decisions linked to it, which emanated from the White House. Congress needed to deal with the fact that the decade before had been marked by weak presidencies and strong congressional leadership, from the old guard of Henry Clay, John Calhoun, and Daniel Webster to new movers and shakers such as Stephen Douglas. But sectionalism, which would explode into war with the election of Abraham Lincoln, compromised the ability of people like Douglas to create a true consensus in Congress. The result was a vacuum of power that resulted in tension between a legislature attempting to assert itself, a presidency manned by weak and indecisive figures, and a Supreme Court attempting to hold on to archaic views of government and society.

Following the election of 1860, the key difference was the man in the White House, Abraham Lincoln. Part of this difference, and the diminution of Congress, was the authority that Lincoln seized as commander in chief under Article II of the Constitution. Beyond Congress's power to declare war, the legislative role seemed to be limited in wartime. The other powers inherent in wartime—the power to raise and support armies and the power to make rules for government and regulation—were not highly empowering.

Most Democratic members of Congress represented southern states. Upon the secession of most of those states from the Union, the majority of Democrats who represented them in Congress departed, leaving Republicans in control of both houses. Those Democrats who were left in Congress remembered that failure to support the supply of troops during the War of 1812 helped speed the demise of the Federalist Party. Thus, all effective opposition to House and Senate Republicans was cut off. As a result, Congress could move forward aggressively and cohesively in performing its limited wartime role.

The first Civil War Congress convened in July 1861 as a special session called by President Lincoln because of the Civil War. There were questions about whether the president had exceeded or extended presidential power unconstitutionally and to the detriment of the Congress. He expanded his power when Congress was not in session, increasing the size of the army without any congressional appropriations and expending funds in ways other than Congress had designated without new authorizing legislation.

The main questions formed around Lincoln's suspension of the writ of habeas corpus, which most people regarded as a prerogative of the legislative branch, not the executive. Lincoln awkwardly acknowledged this by noting to Congress that he had acted in a manner needed because of the emergency and because Congress was not in session. He told Congress he had no doubt they would "readily ratify" his actions. Congress dutifully obeyed.

The most memorable part of the special session was the passage of the Crittenden Resolution. Sponsored by John J. Crittenden of Kentucky, the resolution declared the purpose of the Civil War to be to preserve the Union, to "defend and maintain the supremacy of the Constitution." It was peppered with phrases such as "established institutions" and "rights of the . . . states," which were seen as thinly veiled allusions to slavery. In the end, the resolution was a promise not to touch the institution of slavery at the conclusion of the war. The resolution passed the Senate 30–5 and the House 117–2. While southern states repeatedly pointed to this action in the postwar period, Republicans tried to forget that they had passed it. It was probably passed primarily to reassure the border states so they would not secede (it was passed days after the shocking Union loss at Bull Run) and thereby give what could only be seen as a decided edge to the Confederacy. It was a political move made to secure the war effort rather than to secure the institution of slavery.

In the following months and years, no real consensus emerged regarding war aims, and the Crittenden Resolution went down to defeat in the House when it was up for reaffirmation during the regular session at the end of 1861. Rather, the year-end session of Congress was filled with acrimonious debate over confiscating property of slaveholders.

In subsequent sessions Congress, because of the lack of a major opposition, managed to push through most planks of the Republican platform. In contrast to such laws as the Legal Tender Act (1862) and the Homestead Act (1862), many congressional measures were driven by the war effort at the behest of the executive branch. Pressure from the Treasury Department led Congress to create a national banking system, which permanently replaced the myriad of paper notes issued by local banks with a national currency.

Despite these numerous policy successes, domination by one party saw the rise of factionalism within the party. As during the Era of Good Feelings, the lack of any real opposition saw the fragmentation of the party in power and growing tension between that party and the President. The proceedings of the Joint Committee on the Conduct of the War highlighted these tensions. Run by Radical Republicans and originally charged with investigating Union military defeats, it proceeded to question military commanders and published several volumes on military defeat, misconduct, and scandal during the war. The highly partisan investigations were more like witch hunts than fair inquiries.

Some historians have suggested the committee was the product of a presidential system in which failures in the prosecution of the war left Congress no chance to challenge it except by the mechanism of investigation. In a parliamentary system, the steady stream of defeats that faced the Union in the early part of the war would probably have resulted in the fall of the government and a new administration. In the United States, defeat after defeat left Congress frustrated with the president and the military hierarchy. The conflict reiterated the weakness of Congress in wartime (a weakness played out in every conflict since). The only apparent congressional power was publishing reports at the least and destroying a career at the most. Attempts to meddle with military policy were disastrous and were regularly repelled by the administration. Conversely, some historians argue that the Civil War and the Joint Committee marked a new era and a new type of warfare in which generals on the front lines had to be cognizant of the politicians and public opinion in the rear.

Civil War all but eliminated the South from national politics. From 1861 to 1869 most of the sixty-six House seats held by the eleven states of the Confederacy sat vacant. War also emasculated the Democratic Party outside the South, since the party was linked to the southern cause and suffered as a result. This weakness helped Republicans maintain control in the House until 1875 (and in the Senate until 1879).

Dominating the President during Reconstruction

At the same time, the war and its aftermath gave rise to bitter conflict between Congress and President Johnson, leading to his impeachment in 1868, followed by a prolonged period of legislative dominance. The three decades starting with the Civil War saw the expansion of House membership, an intensification of House efforts to control government spending, an increase in the number and power of House committees, and a continuing struggle to adapt the rules of the House to its legislative purposes.

Lincoln assumed unprecedented powers during the Civil War at a time when both houses were dominated by Republican majorities that were in turn dominated by radicals committed to the Whig doctrine of legislative supremacy. Conflicts between Lincoln and Congress were sharpest over the issue of Reconstruction. Lincoln, who held that the Confederate states had never left the Union, was prepared to restore their political rights as quickly as possible, in sharp contrast to the Radical Republicans, who were determined both to punish the southern states and to reshape the national power structure that had existed prior to the war. Most importantly, the Radicals insisted that the readmission of the southern states and their reconstruction were legislative responsibilities.

When Lincoln set up new governments in Louisiana, Tennessee, and Arkansas, Congress rejected their readmission to the Union, and Radical Republicans in the House passed the Wade-Davis Manifesto, asserting the paramount authority of Congress. If the president wanted Congress's support, it mandated that "he must contain himself to his executive duties—to obey and execute, not make the laws—to suppress by arms armed rebellion, and leave political reorganization to Congress." Lincoln pocket vetoed the bill after Congress adjourned in 1864.

The death of Lincoln gave new life to the Radical leadership, which moved to control all aspects of Reconstruction and quash all attempts by President Johnson, Lincoln's successor, to direct it. Openly sympathetic to the South, Johnson vetoed numerous bills whose effects would be to give Congress full control over Reconstruction and to strip the president of much of his authority.

One of these measures was the Tenure of Office Act of 1867, passed over Johnson's veto to prevent him from firing Secretary of War Edwin Stanton. The law made it a high misdemeanor to remove without the Senate's approval any official whose nomination had been confirmed by the Senate. After Johnson, who deemed the law to be unconstitutional, suspended Stanton from office, the House voted 126–47 to impeach him. The Senate then tried him, where conviction fell one vote short of the two-thirds majority required by the Constitution. (The Tenure of Office Act was amended during the Grant Administration and repealed in 1887. In 1926 the U.S. Supreme Court ruled the law unconstitutional.) This episode saw new House leadership emerge and consolidate as part of the fight to remove the president and set the agenda for Reconstruction.

THE LATE-NINETEENTH CENTURY: CONTINUED LEGISLATIVE DOMINANCE

With expenditures rising from $63 million in 1860 to $1.3 billion in 1865, the Civil War led to renewed efforts by the House to control federal expenditures by a more careful exercise of its power over appropriations. Until then the Committee on Ways and Means had handled all supply as well as revenue bills, in addition to bills on monetary matters. But in 1865 the House transferred some of these responsibilities to two new standing committees: the Committee on Appropriations and the Committee on Banking and Currency.

In the wake of the Civil War, and in the expectation that massive expenditures during Reconstruction would ensue, Congress now began to tighten controls on spending. Although Congress continued to make lump sum appropriations to the army and the navy, it specified in greater detail the amounts and purposes for which the civilian departments and agencies could spend money, limiting their ability to transfer funds and demanding the return of unspent monies. These efforts helped to keep federal expenditures below three hundred million dollars in every year except one from 1871 to 1890. It also served to rein in the executive and inhibit presidential prerogative.

The House's power of the purse was exercised to another end during Rutherford B. Hayes's administration. Democrats controlled the House during the Forty-Fifth Congress (1877–1879) and won control of both chambers in the Forty-Sixth, but by margins too small to override a veto. So, in their attempts to repeal certain laws, the Democrats revived the practice of adding legislative riders to appropriation bills in the hope of forcing the president to reject them. But Hayes vetoed a series of such bills, seeing the tactic for what it was, an attempt by the House to coerce the executive without the need to override his veto. Eventually, House Democrats conceded this and passed the appropriations bills without the riders.

The battle over Reconstruction was between Johnson and Congress. Whether Lincoln would have been able to withstand confrontations with the Radical Republicans will never be known, but it is clear that Johnson's style helped galvanize opposition generally and also brought together disparate elements in Congress. Johnson repeatedly acted in a manner that irritated and angered Congress. Rather than call it into special session to deal with Reconstruction issues, he ignored it. Johnson acted on his own and began to formulate and institute policy independent of Congress. He announced and put into effect his pardon and amnesty policies and his program for readmitting the former Confederate states. This audacity only served to outrage Congress, which upon meeting in the winter of 1865, declared itself to be the country's policy making body and repudiated Johnson's actions.

The result was the establishment of the Joint Committee of Fifteen on Reconstruction. It tried to assert power in a way similar to a British-style cabinet and produced an alternative congressional plan for Reconstruction that was passed over presidential vetoes. Congress moved to seize executive power by the Tenure of Office Act and accentuated its power by impeaching President Johnson. Although coming up one vote shy of removing him from office, Congress effectively emasculated his power and assumed the driver's seat in postwar policy.

In many ways Congress reached its pinnacle of power in this post–Civil War period. It was a rare time in American history when Congress enacted a comprehensive program to deal with the major issues of the day over the active opposition of a determined president. Although the Contract with America promoted by the Republican Congresses of the 1990s resembled this type of legislative initiative, in that case President Bill Clinton, while frequently at odds with Congress, often worked with it. In the end, however, Congress in both cases challenged the president with impeachment.

Under President Ulysses Grant Congress asserted even greater authority. Grant was happy to let Congress run Reconstruction and even allowed the Senate to control patronage appointments, including Cabinet selections. However, the executive could sink only to a certain point, so it is not surprising that fol-

lowing Grant, the pendulum began to swing back the other way, albeit ever so slowly.

Presidents Hayes, James Garfield, and Grover Cleveland all tried to wrestle patronage authority away from the Senate. Hayes attempted to control policy by vetoing the various riders on appropriation bills. The result was a check on the growing power of Congress and the eventual repeal of the Tenure of Office Act.

The last quarter of the nineteenth century featured conservative presidents who failed to initiate major programs. While the two issues of currency and tariff dominated most of the election campaigns, and voters turned out in record numbers, issues often took a backseat to the parties, rallies, parades, and picnics that dominated the campaigns. And while the presidents recommended the enactment of measures to carry out their party platforms, once they had done so, they left it to Congress to work out the legislation. Grover Cleveland was the lone exception, but in the end he too acquiesced, and Congress was able to push through the policies it wanted.

Congress dominated the domestic agenda during this period, and it was under congressional leadership that laws such as the Interstate Commerce Act (1887) were passed. During this period the president was seen as the key force behind only one out of thirteen major legislative measures (the Silver Purchase Repeal Act of 1893). While pressure groups helped initiate two others, Congress was responsible for the bulk of legilsation.

During the late nineteenth century, members of the House and Senate would probably have been shocked had the president communicated with them regarding policy initiatives. The purpose of a visit to the White House by a senator or representative was for the legislator to give advice to the president, not to receive it. The strong-arm tactics of the executive so common in the twentieth century would have been seen as beyond the pale in the late nineteenth. Thus, it was not uncommon to view someone other than the president as the leader of his party. It was Congress that asserted and expanded party authority. Woodrow Wilson commented that the government of the United States was best described as a government of the standing committees' chairs in Congress.

However, any thought that Congress could permanently overwhelm the other branches of government was probably unrealistic. The inability of Congress to claim a permanent place at the top of the pyramid was in large part due to the checks and balances built into the system, which created a system that inhibited the flow of power between the branches. It was also due in part to the inherent weakness of Congress's structure. A major disadvantage was the existence of two houses, which helped exacerbate other flaws in the system. By the late nineteenth century, Congress also suffered from its increasing decentralization into independent committees, a lack of unifying leadership, and general irresponsibility in legislating. Finally, the lack of a coherent program and the ram-

pant corruption that filled the halls of politics from the local machines such as Tammany Hall to the floors of the House and Senate all compromised Congress's ability to grab the mantle of power and hold it.

STRONG PRESIDENTS IN THE EARLY TWENTIETH CENTURY

These shortcomings did not mean that Congress was slipping into total dysfunction and conceding all to the other branches. In fact, Congress managed to overcome many of these weaknesses through the instituting of some internal discipline and the emergence of strong leaders. Within the House, power had been gradually accruing to the Speaker of the House. On the other hand, this power was mitigated by the emergence of a strong president in the person of Teddy Roosevelt. Thus, despite the growing power and organization of Congress, the collision between the two branches resulted in the emergence of a strong executive and an ensuing shift of authority to the president.

In the nineteenth century, presidents who believed in a strong executive were the exception. Starting with Roosevelt, the opposite was true in the twentieth century. One of the reasons for this shift was the appearance of strong personalities in the White House who succeeded in dominating the political arena. The presidents who exerted forceful leadership won the most fervent support. When Americans look to the past, it is

Theodore Roosevelt waves to the crowd during his campaign tour in New Jersey, 1912. (Library of Congress)

strong presidents who are remembered and honored, not strong Congresses or congressional leadership, and weaker presidents are forgotten. In times of crisis, people look for leadership, and in the eyes of the American public that leadership resides in the White House, not at the other end of Pennsylvania Avenue.

At the century's start, Teddy Roosevelt established the notion of the "bully pulpit," using the presidency as a platform to institute his ideas and his policy. He proclaimed one should "talk softly but carry a big stick," indicating how he thought it

best to get things done. However, although a strong president, he had to contend with a very conservative Congress dominated by entrenched conservatives that was strong in leadership and organization. Rarely did he directly challenge the ideologically hostile Republican leadership of the Congress until the end of his second term, by which point executive-legislative relations had badly disintegrated. Before that he had relied on negotiation with less than stellar results.

In those areas where Roosevelt did not need Congress, he employed executive action, bypassing it. In this way he created national forests from the public lands, initiated antitrust prosecutions, settled a coal strike through a threat to seize the mines, and took foreign policy initiatives. These actions increased tension between him and Congress. During his first term it adopted a resolution requesting him to file copies of his executive orders and cite the legal authority on which they were based. It also established a commission of lawyers to pass on their legality, but Roosevelt ignored the resolution.

Roosevelt's successor, William H. Taft, paid the price for Roosevelt's bluster. He inherited the rocky relationship between the executive and the legislature, and while Taft's actions were far more modest than those of his predecessor, his failure to "handle" Congress cost him in the 1912 election. Taft was elected in essence to get certain laws passed, but because of congressional intransigence, he failed to do so.

Woodrow Wilson believed that the U.S. government should be like the British parliamentary system and considered it his duty to dominate and dictate to Congress. He wrote extensively on the importance of leadership in the American system and that this leadership should come from the presidency. He modeled himself after Jefferson. Unlike Teddy Roosevelt, he had with him a Progressive majority in Congress that supported his programs. Even the conservative Democrats, in the interest of party loyalty, supported him at first, so that by the end of Wilson's second term, the balance had again been upset so that the president once more overshadowed Congress. While much of this power accrued in response to the needs of World War I, the public reacted in a hostile fashion, and by the end of his presidency, a strong reaction was brewing.

THE 1920s: A REVIVED CONGRESS

The 1920s signaled an active Congress. In the wake of Wilson's demise and three successive Republican presidents, Congress pushed itself forward. It overrode two presidential vetoes, initiated two amendments to the Constitution, attempted to regulate the American population's behavior via Prohibition, became isolationist, reinvigorated the ideas of laissez-faire, and expanded the authority of the federal government.

By the time Wilson left the White House, the American people were ready for a less assertive presidency. The steady flow of power to the White House at the expense of Congress halted for a decade as America turned back on itself with policies and ideology that pointed toward late nineteenth-century America rather than America a quarter of the way through a new century with a world war in its past. But in fact it was no longer 1890, and all three presidents of the 1920s, while conservative in their approach, were not nineteenth-century Whigs. In fact, they appeared ambivalent, consciously trying to steer a middle course between the extreme activism of Wilson and the passivity that had destroyed Taft. In the end, this middle-of-the-road approach created a government unwilling or unable to deal with the exigencies of both the rapidly changing face of America in the 1920s and the economic catastrophe of the 1930s.

In 1920 Warren Harding began his presidency by denouncing "executive dictatorship" and promising not to interfere, as Wilson had, in the legislative process. Harding did not stick to this affirmation completely, as when he intervened directly by appearing before the Senate during consideration of a soldier's bonus bill. On balance, however, his occasional intervention did not amount to leading Congress. The next president, Calvin Coolidge, remarked that it was not his job or duty to try to convince senators or representatives how to vote. Coolidge also believed that a president should not be vindictive and act negatively against those who voted against the president's wishes. Nevertheless, Coolidge frequently used his veto. Like Coolidge, President Herbert Hoover failed to exert leadership to get legislation enacted. He wanted limited tariff revision, but when Congress asserted itself and pushed a high tariff, Hoover backed off. By the end of his term, the Democrats had captured the lower house of Congress and national policy was on the whole deadlocked. On the rare occasion when Hoover did step forward, as when he proposed the Reconstruction Finance Corporation to battle the Depression, Congress passed it.

CLASHES WITH FDR

The Great Depression meant a Congress more than willing to fall into step with the president until so challenged that it lashed back. Ironically, while the New Deal is remembered for the dominating figure of Franklin Roosevelt, during the first one hundred days in 1933, only two of the fifteen programs put forth emanated from the White House. Except for the Civilian Conservation Corps and the Economy Act, the programs for the most part originated in Congress. No matter where the idea for the legislation started, Congress responded to the president's call, and while critics arose, for the most part they did not challenge presidential prerogative, especially during the first two terms. Comparing the Depression to the crisis of war, Roosevelt argued that, as in wartime, the president needed to exert a degree of power that would not be acceptable in peacetime. Thus, Roosevelt charged forward and the Congress followed. And while there is no doubt that Congress took initiatives and put forth programs, it did so in concert with, not at odds with, the White House. With perhaps the exception of Woodrow Wilson, Roosevelt involved himself more directly in lawmaking than any of his predecessors. He helped coordinate legislative activity through public support and fireside chats. However, it should not be forgotten that as active as Roosevelt was, successors such as Lyndon Johnson and Bill Clinton were much more active and carved out large legislative roles for themselves.

Like his successors, Roosevelt at times pushed too far and was stopped by Congress. Confrontation between Congress and the president during FDR's four terms came to a head over Roosevelt's

Court-packing plan. Frustrated at the Supreme Court's continued striking down of New Deal legislation, Roosevelt proposed a solution by asking Congress to empower him to appoint an additional justice to the Supreme Court for every justice over seventy who did not retire. In contrast to the way he handled a great deal of New Deal legislation, FDR failed to consult with Congress prior to the proposal. The plan was a massive miscalculation, and Congress rebelled. Heavy-handed efforts by Roosevelt did not help, and Congress refused to adopt the scheme. Coupled with this was the congressional refusal to accept a presidential proposal to reorganize the executive branch in light of the growing number of federal agencies. Fear of the accrual of power in the executive branch created a backlash in which Congress turned a more critical eye toward FDR's New Deal programs.

The debate over packing the Court taught FDR important lessons, and for subsequent programs such as Lend-Lease, he garnered congressional support before attempting to push through his programs. And with the attack on Pearl Harbor, Congress's prestige began to fade. World War II saw the relationship between the president and Congress deteriorate to a degree. Congress acceded to most wartime measures, granting the president tremendous authority to prosecute the conflict and manage the economy. However, despite these concessions, acrimony rose as Republicans, seemingly in the minority forever, grew frustrated, while southern Democrats grew fearful that presidential policies would undermine white supremacy in the South.

Perhaps the culmination of this conflict occurred in February 1944 over a tax bill passed by both houses. Among other shortcomings that FDR saw in the bill, he thought the level of taxation was insufficient. And while possibly correct in his criticisms, he proceeded to express his dissatisfaction in a stinging veto message that challenged the Democratic leadership's integrity. In response, Alben Barkley, the Senate majority leader and normally a stalwart FDR supporter, resigned in protest. Congress then overrode the veto and reelected Barkley to his old post.

CONGRESS STRUGGLES TO REGAIN POWER

Nevertheless, it was under Franklin Delano Roosevelt that the power of the presidency soared, and he showed how a strong president could more often than not control Congress and the nation's agenda. Each of Roosevelt's successors accepted his legacy and moved it forward. Harry Truman aggressively used presidential powers in pursuing the Korean War, impounding funds and seizing the steel mills. Dwight Eisenhower continued the practice of presenting a comprehensive legislative program and also employed aggressive executive action in cases such as the 1957 desegregation crisis in Little Rock. However, as illustrated by President John F. Kennedy's failure to move forward much of his domestic legislation on civil rights and education, Congress was not simply a foil to be manipulated by presidential will. Strong congressional leadership could and did sometimes stand up to presidential initiatives.

Nevertheless, by the time of Richard Nixon's inauguration in 1968, strong political leadership based in the White House was the standard firmly implanted in American political culture. The modern aggrandizement of power to the presidency was the product of both intentional and unintentional acts of the legislature. Congress had to consent at times because it had to pass the laws that in essence stripped it of its authority.

More than that, however, much of the transfer of power was initiated by the legislative branch itself. In the last half of the twentieth century, as Congress saw that its power had both subtly and not so subtly been appropriated, it sought to regain that authority.

Watergate

Two great pushes to reclaim this authority were connected to Vietnam and Watergate. Vietnam presented Congress with a unique challenge to participate in foreign policy. Congress was initially

Members of the Senate Select Committee on Presidential Campaign Activities convene in the Senate Caucus Room in May 1973 to hear testimony related to the break-in at the Watergate complex. The public hearings that became known as the "Watergate hearings" began on May 17, 1973, and lasted until August 7, 1973. All 319 hours of proceedings were televised. (Library of Congress)

criticized for being slow to act, but ultimately it did respond. Over a presidential veto, Congress enacted the War Powers Act of 1973, marking the first time in history that Congress defined and limited the president's power to make war.

Also, Congress investigated the Nixon presidency regarding the abuses of presidential power in the matter of Watergate. The Senate Watergate committee uncovered the existence of incriminating White House tape recordings. Nixon's struggle to deny special prosecutor Archibald Cox access to the tapes resulted in the president's firing Cox on October 20, 1973. Attorney General Elliot Richardson resigned rather that carry out the White House order to dismiss Cox, and Deputy Attorney General William D. Ruckelshaus was fired after he, too, refused to execute the order.

Responding to an enormous outcry over these events, called the Saturday Night Massacre, House Democratic leaders met October 22 with Speaker Carl Albert and agreed to have the House Judiciary Committee begin an inquiry into grounds for impeachment. Ten months later, after the committee had voted three articles of impeachment, Nixon became the first president to resign from office.

Watergate represented a critical moment in congressional and constitutional history and the politics of the United States. It marked an attempt, albeit not an entirely successful one, by the legislative branch to restructure the balance of power in Washington. Coupled with the aftershocks of the Vietnam War, Watergate undercut American faith in the idea

of the imperial presidency and restored some congressional leadership in a time of flux and disorientation following the upheaval of the 1960s.

Foreign Affairs

In this period, the constant tensions that existed between the White House and Congress regarding foreign affairs and war powers were reiterated. In the early 1970s, Congress seized upon disillusion over the Vietnam War as an opportunity to try to reclaim power in foreign policy and war making that it thought had been wrongfully seized by the executive branch.

The Constitution set the stage for this conflict by making the president commander in chief, yet giving the Congress the power to declare war. What each of those duties entails is open to interpretation, and as Lincoln noted during the Civil War, he was not looking to circumvent Congress but merely to execute the powers given to him. In the early twenty-first century, President George W. Bush came under heavy criticism for authorizing warrantless wiretaps and argued that he had the authority as commander in chief to take such actions. He was not trying to dodge Congress, but merely acted where he could and they could not.

World War I saw Congress and the executive both work together and butt heads. At times Congress was willing to work with President Wilson, even granting broad swaths of power to the president such as in the Lever Food Control Act of 1917. Wilson argued it was important that great power was placed in his hands and with that legislation Congress authorized the president to regulate the price, production, transportation, and allocation of feeds, food, fuel, beverages, and distilled spirits for the remainder of World War I. Other pieces of legislation like the Overman Act gave Wilson unprecedented control over the war effort, from governmental powers down to production powers.

Despite the seeming congruence between the two branches over a variety of issues, entering the war was not a given: whether or not to engage in the European conflict was hotly debated. In the end, convincing Congress to declare war was the easy part. The lopsided approval of the war concealed many congressional concerns that would eventually emerge. A thin majority in Congress and the factionalization of the Democratic Party crippled Wilson's ability to control Congress and get his wartime agenda through, creating conflict between recalcitrant Republicans and the White House.

The first example of conflict between Congress and the president was over the effort to raise an army. Many in Congress feared a draft would give too much power to the federal government, especially the executive, and antagonists such as Theodore Roosevelt called for an all-volunteer army. Republicans jumped into the fray and helped create partisan controversy in almost every aspect of the effort to place the nation on a war footing.

The war effort bogged down so badly that by January 1918, five major investigations of it were under way on Capitol Hill. The culmination of executive-legislative wrangling came over the Treaty of Versailles. President Wilson's snubbing of Henry Cabot Lodge, the chairman of the Senate Foreign Relations Committee, by not inviting him to Paris to participate in negotiations doomed the treaty at home. In an attempt to circumvent both Lodge and Congress as a whole, Wilson sought to gain the support of the American people. He embarked on a nationwide tour to sell the treaty and its League of Nations. His attempt to force the treaty through was short-circuited when he fell ill and then suffered a stroke in October 1919. With Wilson out of the way, Lodge easily scuttled the treaty.

Unquestionably, the executive branch largely held sway in foreign policy matters. The Supreme Court acknowledged the predominant role of the president in such matters in a variety of cases, but most notably in *United States* v. *Curtiss-Wright Export Corporation* (1936). In that case the Court declared power over foreign affairs was "plenary and exclusive power of the President as the sole organ of the federal government in the field of international relations—a power which does not require as a basis for its exercise an act of Congress." This assertion opened the door for congressional acquiescence or at least silence on many occasions.

War Powers Resolution: The Historical Background

Both World Wars I and II saw Congress cede to the president certain authority to run the wars, but more importantly, they gathered power into the federal government as a whole for prosecuting the conflicts. Subsequently, the open-ended nature of presidential power during the Vietnam War prompted Congress to take stock of its institutional and constitutional duties in times of war or conflict. Also, in an attempt to prevent such an extension of executive power again, Congress passed the War Powers Act of 1973, supposedly designed to reassert congressional power and reinforce the checks on the executive's ability to deploy American military forces.

The statute was drafted in a manner that raised grave constitutional questions. Some commentators of the day argued that it posed one of the most serious constitutional threats to the U.S. political system since the ratification of the Constitution. It was also suggested by some that rather than reasserting a balance between executive and legislative powers, it shifted the imbalance in the legislature's favor and led Congress to think it had more authority where in reality it limited congressional power even more.

Since the passage of the act, the White House has denied that it needs to accede to its dictates, and the president has taken a growing number of unilateral actions with few legislative constraints. After September 11, 2001, President Bush placed American troops into Afghanistan and Iraq on the basis of open-ended joint resolutions passed by Congress similar to the Gulf of Tonkin Resolution. The specter of a president rapidly expanding his authority to the chagrin of Congress mirrored the use of power by Presidents Johnson and Nixon

under the Gulf of Tonkin Resolution. The inclusion in the Constitution of the congressional power to declare war was an apparent attempt by the Framers to inhibit the ability of the president to wage war unchecked, but the post-Vietnam era has seen American military forces moved more and more with only a cursory check by the Congress.

Part of the increase in war-making power that Congress sought to check in 1973 can be attributed to the post–World War II international agreements, most notably those establishing the United Nations and the North Atlantic Treaty Organization (NATO). Now the president could go to those organizations to get the necessary authorization to move forces into hostile areas. Harry Truman in Korea, Bill Clinton in the Balkans, and George H. W. Bush in Iraq all appealed to those organizations, evading the need to gain congressional approval and, some would argue, circumventing the Constitution in the process.

For almost the first two centuries of U.S. history, it was generally acknowledged that only Congress could place American troops on the offensive and instigate hostilities. The president was not emasculated in his role as commander in chief and obviously had authority to take military action without congressional approval in some circumstances, for example, to "repel sudden attacks." However, with the Communist invasion of South Korea, President Truman used an opening that enabled him to do an end run around Congress and engage United States troops in a major conflict. He circumvented Congress by appealing to the

Representatives from twelve nations convene in Washington, D.C., to sign the North Atlantic Treaty on April 4, 1949. (NATO Photos)

United Nations Security Council, and while technically it was a UN force that did battle in Korea, the bulk of the troops and casualties were American. All of this happened without official congressional approval, which had been given in the two world wars.

Like the UN charter, the various post–World War II mutual security pacts the United States entered into, like NATO and the Southeast Asia Treaty Organization (SEATO), obligated U.S. troops to engage under certain condi-

tions, none of which required a direct appeal to Congress. While this seemed to circumvent the constitutional requirement of congressional approval, the ratification of such treaties by the Senate would seem to suggest that congressional approval was implicit in such unilateral actions. Thus, the last half of the twentieth century saw major American deployments of troops (Truman in Korea; George H. W. Bush in Iraq; Clinton in Haiti, Bosnia, and Kosovo) in alignment with the mutual security treaties and smaller extensions of U.S. forces, not necessarily triggered by those treaties, but nonetheless sidestepping Congress (Eisenhower in Lebanon; Johnson in the Dominican Republic; Reagan in Lebanon, Grenada, and Panama).

This demise of congressional power regarding war started with the ratification of the UN Charter. During the Senate debate over it, Truman reassured Congress that all UN actions would have to be approved by both houses of Congress. The UN Participation Act of 1945 explicitly stated that American troops could only be committed "subject to the approval of the Congress by appropriate act or joint resolution." Despite this apparently explicit wording, Truman sent troops into Korea without the seemingly requisite congressional resolution.

During the Korean War, the Supreme Court noted that the president's power as commander in chief is not absolute and approved the right of Congress to limit presidential power in that regard. When President Truman tried to take over the steel mills after a strike by steel workers, the Court rebuffed his reliance on presidential authority. In *Youngstown Company v. Sawyer* (1952), the Court asserted that the president's authority was limited to those acts that were either clearly defined by the Constitution or had been explicitly granted by Congress. Truman argued that he had the authority to seize the mills to avoid the nationwide strike under his power as commander in chief because of the threat to national defense such a strike would incur. As Justice Robert Jackson wrote in his concurrence, the president cannot act when Congress

has explicitly or implicitly denied such power to do so. Jackson continued that unlimited executive power, unchecked by the legislature in any circumstance, harkened back to the days of George III and must have been what the Framers were thinking of when they created the system of checks and balances. In addition to the general prerogative of presidents as commander in chief and their authority relating to UN military actions, the other mechanism they have relied on are treaties that demand U.S. military involvement in certain circumstances. The two greatest examples of this, both of which have resulted in large movements of the American military, are connected to NATO and SEATO obligations. However, the treaties establishing both organizations note that the pacts are not meant to be means of avoiding the normal constitutional process by which a country goes to war.

In August 1964 President Johnson did not act unilaterally but asked Congress for authority to engage North Vietnam. Although questions were raised about the justifications given for the need to extend American involvement in Vietnam, Congress approved American involvement with passage of the Gulf of Tonkin Resolution. It was an open-ended grant of authority to the president to extend American military forces with no apparent limits. The massive escalation that ensued reflected this understanding by the president. The resulting failure of Congress to rein in the expansion of the war under Johnson and later under Nixon as he moved into Laos and Cambodia led to hearings before the

Senate Committee on Foreign Relations at the urging of its chairman, Arkansas senator J. William Fulbright. The 1967 hearings expressed the fears of many members of Congress about the apparent lack of congressional checks on the executive. In response to these hearings and to growing congressional questions about the war in Vietnam, the Senate passed the National Commitments Resolution, which provided that a commitment of military or financial resources to other countries required congressional action of some kind. Legally, the resolution meant nothing, as it had no binding effect. Philosophically, it expressed the congressional desire to shore up its own powers and restrain those of the executive branch.

War Powers Act: Passage

Apparent regrets over the Gulf of Tonkin Resolution surfaced as Congress moved to pass the War Powers Act. A Democratic Congress eager to reassert authority and a Nixon White House jealous of its ability to control and manipulate foreign policy, from its diplomatic to its military dimensions, faced off against each other. The stated purpose of the War Powers Act was to "fulfill the intent of the framers of the Constitution and to insure that the collective judgment" of both branches of government would have input into the decision to commit U.S. troops to combat. It is apparent that the Act failed to create such a partnership and did not successfully reassert congressional authority.

One of the reasons the War Powers Act failed to accomplish its purpose was the wrangling between the House and the Senate in the drafting of the act. The House was far more willing to recognize that the president, in certain circumstances, had to deal with emergency situations. And while the Supreme Court during the Korean War had apparently checked some of the executive's wartime powers when it denied President Truman the right to seize the steel mills, the House was still willing to say that absent explicit denial of a certain power, as with Truman's attempt to take over the mills, the president had a certain leeway as commander in chief. To limit that authority too much—to try to define exact situations when the president could and could not engage the American military—was impractical. Rather, the House favored general language that demanded that the president, "whenever feasible," consult with the Congress prior to sending American forces to war. The House version also asked that when the president committed U.S. forces without congressional sanction, the White House report the circumstances that demanded the sending of U.S. troops; the authority (either the Constitution, a statute, or a treaty) under which the executive had acted; why prior congressional approval had not been sought; and, finally, the scope of the involvement.

The Senate balked at giving the president what appeared to be wide authority to act without congressional approval. By the early 1970s it was obvious that the chief executive could engage American troops in a conflict very quickly, forcing Congress's hand afterward into rubber-stamping the executive action. Led by senators Tom Eagleton, Democrat of Missouri, Jacob Javits, Republican of New York, and John Stennis, Democrat of Mississippi, the Senate refused to sign on to the House version. The House ceded to Senate pressure and altered its measure to demand that if Congress did not approve of the president's action (that is, adopt a declaration of war) within 120 days, the president had to end U.S. involvement and withdraw troops. The House bill also allowed Congress, by concurrent resolution, to direct the president to disengage at any time during the 120-day period.

While the House version focused on reining in the president once action had commenced, the Senate was more concerned with restraining the hand of the president prior to the initial engagement. The Senate version attempted to delineate the specific instances and conditions under which it would be permissible for the president to act without prior congressional approval. Thus, the Senate version of the bill stipulated that armed forces could be used without congressional sanction in only three circumstances: first, to repel an attack on the United States, to retaliate in case of such an attack, or to forestall the direct and imminent threat of such an attack (with the definition of "United States" including not just the U.S. proper, but all territories and possessions of the United States); second, to repel an armed attack against U.S. forces outside the United States; and third, to rescue endangered American citizens in foreign countries or at sea.

Arguably, the first circumstance was in line with the original intent of the Framers. The second and third seemed to reflect the changing nature of the world and exigencies created by the concepts of defensive war, the existence of American installations and troops all over the world, and various treaty obligations. The final circumstance seemed merely to restate what presidents had always done in the past: use American forces to protect and rescue American citizens and property overseas, as Jefferson did in battling the Tripoli pirates.

The Senate resolution was far less generous with the amount of time given the president: it gave him a window of only thirty days. At that point congressional approval was needed if American involvement was to continue. This requirement could be avoided and the military operations could be continued if the president (and only the president) determined "that unavoidable military necessity respecting the safety" of the armed forces required their continued use for the purpose of bringing about a prompt disengagement.

The compromise between the two houses resulted in a bill that seemed to gut all the checks proposed by both houses. Most importantly, the compromise resolution gave the president unilateral authority for from sixty to ninety days. No reason had to be submitted to Congress. The president could go to war anywhere, at any time, without offering any justification. All he had to do was report to Congress when he could and consult with lawmakers whenever possible.

Several senators and representatives expressed dismay at the resulting resolution. They said it did not do what had been originally proposed. Instead of enhancing congressional authority and limiting the executive, it actually did the reverse, giving the president power that, some stated, was at odds with the Constitution. Despite various protests, the Act easily passed both houses, with greater support from Democrats than Republicans. It was apparent that despite the objections just noted, most saw it as a major step toward restricting presidential power, rather than expanding it.

That was President Nixon's view, and he vetoed the bill, asserting that it was impractical and dangerous to define explicitly, via statute, how the president and Congress should take the country to war. He also felt the bill represented an unconstitutional expansion of congressional power into executive authority. However, his veto was overridden, with several senators and representatives stating the importance of the legislation in controlling the president's ability unilaterally to engage the American people in armed conflict, with tremendous loss of life, without the check of the people through Congress.

The War Powers Act enabled the president to use military force for up to ninety days without seeking congressional authority. It also required the president to submit reports to Congress and consult with members of the legislature "in every possible instance."

War Powers Act: Consequences

Since the passage of the War Powers Act, every president has denied its constitutionality and the need for the executive to accede to its demands. In the years immediately following its passage, Presidents Gerald Ford and Jimmy Carter managed to avoid major confrontations and thus the need to resort to the mechanisms outlined in the Act. Ford spent most of his time disengaging the U.S. military from Vietnam and introduced troops into a hostile situation only during the capture of the *Mayaguez.* Carter's sole attempt to use the military was in the unsuccessful attempt to rescue U.S. hostages in Iran. Both cases, however, seemed to fall well within the traditional powers ascribed to the executive branch and were not the kinds of actions that the War Powers Act was meant to prevent. With the election of Ronald Reagan, the situation changed.

The inefficacy of the War Powers Act became readily apparent under President Reagan. He repeatedly used American forces in Lebanon, Grenada, air strikes over Libya, and extensive naval operations in the Persian Gulf. All of these would seem to be the types of actions that the Act was designed to bring Congress into, yet in each case Reagan denied a need to go to Congress. One of the impacts of the Act was that legislators challenged presidential actions in the courts. Four times during the 1980s, members of Congress challenged President Reagan not via congressional actions but via the judicial system. When Reagan introduced military advisers into

El Salvador early in his presidency, he denied the need to consult with Congress because American forces were not introduced with the intent to engage in hostilities. The federal courts begged the question in *Crockett v. Reagan* (1982), denying their ability to resolve the question at hand, namely, the facts of the military situation in El Salvador.

Two years later, the 1982 invasion of Grenada was challenged in *Conyers v. Reagan* (1984). A federal court backed off, claiming the issue was moot because the action the suit sought to enjoin, the invasion of Grenada, was over. While the court did comment that the executive-legislative relationship was an interesting one, it was not willing to comment or rule on it at that time.

The fundamental assumption of the War Powers Act is that at some point a president must consult with Congress to garner the authority either to introduce American troops into a hostile environment or to continue to engage troops. One of its goals was to stop the president from circumventing congressional authority via the invoking of treaties. President George H. W. Bush apparently scuttled this hope in 1990 when he appealed to the UN Security Council following the Iraqi invasion of Kuwait. Secretary of Defense Dick Cheney testified before Congress that President Bush did not need any additional authorization from Congress. The House Democratic Caucus reacted swiftly, condemning such an interpretation. This resulted in a challenge in the federal courts to the United States–led war in the Persian Gulf.

In *Dellums v. Bush* (1990) the United States District Court for the District of Columbia refused to hear the challenge on the basis of "ripeness" (military operations had not yet begun). If the president "had the sole power to determine that any particular offensive military operation no matter how vast, does not constitute war-making [unless U.S. forces engage in an] offensive military attack, the congressional power to declare war will be at the mercy of a semantic decision by the Executive. Such an interpretation "would evade the plain language of the Constitution and it cannot stand."

The senior president Bush, in an apparent concession to the dictates of the War Powers Act, asked Congress for legislation authorizing the use of force in the Gulf. Congress did so. However, in signing the bill, President Bush clearly stated that he was neither conceding the constitutionality of the War Powers Act nor limiting the ability of the president to "use the armed forces to defend vital U.S. interests."

Following the leads of Presidents Truman and the senior Bush, President Clinton also relied on the United Nations to authorize American military involvement. In October 1993, after armed civilians on the island of Haiti prevented approximately 600 American troops from landing, Clinton threatened military force. Congress debated a resolution that would limit the president's actions, but nothing binding was passed.

In July 1994 the Security Council adopted a resolution "inviting" all states, especially those in the Western Hemisphere, to use "all necessary means" to remove those then in control in Haiti. The Senate responded by passing a non-binding resolution 100–0. In the resolution the Senate stated the Security Council resolution could not authorize U.S. troops in Haiti, or it would violate the Constitution and the War Powers Act. In a nationally televised address, Clinton referred to the UN language in expressing his intent to engage U.S. forces and lead a multinational force to resolve the problems in Haiti. At no time did he refer to the need or desire to consult with Congress. While an invasion became unnecessary as the problem was resolved through diplomatic means, the United States still sent 20,000 troops to provide stability for the new regime. An attempt at a resolution to provide retroactive authorization was rejected in favor of language that asserted Clinton "should have sought and welcomed Congressional approval" before any forces had been deployed. Even those who voted against it suggested that the president should have asked for congressional approval.

Twice during his presidency, Clinton appealed to NATO to authorize military action. Both cases revolved around sending U.S. troops into the Balkans: Bosnia in 1994–1995 and Kosovo in 1999. At no time did he appeal to Congress for the authority to take such actions. At no point was it necessary for Congress to act, he argued. At no point did Congress challenge this interpretation and contest his authority to carry out the air strikes.

Following the bombing raids, Clinton ordered the deployment of twenty thousand American ground troops into Bosnia. The president did not attempt to obtain authority from Congress, arguing he did not need to because his authority to move American troops into the Balkans came from U.S. membership in NATO. This time Congress debated various bills and resolutions to limit the action but failed to pass any. The best Congress could manage were meaningless nonbinding resolutions that demanded that U.S. troops not be deployed without congressional approval. However, when the time came to pass resolutions that would bind the president, members of both houses bailed out.

Clinton effectively combined Security Council resolutions and NATO provisions to justify actions in Bosnia. Failure to get UN support for action in Kosovo left him to rely totally on NATO, with the result that the United States joined NATO, mostly in an air capacity, in its bombing of Belgrade and insertion of troops into Kosovo. The purpose of the War Powers Resolution, to restrain the president from acting without congressional authority, appeared to be thwarted. However, when Congress had the opportunity to step up and challenge the chief executive, it failed to act, so the efficacy of the resolution was still truly untested.

As U.S. forces readied themselves to begin air strikes against Serbia, the House adopted a resolution to authorize the presence of U.S. forces as part of a NATO peacekeeping operation. Many senators opposed military action. They expected a peace agreement between Serbia and Kosovo, but while Kosovo accepted the NATO plan, it was rejected by the Serbs. By the time of the Senate vote, negotiations had collapsed and war was imminent. The Senate then decided in favor of military air operations and missile strikes against Serbia (and Montenegro). In contrast, the House voted on a series of resolutions. The first one, passed 249–180, prohibited the use of any appropriated funds for ground forces in the Balkans. A second resolution demanding the removal of U.S. forces failed, and a third calling for a declaration of war against Yugoslavia also failed. A final fourth vote to authorize air operations failed on a tie vote. A number of Senate resolutions to either authorize the war or require Clinton to seek approval from Congress were tabled. In the meantime, ignoring Congressional sentiments, or lack thereof, U.S. forces went to the Balkans and President Clinton was able to act pretty much at will without congressional approval.

Again lawmakers went to court. In *Campbell v. Clinton* (2000), various members of Congress filed suit seeking a declaration by the Court that the president had violated the War Powers Clause of the Constitution and the War Powers Resolution by directing United States forces' participation in NATO air strikes against Serbia without congressional authorization. The D.C. Circuit Court refused to rule, arguing that the members of Congress had no standing. It also said that it could not act because the War

Powers Resolution had never been triggered and that thus the issue was a political question, outside the purview of the judiciary. As the Court noted, there is no "test for war." If a judge cannot determine what constitutes war, how can the court determine if the War Powers Act has been violated? And the court said that while the Constitution grants Congress the power to declare war, that is not necessarily the same as the power to determine whether U.S. forces will fight in a war.

Terrorism

Since the Clinton presidency, the most pressing question concerning the war power involves the U.S. response to terrorism. Several times during the Clinton Administration, U.S. forces were directed against nations that supported terrorist acts or seemed to be capable of developing weapons of mass destruction. Early during his term of office, Clinton launched air strikes against Iraq to retaliate for the plan of that country's regime to assassinate the former president, George H. W. Bush. He stated that the reason for the strikes was "to send a message to those who engage in state-sponsored terrorism."

Additional actions were taken against Iraq in 1996 with the launching of cruise missiles in response to Iraqi actions against the Kurds and the use of additional military action in 1998 for Saddam Hussein's denial of access to UN inspectors. Clinton also ordered strikes against Afghanistan and the Sudan in retaliation for bombings of U.S. embassies

On September 20, 2001, President George W. Bush addresses a joint session of Congress on Capitol Hill in Washington, D.C., to prepare Americans for a long, deadly, and often covert war against elusive terrorists. Sitting behind Bush are Sen. Robert Byrd (right), president pro-tem of the Senate, and Speaker of the House Dennis Hastert (left). (AP/Wide World Photos)

in east Africa. In all of these cases, no congressional approval was asked for or given.

Terrorism gave the president far more flexibility to act than the traditional powers of the president. Apparent imminent danger constituted a situation where Congress would be hard-pressed to challenge presidential authority.

In the wake of the September 11, 2001, terrorist attacks on New York and Wash-

ington, D.C., the shift of power to the president was obvious. Congress quickly followed the attacks with a broad joint resolution authorizing President George W. Bush to use all "necessary and appropriate force" against the nations, organizations, and persons responsible in any way for the attacks of September 11 "in order to prevent any future acts of international terrorism against the United States by such nations, organizations or persons." Under this authority, President Bush sent U.S. forces into Afghanistan in conjunction with NATO.

Next on the administration's agenda was Iraq. Originally, President Bush pursued three separate arguments: (1) he could send troops because of American interests through his power as commander in chief; (2) he did not need to get additional authorization from Congress to send U.S. troops into Iraq because the original resolution validating American troops in Afghanistan could easily be extended to the situation in Iraq; and (3) the original authorization passed ten years previously for his father was still valid for future operations authorized by the UN Security Council. All of these arguments became moot when Congress passed a resolution authorizing American military force against Iraq. Prior to asking Congress for such authorization, Bush repeatedly noted that he did not need to do so.

Congress reacted to its Gulf of Tonkin authorization in 1964, seen in retrospect as far too open-ended a grant of authority, with the passage of the War Powers Resolution of 1973. In the succeeding decades, however, Congress repeatedly failed to assert itself strongly, opening the door for still greater presidential authority. Finally, it repeated its supposed mistake of 1964 with a wide-ranging authorization that has seen the president move beyond the mere use of military force to argue that such authorization enabled him to sanction warrantless wiretaps by the National Security Agency in apparent direct contradiction of prior congressional disapproval of such wiretaps under the Foreign Intelligence Surveillance Act.

CONGRESS AND THE SUPREME COURT

In contrast to conflicts with the president, when Congress and the Supreme Court face off the controversy is more constrained. These two bodies are more likely to acknowledge the other's authority.

Suppose the Supreme Court rules that a law is unconstitutional and that the ruling is based squarely on the Court's conclusions from facts placed in evidence. Then Congress passes a new law that is directly contrary to the Court's decision, because Congress draws a conflicting conclusion from the same facts. A key constitutional question turns on whose view of the facts is correct. Whose view of the evidence should win out?

It is an interesting question. Courts routinely draw conclusions from facts, but so do legislatures. Indeed, in some cases legislatures are better than courts at surveying facts. Thus, the issue is not one of basic competence but of authority. Which branch of the federal government, the judicial or the legislative, has the power to impose its interpretation of facts on the other when that interpretation governs how a question of constitutional law will be resolved?

One of the most discredited periods in Supreme Court history was the early 1900s, when the Court in some cases arguably acted as a superlegislature. The Court oversaw state and federal legislation, and in striking down laws, it often second-guessed the legislative rationales or narrowly interpreted congressional power so as to restrict the power of the government to act. In the most famous case of that era, *Lochner v. New York* (1905), the Supreme Court ruled that a New York State law setting a maximum number of hours a baker could work was unconstitutional. In part, the Court rejected the New York legislature's rationale for the law, acting like a superlegislature. Actions such as this inhibited legislative attempts (at the both the state and federal level) to effect reforms in society. Justice Holmes chastised the Court, stating that "the Fourteenth Amendment does not enact Mr. Herbert Spencer's Social Statistics" and that

> a constitution is not intended to embody a particular economic theory, whether of paternalism and the organic relation of the citizen to the State or of *laissez faire.* It is made for people of fundamentally differing views, and the accident of our finding certain opinions natural and familiar or novel and even shocking ought not to conclude our judgment upon the question whether statutes embodying them conflict with the Constitution of the United States.

The Court's job was to interpret the law, not rule on its efficacy. This became especially problematic in the 1930s during the Depression. Eventually, the Court, in essence, backed off—giving Congress a free rein in the economic sphere. However, in retiring from overseeing the con-

gressional actions under Congress's commerce authority, it suggested, in a famous footnote in *United States v. Caroline Products Co.* (1938), that in the area of civil liberties and civil rights, a more exacting scrutiny would be pursued. Toward the end of the twentieth century, the Court began to rethink its rationale regarding the commerce power. Two cases at the end of the twentieth century, *United States v. Morrison* (2000) and *United States v. Lopez* (1995), challenged what had been an almost unfettered use of commerce authority by the Congress. This new view was fueled by a conservative Court with a reinvigorated vision of federalism that was very eager to restrict federal powers, especially congressional authority over what were considered traditionally local matters. Also, Congress challenged Court opinions that struck down various laws as being reminiscent of *Lochner.*

For example, in *Stenberg v. Carhart* (2000) the Supreme Court struck down Nebraska's ban on "partial-birth" abortions, in medical terms "dilation and extraction" (D&X). The Court based its ruling on the fact that many in the medical community thought D&X was a safer procedure for some women than the other procedure at issue in *Stenberg.* Yet, the Court noted, the Nebraska law contained no "health exception." Accordingly, the Court, based on this medical evidence, found the ban to be an "undue burden" on the constitutional right of abortion.

Congress reacted strongly, passing a federal partial-birth abortion bill but instead of incorporating the Court's "suggestion" that a health exception be included, the new law had no such exception. Criticizing the Court for overstepping its bounds, the new law incorporated findings that contradicted the Supreme Court's review of the medical evidence. The conflict presented the question of whose evidence took precedence, Congress's finding that D&X "is never necessary to preserve the health of a woman" or the Court's ruling that it sometimes is. This raised serious constitutional questions. Should the Supreme Court defer to Congress's view of the medical evidence? Or should the Court stand by its own analysis, which led it to conclude that the Nebraska law was flawed?

A similar situation arose in *City of Boerne v. Flores* (1997). In *Boerne* the Court ruled that Congress had overstepped its authority by passing the Religious Freedom Restoration Act, which in essence trumped an earlier Supreme Court ruling (*Employment Division, Department of Human Resources of Oregon v. Smith* [1990]). Critics noted that Congress was not only challenging the Court's authority, but emasculating it.

The issue is whether Congress may "overrule" a Supreme Court opinion. The Court has argued that when a question of constitutional law turns on what the "true facts" are, congressional "findings" cannot make something true that is not true. By ruling in such a manner, the Court suggests it is not returning to the discredited philosophy of the *Lochner* era at the turn of the twentieth century, but is rather providing a proper check on a branch of government that is exceeding its constitutional mandate. In these cases the Court argues that it is not challenging the facts presented by Congress, but rather a rationale that uses a tenuous set of facts.

As noted above, a case that strove to make this distinction, and in so doing struck down a major piece of Congressional legislation, was *United States v. Morrison* (2000). When Congress passed the Violence against Women Act (VAWA) (1994), it did so by its authority under the Commerce Clause. Congress's rationale was that gender-motivated violence affected interstate commerce. The Court rejected this justification and ruled the act unconstitutional for being outside the scope of congressional commerce authority.

Congress suspected that when VAWA got to the Supreme Court, the Commerce Clause would be a problem. The Rehnquist Court focused on federalism concerns. From Chief Justice William Rehnquist's first days on the Court, he had sought to reinvigorate the Tenth Amendment. In 1995 *United States v. Lopez* had denied Congress the authority to regulate firearms on school property. This decision reflected the strongly held view by the more conservative wing of the Court that certain issues were best dealt with at the state rather than the federal level. Violent crimes, of course, were typically addressed by state, not federal law—including violence directed against women.

Congress resolved to tackle the anticipated constitutional problem with VAWA by making explicit findings that gender-motivated violence affected interstate commerce. Congress's fact-finding established to its satisfaction a connection between violence against women and interstate commerce. As the Court stressed in *Morrison*, however, the ultimate issue of whether something affects interstate commerce is a constitutional question. Just saying it is connected to interstate commerce does not make it so. This was a constitutional matter that the Court had to decide. If the Court did not have the authority to do so, then what purpose did it serve? The Court harkened back to Chief Justice John Marshall and *Marbury v. Madison* (1803), which noted that the job of assessing congressional statutes to see if they are consistent with the Constitution was the Supreme Court's special province.

For these reasons, the Court held in *Morrison* that Congress's finding that something affects interstate commerce "does not necessarily make it so." Another example of the Court blocking Congress was its declaration that Congress could not do an end run around a Court decision by changing the law. In *Dickerson v. United States* (1999) the Court, in a seven to two decision, rejected Congress's effort to overrule the *Miranda* decision. Chief Justice Rehnquist emphasized that "Miranda announced a constitutional rule that Congress may not supersede legislatively. We decline to overrule Miranda ourselves." (In fact, the only way for the Congress to "overrule" a Supreme Court decision is to propose to the states an amendment to the Constitution. This in essence was done when after the Civil War, with the Thirteenth, Fourteenth, and Fifteenth Amendments effectively voiding the *Dred Scott* decision of 1857.)

But these battles between the Court and Congress, while spirited at times, are in essence part of the checks and balances system that was established in part to prevent Congress from overstepping its authority. Congress, and the executive as well, concedes to the Supreme Court the authority to strike down their actions.

CENSURE

Congress's efforts to rein in the other two branches by methods outside the legislative process often create the most contentious interactions between the three branches. Such confrontational interfaces occur when Congress attempts to discipline or remove members of the executive and judicial branches by a censure resolution or, in more extreme cases, impeachment.

In the last decade of the twentieth century, some members of Congress argued that President Clinton's actions in the Monica Lewinsky affair warranted censuring by the legislature. In opposing a censure of President Clinton, many Republicans argued that the Constitution contains no words allowing Congress to take that step, whereas the Constitution makes specific provision for impeachment. Their argument made sense in light of the historical use of censure.

Censure is a seldom-used procedure in part because it merely condemns persons publicly (whether president, judge, or member of Congress), allowing them to stay in office. Thus, after the Senate investigated and censured Sen. Joseph Mc-

Carthy in 1954, he stayed in the Senate and served out his term. The earliest legislative attempt to censure a president occurred in 1800, when the House of Representatives debated for two weeks over whether to censure President John Adams for "a dangerous interference of the Executive with Judicial decisions."

The censure of Adams revolved around a seaman named Jonathan Robbins, who was on trial for murder in South Carolina. The British navy also had a claim on Robbins (who claimed he was a fugitive named Thomas Nash). Adams ordered South Carolina authorities to turn Robbins over to the English. Adams was attacked as subverting the U.S. judicial process, and a House investigation began. Relevant papers were demanded from the executive and a resolution was put forth saying Adams's behavior "exposes the administration thereof to suspicion and reproach." The resolution was described by its sponsor as a censure of the president.

From the first, some members argued that the House did not have the power to censure the president, only to impeach, but there was little other discussion about whether such legislative action was constitutional. The problem, as noted by Rep. John Nichols of Virginia, was that Adams's conduct might not warrant impeachment but was, however, definitely improper and deserved some response by Congress. Rep. James A. Bayard of Delaware was more generous in his assessment of House power and argued he had "no doubt of the competency of the House either to impeach, to censure or to approbate the conduct of

the Executive, and of course both the resolutions were in their power." Future chief justice John Marshall defended Adams. However, Marshall, who had been at Virginia's ratification convention in 1788, did not question the legality of the censure resolution.

Albert Gallatin of Pennsylvania, a critic of Adams, argued Adams had undertaken an "injurious" act which "might be of censure where the same act committed with a criminal intent would be impeachable." He contended that the House "had as much power to disapprove and censure" as it did to impeach. Eventually, the House voted 65–35 against the censure resolution.

The House challenged Andrew Jackson in the wake of the fight over the Bank of the United States. The censure of Jackson reflected deep political divisions between the Congress and the presidency. In the long political struggle that followed the defeat of the Bank, Jackson's enemies blamed him for the Depression that followed and generally for his obstinate attitude and, according to Rep. John Quincy Adams, "a tone of insolence and insult" in his dealings with Congress.

On March 28, 1834, the Senate voted its disapproval, 28–18, of the president's removal of federal funds from the Bank, which it said was beyond his powers. The resolution did not contain the word "censure," but most historians consider the measure a censure. No matter: three years later, Jackson's allies took control of the Senate and revoked the resolution. Some historians argue that the censure movement against Jackson resulted in positive gains for the president rather than the negative impact hoped for by the Senate.

Three other resolutions during the antebellum period and the Civil War failed to take hold. John Tyler became the first vice president to succeed to the presidency when William Henry Harrison died on April 6, 1841, after only a month in office. In 1842 Tyler vetoed two tariff bills favored by his Whig Party. His Cabinet resigned, his own party expelled him, and a resolution was introduced in the House to investigate him for purposes of possible impeachment. That measure, the first presidential impeachment proceeding ever introduced in Congress, was defeated in January 1843. However, Tyler's political power was crippled, and he failed to win his party's renomination in 1844.

The House challenged James Buchanan twice, once with his secretary of the navy for corruption in the awarding of contracts and again after he was out of office for failure to halt Confederate secession. In the first case, the navy secretary awarded contracts to his relatives and Buchanan signed off on one of them. Upon the introduction of the censure resolution, Rep. Thomas Stanley Bocock of Virginia argued it was outside the scope of congressional power. On "what page," he asked, "of the Constitution do you find the power in this House to pass censure on the President of the United States?" Others also questioned the House's authority to take such action and claimed that it breached the separation of powers and infringed "upon the high prerogatives of the Executive Department of the Government." However, the House still adopted the resolution, 106–61.

President Buchanan, who served from 1857 to 1861, did not think the southern states had a right to leave the Union, but neither did he think the federal government had the power to do anything about it. By the time he left the White House with the accession of Abraham Lincoln, who had rather different ideas about secession and preserving the Union, seven states had seceded and civil war was inevitable. In 1862 the Senate debated a measure of "condemnation and censure" against Buchanan for his failure to prevent secession. The measure was tabled.

The most recent attempts to censure a president were aimed at Richard Nixon and Bill Clinton. The censure movements against Nixon, in the context of Watergate in 1973 and 1974, condemned Nixon for the "Saturday Night Massacre" of October 1973 and for actions beyond his authority in 1974. The president's resignation made them moot, and in light of the impending impeachment on the eve of his resignation, the memory of the censure attempts has faded.

IMPEACHMENTS

Censure aside, the most potent power the Congress holds against the executive and judicial branches, as noted above, is the power of impeachment. The process of impeachment seems simple enough, but as evidenced by history, the actual implementation becomes difficult, lengthy, and contentious. At the time of the drafting of the Constitution, impeachment was an established process in English law and government. The Founding Fathers incorporated the process, with modifications, into the framework for government. However, it is only the idea and the basic who's, why's, and how's, not the intricate procedural processes, that are explained. Those have evolved and are included in the internal rules of the House and Senate.

Removing an official from office requires two basic steps: (1) a formal accusation, or impeachment, by the House of Representatives, and (2) a trial and conviction by the Senate. Impeachment requires a majority vote of the House; conviction is more difficult, requiring a two-thirds vote by the Senate. The vice president presides over the Senate proceedings in the case of all officials except the president, whose trial is presided over by the chief justice of the Supreme Court.

Article II, Section 4 designates who may be impeached: "The President, Vice-President, and all civil officers of the United States." This includes federal judges. (Congress cannot impeach its own members; a separate process must be followed to remove a member from his or her seat.) Article II , Section 4 also specifies the reasons for which an official may be impeached and removed: "on Impeachment for, and conviction of, treason, bribery, or other high crimes or misdemeanors."

The implication of these words is that impeachment does not equal crime in the sense of the criminal law, and is therefore not purely a matter of criminal law. All crimes do not qualify as impeachable offenses. The ambiguous phrase, "high crimes and misdemeanors," leaves the standard undefined. This was evident in the debates over the first impeachment; there was no sure meaning of these terms, even by the men who were alive during their formulation.

"High crimes and misdemeanors" covers a vast amount of territory. Abuse of power and serious misconduct in office fit this category, but despite the political wrangling that encompassed the impeachment hearings of President Clinton, it can be strongly argued that the Founders disapproved of the idea of using partisan conflict as a ground for impeachment. To further confuse manners, the term "misdemeanor" does not correspond to the modern definition, which denotes it as a less serious (something less than a felony) infraction or common law criminal offense.

While bribery, perjury, and treason appear to be less ambiguous grounds for impeachment and removal, even they raise questions. During the impeachment hearings of President Clinton, there was a battle over whether perjury committed while Clinton was not acting as president qualified as a reason for impeachment.

Several impeachment cases have confused political animosity with genuine crimes. The political nature of Congress makes it difficult at times to separate the politics from the trial, yet because Congress is responsible for indicting, trying, and convicting public officials, it is theoretically necessary for the legislative branch to cast aside its political nature and adopt a judicial role.

The process of impeachment follows a series of steps, outlined by the Constitution. Article I, Section 2, paragraph 5 states: "The House of Representatives . . . shall have the sole power of impeachment." The House formulates the charge against the official and reduces it to writing.

The power of impeachment is, in essence, the power of Congress to indict and try an official. There are two parts to the impeachment process. First, as in an ordinary criminal trial, an indictment (or in some states an information) officially charges an individual before he or she appears in court for a formal trial. In the impeachment process, the House Judiciary Committee conducts an investigation, gathers evidence, and deliberates over whether to initiate an impeachment inquiry.

Following the investigation, if the evidence warrants such action, the House debates and considers any resolutions put forth from the Judiciary Committee and assembles the evidence into individual indictments or charges known as articles of impeachment. Each article requires a majority vote of the House before it is passed on to the Senate. Once an article is approved, the official is considered impeached and subject to trial.

The next step is defined in Article I, Section 3, paragraph 6: "The Senate shall have the sole power to try all impeachments. When sitting for that purpose,

they shall be on oath or affirmation. When the President of the United States is tried, the Chief Justice shall preside: And no person shall be convicted without the concurrence of two thirds of the members present."

The Senate holds a trial on the articles of impeachment, sitting as a court. The Senate establishes its own procedure as to how it will consider evidence and hear witnesses. House managers conduct the trial, which is held in the well of the Senate. In *Nixon v. United States* (1993), regarding the impeachment trial of a federal judge, the Supreme Court ruled that the application of the phrase "sole power to try all impeachments" was not justiciable. The Court ruled that the process and procedure for impeachment lies solely within the purview of the legislature. The officer subject to an impeachment proceeding has no appeal to a federal court, and the decision of the Congress is final.

As Article I, Section 3, paragraph 7 states, "Judgment in cases of impeachment shall not extend further than to removal from office, and disqualification to hold and enjoy any office of honor, trust or profit under the United States: but the party convicted shall nevertheless be liable and subject to indictment, trial, judgment and punishment, according to law." Because it is not an official court of law, that is, a part of the judicial branch, an impeachment and removal does not activate the double jeopardy clause of the Fifth Amendment. The former officer may face criminal indictments and trials for the same conduct that led to her or his impeachment and removal from office.

In the history of the United States, the House has impeached sixteen people. These sixteen represent members of all three branches of the federal government, including one Supreme Court justice, eleven federal judges, one senator, one Cabinet member, and two presidents. Seven of this group were convicted and removed by the Senate, all federal judges. The threat of impeachment can also be efficacious, as some members of the government have resigned rather than face congressional scrutiny, most notably President Richard Nixon, who resigned in 1974 to avoid what would have most likely been a conviction.

In 1797 Sen. William Blount became the first person to be impeached by the House. He was accused of conspiring with Britain to seize Spanish territory in North America. The impeachment was dismissed by the Senate in early 1799 because it decided impeachment was a mechanism to be used as a check against the other two branches of government, not members of Congress. It was noted that other avenues are open to the Senate and the House when they want to discipline their own members, one of which the Senate promptly used by expelling Blount.

The first person impeached and convicted was Judge John Pickering of New Hampshire. His transgressions included drunkenness and unlawful rulings, with some saying he was insane. In 1804 he was removed from the bench.

Pickering's conviction was part of an attempt by the newly dominant Jeffersonian Republicans to raid the federal bench and remove Federalist judges, with their eyes on the big prize, the chief justice of the U.S. Supreme Court, John Marshall. After Pickering, the Democratic-Republican–controlled Congress attacked Associate Justice Samuel Chase. The House impeached Chase for what it called judicial bias, but he was acquitted by the Senate at trial in March 1805. Failure to remove Chase had two important historical consequences. First, the inability to get the associate justice meant that the chief justice was not a feasible target, so the Democratic-Republicans began to focus their energies elsewhere in their continuing attempts to dismantle various Federalist programs and influences. Second, and perhaps more importantly, it established that impeachment should not be used for purely political reasons or because of dissatisfaction with the job an individual was doing, but should be reserved for far more serious reasons. The impeachment clause of the Constitution, including the words "crimes and misdemeanors," seemed to suggest actions that were illegal, such as bribery, perjury, treason, and deeds that seemed to offend the Constitution.

Presidential Impeachments

By the beginning of the twenty-first century, while only two presidents had actually been impeached and gone to trial before the Senate, nine different presidents had had impeachment charges filed against them in the House. They were John Tyler, Andrew Johnson, Grover Cleveland, Herbert Hoover, Harry S. Truman, Richard M. Nixon, Ronald Reagan, George H. W. Bush, and Bill Clinton. In the wake of the Clinton impeachment in 1998, which in defiance of the lessons of the Chase impeachment was fueled by political animosities, and with growing popular resentment against the war in Iraq and its architect, President George W. Bush, cries of impeachment again arose. However, in part as a result of lessons learned during the Clinton impeachment about how draining and divisive the process was, only a minority of members of Congress and the public supported the call for impeachment. Attempts in the Senate and House to impeach or censure the president regularly failed to gain any momentum, and the coming of the 2008 election, which would end the Bush presidency, sealed the fate of such moves.

Of the nine presidential impeachment charges put forth, only two have moved forward to actual impeachment by the House. The two presidents involved, Andrew Johnson and Bill Clinton, are the only presidents to have faced a Senate trial.

The Johnson Impeachment

Johnson, who assumed the presidency following the assassination of Abraham Lincoln, was a southern Democrat from Tennessee. He was a weak president, with very little clout in a Congress dominated by Radical Republicans. His mild

Reconstruction policy put him at serious odds with the movers and shakers in the Congress, who rejected his lenient attitude toward the defeated Confederacy. Johnson further antagonized Congress by vetoing several pieces of legislation tied to the Republican plan for Reconstruction, including the Civil Rights Act of 1866, and by vigorously opposing the Fourteenth Amendment.

Radical Republicans, while realizing that Johnson's power was limited, still acknowledged that he had power and feared he would emasculate the victory won by the Civil War. To try to keep supporters of the Radical Republicans in the administration by preventing Johnson from removing them and replacing them with people more sympathetic to his own agenda, Congress passed the Tenure of Office Act in 1867 over Johnson's veto. This act prevented the president from removing members of his administration who had obtained their jobs through Senate approval; in particular, it was aimed at keeping Secretary of War Edwin Stanton in office. Stanton, an important part of the Lincoln Administration, was a supporter of Radical Republican interests and helped to mitigate actions by Johnson that ran counter to those interests.

With his veto of the law overridden and his authority challenged, Johnson wasted little time before contesting the law. The president was at odds with Stanton over a variety of issues, most notably actions surrounding the execution of the assassin involved in the murder of President Lincoln. Johnson believed Stanton had deceived him, and in addition, he was tired of the secretary of war's obstructionist activities when it came to the White House's plans for Reconstruction. Johnson's firing of Stanton, in defiance of the Tenure of Office Act, provided the foundation for his impeachment in 1868. The House passed and presented eleven articles of impeachment to the Senate. The best chance for conviction seemed to rest with the eleventh article, which charged the president with attempting to prevent Stanton from resuming his office after the Senate disapproved his suspension. Most of the other articles seemed far more political, rooted in policy disagreements along party lines rather than what was perceived by some critics as proper challenges. However, the vote in the Senate on article eleven came up one short of the needed two-thirds majority, and Johnson was acquitted in the spring of 1868. In retrospect, many historians argue that the Johnson impeachment hearings were a poor attempt to impeach a president because of weak charges, rooted mostly in party hostility toward him. The very law that was used as the basis of the impeachment was partly repealed two decades later and was finally declared unconstitutional by the Supreme Court in 1926.

The Clinton Impeachment

Bill Clinton's impeachment was reminiscent of the Johnson impeachment in that political issues often muddied the waters concerning exactly what Clinton had done that was an impeachable offense. In contrast to the Johnson affair, the roots of Clinton's impeachment reached back to the days when he was governor of Arkansas and involved character issues rather than abuse of power in office, including a claim of sexual harassment by a former state employee. Steeped in sexual liaisons and some suspect real estate dealings, the impeachment of Clinton sprang from his apparent perjury about his relationship with White House intern Monica Lewinsky, and following his appearance before a federal grand jury, the push for impeachment grew.

Clinton's admission that he had lied to the American public about the Lewinsky affair helped create a political feeding frenzy as lines were sharply drawn along party lines over whether or not Clinton's conduct warranted impeachment. In late August 1998, Clinton's presidency seemed to be in great danger. Kenneth Starr, who had been conducting an independent counsel investigation of the president, was required by law to present the House with "any substantial and credible information" that might provide a ground for impeachment. Starr's report outlined the case for eleven counts against Clinton, including perjury in his Paula Jones and grand jury depositions, obstruction of justice, and one count asserting abuse of office. Responsibility for recommending action on impeachment fell to the House Judiciary Committee. Following a review of the evidence, the committee voted 21–16 along party lines to authorize a full impeachment inquiry. Many Democrats on the committee, arguing the behavior was not an impeachable offense and concerned "lying about sex," favored censure, rather than impeachment. The committee's decision to impeach was ratified by the full House three days later, with thirty-one Democrats joining the majority. After the midterm elections of 1998, in which the Democrats gained seats in the House despite the possibility of impending impeachment, the investigation moved forward, with the Judiciary Committee considering the evidence in trying to determine if Clinton's indiscretions constituted impeachable behavior. Finally, the committee approved four articles of impeachment, sending them to the whole House.

Vigorous debate over the constitutionality of the proceedings took place on the House floor. Finally, the House voted on December 19, 1998, along strict party lines, to approve two of the four articles: grand jury perjury and obstruction of justice.

Immediately following House passage of the articles, President Clinton advocated that we "stop the politics of personal destruction. We must," he said, "get rid of the poisonous venom of excessive partisanship, obsessive animosity, and uncontrolled anger." Americans agreed with the president, and polls showed 60 percent of Americans opposed impeachment.

With the approval of the articles, the Senate approved a bipartisan plan (passed by a unanimous vote of all senators) for procedural rules to govern the trial. Each side would get twenty-four hours to present its case without witnesses. The senators would then have two days for a question-and-answer session of those who presented the case, including the president. Following debate and deliberation, the Senate would vote on motions to dismiss or approve requests for witnesses. Although Senate Republicans lobbied hard, they were unable to garner the needed two-thirds vote to convict the president; neither count came even close to the needed number. On the perjury count, ten Republicans crossed the aisle so that a total of fifty-five senators voted not guilty. The second charge, obstruction of justice, saw the Senate split right down the middle, 50–50, with five Republicans voting with the Democrats.

The Clinton impeachment showed how the process of trying to remove an individual, especially a president, can bring government to a halt. The attention of Congress turns to the trial and little work gets done. Thus, as noted above, few impeachments make it to trial, and often officials resign rather than face congressional scrutiny and the embarrassment of a public trial.

Nixon's Resignation

Perhaps the most notorious of this latter group was President Richard Nixon. There was little question that Nixon had crossed the bridge and was ripe for impeachment. His participation in and possible direction of the cover-up of the break-in at the Watergate Hotel, the headquarters of the Democratic Party, during the 1972 election campaign, left no doubt as to his ripeness for impeachment. In July 1974 the House Judiciary Committee, in the face of growing evidence, issued three articles of impeachment. The articles, focusing on his abuse of presidential authority and power, indicted him for illegal wiretapping, misuse of the CIA, perjury, bribery, obstruction of justice, and other abuses. The final lines of the third article asserted that "Richard M. Nixon has acted in a manner contrary to his trust as president and subversive of constitutional government, to the great prejudice of the cause of law and justice, and to the manifest injury of the people of the United States." There was little question that he would be impeached by the House and convicted by the Senate. In the face of what was obviously going to be a humiliating trial, Nixon resigned eleven days after the House committee voted articles of impeachment.

Nixon's impeachment contrasted deeply with the Johnson and Clinton affairs in its relative lack of partisan overtones. While supporters of the president did exist, impeachment pressure built from both sides of the aisle. The charges the articles put forth unquestionably qualified as "high crimes and misdemeanors." Perhaps the greatest difference from the Johnson and Clinton cases was that Nixon's actions seemed to challenge the Constitution itself and bring harm to the office of the president; he used that office to cripple and frustrate constitutional government. In contrast, the Johnson impeachment was fueled mostly by the personal hostility between the president and the Radical Republicans, and Clinton's hearings seemed to be far more personal and about his actions as an individual, which as despica-

ble as they may have been, did not seem to corrupt the office itself.

While some historians argue that Johnson's actions against Stanton could be perceived as impeachable offenses, political conflicts overshadowed any perceived constitutional abuses. On the other hand, Nixon's actions used the office of the president seemingly to twist the balance of power and do damage to the constitutional structure. Ironically, of the three presidents, the best case for impeachment was that against Nixon, who was not impeached.

The reality is that conflict between Congress and the other branches of government often devolves into petty politics. Therefore, how one perceives what a judicial or executive official has done and how evidence in an impeachment case is viewed is a very political matter.

However, while impeachment is an extraordinary remedy, it has shown itself to be an ordinary aspect of the system of checks and balances. The power of the branch of government to which the accused belongs has strengthened and weakened independently of impeachment proceedings, especially in the case of the president. Following the Johnson presidency, executive weaknesses were as much inherent in the qualities of the successor, Ulysses S. Grant, as resulting from any damage caused to the office by Johnson's impeachment and trial. While Nixon's transgressions damaged the Republican Party, they by no means compromised executive power, and following the Clinton imbroglio, it was readily apparent that the presidency under George W. Bush was anything but weakened.

In the end, Congress asserts itself against the other two branches through the normal legislative process as well as the extraordinary one. In either case, the collisions of the three branches serve to validate and celebrate the three-part system of government rather than compromise and diminish it.

FURTHER READING

Bazan, Elizabeth B. *CRS Report for Congress: Impeachment: An Overview of Constitutional Provisions, Procedure, and Practice.* Damascus, MD: Penny Hill Press, February 14, 1995.

Bazan, Elizabeth B. *CRS Report for Congress: Impeachment: An Overview of Constitutional Provisions, Procedure, and Practice.* Damascus, MD: Penny Hill Press, February 27, 1998.

Bond, R. Jon, and Richard Fleisher. *The President in the Legislative Arena.* Chicago: University of Chicago Press, 1992.

Burgess, Susan R. *Contest for Constitutional Authority: The Abortion and War Power Debates.* Lawrence, KS: University Press of Kansas, 1992.

Collier, Ellen C. *CRS Report for Congress: Foreign Policy Roles of the President and Congress.* Damascus, MD: Penny Hill Press, January 6, 1993.

Doyle, Charles. *CRS Report for Congress: Impeachment Grounds: A Collection of Selected Materials.* Damascus, MD: Penny Hill Press, October 29, 1998.

Doyle, Charles. *CRS Report for Congress: Impeachment Grounds.* Part 1, *Pre-Constitutional Convention Materials.* Damascus, MD: Penny Hill Press, October 30, 1998.

Doyle, Charles. *CRS Report for Congress: Impeachment Grounds.* Part 2, *Selected Constitutional Convention Materials.* Damascus, MD: Penny Hill Press, October 30, 1998.

Doyle, Charles. *CRS Report for Congress: Impeachment Grounds.* Part 3, *Hamilton, Wilson, and Story.* Damascus, MD: Penny Hill Press, October 30, 1998.

Doyle, Charles. *CRS Report for Congress: Impeachment Grounds.* Part 4a, *Articles of Past Impeachments.* Damascus, MD: Penny Hill Press, October 30, 1998.

Doyle, Charles. *CRS Report for Congress: Impeachment Grounds.* Part 4b, *Articles of Past Impeachments.* Damascus, MD: Penny Hill Press, October 30, 1998.

Doyle, Charles. *CRS Report for Congress: Impeachment Grounds.* Part 5, *Selected Douglas/Nixon Inquiry Materials.* Damascus, MD: Penny Hill Press, October 30, 1998.

Doyle, Charles. *CRS Report for Congress: Impeachment Grounds.* Part 6, *Quotes from Sundry Commentators.* Damascus, MD: Penny Hill Press, October 30, 1998.

Fischer, Louis. *CRS Report for Congress: Congressional Checks on the Judiciary.* Damascus, MD: Penny Hill Press, April 29, 1997.

Grimmett, Richard F. *CRS Report for Congress: Foreign Policy Roles of the President and Congress.* Damascus, MD: Penny Hill Press, June 1, 1999.

Halstead, T. J. *CRS Report for Congress: An Overview of the Impeachment Process.* Damascus, MD: Penny Hill Press, April 20, 2005.

Huckabee, David C. *CRS Report for Congress: Impeachment: Days and Dates of Consideration in the House and Senate.* Damascus, MD: Penny Hill Press, April 25, 2000.

Huckabee, David C., Paul S. Runquist, and Thomas H. Neale. *CRS Report for Congress: Impeachment: Frequently Asked Questions.* Damascus, MD: Penny Hill Press, January 8, 1999.

Jones, Charles O. *Separate But Equal: Congress and the Presidency.* 2nd ed. Chappaqua, NY: Chatham House, 1999.

Maskell, Jack. *CRS Report for Congress: Censure of the President by Congress.* Damascus, MD: Penny Hill Press, December 8, 1998.

Maskell, Jack, and Richard S. Beth. *CRS Report for Congress: "No Confidence" Votes and Other Forms of Congressional Censure of Public Officials.* Damascus, MD: Penny Hill Press, June 11, 2007.

Oleszek, Walter. *CRS Report for Congress: Congress and the Courts: Current Policy Issues.* Damascus, MD: Penny Hill Press, September 20, 2005.

Stathis, Stephen W. and David C. Hucakbee. *CRS Report for Congress: Congressional Resolutions on Presidential Impeachment: A Historical Overview.* Damascus, MD: Penny Hill Press, September 16, 1998.

Thurber, James A., ed. *Rivals for Power: Presidential-Congressional Relations.* 3rd ed. Lanham, MD: Rowman & Littlefield, 2003.

Westerfield, Donald L. *War Powers: The President, the Congress and the Question of War.* Westport, CT: Praeger, 1996.

GLOSSARY OF CONCEPTS AND PEOPLE

act: Legislation (a bill or joint resolution, *see* below) that has passed both chambers of Congress in identical form and been signed into law by the president or passed over his veto, thus becoming law.

Adams, John Quincy: (MA) (Senate 1803–1808, Federalist; House 1831–1848, Whig) Served first in the Senate, resigning in 1808 upon leaving the Federalist Party. He served one term as president of the United States, returning to government in the House of Representatives three years after being defeated in 1828 for reelection as president. He became an important voice against slavery in the House and despite the gag rule managed to introduce numerous petitions protesting slavery and the slave trade. He was also an instrumental player in the *Amistad* incident in 1841, arguing for the slaves' freedom. He suffered a stroke and died in 1848.

advice and consent: Under the Constitution, presidential nominations for executive and judicial posts take effect only when confirmed by the Senate; international treaties become effective only when the Senate approves them by a two-thirds vote.

Albert, Carl: (OK) (House 1947–1977, Democrat) Speaker of the House from 1971 to 1977, he also served as House majority whip and majority leader and helped push through the Democratic agenda in the House, including Medicare. He chaired the chaotic 1968 Democratic Convention in Chicago. He eventually retired in 1977 in the wake of scandal.

Aldrich, Nelson: (RI) (Senate 1881–1911, Republican) A stalwart opponent to Theodore Roosevelt and a key member of the Senate Finance Committee, helping set tariffs. His intransigence prompted calls for the direct election of senators and the eventual passage of the Seventeenth Amendment.

Allison, William Boyd: (IA) (House 1863–1870; Senate 1873–1908, Republican) Chair of the powerful Senate Appropriations Committee for twenty-five years of his Senate tenure. He was part of a powerful group of four Senate chairmen who dominated and controlled Congress at the turn of the twentieth century. A strong supporter of business, particularly industrial and railroad interests, he favored "hard money" policies and high protective tariffs. He was a target of the early-twentieth-century muckrakers, and antagonism toward him served as a catalyst in the push for the Seventeenth Amendment.

amendment: A proposal to change the text of pending legislation. Any alteration of the text, whether in part or wholesale, must be done by amendment and then agreed to.

amendment in the nature of a substitute: An amendment that would strike out the entire text of a bill or other measure and insert a different full text.

apportionment: The distribution of seats in the House based on population. Seats in the House of Representatives are apportioned to the states on the basis of their population after every ten-year Census.

Armey, Dick: (TX) (House 1985–2003, Republican) As House Republican Conference chairman, joined Newt Gingrich in 1994 in creating the Contract with America and helping the Republican Party retake Congress. In the wake of the victory, he assumed the role of House majority leader, gaining great power and leading the Republican charge in the 1990s.

Baker, Howard, Jr.: (TN) (Senate 1967–1985, Republican) Nicknamed the "Great Conciliator," Baker was one of the more successful members of Congress in brokering agreements and getting legislation enacted without resorting to vitriol. He spent two terms as Senate minority leader (1977–1981) and two as majority leader (1981–1985). He was the ranking minority member on the Watergate Committee, asking the famous question, "What did the president know and when did he know it?"

Barkley, Alben W: (KY) (House 1913–1926; Senate 1927–1949, 1955–1956, Democrat) Began life as a Wilson Democrat in the House, becoming an ardent supporter of Franklin Delano Roosevelt and the New Deal in the Senate, and as Senate majority leader was often FDR's spokesman on the Hill. He broke with the president in 1944 over a tax bill and resigned his leadership position. He was reelected to the post and left the Senate to serve as vice president of the United States, where he presided regularly over the Senate, returning as a senator for one more term in 1955, until he died in 1956.

Bayh, Birch: (IN) (Senate 1963–1981, Democrat) Important player in the battle for women's rights in the 1970s, he was influential in the passage of Title IX, helping women gain equal opportunities in sports in public education. He served as the chairman of the Senate Subcommittee on Constitutional Amendments and was the main architect of both the Twenty-fifth Amendment (establishing the rules for presidential succession) and the Twenty-sixth Amendment (giving eighteen-year-olds the right to vote). He also helped create the Equal Rights Amendment but failed to get it ratified and worked hard, but unsuccessfully, to eliminate the Electoral College.

Benton, Thomas Hart: (MO) (Senate, 1821–1851: 1821–1824, Democratic-Republican; 1825–1851, Democrat) A strong supporter of President Andrew Jackson, led the Jackson forces in the Senate. In 1837, after Jackson was censured by the Senate, Benton, who had opposed the original censure movement, engineered the successful move to expunge the resolution from the Senate journal. In 1850 Benton was also involved in one of the Senate's explosive incidents when Mississippi senator Henry Foote pulled a gun on him and threatened to shoot him.

bicameral: Any legislative body, like the U.S. Congress, that consists of two separate chambers, or houses.

Bilbo, Theodore G.: (MS) (Senate 1935–1947, Democrat) A strong supporter of Franklin Delano Roosevelt's New Deal, he also was a strong backer of racist policies, supporting segregation and white supremacist attitudes. He pushed for the deportation of black Americans to Africa and was outspoken about his membership in the Ku Klux Klan. Bilbo worked against implementing the Fourteenth and Fifteenth Amendments and played a large role in filibustering an antilynching law that reached the Senate in 1938. His racist views came back to haunt him when, in 1946, the Republicans gained control of the Senate and refused to seat him.

bill: The primary mechanism used by senators and representatives for introducing their proposals (enacting or repealing laws, for example). Bills are designated either H.R. 1, H.R. 2 or S. 1, S. 2, and so on, depending on the order in which they are introduced. Bills can be public or private.

bipartisanship: Cooperation between the two parties.

Blaine, James G.: (ME) (House 1863–1876; Senate 1876–1881, Republican) One of the most powerful men in American politics in the second half of the nineteenth century, serving in both the House and the Senate, twice as secretary of state, and for two years as Speaker of the House and making two runs at the White House. He helped found the Republican Party. He proposed a constitutional amendment that would have forbade the use of public funds for religious schools. While it was defeated at the national level, such laws were adopted by many states.

Blount, William: (TN) (Senate 1796–1797, Democratic-Republican) One of Tennessee's first senators and a driving force in securing statehood for the territory. He did not last long in the Senate, being the first person to be expelled from the chamber and the only senator every impeached by the House.

Brooke, Edward: (MA) (Senate 1967–1979, Republican) The first African American elected to the Senate by popular vote. One of the more than twenty senators in history to receive the Presidential Medal of Freedom.

Brooks, Preston: (SC) (House 1853–1856, Democrat) Famed for his brutal assault on Senator Charles Sumner. He walked up on Sumner from behind, caning him and then leaving him in a pool of blood on the floor of the Senate.

Byrd, Robert C.: (WV) (House 1953–1959; Senate 1959–, Democrat) As of 2008, he is the longest-serving member in the history of the Senate and the longest-serving and oldest member of Congress. He has been president pro tempore (in the 110th Congress), Senate Conference secretary, majority whip, and twice majority leader.

Calhoun, John C.: (SC) (House 1811–1818, Democratic-Republican; Senate 1832–1843, 1845–1850, Democrat) Part of the Great Triumvirate of politicians, along with Daniel Webster and Henry Clay, who drove antebellum politics. He started his political life as a nationalist and supported the War of 1812 with England and internal improvements funded by the national government. In the 1820s he rejected nationalism (although always claiming to be a Unionist) in favor of states' rights, and in the early 1830s he broke with his former ally, Andrew Jackson, over the issue of tariffs. In his view of states' rights, states had the right to nullify federal laws that they deemed unconstitutional. He also propagated the idea of slavery as a positive good rather than a necessary evil.

Cannon, Joseph G.: (IL) (House 1873–1891, 1893–1913, Republican) Speaker of the House from 1903 to 1911 and the second-longest-serving Republican Speaker in congressional history. Known as "Uncle Joe," he ruled the House with an iron fist and is considered one of the most powerful Speakers in history. His uncompromising control led to a revolt among both Democrats and Republicans in 1910 that stripped the Speaker of many powers, including the chairmanship of the House Rules Committee.

Caraway, Hattie: (AK) (Senate 1931–1945, Democrat): Originally appointed to the Senate to take the seat vacated by her husband, Thaddeus Caraway, she was the second woman to serve in the Senate. She became the first woman elected to the upper chamber in 1932. Caraway also became the first woman to chair a Senate committee in 1933 and the first woman to preside over the Senate in 1943.

caucus: Conference of party members in Congress.

Chavez, Dennis: (NM) (House 1931–1934; Senate 1935–1962, Democrat) First American-born Hispanic senator. He introduced several civil rights bills, including the Fair Employment Practices Commission Bill, and was one of the first senators to denounce Joseph McCarthy.

Chisholm, Shirley: (NY) (House 1969–1983, Democrat) The first African American woman elected to Congress. She also was the first African American candidate for president of the United States and until 2008 came closer than any woman to running for president as the candidate of a major party.

Church, Frank: (ID) (Senate 1957–1981, Democrat) Important player in American foreign policy during the 1970s. He was one of the first senators publicly to oppose the Vietnam War and wrote two measures to bring the war to an end. He gained national recognition for hearings he held investigating activities by the FBI and CIA, culminating in the passage of the Foreign Intelligence Surveillance Act (FISA).

Clay, Henry: (KY) (House 1811–1826, Democratic-Republican; Senate: 1805–1810, Democratic-Republican; 1831–1836, Anti-Jacksonian; 1837–1852, Whig) One of the dominant figures in antebellum politics as Speaker of the House, a leader in the Senate, and secretary of state. Part of the Great Triumvirate, along with Daniel Webster and John C. Calhoun, he was known as the "Great Compromiser" and helped engineer a series of compromises beginning with the Missouri Compromise in 1820 to resolve sectional conflict. He helped found and lead the Whig Party and advocated nationalistic programs like the American System that emphasized internal improvements sponsored by the federal government. In 1957 he was named one of the five greatest senators in American history.

clean bill: After amendments have been made to a bill, with the consent of the committee, the chair can consolidate the proposed legislation, combining the original elements and amendments and reintroducing it as a clean bill. This is done so it can be considered as a whole, rather than by each individual amendment. Its goal is to speed up Senate action.

clerk of the House: The chief administrative officer of the House of Representatives, responsible for much of its administrative business. His or her duties correspond to those of the secretary of the Senate.

cloakroom: Long narrow rooms adjacent to the House and Senate chambers. Each party has one for private conversations, to make phone calls, to get snacks, and so on.

closed rule: A House rule that forbids any member from adding an amendment to a bill under consideration, unless the person making the proposal is a member of the committee reporting the bill.

cloture: The procedure by which the Senate can end a filibuster. It is a motion that cuts off or chokes off debate. It takes sixty votes to invoke cloture. A successful cloture vote guarantees that the debated proposal will get a vote on final passage. Once adopted, it does not terminate debate immediately. Rather, thirty additional hours, if needed, are provided for further debate. Rarely does the Senate use the extra time.

committee report: All materials reported out of committee are accompanied by a report that explains the proposed piece of legislation and arguments for and against it.

committees: Groups in the House and Senate that do the bulk of the work. They initially review all proposed legislation and make decisions on whether legislation should be considered further either in a subcommittee or by the chamber as a whole. Each committee has a specific jurisdiction, based on policy issues, although there may be some overlapping areas of concern. Both houses have approximately twenty standing committees in addition to various subcommittees, select committees, and joint committees. Each member of the House works on an average of two committees. Senators serve on approximately four.

concurrent resolution: Passed by both the Senate and the House, it is not presented to the president and does not have the force of law (in contrast to a joint resolution). Concurrent resolutions are often used to deal with administrative matters that may affect both houses, like a budget resolution, a time for adjournment, an expression of the sense of Congress on a certain issue, the creation of temporary joint committees, and so on.

conference committee: A temporary, ad hoc panel composed of House and Senate negotiators. It is formed to resolve differences that arise when different versions of the same bill are passed by both chambers. Any new compromise bill must be approved by both houses and then forwarded to the president, like any other pending legislation.

confirmation: The constitutionally required consent of the Senate to appointments of high-level executive officials and federal judges by the president.

Congressional Record: The daily printed account of proceedings in both the House and Senate. It contains everything said on the floor of the House and Senate. (Prior to publication, members have the opportunity to edit and revise statements they have made and to insert text.) It contains all roll-call votes conducted each day. It is published by the Government Printing Office.

Conkling, Roscoe: (NY) (House 1859–1862, 1865–1866; Senate 1867–1882, Republican) An important part of the New York political machine in the late nineteenth century, his feud with President James Garfield over patronage ended in the assassination of Garfield, the crashing halt of Conkling's political career, and passage of the Civil Service Act in an attempt to end the abuses of patronage.

Crittenden, John J.: (KY) (Senate 1817–1819, Democratic-Republican; 1835–1841, 1842–1848, Whig; 1855–1861, American; 1861–1862, Unionist) Famous for the last-minute sectional compromise that bears his name. He proposed it to prevent a civil war that saw one son on each side of the conflict. It contained six constitutional amendments that would have made the Missouri Compromise permanent, denied Congress the power to interrupt the interstate slave trade, obligated Congress to reimburse those who lost slaves due to failed enforcement of fugitive slave laws, guaranteed the permanence of the constitutional provisions regarding fugitive slaves and the three-fifths compromise, and guaranteed that Congress could not interfere with slavery in the southern states. It was rejected by the Republican Party and never came to a vote.

DeLay, Tom: (TX) (House 1985–2006, Republican) Served as both deputy minority whip and majority whip. He was instrumental in the Republican revolution in the 1990s and helped initiate the K Street Project. He helped orchestrate the impeachment of President Bill Clinton in 1998. DeLay became a powerful force in Congress, uniting Republicans behind President George W. Bush's agenda in the wake of the 2000 election. Elected majority leader in 2002, he helped orchestrate redistricting in Texas to aid Republicans in upcoming elections. He eventually was forced to resign from the House after a grand jury indicted him for campaign fraud and indiscretions connected to the Abramoff scandal.

delegates: Legislators who vote based on the view of their constituents, even if it is at odds with their personal choice.

Dirksen, Everett: (IL) (House 1933–1948; Senate 1951–1970, Republican) Served eight terms in the House until health problems forced him to retire from government. He returned three years later to the Senate and was minority leader in 1959–1969. His influence helped pass the Civil Rights Act of 1964 by virtue of his support for cloture to end the filibuster that had stalled it. He was one of the most powerful men in the Senate during his tenure, and one of the first to broadcast televised opposition speeches to counter the president's State of the Union Address.

discharge petition: Procedural mechanism to get a bill out of committee in the House. A majority of the members of the House must sign it.

discharge resolution: A special motion in the Senate that any senator may introduce to relieve a committee from consideration of a bill before it. The resolution can be called up for Senate approval or disapproval in the same manner as any other Senate business.

divided party government: When one party controls the White House and another party controls one or both houses of Congress.

Douglas, Stephen A.: (IL) (House 1843–1846; Senate 1847–1862, Democrat): Known as the "Little Giant," was a leading political figure in the decade prior to the Civil War. He engineered the passage of the Compromise of 1850 and the Kansas-Nebraska Act of 1854 as attempts to stall sectional conflict and division. However, much to his chagrin, both actions helped fuel growing discontent and create the Republican Party and the emergence of Abraham Lincoln. He engaged in a famous series of debates with Abraham Lincoln during the election of 1858. His rejection of attempts to institute a federal slave code helped split the Democratic Party irreparably.

Drinan, Father Robert: (MA) (House 1971–1981, Democrat) Originally elected to the House on an anti–Vietnam War platform, he was the first Roman Catholic priest to serve in Congress. He was the first member of Congress to call for the impeachment of President Richard Nixon. He did so not in the wake of the Watergate break-in, but rather for the secret bombing of Cambodia. However, the House Judiciary Committee voted against including that charge in the articles of impeachment that were approved and reported to the full House. Despite being a priest, he regularly drew the ire of the Catholic Church hierarchy because of his support for abortion rights. His political career ended when Pope John Paul II demanded that priests not participate in electoral politics.

elastic clause: *see* Necessary and Proper Clause

enacting clause: Key phrase in bills beginning "Be it enacted by the Senate and House of Representatives. . . ." It notes the authority by which Congress passes the bill. No potential legislation can move forward without such a clause. A successful motion to strike it from legislation kills the measure.

engrossed bill/engrossed measure: The version of a bill that has passed one house of Congress and is then sent to the other. It notes all changes that have been made to the original version.

enrolled act: Final version of a bill (or resolution) approved by both houses and certified by an officer of the chamber of origin (clerk of the House or secretary of the Senate). It is printed on parchment paper and forwarded for signatures by the Speaker of the House, the president pro tempore of the Senate, and the president of the United States.

enumerated powers: powers given explicitly to Congress in Article I of the Constitution.

Ervin, Sam: (NC) (House 1945–1946; Senate 1953–1974, Democrat) A constitutional expert, achieved national attention as the chair of the Watergate Committee that investigated President Richard Nixon during the early 1970s in the wake of the Watergate break-in. He chaired the televised hearings and was an important force in the events leading to Nixon's resignation.

ex officio: Literally, "by virtue of office." In both chambers it means that the chair and ranking member of a committee are considered to be members of all the committee's subcommittees. This means they have the right to participate in all subcommittee meetings.

expulsion: Under the Constitution, the House or the Senate can expel one of its members. Expulsion requires a two-thirds vote, and it is limited to misconduct while in office, not anything done prior to election. It has rarely been used in the history of Congress, as both chambers tend to defer to the voters or to courts of law regarding whether or not a member should be unseated.

Felton, Rebecca Lattimer: (GA) (Senate 1921–1922, Democrat) Appointed to fill a vacancy, she was the first woman to serve in the Senate, although her term lasted for only twenty-four hours.

filibuster: The term applied to extended debate in the Senate. It is a product of the rule of unlimited debate in that chamber. It is used as a delaying tactic. Refusal to give up the floor prevents business from moving forward and halts pending legislation.

floor leaders: The members of Congress responsible for shepherding a bill through the legislative process. They are usually the chairman or ranking minority member of the committee or subcommittee that considered the bill before it reached the floor.

Ford, Gerald: (MI) (House 1949–1973, Republican) In the early 1960s he assumed leadership positions including chairman of the House Republican Conference, making him the third-ranking party member. In 1963 Ford was a leader of the Young Turks, a group of disgruntled young Republicans. Two years later he was elected minority leader, a position he held until he left the House to become vice president in 1973. He played an important part in the Republican opposition to President Lyndon Johnson's domestic programs and foreign policy, including Vietnam. Ford's loyalty to President Richard Nixon saw him become the first man to assume the vice presidency under the Twenty-fifth Amendment and eventually president following Nixon's resignation.

franking privilege: Free mail service for senators and representatives.

Fulbright, J. William: (AK) (House 1943–1944; Senate 1945–1974, Democrat) Served as chairman of the Senate Foreign Relations Committee from 1959 to 1974. He sponsored the Fulbright Scholars Act, which grants money to Americans to study overseas and brings foreign scholars to the United States. In 1964 he shepherded the Gulf of Tonkin Resolution through Congress, giving President Lyndon Johnson the authority to escalate the war in Vietnam. Eventually, he reversed his view of the war and led nationally televised hearings on the conflict.

germane: Something relevant to the subject of the pending bill. An amendment is either germane or nongermane. Being germane is not a requirement in the Senate; Senate rules permit senators to offer amendments to any bill on any subject. In the House, all amendments must be germane. Exceptions can be made by special rule.

gerrymandering: Drawing legislative district boundary lines for the benefit of one political party. It is usually controlled by the majority party and done to create "safe seats" for incumbents.

Gingrich, Newt: (GA) (House 1979–1999, Republican) Speaker of the House from 1995 to 1999. He was the leader of the House conservatives from the early 1980s and led the charge against Democratic control of the House, forcing the resignation of Jim Wright as Speaker in 1989. He led the Republican revolution with his "Contract with America," championing a balanced budget amendment, welfare restrictions and reform, and term limits. His successful overthrow of Democratic control made him the first Republican Speaker in forty years in 1995. He was eventually investigated for campaign funding violations and resigned his seat in 1999.

Goldwater, Barry: (AZ) (Senate 1953–1965, 1969–1987, Republican) Known as "Mr. Conservative," Goldwater is often credited with the resurgence of Republican conservative thought. He was a staunch opponent of the New Deal and liberal Democrats but also challenged Republican leadership to stick to conservative principles. After losing the presidential election in 1964, he retired from politics until 1968, when he was returned to the Senate. He became the spokesman for the conservative wing of the Republican Party, supporting the war in Vietnam and President Richard Nixon's foreign policy while critical of his domestic agenda. Ronald Reagan adopted much of the Goldwater ideology to win the presidency in 1980, but like others before him, failed to win Goldwater over on matters of social policy. Goldwater's conservatism always belied his emphasis on individual choice, his later support of gay rights and abortion rights, and his overall rejection of government-enforced morality.

Graham, Lindsey: (SC) (House 1995–2003; Senate 2003–, Republican) Upon entering Congress Graham became an important member of the Judiciary Committee and rose to power during President Bill Clinton's impeachment. He achieved national attention as one of the House managers who prosecuted Clinton in the Senate trial.

hearings: Formal proceedings held by committees (or subcommittees). Members invite witnesses to testify and provide information and opinions on matters of interest to the committee, usually in regard to their support of or opposition to a bill.

Helms, Jesse: (NC) (Senate 1973–2003, Republican) Helms was the first Republican elected to the Senate from North Carolina in the twentieth century. He was a leading conservative in the Senate, who as chairman of the Senate Agriculture Committee lobbied strongly for the tobacco industry. At times Helms seemed like an anachronism, with his anti–United Nations, anti-Communist, antigovernment, antigay, antispending, antiwelfare, anti–arms control, anti–foreign aid, and promilitary positions. He tended to be more of an opponent to a variety of programs, often blocking legislation and appointments, than an advocate who introduced legislation to support his viewpoint. Helms died in July 2008.

hold: Procedural move in the Senate in which a member temporarily blocks a bill or nomination.

hopper: Box on House clerk's desk where members deposit bills and resolutions to introduce them. In the Senate there is no box. Senators hand their bill to a clerk at the rostrum.

impeachment: Part of the system of checks and balances in the Constitution, by which Congress can remove members of the government for "treason, bribery, or other high crimes and misdemeanors." The House votes on the charges, and the trial takes place in the Senate, with the members of that body serving as the jury.

incumbent: Current officeholder.

Inouye, Daniel: (HI) (House 1959–1963; Senate 1963–, Democrat) As of 2008, the third most tenured senator. Upon Hawaii's entrance into the Union as a state, he was its first representative in the House and is the first Japanese American to serve in the House and the Senate.

Johnson, Lyndon: (TX) (House, 1937–1949; Senate 1949–1960, Democrat) Originally elected to the House out of rural Texas as a New Deal Democrat, he was a strong supporter of FDR. After a little over a decade in the House, he won election to the Senate in a very close election and proceeded to establish his power base by aligning with senior senators, most notably Richard Russell, the most powerful man in the Senate. Johnson quickly worked his way into a leadership position when he was elected minority leader in 1953. He was the least senior senator ever elected to that position. His first action was to abolish the seniority system for committee appointments while retaining it for committee chairs. When the Democrats took control of the Senate the next year, he became the youngest majority leader in history, and one of the most powerful and effective ones. Johnson worked with both the Speaker of the House, Sam Rayburn, and President Dwight Eisenhower to avoid excessive political partisanship and pass much of Eisenhower's domestic and foreign agenda. In the wake of *Brown v. Board of Education* (1954), he was one of only three southern politicians who refused to sign the Southern Manifesto protesting the decision. Although he did help scuttle a civil rights bill in 1956, he was a major force in the passage of the first civil rights legislation adopted by the Senate since Reconstruction, the Civil Rights Act of 1957.

joint committee: Committee including membership from both houses of Congress, with equal numbers of House and Senate members. Joint committees are usually established with narrow jurisdictions that include administrative duties or conducting research and issuing studies. They do not consider or report legislation.

joint resolution: Designated as H.J. Res. or S.J. Res. It must be passed by both houses and signed by the president, just like a bill. If approved it has the force of law. Joint resolutions tend to deal with limited matters, such as the correction of errors in existing law, continuing appropriations, a single appropriation, or the establishment of permanent joint committees. Joint resolutions can be used to propose constitutional amendments. In these cases, presidential approval is not necessary, and the amendment takes effect when ratified by three-quarters of the states.

joint session: When the House and Senate meet together to conduct formal business or to hear an address by the president of the United States.

Jordan, Barbara: (TX) (House 1973–1979, Democrat) In 1972 she became the first black woman from a southern state elected to the House. She was also the first black woman to deliver the keynote address at the Democratic National Convention, giving what some people consider the greatest convention keynote speech in history.

Journal: The official record of the proceedings of the House and Senate. The keeping of such records is mandated by the Constitution. It is similar to the minutes of a meeting. Each chamber has a clerk who keeps the Journal noting the business of the day, including roll-call votes and all motions and amendments adopted. Unlike the Congressional Record, the Journal does not record debates.

Kennedy, Edward "Ted": (MA) (Senate 1961–, Democrat) Perhaps most famous for the tragedy that has surrounded his family, he has nevertheless carved out a long-important role in the Senate. Originally, he assumed his seat to finish the term of his brother, John, and was then elected eight more times. He is know for his liberal stances, especially on social issues dealing with education and health care. His personal life has been filled with scandal, including a 1969 car accident where his companion, a young woman named Mary Jo Kopechne, died when he drove the car off a bridge at Chappaquiddick. The voters responded positively, and Kennedy stayed in office. Since then he has been a steady opponent to Republican presidents and a staunch advocate of national health, tax reform, and improved education.

La Follette, Robert M., Sr.: (WI) (House 1885–1890; Senate 1905–1925, Republican) Known as "Battling Bob," he was named by a Senate committee as one of the five greatest senators of all time. La Follette was a champion of the Progressive cause. He pushed for regulation of the railroads, direct election of senators, and protection for workers while opposing entry into World War I and condemning restrictions on civil liberties both during and after the war. He initiated the investigation that led to the Teapot Dome scandal. La Follette's views were summed up in his run for the presidency in 1924, when the Progressive ticket he headed stood for government ownership of railroads and utilities, cheap credit for farmers, support of labor unions, elimination of child labor, and increased protection of civil liberties. On the foreign front, he pushed for an end to American imperialism, especially in Latin America, and backed the demand that a national vote be required before the country ever went to war again.

La Follette, Robert M., Jr.: (WI) (Senate 1925–1934, Republican; 1934–1947, Progressive) Despite his Republican roots, La Follette championed liberal causes, especially in the areas of civil liberties and labor issues. The son of La Follette Sr.—Battling Bob— whom he replaced, La Follette Jr. won election in his own right three times. He argued for farm relief, the right of labor to organize, and reform of the tax system. On foreign relations he took an antiwar view, making him an isolationist prior to the outbreak of World War II and one of the founders of the America First Committee. One of his last actions in the Senate was the drafting and passage of the Legislative Reorganization Act of 1946, helping streamline Senate procedures. He eventually lost his seat in a primary to Joseph McCarthy, which began a downward spiral culminating in La Follette's suicide in 1953.

lame duck: After an election, when Congress convenes, any member who has not been reelected or will not be returning in the new session is a lame duck.

law, public law, private law: A law is any legislation passed by both the House and the Senate and signed by the president or passed over his veto. Public laws affect the country as a whole. Private laws affect single entities (that is, one individual or institution).

Lodge, Henry Cabot: (MA) (House 1887–1892; Senate 1892–1924, Republican) Lodge was a hard-core Republican and staunch patriot. He served as president pro tempore and chair of the Republican Conference, placing him in positions of great power. As the chair of the Senate Foreign Relations Committee, he vehemently opposed President Woodrow Wilson and the Treaty of Versailles. Miffed at what he perceived as Wilson's ignoring of him, Lodge managed to block the treaty in the Senate and therefore the subsequent participation of the United States in the League of Nations.

logrolling: The bargaining and vote trading that takes place between members of Congress.

Long, Huey: (LA) (Senate 1931–1936, Democrat) Nicknamed the "Kingfish," he favored radical populist policies, originally supporting FDR and his New Deal. In the Senate, as his power grew he began to challenge the president, and as early as 1933 he opposed New Deal programs such as the National Recovery Act and led a three-week filibuster against the Glass-Steagall Banking Act. The next year he introduced his Share the Wealth program, which argued for a radical redistribution of wealth through a new tax code; huge aid grants for education, the elderly, veterans, and farmers; and a work week of thirty hours. In the wake of the rejection of his program, Long mounted a national campaign to oppose Roosevelt and the Democratic Party. Some historians credit his pressure on the White House as being the inspiration behind the more liberal New Deal programs such as Social Security and the Works Progress Administration. Long's challenge was cut short by an assassin's bullet in September 1935.

Lott, Trent: (LA) (House 1973–1988; Senate 1989–2007, Republican) One of the first Republicans (along with William Cochran) elected to Congress from Mississippi since Reconstruction. In the House he served as minority whip, the first southern Republican to rise to such a high leadership position. He moved to the Senate in 1988, became majority whip in 1995, and assumed the majority leadership position in 1996. He played a major role in the impeachment of President Bill Clinton, when despite the apparent lack of votes, he proceeded with the trial. He fell from grace when, at a party for Strom Thurmond in 2002, he remarked, "When Strom Thurmond ran for president, we voted for him. We're proud of it. And if the rest of the country had followed our lead, we wouldn't have had all these problems over the years, either." Thurmond had run on a segregationist Dixiecrat ticket, and the ensuing firestorm around Lott's comments forced him to resign his leadership position. He regained power in 2007 when he was named minority whip. However, he retired near the end of the year.

Madison, James: (VA) (House 1789–1796, Anti-Administration, Democratic-Republican) A leader of the early House of Representatives, at first he worked with President George Washington in organizing the new government. He was an important architect of the Constitution, and in the First Congress, he authored the amendments that became the Bill of Rights. He eventually teamed up with Thomas Jefferson to challenge the Federalist Party's policies.

majority leader: In the House, the leader of the majority party and the second most powerful member in the chamber. Elected by the party caucus. In the Senate, the leader of the majority party, elected by party members, who performs functions similar to those of Speaker in the House.

Mansfield, Mike: (MT) (Senate 1953–1977, Democrat) Followed Lyndon Johnson as Senate majority leader, becoming the longest-serving majority leader in the history of the Senate. With a very different style from Johnson that did not resemble the latter's "master of the Senate" style, Mansfield was far more permissive, much to the dismay of some of his colleagues, including Johnson. Nevertheless, he played an important part in pushing the legislation of the Great Society and helped break the filibuster in 1964 against the Civil Rights Act.

markup: The process by which congressional committees and subcommittees debate, amend, and rewrite proposed legislation.

McCarthy, Joseph: (WI) (Senate 1947–1957, Republican) Had a fairly undistinguished career in politics until he garnered national attention with a speech in Wheeling, West Virginia, in 1950, accusing the State Department of being overrun with Communists. McCarthy used his anti-Communist rhetoric to gain a national platform, and he continued to make accusations, even when he had little facts to base those accusations on. He doggedly pursued Communists in the government, and the early 1950s became known as the McCarthy Era. Televised hearings of his investigation of the army were the beginning of his fall. In 1954, with the Democrats back in control of the Senate, he was formally "condemned" by that chamber. While it was not officially a censure, the official Senate documents note it as such. This was only the fourth time in history that the Senate exercised such power against one of its members. Following the rebuke, McCarthy's power waned, he was ostracized by his colleagues, and eventually died in 1957 from heavy drinking that led to cirrhosis of the liver.

minority leader: Leader of the minority party or the party not in power in either house.

Necessary and Proper Clause: The final, eighteenth clause of Article I, Section 8 of the Constitution, stating that Congress can "make all laws which shall be necessary and proper for carrying into Execution the foregoing Powers." Over time it has been the window to expansive congressional power, especially under the Commerce, Spending, and Taxing clauses.

Nixon, Richard: (CA) (House 1946–1950; Senate 1950–1952, Republican) Nixon made his first claim to fame as a member of the House Un-American Activities Committee (HUAC), participating in that panel's investigation of Alger Hiss in the late 1940s. He was elected to the Senate based on a vicious red-baiting campaign against Helen Gahagan Douglas, accusing her of sympathizing with Communists. While he labeled her the "pink lady," she dubbed him "Tricky Dick." He left the Senate to run for vice president on Dwight Eisenhower's ticket in the 1952 election.

nongermane amendment: An amendment that is not of the same subject matter as the bill to which it is offered as an attachment. In the Senate it is often referred to as a rider.

O'Neill, Thomas "Tip": (MA) (House 1953–1986, Democrat) Originally entered the House taking the seat vacated by Senator-elect John F. Kennedy. He quickly became a leading player in House politics, assuming a position on the important House Rules Committee in his second term. In 1971 he became majority whip and two years later was chosen majority leader, leaving him at the head of the fight in the House for the impeachment of President Richard Nixon. With the demise of Carl Albert as Speaker due to scandal, O'Neill assumed that position in 1977. Although a powerful speaker with a large majority, O'Neill struggled at times to put forth the Democratic agenda. A sharp critic of President Ronald Reagan's policies, he was subjected to bitter Republican attacks in the early 1980s.

open rule: Permits any amendment to a bill under consideration on the floor of the House, within the allotted time.

override: When Congress reverses a presidential veto. A two-thirds majority is required in both houses to overturn such a presidential action.

pocket veto: When the president takes no action on a bill for ten days and Congress is in adjournment, the bill is considered vetoed, does not become law, and is not returned to the Congress for a possible override.

pork barreling: Legislation designed to direct government benefits such as jobs, bridges, highways, dams, military installations, government projects, and so on to a particular district, used as political patronage.

Powell, Adam Clayton: (NY) (House 1945–1972, Democrat) The first black member of Congress from New York. He focused on eradicating racial segregation, especially in public school systems and the military. He served on the Education and Labor Committee and became its chairman in 1960. That leadership position enabled him to play a key role in passage of a minimum wage act, antipoverty acts, and other major pieces of social legislation, especially those connected to Johnson's Great Society. Despite these accomplishments, Powell made many enemies both in and out of Congress. He was cited for contempt of court in 1966 for refusing to pay damages from a lawsuit, and in 1967 the House refused to seat him. He was finally admitted to the House but denied his committee chairmanship and stripped of his seniority. In 1969 the Supreme Court of the United States ruled he had been unconstitutionally denied his position. He failed to win the Democratic primary in 1970, however, and retired to the island of Bimini.

president of the Senate: The vice president of the United States. In actual practice, because the vice president rarely attends meetings of the Senate, presiding duties are performed by a designated substitute, either the president pro tempore of the Senate or a majority party senator filling in for a while in the chair.

president pro tempore: The "president for a time" is elected by the Senate and is, by custom, the senator of the majority party with the longest record of continuous service. He or she acts as the chair when the vice president is not present.

private law: Legislation passed to the benefit of a single entity, not the nation as a whole.

Proxmire, William: (WI) (Senate 1957–1989, Democrat) Holds the record for consecutive roll-call votes cast at 10,252. An early critic of the Vietnam War, he challenged both Presidents Lyndon Johnson and Richard Nixon over foreign policy. As a member of the Senate Armed Services Committee, he focused on waste in the military and was a critic of much pork barrel legislation concerning the armed forces. He introduced the Golden Fleece Award to focus attention on wasteful government spending. He was an early advocate of campaign finance reform and worked hard to get the United States to ratify the Convention on Prevention and Punishment of the Crime of Genocide.

public law: General legislation passed by Congress that applies to the whole Union.

quorum: The number of members who must be present before business can be conducted. In the House the quorum is 218. (The number is only 100 when the House meets as a Committee of the Whole.) In the Senate fifty-one members must be present. There, business is often conducted in the absence of one, unless a point of order is raised.

quorum call: Calling the roll to see if a quorum is present so business can be conducted.

Rankin, Jeannette: (MT) (House 1917–1919, 1941–1943, Republican) First woman elected to Congress. She voted against entry into World War I. That vote, combined with her "radical" views on trade union rights, equal pay for women, and birth control, led to her exit from Congress after one term. She reentered Congress in the early 1940s and was the only person in either chamber to vote against entry into World War II.

ranking minority member: The minority party committee member with the most seniority.

Rayburn, Sam: (TX) (House 1913–1961, Democrat) At the time of his death in 1961, he had served longer in the House than any other member. He held the position of Speaker through every Democratic-controlled Congress between 1940 and 1961 (1940–1947, 1949–1953, 1955–1961). On three different occasions he was chairman of the Democratic National Convention (1948, 1952, 1956). Rayburn was a key figure in pushing through much of FDR's New Deal legislation in the late 1930s. He helped solidify support for World War II, supported Harry Truman's programs, and teamed with Lyndon Johnson during the Eisenhower Administration. Rayburn's support was crucial to Johnson's quest for the White House in 1960.

reapportionment: The practice of redrawing congressional district lines and adjusting the number of representatives in the House for each state.

Reed, Thomas: (ME) (House 1877–1900, Republican) Served as the Speaker of the House during 1889–1891 and 1895–1899. As Speaker he introduced what came to be known as the Reed Rules in 1890. Under these rules, Reed could strong-arm votes, most importantly by determining quorum in the House by counting members who were present, rather than only those who voted, undercutting those members who tried to stymie legislation by abstaining. These rules dramatically increased the power of the Speaker. Through his enlarged power he regularly prevented minority party members from obstructing legislation and was able to push a conservative Republican agenda through. The Reed Rules paved the way for the ascendancy of "Uncle Joe" Cannon.

restricted rule: Allows only those amendments specified to be added to a bill under consideration in the House.

Revels, Hiram: (MS) (Senate 1869–1870, Republican) He was the first African American to serve in the Senate, sent by the state legislature to fill a vacated seat.

rider: Amendment to a bill that may or may not be germane to the bill's purposes.

roll-call vote: When the full House or Senate votes and each individual member's votes are recorded and made public.

Rostenkowski, Dan: (IL) (House 1959–1995, Democrat) Rostenkowski was an important congressional power broker who eventually chaired the important House Ways and Means Committee, helping determine tax and trade policy from 1981 until his untimely exit in 1995. His career came to a grinding halt when he was indicted on seventeen felony charges during a scandal dealing with the House post office. He pleaded guilty in April 1996 to two counts of misuse of public funds and was sentenced to seventeen months in federal prison. He was released in 1997. His corruption (and that of others) helped fuel the Republican call for the Contract with America.

rules: The House has twenty-eight permanent standing rules that govern its procedures. The various rules that direct legislative procedure come from a variety of sources, including precedent, rule-making provisions in certain laws, and the U.S. Constitution. Robert's Rules of Order do not govern House procedure. House rules that have developed over time are unique to the House. In the Senate there are forty-three permanent rules. Senate rules are also the products of precedent, rule-making provisions, and the Constitution.

Russell, Richard: (GA) (Senate 1931–1971, Democrat) A strong supporter of the military, agriculture, and racial segregation. He championed programs that included the Agricultural Adjustment Act, the Farm Security Act, the National School Lunch Act, federal farm relief, and soil conservation. Despite his support of the military, he opposed sending troops to Vietnam. He was a member of the Warren Commission in the wake of the assassination of John F. Kennedy. One of his great negative legacies was his role as the leader of the anti–civil rights forces in the Senate—the southern bloc. As a leader of that faction, he championed states' rights and segregation, breaking with his protégé, Lyndon Johnson.

select or special committee: A committee established for a limited time to perform a particular study or investigation. These committees might be given or denied authority to report legislation to their respective houses.

seniority: Custom that defers to those members of Congress who have served the longest period of time in making selections for chair or ranking minority member of a committee. It has greater impact in the Senate than the House.

sergeant at arms: The law enforcement officer for each house of Congress, charged with keeping order.

Smith, Margaret Chase: (ME) (House 1939–1948; Senate 1949–1972, Republican) The first woman to serve in both houses of Congress. One of Smith's strengths was that she did not focus just on women's issues but also was very active on the Senate Armed Services Committee, influencing foreign policy and military affairs. She came to national attention in 1950 as the first senator to challenge Joseph McCarthy and his tactics. Her Declaration of Conscience brought her so much attention she was considered as a possible vice presidential candidate on the 1952 Republican ticket. She did make a run at the presidency in 1964, when she became the first woman to ever have her name placed in nomination for the presidency.

Southern Bloc: The name given to a group of conservative southern Democratic senators, joined by one Republican, John Tower of Texas, who tried to block government efforts to end segregation and desegregate the South. Led by Richard Russell of Georgia, they unsuccessfully tried to stop the Civil Rights Act of 1964.

Speaker of the House: Presiding officer of the House of Representatives, and ostensibly the most powerful figure, because he or she is chosen by the majority party. Also, third in line for the presidency, after the vice president.

special or select committee: Committee established for a specific purpose, often to conduct an investigation or study a specific problem.

standing committees: Permanent committees in the House and Senate that deal with matters within a specific subject area like agriculture, foreign affairs, education, and so on and that decide if and when legislation will move forward for consideration.

Stevens, Thaddeus: (PA) (House 1849–1852, Whig; 1859–1868, Republican) A leader of the Radical Republicans in the House before, during, and after the Civil War, Stevens was an ardent abolitionist who worked assiduously against what he perceived as a conspiracy of slave power forces to undermine American liberty. During the Civil War, Stevens—chairman of the Ways and Means Committee—was one of the most powerful men in the House, dominating debates over Reconstruction and helping to draft the Fourteenth Amendment and the Reconstruction Act of 1867. He proposed taking southern plantations from their owners and distributing the land to former slaves. He led the charge to impeach President Andrew Johnson in 1868.

subcommittees: Subunits of a committee established for the purpose of dividing the committee's workload. They deal with issues before the full committee does, and any of their recommendations must be approved by the full standing committee before submission to the floor of the House or Senate.

Sumner, Charles: (MA) (Senate 1851–1856, Free Soil; 1857–1874, Republican) Involved in a variety of antebellum reform movements, including abolitionism. He was an opponent of Sen. Stephen Douglas and the Kansas-Nebraska Act of 1854. In the midst of violence in Kansas, he gave one of the great speeches of congressional history in May 1856 titled "The Crime against Kansas." Part of the speech ridiculed Sen. Andrew Butler of South Carolina, who was not in attendance. In retaliation, two days later Butler's nephew, Preston Brooks, clubbed Sumner senseless. It took Sumner three years to recover, but he was reelected. Leading the Radical Republicans in the Senate, Sumner felt that Reconstruction was purely the province of Congress, and working with Thaddeus Stevens in the House, he led the forces attempting to convict President Andrew Johnson on impeachment.

Taft, Robert: (OH) (Senate 1939–1953, Republican) Nicknamed "Mr. Republican" for his domination of the Senate and the party. He was an ardent opponent of FDR's New Deal and sponsored one of the most important pieces of labor legislation in American history, the Taft-Hartley Labor Relations Act of 1947. He tried three times to get the Republican nomination for the presidency but never received it. He became majority leader of the Senate in 1953, just before he died of cancer.

Thurmond, Strom: (SC) (Senate 1954–1964, Democrat; 1964–2003, Republican) Prior to his time in the Senate, Thurmond was nominated for president by the States' Rights Democrats (Dixiecrats). This group consisted of southerners who objected to President Harry Truman because of his civil rights initiative. Although he won thirty-nine electoral votes and expressed his distaste for the Democratic Party, he campaigned successfully for the Senate as a write-in candidate in 1954. He was the originator of the Southern Manifesto of 1956 that condemned the U.S. Supreme Court for its historic ruling in *Brown v. Board of Education* (1954). He holds the record for the longest filibuster in Senate history by speaking for twenty-four hours and eighteen minutes against the Civil Rights Act of 1957. Disenchanted with the Democrats, in 1964 he switched parties and supported Barry Goldwater in his unsuccessful attempt to win the presidency. Thurmond also helped orchestrate the "southern strategy" that helped put Richard Nixon in the White House in 1968 and culminated in the 2004 presidential election, when the Republican nominee won all the southern states. In 1996 he became the oldest sitting senator and in 1997 the longest serving. It was revealed after his death that despite his ardent segregationist position, he had fathered a daughter with his African American maid in 1925.

trustees: Legislators who vote based on their own conscience and values, not necessarily at the behest of their constituency.

unanimous consent: A process used to speed up consideration of noncontroversial measures on the House floor. Proceedings of the House or actions on legislation often take place by unanimous consent of the House (that is, without objection by any member).

unanimous consent agreements: Agreements negotiated among senators by the majority and minority leaders to limit debate on a specified measure, to restrict amendments to it, and to waive points of order. Require the consent of every senator. These agreements, also called "time agreements," are the Senate parallel to "special rules" from the House Rules Committee.

veto: Presidential action that rejects a bill or joint resolution.

Wagner, Robert: (NY) (Senate 1927–1949, Democrat) A strong supporter of labor during his time in the Senate and a strong supporter of the New Deal. He sponsored the National Industrial Recovery Act (1933), which provided for a minimum wage and maximum hours, the Social Security Act of 1935, and the National Labor Relations Act (1935), also known as the Wagner Act. The latter was probably the most progressive piece of labor legislation in American history, guaranteeing labor's right to organize and strike.

Watts, J. C.: (OK) (House 1995–2003, Republican) First black member of Congress to refuse to join the Congressional Black Caucus. Extremely critical of black Democratic leadership, he constantly accused caucus members of selling out African Americans by making them dependent upon government largesse. He gained national attention when he delivered the Republican response to President Bill Clinton's State of the Union Address in 1997. The following year he assumed the fourth highest party leadership position in the House as the chairman of the House Republican Conference.

Webster, Daniel: (NH, MA) (House 1813–1816, 1823–1828, Federalist; Senate 1827–1836, Anti-Jacksonian; 1837–1840, Whig; 1845–1850, Whig) Known as the "Great Orator" and one of the three men who made up the Great Triumvirate, along with Henry Clay and John C. Calhoun. Webster started his political career in the House as a Federalist and a staunch opponent of the War of 1812, often obstructing war legislation. He was a proponent of a national bank and opposed protective tariffs. His second stint in Congress left him supporting federal internal improvements and President John Quincy Adams. Upon his election to the Senate in 1827, he reversed his position to support a protective tariff, helping pass the Tariff of Abominations that triggered the Nullification Crisis of the 1830s. It was at this time that he gained his reputation as the Great Orator. His last great speech in the Senate was in support of the Compromise of 1850.

whip: The member in either chamber in charge of organizing party unity by acting as the liaison between the party leadership and the rank and file, supplying membership with needed information for upcoming votes and counting prospective votes.

Wilmot, David: (PA) (House, 1845–1850, Democrat; Senate 1861–1862, Republican) Helped trigger a heightening of sectional conflict when he proposed a rider to an appropriations bill. The rider, known as the Wilmot Proviso, would have prevented the spread of slavery into the territories. Although defeated, it ignited strong southern protest and paved the way to the Compromise of 1850.

Wright, Jim: (TX) (House 1955–1991, Democrat) Rose to prominence in the House as majority leader from 1976 until elected Speaker in 1987. His tenure as Speaker was short, as he resigned after two years amid charges of unethical conduct.

DOCUMENTS

JOHN ADAMS, *THOUGHTS ON GOVERNMENT* (1776)

After hostilities had broken out, and before the official Declaration of Independence, Adams ruminated over what was the best form of government, and how it should be constructed. He commented heavily on the need for a strong assembly, and what the scope of its power should be.

. . . We ought to consider, what is the end of government, before we determine which is the best form. Upon this point all speculative politicians will agree, that the happiness of society is the end of government, as all Divines and moral Philosophers will agree that the happiness of the individual is the end of man. From this principle it will follow, that the form of government, which communicates ease, comfort, security, or in one word happiness to the greatest number of persons, and in the greatest degree, is the best. . . .

If there is a form of government then, whose principle and foundation is virtue, will not every sober man acknowledge it better calculated to promote the general happiness than any other form?

Fear is the foundation of most governments; but is so sordid and brutal a passion, and renders men, in whose breasts it predominates, so stupid, and miserable, that Americans will not be likely to approve of any political institution which is founded on it.

Honor is truly sacred, but holds a lower rank in the scale of moral excellence than virtue. Indeed the former is but a part of the latter, and consequently has not equal pretensions to support a frame of government productive of human happiness. The foundation of every government is some principle or passion in the minds of the people. The noblest principles and most generous affections in our nature, then, have the fairest chance to support the noblest and most generous models of government . . .

As good government is an empire of laws, how shall your laws be made? In a large society, inhabiting an extensive country, it is impossible that the whole should assemble to make laws: The first necessary step, then, is, to depute power from the many to a few of the most wise and good. But by what rules shall you chuse your representatives? Agree upon the number and qualifications of persons, who shall have the benefit of choosing, or annex this priviledge to the inhabitants of a certain extent of ground.

The principal difficulty lies, and the greatest care should be employed in constituting this Representative Assembly. It should be in miniature, an exact portrait of the people at large. It should think, feel, reason, and act like them. That it may be the interest of this Assembly to do strict justice at all times, it should be an equal representation, or in other words equal interest among the people should have equal interest in it. Great care should be taken to effect this, and to prevent unfair, partial, and corrupt elections. Such regulations, however, may be better made in times of greater tranquility than the present, and they will spring up of themselves naturally, when all the powers of government come to be in the hands of the people's friends. At present it will be safest to proceed in all established modes to which the people have been familiarised by habit.

A representation of the people in one assembly being obtained, a question arises whether all the powers of government, legislative, executive, and judicial, shall be left in this body? I think a people cannot be long free, nor ever happy, whose government is in one Assembly. My reasons for this opinion are as follow.

1. A single Assembly is liable to all the vices, follies and frailties of an individual. Subject to fits of humour, starts of passion, flights of enthusiasm, partialities of prejudice, and consequently productive of hasty results and absurd judgments: And all these errors ought to be corrected and defects supplied by some controuling power.
2. A single Assembly is apt to be avaricious, and in time will not scruple to exempt itself from burthens which it will lay, without compunction, on its constituents.
3. A single Assembly is apt to grow ambitious, and after a time will not hesitate to vote itself perpetual. This was one fault of the long parliament, but more remarkably of Holland, whose Assembly first voted themselves from annual to septennial, then for life, and after a course of years, that all vacancies happening by death, or otherwise, should be filled by themselves, without any application to constituents at all.
4. A Representative Assembly, altho' extremely well qualified, and absolutely necessary as a branch of the legislature, is unfit to exercise the executive power, for want of two essential properties, secrecy and dispatch.
5. A Representative Assembly is still less qualified for the judicial power; because it is too numerous, too slow, and too little skilled in the laws.
6. Because a single Assembly, possessed of all the powers of government, would make arbitrary laws for their own interest, execute all laws arbitrarily for their own interest, and adjudge all controversies in their own favour.

But shall the whole power of legislation rest in one Assembly? Most of the foregoing reasons apply equally to prove that the legislative power ought to be more complex— to which we may add, that if the legislative power is wholly in one Assembly, and the executive in another, or in a single person, these two powers will oppose and enervate upon each other, until the contest shall end in war, and the whole power, legislative and executive, be usurped by the strongest. . . .

To avoid these dangers let a [distinct] Assembly be constituted, as a mediator between the two extreme branches of the legislature, that which represents the people and that which is vested with the executive power.

Let the Representative Assembly then elect by ballot, from among themselves or their constituents, or both, a distinct Assembly, which for the sake of perspicuity we will call a Council. It may consist of any number you please, say twenty or thirty, and should have a free and independent exercise of its judgment, and consequently a negative voice in the legislature.

These two bodies thus constituted, and made integral parts of the legislature, let them unite, and by joint ballot choose a Governor, who, after being stripped of most of those badges of domination called prerogatives, should have a free and independent exercise of his judgment, and be made also an integral part of the legislature. This I know is liable to objections, and if you please you may make him only President of the Council, as in Connecticut: But as the Governor is to be invested with the executive power, with consent of Council, I think he ought to have a negative upon the legislative. If he is annually elective, as he ought to be, he will always have so much reverence and affection for the People, their Representatives and Councillors, that although you give him an independent exercise of his judgment, he will seldom use it in opposition to the two Houses, except in cases the public utility of which would be conspicuous, and some such cases would happen. . . .

A Constitution, founded on these principles, introduces knowledge among the People, and inspires them with a conscious dignity, becoming Freemen. A general emulation takes place, which causes good humour, sociability, good manners, and good morals to be general. That elevation of sentiment, inspired by such a government, makes the common people brave and enterprizing. That ambition which is inspired by it makes them sober, industrious and frugal. You will find among them some elegance, perhaps, but more solidity; a little pleasure, but a great deal of business—some politeness, but more civility. If you compare such a country with the regions of domination, whether Monarchial or Aristocratical, you will fancy yourself in Arcadia or Elisium.

If the Colonies should assume governments separately, they should be left entirely to their own choice of the forms, and if a Continental Constitution should be formed, it should be a Congress, containing a fair and adequate Representation of the Colonies, and its authority should sacredly be confined to these cases, viz. war, trade, disputes between Colony and Colony, the Post-Office, and the unappropriated lands of the Crown, as they used to be called.

These Colonies, under such forms of government, and in such a union, would be unconquerable by all the Monarchies of Europe. . . .

Source: *The Founders Constitution*, web edition. University of Chicago Press and the Liberty Fund. Philip B. Kurland and Ralph Lerner, eds. http://press-pubs.uchicago.edu/founders/documents/v1ch4s5.html

UNITED STATES CONSTITUTION (1787), ARTICLE I (EXCERPTS)

The Constitution lays out the basic power of Congress in Article I. While the Constitution seems to be explicit in creating a government of limited powers, as was evident very early on, the last clause of Section 8, the "necessary and proper" clause, opened the door for expansion of congressional and thus federal power. Much of Article I, and the powers expressed, are responses to inadequacies and shortcomings exhibited in the Articles of Confederation, which the Constitution replaced.

Article 1

Section 1: All legislative Powers herein granted shall be vested in a Congress of the United States, which shall consist of a Senate and House of Representatives.

Section 2, paragraph 5: The House of Representatives shall chuse their Speaker and other Officers; and shall have the sole Power of Impeachment.

Section 3, paragraph 6: The Senate shall have the sole Power to try all Impeachments. When sitting for that Purpose, they shall be on Oath or Affirmation. When the President of the United States is tried, the Chief Justice shall preside: And no Person shall be convicted without the Concurrence of two thirds of the Members present.

paragraph 7: Judgment in Cases of Impeachment shall not extend further than to removal from Office, and disqualification to hold and enjoy any Office of honor, Trust or Profit under the United States: but the Party convicted shall nevertheless be liable and subject to Indictment, Trial, Judgment and Punishment, according to Law.

Section 7, paragraph 1: All Bills for raising Revenue shall originate in the House of Representatives; but the Senate may propose or concur with Amendments as on other Bills.

paragraph 2: Every Bill which shall have passed the House of Representatives and the Senate, shall, before it become a Law, be presented to the President of the United States; If he approve he shall sign it, but if not he shall return it, with his Objections to that House in which it shall have originated, who shall enter the Objections at large on their Journal, and proceed to reconsider it. If after such Reconsideration two thirds of that House shall agree to pass the Bill, it shall be sent, together with the Objections, to the other House, by which it shall likewise be reconsidered, and if approved by two thirds of that House, it shall become a Law. But in all such Cases the Votes of both Houses shall be determined by Yeas and Nays, and the Names of the Persons voting for and against the Bill shall be entered on the Journal of each House respectively. If any Bill shall not be returned by the President within ten Days (Sundays excepted) after it shall have been presented to him, the Same shall be a Law, in like Manner as if he had signed it, unless the Congress by their Adjournment prevent its Return, in which Case it shall not be a Law.

Section. 8, paragraph 1: The Congress shall have Power To lay and collect Taxes, Duties, Imposts and Excises, to pay the Debts and provide for the common Defence and general Welfare of the United States; but all Duties, Imposts and Excises shall be uniform throughout the United States;

paragraph 2: To borrow Money on the credit of the United States;

paragraph 3: To regulate Commerce with foreign Nations, and among the several States, and with the Indian Tribes;

paragraph 4: To establish an uniform Rule of Naturalization, and uniform Laws on the subject of Bankruptcies throughout the United States;

paragraph 5: To coin Money, regulate the Value thereof, and of foreign Coin, and fix the Standard of Weights and Measures;

paragraph 6: To provide for the Punishment of counterfeiting the Securities and current Coin of the United States;

paragraph 7: To establish Post Offices and post Roads;

paragraph 8: To promote the Progress of Science and useful Arts, by securing for limited Times to Authors and Inventors the exclusive Right to their respective Writings and Discoveries;

paragraph 9: To constitute Tribunals inferior to the supreme Court;

paragraph 10: To define and punish Piracies and Felonies committed on the high Seas, and Offences against the Law of Nations;

paragraph 11: To declare War, grant Letters of Marque and Reprisal, and make Rules concerning Captures on Land and Water;

paragraph 12: To raise and support Armies, but no Appropriation of Money to that Use shall be for a longer Term than two Years;

paragraph 13: To provide and maintain a Navy;

paragraph 14: To make Rules for the Government and Regulation of the land and naval Forces;

paragraph 15: To provide for calling forth the Militia to execute the Laws of the Union, suppress Insurrections and repel Invasions;

paragraph 16: To provide for organizing, arming, and disciplining, the Militia, and for governing such Part of them as may be employed in the Service of the United States, reserving to the States respectively, the Appointment of the Officers, and the Authority of training the Militia according to the discipline prescribed by Congress;

paragraph 17: To exercise exclusive Legislation in all Cases whatsoever, over such District (not exceeding ten Miles square) as may, by Cession of particular States, and the Acceptance of Congress, become the Seat of the Government of the United States, and to exercise like Authority over all Places purchased by the Consent of the Legislature of the State in which the Same shall be, for the Erection of Forts, Magazines, Arsenals, dock-Yards, and other needful Buildings;—And

paragraph 18: To make all Laws which shall be necessary and proper for carrying into Execution the foregoing Powers, and all other Powers vested by this Constitution in the Government of the United States, or in any Department or Officer thereof.

Thomas Jefferson, "Opinion on the Constitutionality of a National Bank" (1791)

In the wake of Hamilton's proposal to create a national bank, great debate arose over how much power the Congress had to legislate, especially in terms of the "necessary and proper" clause of Article I, Section 8. President Washington asked Thomas Jefferson and Alexander Hamilton to submit opinions to him. The two arguments are classic expositions on how to interpret the Constitution, from Jefferson's strict construction model, to Hamilton's loose interpretative model. Hamilton's position won the day and helped establish the power of Congress to legislate in a broad manner, under its Article I powers.

I consider the foundation of the Constitution as laid on this ground: That "all powers not delegated to the United States, by the Constitution, nor prohibited by it to the States, are reserved to the States or to the people." To take a single step beyond the boundaries thus specially drawn around the powers of Congress, is to take possession of a boundless field of power, no longer susceptible of any definition.

The incorporation of a bank, and the powers assumed by this bill, have not, in my opinion, been delegated to the United States, by the Constitution.

I.   They are not among the powers specially enumerated: for these are: 1st A power to lay taxes for the purpose of paying the debts of the United States; but no debt is paid by this bill, nor any tax laid. Were it a bill to raise money, its origination in the Senate would condemn it by the Constitution.

1.   A power to *lay taxes* for the purpose of paying the debts of the U.S. But no debt is paid by this bill, nor any tax laid. Were it a bill to raise money, it's origination in the Senate would condemn it by the constitution.

2.   "To borrow money." But this bill neither borrows money nor ensures the borrowing it. The proprietors of the bank will be just as free as any other money holders, to lend or not to lend their money to the public. The operation proposed in the bill first, to lend them two millions, and then to borrow them back again, cannot change the nature of the latter act, which will still be a payment, and not a loan, call it by what name you please.

3.   To "regulate commerce with foreign nations, and among the States, and with the Indian tribes." To erect a bank, and to regulate commerce, are very different acts. He who erects a bank, creates a subject of commerce in its bills, so does he who makes a bushel of wheat, or digs a dollar out of the mines; yet neither of these persons regulates commerce thereby. To make a thing which may be bought and sold, is not to prescribe regulations for buying and selling. Besides, if this was an exercise of the power of regulating commerce, it would be void, as extending as much to the internal commerce of every State, as to its external. For the power given to Congress by the Constitution does not extend to the internal regulation of the commerce of a

State, (that is to say of the commerce between citizen and citizen,) which remain exclusively with its own legislature; but to its external commerce only, that is to say, its commerce with another State, or with foreign nations, or with the Indian tribes. Accordingly the bill does not propose the measure as a regulation of trace, but as "productive of considerable advantages to trade." Still less are these powers covered by any other of the special enumerations.

II. Nor are they within either of the general phrases, which are the two following:

1. To lay taxes to provide for the general welfare of the United States, that is to say, "to lay taxes for *the purpose of* providing for the general welfare." For the laying of taxes is the *power,* and the general welfare the *purpose* for which the power is to be exercised. They are not to lay taxes *ad libitum for any purpose they please;* but only *to pay the debts or provide for the welfare of the Union.* In like manner, they are not *to do anything they please* to provide for the general welfare, but only to *lay taxes* for that purpose. To consider the latter phrase, not as describing the purpose of the first, but as giving a distinct and independent power to do any act they please, which might be for the good of the Union, would render all the preceding and subsequent enumerations of power completely useless.

   It would reduce the whole instrument to a single phrase, that of instituting a Congress with power to do whatever would be for the good of the United States; and, as they would be the sole judges of the good or evil, it would be also a power to do whatever evil they please.

   It is an established rule of construction where a phrase will bear either of two meanings, to give it that which will allow some meaning to the other parts of the instrument, and not that which would render all the others useless. Certainly no such universal power was meant to be given them. It was intended to lace them up straitly within the enumerated powers, and those without which, as means, these powers could not be carried into effect. It is known that the very power now proposed *as a means* was rejected as *an end* by the Convention which formed the Constitution. A proposition was made to them to authorize Congress to open canals, and an amendatory one to empower them to incorporate. But the whole was rejected, and one of the reasons for rejection urged in debate was, that then they would have a power to erect a bank, which would render the great cities, where there were prejudices and jealousies on the subject, adverse to the reception of the Constitution.

2. The second general phrase is, "to make all laws *necessary* and proper for carrying into execution the enumerated powers." But they can all be carried into execution without a bank. A bank therefore is not *necessary,* and consequently not authorized by this phrase.

It has been urged that a bank will give great facility or convenience in the collection of taxes, Suppose this were true: yet the Constitution allows only the means which are "*necessary*," not those which are merely "convenient" for effecting the enumerated powers. If such a latitude of construction be allowed to this phrase as to give any non-enumerated power, it will go to everyone, for there is not one which ingenuity may not torture into a *convenience* in some instance *or other*, to *some one* of so long a list of enumerated powers. It would swallow up all the delegated powers, and reduce the whole to one power, as before observed. Therefore it was that the Constitution restrained them to the *necessary* means, that is to say, to those means without which the grant of power would be nugatory.

But let us examine this convenience and see what it is. The report on this subject, page 3, states the only *general* convenience to be, the preventing the transportation and re-transportation of money between the States and the treasury, (for I pass over the increase of circulating medium, ascribed to it as a want, and which, according to my ideas of paper money, is clearly a demerit.) Every State will have to pay a sum of tax money into the treasury; and the treasury will have to pay, in every State, a part of the interest on the public debt, and salaries to the officers of government resident in that State. In most of the States there will still be a surplus of tax money to come up to the seat of government for the officers residing there. The payments of interest and salary in each State may he made by treasury orders on the State collector. This will take up the greater part of the money he has collected in his State, and consequently prevent the great mass of it from being drawn out of the State. If there be a balance of commerce in favor of that State against the one in which the government resides, the surplus of taxes will be remitted by the bills of exchange drawn for that commercial balance. And so it must be if there was a bank. But if there be no balance of commerce, either direct or circuitous, all the banks in the world could not bring up the surplus of taxes, but in the form of money. Treasury orders then, and bills of exchange may prevent the displacement of the main mass of the money collected, without the aid of any bank; and where these fail, it cannot be prevented even with that aid.

Perhaps, indeed, bank bills may be a more *convenient* vehicle than treasury orders. But a little *difference* in the degree of *convenience* cannot constitute the necessity which the Constitution makes the ground for assuming any non-enumerated power.

Besides, the existing banks will, without a doubt, enter into arrangements for lending their agency, and the more favorable, as there will be a competition among them for it; whereas the bill delivers us up bound to the national bank, who are free to refuse all arrangement, but on their own terms, and the public not free, on such refusal, to employ any other bank. That of Philadelphia I believe, now does this business, by their post-notes, which, by an arrangement with the treasury, are paid by any State collector to whom they are presented. This expedient alone suffices to prevent the existence of that *necessity* which may justify the assumption of a non-enumerated power as a means for carrying into effect an enumerated one. The thing may be done, and has been done, and well done, without this assumption, therefore it does not stand on that degree of *necessity* which can honestly justify it.

It may be said that a bank whose bills would have a currency all over the States, would be more convenient than one whose currency is limited to a single State. So it would be still more convenient that there should be a bank, whose bills should have a currency all over the world. But it does not follow from this superior conveniency, that there exists anywhere a power to establish such a bank; or that the world may not go on very well without it.

Can it be thought that the Constitution intended that for a shade or two of *convenience*, more or less, Congress should be authorized to break down the most ancient and fundamental laws of the several States; such as those against Mortmain, the laws of Alienage, the rules of descent, the acts of distribution, the laws of escheat and forfeiture, the laws of monopoly? Nothing but a necessity invincible by any other means, can justify such a prostitution of laws, which constitute the pillars of our whole system of jurisprudence. Will Congress be too strait-laced to carry the Constitution into honest effect, unless they may pass over the foundation-laws of the State government for the slightest convenience of theirs ?

The negative of the President is the shield provided by the Constitution to protect against the invasions of the legislature: 1. The right of the Executive. 2. Of the Judiciary. 3. Of the States and State legislatures. The present is the case of a right remaining exclusively with the States, and consequently one of those intended by the Constitution to be placed under its protection,

It must be added, however, that unless the President's mind on a view of everything which is urged for and against this bill, is tolerably clear that it is unauthorized by the Constitution; if the pro and the con hang so even as to balance his judgment, a just respect for the wisdom of the legislature would naturally decide the balance in favor of their opinion. It is chiefly for cases where they are clearly misled by error, ambition, or interest, that the Constitution has placed a check in the negative of the President.

Source: The Avalon Project at Yale Law School. http://www.yale.edu/lawweb/avalon/amerdoc/bank-tj.htm

ALEXANDER HAMILTON, "OPINION AS TO THE CONSTITUTIONALITY OF THE BANK OF THE UNITED STATES" (1791)

The Secretary of the Treasury having perused with attention the papers containing the opinions of the Secretary of State and Attorney General, concerning the constitutionality of the bill for establishing a National Bank, proceeds, according to the order of the President, to submit the reasons which have induced him to entertain a different opinion. . . .

In entering upon the argument, it ought to be premised that the objections of the Secretary of State and Attorney General are founded on a general denial of the authority of the United States to erect corporations. The latter, indeed, expressly admits, that if there be anything in the bill which is not warranted by the Constitution, it is the clause of incorporation.

Now it appears to the Secretary of the Treasury that this general principle is inherent in the very definition of government, and essential to every step of progress to be made by that of the United States, namely: That every power vested in a government is in its nature sovereign, and includes, by force of the term, a right to employ all the means requisite and fairly applicable to the attainment of the ends of such power, and which are not precluded by restrictions and exceptions specified in the Constitution, or not immoral, or not contrary to the essential ends of political society.

This principle, in its application to government in general, would be admitted as an axiom; and it will be incumbent upon those who may incline to deny it, to prove a distinction, and to show that a rule which, in the general system of things, is essential to the preservation of the social order, is inapplicable to the United States.

The circumstance that the powers of sovereignty are in this country divided between the National and State governments, does not afford the distinction required. It does not follow from this, that each of the portion of powers delegated to the one or to the other, is not sovereign with regard to its proper objects. It will only follow from it, that each has sovereign power as to certain things, and not as to other things. To deny that the government of the United States has sovereign power, as to its declared purposes and trusts, because its power does not extend to all cases would be equally to deny that the State governments have sovereign power in any case, because their power does not extend to every case. The tenth section of the first article of the Constitution exhibits a long list of very important things which they may not do. And thus the United States would furnish the singular spectacle of a political society without sovereignty, or of a people governed, without government.

If it would be necessary to bring proof to a proposition so clear, as that which affirms that the powers of the federal government, as to its objects, were sovereign, there is a clause of its Constitution which would be decisive. It is that which declares that the Constitution, and the laws of the United States made in pursuance of it, and all treaties made, or which shall be made, under their authority, shall be the serene law of the land. The power which can create the supreme law of the land in any case, is doubtless sovereign as to such case.

This general and indisputable principle puts at once an end to the abstract question, whether the United States have power to erect a corporation; that is to say, to give a legal or artificial capacity to one or more persons, distinct from the natural. For it is unquestionably incident to sovereign power to erect corporations, and consequently to that of the United States, in relation to the objects intrusted to the management of the government. The difference is this: where the authority of the government is general, it can create corporations in ad cases, where it is confined to certain branches of legislation, it can create corporations only in those cases. . . .

It is not denied that there are implied as well as express powers, and that the former are as effectually delegated as the latter. And for the sake of accuracy it shall be mentioned, that there is another class of powers, which may be properly denominated resting powers. It will not be doubted, that if the United States should make a conquest of any of the territories of its neighbors, they would possess sovereign jurisdiction over the conquered territory. This would be rather a result, from the whole mass of the powers of the government, and from the nature of political society, than a consequence of either of the powers specially enumerated. . . .

Another argument made use of by the Secretary of State is, the rejection of a proposition by the Convention to empower Congress to make corporations, either generally, or for some special purpose.

What was the precise nature or extent of this proposition, or what the reasons for refusing it, is not ascertained by any authentic document, or even by accurate recollection. . . .

To establish such a right, it remains to show the relation of such an institution to one or more of the specified powers of the government. Accordingly it is affirmed that it has a relation, more or less direct, to the power of collecting taxes, to that of borrowing money, to that of regulating trade between the States, and to those of raising and maintaining fleets and armies. To the two former the relation Nay be said to be immediate; and in the last place it will be argued, that it is clearly within the provision which authorizes the making of all needful rules and regulations concerning the property of the United States, as the same has been practiced upon by the government.

A bank relates to the collection of taxes in two ways indirectly, by increasing the quantity of circulating medium and quickening circulation, which facilitates the means of paying directly, by creating a convenient! species of medium in which they are to be paid.

To designate or appoint the money or thing in which taxes are to be paid, is not only a proper, but a necessary exercise of the power of collecting them. . . .

A bank has a direct relation to the power of borrowing money, because it is an usual, and in sudden emergencies an essential, instrument in the obtaining of loans to government. . . .

The Secretary of State objects to the relation here insisted upon by the following mode of reasoning: To erect a bank, says he, and to regulate commerce, are very different acts. . . . To make a thing which may be bought and sold, is not to prescribe regulations for buying and selling.

This making the regulation of commerce to consist in prescribing rules for buying and selling this, indeed, is a species of regulation of trade, [but] is one which falls more aptly within the province of the local jurisdictions than within that of the general government, whose care they must be presumed to have been intended to be directed to those general political arrangements concerning trade on which its aggregated interests depend, rather than to the details of buying and selling. Accordingly, such only are the regulations to be found in the laws of the United States whose objects are to give encouragement to the enterprise of our own merchants, and to advance our navigation and manufactures. And it is in reference to these general relations of commerce, that an establishment which furnishes facilities to circulation, and a convenient medium of exchange and alienation, is to be regarded as a regulation of trade.

The Secretary of State further argues, that if this was a regulation of commerce, it would be void, as extending as much to the internal commerce of every State as to its external. But what regulation of commerce does not extend to the internal commerce of every State? What are all the duties upon imported articles amounting to prohibitions, but so many bounties upon domestic manufactures, affecting the interests of different classes of citizens, in different ways? What are all the provisions in the Coasting Acts which relate to the trade between district and district of the same State? In short, what regulation of trade between the States but must affect the internal trade of each State? What can operate upon the whole, but must extend to every part? . . .

A hope is entertained that it has, by this time, been made to appear, to the satisfaction of the President, that a bank has a natural relation to the power of collecting taxes—to that of regulating trade—to that of providing for the common defense and that, as the bill under consideration contemplates the government in the light of a joint proprietor of the stock of the bank, it brings the case within the provision of the clause of the Constitution which immediately respects the property of the United States.

Under a conviction that such a relation subsists, the Secretary of the Treasury, with all deference, conceives that it will result as a necessary consequence from the position that all the special powers of government are sovereign, as to the proper objects that the incorporation of a bank is a constitutional measure, and that the objections taken to the bill, in this respect, are ill-founded . . .

Source: The Avalon Project at Yale Law School. http://www.yale.edu/lawweb/avalon/amerdoc/bank-ah.htm

MARBURY V. MADISON (1803)

First example of the Supreme Court declaring an Act of Congress unconstitutional. It not only established the Supreme Court's right to judicial review, but it put the Congress on notice that its power could be checked and negated if it overstepped its constitutional boundaries. In this case, because the Congress by legislative act had altered the terms of the Supreme Court's original jurisdiction, as prescribed by the Constitution, the law was declared unconstitutional, and therefore void.

Mr. Chief Justice MARSHALL delivered the opinion of the court. . . .

The act to establish the judicial courts of the United States authorizes the supreme court 'to issue writs of mandamus, in cases warranted by the principles and usages of law, to any courts appointed, or persons holding office, under the authority of the United States.'

The secretary of state, being a person, holding an office under the authority of the United States, is precisely within the letter of the description; and if this court is not authorized to issue a writ of mandamus to such an officer, it must be because the law is unconstitutional, and therefore absolutely incapable of conferring the authority, and assigning the duties which its words purport to confer and assign.

The constitution vests the whole judicial power of the United States in one supreme court, and such inferior courts as congress shall, from time to time, ordain and establish. This power is expressly extended to all cases arising under the laws of the United States; and consequently, in some form, may be exercised over the present case; because the right claimed is given by a law of the United States.

In the distribution of this power it is declared that 'the supreme court shall have original jurisdiction in all cases affecting ambassadors, other public ministers and consuls, and those in which a state shall be a party. In all other cases, the supreme court shall have appellate jurisdiction.'

It has been insisted at the bar, that as the original grant of jurisdiction to the supreme and inferior courts is general, and the clause, assigning original jurisdiction to the supreme court, contains no negative or restrictive words; the power remains to the legislature to assign original jurisdiction to that court in other cases than those specified in the article which has been recited; provided those cases belong to the judicial power of the United States.

If it had been intended to leave it in the discretion of the legislature to apportion the judicial power between the supreme and inferior courts according to the will of that body, it would certainly have been useless to have proceeded further than to have defined the judicial power, and the tribunals in which it should be vested. The subsequent part of the section is mere surplusage, is entirely without meaning, if such is to be the construction. If congress remains at liberty to give this court appellate jurisdiction, where the constitution has declared their jurisdiction shall be original; and original jurisdiction where the constitution has declared it shall be appellate; the distribution of jurisdiction made in the constitution, is form without substance.

Affirmative words are often, in their operation, negative of other objects than those affirmed; and in this case, a negative or exclusive sense must be given to them or they have no operation at all.

It cannot be presumed that any clause in the constitution is intended to be without effect; and therefore such construction is inadmissible, unless the words require it.

If the solicitude of the convention, respecting our peace with foreign powers, induced a provision that the supreme court should take original jurisdiction in cases which might be supposed to affect them; yet the clause would have proceeded no further than to provide for such cases, if no further restriction on the powers of congress had been intended. That they should have appellate jurisdiction in all other cases, with such exceptions as congress might make, is no restriction; unless the words be deemed exclusive of original jurisdiction.

When an instrument organizing fundamentally a judicial system, divides it into one supreme, and so many inferior courts as the legislature may ordain and establish; then enumerates its powers, and proceeds so far to distribute them, as to define the jurisdiction of the supreme court by declaring the cases in which it shall take original jurisdiction, and that in others it shall take appellate jurisdiction, the plain import of the words seems to be, that in one class of cases its jurisdiction is original, and not appellate; in the other it is appellate, and not original. If any other construction would render the clause inoperative, that is an additional reason for rejecting such other construction, and for adhering to the obvious meaning.

To enable this court then to issue a mandamus, it must be shown to be an exercise of appellate jurisdiction, or to be necessary to enable them to exercise appellate jurisdiction.

It has been stated at the bar that the appellate jurisdiction may be exercised in a variety of forms, and that if it be the will of the legislature that a mandamus should be used for that purpose, that will must be obeyed. This is true; yet the jurisdiction must be appellate, not original.

It is the essential criterion of appellate jurisdiction, that it revises and corrects the proceedings in a cause already instituted, and does not create that case. Although, therefore, a mandamus may be directed to courts, yet to issue such a writ to an officer for the delivery of a paper, is in effect the same as to sustain an original action for that paper, and therefore seems not to belong to appellate, but to original jurisdiction. Neither is it necessary in such a case as this, to enable the court to exercise its appellate jurisdiction.

The authority, therefore, given to the supreme court, by the act establishing the judicial courts of the United States, to issue writs of mandamus to public officers, appears not to be warranted by the constitution; and it becomes necessary to inquire whether a jurisdiction, so conferred, can be exercised.

The question, whether an act, repugnant to the constitution, can become the law of the land, is a question deeply interesting to the United States; but, happily, not of an intricacy proportioned to its interest. It seems only necessary to recognise certain principles, supposed to have been long and well established, to decide it.

That the people have an original right to establish, for their future government, such principles as, in their opinion, shall most conduce to their own happiness, is the basis on which the whole American fabric has been erected. The exercise of this original right is a very great exertion; nor can it nor ought it to be frequently repeated. The principles, therefore, so established are deemed fundamental. And as the authority, from which they proceed, is supreme, and can seldom act, they are designed to be permanent.

This original and supreme will organizes the government, and assigns to different departments their respective powers. It may either stop here; or establish certain limits not to be transcended by those departments.

The government of the United States is of the latter description. The powers of the legislature are defined and limited; and that those limits may not be mistaken or forgotten, the constitution is written. To what purpose are powers limited, and to what purpose is that limitation committed to writing; if these limits may, at any time, be passed by those intended to be restrained? The distinction between a government with limited and unlimited powers is abolished, if those limits do not confine the persons on whom they are imposed, and if acts prohibited and acts allowed are of equal obligation. It is a proposition too plain to be contested, that the constitution controls any legislative act repugnant to it; or, that the legislature may alter the constitution by an ordinary act.

Between these alternatives there is no middle ground. The constitution is either a superior, paramount law, unchangeable by ordinary means, or it is on a level with ordinary legislative acts, and like other acts, is alterable when the legislature shall please to alter it.

If the former part of the alternative be true, then a legislative act contrary to the constitution is not law: if the latter part be true, then written constitutions are absurd attempts, on the part of the people, to limit a power in its own nature illimitable.

Certainly all those who have framed written constitutions contemplate them as forming the fundamental and paramount law of the nation, and consequently the theory of every such government must be, that an act of the legislature repugnant to the constitution is void.

This theory is essentially attached to a written constitution, and is consequently to be considered by this court as one of the fundamental principles of our society. It is not therefore to be lost sight of in the further consideration of this subject.

If an act of the legislature, repugnant to the constitution, is void, does it, notwithstanding its invalidity, bind the courts and oblige them to give it effect? Or, in other words, though it be not law, does it constitute a rule as operative as if it was a law? This would be to overthrow in fact what was established in theory; and would seem, at first view, an absurdity too gross to be insisted on. It shall, however, receive a more attentive consideration.

It is emphatically the province and duty of the judicial department to say what the law is. Those who apply the rule to particular cases, must of necessity expound and interpret that rule. If two laws conflict with each other, the courts must decide on the operation of each.

So if a law be in opposition to the constitution: if both the law and the constitution apply to a particular case, so that the court must either decide that case conformably to the law, disregarding the constitution; or conformably to the constitution, disregarding the law: the court must determine which of these conflicting rules governs the case. This is of the very essence of judicial duty.

If then the courts are to regard the constitution; and the constitution is superior to any ordinary act of the legislature; the constitution, and not such ordinary act, must govern the case to which they both apply.

Those then who controvert the principle that the constitution is to be considered, in court, as a paramount law, are reduced to the necessity of maintaining that courts must close their eyes on the constitution, and see only the law.

This doctrine would subvert the very foundation of all written constitutions. It would declare that an act, which, according to the principles and theory of our government, is entirely void, is yet, in practice, completely obligatory. It would declare, that if the legislature shall do what is expressly forbidden, such act, notwithstanding the express prohibition, is in reality effectual. It would be giving to the legislature a practical and real omnipotence with the same breath which professes to restrict their powers within narrow limits. It is prescribing limits, and declaring that those limits may be passed at pleasure.

That it thus reduces to nothing what we have deemed the greatest improvement on political institutions—a written constitution, would of itself be sufficient, in America where written constitutions have been viewed with so much reverence, for rejecting the construction. But the peculiar expressions of the constitution of the United States furnish additional arguments in favour of its rejection.

The judicial power of the United States is extended to all cases arising under the constitution. Could it be the intention of those who gave this power, to say that, in using it, the constitution should not be looked into? That a case arising under the constitution should be decided without examining the instrument under which it arises?

This is too extravagant to be maintained.

In some cases then, the constitution must be looked into by the judges. And if they can open it at all, what part of it are they forbidden to read, or to obey?

There are many other parts of the constitution which serve to illustrate this subject.

It is declared that 'no tax or duty shall be laid on articles exported from any state.' Suppose a duty on the export of cotton, of tobacco, or of flour; and a suit instituted to recover it. Ought judgment to be rendered in such a case? ought the judges to close their eyes on the constitution, and only see the law.

The constitution declares that 'no bill of attainder or ex post facto law shall be passed.'

If, however, such a bill should be passed and a person should be prosecuted under it, must the court condemn to death those victims whom the constitution endeavours to preserve?

'No person,' says the constitution, 'shall be convicted of treason unless on the testimony of two witnesses to the same overt act, or on confession in open court.'

Here the language of the constitution is addressed especially to the courts. It prescribes, directly for them, a rule of evidence not to be departed from. If the legislature should change that rule, and declare one witness, or a confession out of court, sufficient for conviction, must the constitutional principle yield to the legislative act?

From these and many other selections which might be made, it is apparent, that the framers of the constitution contemplated that instrument as a rule for the government of courts, as well as of the legislature.

Why otherwise does it direct the judges to take an oath to support it? This oath certainly applies, in an especial manner, to their conduct in their official character. How immoral to impose it on them, if they were to be used as the instruments, and the knowing instruments, for violating what they swear to support!

The oath of office, too, imposed by the legislature, is completely demonstrative of the legislative opinion on this subject. It is in these words: 'I do solemnly swear that I will administer justice without respect to persons, and do equal right to the poor and to the rich; and that I will faithfully and impartially discharge all the duties incumbent on me as according to the best of my abilities and understanding, agreeably to the constitution and laws of the United States.'

Why does a judge swear to discharge his duties agreeably to the constitution of the United States, if that constitution forms no rule for his government? if it is closed upon him and cannot be inspected by him.

If such be the real state of things, this is worse than solemn mockery. To prescribe, or to take this oath, becomes equally a crime.

It is also not entirely unworthy of observation, that in declaring what shall be the supreme law of the land, the constitution itself is first mentioned; and not the laws of the United States generally, but those only which shall be made in pursuance of the constitution, have that rank.

Thus, the particular phraseology of the constitution of the United States confirms and strengthens the principle, supposed to be essential to all written constitutions, that a law repugnant to the constitution is void, and that courts, as well as other departments, are bound by that instrument.

Source: Findlaw. http://caselaw.lp.findlaw.com/scripts/getcase.pl?court=US&vol=5&invol=137

McCulloch v. Maryland (1819)

In this case, Chief Justice Marshall reiterated Hamilton's position on the interpretation of the elastic clause and upholding Congressional authority to charter a bank. He also established the supremacy of the federal government and therefore Congress in passing laws. It is important to note that this case by no means ended the debate over the scope of national power, but rather was one of many cases to reflect upon federalism, and the nature or power within the structure.

The first question made in the cause is—has congress power to incorporate a bank? It has been truly said, that this can scarcely be considered as an open question, entirely unprejudiced by the former proceedings of the nation respecting it. The principle now contested was introduced at a very early period of our history, has been recognised by many successive legislatures, and has been acted upon by the judicial department, in cases of peculiar delicacy, as a law of undoubted obligation. . . .

The power now contested was exercised by the first congress elected under the present constitution. The bill for incorporating the Bank of the United States did not steal upon an unsuspecting legislature, and pass unobserved. Its principle was completely understood, and was opposed with equal zeal and ability. After being resisted, first, in the fair and open field of debate, and afterwards, in the executive cabinet, with as much persevering talent as any measure has ever experienced, and being supported by arguments which convinced minds as pure and as intelligent as this country can boast, it became a law. The original act was permitted to expire; but a short experience of the embarrassments to which the refusal to revive it exposed the government, convinced those who were most prejudiced against the measure of its necessity, and induced the passage of the present law. It would require no ordinary share of intrepidity, to assert that a measure adopted under these circumstances, was a bold and plain usurpation, to which the constitution gave no countenance. These observations belong to the cause; but they are not made under the impression, that, were the question entirely new, the law would be found irreconcilable with the constitution.

In discussing this question, the counsel for the state of Maryland have deemed it of some importance, in the construction of the constitution, to consider that instrument, not as emanating from the people, but as the act of sovereign and independent states. The powers of the general government, it has been said, are delegated by the states, who alone are truly sovereign; and must be exercised in subordination to the states, who alone possess supreme dominion. It would be difficult to sustain this proposition. The convention which framed the constitution was indeed elected by the state legislatures. But the instrument, when it came from their hands, was a mere proposal, without obligation, or pretensions to it. It was reported to the then existing congress of the United States, with a request that it might 'be submitted to a convention of delegates, chosen in each state by the people thereof, under the recommendation of its legislature, for their assent and ratification.' This mode of proceeding was adopted; and by the convention, by congress, and by the state legislatures, the instrument was submitted to the people. They acted upon it in the only manner in which they can act safely, effectively and wisely, on such a subject, by assembling in convention. It is true, they assembled in their several states—and where else should they have assembled? No political dreamer was ever wild enough to think of breaking down the lines which separate the states, and of compounding the American people into one common mass. Of consequence, when they act, they act in their states. But the measures they adopt do not, on that account, cease to be the measures of the people themselves, or become the measures of the state governments.

From these conventions, the constitution derives its whole authority. The government proceeds directly from the people; is 'ordained and established,' in the name of the people; and is declared to be ordained, 'in order to form a more perfect union, establish justice, insure domestic tranquillity, and secure the blessings of liberty to themselves and to their posterity.' The assent of the states, in their sovereign capacity, is implied, in calling a convention, and thus submitting that instrument to the people. But the people were at perfect liberty to accept or reject it; and their act was final. It required not the affirmance, and could not be negatived, by the state governments. The constitution, when thus adopted, was of complete obligation, and bound the state sovereignties. . . .

Among the enumerated powers, we do not find that of establishing a bank or creating a corporation. But there is no phrase in the instrument which, like the articles of confederation, excludes incidental or implied powers; and which requires that everything granted shall be expressly and minutely described. Even the 10th amendment, which was framed for the purpose of quieting the excessive jealousies which had been excited, omits the word 'expressly,' and declares only, that the powers 'not delegated to the United States, nor prohibited to the states, are reserved to the states or to the people;' thus leaving the question, whether the particular power which may become the subject of contest, has been delegated to the one government, or prohibited to the other, to depend on a fair construction of the whole instrument. The men who drew and adopted this amendment had experienced the embarrassments resulting from the insertion of this word in the articles of confederation, and probably omitted it, to avoid those embarrassments. A constitution, to contain an accurate detail of all the subdivisions of which its great powers will admit, and of all the means by which they may be carried into execution, would partake of the prolixity of a legal code, and could scarcely be embraced by the human mind. It would, probably, never be understood by the public. Its nature, therefore, requires, that only its great outlines should be marked, its important objects designated, and the minor ingredients which compose those objects, be deduced from the nature of the objects themselves. That this idea was entertained by the framers of the American constitution, is not only to be inferred from the nature of the instrument, but from the language. Why else were some of the limitations, found in the 9th section of the 1st article, introduced? It is also, in some degree, warranted, by their having omitted to use any restrictive term which might prevent its receiving a fair and just interpretation. In considering this question, then, we must never forget that it is a constitution we are expounding.

Although, among the enumerated powers of government, we do not find the word 'bank' or 'incorporation,' we find the great powers, to lay and collect taxes; to borrow money; to regulate commerce; to declare and conduct a war; and to raise and support armies and navies. The sword and the purse, all the external relations, and no inconsiderable portion of the industry of the nation, are intrusted to its government. It can never be pretended, that these vast powers draw after them others of inferior importance, merely because they are inferior. Such an idea can never be advanced. But it may with great reason be contended, that a government, intrusted with such ample powers, on the due execution of which the happiness and prosperity of the nation so vitally depends, must also be intrusted with ample means for their execution. The power being given, it is the interest of the nation to facilitate its execution. It can never be their interest, and cannot be presumed to have been their intention, to clog and embarrass its execution, by withholding the most appropriate means. Throughout this vast republic, from the St. Croix to the Gulf of Mexico, from the Atlantic to the Pacific, revenue is to be collected and expended, armies are to be marched and supported. The exigencies of the nation may require, that the treasure raised in the north should be transported to the south, that raised in the east, conveyed to the west, or that this order should be reversed. Is that construction of the constitution to be preferred, which would render these operations difficult, hazardous and expensive? Can we adopt that construction (unless the words imperiously require it), which would impute to the framers of that instrument, when granting these powers for the public good, the intention of impeding their exercise, by withholding a choice of means? If, indeed, such be the mandate of the constitution, we have only to obey; but that instrument does not profess to enumerate the means by which the powers it confers may be executed; nor does it prohibit the creation of a corporation, if the existence of such a being be essential, to the beneficial exercise of those powers. It is, then, the subject of fair inquiry, how far such means may be employed.

It is not denied, that the powers given to the government imply the ordinary means of execution. That, for example, of raising revenue, and applying it to national purposes, is admitted to imply the power of conveying money from place to place, as the exigencies of the nation may require, and of employing the usual means of conveyance. But it is denied, that the government has its choice of means; or, that it may employ the most convenient means, if, to employ them, it be necessary to erect a corporation. On what foundation does this argument rest? On this alone: the power of creating a corporation, is one appertaining to sovereignty, and is not expressly conferred on congress. This is true. But all legislative powers appertain to sovereignty. The original power of giving the law on any subject whatever, is a sovereign power; and if the government of the Union is restrained from creating a corporation, as a means for performing its functions, on the single reason that the creation of a corporation is an act of sovereignty; if the sufficiency of this reason be acknowledged, there would be some difficulty in sustaining the authority of congress to pass other laws for the accomplishment of the same objects. The government which has a right to do an act, and has imposed on it, the duty of performing that act, must, according to the dictates of reason, be allowed to select the means; and those who contend that it may not select any appropriate means, that one particular mode of effecting the object is excepted, take upon themselves the burden of establishing that exception.

The creation of a corporation, it is said, appertains to sovereignty. This is admitted. But to what portion of sovereignty does it appertain? Does it belong to one more than to another? In America, the powers of sovereignty are divided between the government of the Union, and those of the states. They are each sovereign, with respect to the objects committed to it, and neither sovereign, with respect to the objects committed to the other. We cannot comprehend that train of reasoning, which would maintain, that the extent of power granted by the people is to be ascertained, not by the nature and terms of the grant, but by its date. Some state constitutions were formed before, some since that of the United States. We cannot believe, that their relation to each other is in any degree dependent upon this circumstance. Their respective powers must, we think, be precisely the same, as if they had been formed at the same time. Had they been formed at the same time, and had the people conferred on the general government the power contained in the constitution, and on the states the whole residuum of power, would it have been asserted, that the government of the Union was not sovereign, with respect to those objects which were intrusted to it, in relation to which its laws were declared to be supreme? If this could not have been asserted, we cannot well comprehend the process of reasoning which maintains, that a power appertaining to sovereignty cannot be connected with that vast portion of it which is granted to the general government, so far as it is calculated to subserve the legitimate objects of that government. The power of creating a corporation, though appertaining to sovereignty, is not, like the power of making war, or levying taxes, or of regulating commerce, a great substantive and independent power, which cannot be implied as incidental to other powers, or used as a means of executing them. It is never the end for which other powers are exercised, but a means by which other objects are accomplished. No contributions are made to charity, for the sake of an incorporation, but a corporation is created to administer the charity; no seminary of learning is instituted, in order to be incorporated, but the corporate character is conferred to subserve the purposes of education. No city was ever built, with the sole object of being incorporated, but is incorporated as affording the best means of being well governed. The power of creating a corporation is never used for its own sake, but for the purpose of effecting something else. No sufficient reason is, therefore, perceived, why it may not pass as incidental to those powers which are expressly given, if it be a direct mode of executing them.

But the constitution of the United States has not left the right of congress to employ the necessary means, for the execution of the powers conferred on the government, to general reasoning. To its enumeration of powers is added, that of making 'all laws which shall be necessary and proper, for carrying into execution the foregoing powers, and all other powers vested by this constitution, in the government of the United States, or in any department thereof.' The counsel for the state of Maryland have urged various arguments, to prove that this clause, though, in terms, a grant of power, is not so, in effect; but is really restrictive of the general right, which might otherwise be implied, of selecting means for executing the enumerated powers. In support of this proposition, they have found it necessary to contend, that this clause was inserted for the purpose of conferring on congress the power of making laws. That, without it, doubts might be entertained, whether congress could exercise its powers in the form of legislation. . . .

But the argument on which most reliance is placed, is drawn from that peculiar language of this clause. Congress is not empowered by it to make all laws, which may have relation to the powers confered [sic] on the government, but such only as may be 'necessary and proper' for carrying them into execution. The word 'necessary' is considered as controlling the whole sentence, and as limiting the right to pass laws for the execution of the granted powers, to such as are indispensable, and without which the power would be nugatory. That it excludes the choice of means, and leaves to congress, in each case, that only which is most direct and simple.

Is it true, that this is the sense in which the word 'necessary' is always used? Does it always import an absolute physical necessity, so strong, that one thing to which another may be termed necessary, cannot exist without that other? We think it does not. If reference be had to its use, in the common affairs of the world, or in approved authors, we find that it frequently imports no more than that one thing is convenient, or useful, or essential to another. To employ the means necessary to an end, is generally understood as employing any means calculated to produce the end, and not as being confined to those single means, without which the end would be entirely unattainable. Such is the character of human language, that no word conveys to the mind, in all situations, one single definite idea; and nothing is more common than to use words in a figurative sense. Almost all compositions contain words, which, taken in their rigorous sense, would convey a meaning different from that which is obviously intended. It is essential to just construction, that many words which import something excessive, should be understood in a more mitigated sense—in that sense which common usage justifies. The word 'necessary' is of this description. It has not a fixed character, peculiar to itself. It admits of all degrees of comparison; and is often connected with other words, which increase or diminish the impression the mind receives of the urgency it imports. A thing may be necessary, very necessary, absolutely or indispensably necessary. To no mind would the same idea be conveyed by these several phrases. The comment on the word is well illustrated by the passage cited at the bar, from the 10th section of the 1st article of the constitution. It is, we think, impossible to compare the sentence which prohibits a state from laying 'imposts, or duties on imports or exports, except what may be absolutely necessary for executing its inspection laws,' with that which authorizes congress 'to make all laws which shall be necessary and proper for carrying into execution' the powers of the general government, without feeling a conviction, that the convention understood itself to change materially the meaning of the word 'necessary,' by prefixing the word 'absolutely.' This word, then, like others, is used in various senses;

and, in its construction, the subject, the context, the intention of the person using them, are all to be taken into view.

Let this be done in the case under consideration. The subject is the execution of those great powers on which the welfare of a nation essentially depends. It must have been the intention of those who gave these powers, to insure, so far as human prudence could insure, their beneficial execution. This could not be done, by confiding the choice of means to such narrow limits as not to leave it in the power of congress to adopt any which might be appropriate, and which were conducive to the end. This provision is made in a constitution, intended to endure for ages to come, and consequently, to be adapted to the various crises of human affairs. To have prescribed the means by which government should, in all future time, execute its powers, would have been to change, entirely, the character of the instrument, and give it the properties of a legal code. It would have been an unwise attempt to provide, by immutable rules, for exigencies which, if foreseen at all, must have been seen dimly, and which can be best provided for as they occur. To have declared, that the best means shall not be used, but those alone, without which the power given would be nugatory, would have been to deprive the legislature of the capacity to avail itself of experience, to exercise its reason, and to accommodate its legislation to circumstances. If we apply this principle of construction to any of the powers of the government, we shall find it so pernicious in its operation that we shall be compelled to discard it. . . .

The result of the most careful and attentive consideration bestowed upon this clause is, that if it does not enlarge, it cannot be construed to restrain the powers of congress, or to impair the right of the legislature to exercise its best judgment in the selection of measures to carry into execution the constitutional powers of the government. If no other motive for its insertion can be suggested, a sufficient one is found in the desire to remove all doubts respecting the right to legislate on that vast mass of incidental powers which must be involved in the constitution, if that instrument be not a splendid bauble.

We admit, as all must admit, that the powers of the government are limited, and that its limits are not to be transcended. But we think the sound construction of the constitution must allow to the national legislature that discretion, with respect to the means by which the powers it confers are to be carried into execution, which will enable that body to perform the high duties assigned to it, in the manner most beneficial to the people. Let the end be legitimate, let it be within the scope of the constitution, and all means which are appropriate, which are plainly adapted to that end, which are not prohibited, but consist with the letter and spirit of the constitution, are constitutional. . . .

Should congress, in the execution of its powers, adopt measures which are prohibited by the constitution; or should congress, under the pretext of executing its powers, pass laws for the accomplishment of objects not intrusted to the government; it would become the painful duty of this tribunal, should a case requiring such a decision come before it, to say, that such an act was not the law of the land. But where the law is not prohibited, and is really calculated to effect any of the objects intrusted to the government, to undertake here to inquire into the decree of its necessity, would be to pass the line which circumscribes the judicial department, and to tread on legislative ground. This court disclaims all pretensions to such a power.

After this declaration, it can scarcely be necessary to say, that the existence of state banks can have no possible influence on the question. No trace is to be found in the constitution, of an intention to create a dependence of the government of the Union on those of the states, for the execution of the great powers assigned to it. Its means are adequate to its ends; and on those means alone was it expected to rely for the accomplishment of its ends. To impose on it the necessity of resorting to means which it cannot control, which another government may furnish or withhold, would render its course precarious, the result of its measures uncertain, and create a dependence on other governments, which might disappoint its most important designs, and is incompatible with the language of the constitution. But were it otherwise, the choice of means implies a right to choose a national bank in preference to state banks, and congress alone can make the election.

After the most deliberate consideration, it is the unanimous and decided opinion of this court, that the act to incorporate the Bank of the United States is a law made in pursuance of the constitution, and is a part of the supreme law of the land. . . .

Source: Findlaw.com. http://caselaw.lp.findlaw.com/scripts/getcase.pl?court=US &vol=17&invol=316

GIBBONS V. OGDEN (1824)

Another important decision of the early Supreme Court by Chief Justice John Marshall read the federal commerce clause in a broad manner that emphasized not only the scope of congressional power, but that that power overrode a conflicting state law. Whereas McCulloch had provided an opportunity to expand upon the nature of implied power under the "necessary and proper clause," this decision helped define explicit congressional power to regulate interstate commerce.

In this case, the New York Assembly granted a monopoly for navigation of the Hudson River, by steamboat, between New York and New Jersey. Thomas Gibbons attempted to break the monopoly granted to Aaron Ogden by garnering a federal license, in contrast to Ogden's state license. Gibbons argued that the federal license took precedence over the state license. Chief Justice Marshall ruled in favor of Gibbons, and in so doing he took an expansive view of national power and Congress's right to legislate about interstate commerce.

Mr. Chief Justice MARSHALL delivered the opinion of the Court . . .

[The] Constitution contains an enumeration of powers expressly granted by the people to their government. It has been said that these powers ought to be construed strictly. But why ought they to be so construed? Is there one sentence in the Constitution which gives countenance to this rule? In the last of the enumerated powers, that which grants expressly the means for carrying all others into execution, Congress is authorized "to make all laws which shall be necessary and proper" for the purpose. But this limitation on the means which may be used is not extended to the powers which are conferred, nor is there one sentence in the Constitution which has been pointed out by the gentlemen of the bar or which we have been able to discern that prescribes this rule. We do not, therefore, think ourselves justified in adopting it. What do gentlemen mean by a "strict construction?" If they contend only against that enlarged construction, which would extend words beyond their natural and obvious import, we might question the application of the term, but should not controvert the principle. If they contend for that narrow construction which, in support or some theory not to be found in the Constitution, would deny to the government those powers which the words of the grant, as usually understood, import, and which are consistent with the general views and objects of the instrument; for that narrow construction which would cripple the government and render it unequal to the object for which it is declared to be instituted, and to which the powers given, as fairly understood, render it competent; then we cannot perceive the propriety of this strict construction, nor adopt it as the rule by which the Constitution is to be expounded. As men whose intentions require no concealment generally employ the words which most directly and aptly express the ideas they intend to convey, the enlightened patriots who framed our Constitution, and the people who adopted it, must be understood to have employed words in their natural sense, and to have intended what they have said. If, from the imperfection of human language, there should be serious doubts respecting the extent of any given power, it is a well settled rule that the objects for which it was given, especially when those objects are expressed in the instrument itself, should have great influence in the construction. We know of no reason for excluding this rule from the present case. The grant does not convey power which might be beneficial to the grantor if retained by himself, or which can enure solely to the benefit of the grantee, but is an investment of power for the general advantage, in the hands of agents selected for that purpose, which power can never be exercised by the people themselves, but must be placed in the hands of agents or lie dormant. We know of no rule for construing the extent of such powers other than is given by the language of the instrument which confers them, taken in connexion with the purposes for which they were conferred.

The words are, "Congress shall have power to regulate commerce with foreign nations, and among the several States, and with the Indian tribes."

The subject to be regulated is commerce, and our Constitution being, as was aptly said at the bar, one of enumeration, and not of definition, to ascertain the extent of the power, it becomes necessary to settle the meaning of the word. The counsel for the appellee would limit it to traffic, to buying and selling, or the interchange of commodities, and do not admit that it comprehends navigation. This would restrict a general term, applicable to many objects, to one of its significations. Commerce, undoubtedly, is traffic, but it is something more: it is intercourse. It describes the commercial intercourse between nations, and parts of nations, in all its branches, and is regulated by prescribing rules for carrying on that intercourse. The mind can scarcely conceive a system for regulating commerce between nations which shall exclude all laws concerning navigation, which shall be silent on the admission of the vessels of the one nation into the ports of the other, and be confined to prescribing rules for the conduct of individuals in the actual employment of buying and selling or of barter.

If commerce does not include navigation, the government of the Union has no direct power over that subject, and can make no law prescribing what shall constitute American vessels or requiring that they shall be navigated by American seamen. Yet this power has been exercised from the commencement of the government, has been exercised with the consent of all, and has been understood by all to be a commercial regulation. All America understands, and has uniformly understood, the word "commerce" to comprehend navigation. It was so understood, and must have been so understood, when the Constitution was framed. The power over commerce, including navigation, was one of the primary objects for which the people of America adopted their government, and must have been contemplated in forming it. The convention must have used the word in that sense, because all have understood it in that sense, and the attempt to restrict it comes too late.

If the opinion that "commerce," as the word is used in the Constitution, comprehends navigation also, requires any additional confirmation, that additional confirmation is, we think, furnished by the words of the instrument itself.

It is a rule of construction acknowledged by all that the exceptions from a power mark its extent, for it would be absurd, as well as useless, to except from a granted power that which was not granted—that which the words of the grant could not comprehend. If, then, there are in the Constitution plain exceptions from the power over navigation, plain inhibitions to the exercise of that power in a particular way, it is a proof that those who made these exceptions, and prescribed these inhibitions, understood the power to which they applied as being granted. . . .

The word used in the Constitution, then, comprehends, and has been always understood to comprehend, navigation within its meaning, and a power to regulate navigation is as expressly granted as if that term had been added to the word "commerce."

To what commerce does this power extend? The Constitution informs us, to commerce "with foreign nations, and among the several States, and with the Indian tribes."

It has, we believe, been universally admitted that these words comprehend every species of commercial intercourse between the United States and foreign nations. No sort of trade can be carried on between this country and any other to which this power does not extend. It has been truly said that "commerce," as the word is used in the Constitution, is a unit every part of which is indicated by the term.

If this be the admitted meaning of the word in its application to foreign nations, it must carry the same meaning throughout the sentence, and remain a unit, unless there be some plain intelligible cause which alters it.

The subject to which the power is next applied is to commerce "among the several States." The word "among" means intermingled with. A thing which is among others is intermingled with them. Commerce among the States cannot stop at the external boundary line of each State, but may be introduced into the interior.

It is not intended to say that these words comprehend that commerce which is completely internal, which is carried on between man and man in a State, or between different parts of the same State, and which does not extend to or affect other States. Such a power would be inconvenient, and is certainly unnecessary.

Comprehensive as the word "among" is, it may very properly be restricted to that commerce which concerns more States than one. The phrase is not one which would probably have been selected to indicate the completely interior traffic of a State, because it is not an apt phrase for that purpose, and the enumeration of the particular classes of commerce to which the power was to be extended would not have been made had the intention been to extend the power to every description. The enumeration presupposes something not enumerated, and that something, if we regard the language or the subject of the sentence, must be the exclusively internal commerce of a State. The genius and character of the whole government seem to be that its action is to be applied to all the external concerns of the nation, and to those internal concerns which affect the States generally, but not to those which are completely within a particular State, which do not affect other States, and with which it is not necessary to interfere for the purpose of executing some of the general powers of the government. The completely internal commerce of a State, then, may be considered as reserved for the State itself.

But, in regulating commerce with foreign nations, the power of Congress does not stop at the jurisdictional lines of the several States. It would be a very useless power if it could not pass those lines. The commerce of the United States with foreign nations is that of the whole United States. Every district has a right to participate in it. The deep streams which penetrate our country in every direction pass through the interior of almost every State in the Union, and furnish the means of exercising this right. If Congress has the power to regulate it, that power must be exercised whenever the subject exists. If it exists within the States, if a foreign voyage may commence or terminate at a port within a State, then the power of Congress may be exercised within a State.

This principle is, if possible, still more clear, when applied to commerce "among the several States." They either join each other, in which case they are separated by a mathematical line, or they are remote from each other, in which case other States lie between them. What is commerce "among" them, and how is it to be conducted? Can a trading expedition between two adjoining States, commence and terminate outside of each? And if the trading intercourse be between two States remote from each other, must it not commence in one, terminate in the other, and probably pass through a third? Commerce among the States must, of necessity, be commerce with the States. In the regulation of trade with the Indian tribes, the action of the law, especially when the Constitution was made, was chiefly within a State. The power of Congress, then, whatever it may be, must be exercised within the territorial jurisdiction of the several States. The sense of the nation on this subject is unequivocally manifested by the provisions made in the laws for transporting goods by land between Baltimore and Providence, between New York and Philadelphia, and between Philadelphia and Baltimore.

We are now arrived at the inquiry—What is this power?

It is the power to regulate, that is, to prescribe the rule by which commerce is to be governed. This power, like all others vested in Congress, is complete in itself, may be exercised to its utmost extent, and acknowledges no limitations other than are prescribed in the Constitution. These are expressed in plain terms, and do not affect the questions which arise in this case, or which have been discussed at the bar. If, as has always been understood, the sovereignty of Congress, though limited to specified objects, is plenary as to those objects, the power over commerce with foreign nations, and among the several States, is vested in Congress as absolutely as it would be in a single government, having in its Constitution the same restrictions on the exercise of the power as are found in the Constitution of the United States. The wisdom and the discretion of Congress, their identity with the people, and the influence which their constituents possess at elections are, in this, as in many other instances, as that, for example, of declaring war, the sole restraints on which they have relied, to secure them from its abuse. They are the restraints on which the people must often they solely [sic], in all representative governments.

The power of Congress, then, comprehends navigation, within the limits of every State in the Union, so far as that navigation may be in any manner connected with "commerce with foreign nations, or among the several States, or with the Indian tribes." It may, of consequence, pass the jurisdictional line of New York and act upon the very waters to which the prohibition now under consideration applies. . . .

In argument, however, it has been contended that, if a law passed by a State, in the exercise of its acknowledged sovereignty, comes into conflict with a law passed by Congress in pursuance of the Constitution, they affect the subject and each other like equal opposing powers.

But the framers of our Constitution foresaw this state of things, and provided for it by declaring the supremacy not only of itself, but of the laws made in pursuance of it. The nullity of any act inconsistent with the Constitution is produced by the declaration that the Constitution is the supreme law. The appropriate application of that part of the clause which confers the same supremacy on laws and treaties is to such acts of the State Legislatures as do not transcend their powers, but, though enacted in the execution of acknowledged State powers, interfere with, or are contrary to, the laws of Congress made in pursuance of the Constitution or some treaty made under the authority of the United States. In every such case, the act of Congress or the treaty is supreme, and the law of the State, though enacted in the exercise of powers not controverted, must yield to it.

In pursuing this inquiry at the bar, it has been said that the Constitution does not confer the right of intercourse between State and State. That right derives its source from those laws whose authority is acknowledged by civilized man throughout the world. This is true. The Constitution found it an existing right, and gave to Congress the power to regulate it. In the exercise of this power, Congress has passed "an act for enrolling or licensing ships or vessels to be employed in the coasting trade and fisheries, and for regulating the same." The counsel for the respondent contend that this act does not give the right to sail from port to port, but confines itself to regulating a preexisting right so far only as to confer certain privileges on enrolled and licensed vessels in its exercise.

It will at once occur that, when a Legislature attaches certain privileges and exemptions to the exercise of a right over which its control is absolute, the law must imply a power to exercise the right. The privileges are gone if the right itself be annihilated. It would be contrary to all reason, and to the course of human affairs, to say that a State is unable to strip a vessel of the particular privileges attendant on the exercise of a right, and yet may annul the right itself; that the State of New York cannot prevent an enrolled and licensed vessel, proceeding from Elizabethtown, in New Jersey, to New York, from enjoying, in her course, and on her entrance into port, all the privileges conferred by the act of Congress, but can shut her up in her own port, and prohibit altogether her entering the waters and ports of another State. To the Court, it seems very clear that the whole act on the subject of the coasting trade, according to those principles which govern the construction of statutes, implies unequivocally an authority to licensed vessels to carry on the coasting trade.

But we will proceed briefly to notice those sections which bear more directly on the subject.

The first section declares that vessels enrolled by virtue of a previous law, and certain other vessels enrolled as described in that act, and having a license in force, as is by the act required, and no others, shall be deemed ships or vessels of the United States, entitled to the privileges of ships or vessels employed in the coasting trade.

This section seems to the Court to contain a positive enactment that the vessels it describes shall be entitled to the privileges of ships or vessels employed in the coasting trade. These privileges cannot be separated from the trade and cannot be enjoyed unless the trade may be prosecuted. The grant of the privilege is an idle, empty form, conveying nothing, unless it convey the right to which the privilege is attached and in the exercise of which its whole value consists. To construe these words otherwise than as entitling the ships or vessels described to carry on the coasting trade would be, we think, to disregard the apparent intent of the act.

The fourth section directs the proper officer to grant to a vessel qualified to receive it, "a license for carrying on the coasting trade," and prescribes its form. After reciting the compliance of the applicant with the previous requisites of the law, the operative words of the instrument are,

license is hereby granted for the said steamboat *Bellona* to be employed in carrying on the coasting trade for one year from the date hereof, and no longer.

These are not the words of the officer, they are the words of the legislature, and convey as explicitly the authority the act intended to give, and operate as effectually, as if they had been inserted in any other part of the act, than in the license itself.

The word "license" means permission or authority, and a license to do any particular thing is a permission or authority to do that thing, and if granted by a person having power to grant it, transfers to the grantee the right to do whatever it purports to authorize. It certainly transfers to him all the right which the grantor can transfer, to do what is within the terms of the license.

Would the validity or effect of such an instrument be questioned by the respondent, if executed by persons claiming regularly under the laws of New York?

The license must be understood to be what it purports to be, a legislative authority to the steamboat *Bellona* "to be employed in carrying on the coasting trade, for one year from this date."

It has been denied that these words authorize a voyage from New Jersey to New York. It is true that no ports are specified, but it is equally true that the words used are perfectly intelligible, and do confer such authority as unquestionably as if the ports had been mentioned. The coasting trade is a term well understood. The law has defined it, and all know its meaning perfectly. The act describes with great minuteness the various operations of a vessel engaged in it, and it cannot, we think, be doubted that a voyage from New Jersey to New York is one of those operations.

Notwithstanding the decided language of the license, it has also been maintained that it gives no right to trade, and that its sole purpose is to confer the American character.

The answer given to this argument that the American character is conferred by the enrollment, and not by the license, is, we think, founded too clearly in the words of the law to require the support of any additional observations. The enrollment of vessels designed for the coasting trade corresponds precisely with the registration of vessels designed for the foreign trade, and requires every circumstance which can constitute the American character. The license can be granted only to vessels already enrolled, if they be of the burthen of twenty tons and upwards, and requires no circumstance essential to the American character. The object of the license, then, cannot be to ascertain the character of the vessel, but to do what it professes to do—that is, to give permission to a vessel already proved by her enrollment to be American, to carry on the coasting trade.

But if the license be a permit to carry on the coasting trade, the respondent denies that these boats were engaged in that trade, or that the decree under consideration has restrained them from prosecuting it. The boats of the appellant were, we are told, employed in the transportation of passengers, and this is no part of that commerce which Congress may regulate.

If, as our whole course of legislation on this subject shows, the power of Congress has been universally understood in America to comprehend navigation, it is a very persuasive, if not a conclusive, argument to prove that the construction is correct, and if it be correct, no clear distinction is perceived between the power to regulate vessels employed in transporting men for hire and property for hire. The subject is transferred to Congress, and no exception to the grant can be admitted which is not proved by the words or the nature of the thing. A coasting vessel employed in the transportation of passengers is as much a portion of the American marine as one employed in the transportation of a cargo, and no reason is perceived why such vessel should be withdrawn from the regulating power of that government which has been thought best fitted for the purpose generally. The provisions of the law respecting native seamen and respecting ownership are as applicable to vessels carrying men as to vessels carrying manufactures, and no reason is perceived why the power over the subject should not be placed in the same hands. The argument urged at the bar rests on the foundation that the power of Congress does not extend to navigation as a branch of commerce, and can only be applied to that subject incidentally and occasionally. But if that foundation be removed, we must show some plain, intelligible distinction, supported by the Constitution or by reason, for discriminating between the power of Congress over vessels employed in navigating the same seas. We can perceive no such distinction.

If we refer to the Constitution, the inference to be drawn from it is rather against the distinction. The section which restrains Congress from prohibiting the migration or importation of such persons as any of the States may think proper to admit until the year 1808 has always been considered as an exception from the power to regulate commerce, and certainly seems to class migration with importation. Migration applies as appropriately to voluntary as importation does to involuntary arrivals, and, so far as an exception from a power proves its existence, this section proves that the power to regulate commerce applies equally to the regulation of vessels employed in transporting men, who pass from place to place voluntarily, and to those who pass involuntarily.

If the power reside in Congress, as a portion of the general grant to regulate commerce, then acts applying that power to vessels generally must be construed as comprehending all vessels. If none appear to be excluded by the language of the act, none can be excluded by construction. . . .

The laws of Congress for the regulation of commerce do not look to the principle by which vessels are moved. That subject is left entirely to individual discretion, and, in that vast and complex system of legislative enactment concerning it, which embraces everything that the Legislature thought it necessary to notice, there is not, we believe, one word respecting the peculiar principle by which vessels are propelled through the water, except what may be found in a single act granting a particular privilege to steamboats. With this exception, every act, either prescribing duties or granting privileges, applies to every vessel, whether navigated by the instrumentality of wind or fire, of sails or machinery. The whole weight of proof, then, is thrown upon him who would introduce a distinction to which the words of the law give no countenance.

If a real difference could be admitted to exist between vessels carrying passengers and others, it has already been observed that there is no fact in this case which can bring up that question. And, if the occupation of steamboats be a matter of such general notoriety that the Court may be presumed to know it, although not specially informed by the record, then we deny that the transportation of passengers is their exclusive occupation. It is a matter of general history that, in our western waters, their principal employment is the transportation of merchandise, and all know that, in the waters of the Atlantic, they are frequently so employed.

But all inquiry into this subject seems to the Court to be put completely at rest by the act already mentioned, entitled, "An act for the enrolling and licensing of steamboats."

This act authorizes a steamboat employed, or intended to be employed, only in a river or bay of the United States, owned wholly or in part by an alien, resident within the United States, to be enrolled and licensed as if the same belonged to a citizen of the United States.

This act demonstrates the opinion of Congress that steamboats may be enrolled and licensed, in common with vessels using sails. They are, of course, entitled to the same privileges, and can no more be restrained from navigating waters and entering ports which are free to such vessels than if they were wafted on their voyage by the winds, instead of being propelled by the agency of fire. The one element may be as legitimately used as the other for every commercial purpose authorized by the laws of the Union, and the act of a State inhibiting the use of either to any vessel having a license under the act of Congress comes, we think, in direct collision with that act.

As this decides the cause, it is unnecessary to enter in an examination of that part of the Constitution which empowers Congress to promote the progress of science and the useful arts.

The Court is aware that, in stating the train of reasoning by which we have been conducted to this result, much time has been consumed in the attempt to demonstrate propositions which may have been thought axioms. It is felt that the tediousness inseparable from the endeavour to prove that which is already clear is imputable to a considerable part of this opinion. But it was unavoidable. The conclusion to which we have come depends on a chain of principles which it was necessary to preserve unbroken, and although some of them were thought nearly self-evident, the magnitude of the question, the weight of character belonging to those from whose judgment we dissent, and the argument at the bar demanded that we should assume nothing.

Powerful and ingenious minds, taking as postulates that the powers expressly granted to the government of the Union are to be contracted by construction into the narrowest possible compass and that the original powers of the States are retained if any possible construction will retain them may, by a course of well digested but refined and metaphysical reasoning founded on these premises, explain away the Constitution of our country and leave it a magnificent structure indeed to look at, but totally unfit for use. They may so entangle and perplex the understanding as to obscure principles which were before thought quite plain, and induce doubts where, if the mind were to pursue its own course, none would be perceived. In such a case, it is peculiarly necessary to recur to safe and fundamental principles to sustain those principles, and when sustained, to make them the tests of the arguments to be examined.

Source: Findlaw.com. http://caselaw.lp.findlaw.com/scripts/getcase.pl?court=US &vol=22&invol=1

ANDREW JACKSON, "VETO OF MAYSVILLE ROAD BILL" (1830)

Henry Clay, one of the early leaders of Congress, was a strong proponent of the American System. This included an expansive program of internal improvements, which which became enmeshed with the ongoing debate over the extent of national power. Jackson's veto discussed the relationship of the federal to state government and the power of Congress in that debate. Jackson vetoed the bill on the grounds that the Constitution forbade Congress from federally funding local improvements.

To the House of Representatives:

Gentlemen, I have maturely considered the bill proposing to authorize a "subscription of stock in the Maysville . . . Road Company" and now return the same to the House of Representatives, in which it originated, with my objections to its passage. . . .

Such grants [of money by the federal government] have always been [passed] under the control of the general principle that the works which might be thus aided should be "of a general, not local, national, not State," character. A disregard of this distinction would of necessity lead to the subversion of the federal system. . . . I am not able to view [the Maysville Road Bill] in any other light than as a measure of purely local character. . . . It has no connection with any established system of improvements; [and] is exclusively within the limits of a State [Kentucky]. . . .

As great as this object [goal of internal improvements] undoubtedly is, it is not the only one which demands the fostering care of the government. The preservation and success of the republican principle rest with us. To elevate its character and its influence rank among our most important duties, and the best means to accomplish this desirable end are those which will rivet the attachment of our citizens to the Government of their choice by the comparative lightness of their public burthens [burdens] and by the attraction which the superior success of its operations will present to the admiration and respect of the world. Through the favor of an overruling and indulgent Providence our country is blessed with a general prosperity and our citizens exempted from the pressure of taxation, which other less favored portions of the human family are obliged to bear; yet it is true that many of the taxes collected from our citizens through the medium of imposts have for a considerable period been onerous. In many particulars these taxes have borne severely upon the laboring and less prosperous classes of the community, being imposed on the necessaries of life, and this, too, in cases where the burden was not relieved by the consciousness that it would ultimately contribute to make us independent of foreign nation articles of prime necessity by the encouragement of growth and manufacture at home. They have been cheerfully borne because they were thought to be necessary to the support of government and the payments of debts unavoidably incurred in the acquisition and maintenance of our national rights and liberties. But have we a right to calculate on the same cheerful acquiescence when it is known that the necessity for their continuance would cease were it not for irregular, improvident, and unequal appropriations of public funds? . . .

How gratifying the effect of presenting to the world the sublime spectacle of a Republic of more than 12,000,000 happy people, in the fifty-fourth year of her existence, after having passed through two protracted wars one for the acquisition and the other for the maintenance of liberty free from debt and all her immense resources unfettered! What a salutary influence would not such an exhibition exercise upon the cause of liberal principles and free government throughout the world! Would we not find ourselves in its effect an additional guarantee that our political institutions will be transmitted to the most remote posterity without decay? A course of policy destined to witness events like these cannot be benefited by a legislation which tolerates a scramble for appropriations that have no relation to any general system of improvement, and whose good effects must of necessity be very limited. . . .

If different impressions are entertained in any quarter; if it is expected that the people of this country, reckless of their constitutional obligations, will prefer their local interest to the principles of the Union . . . indeed has the world but little to hope from the example of free government. When an honest observance of constitutional compacts cannot be obtained from communities like ours, it need not be anticipated elsewhere . . . and the degrading truth that man is unfit for self-government [will be] admitted. And this will be the case if expediency be made a rule of construction in interpreting the Constitution. Power in no government could desire a better shield for the insidious advances which it is ever ready to make upon the checks that are designed to restrain its action.

Source: Andrew Jackson, "Veto of Maysville Road Bill" (1830). http://www.pinzler.com/ushistory/vetoofmaysupp.html

ANDREW JACKSON, "VETO MESSAGE REGARDING THE BANK OF THE UNITED STATES" (1832)

Jackson again used his veto power to stymie congressional desires by declaring, despite Chief Justice Marshall's pronouncement, over a decade earlier, that a national bank was outside the scope of congressional commerce authority.

To the Senate.

The bill "to modify and continue" the act entitled "An act to incorporate the subscribers to the Bank of the United States" was presented to me on the 4th July instant. Having considered it with that solemn regard to the principles of the Constitution which the day was calculated to inspire, and come to the conclusion that it ought not to become a law, I herewith return it to the Senate, in which it originated, with my objections.

A bank of the United States is in many respects convenient for the Government and useful to the people. Entertaining this opinion, and deeply impressed with the belief that some of the powers and privileges possessed by the existing bank are unauthorized by the Constitution, subversive of the rights of the States, and dangerous to the liberties of the people, I felt it my duty at an early period of my Administration to call the attention of Congress to the practicability of organizing an institution combining all its advantages and obviating these objections. I sincerely regret that in the act before me I can perceive none of those modifications of the bank charter which are necessary, in my opinion, to make it compatible with justice, with sound policy, or with the Constitution of our country.

The present corporate body, denominated the president, directors, and company of the Bank of the United States, will have existed at the time this act is intended to take effect twenty years. It enjoys an exclusive privilege of banking under the authority of the General Government, a monopoly of its favor and support, and, as a necessary consequence, almost a monopoly of the foreign and domestic exchange. The powers, privileges, and favors bestowed upon it in the original charter, by increasing the value of the stock far above its par value, operated as a gratuity of many millions to the stockholders.

An apology may be found for the failure to guard against this result in the consideration that the effect of the original act of incorporation could not be certainly foreseen at the time of its passage. The act before me proposes another gratuity to the holders of the same stock, and in many cases to the same men, of at least seven millions more. This donation finds no apology in any uncertainty as to the effect of the act. On all hands it is conceded that its passage will increase at least so or 30 per cent more the market price of the stock, subject to the payment of the annuity of $200,000 per year secured by the act, thus adding in a moment one-fourth to its par value. It is not our own citizens only who are to receive the bounty of our Government. More than eight millions of the stock of this bank are held by foreigners. By this act the American Republic proposes virtually to make them a present of some millions of dollars. For these gratuities to foreigners and to some of our own opulent citizens the act secures no equivalent whatever. They are the certain gains of the present stockholders under the operation of this act, after making full allowance for the payment of the bonus.

Every monopoly and all exclusive privileges are granted at the expense of the public, which ought to receive a fair equivalent. The many millions which this act proposes to bestow on the stockholders of the existing bank must come directly or indirectly out of the earnings of the American people. It is due to them, therefore, if their Government sell monopolies and exclusive privileges, that they should at least exact for them as much as they are worth in open market. The value of the monopoly in this case may be correctly ascertained. The twenty-eight millions of stock would probably be at an advance of 50 per cent, and command in market at least $42,000,000, subject to the payment of the present bonus. The present value of the monopoly, therefore, is $17,000,000, and this the act proposes to sell for three millions, payable in fifteen annual installments of $200,000 each.

It is not conceivable how the present stockholders can have any claim to the special favor of the Government. The present corporation has enjoyed its monopoly during the period stipulated in the original contract. If we must have such a corporation, why should not the Government sell out the whole stock and thus secure to the people the full market value of the privileges granted? Why should not Congress create and sell twenty-eight millions of stock, incorporating the purchasers with all the powers and privileges secured in this act and putting the premium upon the sales into the Treasury?

But this act does not permit competition in the purchase of this monopoly. It seems to be predicated on the erroneous idea that the present stockholders have a prescriptive right not only to the favor but to the bounty of Government. It appears that more than a fourth part of the stock is held by foreigners and the residue is held by a few hundred of our own citizens, chiefly of the richest class. For their benefit does this act exclude the whole American people from competition in the purchase of this monopoly and dispose of it for many millions less than it is worth. This seems the less excusable because some of our citizens not now stockholders petitioned that the door of competition might be opened, and offered to take a charter on terms much more favorable to the Government and country.

But this proposition, although made by men whose aggregate wealth is believed to be equal to all the private stock in the existing bank, has been set aside, and the bounty of our Government is proposed to be again bestowed on the few who have been fortunate enough to secure the stock and at this moment wield the power of the existing institution. I can not perceive the justice or policy of this course. If our Government must sell monopolies, it would seem to be its duty to take nothing less than their full value, and if gratuities must be made once in fifteen or twenty years let them not be bestowed on the subjects of a foreign government nor upon a designated and favored class of men in our own country. It is but justice and good policy, as far as the nature of the case will admit, to confine our favors to our own fellow-citizens, and let each in his turn enjoy an opportunity to profit by our bounty. In the bearings of the act before me upon these points I find ample reasons why it should not become a law.

It has been urged as an argument in favor of rechartering the present bank that the calling in its loans will produce great embarrassment and distress. The time allowed to close its concerns is ample, and if it has been well managed its pressure will be light, and heavy only in case its management has been bad. If, therefore, it shall produce distress, the fault will be its own, and it would furnish a reason against renewing a power which has been so obviously abused. But will there ever be a time when this reason will be less powerful? To acknowledge its force is to admit that the bank ought to be perpetual, and as a consequence the present stockholders and those inheriting their rights as successors be established a privileged order, clothed both with great political power and enjoying immense pecuniary advantages from their connection with the Government.

The modifications of the existing charter proposed by this act are not such, in my view, as make it consistent with the rights of the States or the liberties of the people. The qualification of the right of the bank to hold real estate, the limitation of its power to establish branches, and the power reserved to Congress to forbid the circulation of small notes are restrictions comparatively of little value or importance. All the objectionable principles of the existing corporation, and most of its odious features, are retained without alleviation.

The fourth section provides "that the notes or bills of the said corporation, although the same be, on the faces thereof, respectively made payable at one place only, shall nevertheless be received by the said corporation at the bank or at any of the offices of discount and deposit thereof if tendered in liquidation or payment of any balance or balances due to said corporation or to such office of discount and deposit from any other incorporated bank." This provision secures to the State banks a legal privilege in the Bank of the United States which is withheld from all private citizens. If a State bank in Philadelphia owe the Bank of the United States and have notes issued by the St. Louis branch, it can pay the debt with those notes, but if a merchant, mechanic, or other private citizen be in like circumstances he can not by law pay his debt with those notes, but must sell them at a discount or send them to St. Louis to be cashed. This boon conceded to the State banks, though not unjust in itself, is most odious because it does not measure out equal justice to the high and the low, the rich and the poor. To the extent of its practical effect it is a bond of union among the banking establishments of the nation, erecting them into an interest separate from that of the people, and its necessary tendency is to unite the Bank of the United States and the State banks in any measure which may be thought conducive to their common interest.

The ninth section of the act recognizes principles of worse tendency than any provision of the present charter.

It enacts that "the cashier of the bank shall annually report to the Secretary of the Treasury the names of all stockholders who are not resident citizens of the United States, and on the application of the treasurer of any State shall make out and transmit to such treasurer a list of stockholders residing in or citizens of such State, with the amount of stock owned by each." Although this provision, taken in connection with a decision of the Supreme Court, surrenders, by its silence, the right of the States to tax the banking institutions created by this corporation under the name of branches throughout the Union, it is evidently intended to be construed as a concession of their right to tax that portion of the stock which may be held by their own citizens and residents. In this light, if the act becomes a law, it will be understood by the States, who will probably proceed to levy a tax equal to that paid upon the stock of banks incorporated by themselves. In some States that tax is now I [one] per cent, either on the capital or on the shares, and that may be assumed as the amount which all citizen or resident stockholders would be taxed under the operation of this act. As it is only the stock held in the States and not that employed within them which would be subject to taxation, and as the names of foreign stockholders are not to be reported to the treasurers of the States, it is obvious that the stock held by them will be exempt from this burden. Their annual profits will therefore be I [one] per cent more than the citizen stockholders, and as the annual dividends of the bank may be safely estimated at 7 per cent, the stock will be worth 10 or 15 per cent more to foreigners than to citizens of the United States. To appreciate the effects which this state of things will produce, we must take a brief review of the operations and present condition of the Bank of the United States.

By documents submitted to Congress at the present session it appears that on the 1st of January, 1832, of the twenty-eight millions of private stock in the corporation, $8,405,500 were held by foreigners, mostly of Great Britain. The amount of stock held in the nine Western and Southwestern States is $140,200, and in the four Southern States is $5,623,100, and in the Middle and Eastern States is about $13,522,000. The profits of the bank in 1831, as shown in a statement to Congress, were about $3,455,598; of this there accrued in the nine western States about $1,640,048; in the four Southern States about $352,507, and in the Middle and Eastern States about $1,463,041. As little stock is held in the West, it is obvious that the debt of the people in that section to the bank is principally a debt to the Eastern and foreign stockholders; that the interest they pay upon it is carried into the Eastern States and into Europe, and that it is a burden upon their industry and a drain of their currency, which no country can bear without inconvenience and occasional distress. To meet this burden and equalize the exchange operations of the bank, the amount of specie drawn from those States through its branches within the last two years, as shown by its official reports, was about $6,000,000. More than half a million of this amount does not stop in the Eastern States, but passes on to Europe to pay the dividends of the foreign stockholders. In the principle of taxation recognized by this act the Western States find no adequate compensation for this perpetual burden on their industry and drain of their currency. The branch bank at Mobile made last year $95,140, yet under the provisions of this act the State of Alabama can raise no revenue from these profitable operations, because not a share of the stock is held by any of her citizens. Mississippi and Missouri are in the same condition in relation to the branches at Natchez and St. Louis, and such, in a greater or less degree, is the condition of every Western State. The tendency of the plan of taxation which this act proposes will be to place the whole United States in the same relation to foreign countries which the Western States now bear to the Eastern. When by a tax on resident stockholders the stock of this bank is made worth 10 or 15 per cent more to foreigners than to residents, most of it will inevitably leave the country.

Thus will this provision in its practical effect deprive the Eastern as well as the Southern and Western States of the means of raising a revenue from the extension of business and great profits of this institution. It will make the American people debtors to aliens in nearly the whole amount due to this bank, and send across the Atlantic from two to five millions of specie every year to pay the bank dividends.

In another of its bearings this provision is fraught with danger. Of the twenty-five directors of this bank five are chosen by the Government and twenty by the citizen stockholders. From all voice in these elections the foreign stockholders are excluded by the charter. In proportion, therefore, as the stock is transferred to foreign holders the extent of suffrage in the choice of directors is curtailed. Already is almost a third of the stock in foreign hands and not represented in elections. It is constantly passing out of the country, and this act will accelerate its departure. The entire control of the institution would necessarily fall into the hands of a few citizen stockholders, and the ease with which the object would be accomplished would be a temptation to designing men to secure that control in their own hands by monopolizing the remaining stock. There is danger that a president and directors would then be able to elect themselves from year to year, and without responsibility or control manage the whole concerns of the bank during the existence of its charter. It is easy to conceive that great evils to our country and its institutions . . . [might] flow from such a concentration of power in the hands of a few men irresponsible to the people.

Is there no danger to our liberty and independence in a bank that in its nature has so little to bind it to our country? The president of the bank has told us that most of the State banks exist by its forbearance. Should its influence become concentered [sic], as it may under the operation of such an act as this, in the hands of a self-elected directory whose interests are identified with those of the foreign stockholders, will there not be cause to tremble for the purity of our elections in peace and for the independence of our country in war? Their power would be great whenever they might choose to exert it; but if this monopoly were regularly renewed every fifteen or twenty years on terms proposed by themselves, they might seldom in peace put forth their strength to influence elections or control the affairs of the nation. But if any private citizen or public functionary should interpose to curtail its powers or prevent a renewal of its privileges, it can not be doubted that he would be made to feel its influence.

Should the stock of the bank principally pass into the hands of the subjects of a foreign country, and we should unfortunately become involved in a war with that country, what would be our condition? Of the course which would be pursued by a bank almost wholly owned by the subjects of a foreign power, and managed by those whose interests, if not affections, would run in the same direction there can be no doubt. All its operations within would be in aid of the hostile fleets and armies without. Controlling our currency, receiving our public moneys, and holding thousands of our citizens in dependence, it would be more formidable and dangerous than the naval and military power of the enemy.

If we must have a bank with private stockholders, every consideration of sound policy and every impulse of American feeling admonishes that it should be *purely American*. Its stockholders should be composed exclusively of our own citizens, who at least ought to be friendly to our Government and willing to support it in times of difficulty and danger. So abundant is domestic capital that competition in subscribing for the stock of local banks has recently led almost to riots. To a bank exclusively of American stockholders, possessing the powers and privileges granted by this act, subscriptions for $200,000,000 could be readily obtained. Instead of sending abroad the stock of the bank in which the Government must deposit its funds and on which it must rely to sustain its credit in times of emergency, it would rather seem to be expedient to prohibit its sale to aliens under penalty of absolute forfeiture.

It is maintained by the advocates of the bank that its constitutionality in all its features ought to be considered as settled by precedent and by the decision of the Supreme Court. To this conclusion I can not assent. Mere precedent is a dangerous source of authority, and should not be regarded as deciding questions of constitutional power except where the acquiescence of the people and the States can be considered as well settled. So far from this being the case on this subject, an argument against the bank might be based on precedent. One Congress, in 1791, decided in favor of a bank; another, in 1811, decided against it. One Congress, in 1815, decided against a bank; another, in 1816, decided in its favor. Prior to the present Congress, therefore, the precedents drawn from that source were equal. If we resort to the States, the expressions of legislative, judicial, and executive opinions against the bank have been probably to those in its favor as 4 to 1. There is nothing in precedent, therefore, which, if its authority were admitted, ought to weigh in favor of the act before me.

If the opinion of the Supreme Court covered the whole ground of this act, it ought not to control the coordinate authorities of this Government. The Congress, the Executive, and the Court must each for itself be guided by its own opinion of the Constitution. Each public officer who takes an oath to support the Constitution swears that he will support it as he understands it, and not as it is understood by others. It is as much the duty of the House of Representatives, of the Senate, and of the President to decide upon the constitutionality of any bill or resolution which may be presented to them for passage or approval as it is of the supreme judges when it may be brought before them for judicial decision. The opinion of the judges has no more authority over Congress than the opinion of Congress has over the judges, and on that point the President is independent of both. The authority of the Supreme Court must not, therefore, be permitted to control the Congress or the Executive when acting in their legislative capacities, but to have only such influence as the force of their reasoning may deserve.

But in the case relied upon the Supreme Court have not decided that all the features of this corporation are compatible with the Constitution. It is true that the court have said that the law incorporating the bank is a constitutional exercise of power by Congress; but taking into view the whole opinion of the court and the reasoning by which they have come to that conclusion, I understand them to have decided that inasmuch as a bank is an appropriate means for carrying into effect the enumerated powers of the General Government, therefore the law incorporating it is in accordance with that provision of the Constitution which declares that Congress shall have power " to make all laws which shall be necessary and proper for carrying those powers into execution." Having satisfied themselves that the word *"necessary"* in the Constitution means *needful," "requisite," "essential," "conducive to,"* and that "a bank" is a convenient, a useful, and essential instrument in the prosecution of the Government's "fiscal operations," they conclude that to "use one must be within the discretion of Congress " and that "the act to incorporate the Bank of the United States is a law made in pursuance of the Constitution"; "but," say they, *"where the law is not prohibited and is really calculated to effect any of the objects intrusted to the Government, to undertake here to inquire into the degree of its necessity would be to pass the line which circumscribes the judicial department and to tread on legislative ground."*

The principle here affirmed is that the "degree of its necessity," involving all the details of a banking institution, is a question exclusively for legislative consideration. A bank is constitutional, but it is the province of the Legislature to determine whether this or that particular power, privilege, or exemption is "necessary and proper" to enable the bank to discharge its duties to the Government, and from their decision there is no appeal to the courts of justice. Under the decision of the Supreme Court, therefore, it is the exclusive province of Congress and the President to decide whether the particular features of this act are *necessary* and *proper* in order to enable the bank to perform conveniently and efficiently the public duties assigned to it as a fiscal agent, and therefore constitutional, or *unnecessary* and *improper,* and therefore unconstitutional.

Without commenting on the general principle affirmed by the Supreme Court, let us examine the details of this act in accordance with the rule of legislative action which they have laid down. It will be found that many of the powers and privileges conferred on it can not be supposed necessary for the purpose for which it is proposed to be created, and are not, therefore, means necessary to attain the end in view, and consequently not justified by the Constitution.

The original act of incorporation, section 2I [sic], enacts "that no other bank shall be established by any future law of the United States during the continuance of the corporation hereby created, for which the faith of the United States is hereby pledged: *Provided,* Congress may renew existing charters for banks within the District of Columbia not increasing the capital thereof, and may also establish any other bank or banks in said District with capitals not exceeding in the whole $6,000,000 if they shall deem it expedient." This provision is continued in force by the act before me fifteen years from the ad of March, 1836.

If Congress possessed the power to establish one bank, they had power to establish more than one if in their opinion two or more banks had been "necessary" to facilitate the execution of the powers delegated to them in the Constitution. If they possessed the power to establish a second bank, it was a power derived from the Constitution to be exercised from time to time, and at any time when the interests of the country or the emergencies of the Government might make it expedient. It was possessed by one Congress as well as another, and by all Congresses alike, and alike at every session. But the Congress of 1816 have taken it away from their successors for twenty years, and the Congress of 1832 proposes to abolish it for fifteen years more. It can not be *"necessary"* or *"proper"* for Congress to barter away or divest themselves of any of the powers vested in them by the Constitution to be exercised for the public good. It is not "necessary" to the efficiency of the bank, nor is it *"proper"* in relation to themselves and their successors. They may *properly* use the discretion vested in them, but they may not limit the discretion of their successors. This restriction on themselves and grant of a monopoly to the bank is therefore unconstitutional.

In another point of view this provision is a palpable attempt to amend the Constitution by an act of legislation. The Constitution declares that "the Congress shall have power to exercise exclusive legislation in all cases whatsoever" over the District of Columbia. Its constitutional power, therefore, to establish banks in the District of

Columbia and increase their capital at will is unlimited and uncontrollable by any other power than that which gave authority to the Constitution. Yet this act declares that Congress shall not increase the capital of existing banks, nor create other banks with capitals exceeding in the whole $6,000,000. The Constitution declares that Congress *shall* have power to exercise exclusive legislation over this District *"in all cases whatsoever,"* and this act declares they shall not. Which is the supreme law of the land? This provision can not be *"necessary"* or *"proper"* or *constitutional* unless the absurdity be admitted that whenever it be "necessary and proper" in the opinion of Congress they have a right to barter away one portion of the powers vested in them by the Constitution as a means of executing the rest.

On two subjects only does the Constitution recognize in Congress the power to grant exclusive privileges or monopolies. It declares that "Congress shall have power to promote the progress of science and useful arts by securing for limited times to authors and inventors the exclusive right to their respective writings and discoveries." Out of this express delegation of power have grown our laws of patents and copyrights. As the Constitution expressly delegates to Congress the power to grant exclusive privileges in these cases as the means of executing the substantive power "to promote the progress of science and useful arts," it is consistent with the fair rules of construction to conclude that such a power was not intended to be granted as a means of accomplishing any other end. On every other subject which comes within the scope of Congressional power there is an ever-living discretion in the use of proper means, which can not be restricted or abolished without an amendment of the Constitution. Every act of Congress, therefore, which attempts by grants of monopolies or sale of exclusive privileges for a limited time, or a time without limit, to restrict or extinguish its own discretion in the choice of means to execute its delegated powers is equivalent to a legislative amendment of the Constitution, and palpably unconstitutional.

This act authorizes and encourages transfers of its stock to foreigners and grants them an exemption from all State and national taxation. So far from being *"necessary and proper"* that the bank should possess this power to make it a safe and efficient agent of the Government in its fiscal operations, it is calculated to convert the Bank of the United States into a foreign bank, to impoverish our people in time of peace, to disseminate a foreign influence through every section of the Republic, and in war to endanger our independence.

The several States reserved the power at the formation of the Constitution to regulate and control titles and transfers of real property, and most, if not all, of them have laws disqualifying aliens from acquiring or holding lands within their limits. But this act, in disregard of the undoubted right of the States to prescribe such disqualifications, gives to aliens stockholders in this bank an interest and title, as members of the corporation, to all the real property it may acquire within any of the States of this Union. This privilege granted to aliens is not *"necessary"* to enable the bank to perform its public duties, nor in any sense *"proper,"* because it is vitally subversive of the rights of the States.

The Government of the United States have no constitutional power to purchase lands within the States except "for the erection of forts, magazines, arsenals, dockyards, and other needful buildings," and even for these objects only "by the consent of the legislature of the State in which the same shall be." By making themselves stockholders in the bank and granting to the corporation the power to purchase lands for other purposes they assume a power not granted in the Constitution and grant to others what they do not themselves possess. It is not *necessary* to the receiving, safe-keeping, or transmission of the funds of the Government that the bank should possess this power, and it is not *proper* that Congress should thus enlarge the powers delegated to them in the Constitution.

The old Bank of the United States possessed a capital of only $11,000,000, which was found fully sufficient to enable it with dispatch and safety to perform all the functions required of it by the Government. The capital of the present bank is $35,000,000—at least twenty-four [million] more than experience has proved to be *necessary* to enable a bank to perform its public functions. The public debt which existed during the period of the old bank and on the establishment of the new has been nearly paid off, and our revenue will soon be reduced. This increase of capital is therefore not for public but for private purposes.

The Government is the only *"proper"* judge where its agents should reside and keep their offices, because it best knows where their presence will be *"necessary."* It can not, therefore, be *"necessary"* or *"proper"* to authorize the bank to locate branches where it pleases to perform the public service, without consulting the Government, and contrary to its will. The principle laid down by the Supreme Court concedes that Congress can not establish a bank for purposes of private speculation and gain, but only as a means of executing the delegated powers of the General Government. By the same principle a branch bank can not constitutionally be established for other than public purposes. The power which this act gives to establish two branches in any State, without the injunction or request of the Government and for other than public purposes, is not *"necessary"* to the due *execution* of the powers delegated to Congress.

The bonus which is exacted from the bank is a confession upon the face of the act that the powers granted by it are greater than are *"necessary"* to its character of a fiscal agent. The Government does not tax its officers and agents for the privilege of serving it. The bonus of a million and a half required by the original charter and that of three millions proposed by this act are not exacted for the privilege of giving "the necessary facilities for transferring the public funds from place to place within the United States or the Territories thereof, and for distributing the same in payment of the public creditors without charging commission or claiming allowance on account of the difference of exchange," as required by the act of incorporation, but for something more beneficial to the stockholders. The original act declares that it (the bonus) is granted "in consideration of the exclusive privileges and benefits conferred by this act upon the said bank," and the act before me declares it to be "in consideration of the exclusive benefits and privileges continued by this act to the said corporation for fifteen years, as aforesaid." It is therefore for "exclusive privileges and benefits" conferred for their own use and emolument, and not for the advantage of the Government, that a bonus is exacted. These surplus powers for which the bank is required to pay can not surely be *"necessary"* to make it the fiscal agent of the Treasury. If they were, the exaction of a bonus for them would not be *"proper."*

It is maintained by some that the bank is a means of executing the constitutional power "to coin money and regulate the value thereof." Congress have established a mint to coin money and passed laws to regulate the value thereof. The money so coined, with its value so regulated, and such foreign coins as Congress may adopt are the only currency known to the Constitution. But if they have other power to regulate the currency, it was conferred to be exercised by themselves, and not to be transferred to a corporation. If the bank be established for that purpose, with a charter unalterable without its consent, Congress have parted with their power for a term of years, during which the Constitution is a dead letter. It is neither necessary nor proper to transfer its legislative power to such a bank, and therefore unconstitutional.

By its silence, considered in connection with the decision of the Supreme Court in the case of McCulloch against the State of Maryland, this act takes from the States the power to tax a portion of the banking business carried on within their limits, in subversion of one of the strongest barriers which secured them against Federal encroachments. Banking, like farming, manufacturing, or any other occupation or profession, is a *business*, the right to follow which is not originally derived from the laws. Every citizen and every company of citizens in all of our States possessed the right until the State legislatures deemed it good policy to prohibit private banking by law. If the prohibitory State laws were now repealed, every citizen would again possess the right. The State banks are a qualified restoration of the right which has been taken away by the laws against banking, guarded by such provisions and limitations as in the opinion of the State legislatures the public interest requires. These corporations, unless there be an exemption in their charter, are, like private bankers and banking companies, subject to State taxation. The manner in which these taxes shall be laid depends wholly on legislative discretion. It may be upon the bank, upon the stock, upon the profits, or in any other mode which the sovereign power shall will.

Upon the formation of the Constitution the States guarded their taxing power with peculiar jealousy. They surrendered it only as it regards imports and exports. In relation to every other object within their jurisdiction, whether persons, property, business, or professions, it was secured in as ample a manner as it was before possessed. All persons, though United States officers, are liable to a poll tax by the States within which they reside. The lands of the United States are liable to the usual land tax, except in the new States, from whom agreements that they will not tax unsold lands are exacted when they are admitted into the Union. Horses, wagons, any beasts or vehicles, tools, or property belonging to private citizens, though employed in the service of the United States, are subject to State taxation. Every private business, whether carried on by an officer of the General Government or not, whether it be mixed with public concerns or not, even if it be carried on by the Government of the United States itself, separately or in partnership, falls within the scope of the taxing power of the State. Nothing comes more fully within it than banks and the business of banking, by whomsoever instituted and carried on. Over this whole subject-matter it is just as absolute, unlimited, and uncontrollable as if the Constitution had never been adopted, because in the formation of that instrument it was reserved without qualification.

The principle is conceded that the States can not rightfully tax the operations of the General Government. They can not tax the money of the Government deposited in the State banks, nor the agency of those banks in remitting it; but will any man maintain that their mere selection to perform this public service for the General Government would exempt the State banks and their ordinary business from State taxation? Had the United States, instead of establishing a bank at Philadelphia, employed a private banker to keep and transmit their funds, would it have deprived Pennsylvania of the right to tax his bank and his usual banking operations? It will not be pretended. Upon what principal, then, are the banking establishments of the Bank of the United States and their usual banking operations to be exempted from taxation? It is not their public agency or the deposits of the Government which the States claim a right to tax, but their banks and their banking powers, instituted and exercised within State jurisdiction for their private emolument—those powers and privileges for which they pay a bonus, and which the States tax in their own banks. The exercise of these powers within a State, no matter by whom or under what authority, whether by private citizens in their original right, by corporate bodies created by the States, by foreigners or the agents of foreign governments located within their limits, forms a legitimate object of State taxation. From this and like sources, from the persons, property, and business that are found residing, located, or carried on under their jurisdiction, must the States, since the surrender of their right to raise a revenue from imports and exports, draw all the money necessary for the support of their governments and the maintenance of their independence. There is no more appropriate subject of taxation than banks, banking, and bank stocks, and none to which the States ought more pertinaciously to cling.

It can not be *necessary* to the character of the bank as a fiscal agent of the Government that its private business should be exempted from that taxation to which all the State banks are liable, nor can I conceive it *"proper"* that the substantive and most essential powers reserved by the States shall be thus attacked and annihilated as a means of executing the powers delegated to the General Government. It may be safely assumed that none of those sages who had an agency in forming or adopting our Constitution ever imagined that any portion of the taxing power of the States not prohibited to them nor delegated to Congress was to be swept away and annihilated as a means of executing certain powers delegated to Congress.

If our power over means is so absolute that the Supreme Court will not call in question the constitutionality of an act of Congress the subject of which "is not prohibited, and is really calculated to effect any of the objects intrusted to the Government," although, as in the case before me, it takes away powers expressly granted to Congress and rights scrupulously reserved to the States, it becomes us to proceed in our legislation with the utmost caution. Though not directly, our own powers and the rights of the States may be indirectly legislated away in the use of means to execute substantive powers. We may not enact that Congress shall not have the power of exclusive legislation over the District of Columbia, but we may pledge the faith of the United States that as a means of executing other powers it shall not be exercised for twenty years or forever. We may not pass an act prohibiting the States to tax the banking business carried on within their limits, but we may, as a means of executing our powers over other objects, place that business in the hands of our agents and then declare it exempt from State taxation in their hands. Thus may our own powers and the rights of the States, which we can not directly curtail or invade, be frittered away and extinguished in the use of means employed by us to execute other powers. That a bank of the United States, competent to all the duties which may be required by the Government, might be so organized as not to infringe on our own delegated powers or the reserved rights of the States I do not entertain a doubt. Had the Executive been called upon to furnish the project of such an institution, the duty would have been cheerfully performed. In the absence of such a call it was obviously proper that he should confine himself to pointing out those prominent features in the act presented which in his opinion make it incompatible with the Constitution and sound policy. A general discussion will now take place, eliciting new light and settling important principles; and a new Congress, elected in the midst of such discussion, and furnishing an equal representation of the people according to the last census, will bear to the Capitol the verdict of public opinion, and, I doubt not, bring this important question to a satisfactory result.

Under such circumstances the bank comes forward and asks a renewal of its charter for a term of fifteen years upon conditions which not only operate as a gratuity to the stockholders of many millions of dollars, but will sanction any abuses and legalize any encroachments.

Suspicions are entertained and charges are made of gross abuse and violation of its charter. An investigation unwillingly conceded and so restricted in time as necessarily to make it incomplete and unsatisfactory discloses enough to excite suspicion and alarm. In the practices of the principal bank partially unveiled, in the absence of important witnesses, and in numerous charges confidently made and as yet wholly uninvestigated there was enough to induce a majority of the committee of investigation—a committee which was selected from the most able and honorable members of the House of Representatives—to recommend a suspension of further action upon the bill and a prosecution of the inquiry. As the charter had yet four years to run, and as a renewal now was not necessary to the successful prosecution of its business, it was to have been expected that the bank itself, conscious of its purity and proud of its character, would have withdrawn its application for the present, and demanded the severest scrutiny into all its transactions. In their declining to do so there seems to be an additional reason why the functionaries of the Government should proceed with less haste and more caution in the renewal of their monopoly.

The bank is professedly established as an agent of the executive branch of the Government, and its constitutionality is maintained on that ground. Neither upon the propriety of present action nor upon the provisions of this act was the Executive consulted. It has had no opportunity to say that it neither needs nor wants an agent clothed with such powers and favored by such exemptions. There is nothing in its legitimate functions which makes it necessary or proper. Whatever interest or influence, whether public or private, has given birth to this act, it can not be found either in the wishes or necessities of the executive department, by which present action is deemed premature, and the powers conferred upon its agent not only unnecessary, but dangerous to the Government and country.

It is to be regretted that the rich and powerful too often bend the acts of government to their selfish purposes. Distinctions in society will always exist under every just government. Equality of talents, of education, or of wealth can not be produced by human institutions. In the full enjoyment of the gifts of Heaven and the fruits of superior industry, economy, and virtue, every man is equally entitled to protection by law; but when the laws undertake to add to these natural and just advantages artificial distinctions, to grant titles, gratuities, and exclusive privileges, to make the rich richer and the potent more powerful, the humble members of society—the farmers, mechanics, and laborers—who have neither the time nor the means of securing like favors to themselves, have a right to complain of the injustice of their Government. There are no necessary evils in government. Its evils exist only in its abuses. If it would confine itself to equal protection, and, as Heaven does its rains, shower its favors alike on the high and the low, the rich and the poor, it would be an unqualified blessing. In the act before me there seems to be a wide and unnecessary departure from these just principles.

Nor is our Government to be maintained or our Union preserved by invasions of the rights and powers of the several States. In thus attempting to make our General Government strong we make it weak. Its true strength consists in leaving individuals and States as much as possible to themselves—in making itself felt, not in its power, but in its beneficence; not in its control, but in its protection; not in binding the States more closely to the center, but leaving each to move unobstructed in its proper orbit.

Experience should teach us wisdom. Most of the difficulties our Government now encounters and most of the dangers which impend over our Union have sprung from an abandonment of the legitimate objects of Government by our national legislation, and the adoption of such principles as are embodied in this act. Many of our rich men have not been content with equal protection and equal benefits, but have besought us to make them richer by act of Congress. By attempting to gratify their desires we have in the results of our legislation arrayed section against section, interest against interest, and man against man, in a fearful commotion which threatens to shake the foundations of our Union. It is time to pause in our career to review our principles, and if possible revive that devoted patriotism and spirit of compromise which distinguished the sages of the Revolution and the fathers of our Union. If we can not at once, in justice to interests vested under improvident legislation, make our Government what it ought to be, we can at least take a stand against all new grants of monopolies and exclusive privileges, against any prostitution of our Government to the advancement of the few at the expense of the many, and in favor of compromise and gradual reform in our code of laws and system of political economy.

I have now done my duty to my country. If sustained by my fellow citizens, I shall be grateful and happy; if not, I shall find in the motives which impel me ample grounds for contentment and peace. In the difficulties which surround us and the dangers which threaten our institutions there is cause for neither dismay nor alarm. For relief and deliverance let us firmly rely on that kind Providence which I am sure watches with peculiar care over the destinies of our Republic, and on the intelligence and wisdom of our countrymen. Through His abundant goodness and their patriotic devotion our liberty and Union will be preserved.

—Andrew Jackson.

Source: The Avalon Project at Yale Law School. http://www.yale.edu/lawweb/avalon/presiden/veto/ajveto01.htm

JOINT RESOLUTION OF THE CONGRESS OF THE UNITED STATES (MARCH 1, 1845)

Joint resolution issued by the Congress under pressure from President John Tyler, after the Senate rejected a treaty to annex Texas in 1844. By annexing Texas via a joint resolution rather than a formal treaty, Congress was able to move forward on a simple majority rather than the two-thirds vote necessary for ratification of a treaty.

28th Congress, Second Session

Begun and held at the city of Washington, in the District of Columbia, on Monday the second day of December, eighteen hundred and forty-four.

Joint Resolution for annexing Texas to the United States.

Resolved by the Senate and House of Representatives of the United States of America in Congress assembled, That Congress doth consent that the territory properly included within, and rightfully belonging to the Republic of Texas, may be erected into a new state, to be called the state of Texas, with a republican form of government, to be adopted by the people of said republic, by deputies in Convention assembled, with the consent of the existing government, in order that the same may be admitted as one of the states of this Union.

2. And be it further resolved, That the foregoing consent of Congress is given upon the following conditions, and with the following guarantees, to wit: First-said state to be formed, subject to the adjustment by this government of all questions of boundary that may arise with other governments; and the constitution thereof, with the proper evidence of its adoption by the people of said republic of Texas, shall be transmitted to the President of the United States, to be laid before Congress for its final action, on or before the first day of January, one thousand eight hundred and forty-six. Second-said

state, when admitted into the Union, after ceding to the United States all public edifices, fortifications, barracks, ports and harbors, navy and navy-yards, docks, magazines, arms, armaments, and all other property and means pertaining to the public defence belonging to said republic of Texas, shall retain all the public funds, debts, taxes, and dues of every kind which may belong to or be due and owing said republic; and shall also retain all the vacant and unappropriated lands lying within its limits, to be applied to the payment of the debts and liabilities of said republic of Texas; and the residue of said lands, after discharging said debts and liabilities, to be disposed of as said state may direct; but in no event are said debts and liabilities to become a charge upon the government of the United States. Third-New states, of convenient size, not exceeding four in number, in addition to said state of Texas, and having sufficient population, may hereafter, by the consent of said state, be formed out of the territory thereof, which shall be entitled to admission under the provisions of the federal constitution. And such states as may be formed out of that portion of said territory lying south of thirty-six degrees thirty minutes north latitude, commonly known as the Missouri compromise line, shall be admitted into the Union with or without slavery, as the people of each state asking admission may desire. And in such state or states as shall be formed out of said territory north of said Missouri compromise line, slavery, or involuntary servitude, (except for crime,) shall be prohibited.

3. And be it further resolved, That if the President of the United States shall in his judgment and discretion deem it most advisable, instead of proceeding to submit the foregoing resolution to the Republic of Texas, as an overture on the part of the United States for admission, to negotiate with that Republic; then, Be it resolved, that a state, to be formed out of the present Republic of Texas, with suitable extent and boundaries, and with two representatives in Congress, until the next apportionment of representation, shall be admitted into the Union, by virtue of this act, on an equal footing with the existing states, as soon as the terms and conditions of such admission, and the cession of the remaining Texan territory to the United States shall be agreed upon by the governments of Texas and the United States: And that the sum of one hundred thousand dollars be, and the same is hereby, appropriated to defray the expenses of missions and negotiations, to agree upon the terms of said admission and cession, either by treaty to be submitted to the Senate, or by articles to be submitted to the two Houses of Congress, as the President may direct.

J W JONES
Speaker of the House of Representatives.
WILLIE P. MANGUM
President, pro tempore, of the Senate.
Approv'd March 1. 1845
JOHN TYLER
Source: The Avalon Project at Yale Law School. http://www.yale.edu/lawweb/avalon/texan01.htm

AMENDMENTS PROPOSED IN CONGRESS BY SENATOR JOHN J. CRITTENDEN (DECEMBER 18, 1860)

A combination of proposed constitutional amendments and congressional resolutions, it was an unsuccessful last-minute attempt by Congress to avert Civil War. Proposed by Sen. John J. Crittenden of Kentucky, it guaranteed the survival of the institution of slavery. Its defeat in the House in January 1861 (113–80) and in the Senate in March (20–19) was the last major attempt to avert Civil War.

Whereas, serious and alarming dissensions have arisen between the Northern and Southern States, concerning the rights and security of the rights of the slaveholding States, and especially their rights in the common territory of the United States; and whereas it is eminently desirable and proper that these dissensions, which now threaten the very existence of this Union, should be permanently quieted and settled by constitutional provisions, which shall do equal justice to all sections, and thereby restore to the people that peace and good will which ought to prevail between all the citizens of the United States: Therefore,

Resolved by the Senate and House of Representatives of the United States of America in Congress assembled (two-thirds of both Houses concurring), That the following articles be, and are hereby, proposed and submitted as amendments to the Constitution of the United States, which shall be valid to all intents and purposes, as part of said Constitution, when ratified by conventions of three-fourths of the several States:

ARTICLE I.

In all the territory of the United States now held, or hereafter acquired, situated north of latitude 36°30′, slavery or involuntary servitude, except as a punishment for crime, is prohibited while such territory shall remain under territorial government. In all the territory south of said line of latitude, slavery of the African race is hereby recognized as existing, and shall not be interfered with by Congress, but shall be protected as property by all the departments of the territorial government during its continuance. And when any Territory, north or south of said line, within such boundaries as Congress may prescribe, shall contain the population requisite for a member of Congress according to the then Federal ratio of representation of the people of the United States, it shall, if its form of government be republican, be admitted into the Union, on an equal footing with the original States, with or without slavery, as the constitution of such new State may provide.

ARTICLE II.

Congress shall have no power to abolish slavery in places under its exclusive jurisdiction, and situate within the limits of States that permit the holding of slaves.

ARTICLE III.

Congress shall have no power to abolish slavery within the District of Columbia, so long as it exists in the adjoining States of Virginia and Maryland, or either, nor without the consent of the inhabitants, nor without just compensation first made to such owners of slaves as do not consent to such abolishment. Nor shall Congress at any time prohibit officers of the Federal Government, or members of Congress, whose duties require them to be in said District, from bringing with them their slaves, and holding them as such, during the time their duties may require them to remain there, and afterward taking them from the District.

ARTICLE IV.

Congress shall have no power to prohibit or hinder the transportation of slaves from one State to another, or to a Territory in which slaves are by law permitted to be held, whether that transportation be by land, navigable rivers, or by the sea.

ARTICLE V.

That in addition to the provisions of the third paragraph of the second section of the fourth article of the Constitution of the United States, Congress shall have power to provide by law, and it shall be its duty so to provide, that the United States shall pay to the owner who shall apply for it, the full value of his fugitive slave in all cases when the marshal or other officer whose duty it was to arrest said fugitive was prevented from so doing by violence or intimidation, or when, after arrest, said fugitive was rescued by force, the owner thereby prevented and obstructed in the pursuit of his remedy for the recovery of his fugitive slave under the said clause of the Constitution and the laws made in pursuance thereof. And in all such cases, when the United States shall pay for such fugitive, they shall have the right, in their own name, to sue the county in which said violence, intimidation, or rescue was committed, and to recover from it, with interest and damages, the amount paid by them for said fugitive slave. And the said county, after it has paid said amount to the United States may, for its indemnity, sue and recover from the wrongdoers or rescuers by whom the owner was prevented from the recovery of his fugitive slave, in like manner as the owner himself might have sued and recovered.

ARTICLE VI.

No future amendment of the Constitution shall affect the five preceding articles; nor the third paragraph of the second section of the first article of the Constitution, nor the third paragraph of the second section of the fourth article of said Constitution and no amendment shall be made to the Constitution which shall authorize or give to Congress any power to abolish or interfere with slavery in any of the States by whose laws it is, or may be allowed or permitted.

And whereas, also, besides these causes of dissension embraced in the foregoing amendments proposed to the Constitution of the United States, there are others which come within the jurisdiction of Congress, as far as its power will extend, to remove all just cause for the popular discontent and agitation which now disturb the peace of the country, and threaten the stability of its institutions: Therefore,

1. Resolved by the Senate and House of Representatives of the United States of America in Congress assembled That the laws now in force for the recovery of fugitive slaves are in strict pursuance of the plain and mandatory provisions of the Constitution, and have been sanctioned as valid and constitutional by the judgment of the Supreme Court of the United States, that the slaveholding States are entitled to the faithful observance and execution of those laws, and that they ought not to be repealed, or so modified or changed as to impair their efficiency; and that laws ought to be made for the punishment of those who attempt by rescue of the slave, or other illegal means, to hinder or defeat the clue execution of said laws,

2. That all State laws which conflict with the fugitive slave acts of Congress, or any other constitutional acts of Congress, or which, in their operation, impede, hinder, or delay the free course and due execution of any of said acts, are null and void by the plain provisions of the Constitution of the United States; yet those State laws, void as they are, have given color to practice, and led to consequences which have obstructed the due administration and execution of acts of Congress, and especially the acts for the delivery of fugitive slaves, and have thereby contributed much to the discord and commotion now prevailing. Congress, therefore, in the present perilous juncture, does not deem it improper respectfully and earnestly to recommend the repeal of those laws to the several States which have enacted them, or such legislative corrections or explanations of them as may prevent their being used or perverted to such mischievous purposes.

3. That the act of the 18th of September, 1850, commonly called the fugitive slave law, ought to be so amended as to make the fee of the commissioner, mentioned in the eighth section of the act equal in amount, in the cases decided by claimant. And to avoid misconstruction, the last clause of the fifth section of said act which authorizes the person holding a warrant for the arrest or detention of a fugitive slave, to summon to his aid the posse comitatus, and which declares it to be the duty of all good citizens to assist him in its execution, ought to be so amended as to expressly limit the authority and duty to cases in which there shall be resistance or danger of resistance or rescue.

4. That the laws for the suppression of the African slave-trade and especially those prohibiting the importation of slaves in the United States, ought to be made effectual, and ought to be thoroughly executed; and all further enactments necessary to those ends ought to be promptly made.

Source: The Avalon Project at Yale Law School. http://www.yale.edu/lawweb/avalon/amerdoc/critten.htm

THE WADE-DAVIS MANIFESTO (AUGUST 5, 1864)

The Wade-Davis Bill represented the first Radical Republican plan for Reconstruction. President Lincoln vetoed it. The bill based Reconstruction on ideas of federalism and republicanism that provided for congressional control and direction in rebuilding the South. Radical Republicans were furious at Lincoln's veto and his far more lenient view of how to treat the former rebels. In response, Benjamin Wade and Henry Winter Davis published the subsequent attack on Lincoln. They accused Lincoln of overstepping his presidential authority and usurping the power of Congress.

We have read without surprise, but not without indignation, the Proclamation of the President of the 8th of July.

The President, by preventing this bill from becoming a law, holds the electoral votes of the Rebel States at the dictation of his personal ambition.

If those votes turn the balance in his favor, is it to be supposed that his competitor, defeated by such means will acquiesce?

If the Rebel majority assert their supremacy in those States, and send votes which elect an enemy of the Government, will we not repel his claims?

And is not that civil war for the Presidency, inaugurated by the votes of Rebel States?

Seriously impressed with these dangers, Congress, "the proper constitutional authority," formally declared that there are no State Governments in the Rebel States, and provided for their erection at a proper time; and both the Senate and the House of Representatives rejected the Senators and Representatives chosen under the authority of what the President calls the Free Constitution and Government of Arkansas.

The President's proclamation "holds for naught" this judgment, and discards the authority of the Supreme Court, and strides headlong toward the anarchy his Proclamation of the 8th of December inaugurated.

If electors for President be allowed to be chosen in either of those States, a sinister light will be cast on the motives which induced the President to "hold for naught" the will of Congress rather than his Government in Louisiana and Arkansas.

That judgment of Congress which the President defies was the exercise of an authority exclusively vested in Congress by the Constitution to determine what is the established Government in a State, and in its own nature and by the highest judicial authority binding on all other departments of the Government.

A more studied outrage on the legislative authority of the people has never been perpetrated.

Congress passed a bill; the President refused to approve it, and then by proclamation puts as much of it in force as he sees fit, and proposes to execute those parts by officers unknown to the laws of the United States and not subject to the confirmation of the Senate!

The bill directed the appointment of Provisional Governors by and with the advice and consent of the Senate.

The President, after defeating the law, proposes to appoint without law, and without the advice and consent of the Senate, Military Governors for the Rebel States!

He has already exercised this dictatorial usurpation in Louisiana, and he defeated the bill to prevent its limitation.

The President has greatly presumed on the forbearance which the supporters of his Administration have so long practiced, in view of the arduous conflict in which we are engaged, and the reckless ferocity of our political opponents.

But he must understand that our support is of a cause and not of a man; that the authority of Congress is paramount and must be respected; that the whole body of the Union men of Congress will not submit to be impeached by him of rash and unconstitutional legislation; and if he wishes our support, he must confine himself to his executive duties—to obey and execute, not make the laws—to suppress by arms armed Rebellion, and leave political reorganization to Congress.

If the supporters of the Government fail to insist on this, they become responsible for the usurpations which they fail to rebuke, and are justly liable to the indignation of the people whose rights and security, committed to their keeping, they sacrifice.

Let them consider the remedy for these usurpations, and, having found it, fearlessly execute it.

Source: AMDOCS: Documents for the Study of American History. http://www.vlib.us/amdocs/texts/1864wade.html

THE CIVIL RIGHTS ACT (1866)

Congress legislated under its new authority derived from the recent ratification of the Thirteenth Amendment outlawing slavery. This law was passed under contentious circumstances. While some of the more radical elements argued that it was important to not just end the institution of slavery, but include provisions in the law that gave meaning to the slaves' freedom, other members of Congress, while supportive of granting civil rights to the freed slaves, questioned whether such laws were within the scope of Congress's power. The result was that two more amendments were passed to guarantee blacks the civil rights they needed, including the right to vote. President Johnson, however, continued to espouse the position that such laws as the Civil Rights Act were outside the scope of congressional authority and vetoed the bill.

An Act to protect all Persons in the United States in their Civil Rights, and furnish the Means of their Vindication.

Be it enacted by the Senate and House of Representatives of the United States of America in Congress assembled, That all persons born in the United States and not subject to any foreign power, excluding Indians not taxed, are hereby declared to be citizens of the United States; and such citizens, of every race and color, without regard to any previous condition of slavery or involuntary servitude, except as a punishment for crime whereof the party shall have been duly convicted, shall have the same right, in every State and Territory in the United States, to make and enforce contracts, to sue, be parties, and give evidence, to inherit, purchase, lease, sell, hold, and convey real and personal property, and to full and equal benefit of all laws and proceedings for the security of person and property, as is enjoyed by white citizens, and shall be subject to like punishment, pains, and penalties, and to none other, any law, statute, ordinance, regulation, or custom, to the contrary notwithstanding.

Sec. 2. And be it further enacted, That any person who, under color of any law, statute, ordinance, regulation, or custom, shall subject, or cause to be subjected, any inhabitant of any State or Territory to the deprivation of any right secured or protected by this act, or to different punishment, pains, or penalties on account of such person having at any time been held in a condition of slavery or involuntary servitude, except as a punishment for crime whereof the party shall have been duly convicted, or by reason of his color or race, than is prescribed for the punishment of white persons, shall be deemed guilty of a misdemeanor, and, on conviction, shall be punished by fine not exceeding one thousand dollars, or imprisonment not exceeding one year, or both, in the discretion of the court.

Sec. 3. And be it further enacted, That the district courts of the United States, within their respective districts, shall have, exclusively of the courts of the several States, cognizance of all crimes and offences committed against the provisions of this act, and also, concurrently with the circuit courts of the United States, of all causes, civil and criminal, affecting persons who are denied or cannot enforce in the courts or judicial tribunals of the State or locality where they may be any of the rights secured to them by the first section of this act; and if any suit or prosecution, civil or criminal, has been or shall be commenced in any State court, against any such person, for any cause whatsoever, or against any officer, civil or military, or other person, for any arrest or imprisonment, trespasses, or wrongs done or committed by virtue or under color of authority derived from this act or the act establishing a Bureau for the relief of Freedmen and Refugees, and all acts amendatory thereof, or for refusing to do any act upon the ground that it would be inconsistent with this act, such defendant shall have the right to remove such cause for trial to the proper district or circuit court in the manner prescribed by the "Act relating to habeas corpus and regulating judicial proceedings in certain cases," approved March three, eighteen hundred and sixty-three, and all act amendatory thereof. The jurisdiction in civil and criminal matters hereby conferred on the district and circuit courts of the United States shall be exercised and enforced in conformity with the laws of the United States, so far as such laws are suitable to carry the same into effect; but in all cases where such laws are not adapted to the object, or are deficient in the provisions necessary to furnish suitable remedies and punish offences against law, the common law, as modified and changed by the constitution and statutes of the State wherein the court having jurisdiction of the cause, civil or criminal, is held, so far as the same is not inconsistent with the Constitution and laws of the United States, shall be extended to and govern said courts in the trial and disposition of such cause, and, if of a criminal nature, in the infliction of punishment on the party found guilty.

Sec. 4. And be it further enacted, That the district attorneys, marshals, and deputy marshals of the United States, the commissioners appointed by the circuit and territorial courts of the United States, with powers of arresting, imprisoning, or bailing offenders against the laws of the United States, the officers and agents of the Freedmen's Bureau, and every other officer who may be specially empowered by the President of the United States, shall be, and they are hereby, specially authorized and required, at the expense of the United States, to institute proceedings against all and every person who shall violate the provisions of this act, and cause him or them to be arrested and imprisoned, or bailed, as the case may be, for trial before such court of the United States or territorial court as by this act has cognizance of the offence. And with a view to affording reasonable protection to all persons in their constitutional rights of equality before the law, without distinction of race or color, or previous condition of slavery or involuntary servitude, except as a punishment for crime, whereof the party shall have been duly convicted, and to the prompt discharge of the duties of this act, it shall be the duty of the circuit courts of the United States and the superior courts of the Territories of the United States, from time to time, to increase the number of commissioners, so as to afford a speedy and convenient means for the arrest and examination of persons charged with a violation of this act; and such commissioners are hereby authorized and required to exercise and discharge all the powers and duties conferred on them by this act, and the same duties with regard to offences created by this act, as they are authorized by law to exercise with regard to other offences against the laws of the United States.

Sec. 5. And be it further enacted, That it shall be the duty of all marshals and deputy marshals to obey and execute all warrants and precepts issued under the provisions of this act, when to them directed; and should any marshal or deputy marshal refuse to receive such warrant or other process when tendered, or to sue all proper means diligently to execute the same, he shall, on conviction thereof, be fined in the sum of one thousand dollars, to the use of the person upon whom the accused is alleged to have committed the offence. And the better to enable the said commissioners to execute their duties faithfully and efficiently, in conformity with the Constitution of the United States and the requirements of this act, they are hereby authorized and empowered, within their counties respectively, to appoint, in writing, under their hands, any one or more suitable persons, from time to time, to execute all such warrants and other process as may be issued by them in the lawful performance of their respective duties; and the persons so appointed to execute any warrant or process as aforesaid shall have authority to summon and call to their aid the bystanders or posse comitatus of the proper county, or such portion of the land or naval forces of the United States, or of the militia, as may be necessary to the performance of the duty with which they are charged, and to insure a faithful observance of the clause of the Constitution which prohibits slavery, in conformity with the provisions of this act; and said warrants shall run and be executed by said officers anywhere in the State or Territory within which they are issued.

Sec. 6. And be it further enacted, That any person who shall knowingly and wilfully obstruct, hinder, or prevent any officer, or other person charged with the execution of any warrant or process issued under the provisions of this act, or any person or persons lawfully assisting him or them, from arresting any person for whose apprehension such warrant or process may have been issued, or shall rescue or attempt to rescue such person from the custody of the officer, other person or persons, or those lawfully assisting as aforesaid, when so arrested pursuant to the authority herein given and declared, or shall aid, abet, or assist any person so arrested as aforesaid, directly or indirectly, to escape from the custody of the officer or other person legally authorized as aforesaid, or shall harbor or conceal any person for whose arrest a warrant or process shall have been issued as aforesaid, so as to prevent his discovery and arrest after notice or knowledge of the fact that a warrant has been issued for the apprehension of such personal [sic], shall, for either of said offences, be subject to a fine not exceeding one thousand dollars, and imprisonment not exceeding six months, by indictment and conviction before the district court of the United States for the district in which said offence may have been committed, or before the proper court of criminal jurisdiction, if committed within any one of the organized Territories of the United States.

Sec. 7. And be it further enacted, That the district attorneys, the marshals, their deputies, and the clerks of the said district and territorial courts shall be paid for their services the like fees as may be allowed to them for similar services in other cases; and in all cases where the proceedings are before a commissioner, he shall be entitled to a fee of ten dollars in full for his services in each case, inclusive of all services incident to such arrest and examination. The person or persons authorized to execute the process to be issued by such commissioners for the arrest of offenders against the provisions of this act shall be entitled to a fee of five dollars for each person he or they may arrest and take before any such commissioner as aforesaid, with such other fees as may be deemed reasonable by such commissioner for such other additional services as may be necessarily performed by him or them, such as attending at the examination, keeping the prisoner in custody, and providing him with food and lodging during his detention, and until the final determination of such commissioner, and in general for performing such other duties as may be required in the premises; such fees to be made up in conformity with the fees usually charged by the officers of the courts of justice within the proper district or county, as near as may be practicable, and paid out of the Treasury of the United States on the certificate of the judge of the district within which the arrest is made, and to be recoverable from the defendant as part of the judgment in case of conviction.

Sec. 8. And be it further enacted, That whenever the President of the United States shall have reason to believe that offences have been or are likely to be committed against the provisions of this act within any judicial district, it shall be lawful for him, in his discretion, to direct the judge, marshal, and district attorney of such district to attend at such place within the district, and for such time as he may designate, for the purpose of the more speedy arrest and trial of persons charged with a violation of this act; and it shall be the duty of every judge or other officer, when any such requisition shall be received by him, to attend at the place and for the time therein designated.

Sec. 9. And be it further enacted, That it shall be lawful for the President of the United States, or such person as he may empower for that purpose, to employ such part of the land or naval forces of the United States, or of the militia, as shall be necessary to prevent the violation and enforce the due execution of this act.

Sec. 10. And be it further enacted, That upon all questions of law arising in any cause under the provisions of this act a final appeal may be taken to the Supreme Court of the United States.

Source: AfricanAmericans.com. http://www.africanamericans.com/CivilRightsAct of1866.htm

ARTICLES OF IMPEACHMENT FOR ANDREW JOHNSON (1868)

The first attempt to impeach the president of the United States formed in the wake of President Johnson's firing of Secretary of War Edwin Stanton, in direct opposition to the Tenure of Office Act, passed to prevent such an action. However, the root of the impeachment really stemmed from the political animosity that Congress, controlled by the Radical Republicans, had toward Johnson over disagreement about Reconstruction and his vetoes of various congressional acts. The impeachment failed because the charges were not well placed and because politics muddled up the process. Johnson escaped being removed from office by one vote. Congress may have lost the battle, but it won the war. For the remainder of his term, Johnson was fairly ineffectual as he continued to veto reconstruction bills only to see Congress override his vetoes.

ARTICLE I.

That said Andrew Johnson, President of the United States, on the 21st day of February, in the year of our Lord, 1868, at Washington, in the District of Columbia, unmindful of the high duties of his office, of his oath of office, and of the requirement of the Constitution that he should take care that the laws be faithfully executed, did unlawfully and in violation of the Constitution and laws of the United States issue and order in writing for the removal of Edwin M. Stanton from the office of Secretary for the Department of War, said Edwin M. Stanton having been theretofore duly appointed and commissioned, by and with the advice and consent of the Senate of the United States, as such Secretary, and said Andrew Johnson, President of the United States, on the 12th day of August, in the year of our Lord 1867, and during the recess of said Senate, having been suspended by his order Edwin M. Stanton from said office, and within twenty days after the first day of the next meeing [sic] of said Senate, that is to say, on the 12th day of December, in the year last aforesaid, having reported to said Senate such suspension, with the evidence and reasons for his action in the case and the name of the person designated to perform the duties of such office temporarily until the next meeting og [sic] the Senate, and said Senate thereafterward, on the 13th day of January, in the year of our Lord 1868, having duly considered the evidence and reasons reported by said Andrew Johnson for said suspension, and having been refused to concur in said suspension, whereby and by force of the provisions of an act entitled "An act regulating the tenure of certain civil offices," passed March 2, 1867, said Edwin M. Stanton did forthwith resume the functions of his office, whereof the said Andrew Johnson had then and there due notice, and said Edwin Stanton, by reason of the premises, on said 21st day of February, being lawfully entitled to hold said office of Secretary for the Department of War, which said order for the removal of said Edwin M. Stanton is, in substance, as follows, that is to say:

EXECUTIVE MANSION,
WASHINGTON, D.C., *February* 21, 1868
   SIR: By virtue of the power and authority vested in me, as President by the Constitution and laws of the United States, you are hereby removed from the office of Secretary for the Department of War, and your functions as such will terminate upon receipt of their communication. You will transfer to Brevet Major-General L. Thomas, Adjutant-General of the Army, who has this day been authorized and empowered to act as Secretary of War ad interim, all books, paper and other public property now in your custody and charge.
   Respectfully yours,   ANDREW JOHNSON.
   To Hon. E. M. Stanton, Secretary of War

   Which order was unlawfully issued, and with intent then are there to violate the act entitled "An act regulating the tenure of certain civil office," passed March 2, 1867; and, with the further intent contrary to the provisions of said act, and in violation thereof, and contrary to the provisions of the Constitution of the United States, and without the advice and consent of the Senate of the United States, the said Senate then and there being in session, to remove said Edwin M. Stanton from the office of Secretary for the Department of War, the said Edwin M. Stanton being then and there Secretary of War, and being then and there in the due and lawful execution of the duties of said office, whereby said Andrew Johnson, President of the United States, did then and there commit, and was guilty of a high misdemeanor in office.
. . .

ARTICLE III.
That said Andrew Johnson, President of the United States, on the 21st day of February, in the year of our Lord 1868, at Washington in the District of Columbia, did commit, and was guilty of a high misdemeanor in office, in this, that, without authority of law, while the Senate of the United States was then and there in session, he did appoint one Lorenzo Thomas to be Secretary for the Department of War, *ad interim*, without the

advice and consent of the Senate, and with intent to violate the Constitution of the United States, no vacancy having happened in said office of Secretary for the Department of War during the recess of the Senate, and no vacancy existing in said office at the time, and which said appointment so made by Andrew Johnson, of said Lorenzo Thomas is in substance as follows, that is to say:

EXECUTIVE MANSION,
WASHINGTON, D.C., *February* 21, 1868
SIR: The Hon. Edwin M. Stanton having been this day removed from office as Secretary for the Department of War, you are hereby authorized and empowered to act as Secretary of War *ad interim*, and will immediately enter upon the discharge of the duties pertaining to that office.
Mr. Stanton has been instructed to transfer to you all the records, books, papers and other public property now in his custody and charge.
Respectfully yours, ANDREW JOHNSON
To Brevet Major-General Lorenzo Thomas, *Adjutant General United States Army, Washington, D.C.*

ARTICLE IV.

That said Andrew Johnson, President of the United States, unmindful of the high duties of his office, and of his oath of office, in violation of the Constitution and laws of the United States, on the 21st day of February, in the year of our Lord 1868, at Washington, in the District of Columbia, did unlawfully conspire with one Lorenzo Thomas, and with other persons to the House of Representatives unknown, with intent by intimidation and threats unlawfully to hinder and prevent Edwin M. Stanton, then and there, the Secretary for the Department of War, duly appointed under the laws of the United States, from holding said office of Secretary for the Department of War, contrary to and in violation of the Constitution of the United States, and of the provisions of an act entitled "An act to define and punish certain conspiracies," approved July 31, 1861, whereby said Andrew Johnson, President of the United States, did then and there commit and was guilty of high crime in office.

ARTICLE V.

That said Andrew Johnson, President of the United States, unmindful of the high duties of his office and of his oath of office, on the 21st of February, in the year of our Lord 1868, and on divers others days and time in said year before the 2d day of March, A.D. 1868, at Washington, in the District of Columbia, did unlawfully conspire with one Lorenzo Thomas, and with other persons in the House of Representatives unknown, to prevent and hinder the execution of an act entitled "An act regulating the tenure of certain civil office," passed March 2, 1867, and in pursuance of said conspiracy, did attempt to prevent Edwin M. Stanton, then and there being Secretary for the Department of War, duly appointed and commissioned under the laws of the United States, from holding said office, whereby the said Andrew Johnson, President of the United States, did then and there commit and was guilty of high misdemeanor in office.

ARTICLE VI.

That said Andrew Johnson, President of the United States, unmindful of the high duties of his office and of his oath of office, on the 21st day of February, in the year of our Lord 1868, at Washington, in the District of Columbia, did unlawfully conspire with one Lorenzo Thomas, by force to seize, take, and possess the property of the United Sates [sic] in the Department of War, and then and there in the custody and charge of Edwin M. Stanton, Secretary for said Department, contrary to the provisions of an act entitled "An act to define and punish certain conspiracies," approved July 31, 1861, and with intent to violate and disregard an act entitled "An act regulating the tenure of certain civil offices," passed March 2, 1867, whereby said Andrew Johnson, President of the United States, did then and there commit a high crime in office.

. . .

ARTICLE IX.

That said Andrew Johnson, President of the United States, on the 22nd day of February, in the year of our Lord 1868, at Washington, in the District of Columbia, in disregard of the Constitution and the laws of the United States, duly enacted, as Commander-in-Chief of the Army of the United States, did bring before himself, then and there William H. Emory, a Major-General by brevet in the Army of the United States, actually in command of the department of Washington, and the military forces thereof, and did and there, as such Commander-in-Chief, declare to, and instruct said Emory, that part of a law of the United States, passed March 2, 1867, entitled "An act for making appropriations for the support of the army for the year ending June 30, 1868, and for other purposes," especially the second section thereof, which provides, among other things, that "all orders and instructions relating to military operations issued by the President or Secretary of War, shall be issued through the General of the Army, and, in case of his inability, through the next in rank," was unconstitutional, and in contravention of the commission of said Emory, and which said provision of law had been theretofore duly and legally promulgated by general order for the government and direction of the Army of the United States, as the said Andrew Johnson then and there well knew, with intent thereby to induce said Emory, in his official capacity as Commander of the department of Washington, to violate the provisions of said act, and to take and receive, act upon and obey such orders as he, the said Andrew Johnson, might make and give, and which should not be issued through the General of the Army of the United States, according to the provisions of said act, and with the further intent thereby to enable him, the said Andrew Johnson, to prevent the execution of an act entitled "An act regulating the tenure of certain civil offices," passed March 2, 1867, and to unlawfully prevent Edwin M. Stanton, then being Secretary for the Department of War, from holding said office and discharging the duties thereof, whereby said Andrew Johnson, President of the United States, did then and there commit, and was guilty of a high misdemeanor in office.

ARTICLE X.

That said Andrew Johnson, President of the United States, unmindful of the high duties of his office and the dignity and proprieties thereof, and of the harmony and courtesies which ought to exist and be maintained between the executive and legislative branches of the Government of the United States, designing and intending to set aside the rightful authorities and powers of Congress, did attempt to bring into disgrace, ridicule, hatred, contempt and reproach the Congress of the United States, and the several branches thereof, to impair and destroy the regard and respect of all the good people of the United States for the Congress and legislative power thereof, (which all officers of the government ought inviolably to preserve and maintain,) and to excite the odium and resentment of all good people of the United States against Congress and the laws by it duly and constitutionally enacted; and in pursuance of his said design and intent, openly and publicly and before divers assemblages of citizens of the United States, convened in divers parts thereof, to meet and receive said Andrew Johnson as the Chief Magistrate of the United States, did, on the 18th day of August, in the year of our Lord 1866, and on divers other days and times, as well before as afterward, make and declare, with a loud voice certain intemperate, inflammatory, and scandalous harangues, and therein utter loud threats and bitter menaces, as well against Congress as the laws of the United States duly enacted thereby, amid the cries, jeers and laughter of the multitudes then assembled in hearing, which are set forth in the several specifications hereinafter written. . . .

Article XI.

That the said Andrew Johnson, President of the United States, unmindful of the high duties of his office and his oath of office, and in disregard of the Constitution and laws of the United States, did, heretofore, to wit:? On the 18th day of August, 1866, at the city of Washington, and in the District of Columbia, by public speech, declare and affirm in substance, that the Thirty-ninth Congress of the United States was not a Congress of the United States authorized by the Constitution to exercise legislative power under the same, but on the contrary, was a Congress of only part of the States, thereby denying and intending to deny, that the legislation of said Congress was valid or obligatory upon him, the said Andrew Johnson, except in so far as he saw fit to approve the same, and also thereby denying the power of the said Thirty-ninth Congress to propose amendments to the Constitution of the United States. And in pursuance of said declaration, the said Andrew John [sic], President of the United States, afterwards, to wit:? On the 21st day of February, 1868, at the city of Washington, D.C., did, unlawfully and in disregard of the requirements of the Constitution that he should take care that the laws be faithfully executed, attempt to prevent the execution of an act entitled "An act regulating the tenure of certain civil office," passed March 2, 1867, by unlawfully devising and contriving and attempting to devise and contrive means by which he should prevent Edwin M. Stanton from forthwith resuming the functions of the office of Secretary for the Department of War, notwithstanding the refusal of the Senate to concur in the suspension theretofore made by the said Andrew Johnson of said Edwin M. Stanton from said office of Secretary for the Department of War; and also by further unlawfully devising and contriving, and attempting to devise and contrive means then and there to prevent the execution of an act entitled "An act making appropriations for the support of the army for the fiscal year ending June 30,1868, and for other purposes," approved March 20, 1867. And also to prevent the execution of an act entitled "An act to provide for the more efficient government of the Rebel States," passed Mach 2, 1867. Whereby the said Andrew Johnson, President of the United States, did then, to wit, on the 21st day of February, 1868, at the city of Washington, commit and was guilty of a high misdemeanor in office.

Source: The History Place. http://www.historyplace.com/unitedstates/impeachments/johnson.htm

SLAUGHTERHOUSE CASES (1873)

The Court interpreted the Fourteenth Amendment for the first time, seriously restricting the scope of congressional power under it. In this case, the Court stated that the amendment applied only to African Americans, for whom it was passed.

Mr. Justice MILLER, now, April 14th, 1873, delivered the opinion of the court.

These cases are brought here by writs of error to the Supreme Court of the State of Louisiana. They arise out of the efforts of the butchers of New Orleans to resist the Crescent City Livestock Landing and Slaughter-House Company in the exercise of certain powers conferred by the charter which created it, and which was granted by the legislature of that State.

The cases named on a preceding page, with others which have been brought here and dismissed by agreement, were all decided by the Supreme Court of Louisiana in favor of the Slaughter-House Company, as we shall hereafter call it for the sake of brevity, and these writs are brought to reverse those decisions.

The records show that the plaintiffs in error relied upon, and asserted throughout the entire course of the litigation in the State courts, that the grant of privileges in the charter of defendant, which they were contesting, was a violation of the most important provisions of the thirteenth and fourteenth articles of amendment of the Constitution of the United States. The jurisdiction and the duty of this court to review the judgment of the State court on those questions is clear, and is imperative.

The statute thus assailed as unconstitutional was passed March 8th, 1869, and is entitled

An act to protect the health of the city of New Orleans, to locate the stock landings and slaughterhouses, and to incorporate the Crescent City Livestock Landing aud Slaughter-House Company.

The first section forbids the landing or slaughtering of animals whose flesh is intended for food within the city of New Orleans and other parishes and boundaries named and defined, or the keeping or establishing any slaughterhouses or abattoirs within those limits except by the corporation thereby created, which is also limited to certain places afterwards mentioned. Suitable penalties are enacted for violations of this prohibition.

The second section designates the corporators, gives the name to the corporation, and confers on it the usual corporate powers.

The third and fourth sections authorize the company to establish and erect within certain territorial limits, therein defined, one or more stockyards, stock landings, and slaughterhouses, and imposes upon it the duty of erecting, on or before the first day of June, 1869, one grand slaughterhouse of sufficient capacity for slaughtering five hundred animals per day.

It declares that the company, after it shall have prepared all the necessary buildings, yards, and other conveniences for that purpose, shall have the sole and exclusive privilege of conducting and carrying on the livestock landing and slaughterhouse business within the limits and privilege granted by the act, and that all such animals shall be landed at the stock landings and slaughtered at the slaughterhouses of the company, and nowhere else. Penalties are enacted for infractions of this provision, and prices fixed for the maximum charges of the company for each steamboat and for each animal landed.

Section five orders the closing up of all other stock landings . . . and slaughterhouses after the first day of June, in the parishes of Orleans, Jefferson, and St. Bernard, and makes it the duty of the company to permit any person to slaughter animals in their slaughterhouses under a heavy penalty for each refusal. Another section fixes a limit to the charges to be made by the company for each animal so slaughtered in their building, and another provides for an inspection of all animals intended to be so slaughtered by an officer appointed by the governor of the State for that purpose.

These are the principal features of the statute, and are all that have any bearing upon the questions to be decided by us.

This statute is denounced not only as creating a monopoly and conferring odious and exclusive privileges upon a small number of persons at the expense of the great body of the community of New Orleans, but it is asserted that it deprives a large and meritorious class of citizens—the whole of the butchers of the city—of the right to exercise their trade, the business to which they have been trained and on which they depend for the support of themselves and their families, and that the unrestricted exercise of the business of butchering is necessary to the daily subsistence of the population of the city.

It is not, and cannot be successfully controverted that it is both the right and the duty of the legislative body—the supreme power of the State or municipality—to prescribe and determine the localities where the business of slaughtering for a great city may be conducted. To do this effectively, it is indispensable that all persons who slaughter animals for food shall do it in those places *and nowhere else.*

It cannot be denied that the statute under consideration is aptly framed to remove from the more densely populated part of the city the noxious slaughterhouses, and large and offensive collections of animals necessarily incident to the slaughtering business of a large city, and to locate them where the convenience, health, and comfort of the people require they shall be located. And it must be conceded that the means adopted by the act for this purpose are appropriate, are stringent, and effectual. But it is said that, in creating a corporation for this purpose, and conferring upon it exclusive privileges—privileges which it is said constitute a monopoly—the legislature has exceeded its power.

The proposition is therefore reduced to these terms: can any exclusive privileges be granted to any of its citizens, or to a corporation, by the legislature of a State?

It may, therefore, be considered as established that the authority of the legislature of Louisiana to pass the present statute is ample unless some restraint in the exercise of that power be found in the constitution of that State or in the amendments to the Constitution of the United States, adopted since the date of the decisions we have already cited.

The plaintiffs in error, accepting this issue, allege that the statute is a violation of the Constitution of the United States in these several particulars:

That it abridges the privileges and immunities of citizens of the United States;

That it denies to the plaintiffs the equal protection of the laws; and,

That it deprives them of their property without due process of law, contrary to the provisions of the first section of the fourteenth article of amendment.

This court is thus called upon for the first time to give construction to these articles.

The institution of African slavery, as it existed in about half the States of the Union, and the contests pervading the public mind for many years between those who desired its curtailment and ultimate extinction and those who desired additional safeguards for its security and perpetuation, culminated in the effort, on the part of most of the States in which slavery existed, to separate from the Federal government and to resist its authority. This constituted the war of the rebellion, and whatever auxiliary causes may have contributed to bring about this war, undoubtedly the overshadowing and efficient cause was African slavery.

The process of restoring to their proper relations with the Federal government and with the other States those which had sided with the rebellion, undertaken under the proclamation of President Johnson in 1865 and before the assembling of Congress, developed the fact that, notwithstanding the formal recognition by those States of the abolition of slavery, the condition of the slave race would, without further protection of the Federal government, be almost as bad as it was before. Among the first acts of legislation adopted by several of the States in the legislative bodies which claimed to be in their normal relations with the Federal government were laws which imposed upon the colored race onerous disabilities and burdens and curtailed their rights in the pursuit of life, liberty, and property to such an extent that their freedom was of little value, while they had lost the protection which they had received from their former owners from motives both of interest and humanity.

These circumstances, whatever of falsehood or misconception may have been mingled with their presentation, forced upon the statesmen who had conducted the Federal government in safety through the crisis of the rebellion, and who supposed that, by the thirteenth article of amendment, they had secured the result of their labors, the conviction that something more was necessary in the way of constitutional protection to the unfortunate race who had suffered so much. They accordingly passed through Congress the proposition for the fourteenth amendment, and they declined to treat as restored to their full participation in the government of the Union the States which had been in insurrection until they ratified that article by a formal vote of their legislative bodies.

Before we proceed to examine more critically the provisions of this amendment, on which the plaintiffs in error rely, let us complete and dismiss the history of the recent amendments, as that history relates to the general purpose which pervades them all. A few years' experience satisfied the thoughtful men who had been the authors of the other two amendments that, notwithstanding the restraints of those articles on the States and the laws passed under the additional powers granted to Congress, these were inadequate for the protection of life, liberty, and property, without which freedom to the slave was no boon. They were in all those States denied the right of suffrage. The laws were administered by the white man alone. It was urged that a race of men distinctively marked, as was the negro, living in the midst of another and dominant race, could never be fully secured in their person and their property without the right of suffrage.

Hence, the fifteenth amendment, which declares that the right of a citizen of the United States to vote shall not be denied or abridged by any State on account of race, color, or previous condition of servitude.

The negro having, by the fourteenth amendment, been declared to be a citizen of the United States, is thus made a voter in every State of the Union.

We repeat, then, in the light of this recapitulation of events, almost too recent to be called history, but which are familiar to us all, and on the most casual examination of the language of these amendments, no one can fail to be impressed with the one pervading purpose found in them all, lying at the foundation of each, and without which none of them would have been even suggested; we mean the freedom of the slave race, the security and firm establishment of that freedom, and the protection of the newly made freeman and citizen from the oppressions of those who had formerly exercised unlimited dominion over him.

But what we do say, and what we wish to be understood, is that, in any fair and just construction of any section or phrase of these amendments, it is necessary to look to the purpose which we have said was the pervading spirit of them all, the evil which they were designed to remedy, and the process of continued addition to the Constitution, until that purpose was supposed to be accomplished as far as constitutional law can accomplish it.

The first section of the fourteenth article to which our attention is more specially invited opens with a definition of citizenship—not only citizenship of the United States, but citizenship of the States. No such definition was previously found in the Constitution, nor had any attempt been made to define it by act of Congress.

To remove this difficulty primarily, and to establish clear and comprehensive definition of citizenship which should declare what should constitute citizenship of the United States and also citizenship of a State, the first clause of the first section was framed.

All persons born or naturalized in the United States, and subject to the jurisdiction thereof, are citizens of the United States and of the State wherein they reside.

That its main purpose was to establish the citizenship of the negro can admit of no doubt.

The next observation is more important in view of the arguments of counsel in the present case. It is that the distinction between citizenship of the United States and citizenship of a State is clearly recognized and established. Not only may a man be a citizen of the United States without being a citizen of a State, but an important element is necessary to convert the former into the latter. He must reside within the State to make him a citizen of it, but it is only necessary that he should be born or naturalized in the United States to be a citizen of the Union.

It is quite clear, then, that there is a citizenship of the United States, and a citizenship of a State, which are distinct from each other, and which depend upon different characteristics or circumstances in the individual.

We think this distinction and its explicit recognition in this amendment of great weight in this argument, because the next paragraph of this same section, which is the one mainly relied on by the plaintiffs in error, speaks only of privileges and immunities of citizens of the United States, and does not speak of those of citizens of the several States. The argument, however, in favor of the plaintiffs rests wholly on the assumption that the citizenship is the same, and the privileges and immunities guaranteed by the clause are the same.

The language is, "No State shall make or enforce any law which shall abridge the privileges or immunities of citizens of *the United States.*" It is a little remarkable, if this clause was intended as a protection to the citizen of a State against the legislative power of his own State, that the word citizen of the State should be left out when it is so carefully used, and used in contradistinction to citizens of the United States in the very sentence which precedes it. It is too clear for argument that the change in phraseology was adopted understandingly and, with a purpose.

Of the privileges and immunities of the citizen of the United States, and of the privileges and immunities of the citizen of the State, and what they respectively are, we will presently consider; but we wish to state here that it is only the former which are placed by this clause under the protection of the Federal Constitution, and that the latter, whatever they may be, are not intended to have any additional protection by this paragraph of the amendment.

If, then, there is a difference between the privileges and immunities belonging to a citizen of the United States as such and those belonging to the citizen of the State as such, the latter must rest for their security and protection where they have heretofore rested, for they are not embraced by this paragraph of the amendment.

The constitutional provision there alluded to did not create those rights, which it called privileges and immunities of citizens of the States. It threw around them in that clause no security for the citizen of the State in which they were claimed or exercised. Nor did it profess to control the power of the State governments over the rights of its own citizens.

Its sole purpose was to declare to the several States that, whatever those rights, as you grant or establish them to your own citizens, or as you limit or qualify or impose restrictions on their exercise, the same, neither more nor less, shall be the measure of the rights of citizens of other States within your jurisdiction.

It would be the vainest show of learning to attempt to prove by citations of authority that, up to the adoption of the recent amendments, no claim or pretence was set up that those rights depended on the Federal government for their existence or protection beyond the very few express limitations which the Federal Constitution imposed upon the States—such, for instance, as the prohibition against *ex post facto* laws, bills of attainder, and laws impairing the obligation of contracts. *But, with the exception of these and a few other restrictions, the entire domain of the privileges and immunities of citizens of the States, as above defined, lay within the constitutional and legislative power of the States, and without that of the Federal government.* Was it the purpose of the fourteenth amendment, by the simple declaration that no State should make or enforce any law which shall abridge the privileges and immunities of citizens of the United States, to transfer the security and protection of all the civil rights which we have mentioned, from the States to the Federal government? And where it is declared that Congress Shall have the power to enforce that article, was it intended to bring within the power of Congress the entire domain of civil rights heretofore belonging exclusively to the States?

We are convinced that no such results were intended by the Congress which proposed these amendments, nor by the legislatures of the States which ratified them.

Having shown that the privileges and immunities relied on in the argument are those which belong to citizens of the States as such, and that they are left to the State governments for security and protection, and not by this article placed under the special care of the Federal government, we may hold ourselves excused from defining the privileges and immunities of citizens of the United States which no State can abridge until some case involving those privileges may make it necessary to do so.

The argument has not been much pressed in these cases that the defendant's charter deprives the plaintiffs of their property without due process of law, or that it denies to them the equal protection of the law. The first of these paragraphs has been in the Constitution since the adoption of the fifth amendment, as a restraint upon the Federal power. It is also to be found in some form of expression in the constitutions of nearly all the States as a restraint upon the power of the States. This law, then, has practically been the same as it now is during the existence of the government, except so far as the present amendment may place the restraining power over the States in this matter in the hands of the Federal government.

We are not without judicial interpretation, therefore, both State and National, of the meaning of this clause. And it . . . is sufficient to say that under no construction of that provision that we have ever seen, or any that we deem admissible, can the restraint imposed by the State of Louisiana upon the exercise of their trade by the butchers of New Orleans be held to be a deprivation of property within the meaning of that provision.

"Nor shall any State deny to any person within its jurisdiction the equal protection of the laws."

In the light of the history of these amendments, and the pervading purpose of them, which we have already discussed, it is not difficult to give a meaning to this clause. The existence of laws in the States where the newly emancipated negroes resided, which discriminated with gross injustice and hardship against them as a class, was the evil to be remedied by this clause, and by it such laws are forbidden.

If, however, the States did not conform their laws to its requirements, then by the fifth section of the article of amendment Congress was authorized to enforce it by suitable legislation. We doubt very much whether any action of a State not directed by way of discrimination against the negroes as a class, or on account of their race, will ever be held to come within the purview of this provision. It is so clearly a provision for that race and that emergency that a strong case would be necessary for its application to any other.

The judgments of the Supreme Court of Louisiana in these cases are

AFFIRMED.

Source: Justia.com – US Supreme Court Center. http://supreme.justia.com/us/83/36/case.html

CIVIL RIGHTS CASES (1883)

Judicial challenge to the Civil Rights Act of 1875, which attempted to guarantee civil equality to the former slaves. The bill was passed under the authority granted Congress in Section 5 of the Fourteenth Amendment, the section that gave Congress the power to enforce the rest of the amendment. However, the Supreme Court denied that Congress had power to act in an affirmative manner to enforce the amendment; rather, Congress could only act in a reactive manner. In other words, Congress was limited to act only when the states had acted in a manner that denied African Americans rights guaranteed by the Fourteenth Amendment. Absent state action, no congressional action was permitted. It shut the door on congressional action to limit discrimination until the 1960s.

MR. JUSTICE BRADLEY delivered the opinion of the court. After stating the facts in the above language, he continued:

It is obvious that the primary and important question in all . . . the cases is the constitutionality of the law, for if the law is unconstitutional, none of the prosecutions can stand.

The sections of the law referred to provide as follows:

SEC. 1. That all persons within the jurisdiction of the United States shall be entitled to the full and equal enjoyment of the accommodations, advantages, facilities, and privileges of inns, public conveyances on land or water, theatres, and other places of public amusement, subject only to the conditions and limitations established by law and applicable alike to citizens of every race and color, regardless of any previous condition of servitude.

SEC. 2. That any person who shall violate the foregoing section by denying to any citizen, except for reasons by law applicable to citizens of every race and color, and regardless of any previous condition of servitude, the full enjoyment of any of the accommodations, advantages, facilities, or privileges in said section enumerated, or by aiding or inciting such denial, shall for every such offence, forfeit and pay the sum of five hundred dollars to the person aggrieved thereby, to be recovered in an action of debt, with full costs, and shall also, for every such offence, be deemed guilty of a misdemeanor, and, upon conviction thereof, shall be fined not less than five hundred nor more than one thousand dollars, or shall be imprisoned not less than thirty days nor more than one year, *Provided*, That all persons may elect to sue for the penalty aforesaid, or to proceed under their rights at common law and by State statutes, and having so elected to proceed in the one mode or the other, their right to proceed in the other jurisdiction shall be barred. But this provision shall not apply to criminal proceedings, either under this act or the criminal law of any State; *and provided further,* that a judgment for the penalty in favor of the party aggrieved, or a judgment upon an indictment, shall be a bar to either prosecution respectively.

Are these sections constitutional? The first section, which is the principal one, cannot be fairly understood without attending to the last clause, which qualifies the preceding part.

The essence of the law is not to declare broadly that all persons shall be entitled to the full and equal enjoyment of the accommodations, advantages, facilities, and privileges of inns, public conveyances, and theatres, but that such enjoyment shall not be subject to any conditions applicable only to citizens of a particular race or color, or who had been in a previous condition of servitude. In other words, it is the purpose of the law to declare that, in the enjoyment of the accommodations and privileges of inns, public conveyances, theatres, and other places of public amusement, no distinction shall be made between citizens of different race or color or between those who have, and those who have not, been slaves. Its effect is to declare that, in all inns, public conveyances, and places of amusement, colored citizens, whether formerly slaves or not, and citizens of other races, shall have the same accommodations and privileges in all inns, public conveyances, and places of amusement as are enjoyed by white citizens, and vice versa. The second section makes it a penal offence in any person to deny to any citizen of any race or color, regardless of previous servitude, any of the accommodations or privileges mentioned in the first section.

Has Congress constitutional power to make such a law? The first section of the Fourteenth Amendment (which is the one relied on), after declaring who shall be citizens of the United States, and of the several States, is prohibitory in its character, and prohibitory upon the States. It declares that:

No State shall make or enforce any law which shall abridge the privileges or immunities of citizens of the United States; nor shall any State deprive any person of life, liberty, or property without due process of law; nor deny to any person within its jurisdiction the equal protection of the laws.

It is State action of a particular character that is prohibited. Individual invasion of individual rights is not the subject matter of the amendment. It has a deeper and broader scope. It nullifies and makes void all State legislation, and State action of every kind, which impairs the privileges and immunities of citizens of the United States or which injures them in life, liberty or property without due process of law, or which denies to any of them the equal protection of the laws. It does not invest Congress with power to legislate upon subjects which are within the domain of State legislation, but to provide modes of relief against State legislation, or State action, of the kind referred to. It does not authorize Congress to create a code of municipal law for the regulation of private rights, but to provide modes of redress against the operation of State laws and the action of State officers executive or judicial when these are subversive of the fundamental rights specified in the amendment.

And so, in the present case, until some State law has been passed, or some State action through its officers or agents has been taken, adverse to the rights of citizens sought to be protected by the Fourteenth Amendment, no legislation of the United States under said amendment, nor any proceeding under such legislation, can be called into activity, for the prohibitions of the amendment are against State laws and acts done under State authority. In fine, the legislation which Congress is authorized to adopt in this behalf is not general legislation upon the rights of the citizen, but corrective legislation, that is, such as may be necessary and proper for counteracting such laws as the States may adopt or enforce, and which, by the amendment, they are prohibited from making or enforcing, or such acts and proceedings as the States may commit or take, and which, by the amendment, they are prohibited from committing or taking.

An inspection of the law shows that it makes no reference whatever to any supposed or apprehended violation of the Fourteenth Amendment on the part of the States. It is not predicated on any such view. It proceeds *ex directo* to declare that certain acts committed by individuals shall be deemed offences, and shall be prosecuted and punished by proceedings in the courts of the United States. It does not profess to be corrective of any constitutional wrong committed by the States; it does not make its operation to depend upon any such wrong committed. It applies equally to cases arising in States which have the justest laws respecting the personal rights of citizens, and whose authorities are ever ready to enforce such laws, as to those which arise in States that may have violated the prohibition of the amendment. In other words, it steps into the domain of local jurisprudence, and lays down rules for the conduct of individuals in society towards each other, and imposes sanctions for the enforcement of those rules, without referring in any manner to any supposed action of the State or its authorities.

On the whole, we are of opinion that no countenance of authority for the passage of the law in question can be found in either the Thirteenth or Fourteenth Amendment of the Constitution, and no other ground of authority for its passage being suggested, it must necessarily be declared void, at least so far as its operation in the several States is concerned.

This conclusion disposes of the cases now under consideration. In the cases, the answer to be given will be that the first and second sections of the act of Congress of March 1st, 1875, entitled "An Act to protect all citizens in their civil and legal rights," are unconstitutional and void, and that judgment should be rendered upon the several indictments in those cases accordingly.

And it is so ordered

Source: Justia.com – US Supreme Court Center. http://supreme.justia.com/us/109/3/case.html

WABASH, ST. L. & P. RY. CO. V. PEOPLE OF STATE OF ILLINOIS (1886)

Court case struck down state regulation of railroads and led to the creation of the Interstate Commerce Commission. It compromised earlier decisions such as Munn v. Illinois *(1877), which had allowed such state regulation. Wabash prohibited the long haul, short haul clauses that plagued interstate transportation, as an infringement on Congress's exclusive power under the Commerce Clause.*

JUSTICE MILLER delivered the opinion of the Court

In *Munn v. Illinois:* "We come now to consider the effect upon this statute of the power of congress to regulate commerce. It was very properly said in Case of state Tax on Railway Gross Receipts, 15 Wall. 293, that 'it is not everything that affects commerce that amounts to a regulation of it, within the meaning of the constitution.' warehouses of these plaintiffs in error are situated, and their business carried on, exclusively within the limits of the state of Illinois. They are used as instruments by those engaged in state as well as those engaged in interstate commerce, but they are no more necessarily a part of commerce itself than the dray or cart by which, but for them, grain would be transferred from one railroad station to another. Incidentally they may become connected with interstate commerce, but not necessarily so. Their regulation is a thing of domestic concern, and, certainly, until congress acts in reference to their interstate relations, the state may exercise all the powers of government over them, even though in so doing it may indirectly operate upon commerce outside its immediate jurisdiction. We do not say that a case may not arise in which it will be found that a state, under the form of regulating its own affairs, has encroached upon the exclusive domain of congress in respect to interstate commerce; but we do say that upon the facts as they are represented to us in this record, that has not been done. . . ."

The question of the right of the state to regulate the rates of fares and tolls on railroads, and how far that right was affected by the commerce clause of the constitution of the United States, was presented to the court in those cases. And it must be admitted that, in a general way, the court treated the cases then before it as belonging to that class of regulations of commerce which, like pilotage, bridging navigable rivers, and many others, could be acted upon by the states, in the absence of any legislation by congress on the same subject. . . .

The great question to be decided, and which was decided, and which was argued in all those cases, was the right of the state within which a railroad company did business to regulate or limit the amount of any of these traffic charges. . . .

It cannot be too strongly insisted upon that the right of continuous transportation, from one end of the country to the other, is essential, in modern times, to that freedom of commerce, from the restraints which the states might choose to impose upon it, that the commerce clause was intended to secure. This clause, giving to congress the power to regulate commerce among the states, and with foreign nations, as this court has said before, was among the most important of the subjects which prompted the formation of the Constitution. . . . And it would be a very feeble and almost useless provision, but poorly adapted to secure the entire freedom of commerce among the states which was deemed essential to a more perfect union by the framers of the constitution, if, at every stage of the transportation of goods and chattels through the country, the state within whose limits a part of this transportation must be done could impose regulations concerning the price, compensation, or taxation, or any other restrictive regulation interfering with and seriously embarrassing this commerce.

The argument on this subject can never be better stated than it is by Chief Justice MARSHALL in *Gibbons v. Ogden.* . . . He there demonstrates that commerce among the states, like commerce with foreign nations, is necessarily a commerce which crosses state lines, and extends into the states, and the power of congress to regulate it exists wherever that commerce is found. Speaking of navigation as an element of commerce, which it is only as a means of transportation, now largely superseded by railroads. . . .

We must therefore hold that it is not, and never has been, the deliberate opinion of a majority of this court that a statute of a state which attempts to regulate the fares and charges by railroad companies within its limits, for a transportation which constitutes a part of commerce among the states, is a valid law.

Let us see precisely what is the degree of interference with transportation of property or persons from one state to another which this statute proposes. A citizen of New York has goods which he desires to have transported by the railroad companies from that city to the interior of the state of Illinois. A continuous line of rail over which a car loaded with these goods can be carried, and is carried habitually, connects the place of shipment with the place of delivery. He undertakes to make a contract with a person engaged in the carrying business at the end of this route from whence the goods are to start, and he is told by the carrier: "I am free to make a fair and reasonable contract for this carriage to the line of the state of Illinois, but when the car which carries these goods is to cross the line of that state, pursuing at the same time this continuous track, I am met by a law of Illinois which forbids me to make a free contract concerning this transportation within that state, and subjects me to certain rules by which I am to be governed as to the charges which the same railroad company in Illinois may make, or has made, with reference to other persons and other places of delivery." So that while that carrier might be willing to carry these goods from the city of New York to the city of Peoria at the rate of 15 cents per hundred pounds, he is not permitted to do so, because the Illinois railroad company has already charged at the rage of 25 cents per hundred pounds for carriage to Gilman, in Illinois, which is 86 miles shorter than the distance to Peoria. So, also, in the present case, the owner of corn, the principal product of the country, desiring to transport it from Peoria, in Illinois, to New York, finds a railroad company willing to do this at the rate of 15 cents per hundred pounds for a car-load, but is compelled to pay at the rate of 25 cents per hundred pounds, because the railroad company has received from a person residing at Gilman 25 cents per hundred pounds for the transportation of a car-load of the same class of freight over the same line of road from Gilman to New York. This is the result of the statute of Illinois, in its endeavor to prevent unjust discrimination, as construed by the supreme court of that state. The effect of it is that whatever may be the rate of transportation per mile charged by the railroad company from Gilman to Sheldon, a distance of 23 miles, in which the loading and the unloading of the freight is the largest expense incurred by the railroad company, the same rate per mile must be charged from Peoria to the city of New York. The obvious injustice of such a rule as this, which railroad companies are by heavy penalties compelled to conform to, in regard to commerce among the states, when applied to transportation which includes Illinois in a long line of carriage through several states, shows the value of the constitutional provision which confides the power of regulating interstate commerce to the congress of the United States, whose enlarged view of the interests of all the states, and of the railroads concerned, better fits it to establish just and equitable rules.

Of the justice or propriety of the principle which lies at the foundation of the Illinois statute it is not the province of this court to speak. As restricted to a transportation which begins and ends within the limits of the state, it may be very just and equitable, and it certainly is the province of the state legislature to determine that question; but when it is attempted to apply to transportation through an entire series of states a principle of this kind, and each one of the states shall attempt to establish its own rates of transportation, its own methods to prevent discrimination in rates, or to permit it, the deleterious influence upon the freedom of commerce among the states, and upon the transit of goods through those states, cannot be overestimated. That this species of regulation is one which must be, if established at all, of a general and national character, and cannot be safely and wisely remitted to local rules and local regulations, we think is clear from what has already been said. And if it be a regulation of commerce, as we think we have demonstrated it is, and as the Illinois court concedes it to be, it must be of that national character; and the regulation can only appropriately exist by general rules and principles, which demand that it should be done by the congress of the United States under the commerce clause of the Constitution.

The judgment of the supreme court of Illinois is therefore reversed, and the case remanded to that court for further proceedings in conformity with this opinion.

Source: Justia.com – US Supreme Court Center. http://supreme.justia.com/us/ 118/557/case.html

THE INTERSTATE COMMERCE ACT (1887)

Spurred on by the Court's decision in Wabash, St. Louis & Pacific Ry. Co. v. Illinois *(1886), which denied the states the authority to regulate the railroads, as they had done for the past decade, dating back to* Munn v. Illinois *(1877). The result was the attempt by Congress to institute some regulation over the railroads in response to the growing Grange movement.*

Be it enacted . . . , That the provisions of this act shall apply to any common carrier or carriers engaged in the transportation of passengers or property wholly by railroad, or partly by railroad and partly by water when both are used, under a common control, management, or arrangement, for a continuous carriage or shipment, from one State or Territory of the United States, or the District of Columbia, or from any place in the United States through a foreign country to any other place in the United States, and also to the transportation in like manner of property shipped from any place in the United States to a foreign country and carried from such place to a port of transshipment, or shipped from a foreign country to any other place in the United States, and also to the transportation in like manner of property shipped from any place in the United States to a foreign country and carried from such place to a port of entry either in the United States or an adjacent foreign country: *Provided, however,* That the provisions of this act shall not apply to the transportation of passengers or property, or to the receiving, delivering, storage, or handling of property, wholly within one State, and not shipped to or from a foreign country from or to any State or Territory as aforesaid.

The term "railroad" as used in this act shall include all bridges and ferries used or operated in connection with any railroad, and also all the road in use by any corporation operating a railroad, whether owned or operated under a contract, agreement, or lease; and the term "transportation" shall include all instrumentalities of shipment or carriage.

All charges made for any service rendered or to be rendered in the transportation of passengers or property as aforesaid, or in connection therewith, or for the receiving, delivering, storage, or handling of such property, shall be reasonable and just; and every unjust and unreasonable charge for such service is prohibited and declared to be unlawful.

Sec. 2. That if any common carrier subject to the provisions of this act shall, directly or indirectly, by any special rate, rebate, drawback, or other device, charge, demand, collect, or receive from any person or persons a greater or less compensation for any service rendered, or to be rendered, in the transportation of passengers or property, subject to the provisions of this act, than it charges, demands, collects, or receives from any other person or persons for doing for him or them a like and contemporaneous service in the transportation of a like kind of traffic under substantially similar circumstances and conditions, such common carrier shall be deemed guilty of unjust discrimination, which is hereby prohibited and declared to be unlawful.

Sec. 3. That it shall be unlawful for any common carrier subject to the provisions of this act to make or give any undue or unreasonable preference or advantage to any particular person, company, firm, corporation, or locality, or any particular description of traffic, in any respect whatsoever, or to subject any particular person, company, firm, corporation, or locality, or any particular description of traffic, to any undue or unreasonable prejudice or disadvantage in any respect whatsoever.

Every common carrier subject to the provisions of this act shall, according to their respective powers, afford all reasonable, proper, and equal facilities for the interchange of traffic between their respective lines, and for the receiving, forwarding, and delivering of passengers and property to and from their several lines and those connecting therewith, and shall not discriminate in their rates and charges between such connecting lines; but this shall not be construed as requiring any such common carrier to give the use of its tracks or terminal facilities to another carrier engaged in like business.

Sec. 4. That it shall be unlawful for any common carrier subject to the provisions of this act to charge or receive any greater compensation in the aggregate for the transportation of passengers or of like kind of property, under substantially similar circumstances and conditions, for a shorter than for a longer distance over the same line, in the same direction, the shorter being included within the longer distance; but this shall not be construed as authorizing any common carrier within the terms of this act to charge and receive as great compensation for a shorter as for a longer distance: *Provided, however,* That upon application to the Commission appointed under the provisions of this act, such common carrier may, in special cases, after investigation by the Commission, be authorized to charge less for longer than for shorter distances for the transportation of passengers or property; and the Commission may from time to time prescribe the extent to which such designated common carrier may be relieved from the operation of this section of this act.

Sec. 5. That it shall be unlawful for any common carrier subject to the provisions of this act to enter into any contract, agreement, or combination with any other common carrier or carriers for the pooling of freights of different and competing railroads, or to divide between them the aggregate or net proceeds of the earnings of such railroads, or any portion thereof; and in any case of an agreement for the pooling of freights as aforesaid, each day of its continuation shall be deemed a separate offense.

Sec. 6. That every common carrier subject to the provisions of this act shall print and keep for public inspection schedules showing the rates and fares and charges for the transportation of passengers and property which any such common carrier has established and which are in force at the time upon its railroad, as defined by the first section of this act. . . .

No advance shall be made in the rates, fares, and charges which have been established and published as aforesaid by any common carrier in compliance with the requirements of this section, except after ten days' public notice, which shall plainly state the changes proposed to be made in the schedule then in force, and the time when the increased rates, fares, or charges will go into effect. . . .

And when any such common carrier shall have established and published its rates, fares, and charges in compliance with the provisions of this section, it shall be unlawful for such common carrier to charge, demand, collect, or receive from any person or persons a greater or less compensation for the transportation of passengers or property, or for any services in connection therewith, than is specified in such published schedule of rates, fares, and charges as may at the time be in force.

Every common carrier subject to the provisions of this act shall file with the Commission hereinafter provided for copies of its schedules of rates, fares, and charges which have been established and published in compliance with the requirements of this section, and shall promptly notify said Commission of all changes made in the same. Every such common carrier shall also file with said Commission copies of all contracts, agreements, or arrangements with other common carriers in relation to any traffic affected by the provisions of this act to which it may be a party. . . .

Sec. 9. That any person or persons claiming to be damaged by any common carrier subject to the provisions of this act may either make complaint to the Commission as hereinafter provided for, or may bring suit in his or their own behalf for the recovery of the damages for which such common carrier may be liable under the provisions of this act, in any district or circuit court of the United States of competent jurisdiction. . . .

Sec. 10. That any common carrier subject to the provisions of this act, or, wherever such common carrier is a corporation, any director or officer thereof, or any receiver, trustee, lessee, agent, or person acting for or employed by such corporation, who, alone or with any other corporation, company, person, or party, . . . shall be guilty of any infraction of this act, or shall aid or abet therein, shall be deemed guilty of a misdemeanor, and shall, upon conviction thereof in any district court of the United States within the jurisdiction of which such offense was committed, be subject to a fine of not to exceed five thousand dollars for each offense.

Sec. 11. That a Commission is hereby created and established to be known as the Inter-State Commerce Commission, which shall be composed of five Commissioners, who shall be appointed by the President, by and with the advice and consent of the Senate. The Commissioners first appointed under this act shall continue in office for the term of two, three, four, five, and six years, respectively, from January 1, 1887, the term of each to be designated by the President; but their successors shall be appointed for terms of six years. . . . Any Commissioner may be removed by the President for inefficiency, neglect of duty, or malfeasance in office. Not more than three of the Commissioners shall be appointed from the same political party. No person in the employ of or holding any official relation to any common carrier subject to the provisions of this act, or owning stock or bonds thereof, or who is in any manner pecuniarily interested therein, shall enter upon the duties of or hold such office. Said Commissioners shall not engage in any other business, vocation, or employment. No vacancy in the Commission shall impair the right of the remaining Commissioners to exercise all the powers of the Commission.

Sec. 12. That the Commission hereby created shall have authority to inquire into the management of the business of all common carriers subject to the provisions of this act, and shall keep itself informed as to the manner and method in which the same is conducted, and shall have the right to obtain from such common carriers full and complete information necessary to enable the Commission to perform the duties and carry out the objects for which it was created; and for the purposes of this act the Commission shall have power to require the attendance and testimony of witnesses and the production of all books, papers, tariffs, contracts, agreements, and documents relating to any matter under investigation, and to that end may invoke the aid of any court of the United States in requiring the attendance and testimony of witnesses and the production of books, papers, and documents under the provisions of this section. . . .

Sec. 13. That any person, firm, corporation, or association, or any mercantile, agricultural, or manufacturing society, or any body politic or municipal organization complaining of anything done or omitted to be done by any common carrier subject to the provisions of this act, in contravention of the provisions thereof, may apply to said Commission by petition, which shall briefly state the facts; whereupon a statement of the charges thus made shall be forwarded by the Commission to such common carrier, who shall be called upon to satisfy the complaint or to answer the same in writing within a reasonable time, to be specified by the Commission. . . . If there shall appear to be any reasonable ground for investigating said complaint, it shall be the duty of the Commission to investigate the matters complained of in such manner and by such means as it shall deem proper.

Said Commission shall in like manner investigate any complaint forwarded by the railroad commissioner or railroad commission of any State or Territory, at the request of such commissioner or commission, and may institute any inquiry on its own motion in the same manner and to the same effect as though complaint had been made. . . .

Sec. 16. That whenever any common carrier, . . . shall violate or refuse to neglect to obey any lawful order or requirement of the Commission on this act named, it shall be the duty of the Commission, and lawful for any company or person interested in such order or requirement, to apply, in a summary way, by petition, to the circuit court of the United States sitting in equity in the judicial district in which the common carrier complained of has its principal office, or in which the violation or disobedience of such order or requirements shall happen, alleging such violation or disobedience, as the case may be; and the said court shall have power to hear and determine the matter, on such short notice to the common carrier complained of as the court shall deem reasonable. . . .

Sec. 20. That the Commission is hereby authorized to require annual reports from all common carriers subject to the provisions of this act, fix the time and prescribe the manner in which such reports shall be made, and to require from such carriers specific answers to all questions upon which the Commission may need information. Such reports shall also contain such information in relation to rates or regulations concerning fares or freights, or agreements, arrangements, or contracts with other common carriers, as the Commission may require; and the said Commission may, within its discretion, for the purpose of enabling it the better to carry out the purposes of this act, prescribe (if in the opinion of the Commission it is practicable to prescribe such uniformity and methods of keeping accounts) a period of time within which all common carriers subject to the provisions of this act shall have, as near as may be, a uniform system of accounts, and the manner in which such accounts shall be kept. . . .

Source: Historical Documents in United States History. http://www.historicaldocuments.com/InterstateCommerceAct.htm

UNITED STATES V. E. C. KNIGHT CO. (1895)

First decision under the Sherman Antitrust Act (1890), a congressional attempt to control monopolies. Under the decision, the Court perpetuated distinctions regarding congressional commerce power, noting a difference between manufacturing and commerce. This case severely limited congressional power to control the economy by limiting its commerce authority; it emasculated the Sherman Antitrust Act.

Mr. Chief Justice FULLER delivered the opinion of the court.

By the purchase of the stock of the four Philadelphia refineries with shares of its own stock the American Sugar Refining Company acquired nearly complete control of the manufacture of refined sugar within the United States. The bill charged that the contracts under which these purchases were made constituted combinations in restraint of trade, and that in entering into them the defendants combined and conspired to restrain the trade and commerce in refined sugar among the several states and with foreign nations, contrary to the act of congress of July 2, 1890. . . .

The fundamental question is whether, conceding that the existence of a monopoly in manufacture is established by the evidence, that monopoly can be directly suppressed under the act of congress in the mode attempted by this bill.

It cannot be denied that the power of a state to protect the lives, health, and property of its citizens, and to preserve good order and the public morals, 'the power to govern men and things within the limits of its dominion,' is a power originally and always belonging to the states, not surrendered by them to the general government, nor directly restrained by the constitution of the United States, and essentially exclusive. The relief of the citizens of each state from the burden of monopoly and the evils resulting from the restraint of trade among such citizens was left with the states to deal with, and this court has recognized their possession of that power even to the extent of holding that an employment or business carried on by private individuals, when it becomes a matter of such public interest and importance as to create a common charge or burden upon the citizen,—in other words, when it becomes a practical monopoly, to which the citizen is compelled to resort, and by means of which a tribute can be exacted from the community,—is subject to regulation by state legislative power. On the other hand, the power of congress to regulate commerce among the several states is also exclusive. The constitution does not provide that interstate commerce shall be free, but, by the grant of this exclusive power to regulate it, it was left free, except as congress might impose restraints. Therefore it has been determined that the failure of congress to exercise this exclusive power in any case is an expression of its will that the subject shall be free from restrictions or impositions upon it by the several states, and if a law passed by a state in the exercise of its acknowledged powers comes into conflict with that will, the congress and the state cannot occupy the position of equal opposing sovereignties, because the constitution declares its supremacy, and that of the laws passed in pursuance thereof; and that which is not supreme must yield to that which is supreme. "Commerce undoubtedly is traffic," said Chief Justice Marshall, "but it is something more; it is intercourse. It describes the commercial intercourse between nations and parts of nations in all its branches, and is regulated by prescribing rules for carrying on that intercourse." That which belongs to commerce is within the jurisdiction of the United States, but that which does not belong to commerce is within the jurisdiction of the police power of the state. . . .

The argument is that the power to control the manufacture of refined sugar is a monopoly over a necessary of life, to the enjoyment of which by a large part of the population of the United States interstate commerce is indispensable, and that, therefore, the general government, in the exercise of the power to regulate commerce, may repress such monopoly directly, and set aside the instruments which have created it. But this argument cannot be confined to necessaries of life merely, and must include all articles of general consumption. Doubtless the power to control the manufacture of a given thing involves, in a certain sense, the control of its disposition, but this is a secondary, and not the primary, sense; and, although the exercise of that power may result in bringing the operation of commerce into play, it does not control it, and affects it only incidentally and indirectly. Commerce succeeds to manufacture, and is not a part of it. The power to regulate commerce is the power to prescribe the rule by which commerce shall be governed, and is a power independent of the power to suppress monopoly. . . .

The regulation of commerce applies to the subjects of commerce, and not to matters of internal police. Contracts to buy, sell, or exchange goods to be transported among the several states, the transportation and its instrumentalities, and articles bought, sold, or exchanged for the purposes of such transit among the states, or put in the way of transit, may be regulated; but this is because they form part of interstate trade or commerce. The fact that an article is manufactured for export to another state does not of itself make it an article of interstate commerce, and the intent of the manufacturer does not determine the time when the article or product passes from the control of the state and belongs to commerce. . . .

Contracts, combinations, or conspiracies to control domestic enterprise in manufacture, agriculture, mining, production in all its forms, or to raise or lower prices or wages, might unquestionably tend to restrain external as well as domestic trade, but the restraint would be an indirect result, however inevitable, and whatever its extent, and such result would not necessarily determine the object of the contract, combination, or conspiracy.

Again, all the authorities agree that, in order to vitiate a contract or combination, it is not essential that its result should be a complete monopoly; it is sufficient if it really tends to that end, and to deprive the public of the advantages which flow from free competition. Slight reflection will show that, if the national power extends to all contracts and combinations in manufacture, agriculture, mining, and other productive industries, whose ultimate result may affect external commerce, comparatively little of business operations and affairs would be left for state control. . . .

Sugar was refined for sale, and sales were probably made at Philadelphia for consumption, and undoubtedly for resale by the first purchasers throughout Pennsylvania and other states, and refined sugar was also forwarded by the companies to other states for sale. Nevertheless it does not follow that an attempt to monopolize, or the actual monopoly of, the manufacture was an attempt, whether executory or consummated, to monopolize commerce, even though, in order to dispose of the product, the instrumentality of commerce was necessarily invoked.

Decree affirmed.

Mr. Justice HARLAN, dissenting.

The court holds it to be vital in our system of government to recognize and give effect to both the commercial power of the nation and the police powers of the states, to the end that the Union be strengthened, and the autonomy of the states preserved. In this view I entirely concur. . . .

What is commerce among the states? The decisions of this court fully answer the question. "Commerce, undoubtedly, is traffic, but it is something more; it is intercourse." It does not embrace the completely interior traffic of the respective states,—that which is "carried on between man and man in a state, or between different parts of the same state, and which does not extend to or affect other states."—but it does embrace "every species of commercial intercourse" between the United States and foreign nations and among the states, and therefore it includes such traffic or trade, buying, selling, and interchange of commodities, as directly affects or necessarily involves the interests of the people of the United States. "Commerce, as the word is used in the constitution, is a unit," and "cannot stop at the external boundary line of each state, but may be introduced into the interior." "The genius and character of the whole government seem to be that its action is to be applied to all the external concerns of the nation, and to those internal concerns which affect the states generally."

It would seem to be indisputable that no combination of corporations or individuals can, of right, impose unlawful restraints upon interstate trade, whether upon transportation or upon such interstate intercourse and traffic as precede transportation, any more than it can, of right, impose unreasonable restraints upon the completely internal traffic of a state. . . .

The fundamental inquiry in this case is, what, in a legal sense, is an unlawful restraint of trade?. . .

It is the Constitution, the supreme law of the land, which invests congress with power to protect commerce among the states against burdens and exactions arising from unlawful restraints by whatever authority imposed. Surely, a right secured or granted by that instrument is under the protection of the government which that instrument creates. Any combination, therefore, that disturbs or unreasonably obstructs freedom in buying and selling articles manufactured to be sold to persons in other states, or to be carried to other states,—a freedom that cannot exist if the right to buy and sell is fettered by unlawful restraints that crush out competition,—affects, not incidentally, but directly, the people of all the states; and the remedy for such an evil is found only in the exercise of powers confided to a government which, this court has said, was the government of all, exercising powers delegated by all, representing all, acting for all. . . .

The power of congress covers and protects the absolute freedom of such intercourse and trade among the states as may or must succeed manufacture and precede transportation from the place of purchase. . . . Each part of such trade is then under the protection of congress. And yet, by the opinion and judgment in this case, if I do not misapprehend them, congress is without power to protect the commercial intercourse that such purchasing necessarily involves against the restraints and burdens arising from the existence of combinations that meet purchasers, from whatever state they come, with the threat—for it is nothing more nor less than a threat—that they shall not purchase what they desire to purchase, except at the prices fixed by such combinations. . . .

The question here relates to restraints upon the freedom of interstate trade and commerce imposed by illegal combinations. After the fullest consideration I have been able to bestow upon this important question, I find it impossible to refuse my assent to this proposition: Whatever a state may do to protect its completely interior traffic or trade against unlawful restraints, the general government is empowered to do for the protection of the people of all the states—for this purpose, one people—against unlawful restraints imposed upon interstate traffic or trade in articles that are to enter into commerce among the several states. If, as already shown, a state may prevent or suppress a combination, the effect of which is to subject its domestic trade to the restraints necessarily arising from their obtaining the absclute [sic] control of the sale of a particular article in general use by the community, there ought to be no hesitation in allowing to congress the right to suppress a similar combination that imposes a like unlawful restraint upon interstate trade and traffic in that article. While the states retain, because they have never surrendered, full control of their completely internal traffic, it was not intended by the framers of the constitution that any part of interstate commerce should be excluded from the control of congress. Each state can reach and suppress combinations so far as they unlawfully restrain its interior trade, while the national government may reach and suppress them so far as they unlawfully restrain trade among the states. . . .

While the opinion of the court in this case does not declare the act of 1890 to be unconstitutional, it defeats the main object for which it was passed, for it is, in effect, held that the statute would be unconstitutional if interpreted as embracing such unlawful restraints upon the purchasing of goods in one state to be carried to another state as necessarily arise from the existence of combinations formed for the purpose and with the effect, not only of monopolizing the ownership of all such goods in every part of the country, but of controlling the prices for them in all the states. This view of the scope of the act leaves the public, so far as national power is concerned, entirely at the mercy of combinations which arbitrarily control the prices of articles purchased to be transported from one state to another state. I cannot assent to that view. In my judgment, the general government is not placed by the constitution in such a condition of helplessness that it must fold its arms and remain inactive while capital combines, under the name of a corporation, to destroy competition, not in one state only, but throughout the entire country, in the buying and selling of articles—especially the necessaries of life—that go into commerce among the states. The doctrine of the autonomy of the states cannot properly be invoked to justify a denial of power in the national government to meet such an emergency, involving, as it does, that freedom of commercial intercourse among the states which the constitution sought to attain. . . .

For the reasons stated, I dissent from the opinion and judgment of the court.

Source: Justia.com – US Supreme Court Center. http://supreme.justia.com/us/156/1/case.html

UNITED STATES CONSTITUTION—AMENDMENT XVI

In Pollock v. Farmer's Loan & Trust, *the Supreme Court ruled that under the original Constitution, Congress had no power to impose a direct tax on income derived from property. Direct tax on income was an important part of the populist platform and* Pollock *helped crush that move. Almost twenty years later, that case was overruled by this amendment allowing Congress to directly tax the populace's income.*

Passed by Congress July 2, 1909. Ratified February 3, 1913.

Note: Article I, Section 9, of the Constitution was modified by the Sixteenth Amendment. The Congress shall have power to lay and collect taxes on incomes, from whatever source derived, without apportionment among the several States, and without regard to any census or enumeration.

UNITED STATES CONSTITUTION—AMENDMENT XVII

The Framers originally called for senators to be elected by state legislatures. One of the reasons was because the Founders hoped senators elected by local legislatures would focus on the business of national government and national concerns, rather than be subject to the pressure of the local population with more local concerns. This amendment grew out of almost a century of agitation. Growing concerns over corruption, and failure to really respond to needs of the people, resulted in pushes that grew during the populist movement of the late nineteenth century and the progressive movement in the early twentieth.

Passed by Congress May 13, 1912. Ratified April 8, 1913.

Note: Article I, Section 3, of the Constitution was modified by the Seventeenth Amendment.

The Senate of the United States shall be composed of two Senators from each State, elected by the people thereof, for six years; and each Senator shall have one vote. The electors in each State shall have the qualifications requisite for electors of the most numerous branch of the State legislatures.

When vacancies happen in the representation of any State in the Senate, the executive authority of such State shall issue writs of election to fill such vacancies: *Provided,* That the legislature of any State may empower the executive thereof to make temporary appointments until the people fill the vacancies by election as the legislature may direct.

This amendment shall not be so construed as to affect the election or term of any Senator chosen before it becomes valid as part of the Constitution.

SCHECHTER POULTRY CORPORATION V. UNITED STATES (1935)

A unanimous decision by the Supreme Court that struck down an early attempt by Congress to solve the problems of the Great Depression. The National Industrial Recovery Act (1933), one of the first New Deal programs, established a system whereby the president established codes to regulate hours, wages, and ages of workers. These codes were declared unconstitutional, most importantly because Congress could not delegate its law-making authority to the executive branch. In the NIRA the Congress had not established rules or guidelines, but merely ceded that authority to the president.

Mr. Chief Justice HUGHES delivered the opinion of the Court.

First. Two preliminary points are stressed by the government with respect to the appropriate approach to the important questions presented. We are told that the provision of the statute authorizing the adoption of codes must be viewed in the light of the grave national crisis with which Congress was confronted. Undoubtedly, the conditions to which power is addressed are always to be considered when the exercise of power is challenged. Extraordinary conditions may call for extraordinary remedies. But the argument necessarily stops short of an attempt to justify action which lies outside the sphere of constitutional authority. Extraordinary conditions do not create or enlarge constitutional power. The Constitution established a national government with powers deemed to be adequate, as they have proved to be both in war and peace, but these powers of the national government are limited by the constitutional grants. Those who act under these grants are not at liberty to transcend the imposed limits because they believe that more or different power is necessary. Such assertions of extraconstitutional authority were anticipated and precluded by the explicit terms of the Tenth Amendment—"The powers not delegated to the United States by the Constitution, nor prohibited by it to the States, are reserved to the States respectively, or to the people."

The further point is urged that the national crisis demanded a broad and intensive co-operative effort by those engaged in trade and industry, and that this necessary co-operation was sought to be fostered by permitting them to initiate the adoption of codes. But the statutory plan is not simply one for voluntary effort. It does not seek merely to endow voluntary trade or industrial associations or groups with privileges or immunities. It involves the coercive exercise of the lawmaking power. The codes of fair competition which the statute attempts to authorize are codes of laws. If valid, they place all persons within their reach under the obligation of positive law, binding equally those who assent and those who do not assent. Violations of the provisions of the codes are punishable as crimes.

Second. The Question of the Delegation of Legislative Power. . . . The Constitution provides that "All legislative powers herein granted shall be vested in a Congress of the United States, which shall consist of a Senate and House of Representatives." Article 1, 1. And the Congress is authorized "To make all Laws which shall be necessary and proper for carrying into Execution" its general powers. Article 1, 8, par. 18. The Congress is not permitted to abdicate or to transfer to others the essential legislative functions with which it is thus vested. . . .

To summarize and conclude upon this point: Section 3 of the Recovery Act (15 USCA 703) is without precedent. It supplies no standards for any trade, industry, or activity. It does not undertake to prescribe rules of conduct to be applied to particular states of fact determined by appropriate administrative procedure. Instead of prescribing rules of conduct, it authorizes the making of codes to prescribe them. . . . We think that the code-making authority thus conferred is an unconstitutional delegation of legislative power.

Third. The Question of the Application of the Provisions of the Live Poultry Code to Intrastate Transactions. . . .

The undisputed facts thus afford no warrant for the argument that the poultry handled by defendants at their slaughterhouse markets was in a "current" or "flow" of interstate commerce, and was thus subject to congressional regulation. The mere fact that there may be a constant flow of commodities into a state does not mean that the flow continues after the property has arrived and has become commingled with the mass of property within the state and is there held solely for local disposition and use.

So far as the poultry here in question is concerned, the flow in interstate commerce had ceased. The poultry had come to a permanent rest within the state. It was not held, used, or sold by defendants in relation to any further transactions in interstate commerce and was not destined for transportation to other states. Hence decisions which deal with a stream of interstate commerce—where goods come to rest within a state temporarily and are later to go forward in interstate commerce—and with the regulations of transactions involved in that practical continuity of movement, are not applicable here. . . .

Did the defendants' transactions directly "affect" interstate commerce so as to be subject to federal regulation? The power of Congress extends, not only to the regulation of transactions which are part of interstate commerce, but to the protection of that commerce from injury. . . .

In determining how far the federal government may go in controlling intrastate transactions upon the ground that they "affect" interstate commerce, there is a necessary and well-established distinction between direct and indirect effects. The precise line can be drawn only as individual cases arise, but the distinction is clear in principle. Direct effects are illustrated by the railroad cases we have cited, as, e.g., the effect of failure to use prescribed safety appliances on railroads which are the highways of both interstate and intrastate commerce, injury to an employee engaged in interstate transportation by the negligence of an employee engaged in an intrastate movement, the fixing of rates for intrastate transportation which unjustly discriminate against interstate commerce. But where the effect of intrastate transactions upon interstate commerce is merely indirect, such transactions remain within the domain of state power. If the commerce clause were construed to reach all enterprises and transactions which could be said to have an indirect effect upon interstate commerce, the federal authority would embrace practically all the activities of the people, and the authority of the state over its domestic concerns would exist only by sufferance of the federal government. Indeed, on such a theory, even the development of the state's commercial facilities would be subject to federal control. . . .

The distinction between direct and indirect effects has been clearly recognized in the application of the Anti-Trust Act. Where a combination or conspiracy is formed, with the intent to restrain interstate commerce or to monopolize any part of it, the violation of the statute is clear. . . . But, where that intent is absent, and the objectives are limited to intrastate activities, the fact that there may be an indirect effect upon interstate commerce does not subject the parties to the federal statute, notwithstanding its broad provisions. . . .

The question of chief importance relates to the provisions of the code as to the hours and wages of those employed in defendants' slaughterhouse markets. It is plain that these requirements are imposed in order to govern the details of defendants' management of their local business. The persons employed in slaughtering and selling in local trade are not employed in interstate commerce. Their hours and wages have no direct relation to interstate commerce. The question of how many hours these employees should work and what they should be paid differs in no essential respect from similar questions in other local businesses which handle commodities brought into a state and there dealt in as a part of its internal commerce. This appears from an examination of the considerations urged by the government with respect to conditions in the poultry trade. Thus, the government argues that hours and wages affect prices; that slaughterhouse men sell at a small margin above operating costs; that labor represents 50 to 60 per cent of these costs; that a slaughterhouse operator paying lower wages or reducing his cost by exacting long hours of work translates his saving into lower prices; that this results in demands for a cheaper grade of goods: and that the cutting of prices brings about a demoralization of the price structure. Similar conditions may be adduced in relation to other businesses. The argument of the government proves too much. If the federal government may determine the wages and hours of employees in the internal commerce of a state, because of their relation to cost and prices and their indirect effect upon interstate commerce, it would seem that a similar control might be exerted over other elements of cost, also affecting prices, such as the number of employees, rents, advertising, methods of doing business, etc. All the processes of production and distribution that enter into cost could likewise be controlled. If the cost of doing an intrastate business is in itself the permitted object of federal control, the extent of the regulation of cost would be a question of discretion and not of power. . . .

It is not the province of the Court to consider the economic advantages or disadvantages of such a centralized system. It is sufficient to say that the Federal Constitution does not provide for it. Our growth and development have called for wide use of the commerce power of the federal government in its control over the expanded activities of interstate commerce and in protecting that commerce from burdens, interferences, and conspiracies to restrain and monopolize it. But the authority of the federal government may not be pushed to such an extreme as to destroy the distinction, which the commerce clause itself establishes, between commerce "among the several States" and the internal concerns of a state. The same answer must be made to the contention that is based upon the serious economic situation which led to the passage of the Recovery Act—the fall in prices, the decline in wages and employment, and the curtailment of the market for commodities. Stress is laid upon the great importance of maintaining wage distributions which would provide the necessary stimulus in starting "the cumulative forces making for expanding commercial activity." Without in any way disparaging this motive, it is enough to say that the recuperative efforts of the federal government must be made in a manner consistent with the authority granted by the Constitution. . . .

Mr. Justice CARDOZO (concurring).

The delegated power of legislation which has found expression in this code is not canalized within banks that keep it from overflowing. It is unconfined and vagrant. . . .

This court has held that delegation may be unlawful, though the act to be performed is definite and single, if the necessity, time, and occasion of performance have been left in the end to the discretion of the delegate. . . . I thought that ruling went too far. . . .

If this code had been adopted by Congress itself, and not by the President on the advice of an industrial association, it would even then be void, unless authority to adopt it is included in the grant of power "to regulate commerce with foreign nations, and among the several States." United States Constitution, art. 1, 8, cl. 3.

I find no authority in that grant for the regulation of wages and hours of labor in the intrastate transactions that make up the defendants' business. As to this feature of the case, little can be added to the opinion of the court. There is a view of causation that would obliterate the distinction between what is national and what is local in the activities of commerce. . . . A society such as ours "is an elastic medium which transmits all tremors throughout its territory; the only question is of their size." . . . Activities local in their immediacy do not become interstate and national because of distant repercussions. . . .

Source: Justia.com – US Supreme Court Center. http://supreme.justia.com/us/295/495/case.html

UNITED STATES V. CURTISS-WRIGHT EXPORT CORPORATION (1936)

In contrast to Schechter above, the Court acknowledged a lot more leeway for delegation of authority to the president by Congress in the area of foreign affairs. Curtiss-Wright, in direct violation of a congressional joint resolution and a presidential proclamation, had sold machine guns to Bolivia. The question was did the joint resolution unconstitutionally delegate legislative powers to the executive branch. The Court found no violation. Because the president had special authority in the foreign arena, Congress was allowed to give the president extra discretion in foreign affairs, which it could not do, as noted in Schechter, regarding domestic issues.

Mr. Justice SUTHERLAND delivered the opinion of the Court.

Whether, if the Joint Resolution had related solely to internal affairs, it would be open to the challenge that it constituted an unlawful delegation of legislative power to the Executive, we find it unnecessary to determine. The whole aim of the resolution is to affect a situation entirely external to the United States, and falling within the category of foreign affairs. The determination which we are called to make, therefore, is whether the Joint Resolution, as applied to that situation, is vulnerable to attack under the rule that forbids a delegation of the lawmaking power. In other words, assuming (but not deciding) that the challenged delegation, if it were confined to internal affairs, would be invalid, may it nevertheless be sustained on the ground that its exclusive aim is to afford a remedy for a hurtful condition within foreign territory?

It will contribute to the elucidation of the question if we first consider the differences between the powers of the federal government in respect of foreign or external affairs and those in respect of domestic or internal affairs. That there are differences between them, and that these differences are fundamental, may not be doubted. . . .

It results that the investment of the federal government with the powers of external sovereignty did not depend upon the affirmative grants of the Constitution. The powers to declare and wage war, to conclude peace, to make treaties, to maintain diplomatic relations with other sovereignties, if they had never been mentioned in the Constitution, would have vested in the federal government as necessary concomitants of nationality. . . .

Not only, as we have shown, is the federal power over external affairs in origin and essential character different from that over internal affairs, but participation in the exercise of the power is significantly limited. In this vast external realm, with its important, complicated, delicate and manifold problems, the President alone has the power to speak or listen as a representative of the nation. He makes treaties with the advice and consent of the Senate; but he alone negotiates. Into the field of negotiation the Senate cannot intrude; and Congress itself is powerless to invade it. . . .

It is important to bear in mind that we are here dealing not alone with an authority vested in the President by an exertion of legislative power, but with such an authority plus the very delicate, plenary and exclusive power of the President as the sole organ of the federal government in the field of international relations—a power which does not require as a basis for its exercise an act of Congress, but which, of course, like every other governmental power, must be exercised in subordination to the applicable provisions of the Constitution. It is quite apparent that if, in the maintenance of our international relations, embarrassment—perhaps serious embarrassment—is to be avoided and success for our aims achieved, congressional legislation which is to be made effective through negotiation and inquiry within the international field must often accord to the President a degree of discretion and freedom from statutory restriction which would not be admissible were domestic affairs alone involved. Moreover, he, not Congress, has the better opportunity of knowing the conditions which prevail in foreign countries, and especially is this true in time of war. He has his confidential sources of information. He has his agents in the form of diplomatic, consular and other officials. Secrecy in respect of information gathered by them may be highly necessary, and the premature disclosure of it productive of harmful results. . . .

When the President is to be authorized by legislation to act in respect of a matter intended to affect a situation in foreign territory, the legislator properly bears in mind the important consideration that the form of the President's action—or, indeed, whether he shall act at all—may well depend, among other things, upon the nature of the confidential information which he has or may thereafter receive, or upon the effect which his action may have upon our foreign relations. This consideration, in connection with what we have already said on the subject discloses the unwisdom of requiring Congress in this field of governmental power to lay down narrowly definite standards by which the President is to be governed. . . .

Source: Justia.com – US Supreme Court Center. http://supreme.justia.com/us/299/304/case.html

WEST COAST HOTEL CO. V. PARRISH ET AL. (1936)

The case concerns another attempt by Congress to establish a minimum wage, this time for women. Earlier cases had struck down attempts by Congress to do this, as violating the liberty of contract. It began to open the door to economic regulation under the Commerce Clause by Congress, beginning the trend to overturn three decades of decisions that limited that power through liberty of contract, indirect-direct distinctions about commerce, and the manufacturing-commerce delineation that had crushed congressional attempts to solve problems of the Great Depression.

MR. CHIEF JUSTICE HUGHES delivered the opinion of the Court.

This case presents the question of the constitutional validity of the minimum wage law [for women] of the State of Washington. . . .

The appellant conducts a hotel. The appellee Elsie Parrish was employed as a chambermaid and (with her husband) brought this suit to recover the difference between the wages paid her and the minimum wage fixed pursuant to the state law. The minimum wage was $14.50 per week of 48 hours. The appellant challenged the act as repugnant to the due process clause of the Fourteenth Amendment of the Constitution of the United States. The Supreme Court of the State, reversing the trial court, sustained the statute and directed judgment for the plaintiffs.

The appellant relies upon the decision of this Court in *Adkins* v. *Children's Hospital.* . . .

The principle which must control our decision is not in doubt. The constitutional provision invoked is the due process clause of the Fourteenth Amendment governing the States, as the due process clause invoked in the *Adkins* case governed Congress. In each case the violation alleged by those attacking minimum wage regulation for women is deprivation of freedom of contract. What is this freedom? The Constitution does not speak of freedom of contract. It speaks of liberty and prohibits the deprivation of liberty without due process of law. In prohibiting that deprivation the Constitution does not recognize an absolute and uncontrollable liberty. Liberty in each of its phases has its history and connotation. But the liberty safeguarded is liberty in a social organization which requires the protection of law against the evils which menace the health, safety, morals and welfare of the people. Liberty under the Constitution is thus necessarily subject to the restraints of due process, and regulation which is reasonable in relation to its subject and is adopted in the interests of the community is due process. . . .

We think . . . the *Adkins* case was a departure from the true application of the principles governing the regulation by the State of the relation of employer and employed. . . .

What can be closer to the public interest than the health of women and their protection from unscrupulous and overreaching employers? And if the protection of women is a legitimate end of the exercise of state power, how can it be said that the requirement of the payment of a minimum wage fairly fixed in order to meet the very necessities of existence is not an admissible means to that end? The legislature of the State was clearly entitled to consider the situation of women in employment, the fact that they are in the class receiving the least pay, that their bargaining power is relatively weak, and that they are the ready victims of those who would take advantage of their necessitous circumstances. The legislature was entitled to adopt measures to reduce the evils of the "sweating system," the exploiting of workers at wages so low as to be insufficient to meet the bare cost of living, thus making their very helplessness the occasion of a most injurious competition. The legislature had the right to consider that its minimum wage requirements would be an important aid in carrying out its policy of protection. The adoption of similar requirements by many States evidences a deepseated conviction both as to the presence of the evil and as to the means adapted to check it. Legislative response to that conviction cannot be regarded as arbitrary or capricious, and that is all we have to decide. Even if the wisdom of the policy be regarded as debatable and its effects uncertain, still the legislature is entitled to its judgment.

There is an additional and compelling consideration which recent economic experience has brought into a strong light. The exploitation of a class of workers who are in an unequal position with respect to bargaining power and are thus relatively defenseless against the denial of a living wage is not only detrimental to their health and well being but casts a direct burden for their support upon the community. What these workers lose in wages the taxpayers are called upon to pay. The bare cost of living must be met. We may take judicial notice of the unparalleled demands for relief which arose during the recent period of depression and still continue to an alarming extent despite the degree of economic recovery which has been achieved. It is unnecessary to cite official statistics to establish what is of common knowledge through the length and breadth of the land. While in the instant case no factual brief has been presented, there is no reason to doubt that the State of Washington has encountered the same social problem that is present elsewhere. The community is not bound to provide what is in effect a subsidy for unconscionable employers. The community may direct its law-making power to correct the abuse which springs from their selfish disregard of the public interest. The argument that the legislation in question constitutes an arbitrary discrimination, because it does not extend to men, is unavailing. This Court has frequently held that the legislative authority, acting within its proper field, is not bound to extend its regulation to all cases, which it might possibly reach. The legislature "is free to recognize degrees of harm and it may confine its restrictions to those classes of cases where the need is deemed to be clearest." If "the law presumably hits the evil where it is most felt, it is not to be overthrown because there are other instances to which it might have been applied." There is no "doctrinaire requirement" that the legislation should be couched in all embracing terms. . . .

Our conclusion is that the case of *Adkins* v. *Children's Hospital, supra*, should be, and it is, overruled. The judgment of the Supreme Court of the State of Washington is
   Affirmed.

MR. JUSTICE SUTHERLAND, dissenting:

MR. JUSTICE VAN DEVANTER, MR. JUSTICE McREYNOLDS, MR. JUSTICE BUT-LER and I think the judgment of the court below should be reversed.

The meaning of the Constitution does not change with the ebb and flow of economic events. We frequently are told in more general words that the Constitution must be construed in the light of the present. If by that it is meant that the Constitution is made up of living words that apply to every new condition which they include, the statement is quite true. But to say, if that be intended, that the words of the Constitution mean today what they did not mean when written—that is, that they do not apply to a situation now to which they would have applied then—is to rob that instrument of the essential element which continues it in force as the people have made it until they, and not their official agents, have made it otherwise. . . .

Constitutions can not be changed by events alone. They remain binding as the acts of the people in their sovereign capacity, as the framers of Government, until they are amended or abrogated by the action prescribed by the authority which created them. It is not competent for any department of the Government to change a constitution, or declare it changed, simply because it appears ill adapted to a new state of things. . . .

The judicial function is that of interpretation; it does not include the power of amendment under the guise of interpretation. To miss the point of difference between the two is to miss all that the phrase "supreme law of the land" stands for and to convert what was intended as inescapable and enduring mandates into mere moral reflections.

If the Constitution, intelligently and reasonably construed in the light of these principles, stands in the way of desirable legislation, the blame must rest upon that instrument, and not upon the court for enforcing it according to its terms. The remedy in that situation—and the only true remedy—is to amend the Constitution. . . .

The people by their Constitution created three separate, distinct, independent and co-equal departments of government. The governmental structure rests, and was intended to rest, not upon any one or upon any two, but upon all three of these fundamental pillars. It seems unnecessary to repeat, what so often has been said, that the powers of these departments are different and are to be exercised independently. The differences clearly and definitely appear in the Constitution. Each of the departments is an agent of its creator; and one department is not and cannot be the agent of another. Each is answerable to its creator for what it does, and not to another agent. The view, therefore, of the Executive and of Congress that an act is constitutional is persuasive in a high degree; but it is not controlling.

Coming, then, to a consideration of the Washington statute, it first is to be observed that it is in every substantial respect identical with the statute involved in the *Adkins* case. Such vices as existed in the latter are present in the former. And if the *Adkins* case was properly decided, as we who join in this opinion think it was, it necessarily follows that the Washington statute is invalid.

That the clause of the Fourteenth Amendment which forbids a state to deprive any person of life, liberty or property without due process of law includes freedom of contract is so well settled as to be no longer open to question. . . .

What we said [in *Adkins*] . . . is equally applicable here:

"The law takes account of the necessities of only one party to the contract. It ignores the necessities of the employer by compelling him to pay not less than a certain sum, not only whether the employee is capable of earning it, but irrespective of the ability of his business to sustain the burden, generously leaving him, of course, the privilege of abandoning his business as an alternative for going on at a loss. Within the limits of the minimum sum, he is precluded, under penalty of fine and imprisonment, from adjusting compensation to the differing merits of his employees. It compels him to pay at least the sum fixed in any event, because the employee needs it, but requires no service of equivalent value from the employee. It therefore undertakes to solve but one-half of the problem. The other half is the establishment of a corresponding standard of efficiency, and this forms no part of the policy of the legislation, although in practice the former half without the latter must lead to ultimate failure, in accordance with the inexorable law that no one can continue indefinitely to take out more than he puts in without ultimately exhausting the supply. The law is not confined to the great and powerful employers but embraces those whose bargaining power may be as weak as that of the employee. It takes no account of periods of stress and business depression, of crippling losses, which may leave the employer himself without adequate means of livelihood. To the extent that the sum fixed exceeds the fair value of the services rendered, it amounts to a compulsory exaction from the employer for the support of a partially indigent person, for whose condition there rests upon him no peculiar responsibility, and therefore, in effect, arbitrarily shifts to his shoulders a burden which, if it belongs to anybody, belongs to society as a whole." . . .

Source: Justia.com – US Supreme Court Center. http://supreme.justia.com/us/300/379/case.html

NATIONAL LABOR RELATIONS BOARD V. JONES & LAUGHLIN STEEL CORP. (1937)

Opened the door for congressional regulation of labor, which had previously been declared off limits because it only had an indirect effect on interstate commerce. This case declared the National Labor Relations Act (NLRA) of 1935 to be constitutional. It established that labor-management disputes were directly related to the flow of interstate commerce. The National Labor Relations Board, established by the NLRA, charged Jones & Laughlin for discriminating against union members.

MR. CHIEF JUSTICE HUGHES delivered the opinion of the Court.

The facts as to the nature and scope of the business of the Jones & Laughlin Steel Corporation have been found by the Labor Board and, so far as they are essential to the determination of this controversy, they are not in dispute. The Labor Board has found: The corporation is organized under the laws of Pennsylvania and has its principal office at Pittsburgh. It is engaged in the business of manufacturing iron and steel in plants situated in Pittsburgh and nearby Aliquippa, Pennsylvania. It manufactures and distributes a widely diversified line of steel and pig iron, being the fourth largest producer of steel in the United States. With its subsidiaries—nineteen in number—it is a completely integrated enterprise, owning and operating ore, coal and limestone properties, lake and river transportation facilities and terminal railroads located at its manufacturing plants. It owns or controls mines in Michigan and Minnesota. It operates four ore steamships on the Great Lakes, used in the transportation of ore to its factories. It owns coal mines in Pennsylvania. It operates towboats and steam barges used in carrying coal to its factories. It owns limestone properties in various places in Pennsylvania and West Virginia. It owns the Monongahela connecting railroad which connects the plants of the Pittsburgh works and forms an interconnection with the Pennsylvania, New York Central and Baltimore . . . and Ohio Railroad systems. It owns the Aliquippa and Southern Railroad Company which connects the Aliquippa works with the Pittsburgh and Lake Erie, part of the New York Central system. Much of its product is shipped to its warehouses in Chicago, Detroit, Cincinnati and Memphis,—to the last two places by means of its own barges and transportation equipment. In Long Island City, New York, and in New Orleans it operates structural steel fabricating shops in connection with the warehousing of semi-finished materials sent from its works. Through one of its wholly-owned subsidiaries it owns, leases and operates stores, warehouses and yards for the distribution of equipment and supplies for drilling and operating oil and gas wells and for pipe lines, refineries and pumping stations. It has sales offices in twenty cities in the United States and a wholly-owned subsidiary which is devoted exclusively to distributing its product in Canada. Approximately 75 per cent. of its product is shipped out of Pennsylvania.

Summarizing these operations, the Labor Board concluded that the works in Pittsburgh and Aliquippa "might be likened to the heart of a self-contained, highly integrated body. They draw in the raw materials from Michigan, Minnesota, West Virginia, Pennsylvania in part through arteries and by means controlled by the respondent; they transform the materials and then pump them out to all parts of the nation through the vast mechanism which the respondent has elaborated."

To carry on the activities of the entire steel industry, 33,000 men mine ore, 44,000 men mine coal, 4,000 men quarry limestone, 16,000 men manufacture coke, 343,000 men manufacture steel, and 83,000 men transport its product. Respondent has about 10,000 employees in its Aliquippa plant, which is located in a community of about 30,000 persons. . . .

First. The scope of the Act.—The Act is challenged in its entirety as an attempt to regulate all industry, thus invading the reserved powers of the States over their local concerns. It is asserted that the references in the Act to interstate and foreign commerce are colorable at best; that the Act is not a true regulation of such commerce or of matters which directly affect it but on the contrary has the fundamental object of placing under the compulsory supervision of the federal government all industrial labor relations within the nation. . . .

We think it clear that the National Labor Relations Act may be construed so as to operate within the sphere of constitutional authority. The jurisdiction conferred upon the Board, and invoked in this instance, is found in § 10 (a), which provides:

"SEC. 10 (a). The Board is empowered, as hereinafter provided, to prevent any person from engaging in any unfair labor practice (listed in section 8) affecting commerce."

The critical words of this provision, prescribing the limits of the Board's authority in dealing with the labor practices, are "affecting commerce." The Act specifically defines the "commerce" to which it refers (§ 2(6)):

"The term 'commerce' means trade, traffic, commerce, transportation, or communication among the several States. . . ."

There can be no question that the commerce thus contemplated by the Act (aside from that within a Territory or the District of Columbia) is interstate and foreign commerce in the constitutional sense. The Act also defines the term "affecting commerce" (§ 2 (7)):

"The term 'affecting commerce' means in commerce, or burdening or obstructing commerce or the free flow of commerce, or having led or tending to lead to a labor dispute burdening or obstructing commerce or the free flow of commerce. . . ."

Third. The application of the Act to employees engaged in production. — The principle involved.—Respondent says that whatever may be said of employees engaged in interstate commerce, the industrial relations and activities in the manufacturing department of respondent's enterprise are not subject to federal regulation. The argument rests upon the proposition that manufacturing in itself is not commerce. . . .

The congressional authority to protect interstate commerce from burdens and obstructions is not limited to transactions which can be deemed to be an essential part of a "flow" of interstate or foreign commerce. Burdens and obstructions may be due to injurious action springing from other sources. The fundamental principle is that the power to regulate commerce is the power to enact "all appropriate legislation" for "its protection and advancement" *(The Daniel Ball,* 10 Wall. 557, 564); to adopt measures "to promote its growth and insure its safety" *(Mobile County* v. *Kimball,* 102 U.S. 691, 696, 697); "to foster, protect, control and restrain." *Second Employers' Liability Cases, supra,* p. 47. See *Texas & N.O.R. Co.* v. *Railway Clerks, supra.* That power is plenary and may be exerted to protect interstate commerce "no matter what the source of the dangers which threaten it." *Second Employers' Liability Cases,* p. 51; *Schechter Corp.* v. *United States, supra.* Although activities may be intrastate in character when separately considered, if they have such a close and substantial relation to interstate commerce that their control is essential or appropriate to protect that commerce from burdens and obstructions, Congress cannot be denied the power to exercise that control. *Schechter Corp.* v. *United States, supra.* Undoubtedly the scope of this power must be considered in the light of our dual system of government and may not be extended so as to embrace effects upon interstate commerce so indirect and remote that to embrace them, in view of our complex society, would effectually obliterate the distinction between what is national and what is local and create a completely centralized government. *Id.* The question is necessarily one of degree. . . .

That intrastate activities, by reason of close and intimate relation to interstate commerce, may fall within federal control is demonstrated in the case of carriers who are engaged in both interstate and intrastate transportation. . . .

The close and intimate effect which brings the subject within the reach of federal power may be due to activities in relation to productive industry although the industry when separately viewed is local. . . .

It is thus apparent that the fact that the employees here concerned were engaged in production is not determinative. The question remains as to the effect upon interstate commerce of the labor practice involved. In the *Schechter* case, *supra,* we found that the effect there was so remote as to be beyond the federal power. To find "immediacy or directness" there was to find it "almost everywhere," a result inconsistent with the maintenance of our federal system. . . .

Fourth. Effects of the unfair labor practice in respondent's enterprise.—Giving full weight to respondent's contention with respect to a break in the complete continuity of the "stream of commerce" by reason of respondent's manufacturing operations, the fact remains that the stoppage of those operations by industrial strife would have a most serious effect upon interstate commerce. In view of respondent's far-flung activities, it is idle to say that the effect would be indirect or remote. It is obvious that it would be immediate and might be catastrophic. We are asked to shut our eyes to the plainest facts of our national life and to deal with the question of direct and indirect effects in an intellectual vacuum. Because there may be but indirect and remote effects upon interstate commerce in connection with a host of local enterprises throughout the country, it does not follow that other industrial activities do not have such a close and intimate relation to interstate commerce as to make the presence of industrial strife a matter of the most urgent national concern. When industries organize themselves on a national scale, making their relation to interstate commerce the dominant factor in their activities, how can it be maintained that their industrial labor relations constitute a forbidden field into which Congress may not enter when it is necessary to protect interstate commerce from the paralyzing consequences of industrial war? We have often said that interstate commerce itself is a practical conception. It is equally true that interferences with that commerce must be appraised by a judgment that does not ignore actual experience.

Experience has abundantly demonstrated that the recognition of the right of employees to self-organization and to have representatives of their own choosing for the purpose of collective bargaining is often an essential condition of industrial peace. Refusal to confer and negotiate has been one of the most prolific causes of strife. This is such an outstanding fact in the history of labor disturbances that it is a proper subject of judicial notice and requires no citation of instances. . . .

Our conclusion is that the order of the Board was within its competency and that the Act is valid as here applied. The judgment of the Circuit Court of Appeals is reversed and the cause is remanded for further proceedings in conformity with this opinion.

Reversed.

Source: Justia.com – US Supreme Court Center. http://supreme.justia.com/us/301/1/case.html

STEWARD MACHINE COMPANY V. DAVIS (1937)

Created a wide range of taxing power for Congress. This case validates the Social Security Act (1935), which created a federal payroll tax on employers. The act was challenged as contravening basic federalist principles. The Court held it was a constitutional exercise of congressional power and did not violate the Tenth Amendment by coercing the states to participate in a program against their choosing.

Mr. Justice CARDOZO delivered the opinion of the Court.

The validity of the tax imposed by the Social Security Act (42 U.S.C. A. 301-1305) on employers of eight or more is here to be determined. . . .

First: The tax, which is described in the statute as an excise, is laid with uniformity throughout the United States as a duty, an impost, or an excise upon the relation of employment.

1. We are told that the relation of employment is one so essential to the pursuit of happiness that it may not be burdened with a tax. Appeal is made to history. From the precedents of colonial days, we are supplied with illustrations of excises common in the colonies. . . .

The subject-matter of taxation open to the power of the Congress is as comprehensive as that open to the power of the states, though the method of apportionment may at times be different. "The Congress shall have Power to lay and collect Taxes, Duties, Imposts and Excises." Article 1, 8. If the tax is a direct one, it shall be apportioned according to the census or enumeration. If it is a duty, impost, or excise, it shall be uniform throughout the United States. Together, these classes include every form of tax appropriate to sovereignty. . . . At times taxpayers have contended that Congress is without power to lay an excise on the enjoyment of a privilege created by state law. The contention has been put aside as baseless. Congress may tax the transmission of property by inheritance or will, though the states and not Congress have created the privilege of succession. . . .

2. The tax being an excise, its imposition must conform to the canon of uniformity. . . .

Second: The excise is not invalid under the provisions of the Fifth Amendment by force of its exemptions. The statute does not apply, as we have seen, to employers of less than eight. It does not apply to agricultural labor, or domestic service in a private home or to some other classes of less importance. Petitioner contends that the effect of these restrictions is an arbitrary discrimination vitiating the tax.

The Fifth Amendment unlike the Fourteenth has no equal protection clause. . . . But even the states, though subject to such a clause, are not confined to a formula of rigid uniformity in framing measures of taxation. . . . They may lay an excise on the operations of a particular kind of business, and exempt some other kind of business closely akin thereto. . . . If this latitude of judgment is lawful for the states, it is lawful, a fortiori, in legislation by the Congress, which is subject to restraints less narrow and confining. Quong Wing v. Kirkendall, supra.

The classifications and exemptions directed by the statute now in controversy have support in considerations of policy and practical convenience that cannot be condemned as arbitrary. The classifications and exemptions would therefore be upheld if they had been adopted by a state and the provisions of the Fourteenth Amendment were invoked to annul them. . . .

Third: The excise is not void as involving the coercion of the states in contravention of the Tenth Amendment or of restrictions implicit in our federal form of government. . . .

But before the statute succumbs to an assault upon these lines, . . . there must be a showing . . . that the tax and the credit in combination are weapons of coercion, destroying or impairing the autonomy of the states. . . .

To draw the line intelligently between duress and inducement, there is need to remind ourselves of facts as to the problem of unemployment that are now matters of common knowledge. . . . The fact developed quickly that the states were unable to give the requisite relief. The problem had become national in area and dimensions. There was need of help from the nation if the people were not to starve. It is too late today for the argument to be heard with tolerance that in a crisis so extreme the use of the moneys of the nation to relieve the unemployed and their dependents is a use for any purpose narrower than the promotion of the general welfare. . . .

In the presence of this urgent need for some remedial expedient, the question is to be answered whether the expedient adopted has overlept the bounds of power. The assailants of the statute say that its dominant end and aim is to drive the state Legislatures under the whip of economic pressure into the enactment of unemployment compensation laws at the bidding of the central government. Supporters of the statute say that its operation is not constraint, but the creation of a larger freedom, the states and the nation joining in a co-operative endeavor to avert a common evil. Before Congress acted, unemployment compensation insurance was still, for the most part, a project and no more. . . .

The Social Security Act is an attempt to find a method by which all these public agencies may work together to a common end. Every dollar of the new taxes will continue in all likelihood to be used and needed by the nation as long as states are unwilling, whether through timidity or for other motives, to do what can be done at home. At least the inference is permissible that Congress so believed, though retaining undiminished freedom to spend the money as it pleased. On the other hand, fulfillment of the home duty will be lightened and encouraged by crediting the taxpayer upon his account with the Treasury of the nation to the extent that his contributions under the laws of the locality have simplified or diminished the problem of relief and the probable demand upon the resources of the fisc. Duplicated taxes, or burdens that approach them are recognized hardships that government, state or national, may properly avoid. . . . If Congress believed that the general welfare would better be promoted by relief through local units than by the system then in vogue, the co-operating localities ought not in all fairness to pay a second time.

Who then is coerced through the operation of this statute? Not the taxpayer. He pays in fulfillment of the mandate of the local legislature. Not the state. Even now she does not offer a suggestion that in passing the unemployment law she was affected by duress. . . . The difficulty with the petitioner's contention is that it confuses motive with coercion. "Every tax is in some measure regulatory. To some extent it interposes an economic impediment to the activity taxed as compared with others not taxed." . . . In like manner every rebate from a tax when conditioned upon conduct is in some measure a temptation. But to hold that motive or temptation is equivalent to coercion is to plunge the law in endless difficulties. The outcome of such a doctrine is the acceptance of a philosophical determinism by which choice becomes impossible. Till now the law has been guided by a robust common sense which assumes the freedom of the will as a working hypothesis in the solution of its problems. The wisdom of the hypothesis has illustration in this case. Nothing in the case suggests the exertion of a power akin to undue influence, if we assume that such a concept can ever be applied with fitness to the relations between state and nation. Even on that assumption the location of the point at which pressure turns into compulsion, and ceases to be inducement, would be a question of degree, at times, perhaps, of fact. The point had not been reached when Alabama made her choice. We cannot say that she was acting, not of her unfettered will, but under the strain of a persuasion equivalent to undue influence, when she chose to have relief administered under laws of her own making, by agents of her own selection, instead of under federal laws, administered by federal officers, with all the ensuing evils, at least to many minds, of federal patronage and power. . . .

Fourth: The statute does not call for a surrender by the states of powers essential to their quasi sovereign existence.

The judgment is affirmed.

Separate opinion of Mr. Justice McREYNOLDS.

That portion of the Social Security legislation here under consideration, I think, exceeds the power granted to Congress. It unduly interferes with the orderly government of the state by her own people and otherwise offends the Federal Constitution. . . .

It may be not unreasonably said that the preservation of the States, and the maintenance of their governments, are as much within the design and care of the Constitution as the preservation of the Union and the maintenance of the National Government.

The Constitution, in all its provisions, looks to an indestructible Union, composed of indestructible States. . . .

Unfortunately, the decision just announced opens the way for practical annihilation of this theory; and no cloud of words or ostentatious parade of irrelevant statistics should be permitted to obscure that fact. The invalidity also the destructive tendency of legislation like the act before us were forcefully pointed out by President Franklin Pierce in a veto message sent to the Senate May 3, 1854. . . .

No defense is offered for the legislation under review upon the basis of emergency. The hypothesis is that hereafter it will continuously benefit unemployed members of a class. Forever, so far as we can see, the states are expected to function under federal direction concerning an internal matter. By the sanction of this adventure, the door is open for progressive inauguration of others of like kind under which it can hardly be expected that the states will retain genuine independence of action. And without independent states a Federal Union as contemplated by the Constitution becomes impossible. . . .

Separate opinion of Mr. Justice SUTHERLAND.

With most of what is said in the opinion just handed down, I concur. . . . I agree that the states are not coerced by the federal legislation into adopting unemployment legislation. The provisions of the federal law may operate to induce the state to pass an employment law if it regards such action to be in its interest. But that is not coercion. If the act stopped here, I should accept the conclusion of the court that the legislation is not unconstitutional.

But the question with which I have difficulty is whether the administrative provisions of the act invade the governmental administrative powers of the several states reserved by the Tenth Amendment. . . . The power to tax is vital and fundamental, and, in the highest degree, governmental in character. Without it, the state could not exist. Fundamental also, and no less important, is the governmental power to expend the moneys realized from taxation, and exclusively to administer the laws in respect of the character of the tax and the methods of laying and collecting it and expending the proceeds.

The people of the United States, by their Constitution, have affirmed a division of internal governmental powers between the federal government and the governments of the several states—committing to the first its powers by express grant and necessary implication; to the latter, or to the people, by reservation, "the powers not delegated to the United States by the Constitution, nor prohibited by it to the States." The Constitution thus affirms the complete supremacy and independence of the state within the field of its powers. Carter v. Carter Coal Co., 298 U.S. 238, 295 , 56 S.Ct. 855, 865. The federal government has no more authority to invade that field than the state has to invade the exclusive field of national governmental powers; for, in the oft-repeated words of this court in Texas v. White, 7 Wall. 700, 725, "the preservation of the States, and the maintenance of their governments, are as much within the design and care of the Constitution as the preservation of the Union and the maintenance of the National government." The necessity of preserving each from every form of illegitimate intrusion or interference on the part of the other is so imperative as to require this court, when its judicial power is properly invoked, to view with a careful and discriminating eye any legislation challenged as constituting such an intrusion or interference. . . .

The precise question, therefore, which we are required to answer by an application of these principles is whether the congressional act contemplates a surrender by the state to the federal government, in whole or in part, of any state governmental power to administer its own unemployment law or the state pay roll-tax funds which it has collected for the purposes of that law. An affirmative answer to this question, I think, must be made. . . .

If we are to survive as the United States, the balance between the powers of the nation and those of the states must be maintained. There is grave danger in permitting it to dip in either direction, danger—if there were no other—in the precedent thereby set for further departures from the equipoise. The threat implicit in the present encroachment upon the administrative functions of the states is that greater encroachments, and encroachments upon other functions, will follow.

For the foregoing reasons, I think the judgment below should be reversed.

Mr. Justice VAN DEVANTER joins in this opinion.

Mr. Justice BUTLER, dissenting.

I think that the objections to the challenged enactment expressed in the separate opinions of Mr. Justice McREYNOLDS and Mr. Justice SUTHERLAND are well taken. I am also of opinion that, in principle and as applied to bring about and to gain control over state unemployment compensation, the statutory scheme is repugnant to the Tenth Amendment: "The powers not delegated to the United States by the Constitution, nor prohibited by it to the States, are reserved to the States respectively, or to the people." The Constitution grants to the United States no power to pay unemployed persons or to require the states to enact laws or to raise or disburse money for that purpose. The provisions in question, if not amounting to coercion in a legal sense, are manifestly designed and intended directly to affect state action in the respects specified. And, if valid as so employed, this "tax and credit" device may be made effective to enable federal authorities to induce, if not indeed to compel, state enactments for any purpose within the realm of state power and generally to control state administration of state laws.

Source: Justia.com – US Supreme Court Center. http://supreme.justia.com/us/301/548/case.html

UNITED STATES V. DARBY (1940)

Congress passed the Fair Labor Standards Act in 1938 to extend regulations it had advanced earlier, including minimum wage, maximum hours, and child labor. Any corporation engaging in interstate commerce or producing any goods sold in another state was subject to this act. In contrast to the 5–4 decision in West Coast Hotel, *a unanimous Supreme Court acknowledged congressional commerce power as wide and extensive. The Court harkened back to Marshall's decision in* Gibbons v. Ogden *in 1824 and conceded that the motive and/or purpose of an economic regulation was not something the Court would analyze. As long as something had a significant impact on interstate commerce, Congress could regulate it.*

MR. JUSTICE STONE delivered the opinion of the Court.

The two principal questions raised by the record in this case are, *first,* whether Congress has constitutional power to prohibit the shipment in interstate commerce of lumber manufactured by employees whose wages are less than a prescribed minimum or whose weekly hours of labor at that wage are greater than a prescribed maximum, and, *second,* whether it has power to prohibit the employment of workmen in the production of goods "for interstate commerce" at other than prescribed wages and hours. . . .

The prohibition of shipment of the proscribed goods in interstate commerce. Section 15 (a) (1) prohibits, and the indictment charges, the shipment in interstate commerce, of goods produced for interstate commerce by employees whose wages and hours of employment do not . . . conform to the requirements of the Act. Since this section is not violated unless the commodity shipped has been produced under labor conditions prohibited by § 6 and § 7, the only question arising under the commerce clause with respect to such shipments is whether Congress has the constitutional power to prohibit them.

While manufacture is not of itself interstate commerce, the shipment of manufactured goods interstate is such commerce and the prohibition of such shipment by Congress is indubitably a regulation of the commerce. The power to regulate commerce is the power "to prescribe the rule by which commerce is governed." *Gibbons* v. *Ogden.* It extends not only to those regulations which aid, foster and protect the commerce, but embraces those which prohibit it. . . . It is conceded that the power of Congress to prohibit transportation in interstate commerce includes noxious articles, *Lottery Case, supra; Hipolite Egg Co.* v. *United States,* 220 U.S. 45; cf. *Hoke* v. *United States, supra;* stolen articles, *Brooks* v. *United States,* 267 U.S. 432; kidnapped persons, *Gooch* v. *United States,* 297 U.S. 124, and articles such as intoxicating liquor or convict made goods, traffic in which is forbidden or restricted by the laws of the state of destination. *Kentucky Whip & Collar Co.* v. *Illinois Central R. Co.,* 299 U.S. 334.

But it is said that the present prohibition falls within the scope of none of these categories; that while the prohibition is nominally a regulation of the commerce its motive or purpose is regulation of wages and hours of persons engaged in manufacture, the control of which has been reserved to the states and upon which Georgia and some of the states of destination have placed no restriction; that the effect of the present statute is not to exclude the proscribed articles from interstate commerce in aid of state regulation as in *Kentucky Whip & Collar Co.* v. *Illinois Central R. Co., supra,* but instead, under the guise of a regulation of interstate commerce, it undertakes to regulate wages and hours within the state contrary to the policy of the state which has elected to leave them unregulated.

The power of Congress over interstate commerce "is complete in itself, may be exercised to its utmost extent, and acknowledges no limitations other than are prescribed in the Constitution." *Gibbons* v. *Ogden, supra.* That power can neither be enlarged nor diminished by the exercise or non-exercise of state power. *Kentucky Whip & Collar Co.* v. *Illinois Central R. Co., supra.* Congress, following its own conception of public policy concerning the restrictions which may appropriately be imposed on interstate commerce, is free to exclude from the commerce articles whose use in the states for which they are destined it may conceive to be injurious to the public health, morals or welfare, even though the state has not sought to regulate their use. *Reid* v. *Colorado, supra; Lottery Case, supra; Hipolite Egg Co.* v. *United States, supra; Hoke* v. *United States, supra.*

Such regulation is not a forbidden invasion of state power merely because either its motive or its consequence is to restrict the use of articles of commerce within the states of destination; and is not prohibited unless by other Constitutional provisions. It is no objection to the assertion of the power to regulate interstate commerce that its exercise is attended by the same incidents which attend the exercise of the police power of the states. . . .

The motive and purpose of the present regulation are plainly to make effective the Congressional conception of public policy that interstate commerce should not be made the instrument of competition in the distribution of goods produced under substandard labor conditions, which competition is injurious to the commerce and to the states from and to which the commerce flows. The motive and purpose of a regulation of interstate commerce are matters for the legislative judgment upon the exercise of which the Constitution places no restriction and over which the courts are given no control. *McCray* v. *United States,* . . . "The judicial cannot prescribe to the legislative department of the government limitations upon the exercise of its acknowledged power." *Veazie Bank* v. *Fenno,* 8 Wall. 533. Whatever their motive and purpose, regulations of commerce which do not infringe some constitutional prohibition are within the plenary power conferred on Congress by the Commerce Clause. Subject only to that limitation, presently to be considered, we conclude that the prohibition of the shipment interstate of goods produced under the forbidden substandard labor conditions is within the constitutional authority of Congress.

In the more than a century which has elapsed since the decision of *Gibbons* v. *Ogden,* these principles of constitutional interpretation have been so long and repeatedly recognized by this Court as applicable to the Commerce Clause, that there would be little occasion for repeating them now were it not for the decision of this Court twenty-two years ago in *Hammer* v. *Dagenhart.* In that case it was held by a bare majority of the Court over the powerful and now classic dissent of Mr. Justice Holmes setting forth the fundamental issues involved, that Congress was without power to exclude the products of child labor from interstate commerce. The reasoning and conclusion of the Court's opinion there cannot be reconciled with the conclusion which we have reached, that the power of Congress under the Commerce Clause is plenary to exclude any article from interstate commerce subject only to the specific prohibitions of the Constitution.

Hammer v. *Dagenhart* has not been followed. The distinction on which the decision was rested that congressional power to prohibit interstate commerce is limited to articles which in themselves have some harmful or deleterious property—a distinction which was novel when made and unsupported by any provision of the Constitution—has long since been abandoned. *Brooks* v. *United States, supra; Kentucky Whip & Collar Co.* v. *Illinois Central R. Co., supra; Electric Bond & Share Co.* v. *Securities & Exchange Comm'n,* 303 U.S. 419; *Mulford* v. *Smith,* 307 U.S. 38. The thesis of the opinion that the motive of the prohibition or its effect to control in some measure the use or production within the states of the article thus excluded from the commerce can operate to deprive the regulation of its constitutional authority has long since ceased to have force. *Reid* v. *Colorado, supra; Lottery Case, supra; Hipolite Egg Co.* v. *United States, supra; Seven Cases* v. *United States, supra,* 514; *Hamilton* v. *Kentucky Distilleries & Warehouse Co., supra,* 156; *United States* v. *Carolene Products Co., supra,* 147. And finally we have declared "The authority of the federal government over interstate commerce does not differ in extent or character from that retained by the states over intrastate commerce." *United States* v. *Rock Royal Co-operative,* 307 U.S. 533, 569.

The conclusion is inescapable that *Hammer* v. *Dagenhart,* was a departure from the principles which have prevailed in the interpretation of the Commerce Clause both before and since the decision and that such vitality, as a precedent, as it then had has long since been exhausted. It should be and now is overruled.

Validity of the wage and hour requirements. Section 15 (a) (2) and §§ 6 and 7 require employers to conform to the wage and hour provisions with respect to all employees engaged in the production of goods for interstate commerce. As appellee's employees are not alleged to be "engaged in interstate commerce" the validity of the prohibition turns on the question whether the employment, under other than the prescribed labor standards, of employees engaged in the production of goods for interstate commerce is so related to the commerce and so affects it as to be within the reach of the power of Congress to regulate it. . . .

To answer this question we must at the outset determine whether the particular acts . . . constitute "production for commerce" within the meaning of the statute. . . .

Without attempting to define the precise limits of the phrase, we think the acts alleged in the indictment are within the sweep of the statute. The obvious purpose of the Act was not only to prevent the interstate transportation of the proscribed product, but to stop the initial step toward transportation, production with the purpose of so transporting it. . . .

Congress, having by the present Act adopted the policy of excluding from interstate commerce all goods produced for the commerce which do not conform to the specified labor standards, it may choose the means reasonably adapted to the attainment of the permitted end, even though they involve control of intrastate activities. Such legislation has often been sustained with respect to powers, other than the commerce power granted to the national government, when the means chosen, although not themselves within the granted power, were nevertheless deemed appropriate aids to the accomplishment of some purpose within an admitted power of the national government. . . . A familiar like exercise of power is the regulation of intrastate transactions which are so commingled with or related to interstate commerce that all must be regulated if the interstate commerce is to be effectively controlled. . . .

The evils aimed at by the Act are the spread of substandard labor conditions through the use of the facilities of interstate commerce for competition by the goods so produced with those produced under the prescribed or better labor conditions; and the consequent dislocation of the commerce itself caused by the impairment or destruction of local businesses by competition made effective through interstate commerce. The Act is thus directed at the suppression of a method or kind of competition in interstate commerce which it has in effect condemned as "unfair," as the Clayton Act has condemned other "unfair methods of competition" made effective through interstate commerce. . . .

The means adopted by § 15 (a) (2) for the protection of interstate commerce by the suppression of the production of the condemned goods for interstate commerce is so related to the commerce and so affects it as to be within the reach of the commerce power. . . . Congress, to attain its objective in the suppression of nationwide competition in interstate commerce by goods produced under substandard labor conditions, has made no distinction as to the volume or amount of shipments in the commerce or of production for commerce by any particular shipper or producer. It recognized that in present day industry, competition by a small part may affect the whole and that the total effect of the competition of many small producers may be great. . . .

Our conclusion is unaffected by the Tenth Amendment which provides: "The powers not delegated to the United States by the Constitution, nor prohibited by it to the States, are reserved to the States respectively, or to the people." The amendment states but a truism that all is retained which has not been surrendered. There is nothing in the history of its adoption to suggest that it was more than declaratory of the relationship between the national and state governments as it had been established by the Constitution before the amendment or that its purpose was other than to allay fears that the new national government might seek to exercise powers not granted, and that the states might not be able to exercise fully their reserved powers. . . .

Reversed.

Source: Justia.com – US Supreme Court Center. http://supreme.justia.com/us/312/100/case.html

WICKARD, SECRETARY OF AGRICULTURE, ET AL. v. FILBURN (1942)

The final item in the line of cases that gave Congress almost a carte blanche in terms of economic regulation. Filburn was a small farmer who harvested twelve acres more than his allotment under a Department of Agriculture directive. He claimed he used the excess wheat purely for his own consumption, including feeding his livestock, and therefore it had no relation to interstate commerce and could not be regulated. The Court rejected the production/commerce dichotomy, stating that even though the production and consumption were totally local in character in this case, the fact that it might have a substantial economic effect on interstate commerce brought it under control of Congress under its commerce authority.

MR. JUSTICE JACKSON delivered the opinion of the Court.

The general scheme of the Agricultural Adjustment Act of 1938 as related to wheat is to control the volume moving in interstate and foreign commerce in order to avoid surpluses and shortages and the consequent abnormally low or high wheat prices and obstructions to commerce. . . . Within prescribed limits and by prescribed standards the Secretary of Agriculture is directed to ascertain and proclaim each year a national acreage allotment for the next crop of wheat, which is then apportioned to the states and their counties, and is eventually broken up into allotments for individual farms. . . .

It is urged that under the Commerce Clause of the Constitution, Article I, § 8, clause 3, Congress does not possess the power it has in this instance sought to exercise. The question would merit little consideration since our decision in *United States* v. *Darby*, 312 U.S. 100, . . . sustaining the federal power to regulate production of goods for commerce, except for the fact that this Act extends federal regulation to production not intended in any part for commerce but wholly for consumption on the farm. The Act includes a definition of "market" and its derivatives, so that as related to wheat, in addition to its conventional meaning, it also means to dispose of "by feeding (in any form) to poultry or livestock which, or the products of which, are sold, bartered, or exchanged, or to be so disposed of." Hence, marketing quotas not only embrace all that may be sold without penalty but also what may be consumed on the premises. Wheat produced on excess acreage is designated as "available for marketing" as so defined, and the penalty is imposed thereon. Penalties do not depend upon whether any part of the wheat, either within or without the quota, is sold or intended to be sold. The sum of this is that the Federal Government fixes a quota including all that the farmer may harvest for sale or for his own farm needs, and declares that wheat produced on excess acreage may neither be disposed of nor used except upon payment of the penalty, or except it is stored as required by the Act or delivered to the Secretary of Agriculture.

Appellee says that this is a regulation of production and consumption of wheat. Such activities are, he urges, beyond the reach of Congressional power under the Commerce Clause, since they are local in character, and their effects upon interstate commerce are at most "indirect." In answer the Government argues that the statute regulates neither production nor consumption, but only marketing; and, in the alternative, that if the Act does go beyond the regulation of marketing it is sustainable as a "necessary and proper" implementation of the power of Congress over interstate commerce.

The Government's concern lest the Act be held to be a regulation of production or consumption, rather than of marketing, is attributable to a few dicta and decisions of this Court which might be understood to lay it down that activities such as "production," "manufacturing," and "mining" are strictly "local" and, except in special circumstances which are not present here, cannot be regulated under the commerce power because their effects upon interstate commerce are, as matter of law, only "indirect." Even today, when this power has been held to have great latitude, there is no decision of this Court that such activities may be regulated where no part of the product is intended for interstate commerce or intermingled with the subjects thereof. We believe that a review of the course of decision under the Commerce Clause will make plain, however, that questions of the power of Congress are not to be decided by reference to any formula which would give controlling force to nomenclature such as "production" and "indirect" and foreclose consideration of the actual effects of the activity in question upon interstate commerce. . . .

The Court's recognition of the relevance of the economic effects in the application of the Commerce Clause . . . has made the mechanical application of legal formulas no longer feasible. Once an economic measure of the reach of the power granted to Congress in the Commerce Clause is accepted, questions of federal power cannot be decided simply by finding the activity in question to be "production," nor can consideration of its economic effects be foreclosed by calling them "indirect." The present Chief Justice has said in summary of the present state of the law: "The commerce power is not confined in its exercise to the regulation of commerce among the states. It extends to those activities intrastate which so affect interstate commerce, or the exertion of the power of Congress over it, as to make regulation of them appropriate means to the attainment of a legitimate end, the effective execution of the granted power to regulate interstate commerce. . . . The power of Congress over interstate commerce is plenary and complete in itself, may be exercised to its utmost extent, and acknowledges no limitations other than are prescribed in the Constitution. . . . It follows that no form of state activity can constitutionally thwart the regulatory power granted by the commerce clause to Congress. Hence the reach of that power extends to those intrastate activities which in a substantial way interfere with or obstruct the exercise of the granted power." *United States* v. *Wrightwood*. . . .

Whether the subject of the regulation in question was "production," "consumption," or "marketing" is, therefore, not material for purposes of deciding the question of federal power before us. That an activity is of local character may help in a doubtful case to determine whether Congress intended to reach it. The same consideration might help in determining whether in the absence of Congressional action it would be permissible for the state to exert its power on the subject matter, even though in so doing it to some degree affected interstate commerce. But even if appellee's activity be local and though it may not be regarded as commerce, it may still, whatever its nature, be reached by Congress if it exerts a substantial economic effect on interstate commerce, and this irrespective of whether such effect is what might at some earlier time have been defined as "direct" or "indirect." . . .

The wheat industry has been a problem industry for some years. Largely as a result of increased foreign production and import restrictions, annual exports of wheat and flour from the United States during the ten-year period ending in 1940 averaged less than 10 per cent of total production, while during the 1920's they averaged more than 25 per cent. The decline in the export trade has left a large surplus in production which, in connection with an abnormally large supply of wheat and other grains in recent years, caused congestion in a number of markets; tied up railroad cars; and caused elevators in some instances to turn away grains, and railroads to institute embargoes to prevent further congestion. . . .

In the absence of regulation, the price of wheat in the United States would be much affected by world conditions. During 1941, producers who cooperated with the Agricultural Adjustment program received an average price on the farm of about $1.16 a bushel, as compared with the world market price of 40 cents a bushel. . . .

The effect of consumption of home-grown wheat on interstate commerce is due to the fact that it constitutes the most variable factor in the disappearance of the wheat crop. Consumption on the farm where grown appears to vary in an amount greater than 20 per cent of average production. The total amount of wheat consumed as food varies but relatively little, and use as seed is relatively constant.

The maintenance by government regulation of a price for wheat undoubtedly can be accomplished as effectively by sustaining or increasing the demand as by limiting the supply. The effect of the statute before us is to restrict the amount which may be produced for market and the extent as well to which one may forestall resort to the market by producing to meet his own needs. That appellee's own contribution to the demand for wheat may be trivial by itself is not enough to remove him from the scope of federal regulation where, as here, his contribution, taken together with that of many others similarly situated, is far from trivial. . . .

It is well established by decisions of this Court that the power to regulate commerce includes the power to regulate the prices at which commodities in that commerce are dealt in and practices affecting such prices. One of the primary purposes of the Act in question was to increase the market price of wheat, and to that end to limit the volume thereof that could affect the market. It can hardly be denied that a factor of such volume and variability as home-consumed wheat would have a substantial influence on price and market conditions. This may arise because being in marketable condition such wheat overhangs the market and, if induced by rising prices, tends to flow into the market and check price increases. But if we assume that it is never marketed, it supplies a need of the man who grew it which would otherwise be reflected by purchases in the open market. Home-grown wheat in this sense competes with wheat in commerce. The stimulation of commerce is a use of the regulatory function quite as definitely as prohibitions or restrictions thereon. This record leaves us in no doubt that Congress may properly have considered that wheat consumed on the farm where grown, if wholly outside the scheme of regulation, would have a substantial effect in defeating and obstructing its purpose to stimulate trade therein at increased prices. . . .

III

The statute is also challenged as a deprivation of property without due process of law contrary to the Fifth Amendment, both because of its regulatory effect on the appellee and because of its alleged retroactive effect. . . .

We do not agree. In its effort to control total supply, the Government gave the farmer a choice which was, of course, designed to encourage cooperation and discourage non-cooperation. The farmer who planted within his allotment was in effect guaranteed a minimum return much above what his wheat would have brought if sold on a world market basis. Exemption from the applicability of quotas was made in favor of small producers. The farmer who produced in excess of his quota might escape penalty by delivering his wheat to the Secretary, or by storing it with the privilege of sale without penalty in a later year to fill out his quota, or irrespective of quotas if they are no longer in effect, and he could obtain a loan of 60 per cent of the rate for cooperators, or about 59 cents a bushel, on so much of his wheat as would be subject to penalty if marketed. Finally, he might make other disposition of his wheat, subject to the penalty. It is agreed that as the result of the wheat programs he is able to market his wheat at a price "far above any world price based on the natural reaction of supply and demand." We can hardly find a denial of due process in these circumstances, particularly since it is even doubtful that appellee's burdens under the program outweigh his benefits. It is hardly lack of due process for the Government to regulate that which it subsidizes. . . .

Source: Justia.com – US Supreme Court Center. http://supreme.justia.com/us/317/111/case.html

YOUNGSTOWN SHEET & TUBE CO. ET AL. V. SAWYER [STEEL SEIZURE CASE] (1952)

This case went to the heart of what a president can do regarding a power when Congress has implicitly said he cannot exercise that power. During the Korean War, President Truman, through an executive order, directed the seizing of the country's steel mills. Truman argued that doing this was important for the war effort because of an impending strike by the steelworkers. The immediate question was did the President have the constitutional authority to seize and operate the steel mills. The Court declared that, absent express congressional authorization, the president could not take such an action. The president's military power as commander in chief, under which Truman said he had the authority to seize the mills, did not extend to internal domes-

tic issues such as labor disputes. In particular, Justice Jackson's concurrence defined the powers of Congress and the president when it came to the implied and explicit delegation or denial of authority.

MR. JUSTICE BLACK delivered the opinion of the Court.

We are asked to decide whether the President was acting within his constitutional power when he issued an order directing the Secretary of Commerce to take possession of and operate most of the Nation's steel mills. The mill owners argue that the President's order amounts to lawmaking, a legislative function which the Constitution has expressly confided to the Congress and not to the President. The Government's position is that the order was made on findings of the President that his action was necessary to avert a national catastrophe which would inevitably result from a stoppage of steel production, and that in meeting this grave emergency the President was acting within the aggregate of his constitutional powers as the Nation's Chief Executive and the Commander in Chief of the Armed Forces of the United States. . . .

Two crucial issues have developed: *First.* Should final determination of the constitutional validity of the President's order be made in this case which has proceeded no further than the preliminary injunction stage? *Second.* If so, is the seizure order within the constitutional power of the President? . . .

The President's power, if any, to issue the order must stem either from an act of Congress or from the Constitution itself. There is no statute that expressly authorizes the President to take possession of property as he did here. Nor is there any act of Congress to which our attention has been directed from which such a power can fairly be implied. Indeed, we do not understand the Government to rely on statutory authorization for this seizure. There are two statutes which do authorize the President to take both personal and real property under certain conditions. . . . However, the Government admits that these conditions were not met and that the President's order was not rooted in either of the statutes. . . .

Moreover, the use of the seizure technique to solve labor disputes in order to prevent work stoppages was not only unauthorized by any congressional enactment; prior to this controversy, Congress had refused to adopt that method of settling labor disputes. When the Taft-Hartley Act was under consideration in 1947, Congress rejected an amendment which would have authorized such governmental seizures in cases of emergency. . . . Apparently it was thought that the technique of seizure, like that of compulsory arbitration, would interfere with the process of collective bargaining. Consequently, the plan Congress adopted in that Act did not provide for seizure under any circumstances. Instead, the plan sought to bring about settlements by use of the customary devices of mediation, conciliation, investigation by boards of inquiry, and public reports. In some instances temporary injunctions were authorized to provide cooling-off periods. All this failing, unions were left free to strike. . . .

It is clear that if the President had authority to issue the order he did, it must be found in some provision of the Constitution. And it is not claimed that express constitutional language grants this power to the President. The contention is that presidential power should be implied from the aggregate of his powers under the Constitution. Particular reliance is placed on provisions in Article II which say that "The executive Power shall be vested in a President. . . ."; that "he shall take Care that the Laws be faithfully executed"; and that he "shall be Commander in Chief of the Army and Navy of the United States."

The order cannot properly be sustained as an exercise of the President's military power as Commander in Chief of the Armed Forces. The Government attempts to do so by citing a number of cases upholding broad powers in military commanders engaged in day-to-day fighting in a theater of war. Such cases need not concern us here. Even though "theater of war" be an expanding concept, we cannot with faithfulness to our constitutional system hold that the Commander in Chief of the Armed Forces has the ultimate power as such to take possession of private property in order to keep labor disputes from stopping production. This is a job for the Nation's lawmakers, not for its military authorities.

Nor can the seizure order be sustained because of the several constitutional provisions that grant executive power to the President. In the framework of our Constitution, the President's power to see that the laws are faithfully executed refutes the idea that he is to be a lawmaker. The Constitution limits his functions in the lawmaking process to the recommending of laws he thinks wise and the vetoing of laws he thinks bad. And the Constitution is neither silent nor equivocal about who shall make laws which the President is to execute. The first section of the first article says that "All legislative Powers herein granted shall be vested in a Congress of the United States. . . ." After granting many powers to the Congress, Article I goes on to provide that Congress may "make all Laws which shall be necessary and proper for carrying into Execution the foregoing Powers, and all other Powers vested by this Constitution in the Government of the United States, or in any Department or Officer thereof."

The President's order does not direct that a congressional policy be executed in a manner prescribed by Congress—it directs that a presidential policy be executed in a manner prescribed by the President. The preamble of the order itself, like that of many statutes, sets out reasons why the President believes certain policies should be adopted, proclaims these policies as rules of conduct to be followed, and again, like a statute, authorizes a government official to promulgate additional rules and regulations consistent with the policy proclaimed and needed to carry that policy into execution. The power of Congress to adopt such public policies as those proclaimed by the order is beyond question. It can authorize the taking of private property for public use. It can make laws regulating the relationships between employers and employees, prescribing rules designed to settle labor disputes, and fixing wages and working conditions in certain fields of our economy. The Constitution does not subject this lawmaking power of Congress to presidential or military supervision or control.

It is said that other Presidents without congressional authority have taken possession of private business enterprises in order to settle labor disputes. But even if this be true, Congress has not thereby lost its exclusive constitutional authority to make laws necessary and proper to carry out the powers vested by the Constitution "in the Government of the United States, or any Department or Officer thereof."

The Founders of this Nation entrusted the lawmaking power to the Congress alone in both good and bad times. It would do no good to recall the historical events, the fears of power and the hopes for freedom that lay behind their choice. Such a review would but confirm our holding that this seizure order cannot stand.

The judgment of the District Court is

Affirmed.

MR. JUSTICE FRANKFURTER, concurring.

Before the cares of the White House were his own, President Harding is reported to have said that government after all is a very simple thing. He must have said that, if he said it, as a fleeting inhabitant of fairyland. The opposite is the truth. A constitutional democracy like ours is perhaps the most difficult of man's social arrangements to manage successfully. Our scheme of society is more dependent than any other form of government on knowledge and wisdom and self-discipline for the achievement of its aims. For our democracy implies the reign of reason on the most extensive scale. The Founders of this Nation were not imbued with the modern cynicism that the only thing that history teaches is that it teaches nothing. They acted on the conviction that the experience of man sheds a good deal of light on his nature. It sheds a good deal of light not merely on the need for effective power, if a society is to be at once cohesive and civilized, but also on the need for limitations on the power of governors over the governed.

To that end they rested the structure of our central government on the system of checks and balances. For them the doctrine of separation of powers was not mere theory; it was a felt necessity. Not so long ago it was fashionable to find our system of checks and balances obstructive to effective government. It was easy to ridicule that system as outmoded—too easy. The experience through which the world has passed in our own day has made vivid the realization that the Framers of our Constitution were not inexperienced doctrinaires. . . .

The issue before us can be met, and therefore should be, without attempting to define the President's powers comprehensively. I shall not attempt to delineate what belongs to him by virtue of his office beyond the power even of Congress to contract; what authority belongs to him until Congress acts; what kind of problems may be dealt with either by the Congress or by the President or by both, what power must be exercised by the Congress and cannot be delegated to the President. . . .

It cannot be contended that the President would have had power to issue this order had Congress explicitly negated such authority in formal legislation. Congress has expressed its will to withhold this power from the President as though it had said so in so many words. . . .

The authoritatively expressed purpose of Congress to disallow such power to the President and to require him, when in his mind the occasion arose for such a seizure, to put the matter to Congress and ask for specific authority from it, could not be more decisive if it had been written into §§ 206–210 of the Labor Management Relations Act of 1947. . . .

To be sure, the content of the three authorities of government is not to be derived from an abstract analysis. The areas are partly interacting, not wholly disjointed. The Constitution is a framework for government. Therefore the way the framework has consistently operated fairly establishes that it has operated according to its true nature. Deeply embedded traditional ways of conducting government cannot supplant the Constitution or legislation, but they give meaning to the words of a text or supply them. It is an inadmissibly narrow conception of American constitutional law to confine it to the words of the Constitution and to disregard the gloss which life has written upon them. In short, a systematic, unbroken, executive practice, long pursued to the knowledge of the Congress and never before questioned, engaged in by Presidents who have also sworn to uphold the Constitution, making as it were such exercise of power part of the structure of our government, may be treated as a gloss on "executive Power" vested in the President by § 1 of Art. II.

The list of executive assertions of the power of seizure in circumstances comparable to the present reduces to three in the six-month period from June to December of 1941. We need not split hairs in comparing those actions to the one before us, though much might be said by way of differentiation. Without passing on their validity, as we are not called upon to do, it suffices to say that these three isolated instances do not add up, either in number, scope, duration or contemporaneous legal justification. . . . Nor do they come to us sanctioned by long-continued acquiescence of Congress giving decisive weight to a construction by the Executive of its powers.

MR. JUSTICE DOUGLAS, concurring.

There can be no doubt that the emergency which caused the President to seize these steel plants was one that bore heavily on the country. But the emergency did not create power; it merely marked an occasion when power should be exercised. And the fact that it was necessary that measures be taken to keep steel in production does not mean that the President, rather than the Congress, had the constitutional authority to act. The Congress, as well as the President, is trustee of the national welfare. The President can act more quickly than the Congress. The President with the armed services at his disposal can move with force as well as with speed. All executive power—from the reign of ancient kings to the rule of modern dictators—has the outward appearance of efficiency.

Legislative power, by contrast, is slower to exercise. There must be delay while the ponderous machinery of committees, hearings, and debates is put into motion. That takes time; and while the Congress slowly moves into action, the emergency may take its toll in wages, consumer goods, war production, the standard of living of the people, and perhaps even lives. Legislative action may indeed often be cumbersome, time-consuming, and apparently inefficient. But as Mr. Justice Brandeis stated in his dissent in *Myers* v. *United States*, 272 U.S. 52, 293:

"The doctrine of the separation of powers was adopted by the Convention of 1787, not to promote efficiency but to preclude the exercise of arbitrary power. The purpose was, not to avoid friction, but, by means of the inevitable friction incident to the distribution of the governmental powers among three departments, to save the people from autocracy."

We therefore cannot decide this case by determining which branch of government can deal most expeditiously with the present crisis. The answer must depend on the allocation of powers under the Constitution. That in turn requires an analysis of the conditions giving rise to the seizure and of the seizure itself. . . .

MR. JUSTICE JACKSON, *concurring in the judgment and opinion of the Court.*

A judge, like an executive adviser, may be surprised at the poverty of really useful and unambiguous authority applicable to concrete problems of executive power as they actually present themselves. Just what our forefathers did envision, or would have envisioned had they foreseen modern conditions, must be divined from materials almost as enigmatic as the dreams Joseph was called upon to interpret for Pharaoh. A century and a half of partisan debate and scholarly speculation yields no net result but only supplies more or less apt quotations from respected sources on each side of any question. They largely cancel each other. . . . And court decisions are indecisive because of the judicial practice of dealing with the largest questions in the most narrow way.

The actual art of governing under our Constitution does not and cannot conform to judicial definitions of the power of any of its branches based on isolated clauses or even single Articles torn from context. While the Constitution diffuses power the better to secure liberty, it also contemplates that practice will integrate the dispersed powers into a workable government. It enjoins upon its branches separateness but interdependence, autonomy but reciprocity. Presidential powers are not fixed but fluctuate, depending upon their disjunction or conjunction with those of Congress. We may well begin by a somewhat over-simplified grouping of practical situations in which a President may doubt, or others may challenge, his powers, and by distinguishing roughly the legal consequences of this factor of relativity.

1. When the President acts pursuant to an express or implied authorization of Congress, his authority is at its maximum, for it includes all that he possesses in his own right plus all that Congress can delegate. In these circumstances, and in these only, may he be said (for what it may be worth) to personify the federal sovereignty. If his act is held unconstitutional under these circumstances, it usually means that the Federal Government as an un-

divided whole lacks power. A seizure executed by the President pursuant to an Act of Congress would be supported by the strongest of presumptions and the widest latitude of judicial interpretation, and the burden of persuasion would rest heavily upon any who might attack it.

2. When the President acts in absence of either a congressional grant or denial of authority, he can only rely upon his own independent powers, but there is a zone of twilight in which he and Congress may have concurrent authority, or in which its distribution is uncertain. Therefore, congressional inertia, indifference or quiescence may sometimes, at least as a practical matter, enable, if not invite, measures on independent presidential responsibility. In this area, any actual test of power is likely to depend on the imperatives of events and contemporary imponderables rather than on abstract theories of law.

3. When the President takes measures incompatible with the expressed or implied will of Congress, his power is at its lowest ebb, for then he can rely only upon his own constitutional powers minus any constitutional powers of Congress over the matter. Courts can sustain exclusive presidential control in such a case only by disabling the Congress from acting upon the subject. Presidential claim to a power at once so conclusive and preclusive must be scrutinized with caution, for what is at stake is the equilibrium established by our constitutional system.

Into which of these classifications does this executive seizure of the steel industry fit? It is eliminated from the first by admission, for it is conceded that no congressional authorization exists for this seizure. That takes away also the support of the many precedents and declarations which were made in relation, and must be confined, to this category. . . .

This leaves the current seizure to be justified only by the severe tests under the third grouping, where it can be supported only by any remainder of executive power after subtraction of such powers as Congress may have over the subject. In short, we can sustain the President only by holding that seizure of such strike-bound industries is within his domain and beyond control by Congress. Thus, this Court's first review of such seizures occurs under circumstances which leave presidential power most vulnerable to attack and in the least favorable of possible constitutional postures. . . .

That seems to be the logic of an argument tendered at our bar—that the President having, on his own responsibility, sent American troops abroad derives from that act "affirmative power" to seize the means of producing a supply of steel for them. To quote, "Perhaps the most forceful illustration of the scope of Presidential power in this connection is the fact that American troops in Korea, whose safety and effectiveness are so directly involved here, were sent to the field by an exercise of the President's constitutional powers." Thus, it is said, he has invested himself with "war powers."

I cannot foresee all that it might entail if the Court should indorse this argument. Nothing in our Constitution is plainer than that declaration of a war is entrusted only to Congress. Of course, a state of war may in fact exist without a formal declaration. But no doctrine that the Court could promulgate would seem to me more sinister and alarming than that a President whose conduct of foreign affairs is so largely uncontrolled, and often even is unknown, can vastly enlarge his mastery over the internal affairs of the country by his own commitment of the Nation's armed forces to some foreign venture. . . .

Assuming that we are in a war *de facto*, whether it is or is not a war *de jure*, does that empower the Commander in Chief to seize industries he thinks necessary to supply our army? The Constitution expressly places in Congress power "to raise and *support* Armies" and "to *provide* and *maintain* a Navy." (Emphasis supplied.) This certainly lays upon Congress primary responsibility for supplying the armed forces. Congress alone controls the raising of revenues and their appropriation and may determine in what manner and by what means they shall be spent for military and naval procurement. I suppose no one would doubt that Congress can take over war supply as a Government enterprise. On the other hand, if Congress sees fit to rely on free private enterprise collectively bargaining with free labor for support and maintenance of our armed forces, can the Executive, because of lawful disagreements incidental to that process, seize the facility for operation upon Government-imposed terms?

There are indications that the Constitution did not contemplate that the title Commander in Chief *of the Army and Navy* will constitute him also Commander in Chief of the country, its industries and its inhabitants. He has no monopoly of "war powers," whatever they are. While Congress cannot deprive the President of the command of the army and navy, only Congress can provide him an army or navy to command. It is also empowered to make rules for the "Government and Regulation of land and naval Forces," by which it may to some unknown extent impinge upon even command functions.

That military powers of the Commander in Chief were not to supersede representative government of internal affairs seems obvious from the Constitution and from elementary American history. . . .

In the practical working of our Government we already have evolved a technique within the framework of the Constitution by which normal executive powers may be considerably expanded to meet an emergency. Congress may and has granted extraordinary authorities which lie dormant in normal times but may be called into play by the Executive in war or upon proclamation of a national emergency. . . .

In view of the ease, expedition and safety with which Congress can grant and has granted large emergency powers, certainly ample to embrace this crisis, I am quite unimpressed with the argument that we should affirm possession of them without statute. Such power either has no beginning or it has no end. If it exists, it need submit to no legal restraint. I am not alarmed that it would plunge us straightway into dictatorship, but it is at least a step in that wrong direction.

As to whether there is imperative necessity for such powers, it is relevant to note the gap that exists between the President's paper powers and his real powers. The Constitution does not disclose the measure of the actual controls wielded by the modern presidential office. That instrument must be understood as an Eighteenth-Century sketch of a government hoped for, not as a blueprint of the Government that is. Vast accretions of federal power, eroded from that reserved by the States, have magnified the scope of presidential activity. Subtle shifts take place in the centers of real power that do not show on the face of the Constitution.

Executive power has the advantage of concentration in a single head in whose choice the whole Nation has a part, making him the focus of public hopes and expectations. In drama, magnitude and finality his decisions so far overshadow any others that almost alone he fills the public eye and ear. No other personality in public life can begin to compete with him in access to the public mind through modern methods of communications. By his prestige as head of state and his influence upon public opinion he exerts a leverage upon those who are supposed to check and balance his power which often cancels their effectiveness. . . .

But I have no illusion that any decision by this Court can keep power in the hands of Congress if it is not wise and timely in meeting its problems. A crisis that challenges the President equally, or perhaps primarily, challenges Congress. If not good law, there was worldly wisdom in the maxim attributed to Napoleon that "The tools belong to the man who can use them." We may say that power to legislate for emergencies belongs in the hands of Congress, but only Congress itself can prevent power from slipping through its fingers. . . .

MR. CHIEF JUSTICE VINSON, with whom MR. JUSTICE REED and MR. JUSTICE MINTON join, dissenting.

The President of the United States directed the Secretary of Commerce to take temporary possession of the Nation's steel mills during the existing emergency because "a work stoppage would immediately jeopardize and imperil our national defense and the defense of those joined with us in resisting aggression, and would add to the continuing danger of our soldiers, sailors, and airmen engaged in combat in the field." The District Court ordered the mills returned to their private owners on the ground that the President's action was beyond his powers under the Constitution.

This Court affirms. Some members of the Court are of the view that the President is without power to act in time of crisis in the absence of express statutory authorization. Other members of the Court affirm on the basis of their reading of certain statutes. Because we cannot agree that affirmance is proper on any ground, and because of the transcending importance of the questions presented not only in this critical litigation but also to the powers of the President and of future Presidents to act in time of crisis, we are compelled to register this dissent. . . .

Those who suggest that this is a case involving extraordinary powers should be mindful that these are extraordinary times. A world not yet recovered from the devastation of World War II has been forced to face the threat of another and more terrifying global conflict. . . .

Presidents have taken prompt action to enforce the laws and protect the country whether or not Congress happened to provide in advance for the particular method of execution. At the minimum, the executive actions reviewed herein sustain the action of the President in this case. And many of the cited examples of Presidential practice go far beyond the extent of power necessary to sustain the President's order to seize the steel mills. The fact that temporary executive seizures of industrial . . . plants to meet an emergency have not been directly tested in this Court furnishes not the slightest suggestion that such actions have been illegal. Rather, the fact that Congress and the courts have consistently recognized and given their support to such executive action indicates that such a power of seizure has been accepted throughout our history.

History bears out the genius of the Founding Fathers, who created a Government subject to law but not left subject to inertia when vigor and initiative are required.

Focusing now on the situation confronting the President on the night of April 8, 1952, we cannot but conclude that the President was performing his duty under the Constitution to "take Care that the Laws be faithfully executed"—a duty described by President Benjamin Harrison as "the central idea of the office."

Much of the argument in this case has been directed at straw men. We do not now have before us the case of a President acting solely on the basis of his own notions of the public welfare. Nor is there any question of unlimited executive power in this case. The President himself closed the door to any such claim when he sent his Message to Congress stating his purpose to abide by any action of Congress, whether approving or disapproving his seizure action. Here, the President immediately made sure that Congress was fully informed of the temporary action he had taken only to preserve the legislative programs from destruction until Congress could act.

The absence of a specific statute authorizing seizure of the steel mills as a mode of executing the laws—both the military procurement program and the anti-inflation program—has not until today been thought to prevent the President from executing the laws. . . .

Whatever the extent of Presidential power on more tranquil occasions, and whatever the right of the President to execute legislative programs as he sees fit without reporting the mode of execution to Congress, the single Presidential purpose disclosed on this record is to faithfully execute the laws by acting in an emergency to maintain the status quo, thereby preventing collapse of the legislative programs until Congress could act. The President's action served the same purposes as a judicial stay entered to maintain the status quo in order to preserve the jurisdiction of a court. In his Message to Congress immediately following the seizure, the President explained the necessity of his action in executing the military procurement and anti-inflation legislative programs and expressed his desire to cooperate with any legislative proposals approving, regulating or rejecting the seizure of the steel mills. Consequently, there is no evidence whatever of any Presidential purpose to defy Congress or act in any way inconsistent with the legislative will. . . .

Seizure of plaintiffs' property is not a pleasant undertaking. Similarly unpleasant to a free country are the draft which disrupts the home and military procurement which causes economic dislocation and compels adoption of price controls, wage stabilization and allocation of materials. The President informed Congress that even a temporary Government operation of plaintiffs' properties was "thoroughly distasteful" to him, but was necessary to prevent immediate paralysis of the mobilization program. Presidents have been in the past, and any man worthy of the Office should be in the future, free to take at least interim action necessary to execute legislative programs essential to survival of the Nation. A sturdy judiciary should not be swayed by the unpleasantness or unpopularity of necessary executive action, but must independently determine for itself whether the President was acting, as required by the Constitution, to "take Care that the Laws be faithfully executed."

As the District Judge stated, this is no time for "timorous" judicial action. But neither is this a time for timorous executive action. Faced with the duty of executing the defense programs which Congress had enacted and the disastrous effects that any stoppage in steel production would have on those programs, the President acted to preserve those programs by seizing the steel mills. There is no question that the possession was other than temporary in character and subject to congressional direction—either approving, disapproving or regulating the manner in which the mills were to be administered and returned to the owners. The President immediately informed Congress of his action and clearly stated his intention to abide by the legislative will. No basis for claims of arbitrary action, unlimited powers or dictatorial usurpation of congressional power appears from the facts of this case. On the contrary, judicial, legislative and executive precedents throughout our history demonstrate that in this case the President acted in full conformity with his duties under the Constitution. Accordingly, we would reverse the order of the District Court.

Source: Justia.com – US Supreme Court Center. http://supreme.justia.com/us/343/579/case.html

SOUTHERN DECLARATION ON INTEGRATION (1956)

Signed by 101 members of Congress from the former Confederate states—all members from those states except three senators. It laid out their major objections to Brown v. Board of Education *(1954) and the seeming attempt by the federal government to impose civil rights legislation on local authority. It emphasized states' rights and the limited scope of federal power.*

The unwarranted decision of the Supreme Court in the public school cases is now bearing the fruit always produced when men substitute naked power for established law.

The Founding Fathers gave us a Constitution of checks and balances because they realized the inescapable lesson of history that no man or group of men can be safely entrusted with unlimited power. They framed this Constitution with its provisions for change by amendment in order to secure the fundamentals of government against the dangers of temporary popular passion or the personal predilections of public officeholders.

We regard the decision of the Supreme Court in the school cases as a clear abuse of judicial power. It climaxes a trend in the Federal Judiciary undertaking to legislate, in derogation of the authority of Congress, and to encroach upon the reserved rights of the States and the people.

The original Constitution does not mention education. Neither does the 14th amendment nor any other amendment. The debates preceding the submission of the 14th amendment clearly show that there was no intent that it should affect the system of education maintained by the States. . . .

In the case of *Plessy v. Ferguson* in 1896 the Supreme Court expressly declared that under the 14th amendment no person was denied any of his rights if the States provided separate but equal public facilities. This decision has been followed in many other cases. It is notable that the Supreme Court, speaking through Chief Justice Taft, a former President of the United States, unanimously declared in 1927 in *Lum v. Rice* that the "separate but equal" principle is "within the discretion of the State in regulating its public schools and does not conflict with the 14th amendment."

This interpretation, restated time and again, became a part of the life of the people of many of the States and confirmed their habits, customs, traditions, and way of life. It is founded on elemental humanity and commonsense, for parents should not be deprived by Government of the right to direct the lives and education of their own children.

Though there has been no constitutional amendment or act of Congress changing this established legal principle almost a century old, the Supreme Court of the United States, with no legal basis for such action, undertook to exercise their naked judicial power and substituted their personal political and social ideas for the established law of the land.

This unwarranted exercise of power by the Court, contrary to the Constitution, is creating chaos and confusion in the States principally affected. It is destroying the amicable relations between the white and Negro races that have been created through 90 years of patient effort by the good people of both races. It has planted hatred and suspicion where there has been heretofore friendship and understanding.

Without regard to the consent of the governed, outside agitators are threatening immediate and revolutionary changes in our public-school systems. If done, this is certain to destroy the system of public education in some of the States.

With the gravest concern for the explosive and dangerous condition created by this decision and inflamed by outside meddlers:

We reaffirm our reliance on the Constitution as the fundamental law of the land.

We decry the Supreme Court's encroachments on rights reserved to the States and to the people, contrary to established law, and to the Constitution.

We commend the motives of those States which have declared the intention to resist forced integration by any lawful means.

We appeal to the States and people who are not directly affected by these decisions to consider the constitutional principles involved against the time when they too, on issues vital to them, may be the victims of judicial encroachment.

Even though we constitute a minority in the present Congress, we have full faith that a majority of the American people believe in the dual system of government which has enabled us to achieve our greatness and will in time demand that the reserved rights of the States and of the people be made secure against judicial usurpation.

We pledge ourselves to use all lawful means to bring about a reversal of this decision which is contrary to the Constitution and to prevent the use of force in its implementation.

In this trying period, as we all seek to right this wrong, we appeal to our people not to be provoked by the agitators and troublemakers invading our States and to scrupulously refrain from disorder and lawless acts.

Source: Southern Declaration on Integration (1956). http://www.wwnorton.com/college/history/archive/resources/documents/ch33_03.htm

CIVIL RIGHTS ACT (1964)

The Act outlawed discrimination on the basis of race, color, religion, national origin and sex. Because of questions about the authority to pass such legislation under the Fourteenth Amendment in the Civil Rights Cases *in 1883 the Supreme Court had struck down civil rights legislation. In 1964, the Congress tried again, this time passing laws under its commerce authority. Originally submitted by President Kennedy, it stalled in Congress until his assassination, whereupon President Lyndon Johnson pushed the legislation through despite tremendous opposition from southern representatives, especially in the Senate.*

An Act

To enforce the constitutional right to vote, to confer jurisdiction upon the district courts of the United States to provide injunctive relief against discrimination in public accommodations, to authorize the Attorney General to institute suits to protect constitutional rights in public facilities and public education, to extend the Commission on Civil Rights, to prevent discrimination in federally assisted programs, to establish a Commission on Equal Employment Opportunity, and for other purposes.

Be it enacted by the Senate and House of Representatives of the United States of America in Congress assembled, That this Act may be cited as the "Civil Rights Act of 1964".

TITLE II—INJUNCTIVE RELIEF AGAINST DISCRIMINATION IN PLACES OF PUBLIC ACCOMMODATION

SEC. 201. (a) All persons shall be entitled to the full and equal enjoyment of the goods, services, facilities, and privileges, advantages, and accommodations of any place of public accommodation, as defined in this section, without discrimination or segregation on the ground of race, color, religion, or national origin.

(b) Each of the following establishments which serves the public is a place of public accommodation within the meaning of this title if its operations affect commerce, or if discrimination or segregation by it is supported by State action:

(1) any inn, hotel, motel, or other establishment which provides lodging to transient guests, other than an establishment located within a building which contains not more than five rooms for rent or hire and which is actually occupied by the proprietor of such establishment as his residence;

(2) any restaurant, cafeteria, lunchroom, lunch counter, soda fountain, or other facility principally engaged in selling food for consumption on the premises, including, but not limited to, any such facility located on the premises of any retail establishment; or any gasoline station;

(3) any motion picture house, theater, concert hall, sports arena, stadium or other place of exhibition or entertainment; and

(4) any establishment (A)(i) which is physically located within the premises of any establishment otherwise covered by this subsection, or (ii) within the premises of which is physically located any such covered establishment, and (B) which holds itself out as serving patrons of such covered establishment.

(c) The operations of an establishment affect commerce within the meaning of this title if (1) it is one of the establishments described in paragraph (1) of subsection (b); (2) in the case of an establishment described in paragraph (2) of subsection (b), it serves or offers to serve interstate travelers or a substantial portion of the food which it serves, or gasoline or other products which it sells, has moved in commerce; (3) in the case of an establishment described in paragraph (3) of subsection (b), it customarily presents films, performances, athletic teams, exhibitions, or other sources of entertainment which move in commerce; and (4) in the case of an establishment described in paragraph (4) of subsection (b), it is physically located within the premises of, or there is physically located within its premises, an establishment the operations of which affect commerce within the meaning of this subsection. For purposes of this section, "commerce" means travel, trade, traffic, commerce, transportation, or communication among the several States, or between the District of Columbia and any State, or between any foreign country or any territory or possession and any State or the District of Columbia, or between points in the same State but through any other State or the District of Columbia or a foreign country.

(d) Discrimination or segregation by an establishment is supported by State action within the meaning of this title if such discrimination or segregation (1) is carried on under color of any law, statute, ordinance, or regulation; or (2) is carried on under color of any custom or usage required or enforced by officials of the State or political subdivision thereof; or (3) is required by action of the State or political subdivision thereof.

(e) The provisions of this title shall not apply to a private club or other establishment not in fact open to the public, except to the extent that the facilities of such establishment are made available to the customers or patrons of an establishment within the scope of subsection (b).

SEC. 202. All persons shall be entitled to be free, at any establishment or place, from discrimination or segregation of any kind on the ground of race, color, religion, or national origin, if such discrimination or segregation is or purports to be required by any law, statute, ordinance, regulation, rule, or order of a State or any agency or political subdivision thereof . . .

TITLE III—DESEGREGATION OF PUBLIC FACILITIES

SEC. 301. (a) Whenever the Attorney General receives a complaint in writing signed by an individual to the effect that he is being deprived of or threatened with the loss of his right to the equal protection of the laws, on account of his race, color, religion, or national origin, by being denied equal utilization of any public facility which is owned, operated, or managed by or on behalf of any State or subdivision thereof, other than a public school or public college as defined in section 401 of title IV hereof, and the Attorney General believes the complaint is meritorious and certifies that the signer or signers of such complaint are unable, in his judgment, to initiate and maintain appropriate legal proceedings for relief and that the institution of an action will materially further the orderly progress of desegregation in public facilities, the Attorney General is authorized to institute for or in the name of the United States a civil action in any appropriate district court of the United States against such parties and for such relief as may be appropriate, and such court shall have and shall exercise jurisdiction of proceedings instituted pursuant to this section. The Attorney General may implead as defendants such additional parties as are or become necessary to the grant of effective relief hereunder.

(b) The Attorney General may deem a person or persons unable to initiate and maintain appropriate legal proceedings within the meaning of subsection (a) of this section when such person or persons are unable, either directly or through other interested persons or organizations, to bear the expense of the litigation or to obtain effective legal representation; or whenever he is satisfied that the institution of such litigation would jeopardize the personal safety, employment, or economic standing of such person or persons, their families, or their property.

SEC. 302. In any action or proceeding under this title the United States shall be liable for costs, including a reasonable attorney's fee, the same as a private person.

SEC. 303. Nothing in this title shall affect adversely the right of any person to sue for or obtain relief in any court against discrimination in any facility covered by this title.

SEC. 304. A complaint as used in this title is a writing or document within the meaning of section 1001, title 18, United States Code.

TITLE VI—NONDISCRIMINATION IN FEDERALLY ASSISTED PROGRAMS

SEC. 601. No person in the United States shall, on the ground of race, color, or national origin, be excluded from participation in, be denied the benefits of, or be subjected to discrimination under any program or activity receiving Federal financial assistance . . .

TITLE VII—EQUAL EMPLOYMENT OPPORTUNITY

SEC. 703. (a) It shall be an unlawful employment practice for an employer—
   (1) to fail or refuse to hire or to discharge any individual, or otherwise to discriminate against any individual with respect to his compensation, terms, conditions, or privileges of employment, because of such individual's race, color, religion, sex, or national origin; or
   (2) to limit, segregate, or classify his employees in any way which would deprive or tend to deprive any individual of employment opportunities or otherwise adversely affect his status as an employee, because of such individual's race, color, religion, sex, or national origin.
(b) It shall be an unlawful employment practice for an employment agency to fail or refuse to refer for employment, or otherwise to discriminate against, any individual because of his race, color, religion, sex, or national origin, or to classify or refer for employment any individual on the basis of his race, color, religion, sex, or national origin . . .

EQUAL EMPLOYMENT OPPORTUNITY COMMISSION

SEC. 705. (a) There is hereby created a Commission to be known as the Equal Employment Opportunity Commission, which shall be composed of five members, not more than three of whom shall be members of the same political party, who shall be appointed by the President by and with the advice and consent of the Senate . . .

Source: The Avalon Project at Yale Law School. http://www.yale.edu/lawweb/avalon/statutes/civil_rights_1964.htm

GULF OF TONKIN RESOLUTION (1964)

Upon President Lyndon Johnson's request, Congress authorized the president to use military force in Vietnam. Under the claimed authority of the joint resolution, Presidents Johnson and Richard Nixon justified military escalation and involvement in southeast Asia. The lack of a declaration of war did not inhibit prosecution of the war, and ironically it became the longest military conflict in American history. The failure of Congress to formally declare war raised a host of constitutional problems, including the authority of the president to escalate the war, the right of Congress to call for a draft, the power of Congress to limit the military authority of the president, etc. The Resolution was eventually appealed in 1970.

Public Law 88-408; 78 Stat. 384

JOINT RESOLUTION

To promote the maintenance of international peace and security in southeast Asia.

Whereas naval units of the Communist regime in Vietnam, in violation of the principles of the Charter of the United Nations and of international law, have deliberately and repeatedly attacked United States naval vessels lawfully present in international waters; and have thereby created a serious threat to international peace; and

Whereas these attacks are part of a deliberate and systematic campaign of aggression that the Communist regime in North Vietnam has been waging against its neighbors and the nations joined with them in the collective defense of their freedom; and

Whereas the United States is assisting the peoples of southeast Asia to protect their freedom and has no territorial, military or political ambitions in that area, but desires only that these peoples should be left in peace to work out their own destinies in their own way: Now, therefore, be it

Resolved by the Senate and House of Representatives of the United States of America in Congress assembled, That the Congress approves and supports the determination of the President, as Commander in Chief, to take all necessary measures to repel any armed attack against the forces of the United States and to prevent further aggression.

Sec. 2. The United States regards as vital to its national interest and to world peace the maintenance of international peace and security in southeast Asia. Consonant with the Constitution of the United States and the Charter of the United Nations and in accordance with its obligations under the Southeast Asia Collective Defense Treaty, the United States is, therefore, prepared, as the President determines, to take all necessary steps, including the use of armed force, to assist any member or protocol state of the Southeast Asia Collective Treaty requesting assistance in defense of its freedom.

Sec. 3. This resolution shall expire when the President shall determine that the peace and security of the area is reasonably assured by international conditions created by action of the United Nations or otherwise, except that it may be terminated earlier by concurrent resolution of the Congress.

Approved August 10, 1964.

Source: The Avalon Project at Yale Law School. http://www.yale.edu/lawweb/avalon/tonkin-g.htm

KATZENBACH V. MCCLUNG (1964)

Court case that validated the Civil Rights Act of 1964 and Congress's ability under the Commerce Clause of the Constitution to prevent restaurants from discriminating on the basis of race. The Court ruled that an institution's refusal to serve blacks placed a burden on interstate commerce, thus allowing Congress to impose restrictions. Discrimination was seen as imposing a significant burden on the flow of interstate commerce.

MR. JUSTICE CLARK delivered the opinion of the Court.

This case was argued with *Heart of Atlanta Motel v. United States* . . . in which we upheld the constitutional validity of Title II of the Civil Rights Act of 1964 against an attack by hotels, motels, and like establishments.

2. The Facts.

Ollie's Barbecue is a family-owned restaurant in Birmingham, Alabama, specializing in barbecued meats and homemade pies, with a seating capacity of 220 customers. It is located on a state highway 11 blocks from an interstate one and a somewhat greater distance from railroad and bus stations. The restaurant caters to a family and white-collar trade with a take-out service for Negroes. It employs 36 persons, two-thirds of whom are Negroes.

In the 12 months preceding the passage of the Act, the restaurant purchased locally approximately $150,000 worth of food, $69,683 or 46% of which was meat that it bought from a local supplier who had procured it from outside the State. The District Court expressly found that a substantial portion of the food served in the restaurant had moved in interstate commerce. The restaurant has refused to serve Negroes in its dining accommodations since its original opening in 1927, and since July 2, 1964, it has been operating in violation of the Act. The court below concluded that if it were required to serve Negroes it would lose a substantial amount of business.

On the merits, the District Court held that the Act could not be applied under the Fourteenth Amendment because it was conceded that the State of Alabama was not involved in the refusal of the restaurant to serve Negroes. It was also admitted that the Thirteenth Amendment was authority neither for validating nor for invalidating the Act. As to the Commerce Clause, the court found that it was "an express grant of power to Congress to regulate interstate commerce, which consists of the movement of persons, goods or information from one state to another"; and it found that the clause was also a grant of power "to regulate intrastate activities, but only to the extent that action on its part is necessary or appropriate to the effective execution of its expressly granted power to regulate interstate commerce." There must be, it said, a close and substantial relation between local activities and interstate commerce which requires control of the former in the protection of the latter. The court concluded, however, that the Congress, rather than finding facts sufficient to meet this rule, had legislated a conclusive presumption that a restaurant affects interstate commerce if it serves or offers to serve interstate travelers or if a substantial portion of the food which it serves has moved in commerce. This, the court held, it could not do because there was no demonstrable connection between food purchased in interstate commerce and sold in a restaurant and the conclusion of Congress that discrimination in the restaurant would affect that commerce.

The basic holding in *Heart of Atlanta Motel,* answers many of the contentions made by the appellees. There we outlined the overall purpose and operational plan of Title II and found it a valid exercise of the power to regulate interstate commerce insofar as it requires hotels and motels to serve transients without regard to their race or color. In this case we consider its application to restaurants which serve food a substantial portion of which has moved in commerce.

3. The Act As Applied.
Section 201 (a) of Title II commands that all persons shall be entitled to the full and equal enjoyment of the goods and services of any place of public accommodation without discrimination or segregation on the ground of race, color, religion, or national origin; and 201 (b) defines establishments as places of public accommodation if their operations affect commerce or segregation by them is supported by state action. Sections 201 (b) (2) and (c) place any "restaurant . . . principally engaged in selling food for consumption on the premises" under the Act "if . . . it serves or offers to serve interstate travelers or a substantial portion of the food which it serves . . . has moved in commerce."

Ollie's Barbecue admits that it is covered by these provisions of the Act. The Government makes no contention that the discrimination at the restaurant was supported by the State of Alabama. There is no claim that interstate travelers frequented the restaurant. The sole question, therefore, narrows down to whether Title II, as applied to a restaurant annually receiving about $70,000 worth of food which has moved in commerce, is a valid exercise of the power of Congress. The Government has contended that Congress had ample basis upon which to find that racial discrimination at restaurants which receive from out of state a substantial portion of the food served does, in fact, impose commercial burdens of national magnitude upon interstate commerce. The appellees' major argument is directed to this premise. They urge that no such basis existed. It is to that question that we now turn.

4. The Congressional Hearings.

As we noted in *Heart of Atlanta Motel* both Houses of Congress conducted prolonged hearings on the Act. And, as we said there, while no formal findings were made, which of course are not necessary, it is well that we make mention of the testimony at these hearings the better to understand the problem before Congress and determine whether the Act is a reasonable and appropriate means toward its solution. The record is replete with testimony of the burdens placed on interstate commerce by racial discrimination in restaurants. A comparison of per capita spending by Negroes in restaurants, theaters, and like establishments indicated less spending, after discounting income differences, in areas where discrimination is widely practiced. This condition, which was especially aggravated in the South, was attributed in the testimony of the Under Secretary of Commerce to racial segregation. See Hearings before the Senate Committee on Commerce on S. 1732, 88th Cong., 1st Sess., 695. This diminutive spending springing from a refusal to serve Negroes and their total loss as customers has, regardless of the absence of direct evidence, a close connection to interstate commerce. The fewer customers a restaurant enjoys the less food it sells and consequently the less it buys. S. Rep. No. 872, 88th Cong., 2d Sess., at 19; Senate Commerce Committee Hearings, at 207. In addition, the Attorney General testified that this type of discrimination imposed "an artificial restriction on the market" and interfered [379 U.S. 294, 300] with the flow of merchandise. Id., at 18-19; also, on this point, see testimony of Senator Magnuson, 110 Cong. Rec. 7402-7403. In addition, there were many references to discriminatory situations causing wide unrest and having a depressant effect on general business conditions in the respective communities. See, e.g., Senate Commerce Committee Hearings, at 623–630, 695–700, 1384–1385.

Moreover there was an impressive array of testimony that discrimination in restaurants had a direct and highly restrictive effect upon interstate travel by Negroes. This resulted, it was said, because discriminatory practices prevent Negroes from buying prepared food served on the premises while on a trip, except in isolated and unkempt restaurants and under most unsatisfactory and often unpleasant conditions. This obviously discourages travel and obstructs interstate commerce for one can hardly travel without eating. Likewise, it was said, that discrimination deterred professional, as well as skilled, people from moving into areas where such practices occurred and thereby caused industry to be reluctant to establish there. S. Rep. No. 872, supra, at 18-19.

We believe that this testimony afforded ample basis for the conclusion that established restaurants in such areas sold less interstate goods because of the discrimination, that interstate travel was obstructed directly by it, that business in general suffered and that many new businesses refrained from establishing there as a result of it. Hence the

District Court was in error in concluding that there was no connection between discrimination and the movement of interstate commerce. The court's conclusion that such a connection is outside "common experience" flies in the face of stubborn fact.

It goes without saying that, viewed in isolation, the volume of food purchased by Ollie's Barbecue from sources supplied from out of state was insignificant when [379 U.S. 294, 301] compared with the total foodstuffs moving in commerce. But, as our late Brother Jackson said for the Court in *Wickard v. Filburn* . . .

> "That appellee's own contribution to the demand for wheat may be trivial by itself is not enough to remove him from the scope of federal regulation where, as here, his contribution, taken together with that of many others similarly situated, is far from trivial."

We noted in *Heart of Atlanta Motel* that a number of witnesses attested to the fact that racial discrimination was not merely a state or regional problem but was one of nationwide scope. Against this background, we must conclude that while the focus of the legislation was on the individual restaurant's relation to interstate commerce, Congress appropriately considered the importance of that connection with the knowledge that the discrimination was but "representative of many others throughout the country, the total incidence of which if left unchecked may well become far-reaching in its harm to commerce." Polish Alliance v. Labor Board. . . .

> With this situation spreading as the record shows, Congress was not required to await the total dislocation of commerce. . . .

5. The Power of Congress to Regulate Local Activities.

Article I, 8, cl. 3, confers upon Congress the power "to regulate Commerce . . . among the several States" and Clause 18 of the same Article grants it the power "to make all Laws which shall be necessary and proper for carrying into Execution the foregoing Powers. . . ." This grant, as we have pointed out in *Heart of Atlanta Motel* "extends to those activities intrastate which so affect interstate commerce, or the exertion of the power of Congress over it, as to make regulation of them appropriate means to the attainment of a legitimate end, the effective execution of the granted power to regulate interstate commerce." . . . Much is said about a restaurant business being local but "even if appellee's activity be local and though it may not be regarded as commerce, it may still, whatever its nature, be reached by Congress if it exerts a substantial economic effect on interstate commerce. . . ." *Wickard v. Filburn*. The activities that are beyond the reach of Congress are "those which are completely within a particular State, which do not affect other States, and with which it is not necessary to interfere, for the purpose of executing some of the general powers of the government." *Gibbons v. Ogden*. This rule is as good today as it was when Chief Justice Marshall laid it down almost a century and a half ago.

This Court has held time and again that this power extends to activities of retail establishments, including restaurants, which directly or indirectly burden or obstruct interstate commerce. We have detailed the cases in *Heart of Atlanta Motel*, and will not repeat them here.

Nor are the cases holding that interstate commerce ends when goods come to rest in the State of destination apposite here. That line of cases has been applied with reference to state taxation or regulation but not in the field of federal regulation.

The appellees contend that Congress has arbitrarily created a conclusive presumption that all restaurants meeting the criteria set out in the Act "affect commerce." Stated another way, they object to the omission of a provision for a case-by-case determination—judicial or administrative—that racial discrimination in a particular restaurant affects commerce.

But Congress' action in framing this Act was not unprecedented. In *United States v. Darby* this Court held constitutional the Fair Labor Standards Act of 1938. There Congress determined that the payment of substandard wages to employees engaged in the production of goods for commerce, while not itself commerce, so inhibited it as to be subject to federal regulation. The appellees in that case argued, as do the appellees here, that the Act was invalid because it included no provision for an independent inquiry regarding the effect on commerce of substandard wages in a particular business. (Brief for appellees . . . *United States v. Darby*) But the Court rejected the argument, observing that:

> "Sometimes Congress itself has said that a particular activity affects the commerce, as it did in the present Act, the Safety Appliance Act and the Railway Labor Act. In passing on the validity of legislation of the class last mentioned the only function of courts is to determine whether the particular activity regulated or prohibited is within the reach of the federal power."

Here, as there, Congress has determined for itself that refusals of service to Negroes have imposed burdens both upon the interstate flow of food and upon the movement of products generally. Of course, the mere fact that Congress has said when particular activity shall be deemed to affect commerce does not preclude further examination by this Court. But where we find that the legislators, in light of the facts and testimony before them, have a rational basis for finding a chosen regulatory scheme necessary to the protection of commerce, our investigation is at an end. The only remaining question—one answered in the affirmative by the court below—is whether the particular restaurant either serves or offers to serve interstate travelers or serves food a substantial portion of which has moved in interstate commerce.

The appellees urge that Congress, in passing the Fair Labor Standards Act and the National Labor Relations Act, made specific findings which were embodied in those statutes. Here, of course, Congress has included no formal findings. But their absence is not fatal to the validity of the statute, see *United States v. Carolene Products Co.* for the evidence presented at the hearings fully indicated the nature and effect of the burdens on commerce which Congress meant to alleviate.

Confronted as we are with the facts laid before Congress, we must conclude that it had a rational basis for finding that racial discrimination in restaurants had a direct and adverse effect on the free flow of interstate commerce. Insofar as the sections of the Act here relevant are concerned, 201 (b) (2) and (c), Congress prohibited discrimination only in those establishments having a close tie to interstate commerce, i.e., those, like the McClungs', serving food that has come from out of the State. We think in so doing that Congress acted well within its power to protect and foster commerce in extending the coverage of Title II only to those restaurants offering to serve interstate travelers or serving food, a substantial portion of which has moved in interstate commerce.

The absence of direct evidence connecting discriminatory restaurant service with the flow of interstate food, a factor on which the appellees place much reliance, is not, given the evidence as to the effect of such practices on other aspects of commerce, a crucial matter.

The power of Congress in this field is broad and sweeping; where it keeps within its sphere and violates no express constitutional limitation it has been the rule of this Court, going back almost to the founding days of the Republic, not to interfere. The Civil Rights Act of 1964, as here applied, we find to be plainly appropriate in the resolution of what the Congress found to be a national commercial problem of the first magnitude. We find it in no violation of any express limitations of the Constitution and we therefore declare it valid.

The judgment is therefore

Reversed.

Source: Justia.com – US Supreme Court Center. http://supreme.justia.com/us/379/294/case.html

HEART OF ATLANTA MOTEL, INC. V. UNITED STATES ET AL. (1964)

Decided with Katzenbach, *ruled on Title II of the Civil Rights Act of 1964, which prohibited racial discrimination in hotels, motels, and other places of public accommodation if the operation of those institutions affected commerce. The Heart of Atlanta Motel in Atlanta, Georgia, was a whites-only institution where blacks were not allowed to stay, and so it was charged under the act. The Court ruled that Congress did not exceed its authority under the Commerce Clause, because Congress could regulate local commerce as long as it had a direct and substantial relationship to the flow of interstate commerce. In this case, the fact that black citizens did not have a place to stay would impede their ability to travel from state to state, thus affecting interstate commerce.*

MR. JUSTICE CLARK delivered the opinion of the Court. . . .

The case comes here on admissions and stipulated facts. Appellant owns and operates the Heart of Atlanta Motel which has 216 rooms available to transient guests. The motel is located on Courtland Street, two blocks from downtown Peachtree Street. It is readily accessible to interstate highways 75 and 85 and state highways 23 and 41. Appellant solicits patronage from outside the State of Georgia through various national advertising media, including magazines of national circulation; it maintains over 50 billboards and highway signs within the State, soliciting patronage for the motel; it accepts convention trade from outside Georgia and approximately 75% of its registered guests are from out of State. Prior to passage of the Act the motel had followed a practice of refusing to rent rooms to Negroes, and it alleged that it intended to continue to do so. In an effort to perpetuate that policy this suit was filed.

The appellant contends that Congress in passing this Act exceeded its power to regulate commerce under Art. I, § 8, cl. 3, of the Constitution of the United States; that the Act violates the Fifth Amendment because appellant is deprived of the right to choose its customers and operate its business as it wishes, resulting in a taking of its liberty and property without due process of law and a taking of its property without just compensation; and, finally, that by requiring appellant to rent available rooms to Negroes against its will, Congress is subjecting it to involuntary servitude in contravention of the Thirteenth Amendment.

The appellees counter that the unavailability to Negroes of adequate accommodations interferes significantly with interstate travel, and that Congress, under the Commerce Clause, has power to remove such obstructions and restraints; that the Fifth Amendment does not forbid reasonable regulation and that consequential damage does not constitute a "taking" within the meaning of that amendment; that the Thirteenth Amendment claim fails because it is entirely frivolous to say that an amendment directed to the abolition of human bondage and the removal of widespread disabilities associated with slavery places discrimination in public accommodations beyond the reach of both federal and state law. . . .

The sole question posed is, therefore, the constitutionality of the Civil Rights Act of 1964 as applied to these facts. The legislative history of the Act indicates that Congress based the Act on § 5 and the Equal Protection Clause of the Fourteenth Amendment as well as its power to regulate interstate commerce under Art. I, § 8, cl. 3, of the Constitution.

The Senate Commerce Committee made it quite clear that the fundamental object of Title II was to vindicate "the deprivation of personal dignity that surely accompanies denials of equal access to public establishments." At the same time, however, it noted that such an objective has been and could be readily achieved "by congressional action based on the commerce power of the Constitution." . . . Our study of the legislative record, made in the light of prior cases, has brought us to the conclusion that Congress possessed ample power in this regard, and we have therefore not considered the other grounds relied upon. This is not to say that the remaining authority upon which it acted was not adequate, a question upon which we do not pass, but merely that since the commerce power is sufficient for our decision here we have considered it alone. . . .

In light of our ground for decision, it might be well at the outset to discuss the *Civil Rights Case* which declared provisions of the Civil Rights Act of 1875 unconstitutional. 18 Stat. 335, 336. We think that decision inapposite, and without precedential value in determining the constitutionality of the present Act. . . .

While the Act as adopted carried no congressional findings the record of its passage through each house is replete with evidence of the burdens that discrimination by race or color places upon interstate commerce. . . . This testimony included the fact that our people have become increasingly mobile with millions of people of all races traveling from State to State; that Negroes in particular have been the subject of discrimination in transient accommodations, having to travel great distances to secure the same; that often they have been unable to obtain accommodations and have had to call upon friends to put them up overnight . . . and that these conditions had become so acute as to require the listing of available lodging for Negroes in a special guidebook which was itself "dramatic testimony to the difficulties" Negroes encounter in travel. . . .

The power of Congress to deal with these obstructions depends on the meaning of the Commerce Clause. Its meaning was first enunciated 140 years ago by the great Chief Justice John Marshall in *Gibbons* v. *Ogden*. . . .

The same interest in protecting interstate commerce which led Congress to deal with segregation in interstate carriers and the white-slave traffic has prompted it to extend the exercise of its power to gambling . . . to criminal enterprises . . . to deceptive practices in the sale of products . . . to fraudulent security transactions . . . to misbranding of drugs . . . to wages and hours . . . to members of labor unions . . . to crop control . . . to discrimination against shippers . . . to the protection of small business from injurious price cutting . . . to professional football . . . and to racial discrimination by owners and managers of terminal restaurants. . . .

That Congress was legislating against moral wrongs in many of these areas rendered its enactments no less valid. In framing Title II of this Act Congress was also dealing with what it considered a moral problem. But that fact does not detract from the overwhelming evidence of the disruptive effect that racial discrimination has had on commercial intercourse. It was this burden which empowered Congress to enact appropriate legislation, and, given this basis for the exercise of its power, Congress was not restricted by the fact that the particular obstruction to interstate commerce with which it was dealing was also deemed a moral and social wrong.

It is said that the operation of the motel here is of a purely local character. But, assuming this to be true, "if it is interstate commerce that feels the pinch, it does not matter how local the operation which applies the squeeze." . . .

Thus the power of Congress to promote interstate commerce also includes the power to regulate the local incidents thereof, including local activities in both the States of origin and destination, which might have a substantial and harmful effect upon that commerce. One need only examine the evidence which we have discussed above to see that Congress may—as it has—prohibit racial discrimination by motels serving travelers, however "local" their operations may appear. . . .

It is doubtful if in the long run appellant will suffer economic loss as a result of the Act. Experience is to the contrary where discrimination is completely obliterated as to all public accommodations. But whether this be true or not is of no consequence since this Court has specifically held that the fact that a "member of the class which is regulated may suffer economic losses not shared by others . . . has never been a barrier" to such legislation. . . .

Likewise in a long line of cases this Court has rejected the claim that the prohibition of racial discrimination in public accommodations interferes with personal liberty. . . .

We, therefore, conclude that the action of the Congress in the adoption of the Act as applied here to a motel which concededly serves interstate travelers is within the power granted it by the Commerce Clause of the Constitution, as interpreted by this Court for 140 years. It may be argued that Congress could have pursued other methods to eliminate the obstructions it found in interstate commerce caused by racial discrimination. But this is a matter of policy that rests entirely with the Congress not with the courts. How obstructions in commerce may be removed—what means are to be employed—is within the sound and exclusive discretion of the Congress. It is subject only to one caveat—that the means chosen by it must be reasonably adapted to the end permitted by the Constitution. We cannot say that its choice here was not so adapted. The Constitution requires no more.

Affirmed.

MR. JUSTICE BLACK *concurring* . . .

It requires no novel or strained interpretation of the Commerce Clause to sustain Title II as applied in either of these cases. At least since *Gibbons* v. *Ogden*, 9 Wheat. 1, decided in 1824 in an opinion by Chief Justice John Marshall, it has been uniformly accepted that the power of Congress to regulate commerce among the States is plenary, "complete in itself, may be exercised to its utmost extent, and acknowledges no limitations, other than are prescribed in the constitution." . . . as used in the Commerce Clause to be limited to a narrow, technical concept. It includes not only, as Congress has enumerated in the Act, "travel, trade, traffic, commerce, transportation, or communication," but also all other unitary transactions and activities that take place in more States than one. That some parts or segments of such unitary transactions may take place only in one State cannot, of course, take from Congress its plenary power to regulate them in the national interest. The facilities and instrumentalities used to carry on this commerce, such as railroads, truck lines, ships, rivers, and even highways are also subject to congressional regulation, so far as is necessary to keep interstate traffic upon fair and equal terms.

MR JUSTICE DOUGLAS concurring . . .

Though I join the Court's opinions, I am somewhat reluctant here, as I was in *Edwards* v. *California,* 314 U.S. 160, 177, to rest solely on the Commerce Clause. My reluctance is not due to any conviction that Congress lacks power to regulate commerce in the interests of human rights. It is rather my belief that the right of people to be free of state action that discriminates against them because of race, like the "right of persons to move freely from State to State" (*Edwards* v. *California, supra,* at 177), "occupies a more protected position in our constitutional system than does the movement of cattle, fruit, steel and coal across state lines." *Ibid.* Moreover, when we come to the problem of abatement in *Hamm* v. *City of Rock Hill, post,* p. 306, decided this day, the result reached by the Court is for me much more obvious as a protective measure under the Fourteenth Amendment than under the Commerce Clause. For the former deals with the constitutional status of the individual not with the impact on commerce of local activities or vice versa.

Hence I would prefer to rest on the assertion of legislative power contained in § 5 of the Fourteenth Amendment which states: "The Congress shall have power to enforce, by appropriate legislation, the provisions of this article"—a power which the Court concedes was exercised at least in part in this Act.

MR JUSTICE GOLDBERG concurring . . .

In my concurring opinion in *Bell* v. *Maryland,* 378 U.S. 226, 317, however, I expressed my conviction that § 1 of the Fourteenth Amendment guarantees to all Americans the constitutional right "to be treated as equal members of the community with respect to public accommodations," and that "Congress [has] authority under § 5 of the Fourteenth Amendment, or under the Commerce Clause, Art. I, § 8, to implement the rights protected by § 1 of the Fourteenth Amendment. In the give-and-take of the legislative process, Congress . . . can fashion a law drawing the guidelines necessary and appropriate to facilitate practical administration and to distinguish between genuinely public and private accommodations." The challenged Act is just such a law and, in my view, Congress clearly had authority under both § 5 of the Fourteenth Amendment and the Commerce Clause to enact the Civil Rights Act of 1964.

Source: Justia.com – US Supreme Court Center. http://supreme.justia.com/us/379/241/case.html

VOTING RIGHTS ACT (1965)

Passed under the authority of the Fifteenth Amendment, which outlawed discrimination in voting on the basis of race. Despite the amendment, for almost a century blacks had been systematically excluded from voting in the South through the use of poll taxes, literacy tests, and other manifestations of Jim Crow. Congress responded in the wake of the murder of voting rights activists in Mississippi; Klan activity; the violent attack by Alabama state troopers on peaceful marchers as they crossed the Edmund

Pettus Bridge in Selma, Alabama; the ensuing Selma to Montgomery March; and an appeal by President Johnson. The act strove to dissolve the vestiges of Jim Crow that inhibited black voter participation in the South by giving the federal government proactive tools to solve the problem.

AN ACT To enforce the fifteenth amendment to the Constitution of the United States, and for other purposes.

Be it enacted by the Senate and House of Representatives of the United States of America in Congress assembled, That this Act shall be known as the "Voting Rights Act of 1965."

SEC. 2.

No voting qualification or prerequisite to voting, or standard, practice, or procedure shall be imposed or applied by any State or political subdivision to deny or abridge the right of any citizen of the United States to vote on account of race or color.

SEC. 4.

(a) To assure that the right of citizens of the United States to vote is not denied or abridged on account of race or color, no citizen shall be denied the right to vote in any Federal, State, or local election because of his failure to comply with any test or device in any State with respect to which the determinations have been made under subsection (b) or in any political subdivision with respect to which such determinations have been made as a separate unit, unless the United States District Court for the District of Columbia in an action for a declaratory judgment brought by such State or subdivision against the United States has determined that no such test or device has been used during the five years preceding the filing of the action for the purpose or with the effect of denying or abridging the right to vote on account of race or color: Provided, That no such declaratory judgment shall issue with respect to any plaintiff for a period of five years after the entry of a final judgment of any court of the United States, other than the denial of a declaratory judgment under this section, whether entered prior to or after the enactment of this Act, determining that denials or abridgments of the right to vote on account of race or color through the use of such tests or devices have occurred anywhere in the territory of such plaintiff. An action pursuant to this subsection shall be heard and determined by a court of three judges in accordance with the provisions of section 2284 of title 28 of the United States Code and any appeal shall lie to the Supreme Court. The court shall retain jurisdiction of any action pursuant to this subsection for five years after judgment and shall reopen the action upon motion of the Attorney General alleging that a test or device has been used for the purpose or with the effect of denying or abridging the right to vote on account of race or color.

If the Attorney General determines that he has no reason to believe that any such test or device has been used during the five years preceding the filing of the action for the purpose or with the effect of denying or abridging the right to vote on account of race or color, he shall consent to the entry of such judgment.

(b) The provisions of subsection (a) shall apply in any State or in any political subdivision of a state which (1) the Attorney General determines maintained on November 1, 1964, any test or device, and with respect to which (2) the Director of the Census determines that less than 50 percentum of the persons of voting age residing therein were registered on November 1, 1964, or that less than 50 percentum of such persons voted in the presidential election of November 1964.

A determination or certification of the Attorney General or of the Director of the Census under this section or under section 6 or section 13 shall not be reviewable in any court and shall be effective upon publication in the Federal Register.

(c) The phrase "test or device" shall mean any requirement that a person as a prerequisite for voting or registration for voting (1) demonstrate the ability to read, write, understand, or interpret any matter, (2) demonstrate any educational achievement or his knowledge of any particular subject, (3) possess good moral character, or (4) prove his qualifications by the voucher of registered voters or members of any other class.

(d) For purposes of this section no State or political subdivision shall be determined to have engaged in the use of tests or devices for the purpose or with the effect of denying or abridging the right to vote on account of race or color if (1) incidents of such use have been few in number and have been promptly and effectively corrected by State or local action, (2) the continuing effect of such incidents has been eliminated, and (3) there is no reasonable probability of their recurrence in the future.

(e) (1) Congress hereby declares that to secure the rights under the fourteenth amendment of persons educated in American-flag schools in which the predominant classroom language was other than English, it is necessary to prohibit the States from conditioning the right to vote of such persons on ability to read, write, understand, or interpret any matter in the English language. (2) No person who demonstrates that he has successfully completed the sixth primary grade in a public school in, or a private school accredited by, any State or territory, the District of Columbia, or the Commonwealth of Puerto Rico in which the predominant classroom language was other than English, shall be denied the right to vote in any Federal, State, or local election because of his inability to read, write, understand, or interpret any matter in the English language, except that, in States in which State law provides that a different level of education is presumptive of literacy, he shall demonstrate that he has successfully completed an equivalent level of education in a public school in, or a private school accredited by, any State or territory, the District of Columbia, or the Commonwealth of Puerto Rico in which the predominant classroom language was other than English.

Sec. 5.

Whenever a State or political subdivision with respect to which the prohibitions set forth in section 4(a) are in effect shall enact or seek to administer any voting qualification or prerequisite to voting, or standard, practice, or procedure with respect to voting different from that in force or effect on November 1, 1964, such State or subdivision may institute an action in the United States District Court for the District of Columbia for a declaratory judgment that such qualification, prerequisite, standard, practice, or procedure does not have the purpose and will not have the effect of denying or abridging the right to vote on account of race or color, and unless and until the court enters such judgment no person shall be denied the right to vote for failure to comply with such qualification, prerequisite, standard, practice, or procedure: Provided, That such qualification, prerequisite, standard, practice, or procedure may be enforced without such proceeding if the qualification, prerequisite, standard, practice, or procedure has been submitted by the chief legal officer or other appropriate official of such State or subdivision to the Attorney General and the Attorney General has not interposed an objection within sixty days after such submission, except that neither the Attorney General's failure to object nor a declaratory judgment entered under this section shall bar a subsequent action to enjoin enforcement of such qualification, prerequisite, standard, practice, or procedure. Any action under this section shall be heard and determined by a court of three judges in accordance with the provisions of section 2284 of title 28 of the United States Code and any appeal shall lie to the Supreme Court.

Sec. 6.

Whenever (a) a court has authorized the appointment of examiners pursuant to the provisions of section 3(a), or (b) unless a declaratory judgment has been rendered under section 4(a), the Attorney General certifies with respect to any political subdivision named in, or included within the scope of, determinations made under section 4(b) that (1) he has received complaints in writing from twenty or more residents of such political subdivision alleging that they have been denied the right to vote under color of law on account of race or color, and that he believes such complaints to be meritorious, or (2) that, in his judgment (considering, among other factors, whether the ratio of nonwhite persons to white persons registered to vote within such subdivision appears to him to be reasonably attributable to violations of the fifteenth amendment or whether substantial evidence exists that bona fide efforts are being made within such subdivision to comply with the fifteenth amendment), the appointment of examiners is otherwise necessary to enforce the guarantees of the fifteenth amendment, the Civil Service Commission shall appoint as many examiners for such subdivision as it may deem appropriate to prepare and maintain lists of persons eligible to vote in Federal, State, and local elections. Such examiners, hearing officers provided for in section 9(a), and other persons deemed necessary by the Commission to carry out the provisions and purposes of this Act shall be appointed, compensated, and separated without regard to the provisions of any statute administered by the Civil Service Commission, and service under this Act shall not be considered employment for the purposes of any statute administered by the Civil Service Commission, except the provisions of section 9 of the Act of August 2, 1939, as amended (5 U.S.C. 118i), prohibiting partisan political activity: Provided, That the Commission is authorized, after consulting the head of the appropriate department or agency, to designate suitable persons in the official service of the United States, with their consent, to serve in these positions. Examiners and hearing officers shall have the power to administer oaths.

Sec. 7.

(a) The examiners for each political subdivision shall, at such places as the Civil Service Commission shall by regulation designate, examine applicants concerning their qualifications for voting. An application to an examiner shall be in such form as the Commission may require and shall contain allegations that the applicant is not otherwise registered to vote. (b) Any person whom the examiner finds, in accordance with instructions received under section 9(b), to have the qualifications prescribed by State law not inconsistent with the Constitution and laws of the United States shall promptly be placed on a list of eligible voters. A challenge to such listing may be made in accordance with section 9(a) and shall not be the basis for a prosecution under section 12 of this Act. The examiner shall certify and transmit such list, and any supplements as appropriate, at least once a month, to the offices of the appropriate election officials, with copies to the Attorney General and the attorney general of the State, and any such lists and supplements thereto transmitted during the month shall be available for public inspection on the last business day of the month and, in any event, not later than the forty-fifth day prior to any election. The appropriate State or local election official shall place such names on the official voting list. Any person whose name appears on the examiner's list shall be entitled and allowed to vote in the election district of his residence unless and until the appropriate election officials shall have been notified that such person has been removed from such list in accordance with subsection (d): Provided, That no person shall be entitled to vote in any election by virtue of this Act unless his name shall have been certified and transmitted on such a list to the offices of the appropriate election officials at least forty-five days prior to such election.

(c) The examiner shall issue to each person whose name appears on such a list a certificate evidencing his eligibility to vote.

(d) A person whose name appears on such a list shall be removed therefrom by an examiner if (1) such person has been successfully challenged in accordance with the procedure prescribed in section 9, or (2) he has been determined by an examiner to have lost his eligibility to vote under State law not inconsistent with the Constitution and the laws of the United States.

Sec. 8.

Whenever an examiner is serving under this Act in any political subdivision, the Civil Service Commission may assign, at the request of the Attorney General, one or more persons, who may be officers of the United States, (1) to enter and attend at any place for holding an election in such subdivision for the purpose of observing whether persons who are entitled to vote are being permitted to vote, and (2) to enter and attend at any place for tabulating the votes cast at any election held in such subdivision for the purpose of observing whether votes cast by persons entitled to vote are being properly tabulated. Such persons so assigned shall report to an examiner appointed for such political subdivision, to the Attorney General, and if the appointment of examiners has been authorized pursuant to section 3(a), to the court.

Sec. 9.

(a) Any challenge to a listing on an eligibility list prepared by an examiner shall be heard and determined by a hearing officer appointed by and responsible to the Civil Service Commission and under such rules as the Commission shall by regulation prescribe. Such challenge shall be entertained only if filed at such office within the State as the Civil Service Commission shall by regulation designate, and within ten days after the listing of the challenged person is made available for public inspection, and if supported by (1) the affidavits of at least two persons having personal knowledge of the facts constituting grounds for the challenge, and (2) a certification that a copy of the challenge and affidavits have been served by mail or in person upon the person challenged at his place of residence set out in the application. Such challenge shall be determined within fifteen days after it has been filed. A petition for review of the decision of the hearing officer may be filed in the United States court of appeals for the circuit in which the person challenged resides within fifteen days after service of such decision by mail on the person petitioning for review but no decision of a hearing officer shall be reversed unless clearly erroneous. Any person listed shall be entitled and allowed to vote pending final determination by the hearing officer and by the court (b) The times, places, procedures, and form for application and listing pursuant to this Act and removals from the eligibility lists shall be prescribed by regulations promulgated by the Civil Service Commission and the Commission shall, after consultation with the Attorney General, instruct examiners concerning applicable State law not inconsistent with the Constitution and laws of the United States with respect to (1) the qualifications required for listing, and (2) loss of eligibility to vote.

(c) Upon the request of the applicant or the challenger or on its own motion the Civil Service Commission shall have the power to require by subpoena the attendance and testimony of witnesses and the production of documentary evidence relating to any matter pending before it under the authority of this section. In case of contumacy or refusal to obey a subpoena, any district court of the United States or the United States court of any territory or possession, or the District Court of the United States for the District of Columbia, within the jurisdiction of which said person guilty of contumacy or refusal to obey is found or resides or is domiciled or transacts business, or has appointed an agent for receipt of service of process, upon application by the Attorney General of the United States shall have jurisdiction to issue to such person an order requiring such person to appear before the Commission or a hearing officer, there to produce pertinent, relevant, and nonprivileged documentary evidence if so ordered, or there to give testimony touching the matter under investigation, and any failure to obey such order of the court may be punished by said court as a contempt thereof.

Sec. 10.

(a) The Congress finds that the requirement of the payment of a poll tax as a precondition to voting (i) precludes persons of limited means from voting or imposes unreasonable financial hardship upon such persons as a precondition to their exercise of the franchise, (ii) does not bear a reasonable relationship to any legitimate State interest in the conduct of elections, and (iii) in some areas has the purpose or effect of denying persons the right to vote because of race or color. Upon the basis of these findings, Congress declares that the constitutional right of citizens to vote is denied or abridged in some areas by the requirement of the payment of a poll tax as a precondition to voting.

(b) In the exercise of the powers of Congress under section 5 of the fourteenth amendment and section 2 of the fifteenth amendment, the Attorney General is authorized and directed to institute forthwith in the name of the United States such actions, including actions against States or political subdivisions, for declaratory judgment or injunctive relief against the enforcement of any requirement of the payment of a poll tax as a precondition to voting, or substitute therefor [sic] enacted after November 1, 1964, as will be necessary to implement the declaration of subsection (a) and the purposes of this section.

(c) The district courts of the United States shall have jurisdiction of such actions which shall be heard and determined by a court of three judges in accordance with the provisions of section 2284 of title 28 of the United States Code and any appeal shall lie to the Supreme Court. It shall be the duty of the judges designated to hear the case to assign the case for hearing at the earliest practicable date, to participate in the hearing and determination thereof, and to cause the case to be in every way expedited.

(d) During the pendency of such actions, and thereafter if the courts, notwithstanding this action by the Congress, should declare the requirement of the payment of a poll tax to be constitutional, no citizen of the United States who is a resident of a State or political subdivision with respect to which determinations have been made under subsection 4(b) and a declaratory judgment has not been entered under subsection 4(a), during the first year he becomes otherwise entitled to vote by reason of registration by State or local officials or listing by an examiner, shall be denied the right to vote for failure to pay a poll tax if he tenders payment of such tax for the current year to an examiner or to the appropriate State or local official at least forty-five days prior to election, whether or not such tender would be timely or adequate under State law. An examiner shall have authority to accept such payment from any person authorized by this Act to make an application for listing, and shall issue a receipt for such payment. The examiner shall transmit promptly any such poll tax payment to the office of the State or local official authorized to receive such payment under State law, together with the name and address of the applicant.

Sec. 11.

(a) No person acting under color of law shall fail or refuse to permit any person to vote who is entitled to vote under any provision of this Act or is otherwise qualified to vote, or willfully fail or refuse to tabulate, count, and report such person's vote.

(b) No person, whether acting under color of law or otherwise, shall intimidate, threaten, or coerce, or attempt to intimidate, threaten, or coerce any person for voting or attempting to vote, or intimidate, threaten, or coerce, or attempt to intimidate, threaten, or coerce any person for urging or aiding any person to vote or attempt to vote, or intimidate, threaten, or coerce any person for exercising any powers or duties under section 3(a), 6, 8, 9, 10, or 12(e).

(c) Whoever knowingly or willfully gives false information as to his name, address, or period of residence in the voting district for the purpose of establishing his eligibility to register or vote, or conspires with another individual for the purpose of encouraging his false registration to vote or illegal voting, or pays or offers to pay or accepts payment either for registration to vote or for voting shall be fined not more than $10,000 or imprisoned not more than five years, or both: Provided, however, That this provision shall be applicable only to general, special, or primary elections held solely or in part for the purpose of selecting or electing any candidate for the office of President, Vice President, presidential elector, Member of the United States Senate, Member of the United States House of Representatives, or Delegates or Commissioners from the territories or possessions, or Resident Commissioner of the Commonwealth of Puerto Rico.

(d) Whoever, in any matter within the jurisdiction of an examiner or hearing officer knowingly and willfully falsifies or conceals a material fact, or makes any false, fictitious, or fraudulent statements or representations, or makes or uses any false writing or document knowing the same to contain any false, fictitious, or fraudulent statement or entry, shall be fined not more than $10,000 or imprisoned not more than five years, or both.

Sec. 12.

(a) Whoever shall deprive or attempt to deprive any person of any right secured by section 2, 3, 4, 5, 7, or 10 or shall violate section 11(a) or (b), shall be fined not more than $5,000, or imprisoned not more than five years, or both.

(b) Whoever, within a year following an election in a political subdivision in which an examiner has been appointed (1) destroys, defaces, mutilates, or otherwise alters the marking of a paper ballot which has been cast in such election, or (2) alters any official record of voting in such election tabulated from a voting machine or otherwise, shall be fined not more than $5,000, or imprisoned not more than five years, or both.

(c) Whoever conspires to violate the provisions of subsection (a) or (b) of this section, or interferes with any right secured by section 2, 3 4, 5, 7, 10, or 11(a) or (b) shall be fined not more than $5,000, or imprisoned not more than five years, or both.

(d) Whenever any person has engaged or there are reasonable grounds to believe that any person is about to engage in any act or practice prohibited by section 2, 3, 4, 5, 7, 10, 11, or subsection (b) of this section, the Attorney General may institute for the United States, or in the name of the United States, an action for preventive relief, including an application for a temporary or permanent injunction, restraining order, or other order, and including an order directed to the State and State or local election officials to require them (1) to permit persons listed under this Act to vote and (2) to count such votes.

(e) Whenever in any political subdivision in which there are examiners appointed pursuant to this Act any persons allege to such an examiner within forty-eight hours after the closing of the polls that notwithstanding (1) their listing under this Act or registration by an appropriate election official and (2) their eligibility to vote, they have not been permitted to vote in such election, the examiner shall forthwith notify the Attorney General if such allegations in his opinion appear to be well founded. Upon receipt of such notification, the Attorney General may forthwith file with the district court an application for an order providing for the marking, casting, and counting of the ballots of such persons and requiring the inclusion of their votes in the total vote before the results of such election shall be deemed final and any force or effect given thereto. The district court shall hear and determine such matters immediately after the filing of such application. The remedy provided in this subsection shall not preclude any remedy available under State or Federal law.

(f) The district courts of the United States shall have jurisdiction of proceedings instituted pursuant to this section and shall exercise the same without regard to whether a person asserting rights under the provisions of this Act shall have exhausted any administrative or other remedies that may be provided by law.

Sec. 13.

Listing procedures shall be terminated in any political subdivision of any State (a) with respect to examiners appointed pursuant to clause (b) of section 6 whenever the Attorney General notifies the Civil Service Commission, or whenever the District Court for the District of Columbia determines in an action for declaratory judgment brought by any political subdivision with respect to which the Director of the Census has determined that more than 50 percentum of the nonwhite persons of voting age residing therein are registered to vote, (1) that all persons listed by an examiner for such subdivision have been placed on the appropriate voting registration roll, and (2) that there is no longer reasonable cause to believe that persons will be deprived of or denied the right to vote on account of race or color in such subdivision, and (b), with respect to examiners appointed pursuant to section 3(a), upon order of the authorizing court. A political subdivision may petition the Attorney General for the termination of listing procedures under clause (a) of this section, and may petition the Attorney General to request the Director of the Census to take such survey or census as may be appropriate for the making of the determination provided for in this section. The District Court for the District of Columbia shall have jurisdiction to require such survey or census to be made by the Director of the Census and it shall require him to do so if it deems the Attorney General's refusal to request such survey or census to be arbitrary or unreasonable.

Sec. 14.

(a) All cases of criminal contempt arising under the provisions of this Act shall be governed by section 151 of the Civil Rights Act of 1957 (42 U.S.C.1995).

(b) No court other than the District Court for the District of Columbia or a court of appeals in any proceeding under section 9 shall have jurisdiction to issue any declaratory judgment pursuant to section 4 or section 5 or any restraining order or temporary or permanent injunction against the execution or enforcement of any provision of this Act or any action of any Federal officer or employee pursuant hereto.

(c) (1) The terms "vote" or "voting" shall include all action necessary to make a vote effective in any primary, special, or general election, including, but not limited to, registration, listing pursuant to this Act, or other action required by law prerequisite to voting, casting a ballot, and having such ballot counted properly and included in the appropriate totals of votes cast with respect to candidates for public or party office and propositions for which votes are received in an election. (2) The term "political subdivision" shall mean any county or parish, except that, where registration for voting is not conducted under the supervision of a county or parish, the term shall include any other subdivision of a State which conducts registration for voting.

(d) In any action for a declaratory judgment brought pursuant to section 4 or section 5 of this Act, subpoenas for witnesses who are required to attend the District Court for the District of Columbia may be served in any judicial district of the United States: Provided, That no writ of subpoena shall issue for witnesses without the District of Columbia at a greater distance than one hundred miles from the place of holding court without the permission of the District Court for the District of Columbia being first had upon proper application and cause shown.

Sec. 15.

Section 2004 of the Revised Statutes (42 U.S.C.1971), as amended by section 131 of the Civil Rights Act of 1957 (71 Stat. 637), and amended by section 601 of the Civil Rights Act of 1960 (74 Stat. 90), and as further amended by section 101 of the Civil Rights Act of 1964 (78 Stat. 241), is further amended as follows:

(a) Delete the word "Federal" wherever it appears in subsections (a) and (c); (b) Repeal subsection (f) and designate the present subsections (g) and (h) as (f) and (g), respectively.

Sec. 16.

The Attorney General and the Secretary of Defense, jointly, shall make a full and complete study to determine whether, under the laws or practices of any State or States, there are preconditions to voting, which might tend to result in discrimination against citizens serving in the Armed Forces of the United States seeking to vote. Such officials shall, jointly, make a report to the Congress not later than June 30, 1966, containing the results of such study, together with a list of any States in which such preconditions exist, and shall include in such report such recommendations for legislation as they deem advisable to prevent discrimination in voting against citizens serving in the Armed Forces of the United States.

Sec. 17.

Nothing in this Act shall be construed to deny, impair, or otherwise adversely affect the right to vote of any person registered to vote under the law of any State or political subdivision.

Sec. 18.

There are hereby authorized to be appropriated such sums as are necessary to carry out the provisions of this Act. . . .

Sec. 19.

If any provision of this Act or the application thereof to any person or circumstances is held invalid, the remainder of the Act and the application of the provision to other persons not similarly situated or to other circumstances shall not be affected thereby.

Approved August 6, 1965.

Source: Avalon Project at Yale Law School. http://www.yale.edu/lawweb/avalon/statutes/voting_rights_1965.htm

JOINT RESOLUTION CONCERNING THE WAR POWERS OF CONGRESS AND THE PRESIDENT (1973)

Passed in the final days of the Vietnam War by Congress as an attempt to rein in the power of the president to get the United States involved in another protracted military engagement. When passed, there were many who questioned the constitutional authority of Congress to adopt such an act. Nixon vetoed the resolution, citing its dubious constitutionality. Congress overrode the veto. In its most basic form it requires the president to consult with Congress prior to sending troops overseas into hostile territory. It establishes a timetable of basically 60 days, by the end of which the president must ask for congressional approval or withdraw the troops. Every U.S. president since its inception has questioned its validity and has been accused of violating it.

Resolved by the Senate and the House of Representatives of the United States of America in Congress assembled,

SHORT TITLE

SECTION 1. This joint resolution may be cited as the "War Powers Resolution."
PURPOSE AND POLICY

SEC. 2. (a) It is the purpose of this joint resolution to fulfill the intent of the framers of the Constitution of the United States and insure that the collective judgement of both the Congress and the President will apply to the introduction of United States Armed Forces into hostilities, or into situations where imminent involvement in hostilities is clearly indicated by the circumstances, and to the continued use of such forces in hostilities or in such situations.

(b) Under article I, section 8, of the Constitution, it is specifically provided that the Congress shall have the power to make all laws necessary and proper for carrying into execution, not only its own powers but also all other powers vested by the Constitution in the Government of the United States, or in any department or officer thereof.

(c) The constitutional powers of the President as Commander-in-Chief to introduce United States Armed Forces into hostilities, or into situations where imminent involvement in hostilities is clearly indicated by the circumstances, are exercised only pursuant to (1) a declaration of war, (2) specific statutory authorization, or (3) a national emergency created by attack upon the United States, its territories or possessions, or its armed forces.

CONSULTATION

SEC. 3. The President in every possible instance shall consult with Congress before introducing United States Armed Forces into hostilities or into situation where imminent involvement in hostilities is clearly indicated by the circumstances, and after every such introduction shall consult regularly with the Congress until United States Armed Forces are no longer engaged in hostilities or have been removed from such situations.

REPORTING

SEC. 4. (a) In the absence of a declaration of war, in any case in which United States Armed Forces are introduced—

(1) into hostilities or into situations where imminent involvement in hostilities is clearly indicated by the circumstances;

(2) into the territory, airspace or waters of a foreign nation, while equipped for combat, except for deployments which relate solely to supply, replacement, repair, or training of such forces; or

(3) in numbers which substantially enlarge United States Armed Forces equipped for combat already located in a foreign nation; the president shall submit within 48 hours to the Speaker of the House of Representatives and to the President pro tempore of the Senate a report, in writing, setting forth—

(A) the circumstances necessitating the introduction of United States Armed Forces;

(B) the constitutional and legislative authority under which such introduction took place; and

(C) the estimated scope and duration of the hostilities or involvement.

(b) The President shall provide such other information as the Congress may request in the fulfillment of its constitutional responsibilities with respect to committing the Nation to war and to the use of United States Armed Forces abroad

(c) Whenever United States Armed Forces are introduced into hostilities or into any situation described in subsection (a) of this section, the President shall, so long as such armed forces continue to be engaged in such hostilities or situation, report to the Congress periodically on the status of such hostilities or situation as well as on the scope and duration of such hostilities or situation, but in no event shall he report to the Congress less often than once every six months.

CONGRESSIONAL ACTION

SEC. 5. (a) Each report submitted pursuant to section 4(a)(1) shall be transmitted to the Speaker of the House of Representatives and to the President pro tempore of the Senate on the same calendar day. Each report so transmitted shall be referred to the Committee on Foreign Affairs of the House of Representatives and to the Committee on Foreign Relations of the Senate for appropriate action. If, when the report is transmitted, the Congress has adjourned sine die or has adjourned for any period in excess of three calendar days, the Speaker of the House of Representatives and the President pro tempore of the Senate, if they deem it advisable (or if petitioned by at least 30 percent of the membership of their respective Houses) shall jointly request the President to convene Congress in order that it may consider the report and take appropriate action pursuant to this section.

(b) Within sixty calendar days after a report is submitted or is required to be submitted pursuant to section 4(a)(1), whichever is earlier, the President shall terminate any use of United States Armed Forces with respect to which such report was submitted (or required to be submitted), unless the Congress (1) has declared war or has enacted a specific authorization for such use of United States Armed Forces, (2) has extended by law such sixty-day period, or (3) is physically unable to meet as a result of an armed attack upon the United States. Such sixty-day period shall be extended for not more than an additional thirty days if the President determines and certifies to the Congress in writing that unavoidable military necessity respecting the safety of United States Armed Forces requires the continued use of such armed forces in the course of bringing about a prompt removal of such forces.

(c) Notwithstanding subsection (b), at any time that United States Armed Forces are engaged in hostilities outside the territory of the United States, its possessions and territories without a declaration of war or specific statutory authorization, such forces shall be removed by the President if the Congress so directs by concurrent resolution.

CONGRESSIONAL PRIORITY PROCEDURES FOR JOINT RESOLUTION OR BILL

SEC. 6. (a) Any joint resolution or bill introduced pursuant to section 5(b) at least thirty calendar days before the expiration of the sixty-day period specified in such section shall be referred to the Committee on Foreign Affairs of the House of Representatives or the Committee on Foreign Relations of the Senate, as the case may be, and such committee shall report one such joint resolution or bill, together with its recommendations, not later than twenty-four calendar days before the expiration of the sixty-day period specified in such section, unless such House shall otherwise determine by the yeas and nays.

(b) Any joint resolution or bill so reported shall become the pending business of the House in question (in the case of the Senate the time for debate shall be equally divided between the proponents and the opponents), and shall be voted on within three calendar days thereafter, unless such House shall otherwise determine by yeas and nays.

(c) Such a joint resolution or bill passed by one House shall be referred to the committee of the other House named in subsection (a) and shall be reported out not later than fourteen calendar days before the expiration of the sixty-day period specified in section 5(b). The joint resolution or bill so reported shall become the pending business of the House in question and shall be voted on within three calendar days after it has been reported, unless such House shall otherwise determine by yeas and nays.

(d) In the case of any disagreement between the two Houses of Congress with respect to a joint resolution or bill passed by both Houses, conferees shall be promptly appointed and the committee of conference shall make and file a report with respect to such resolution or bill not later than four calendar days before the expiration of the sixty-day period specified in section 5(b). In the event the conferees are unable to agree within 48 hours, they shall report back to their respective Houses in disagreement. Notwithstanding any rule in either House concerning the printing of conference reports in the Record or concerning any delay in the consideration of such reports, such report shall be acted on by both Houses not later than the expiration of such sixty-day period.

CONGRESSIONAL PRIORITY PROCEDURES FOR CONCURRENT RESOLUTION

SEC. 7. (a) Any concurrent resolution introduced pursuant to section 5(b) at least thirty calendar days before the expiration of the sixty-day period specified in such section shall be referred to the Committee on Foreign Affairs of the House of Representatives or the Committee on Foreign Relations of the Senate, as the case may be, and one such concurrent resolution shall be reported out by such committee together with its recommendations within fifteen calendar days, unless such House shall otherwise determine by the yeas and nays.

(b) Any concurrent resolution so reported shall become the pending business of the House in question (in the case of the Senate the time for debate shall be equally divided between the proponents and the opponents), and shall be voted on within three calendar days thereafter, unless such House shall otherwise determine by yeas and nays.

(c) Such a concurrent resolution passed by one House shall be referred to the committee of the other House named in subsection (a) and shall be reported out by such committee together with its recommendations within fifteen calendar days and shall thereupon become the pending business of such House and shall be voted on within three calendar days after it has been reported, unless such House shall otherwise determine by yeas and nays.

(d) In the case of any disagreement between the two Houses of Congress with respect to a concurrent resolution passed by both Houses, conferees shall be promptly appointed and the committee of conference shall make and file a report with respect to such concurrent resolution within six calendar days after the legislation is referred to the committee of conference. Notwithstanding any rule in either House concerning the printing of conference reports in the Record or concerning any delay in the consideration of such reports, such report shall be acted on by both Houses not later than six calendar days after the conference report is filed. In the event the conferees are unable to agree within 48 hours, they shall report back to their respective Houses in disagreement.

INTERPRETATION OF JOINT RESOLUTION

SEC. 8. (a) Authority to introduce United States Armed Forces into hostilities or into situations wherein involvement in hostilities is clearly indicated by the circumstances shall not be inferred—

(1) from any provision of law (whether or not in effect before the date of the enactment of this joint resolution), including any provision contained in any appropriation Act, unless such provision specifically authorizes the introduction of United States Armed Forces into hostilities or into such situations and stating that it is intended to constitute specific statutory authorization within the meaning of this joint resolution; or

(2) from any treaty heretofore or hereafter ratified unless such treaty is implemented by legislation specifically authorizing the introduction of United States Armed Forces

into hostilities or into such situations and stating that it is intended to constitute specific statutory authorization within the meaning of this joint resolution.

(b) Nothing in this joint resolution shall be construed to require any further specific statutory authorization to permit members of United States Armed Forces to participate jointly with members of the armed forces of one or more foreign countries in the headquarters operations of high-level military commands which were established prior to the date of enactment of this joint resolution and pursuant to the United Nations Charter or any treaty ratified by the United States prior to such date.

(c) For purposes of this joint resolution, the term "introduction of United States Armed Forces" includes the assignment of member of such armed forces to command, coordinate, participate in the movement of, or accompany the regular or irregular military forces of any foreign country or government when such military forces are engaged, or there exists an imminent threat that such forces will become engaged, in hostilities.

(d) Nothing in this joint resolution—

(1) is intended to alter the constitutional authority of the Congress or of the President, or the provision of existing treaties; or

(2) shall be construed as granting any authority to the President with respect to the introduction of United States Armed Forces into hostilities or into situations wherein involvement in hostilities is clearly indicated by the circumstances which authority he would not have had in the absence of this joint resolution.

SEPARABILITY CLAUSE

SEC. 9. If any provision of this joint resolution or the application thereof to any person or circumstance is held invalid, the remainder of the joint resolution and the application of such provision to any other person or circumstance shall not be affected thereby.

EFFECTIVE DATE

SEC. 10. This joint resolution shall take effect on the date of its enactment.

CARL ALBERT

Speaker of the House of Representatives.

JAMES O. EASTLAND

President of the Senate pro tempore.

IN THE HOUSE OF REPRESENTATIVES, U.S.,

November 7, 1973.

The House of Representatives having proceeded to reconsider the resolution (H. J. Res 542) entitled "Joint resolution concerning the war powers of Congress and the President," returned by the President of the United States with his objections, to the House of Representatives, in which it originated, it was

Resolved, That the said resolution pass, two-thirds of the House of Representatives agreeing to pass the same.

Attest:

W. PAT JENNINGS

Clerk.

I certify that this Joint Resolution originated in the House of Representatives.

W. PAT JENNINGS

Clerk.

IN THE SENATE OF THE UNITED STATES

November 7, 1973

The Senate having proceeded to reconsider the joint resolution (H. J. Res. 542) entitled "Joint resolution concerning the war powers of Congress and the President," returned by the President of the United States with his objections to the House of Representatives, in which it originated, it was

Resolved, That the said joint resolution pass, two-thirds of the Senators present having voted in the affirmative.

Attest:

FRANCIS R. VALEO

Secretary.

Source: The Avalon Project at Yale Law School. http://www.yale.edu/lawweb/avalon/warpower.htm

VETO OF WAR POWERS RESOLUTION (1973)

The President's Message to the House of Representatives Returning H.J. Res. 542 Without His Approval. October 24, 1973.

To the House of Representatives:

I hereby return without my approval House Joint Resolution 542—the War Powers Resolution. While I am in accord with the desire of the Congress to assert its proper role in the conduct of our foreign affairs, the restrictions which this resolution would impose upon the authority of the President are both unconstitutional and dangerous to the best interests of our Nation.

The proper roles of the Congress and the Executive in the conduct of foreign affairs have been debated since the founding of our country. Only recently, however, has there been a serious challenge to the wisdom of the Founding Fathers in choosing not to draw a precise and detailed line of demarcation between the foreign policy powers of the two branches.

The Founding Fathers understood the impossibility of foreseeing every contingency that might arise in this complex area. They acknowledged the need for flexibility in responding to changing circumstances. They recognized that foreign policy decisions must be made through close cooperation between the two branches and not through rigidly codified procedures.

These principles remain as valid today as they were when our Constitution was written. Yet House Joint Resolution 542 would violate those principles by defining the President's powers in ways which would strictly limit his constitutional authority.

Clearly Unconstitutional

House Joint Resolution 542 would attempt to take away, by a mere legislative act, authorities which the President has properly exercised under the Constitution for almost 200 years. One of its provisions would automatically cut off certain authorities after sixty days unless the Congress extended them. Another would allow the Congress to eliminate certain authorities merely by the passage of a concurrent resolution—an action which does not normally have the force of law, since it denies the President his constitutional role in approving legislation.

I believe that both these provisions are unconstitutional. The only way in which the constitutional powers of a branch of the Government can be altered is by amending the Constitution—and any attempt to make such alterations by legislation alone is clearly without force.

Undermining Our Foreign Policy

While I firmly believe that a veto of House Joint Resolution 542 is warranted solely on constitutional grounds, I am also deeply disturbed by the practical consequences of this resolution. For it would seriously undermine this Nation's ability to act decisively and convincingly in times of international crisis. As a result, the confidence of our allies in our ability to assist them could be diminished and the respect of our adversaries for our deterrent posture could decline. A permanent and substantial element of unpredictability would be injected into the world's assessment of American behavior, further increasing the likelihood of miscalculation and war.

If this resolution had been in operation, America's effective response to a variety of challenges in recent years would have been vastly complicated or even made impossible. We may well have been unable to respond in the way we did during the Berlin crisis of 1961, the Cuban missile crisis of 1962, the Congo rescue operation in 1964, and the Jordanian crisis of 1970—to mention just a few examples. In addition, our recent actions to bring about a peaceful settlement of the hostilities in the Middle East would have been seriously impaired if this resolution had been in force.

While all the specific consequences of House Joint Resolution 542 cannot yet be predicted, it is clear that it would undercut the ability of the United States to act as an effective influence for peace. For example, the provision automatically cutting off certain authorities after 60 days unless they are extended by the Congress could work to prolong or intensify a crisis. Until the Congress suspended the deadline, there would be at least a chance of United States withdrawal and an adversary would be tempted therefore to postpone serious negotiations until the 60 days were up. Only after the Congress acted would there be a strong incentive for an adversary to negotiate. In addition, the very existence of a deadline could lead to an escalation of hostilities in order to achieve certain objectives before the 60 days expired.

The measure would jeopardize our role as a force for peace in other ways as well. It would, for example, strike from the President's hand a wide range of important peace-keeping tools by eliminating his ability to exercise quiet diplomacy backed by subtle shifts in our military deployments. It would also cast into doubt authorities which Presidents have used to undertake certain humanitarian relief missions in conflict areas, to protect fishing boats from seizure, to deal with ship or aircraft hijackings, and to respond to threats of attack. Not the least of the adverse consequences of this resolution would be the prohibition contained in section 8 against fulfilling our obligations under the NATO treaty as ratified by the Senate. Finally, since the bill is somewhat vague as to when the 60 day rule would apply, it could lead to extreme confusion and dangerous disagreements concerning the prerogatives of the two branches, seriously damaging our ability to respond to international crises.

Failure to Require Positive Congressional Action

I am particularly disturbed by the fact that certain of the President's constitutional powers as Commander in Chief of the Armed Forces would terminate automatically under this resolution 60 days after they were invoked. No overt Congressional action would be required to cut off these powers—they would disappear automatically unless the Congress extended them. In effect, the Congress is here attempting to increase its policy-making role through a provision which requires it to take absolutely no action at all.

In my view, the proper way for the Congress to make known its will on such foreign policy questions is through a positive action, with full debate on the merits of the issue and with each member taking the responsibility of casting a yes or no vote after considering those merits. The authorization and appropriations process represents one of the ways in which such influence can be exercised. I do not, however, believe that the Congress can responsibly contribute its considered, collective judgment on such grave questions without full debate and without a yes or no vote. Yet this is precisely what the joint resolution would allow. It would give every future Congress the ability to handcuff every future President merely by doing nothing and sitting still. In my view, one cannot become a responsible partner unless one is prepared to take responsible action.

Strengthening Cooperation Between the Congress and the Executive Branches

The responsible and effective exercise of the war powers requires the fullest cooperation between the Congress and the Executive and the prudent fulfillment by each branch of its constitutional responsibilities. House Joint Resolution 542 includes certain constructive measures which would foster this process by enhancing the flow of information from the executive branch to the Congress. Section 3, for example, calls for consultations with the Congress before and during the involvement of the United States forces in hostilities abroad. This provision is consistent with the desire of this

Administration for regularized consultations with the Congress in an even wider range of circumstances.

I believe that full and cooperative participation in foreign policy matters by both the executive and the legislative branches could be enhanced by a careful and dispassionate study of their constitutional roles. Helpful proposals for such a study have already been made in the Congress. I would welcome the establishment of a non-partisan commission on the constitutional roles of the Congress and the President in the conduct of foreign affairs. This commission could make a thorough review of the principal constitutional issues in Executive-Congressional relations, including the war powers, the international agreement powers, and the question of Executive privilege, and then submit its recommendations to the President and the Congress. The members of such a commission could be drawn from both parties—and could represent many perspectives including those of the Congress, the executive branch, the legal profession, and the academic community.

This Administration is dedicated to strengthening cooperation between the Congress and the President in the conduct of foreign affairs and to preserving the constitutional prerogatives of both branches of our Government. I know that the Congress shares that goal. A commission on the constitutional roles of the Congress and the President would provide a useful opportunity for both branches to work together toward that common objective.

RICHARD NIXON

The White House,
October 24, 1973.
Source: The American Presidency Project. http://www.presidency.ucsb.edu/ws/index.php?pid=4021

ARTICLES OF IMPEACHMENT OF PRESIDENT NIXON (1974)

Passed in the light of the Watergate scandal, probably no other attempt to impeach a United States president was as well founded. Accused of obstruction of justice, misuse of power, and contempt of Congress, Nixon would probably have been found guilty and removed from office, but he resigned in August 1974. The Nixon impeachment proceedings were characterized by less rancor than the previous impeachment of Andrew Johnson and the subsequent impeachment of Bill Clinton.

Article 1
RESOLVED, That Richard M. Nixon, President of the United States, is impeached for high crimes and misdemeanours, and that the following articles of impeachment to be exhibited to the Senate:
ARTICLES OF IMPEACHMENT EXHIBITED BY THE HOUSE OF REPRESENTATIVES OF THE UNITED STATES OF AMERICA IN THE NAME OF ITSELF AND OF ALL OF THE PEOPLE OF THE UNITED STATES OF AMERICA, AGAINST RICHARD

M. NIXON, PRESIDENT OF THE UNITED STATES OF AMERICA, IN MAINTE-NANCE AND SUPPORT OF ITS IMPEACHMENT AGAINST HIM FOR HIGH CRIMES AND MISDEMEANOURS.

ARTICLE 1

In his conduct of the office of President of the United States, Richard M. Nixon, in violation of his constitutional oath faithfully to execute the office of President of the United States and, to the best of his ability, preserve, protect, and defend the Constitution of the United States, and in violation of his consitutional [sic] duty to take care that the laws be faithfully executed, has prevented, obstructed, and impeded the administration of justice, in that:

On June 17, 1972, and prior thereto, agents of the Committee for the Re-election of the President committed unlawful entry of the headquarters of the Democratic National Committee in Washington, District of Columbia, for the purpose of securing political intelligence. Subsequent thereto, Richard M. Nixon, using the powers of his high office, engaged personally and through his close subordinates and agents, in a course of conduct or plan designed to delay, impede, and obstruct the investigation of such illegal entry; to cover up, conceal and protect those responsible; and to conceal the existence and scope of other unlawful covert activities.

The means used to implement this course of conduct or plan included one or more of the following:

(1) Making or causing to be made false or misleading statements to lawfully authorized investigative officers and employes of the United States.

(2) Withholding relevant and material evidence or information from lawfully authorized investigative officers and employes of the United States.

(3) Approving, condoning, acquiescing in, and counseling witnesses with respect to the giving of false or misleading statements to lawfully authorized investigative officers and employes of the United States and false or misleading testimony in duly instituted judicial and congressional proceedings.

(4) Interfering or endeavoring to interfere with the conduct of investigations by the Department of Justice of the United States, the Federal Bureau of Investigation, the office of Watergate Special Prosecution Force and congressional committees.

(5) Approving, condoning, and acquiescing in, the surreptitious payments of substantial sums of money for the purpose of obtaining the silence or influencing the testimony of witnesses, potential witnesses or individuals who participated in such unlawful entry and other illegal activities.

(6) Endeavoring to misuse the Central Intelligence Agency, an agency of the United States.

(7) Disseminating information received from officers of the Department of Justice of the United States to subjects of investigations conducted by lawfully authorized investigative officers and employes of the United States for the purpose of aiding and assisting such subjects in their attempts to avoid criminal liability.

(8) Making false or misleading public statements for the purpose of deceiving the people of the United States into believing that a thorough and complete investigation has been conducted with respect to allegation of misconduct on the part of personnel of the Executive Branch of the United States and personnel of the Committee for the Re-Election of the President, and that there was no involvement of such personnel in such misconduct; or

(9) Endeavoring to cause prospective defendants, and individuals duly tried and convicted, to expect favored treatment and consideration in return for their silence or false testimony, or rewarding individuals for their silence or false testimony.

In all of this, Richard M. Nixon has acted in a manner contrary to his trust as President and subversive of constitutional government, to the great prejudice of the cause of law and justice and to the manifest injury of the people of the United States.

Wherefore Richard M. Nixon, by such conduct, warrants impeachment and trial, and removal from office.

(Approved by a vote of 27-11 by the House Judiciary Committee on Saturday, July 27, 1974.)

Article 2: Abuse of Power

Using the powers of the office of President of the United States, Richard M. Nixon, in violation of his constitutional oath faithfully to execute the office of President of the United States and, to the best of his ability, preserve, protect, and defend the Constitution of the United States, and in disregard of his constitutional duty to take care that the laws be faithfully executed, has repeatedly engaged in conduct violating the constitutional rights of citizens, impairing the due and proper administration of justice and the conduct of lawful inquiries, or contravening the laws governing agencies of the executive branch and the purposed of these agencies.

This conduct has included one or more of the following:

(1) He has, acting personally and through his subordinated and agents, endeavored to obtain from the Internal Revenue Service, in violation of the constitutional rights of citizens, confidential information contained in income tax returns for purposes not authorized by law, and to cause, in violation of the constitutional rights of citizens, income tax audits or other income tax investigation to be initiated or conducted in a discriminatory manner.

(2) He misused the Federal Bureau of Investigation, the Secret Service, and other executive personnel, in violation or disregard of the constitutional rights of citizens, by directing or authorizing such agencies or personnel to conduct or continue electronic surveillance or other investigations for purposes unrelated to national security, the enforcement of laws, or any other lawful function of his office; he did direct, authorize, or permit the use of information obtained thereby for purposes unrelated to national security, the enforcement of laws, or any other lawful function of his office; and he did direct the concealment of certain records made by the Federal Bureau of Investigation of electronic surveillance.

(3) He has, acting personally and through his subordinates and agents, in violation or disregard of the constitutional rights of citizens, authorized and permitted to be maintained a secret investigative unit within the office of the President, financed in part with money derived from campaign contributions to him, which unlawfully utilized the resources of the Central Intelligence Agency, engaged in covert and unlawful activities, and attempted to prejudice the constitutional right of an accused to a fair trial.

(4) He has failed to take care that the laws were faithfully executed by failing to act when he knew or had reason to know that his close subordinates endeavored to impede and frustrate lawful inquiries by duly constituted executive, judicial and legislative entities concerning the unlawful entry into the headquarters of the Democratic National Committee, and the cover-up thereof, and concerning other unlawful activities including those relating to the confirmation of Richard Kleindienst as attorney general of the United States, the electronic surveillance of private citizens, the break-in into the office of Dr. Lewis Fielding, and the campaign financing practices of the Committee to Re-elect the President.

(5) In disregard of the rule of law: he knowingly misused the executive power by interfering with agencies of the executive branch: including the Federal Bureau of Investigation, the Criminal Division and the Office of Watergate Special Prosecution Force of the Department of Justice, in violation of his duty to take care that the laws be faithfully executed.

In all of this, Richard M. Nixon has acted in a manner contrary to his trust as President and subversive of constitutional government, to the great prejudice of the cause of law and justice and to the manifest injury of the people of the United States.

Wherefore Richard M. Nixon, by such conduct, warrants impeachment and trial, and removal from office.

(Approved 28-10 by the House Judiciary Committee on Monday, July 29, 1974.)

Article 3

In his conduct of the office of President of the United States, Richard M. Nixon, contrary to his oath faithfully to execute the office of President of the United States and, to the best of his ability, preserve, protect, and defend the Constitution of the United States, and in violation of his constitutional duty to take care that the laws be faithfully executed, has failed without lawful cause or excuse to produce papers and things as directed by duly authorized subpoenas issued by the Committee on the Judiciary of the House of Representatives on April 11, 1974, May 15, 1974, May 30, 1974, and June 24, 1974, and willfully disobeyed such subpoenas. The subpoenaed papers and things were deemed necessary by the Committee in order to resolve by direct evidence fundamental, factual questions relating to Presidential direction, knowledge or approval of actions demonstrated by other evidence to be substantial grounds for impeachment of the President. In refusing to produce these papers and things Richard M. Nixon, substituting his judgment as to what materials were necessary for the inquiry, interposed the powers of the Presidency against the the lawful subpoenas of the House of Representatives, thereby assuming to himself functions and judgments necessary to the exercise of the sole power of impeachment vested by the Constitution in the House of Representatives.

In all of this, Richard M. Nixon has acted in a manner contrary to his trust as President and subversive of constitutional government, to the great prejudice of the cause of law and justice, and to the manifest injury of the people of the United States.

Wherefore, Richard M. Nixon, by such conduct, warrants impeachment and trial, and removal from office.

(Approved 21-17 by the House Judiciary Committee on Tuesday, July 30, 1974.)

Source: The History Place. http://www.historyplace.com/unitedstates/impeach ments/nixon.htm

CROCKETT V. REAGAN (1982)

An attempt to enforce the War Powers Resolution and deny President Reagan the authority to send fifty-six military advisers to El Salvador. Led by Michigan representative George W. Crockett Jr., more than a dozen members of Congress sued the president in federal court. The District Court refused to rule, asserting that the issue was a political one and that the court was unable or unequipped to make military and/or foreign policy determinations. The fact-finding necessary for the court to render such a decision was not possible.

MEMORANDUM OPINION AND ORDER

JOYCE HENS GREEN, District Judge.

This case was brought by 29 Members of Congress against Ronald Reagan, individually and in his capacity as President of the United States. . . . Plaintiffs have alleged that defendants have supplied military equipment and aid to the government of El Salvador in violation of the War Powers Clause of the Constitution, the War Powers Resolution, and Section 502B of the Foreign Assistance Act of 1961, 22 U.S.C. § 2304. . . . According to the complaint, in addition to the provision of monetary aid and military equipment, the defendants have dispatched at least 56 members of the United States Armed Forces to El Salvador in aid of the Junta. These forces allegedly are in situations where imminent involvement in hostilities is clearly indicated by the circumstances, and are allegedly taking part in the war effort and assisting in planning operations against the FMLN. . . . Plaintiffs claim that this involvement violates Article 1, Section 8, Clause 11 of the Constitution, granting to Congress the exclusive power to declare war, as implemented by the War Powers Resolution (WPR). The WPR requires that absent a declaration of war, a report be made to the Congress within 48 hours of any time when United States Armed Forces have been introduced into hostilities or into situations where imminent involvement in hostilities is clearly indicated by the circumstances, . . . and that 60 days after a report is submitted or is required to be submitted, the President shall terminate any use of United States Armed Forces unless Congress declares war, enacts a specific authorization for such use of United States Armed Forces, or extends the 60-day period for 30 additional days. No report pursuant to the WPR has been made, and American forces have remained more than 60 days since they allegedly were introduced into a situation of hostilities or imminent hostilities without a declaration of war. . . .

If the merits were reached, the Court would have to decide whether the Resolution is applicable to the American military presence in El Salvador, and if so, what remedial action is appropriate. The Court decides that the cause of action under the WPR in its present posture is non-justiciable because of the nature of the factfinding that would be required, and that the 60-day automatic termination provision is not operative unless a report has been submitted or required to be submitted by Congress or a court.

Although defendants have not emphasized the factual issues, which need not be reached if their motion to dismiss is granted, their pleadings and exhibits do make clear that the position of the government is that the factual circumstances in El Salvador do not trigger the WPR, that is, U.S. Armed Forces have not been "introduced into hostilities or into situations where imminent involvement in hostilities is clearly indicated by the circumstances." Plaintiffs present a significantly different picture of what is actually occurring in El Salvador, and the relationship of U.S. military personnel to it. Although consideration of the merits might reveal disagreements about the meaning of WPR terms such as "imminent involvement in hostilities," the most striking feature of the pleadings at this stage of the case is the discrepancy as to the facts. . . .

Plaintiffs contend that American military personnel in El Salvador are taking part in coordinating the war effort and are assisting in planning specific operations against the FMLN. Also, many of the 56 military personnel are alleged to work in and around areas where there is heavy combat. . . .

More recently, plaintiffs have supplemented their pleadings to bolster their contention that American forces in El Salvador have been introduced into hostilities or imminent hostilities. They rely upon two news articles. The first is to the effect that U.S. Armed Forces are "fighting side by side" with government troops battling against the FMLN. The second concerns a General Accounting Office (GAO) report which reportedly disclosed that U.S. Military personnel in El Salvador are drawing "hostile fire pay," and that a tentative Pentagon ruling that all of El Salvador qualified as a "hostile fire area" was reversed for "policy reasons," possibly to avoid the necessity of reporting to Congress under the WPR. (The actual GPO report has not been submitted.)

In sum, if plaintiffs' allegations are correct, the executive branch does not merely have a different view of the application of the WPR to the facts, but also is distorting the reality of our involvement in El Salvador. This discrepancy as to factual matters is also evident in the contrast between plaintiffs' allegations regarding the human rights situation in El Salvador, and the President's certifications under the Foreign Assistance Act, discussed *infra*. Plaintiffs' allegations, which are to be accepted as true for the purpose of a motion to dismiss, are, at a minimum, disturbing. This nonetheless does not mean that judicial resolution is appropriate to vindicate, allay or obviate plaintiffs' concerns.

The Court concludes that the factfinding that would be necessary to determine whether U.S. forces have been introduced into hostilities or imminent hostilities in El Salvador renders this case in its current posture non-justiciable. The questions as to the nature and extent of the United States' presence in El Salvador and whether a report under the WPR is mandated because our forces have been subject to hostile fire or are taking part in the war effort are appropriate for congressional, not judicial, investigation and determination. Further, in order to determine the application of the 60-day provision, the Court would be required to decide at exactly what point in time U.S. forces had been introduced into hostilities or imminent hostilities, and whether that situation continues to exist. This inquiry would be even more inappropriate for the judiciary.

In *Baker v. Carr* (1962), Justice Brennan identified several categories of "political questions". The question here belongs to the category characterized by a lack of judicially discoverable and manageable standards for resolution. The Court disagrees with defendants that this is the type of political question which involves potential judicial interference with executive discretion in the foreign affairs field. Plaintiffs do not seek relief that would dictate foreign policy but rather to enforce existing law concerning the procedures for decision-making. Moreover, the issue here is not a political question simply because it involves the apportionment of power between the executive and legislative branches. The duty of courts to decide such questions has been repeatedly reaffirmed by the Supreme Court. . . .

However, the question presented does require judicial inquiry into sensitive military matters. Even if the plaintiffs could introduce admissible evidence concerning the state of hostilities in various geographical areas in El Salvador where U.S. forces are stationed and the exact nature of U.S. participation in the conflict (and this information may well be unavailable except through inadmissible newspaper articles), the Court no doubt would be presented conflicting evidence on those issues by defendants. The Court lacks the resources and expertise (which are accessible to the Congress) to resolve disputed questions of fact concerning the military situation in El Salvador. . . .

Admittedly, a case could arise with facts less elusive than these. For example, this Circuit in *Mitchell v. Laird* (D.C. Cir.1973), held that the court could determine the truth of allegations to the effect that the United States had been involved in hostilities in Indo-China for at least seven years, which hostilities had resulted in one million deaths, including those of 50,000 Americans, and for which the United States had spent at least one hundred billion dollars. If such allegations were true, the court stated, it would conclude that the United States was at war in Indo-China. Were a court asked to declare that the War Powers Resolution was applicable to a situation like that in Vietnam, it would be absurd for it to decline to find that U.S. forces had been introduced into hostilities after 50,000 American lives had been lost. However, here the Court faces a dispute as to whether a small number of American military personnel who apparently have suffered no casualties have been introduced into hostilities or imminent hostilities. The subtleties of factfinding in this situation should be left to the political branches. If Congress doubts or disagrees with the Executive's determination that U.S. forces in El Salvador have not been introduced into hostilities or imminent hostilities, it has the resources to investigate the matter and assert its wishes. The Court need not decide here what type of congressional statement or action would constitute an official congressional stance that our involvement in El Salvador is subject to the WPR, because Congress has taken absolutely no action that could be interpreted to have that effect. Certainly, were Congress to pass a resolution to the effect that a report was required under the WPR, or to the effect that the forces should be withdrawn, and the President disregarded it, a constitutional impasse appropriate for judicial resolution would be presented.

Even if the factfinding here did not require resolution of a political question, this Court would not order withdrawal of U.S. forces at this juncture. At most, it could order that a report be filed. This conclusion is based upon the structure and legislative history of the WPR.

The War Powers Resolution, which was considered and enacted as the Vietnam war was coming to an end, was intended to prevent another situation in which a President could gradually build up American involvement in a foreign war without congressional knowledge or approval, eventually presenting Congress with a full-blown undeclared war which on a practical level it was powerless to stop. While Congress always had the power to deny appropriations supporting a military engagement, it found it politically impossible to do so after large numbers of American lives had been placed at risk and American honor committed. The purpose of the WPR was to give Congress both the knowledge and the mechanism needed to reclaim its constitutional power to declare war. In the words of Senator Javits, one of its authors and prime sponsors, the Resolution is an effort to learn from the lessons of the last tragic decade of war in Vietnam which has cost our nation so heavily in blood, treasure, and morale. The War Powers Act would assure that any future decision to commit the United States to any warmaking must be shared in by the Congress to be lawful.

So that Congress would be informed at the outset of any involvement that could potentially lead to war, the Resolution provides for prior consultation (not at issue here), and early reporting whenever any American troops are introduced into a situation of hostilities, or even imminent hostilities, on the President's initiative and without a declaration of war. The President is not to wait until our forces are actually engaged in combat before informing Congress. Further, the automatic cutoff after 60 days was intended to place the burden on the President to seek positive approval from the Congress, rather than to require the Congress positively to disapprove the action, which had proven so politically difficult during the Vietnam war. To give force to congressional power to declare war, Presidential warmaking would not be justified by congressional silence, but only by a congressional initiative to "declare war." Again in Senator Javits' words, "The approach taken in the War Powers Bill reverses the situation by placing the burden on the Executive to come to Congress for specific authority. The sponsors of the Bill believe that this provision [the 60-day automatic cutoff] will provide an important national safeguard against creeping involvement in future Vietnam style wars." . . .

Plaintiffs contend that the Resolution is fully self-executing, designed as it is to prevent involvement in military actions without positive action by Congress. When U.S. forces are introduced into hostilities or a situation of imminent hostilities, the reporting requirement automatically comes into play, and the President violates the law if he does not make the mandated report. Further, whether or not he makes the report, the 60-day period begins to run from the time the report should have been submitted. . . . Thus, according to the plaintiffs, after 62 days (60 days plus the 48 hours before a report is required), whether or not a report has been made, the President is required to withdraw the Armed Forces if Congress has not declared war or enacted a specific authorization for the action. Plaintiffs contend that a court may find the facts as to whether the situation into which American forces have been introduced constitutes hostilities or imminent hostilities, and if it so finds, it may order the President to make the report or to withdraw the forces.

Defendants do not dispute the interpretation of the basic purpose of the WPR presented here and emphasized by plaintiffs. However, they deny that it is self-executing in a situation where a report has not been submitted. They argue that the decision as to whether a situation warrants a report under the WPR is left to the President's discretion in the first instance. In their view, his failure to submit a report does not justify a court action, and the 60-day period does not begin to run from the time he assertedly should have filed the report. Rather, in instances of disagreement between the President and Congress as to whether a report is required, a "second trigger" is needed to bring the WPR into play. Congress must either take action to express its view that the WPR is applicable to the situation and that a report is required, or, if it desires immediate withdrawal of forces, pass a concurrent resolution directing removal of the forces pursuant to § 5(c) of the WPR, 50 U.S.C. § 1544(c). . . .

The Court finds that the legislative scheme did not contemplate court-ordered withdrawal when no report has been filed, but rather, it leaves open the possibility for a court to order that a report be filed or, alternatively, withdrawal 60 days after a report was filed or required to be filed by a court or Congress. The legislative scheme was carefully designed to force congressional consideration of American military involvement abroad once a report is filed. The priority procedures of Section 6 of the Act, assure that a bill or resolution introduced to approve military involvement which has been the subject of a WPR report will be promptly considered by both houses of Congress. Accordingly, while the involvement will automatically terminate after 60 days if either house fails to act or if the two houses are unable to reach an agreement, this can only occur after open and formal consideration of the question by both full houses, provided that at least one member of either house introduces a bill or resolution. In contrast, when no report has been submitted, there will not necessarily be any debate or floor consideration of the issue at all. If plaintiffs' position is correct, total congressional inaction (which perhaps could signify general agreement with the President's appraisal that no report is required) could result in mandatory withdrawal of U.S. forces if a court adjudged that they had been introduced into hostilities or imminent hostilities more than 60 days previously. In all of the extensive debate on the mandatory withdrawal provision, this possibility was never entertained. In fact, Congressman Zablocki, Chairman of the Foreign Affairs Subcommittee on National Security Policy and Scientific Developments which reported out the bill, clearly stated that mandatory withdrawal would not come about without congressional action. Congress would be actively involved in considering legislation either approving or disapproving the President's action virtually as soon as it was introduced, and the ability of any one of the 535 members to trigger the priority procedures would assure that the question came to an eventual up or down vote. Congress would be well aware that if it failed to specifically authorize the involvement, it would terminate after 60 days. However, in a situation where no report has been filed, and the priority procedures would not be invoked, the majority of Congress might not be of the opinion that a specific authorization is necessary for continued involvement and take no action, unaware that this course would result in mandatory withdrawal. In that instance court-ordered withdrawal could thwart the will of the majority of Congress. Therefore, when a report has not been filed, it is consistent with the purposes and structure of the WPR to require further congressional action before the automatic termination provision operates.

The requirement to file a report, however, is a different matter. The mere filing of a report cannot thwart congressional will, but can only supply information to aid congressional decisionmaking. Although the Court need not reach the question because the nature of the factfinding in these circumstances precludes judicial inquiry, it does not foreclose the possibility of a court determination that a report is required under the WPR. If, hypothetically, a court did order a report under the WPR, Congress would then have 60 days to give the matter its full consideration in accordance with the priority procedures of the Resolution before withdrawal would be automatically required. Likewise, if Congress itself requires a report, the 60 days for consideration of whether or not to authorize the action would begin at that point. Of course, Congress can always order immediate withdrawal if it so chooses.

The arguments discussed above convince the Court that the cause must be dismissed. Therefore, it is unnecessary to reach the other asserted bases for dismissal, which include standing, equitable discretion and lack of a private right of action. As already stated, the Court does not decide that all disputes under the War Powers Resolution would be inappropriate for judicial resolution.

IMMIGRATION AND NATURALIZATION SERVICE V. CHADHA ET AL. (1983)

An immigration judge suspended an alien's deportation under the Immigration and Nationality Act. The act gave one house of Congress the authority to overrule a decision by the executive branch to allow a deportable alien to stay in the United States. The immigration judge, following the orders of the House, reopened the deportation proceedings and ordered Chadha deported. The Board of Immigration Appeals dismissed his appeal, holding that it had no power to declare an act of Congress unconstitutional. The Supreme Court held that one-house legislative vetoes are unconstitutional. It focused on separation of powers and the Constitution's requirement of bicameralism and presentment.

CHIEF JUSTICE BURGER delivered the opinion of the Court.

. . . It is also argued that these cases present a nonjusticiable political question because Chadha is merely challenging Congress' authority under the Naturalization Clause, U.S. Const., Art. I, § 8, cl. 4, and the Necessary and Proper Clause, U.S. Const., Art. I, § 8, cl. 18. It is argued that Congress' Art. I power "To establish an uniform Rule of Naturalization," combined with the Necessary and Proper Clause, grants it unreviewable authority over the regulation of aliens. The plenary authority of Congress over aliens under Art. I, § 8, cl. 4, is not open to question, but what is challenged here is whether Congress has chosen a constitutionally permissible means of implementing that power . . . so long as the exercise of that authority does not offend some other constitutional restriction."

A brief review of those factors which may indicate the presence of a nonjusticiable political question satisfies us that our assertion of jurisdiction over these cases does no violence to the political question doctrine. . . .

It is correct that this controversy may, in a sense, be termed "political." But the presence of constitutional issues with significant political overtones does not automatically invoke the political question doctrine. Resolution of litigation challenging the constitutional authority of one of the three branches cannot be evaded by courts because the issues have political implications in the sense urged by Congress. *Marbury* v. *Madison*, was also a "political" case, involving as it did claims under a judicial commission alleged to have been duly signed by the President but not delivered. But "courts cannot reject as 'no law suit' a bona fide controversy as to whether some action denominated 'political' exceeds constitutional authority." *Baker* v. *Carr*, *supra*. . . .

The contentions on standing and justiciability have been fully examined, and we are satisfied the parties are properly before us. The important issues have been fully briefed and [*944] twice argued. . . . The Court's duty in these cases, as Chief Justice Marshall declared in *Cohens* v. *Virginia* is clear:

"Questions may occur which we would gladly avoid; but we cannot avoid them. All we can do is, to exercise our best judgment, and conscientiously to perform our duty."
. . .

III

A

We turn now to the question whether action of one House of Congress under § 244(c)(2) violates strictures of the Constitution. We begin, of course, with the presumption that the challenged statute is valid. Its wisdom is not the concern of the courts; if a challenged action does not violate the Constitution, it must be sustained. . .

By the same token, the fact that a given law or procedure is efficient, convenient, and useful in facilitating functions of government, standing alone, will not save it if it is contrary to the Constitution. Convenience and efficiency are not the primary objectives—or the hallmarks—of democratic government and our inquiry is sharpened rather than blunted by the fact that congressional veto provisions are appearing with increasing frequency in statutes which delegate authority to executive and independent agencies. . . .

JUSTICE WHITE undertakes to make a case for the proposition that the one-House veto is a useful "political invention," and we need not challenge that assertion. We can even concede this utilitarian argument although the long-range political wisdom of this "invention" is arguable. It has been vigorously debated, and it is instructive to compare the views of the protagonists. . . . But policy arguments supporting even useful "political inventions" are subject to the demands of the Constitution which defines powers and, with respect to this subject, sets out just how those powers are to be exercised.

Explicit and unambiguous provisions of the Constitution prescribe and define the respective functions of the Congress and of the Executive in the legislative process. Since the precise terms of those familiar provisions are critical to the resolution of these cases, we set them out verbatim. Article I provides:

"All legislative Powers herein granted shall be vested in a Congress of the United States, which shall consist of a Senate *and* House of Representatives." Art. I, § 1. (Emphasis added.)

"Every Bill which shall have passed the House of Representatives *and* the Senate, *shall*, before it becomes a law, be presented to the President of the United States . . . ." Art. I, § 7, cl. 2. (Emphasis added.)

"*Every* Order, Resolution, or Vote to which the Concurrence of the Senate and House of Representatives may be necessary (except on a question of Adjournment) [*946] *shall be* presented to the President of the United States; and before the Same shall take Effect, *shall be* approved by him, or being disapproved by him, *shall be* repassed by two thirds of the Senate and House of Representatives, according to the Rules and Limitations prescribed in the Case of a Bill." Art. I, § 7, cl. 3. (Emphasis added.)

These provisions of Art. I are integral parts of the constitutional design for the separation of powers. We have recently noted that "[the] principle of separation of powers was not simply an abstract generalization in the minds of the Framers: it was woven into the document that they drafted in Philadelphia in the summer of 1787." . . . Just as we relied on the textual provision of Art. II, § 2, cl. 2, to vindicate the principle of separation of powers in *Buckley*, we see that the purposes underlying the Presentment Clauses, Art. I, § 7, cls. 2, 3, and the bicameral requirement of Art. I, § 1, and § 7, cl. 2, guide our resolution of the important question presented in these cases. The very structure of the Articles delegating and separating powers under Arts. I, II, and III exemplifies the concept of separation of powers, and we now turn to Art. I.

B

The Presentment Clauses

The records of the Constitutional Convention reveal that the requirement that all legislation be presented to the President before becoming law was uniformly accepted by the Framers. n14 Presentment to the President and the Presidential veto were considered so imperative that the draftsmen took special pains to assure that these requirements could not be circumvented. . . .

The decision to provide the President with a limited and qualified power to nullify proposed legislation by veto was based on the profound conviction of the Framers that the powers conferred on Congress were the powers to be most carefully circumscribed. It is beyond doubt that lawmaking was a power to be shared by both Houses and the President. . . .

The President's role in the lawmaking process also reflects the Framers' careful efforts to check whatever propensity a particular Congress might have to enact oppressive, improvident, or ill-considered measures. The President's veto role in the legislative process was described later during public debate on ratification. . . .

We see therefore that the Framers were acutely conscious that the bicameral requirement and the Presentment Clauses would serve essential constitutional functions. The President's participation in the legislative process was to protect the Executive Branch from Congress and to protect the whole people from improvident laws. The division of the Congress into two distinctive bodies assures that the legislative power would be exercised only after opportunity for full study and debate in separate settings. The President's unilateral veto power, in turn, was limited by the power of two-thirds of both Houses of Congress to overrule a veto thereby precluding final arbitrary action of one person. It emerges clearly that the prescription for legislative action in Art. I, §§ 1, 7, represents the Framers' decision that the legislative power of the Federal Government be exercised in accord with a single, finely wrought and exhaustively considered, procedure.

IV

The Constitution sought to divide the delegated powers of the new Federal Government into three defined categories, Legislative, Executive, and Judicial, to assure, as nearly as possible, that each branch of government would confine itself to its assigned responsibility. The hydraulic pressure inherent within each of the separate Branches to exceed the outer limits of its power, even to accomplish desirable objectives, must be resisted.

Although not "hermetically" sealed from one another . . . the powers delegated to the three Branches are functionally identifiable. When any Branch acts, it is presumptively exercising the power the Constitution has delegated to it. . . . When the Executive acts, he presumptively acts in an executive or administrative capacity as defined in Art. II. And when, as here, one House of Congress purports to act, it is presumptively acting within its assigned sphere.

Beginning with this presumption, we must nevertheless establish that the challenged action under § 244(c)(2) is of the kind to which the procedural requirements of Art. I, § 7, apply. Not every action taken by either House is subject to the bicameralism and presentment requirements of Art. I. Whether actions taken by either House are, in law and fact, an exercise of legislative power depends not on their form but upon "whether they contain matter which is properly to be regarded as legislative in its character and effect." S. Rep. No. 1335, 54th Cong., 2d Sess., 8 (1897).

Examination of the action taken here by one House pursuant to § 244(c)(2) reveals that it was essentially legislative in purpose and effect. In purporting to exercise power defined in Art. I, § 8, cl. 4, to "establish an uniform Rule of Naturalization," the House took action that had the purpose and effect of altering the legal rights, duties, and relations of persons, including the Attorney General, Executive Branch officials and Chadha, all outside the Legislative Branch. Section 244(c)(2) purports to authorize one House of Congress to require the Attorney General to deport an individual alien whose deportation otherwise would . . . be canceled under § 244. The one-House veto operated in these cases to overrule the Attorney General and mandate Chadha's deportation; absent the House action, Chadha would remain in the United States. Congress has *acted* and its action has altered Chadha's status. . . .

The nature of the decision implemented by the one-House veto in these cases further manifests its legislative character. After long experience with the clumsy, time-consuming private bill procedure, Congress made a deliberate choice to delegate to the Executive Branch, and specifically to the Attorney General, the authority to allow deportable aliens to remain in this country in certain specified circumstances. It is not disputed that this choice to delegate authority is precisely the kind of decision that can be implemented only in accordance with the procedures set out in Art. I. Disagreement with the Attorney General's decision on Chadha's deportation—that is, Congress' decision to deport Chadha—no less than Congress' original choice to delegate to the Attorney General the authority to make that decision, involves determinations of policy that Congress can implement in only one way; bicameral passage followed by presentment to the President. Congress must abide by its delegation of authority until that delegation is legislatively altered or revoked. . . .

Finally, we see that when the Framers intended to authorize either House of Congress to act alone and outside of its prescribed bicameral legislative role, they narrowly and precisely defined the procedure for such action. . . .

Since it is clear that the action by the House under § 244(c)(2) was not within any of the express constitutional exceptions authorizing one House to act alone, and equally clear that it was an exercise of legislative power, that action was subject to the standards prescribed in Art. I. n22 The bicameral requirement, the Presentment Clauses, the President's veto, and Congress' power to override a veto were intended to erect enduring checks on each Branch and to protect the people from the improvident exercise of power by mandating certain prescribed steps. To preserve those checks, and maintain the separation of powers, the carefully defined limits on the power of each Branch must not be eroded. To accomplish what has been attempted by one House of Congress in this case requires action in conformity with the express procedures of the Constitution's prescription for legislative action: passage by a majority of both Houses and presentment to the President. . . .

The veto authorized by § 244(c)(2) doubtless has been in many respects a convenient shortcut; the "sharing" with the Executive by Congress of its authority over aliens in this manner is, on its face, an appealing compromise. In purely practical terms, it is obviously easier for action to be taken by one House without submission to the President; but it is crystal . . . clear from the records of the Convention, contemporaneous writings and debates, that the Framers ranked other values higher than efficiency. The records of the Convention and debates in the States preceding ratification underscore the common desire to define and limit the exercise of the newly created federal powers affecting the states and the people. There is unmistakable expression of a determination that legislation by the national Congress be a step-by-step, deliberate and deliberative process.

The choices we discern as having been made in the Constitutional Convention impose burdens on governmental processes that often seem clumsy, inefficient, even unworkable, but those hard choices were consciously made by men who had lived under a form of government that permitted arbitrary governmental acts to go unchecked. There is no support in the Constitution or decisions of this Court for the proposition that the cumbersomeness and delays often encountered in complying with explicit constitutional standards may be avoided, either by the Congress or by the President. See *Youngstown Sheet & Tube Co.* v. *Sawyer*, 343 U.S. 579 (1952). With all the obvious flaws of delay, untidiness, and potential for abuse, we have not yet found a better way to preserve freedom than by making the exercise of power subject to the carefully crafted restraints spelled out in the Constitution. . . .

JUSTICE POWELL, concurring in the judgment.

The Court's decision, based on the Presentment Clauses, Art. I, § 7, cls. 2 and 3, apparently will invalidate every use of the legislative veto. The breadth of this holding gives one pause. Congress has included the veto in literally hundreds of statutes, dating back to the 1930's. Congress clearly views this procedure as essential to controlling the delegation of power to administrative agencies. One reasonably may disagree with Congress' assessment of the veto's utility, but the respect due its judgment as a coordinate branch of Government cautions that our holding should be no more extensive than necessary to decide these cases. In my view, the cases may be decided on a narrower ground. When Congress finds that a particular person does not satisfy the statutory criteria for permanent residence in this country it has assumed a judicial function in violation of the principle of separation of powers. Accordingly, I concur only in the judgment. . . .

Chief Justice Marshall observed: "It is the peculiar province of the legislature to prescribe general rules for the government of society; the application of those rules to individuals in society would seem to be the duty of other departments." *Fletcher* v. *Peck*, 6 Cranch 87, 136 (1810). In my view, when Congress undertook to apply its rules to Chadha, it exceeded the scope of its constitutionally prescribed authority. I would not reach the broader question whether legislative vetoes are invalid under the Presentment Clauses.

JUSTICE WHITE, dissenting.

Today the Court not only invalidates § 244(c)(2) of the Immigration and Nationality Act, but also sounds the death knell for nearly 200 other statutory provisions in which Congress has reserved a "legislative veto." For this reason, the Court's decision is of surpassing importance. And it is for this reason that the Court would have been well advised to decide the cases, if possible, on the narrower grounds of separation of powers, leaving for full consideration the constitutionality of other congressional review statutes operating on such varied matters as war powers and agency rulemaking, some of which concern the independent regulatory agencies. . . .

The prominence of the legislative veto mechanism in our contemporary political system and its importance to Congress can hardly be overstated. It has become a central means by which Congress secures the accountability of executive and independent agencies. Without the legislative veto, Congress is faced with a Hobson's choice: either to refrain from delegating the necessary authority, leaving itself with a hopeless task of writing laws with the requisite specificity to cover endless special circumstances across the entire policy landscape, or in the alternative, to abdicate its law-making function to the Executive Branch and independent agencies. To choose the former leaves major national problems unresolved; to opt for the latter risks unaccountable policymaking by those not elected to fill that role. Accordingly, over the past five decades, the legislative veto has been placed in nearly 200 statutes. The device is known in every field of governmental concern: reorganization, budgets, foreign affairs, war powers, and regulation of trade, safety, energy, the environment, and the economy. . . .

For all these reasons, the apparent sweep of the Court's decision today is regretable. The Court's Art. I analysis appears to invalidate all legislative vetoes irrespective of form or subject. Because the legislative veto is commonly found as a check upon rulemaking by administrative agencies and upon broad-based policy decisions of the Executive

Branch, it is particularly unfortunate that the Court reaches its decision in cases involving the exercise of a veto over deportation decisions regarding particular individuals. Courts should always be wary of striking statutes as unconstitutional; to strike an entire class of statutes based on consideration of a somewhat atypical and more readily indictable exemplar of the class is irresponsible. . . .

I do not suggest that all legislative vetoes are necessarily consistent with separation-of-powers principles. A legislative check on an inherently executive function, for example, that of initiating prosecutions, poses an entirely different question. But the legislative veto device here—and in many other settings—is far from an instance of legislative tyranny over the Executive. It is a necessary check on the unavoidably expanding power of the agencies, both Executive and independent, as they engage in exercising authority delegated by Congress.

I regret that I am in disagreement with my colleagues on the fundamental questions that these cases present. But even more I regret the destructive scope of the Court's holding. It reflects a profoundly different conception of the Constitution than that held by the courts which sanctioned the modern administrative state. Today's decision strikes down in one fell swoop provisions in more laws enacted by Congress than the Court has cumulatively invalidated in its history. I fear it will now be more difficult to "[insure] that the fundamental policy decisions in our society will be made not by an appointed official but by the body immediately responsible to the people," . . . I must dissent.

Source: Justia.com – US Supreme Court Center. http://supreme.justia.com/us/462/919/case.html

DELLUMS V. BUSH (1990)

Another challenge to the War Powers Resolution, this time in the context of the first Gulf War under George H. W. Bush. The Supreme Court granted that members of Congress had standing to sue in federal court over whether the president had authority to mobilize and send troops to the Gulf. However, because the troops were not at that point engaged in hostile action, and it was possible they might not engage, the case was not ripe. The issue became moot when Congress approved the insertion of troops to stop the Iraqi invasion of Kuwait.

Harold H. Greene, United States District Judge.

OPINION

This is a lawsuit by a number of members of Congress who request an injunction directed to the President of the United States to prevent him from initiating an offensive attack against Iraq without first securing a declaration of war or other explicit congressional authorization for such action.

The factual background is, briefly, as follows. On August 2, 1990, Iraq invaded the neighboring country of Kuwait. President George Bush almost immediately sent United

States military forces to the Persian Gulf area to deter Iraqi aggression and to preserve the integrity of Saudi Arabia. The United States, generally by presidential order and at times with congressional concurrence, also took other steps, including a blockade of Iraq, which were approved by the United Nations Security Council, and participated in by a great many other nations.

On November 8, 1990, President Bush announced a substantial increase in the Persian Gulf military deployment, raising the troop level significantly above the 230,000 then present in the area. At the same time, the President stated that the objective was to provide "an adequate *offensive* military option" should that be necessary to achieve such goals as the withdrawal of Iraqi forces from Kuwait. Secretary of Defense Richard Cheney likewise referred to the ability of the additional military forces "to conduct *offensive* military operations."

The House of Representatives and the Senate have in various ways expressed their support for the President's past and present actions in the Persian Gulf. However, the Congress was not asked for, and it did not take, action pursuant to Article I, Section 8, Clause 11 of the Constitution "to declare war" on Iraq. On November 19, 1990, the congressional plaintiffs brought this action, which proceeds on the premise that the initiation of offensive United States military action is imminent, that such action would be unlawful in the absence of a declaration of war by the Congress, and that a war without concurrence by the Congress would deprive the congressional plaintiffs of the voice to which they are entitled under the Constitution. . . .

It is appropriate first to sketch out briefly the constitutional and legal framework in which the current controversy arises. Article I, Section 8, Clause 11 of the Constitution grants to the Congress the power "To declare War." To the extent that this unambiguous direction requires construction or explanation, it is provided by the framers' comments that they felt it to be unwise to entrust the momentous power to involve the nation in a war to the President alone; Jefferson explained that he desired "an effectual check to the Dog of war"; James Wilson similarly expressed the expectation that this system would guard against hostilities being initiated by a single man. Even Abraham Lincoln, while a Congressman, said more than half a century later that "*no one man should hold the power of bringing*" war upon us.

The congressional power to declare war does not stand alone, however, but it is accompanied by powers granted to the President. Article II, Section 1, Clause 1 and Section 2 provide that "the executive powers shall be vested in a President of the United States of America," and that "the President shall be Commander in Chief of the Army and Navy. . . ."

It is the position of the Department of Justice on behalf of the President that the simultaneous existence of all these provisions renders it impossible to isolate the war-declaring power. The Department further argues that the design of the Constitution is to have the various war- and military-related provisions construed and acting together, and that their harmonization is a political rather than a legal question. In short, the Department relies on the political question doctrine.

That doctrine is premised both upon the separation of powers and the inherent limits of judicial abilities. . . . In relation to the issues involved in this case, the Department of Justice expands on its basic theme, contending that by their very nature the determination whether certain types of military actions require a declaration of war is not justiciable, but depends instead upon delicate judgments by the political branches. On that view, the question whether an offensive action taken by American armed forces constitutes an act of war (to be initiated by a declaration of war) or an "offensive military attack" (presumably undertaken by the President in his capacity as commander-in-chief) is not one of objective fact but involves an exercise of judgment based upon all the vagaries of foreign affairs and national security. . . . Indeed, the Department contends that there are no judicially discoverable and manageable standards to apply, claiming that only the political branches are able to determine whether or not this country is at war. Such a determination, it is said, is based upon "a political judgment" about the significance of those facts. Under that rationale, a court cannot make an independent determination on this issue because it cannot take adequate account of these political considerations.

This claim on behalf of the Executive is far too sweeping to be accepted by the courts. If the Executive had the sole power to determine that any particular offensive military operation, no matter how vast, does not constitute war-making but only an offensive military attack, the congressional power to declare war will be at the mercy of a semantic decision by the Executive. Such an "interpretation" would evade the plain language of the Constitution, and it cannot stand.

That is not to say that, assuming that the issue is factually close or ambiguous or fraught with intricate technical military and diplomatic baggage, the courts would not defer to the political branches to determine whether or not particular hostilities might qualify as a "war." However, here the forces involved are of such magnitude and significance as to present no serious claim that a war would not ensue if they became engaged in combat, and it is therefore clear that congressional approval is required if Congress desires to become involved. . . .

Notwithstanding these relatively straightforward propositions, the Department goes on to suggest that the issue in this case is still political rather than legal, because in order to resolve the dispute the Court would have to inject itself into foreign affairs, a subject which the Constitution commits to the political branches. That argument, too, must fail.

While the Constitution grants to the political branches, and in particular to the Executive, responsibility for conducting the nation's foreign affairs, it does not follow that the judicial power is excluded from the resolution of cases merely because they may touch upon such affairs. The court must instead look at "the particular question posed" in the case. . . . In fact, courts are routinely deciding cases that touch upon or even have a substantial impact on foreign and defense policy. . . .

The Department's argument also ignores the fact that courts have historically made determinations about whether this country was at war for many other purposes—the construction of treaties, statutes, and even insurance contracts. These judicial determinations of a de facto state of war have occurred even in the absence of a congressional declaration.

Plaintiffs allege in their complaint that 230,000 American troops are currently deployed in Saudi Arabia and the Persian Gulf area, and that by the end of this month the number of American troops in the region will reach 380,000. They also allege, in light of the President's obtaining the support of the United Nations Security Council in a resolution allowing for the use of force against Iraq, that he is planning for an offensive military attack on Iraqi forces.

Given these factual allegations and the legal principles outlined above, the Court has no hesitation in concluding that an offensive entry into Iraq by several hundred thousand United States servicemen under the conditions described above could be described as a "war" within the meaning of Article I, Section 8, Clause 11, of the Constitution. To put it another way: the Court is not prepared to read out of the Constitution the clause granting to the Congress, and to it alone, the authority "to declare war." . . .

The Department of Justice argues next that the plaintiffs lack "standing" to pursue this action.

The Supreme Court has established a two-part test for determining standing under Article III of the Constitution. The plaintiff must allege: (1) that he personally suffered actual or threatened injury, and (2) that the "injury 'fairly can be traced to the challenged action' and 'is likely to be redressed by a favorable decision.'" . . .

The right asserted by the plaintiffs in this case is the right to vote for or against a declaration of war. In view of that subject matter, the right must of necessity be asserted before the President acts; once the President has acted, the asserted right of the members of Congress—to render war action by the President contingent upon a prior congressional declaration of war—is of course lost.

The Department also argues that the threat of injury in this case is not immediate because there is only a "possibility" that the President will initiate war against Iraq, and additionally, that there is no way of knowing before the occurrence of such a possibility whether he would seek a declaration of war from Congress.

That argument, too, must fail, for although it is not entirely fixed what actions the Executive will take towards Iraq and what procedures he will follow with regard to his consultations with Congress, it is clearly more than "unadorned speculation," . . . that the President will go to war by initiating hostilities against Iraq without first obtaining a declaration of war from Congress.

With close to 400,000 United States troops stationed in Saudi Arabia, with all troop rotation and leave provisions suspended, and with the President having acted vigorously on his own as well as through the Secretary of State to obtain from the United Nations Security Council a resolution authorizing the use of all available means to remove Iraqi forces from Kuwait, including the use of force, . . . it is disingenuous for the Department to characterize plaintiffs' allegations as to the imminence of the threat of offensive military action for standing purposes as "remote and conjectural. . . ." For these reasons, the Court concludes that the plaintiffs have adequately alleged a threat of injury in fact necessary to support standing.

Plaintiffs in the instant case . . . cannot gain "substantial relief" by persuasion of their colleagues alone. The "remedies" of cutting off funding to the military or impeaching the President are not available to these plaintiffs either politically or practically. Additionally, these "remedies" would not afford the relief sought by the plaintiffs—which is the guarantee that they will have the opportunity to debate and vote on the wisdom of initiating a military attack against Iraq before the United States military becomes embroiled in belligerency with that nation.

Although, as discussed above, the Court rejects several of defendant's objections to the maintenance of this lawsuit, and concludes that, in principle, an injunction may issue at the request of Members of Congress to prevent the conduct of a war which is about to be carried on without congressional authorization, it does not follow that these plaintiffs are entitled to relief at this juncture. For the plaintiffs are met with a significant obstacle to such relief: the doctrine of ripeness. . . .

In the context of this case, there are two aspects to ripeness, which the Court will now explore. . . .

No one knows the position of the Legislative Branch on the issue of war or peace with Iraq; certainly no one, including this Court, is able to ascertain the congressional position on that issue on the basis of this lawsuit brought by fifty-three members of the House of Representatives and one member of the U.S. Senate. It would be both premature and presumptuous for the Court to render a decision on the issue of whether a declaration of war is required at this time or in the near future when the Congress itself has provided no indication whether it deems such a declaration either necessary, on the one hand, or imprudent, on the other.

For these reasons, this Court has elected to follow the course described by Justice Powell in his concurrence in *Goldwater v. Carter* (1979). In that opinion, Justice Powell provided a test for ripeness in cases involving a confrontation between the legislative and executive branches that is helpful here. In *Goldwater*, President Carter had informed Taiwan that the United States would terminate the mutual defense treaty between the two countries within one year. The President made this announcement without the ratification of the Congress, and members of Congress brought suit claiming that, just as the Constitution required the Senate's ratification of the President's decision to enter into a treaty, so too, congressional ratification was necessary to terminate a treaty.

Justice Powell proposed that "a dispute between Congress and the President is not ready for judicial review unless and until each branch has taken action asserting its constitutional authority." He further explained that in *Goldwater* there had been no such confrontation because there had as yet been no vote in the Senate as to what to do in the face of the President's action to terminate the treaty with Taiwan, and he went on to say that the Judicial Branch should not decide issues affecting the allocation of power between the President and Congress until the political branches reach a constitutional impasse. Otherwise we would encourage small groups or even individual Members of Congress to seek judicial resolution of issues before the normal political process has the opportunity to resolve the conflict. . . . It cannot be said that either the Senate or the House has rejected the President's claim. If the Congress chooses not to confront the President, it is not our task to do so.

Justice Powell's reasoning commends itself to this Court. The consequences of judicial action in the instant case with the facts in their present posture may be drastic, but unnecessarily so. What if the Court issued the injunction requested by the plaintiffs, but it subsequently turned out that a majority of the members of the Legislative Branch were of the view (a) that the President is free as a legal or constitutional matter to proceed with his plans toward Iraq without a congressional declaration of war, . . . or (b) more broadly, that the majority of the members of this Branch, for whatever reason, are content to leave this diplomatically and politically delicate decision to the President?

It would hardly do to have the Court, in effect, force a choice upon the Congress . . . by a blunt injunctive decision, called for by only about ten percent of its membership, to the effect that, unless the rest of the Congress votes in favor of a declaration of war, the President, and the several hundred thousand troops he has dispatched to the Saudi Arabian desert, must be immobilized. Similarly, the President is entitled to be protected from an injunctive order respecting a declaration of war when there is no evidence that this is what the Legislative Branch as such—as distinguished from a fraction thereof—regards as a necessary prerequisite to military moves in the Arabian desert.

All these difficulties are avoided by a requirement that the plaintiffs in an action of this kind be or represent a majority of the Members of the Congress: the majority of the body that under the Constitution is the only one competent to declare war, and therefore also the one with the ability to seek an order from the courts to prevent anyone else, *i.e.*, the Executive, from in effect declaring war. In short, unless the Congress as a whole, or by a majority, is heard from, the controversy here cannot be deemed ripe; it is only if the majority of the Congress seeks relief from an infringement on its constitutional war-declaration power that it may be entitled to receive it. . . .

The second half of the ripeness issue involves the question whether the Executive Branch of government is so clearly committed to immediate military operations that may be equated with a "war" within the meaning of Article I, Section 8, Clause 11, of the Constitution that a judicial decision may properly be rendered regarding the application of that constitutional provision to the current situation.

Plaintiffs assert that the matter is currently ripe for judicial action because the President himself has stated that the present troop build-up is to provide an adequate offensive military option in the area. His successful effort to secure passage of United Nations Resolution 678, which authorizes the use of "all available means" to oust Iraqi forces remaining in Kuwait after January 15, 1991, is said to be an additional fact pointing toward the Executive's intention to initiate military hostilities against Iraq in the near future.

The Department of Justice, on the other hand, points to statements of the President that the troops already in Saudi Arabia are a peacekeeping force to prove that the President might not initiate more offensive military actions. In addition, and more realistically, it is possible that the meetings set for later this month and next between President Bush and the Foreign Minister of Iraq, Tariq Aziz, in Washington, and Secretary of State James Baker and Saddam Hussein in Baghdad, may result in a diplomatic solution to the present situation, and in any event under the U.N. Security Council resolution there will not be resort to force before January 15, 1991.

Given the facts currently available to this Court, it would seem that as of now the Executive Branch has not shown a commitment to a definitive course of action sufficient to support ripeness. In any event, however, a final decision on that issue is not necessary at this time. . . .

ORDERED that plaintiffs' motion for preliminary injunction be and it is hereby denied.

REPUBLICAN CONTRACT WITH AMERICA (1994)

Republicans issued the Contract during the 1994 congressional campaign as a promise to the electorate that, should they be elected, they would institute the programs presented in the document. It was introduced six weeks before the midterm elections and was signed by all but two Republicans in the House and by those Republicans running for office who were not incumbents It was a mix of old and new ideas and met with mixed results. Three proposals became law: the Congressional Accountability Act of 1995; the Unfunded Mandate Reform Act of 1995; and the Paperwork Reduction Act of 1995.

As Republican Members of the House of Representatives and as citizens seeking to join that body we propose not just to change its policies, but even more important, to restore the bonds of trust between the people and their elected representatives.

That is why, in this era of official evasion and posturing, we offer instead a detailed agenda for national renewal, a written commitment with no fine print.

This year's election offers the chance, after four decades of one-party control, to bring to the House a new majority that will transform the way Congress works. That historic change would be the end of government that is too big, too intrusive, and too easy with the public's money. It can be the beginning of a Congress that respects the values and shares the faith of the American family.

Like Lincoln, our first Republican president, we intend to act "with firmness in the right, as God gives us to see the right." To restore accountability to Congress. To end its cycle of scandal and disgrace. To make us all proud again of the way free people govern themselves.

On the first day of the 104th Congress, the new Republican majority will immediately pass the following major reforms, aimed at restoring the faith and trust of the American people in their government:

- **FIRST,** require all laws that apply to the rest of the country also apply equally to the Congress;
- **SECOND,** select a major, independent auditing firm to conduct a comprehensive audit of Congress for waste, fraud or abuse;
- **THIRD,** cut the number of House committees, and cut committee staff by one-third;
- **FOURTH,** limit the terms of all committee chairs;
- **FIFTH,** ban the casting of proxy votes in committee;
- **SIXTH,** require committee meetings to be open to the public;
- **SEVENTH,** require a three-fifths majority vote to pass a tax increase;
- **EIGHTH,** guarantee an honest accounting of our Federal Budget by implementing zero base-line budgeting.

Thereafter, within the first 100 days of the 104th Congress, we shall bring to the House Floor the following bills, each to be given full and open debate, each to be given a clear and fair vote and each to be immediately available this day for public inspection and scrutiny.

1. **THE FISCAL RESPONSIBILITY ACT:** A balanced budget/tax limitation amendment and a legislative line-item veto to restore fiscal responsibility to an out-of-control Congress, requiring them to live under the same budget constraints as families and businesses.
2. **THE TAKING BACK OUR STREETS ACT:** An anti-crime package including stronger truth-in-sentencing, "good faith" exclusionary rule exemptions, effective death penalty provisions, and cuts in social spending from this summer's "crime" bill to fund prison construction and additional law enforcement to keep people secure in their neighborhoods and kids safe in their schools.
3. **THE PERSONAL RESPONSIBILITY ACT:** Discourage illegitimacy and teen pregnancy by prohibiting welfare to minor mothers and denying increased AFDC for additional children while on welfare, cut spending for welfare programs, and enact a tough two-years-and-out provision with work requirements to promote individual responsibility.
4. **THE FAMILY REINFORCEMENT ACT:** Child support enforcement, tax incentives for adoption, strengthening rights of parents in their children's education, stronger child pornography laws, and an elderly dependent care tax credit to reinforce the central role of families in American society.
5. **THE AMERICAN DREAM RESTORATION ACT:** A S500 per child tax credit, begin repeal of the marriage tax penalty, and creation of American Dream Savings Accounts to provide middle class tax relief.
6. **THE NATIONAL SECURITY RESTORATION ACT:** No U.S. troops under U.N. command and restoration of the essential parts of our national security

funding to strengthen our national defense and maintain our credibility around the world.

7. **THE SENIOR CITIZENS FAIRNESS ACT:** Raise the Social Security earnings limit which currently forces seniors out of the work force, repeal the 1993 tax hikes on Social Security benefits and provide tax incentives for private long-term care insurance to let Older Americans keep more of what they have earned over the years.

8. **THE JOB CREATION AND WAGE ENHANCEMENT ACT:** Small business incentives, capital gains cut and indexation, neutral cost recovery, risk assessment/cost-benefit analysis, strengthening the Regulatory Flexibility Act and unfunded mandate reform to create jobs and raise worker wages.

9. **THE COMMON SENSE LEGAL REFORM ACT:** "Loser pays" laws, reasonable limits on punitive damages and reform of product liability laws to stem the endless tide of litigation.

10. **THE CITIZEN LEGISLATURE ACT:** A first-ever vote on term limits to replace career politicians with citizen legislators.

11. **Further, we will instruct** the House Budget Committee to report to the floor and we will work to enact additional budget savings, beyond the budget cuts specifically included in the legislation described above, to ensure that the Federal budget deficit will be less than it would have been without the enactment of these bills.

Respecting the judgment of our fellow citizens as we seek their mandate for reform, we hereby pledge our names to this Contract with America.

Source: REPUBLICAN CONTRACT WITH AMERICA. http://www.house.gov/house/Contract/CONTRACT.html

UNITED STATES, PETITIONER V. ALFONSO LOPEZ, JR. (1995)

The Gun Free School Zones Act of 1990 was declared unconstitutional, thereby limiting congressional commerce power. The law made it a federal offense for anyone to knowingly carry a firearm into a school zone. Because the act did not regulate commercial activity or contain any requirement that the possession of a gun be connected to interstate commerce, the law was declared invalid. In this case a twelfth grader carried a .38 caliber handgun and bullets onto school property. He was confronted and admitted to having the weapon.

CHIEF JUSTICE REHNQUIST delivered the opinion of the Court . . .

We start with first principles. The Constitution creates a Federal Government of enumerated powers. See Art. I, § 8. As James Madison wrote, "the powers delegated by the proposed Constitution to the federal government are few and defined. Those which are to remain in the State governments are numerous and indefinite." The Federalist No. 45. . . . This constitutionally mandated division of authority "was adopted by the Framers to ensure protection of our fundamental liberties." . . . "Just as the separation and independence of the coordinate branches of the Federal Government serve to prevent the accumulation of excessive power in any one branch, a healthy balance of power between the States and the Federal Government will reduce the risk of tyranny and abuse from either front." *Ibid.*

The Constitution delegates to Congress the power "to regulate Commerce with foreign Nations, and among the several States, and with the Indian Tribes." Art. I, § 8, cl. 3. The Court, through Chief Justice Marshall, first defined the nature of Congress' commerce power in *Gibbons* v. *Ogden*, 22 U.S. 1, 9 Wheat. 1, 189-190, 6 L. Ed. 23 (1824):

> "Commerce, undoubtedly, is traffic, but it is something more: it is intercourse. It describes the commercial intercourse between nations, and parts of nations, in all its branches, and is regulated by prescribing rules for carrying on that intercourse."

The commerce power "is the power to regulate; that is, to prescribe the rule by which commerce is to be governed. This power, like all others vested in congress, is complete in itself, may be exercised to its utmost extent, and acknowledges no limitations, other than are prescribed in the constitution." The *Gibbons* Court, however, acknowledged that limitations on the commerce power are inherent in the very language of the Commerce Clause. . . .

For nearly a century thereafter, the Court's Commerce Clause decisions dealt but rarely with the extent of Congress' power, and almost entirely with the Commerce Clause as a limit on state legislation that discriminated against interstate commerce. . .

Jones & Laughlin Steel, Darby, and *Wickard* ushered in an era of Commerce Clause jurisprudence that greatly expanded the previously defined authority of Congress under that Clause. In part, this was a recognition of the great changes that had occurred in the way business was carried on in this country. Enterprises that had once been local or at most regional in nature had become national in scope. But the doctrinal change also reflected a view that earlier Commerce Clause cases artificially had constrained the authority of Congress to regulate interstate commerce.

But even these modern-era precedents which have expanded congressional power under the Commerce Clause confirm that this power is subject to outer limits. In *Jones & Laughlin Steel,* the Court warned that the scope of the interstate commerce power "must be considered in the light of our dual system of government and may not be extended so as to embrace effects upon interstate commerce so indirect and remote that to embrace them, in view of our complex society, would effectually obliterate the distinction between what is national and what is local and create a completely centralized government." . . .

Consistent with this structure, we have identified three broad categories of activity that Congress may regulate under its commerce power. . . . First, Congress may regulate the use of the channels of interstate commerce. See, *e.g., Darby,* 312 U.S. at 114; *Heart of Atlanta Motel, supra,* at 256 ("'The authority of Congress to keep the channels of interstate commerce free from immoral and injurious uses has been frequently sustained, and is no longer open to question.'" . . . "Second, Congress is empowered to regulate and protect the instrumentalities of interstate commerce, or persons or things in interstate commerce, even though the threat may come only from intrastate activities. See, *e.g., Shreveport Rate Cases.* . . . Finally, Congress' commerce authority includes the power to regulate those activities having a substantial relation to interstate commerce, *Jones & Laughlin Steel* . . . those activities that substantially affect interstate commerce.

Within this final category, admittedly, our case law has not been clear whether an activity must "affect" or "substantially affect" interstate commerce in order to be within Congress' power to regulate it under the Commerce Clause. . . . We conclude, consistent with the great weight of our case law, that the proper test requires an analysis of whether the regulated activity "substantially affects" interstate commerce.

We now turn to consider the power of Congress, in the light of this framework, to enact § 922(q). The first two categories of authority may be quickly disposed of: § 922(q) is not a regulation of the use of the channels of interstate commerce, nor is it an attempt to prohibit the interstate transportation of a commodity through the channels of commerce; nor can § 922(q) be justified as a regulation by which Congress has sought to protect an instrumentality of interstate commerce or a thing in interstate commerce. Thus, if § 922(q) is to be sustained, it must be under the third category as a regulation of an activity that substantially affects interstate commerce.

First, . . . Section 922(q) is a criminal statute that by its terms has nothing to do with "commerce" or any sort of economic enterprise, however broadly one might define those terms. Section 922(q) is not an essential part of a larger regulation of economic activity, in which the regulatory scheme could be undercut unless the intrastate activity were regulated. It cannot, therefore, be sustained under our cases upholding regulations of activities that arise out of or are connected with a commercial transaction, which viewed in the aggregate, substantially affects interstate commerce.

Second, § 922(q) contains no jurisdictional element which would ensure, through case-by-case inquiry, that the firearm possession in question affects interstate commerce. . . .

The Government's essential contention . . . is that we may determine here that § 922(q) is valid because possession of a firearm in a local school zone does indeed substantially affect interstate commerce. . . . The Government argues that possession of a firearm in a school zone may result in violent crime and that violent crime can be expected to affect the functioning of the national economy in two ways. First, the costs of violent crime are substantial, and, through the mechanism of insurance, those costs are spread throughout the population. . . . Second, violent crime reduces the willingness of individuals to travel to areas within the country that are perceived to be unsafe. Cf. *Heart of Atlanta Motel*, 379 U.S. at 253. The Government also argues that the presence of guns in schools poses a substantial threat to the educational process by threatening the learning environment. A handicapped educational process, in turn, will result in a less productive citizenry. That, in turn, would have an adverse effect on the Nation's economic well-being. As a result, the Government argues that Congress could rationally have concluded that § 922(q) substantially affects interstate commerce.

We pause to consider the implications of the Government's arguments. The Government admits, under its "costs of crime" reasoning, that Congress could regulate not only all violent crime, but all activities that might lead to violent crime, regardless of how tenuously they relate to interstate commerce. Similarly, under the Government's "national productivity" reasoning, Congress could regulate any activity that it found was related to the economic productivity of individual citizens: family law (including marriage, divorce, and child custody), for example. Under the theories that the Government presents in support of § 922(q), it is difficult to perceive any limitation on federal power, even in areas such as criminal law enforcement or education where States historically have been sovereign. Thus, if we were to accept the Government's arguments, we are hard pressed to posit any activity by an individual that Congress is without power to regulate.

Although JUSTICE BREYER argues that acceptance of the Government's rationales would not authorize a general federal police power, he is unable to identify any activity that the States may regulate but Congress may not. JUSTICE BREYER posits that there might be some limitations on Congress' commerce power, such as family law or certain aspects of education. These suggested limitations, when viewed in light of the dissent's expansive analysis, are devoid of substance. . . .

For instance, if Congress can, pursuant to its Commerce Clause power, regulate activities that adversely affect the learning environment, then, *a fortiori*, it also can regulate the educational process directly. Congress could determine that a school's curriculum has a "significant" effect on the extent of classroom learning. As a result, Congress could mandate a federal curriculum for local elementary and secondary schools because what is taught in local schools has a significant "effect on classroom learning," and that, in turn, has a substantial effect on interstate commerce.

JUSTICE BREYER rejects our reading of precedent and argues that "Congress . . . could rationally conclude that schools fall on the commercial side of the line." . . .

Admittedly, a determination whether an intrastate activity is commercial or noncommercial may in some cases result in legal uncertainty. But, so long as Congress' authority is limited to those powers enumerated in the Constitution, and so long as those enumerated powers are interpreted as having judicially enforceable outer limits, congressional legislation under the Commerce Clause always will engender "legal uncertainty." . . .

The possession of a gun in a local school zone is in no sense an economic activity that might, through repetition elsewhere, substantially affect any sort of interstate commerce. Respondent was a local student at a local school; there is no indication that he had recently moved in interstate commerce, and there is no requirement that his possession of the firearm have any concrete tie to interstate commerce.

To uphold the Government's contentions here, we would have to pile inference upon inference in a manner that would bid fair to convert congressional authority under the Commerce Clause to a general police power of the sort retained by the States. Admittedly, some of our prior cases have taken long steps down that road, giving great deference to congressional action. The broad language in these opinions has suggested the possibility of additional expansion, but we decline here to proceed any further. To do so would require us to conclude that the Constitution's enumeration of powers does not presuppose something not enumerated, cf. *Gibbons* v. *Ogden*, and that there never will be a distinction between what is truly national and what is truly local. . . . This we are unwilling to do.

For the foregoing reasons the judgment of the Court of Appeals is
Affirmed.

JUSTICE BREYER, with whom JUSTICE STEVENS, JUSTICE SOUTER, and JUSTICE GINSBURG join, dissenting . . .

In my view, the statute falls well within the scope of the commerce power as this Court has understood that power over the last half century.

In reaching this conclusion, I apply three basic principles of Commerce Clause interpretation. First, the power to "regulate Commerce . . . among the several States," U.S. Const., Art. I, § 8, cl. 3, encompasses the power to regulate local activities insofar as they significantly affect interstate commerce. See, *e.g., Gibbons* v. *Ogden*. . . .

Second, in determining whether a local activity will likely have a significant effect upon interstate commerce, a court must consider, not the effect of an individual act (a single instance of gun possession), but rather the cumulative effect of all similar instances (*i.e.*, the effect of all guns possessed in or near schools). See, *e.g., Wickard* v. *Filburn*. . . .

Third, the Constitution requires us to judge the connection between a regulated activity and interstate commerce, not directly, but at one remove. Courts must give Congress a degree of leeway in determining the existence of a significant factual connection between the regulated activity and interstate commerce—both because the Constitution delegates the commerce power directly to Congress and because the determination requires an empirical judgment of a kind that a legislature is more likely than a court to make with accuracy. The traditional words "rational basis" capture this leeway. . . . Thus, the specific question before us, as the Court recognizes, is not whether the "regulated activity sufficiently affected interstate commerce," but, rather, whether Congress could have had "*a rational basis*" for so concluding. . . .

Applying these principles to the case at hand, we must ask whether Congress could have had a *rational basis* for finding a significant (or substantial) connection between gun-related school violence and interstate commerce. Or, to put the question in the language of the *explicit* finding that Congress made when it amended this law in 1994: Could Congress rationally have found that "violent crime in school zones," through its effect on the "quality of education," significantly (or substantially) affects "interstate" or "foreign commerce"? . . . As long as one views the commerce connection, not as a "technical legal conception," but as "a practical one," the answer to this question must be yes. Numerous reports and studies—generated both inside and outside government—make clear that Congress could reasonably have found the empirical connection that its law, implicitly or explicitly, asserts. . . .

For one thing, reports, hearings, and other readily available literature make clear that the problem of guns in and around schools is widespread and extremely serious. These materials report, for example, that four percent of American high school students (and six percent of inner-city high school students) carry a gun to school at least occasionally, . . . that 12 percent of urban high school students have had guns fired at them, that 20 percent of those students have been threatened with guns, and that, in any 6-month period, several hundred thousand schoolchildren are victims of violent crimes in or near their schools. . . . And, they report that this widespread violence in schools throughout the Nation significantly interferes with the quality of education in those schools. . . . Based on reports such as these, Congress obviously could have thought that guns and learning are mutually exclusive. . . . Congress could therefore have found a substantial educational problem—teachers unable to teach, students unable to learn— and concluded that guns near schools contribute substantially to the size and scope of that problem.

Having found that guns in schools significantly undermine the quality of education in our Nation's classrooms, Congress could also have found, given the effect of education upon interstate and foreign commerce, that gun-related violence in and around schools is a commercial, as well as a human, problem. Education, although far more than a matter of economics, has long been inextricably intertwined with the Nation's economy. . . .

In recent years the link between secondary education and business has strengthened, becoming both more direct and more important. Scholars on the subject report that technological changes and innovations in management techniques have altered the nature of the workplace so that more jobs now demand greater educational skills. . . .

Increasing global competition also has made primary and secondary education economically more important. . . .

Finally, there is evidence that, today more than ever, many firms base their location decisions upon the presence, or absence, of a work force with a basic education. . . .

The economic links I have just sketched seem fairly obvious. Why then is it not equally obvious, in light of those links, that a widespread, serious, and substantial physical threat to teaching and learning *also* substantially threatens the commerce to which that teaching and learning is inextricably tied? That is to say, guns in the hands of six percent of inner-city high school students and gun-related violence throughout a city's schools must threaten the trade and commerce that those schools support. The only question, then, is whether the latter threat is (to use the majority's terminology) "substantial." The evidence of (1) the *extent* of the gun-related violence problem, (2) the *extent* of the resulting negative effect on classroom learning, see *ibid.*, and (3) the *extent* of the consequent negative commercial effects when taken together, indicate a threat to trade and commerce that is "substantial." At the very least, Congress could rationally have concluded that the links are "substantial."

Specifically, Congress could have found that gun-related violence near the classroom poses a serious economic threat. . . .

The majority's holding—that § 922 falls outside the scope of the Commerce Clause—creates three serious legal problems. First, the majority's holding runs contrary to modern Supreme Court cases that have upheld congressional actions despite connections to interstate or foreign commerce that are less significant than the effect of school violence. . . .

The second legal problem the Court creates comes from its apparent belief that it can reconcile its holding with earlier cases by making a critical distinction between "commercial" and noncommercial "transaction[s]." That is to say, the Court believes the Constitution would distinguish between two local activities, each of which has an identical effect upon interstate commerce, if one, but not the other, is "commercial" in nature. . . .

The third legal problem created by the Court's holding is that it threatens legal uncertainty in an area of law that, until this case, seemed reasonably well settled. Congress has enacted many statutes (more than 100 sections of the United States Code), including criminal statutes (at least 25 sections), that use the words "affecting commerce" to define their scope. . . .

In sum, to find this legislation within the scope of the Commerce Clause would permit "Congress . . . to act in terms of economic . . . realities." . . . It would interpret the Clause as this Court has traditionally interpreted it, with the exception of one wrong turn subsequently corrected. See *Gibbons* v. *Ogden*, (holding that the commerce power extends "to all the external concerns of the nation, and to those internal concerns which affect the States generally"); *United States* v. *Darby*, ("The conclusion is inescapable that *Hammer* v. *Dagenhart* [the child labor case] was a departure from the principles which have prevailed in the interpretation of the Commerce Clause both before and since the decision. . . . It should be and now is overruled"). Upholding this legislation would do no more than simply recognize that Congress had a "rational basis" for finding a significant connection between guns in or near schools and (through their effect on education) the interstate and foreign commerce they threaten. For these reasons, I would reverse the judgment of the Court of Appeals. Respectfully, I dissent.

Source: Justia.com – US Supreme Court Center. http://supreme.justia.com/us/514/549/case.html

CITY OF BOERNE V. P. F. FLORES, ARCHBISHOP OF SAN ANTONIO, AND UNITED STATES (1997)

The Catholic archbishop of San Antonio, Texas, applied for a permit to expand a church. Local zoning authorities denied the permit because it was an historic building. The church sued under the Religious Freedom Restoration Act of 1993. The Court ruled the act unconstitutional as exceeding Congress's power, because Congress could not enforce a constitutional right (in this case under the First Amendment) by changing what the right is, which was claimed to be the case in this instance.

JUSTICE KENNEDY delivered the opinion of the Court.

A decision by local zoning authorities to deny a church a building permit was challenged under the Religious Freedom Restoration Act of 1993 (RFRA), 107 Stat. 1488, 42 U.S.C. § 2000bb *et seq.* The case calls into question the authority of Congress to enact RFRA. We conclude the statute exceeds Congress' power.

II

Congress enacted RFRA in direct response to the Court's decision in *Employment Div., Dept. of Human Resources of Ore.* v. *Smith* (1990). There we considered a Free Exercise Clause claim brought by members of the Native American Church who were denied unemployment benefits when they lost their jobs because they had used peyote. Their practice was to ingest peyote for sacramental purposes, and they challenged an Oregon statute of general applicability which made use of the drug criminal. In evaluating the claim, we declined to apply the balancing test set forth in *Sherbert* v. *Verner* (1963), under which we would have asked whether Oregon's prohibition substantially burdened a religious practice and, if it did, whether the burden was justified by a compelling government interest. . . .

Many criticized the Court's reasoning, and this disagreement resulted in the passage of RFRA. Congress announced:

"(1) The framers of the Constitution, recognizing free exercise of religion as an unalienable right, secured its protection in the First Amendment to the Constitution;

"(2) laws 'neutral' toward religion may burden religious exercise as surely as laws intended to interfere with religious exercise;

"(3) governments should not substantially burden religious exercise without compelling justification;

"(4) in *Employment Division v. Smith* (1990), the Supreme Court virtually eliminated the requirement that the government justify burdens on religious exercise imposed by laws neutral toward religion; and

"(5) the compelling interest test as set forth in prior Federal court rulings is a workable test for striking sensible balances between religious liberty and competing prior governmental interests."

The Act's stated purposes are:

"(1) to restore the compelling interest test as set forth in *Sherbert v. Verner* (1963) and *Wisconsin v. Yoder* (1972) and to guarantee its application in all cases where free exercise of religion is substantially burdened; and

"(2) to provide a claim or defense to persons whose religious exercise is substantially burdened by government."

RFRA prohibits "government" from "substantially burdening" a person's exercise of religion even if the burden results from a rule of general applicability unless the government can demonstrate the burden "(1) is in furtherance of a compelling governmental interest; and (2) is the least restrictive means of furthering that compelling governmental interest." The Act's mandate applies to any "branch, department, agency, instrumentality, and official (or other person acting under color of law) of the United States," as well as to any "State, or . . . subdivision of a State."

III

A

The parties disagree over whether RFRA is a proper exercise of Congress' § 5 power "to enforce" by "appropriate legislation" the constitutional guarantee that no State shall deprive any person of "life, liberty, or property, without due process of law" nor deny any person "equal protection of the laws." . . .

All must acknowledge that § 5 is "a positive grant of legislative power" to Congress, *Katzenbach* v. *Morgan* (1966) . . . Legislation which deters or remedies constitutional violations can fall within the sweep of Congress' enforcement power even if in the process it prohibits conduct which is not itself unconstitutional and intrudes into "legislative spheres of autonomy previously reserved to the States." *Fitzpatrick* v. *Bitzer*, (1976). For example, the Court upheld a suspension of literacy tests and similar voting requirements under Congress' parallel power to enforce the provisions of the Fifteenth Amendment, see U.S. Const., Amdt. 15, § 2, as a measure to combat racial discrimination in voting, *South Carolina* v. *Katzenbach* (1966), despite the facial constitutionality of the tests. . . . We have also concluded that other measures protecting voting rights are within Congress' power to enforce the Fourteenth and Fifteenth Amendments, despite the burdens those measures placed on the States. . . .

It is also true, however, that "as broad as the congressional enforcement power is, it is not unlimited." *Oregon* v. *Mitchell.* In assessing the breadth of § 5's enforcement power, we begin with its text. Congress has been given the power "to enforce" the "provisions of this article." We agree with respondent, of course, that Congress can enact legislation under § 5 enforcing the constitutional right to the free exercise of religion. The "provisions of this article," to which § 5 refers, include the Due Process Clause of the Fourteenth Amendment. Congress' power to enforce the Free Exercise Clause follows from our holding in *Cantwell* v. *Connecticut,* (1940), that the "fundamental concept of liberty embodied in [the Fourteenth Amendment's Due Process Clause] embraces the liberties guaranteed by the First Amendment." . . .

Congress' power under § 5, however, extends only to "enforcing" the provisions of the Fourteenth Amendment. The Court has described this power as "remedial," *South Carolina* v. *Katzenbach, supra,* at 326. The design of the Amendment and the text of § 5 are inconsistent with the suggestion that Congress has the power to decree the substance of the Fourteenth Amendment's restrictions on the States. Legislation which alters the meaning of the Free Exercise Clause cannot be said to be enforcing the Clause. Congress does not enforce a constitutional right by changing what the right is. It has been given the power "to enforce," not the power to determine what constitutes a constitutional violation. Were it not so, what Congress would be enforcing would no longer be, in any meaningful sense, the "provisions of [the Fourteenth Amendment]."

While the line between measures that remedy or prevent unconstitutional actions and measures that make a substantive change in the governing law is not easy to discern, and Congress must have wide latitude in determining where it lies, the distinction exists and must be observed. There must be a congruence and proportionality between the injury to be prevented or remedied and the means adopted to that end. Lacking such a connection, legislation may become substantive in operation and effect. History and our case law support drawing the distinction, one apparent from the text of the Amendment.

1

The Fourteenth Amendment's history confirms the remedial, rather than substantive, nature of the Enforcement Clause.

Any suggestion that Congress has a substantive, non-remedial power under the Fourteenth Amendment is not supported by our case law. In *Oregon* v. *Mitchell,* a majority of the Court concluded Congress had exceeded its enforcement powers by enacting legislation lowering the minimum age of voters from 21 to 18 in state and local elections. . . .

We now turn to consider whether RFRA can be considered enforcement legislation under § 5 of the Fourteenth Amendment.

B

Respondent contends that RFRA is a proper exercise of Congress' remedial or preventive power. The Act, it is said, is a reasonable means of protecting the free exercise of religion as defined by *Smith*. It prevents and remedies laws which are enacted with the unconstitutional object of targeting religious beliefs and practices. See *Church of the Lukumi Babalu Aye, Inc.* v. *Hialeah*, (1993). To avoid the difficulty of proving such violations, it is said, Congress can simply invalidate any law which imposes a substantial burden on a religious practice unless it is justified by a compelling interest and is the least restrictive means of accomplishing that interest. If Congress can prohibit laws with discriminatory effects in order to prevent racial discrimination in violation of the Equal Protection Clause . . . then it can do the same, respondent argues, to promote religious liberty.

While preventive rules are sometimes appropriate remedial measures, there must be a congruence between the means used and the ends to be achieved. The appropriateness of remedial measures must be considered in light of the evil presented. Strong measures appropriate to address one harm may be an unwarranted response to another, lesser one. . . .

Regardless of the state of the legislative record, RFRA cannot be considered remedial, preventive legislation, if those terms are to have any meaning. RFRA is so out of proportion to a supposed remedial or preventive object that it cannot be understood as responsive to, or designed to prevent, unconstitutional behavior. It appears, instead, to attempt a substantive change in constitutional protections. Preventive measures prohibiting certain types of laws may be appropriate when there is reason to believe that many of the laws affected by the congressional enactment have a significant likelihood of being unconstitutional. Remedial legislation under § 5 "should be adapted to the mischief and wrong which the [Fourteenth] Amendment was intended to provide against." *Civil Rights Cases.*

RFRA is not so confined. Sweeping coverage ensures its intrusion at every level of government, displacing laws and prohibiting official actions of almost every description and regardless of subject matter. RFRA's restrictions apply to every agency and official of the Federal, State, and local Governments. RFRA applies to all federal and state law, statutory or otherwise, whether adopted before or after its enactment. § 2000bb-3(a). RFRA has no termination date or termination mechanism. Any law is subject to challenge at any time by any individual who alleges a substantial burden on his or her free exercise of religion.

The reach and scope of RFRA distinguish it from other measures passed under Congress' enforcement power, even in the area of voting rights. In *South Carolina* v. *Katzenbach*, the challenged provisions were confined to those regions of the country where voting discrimination had been most flagrant, and affected a discrete class of state laws, *i.e.*, state voting laws. Furthermore, to ensure that the reach of the Voting Rights Act was limited to those cases in which constitutional violations were most likely (in order to reduce the possibility of overbreadth), the coverage under the Act would terminate "at the behest of States and political subdivisions in which the danger of substantial voting discrimination has not materialized during the preceding five years." . . .

The stringent test RFRA demands of state laws reflects a lack of proportionality or congruence between the means adopted and the legitimate end to be achieved. If an objector can show a substantial burden on his free exercise, the State must demonstrate a compelling governmental interest and show that the law is the least restrictive means of furthering its interest. Claims that a law substantially burdens someone's exercise of religion will often be difficult to contest . . . Laws valid under *Smith* would fall under RFRA without regard to whether they had the object of stifling or punishing free exercise. . . .

The substantial costs RFRA exacts, both in practical terms of imposing a heavy litigation burden on the States and in terms of curtailing their traditional general regulatory power, far exceed any pattern or practice of unconstitutional conduct under the Free Exercise Clause as interpreted in *Smith*. Simply put, RFRA is not designed to identify and counteract state laws likely to be unconstitutional because of their treatment of religion. In most cases, the state laws to which RFRA applies are not ones which will have been motivated by religious bigotry. If a state law disproportionately burdened a particular class of religious observers, this circumstance might be evidence of an impermissible legislative motive. RFRA's substantial burden test, however, is not even a discriminatory effects or disparate impact test. It is a reality of the modern regulatory state that numerous state laws, such as the zoning regulations at issue here, impose a substantial burden on a large class of individuals. When the exercise of religion has been burdened in an incidental way by a law of general application, it does not follow that the persons affected have been burdened any more than other citizens, let alone burdened because of their religious beliefs. In addition, the Act imposes in every case a least restrictive means requirement—a requirement that was not used in the pre-*Smith* jurisprudence RFRA purported to codify—which also indicates that the legislation is broader than is appropriate if the goal is to prevent and remedy constitutional violations. . . .

Broad as the power of Congress is under the Enforcement Clause of the Fourteenth Amendment, RFRA contradicts vital principles necessary to maintain separation of powers and the federal balance. The judgment of the Court of Appeals sustaining the Act's constitutionality is reversed.

It is so ordered.

JUSTICE STEVENS, concurring.

In my opinion, the Religious Freedom Restoration Act of 1993 (RFRA) is a "law respecting an establishment of religion" that violates the First Amendment to the Constitution. . . .

JUSTICE SCALIA, with whom JUSTICE STEVENS joins, concurring in part.

I write to respond briefly to the claim of JUSTICE O'CONNOR's dissent (hereinafter "the dissent") that historical materials support a result contrary to the one reached in *Employment Div., Dept. of Human Resources of Ore.* v. *Smith* (1990). . . . The material that the dissent claims is at odds with *Smith* either has little to say about the issue or is in fact more consistent with *Smith* than with the dissent's interpretation of the Free Exercise Clause. . . .

The dissent first claims that *Smith*'s interpretation of the Free Exercise Clause departs from the understanding reflected in various statutory and constitutional protections of religion enacted by Colonies, States, and Territories in the period leading up to the ratification of the Bill of Rights. But the protections afforded by those enactments are in fact more consistent with *Smith*'s interpretation of free exercise than with the dissent's understanding of it. The Free Exercise Clause, the dissent claims, "is best understood as an affirmative guarantee of the right to participate in religious practices and conduct without impermissible governmental interference, even when such conduct conflicts with a neutral, generally applicable law"; thus, even neutral laws of general application may be invalid if they burden religiously motivated conduct. However, the early "free exercise" enactments cited by the dissent protect only against action that is taken "for" or "in respect of" religion; or action taken "on account of" religion; or "discriminatory" action; or, finally (and unhelpfully for purposes of interpreting "free exercise" in the Federal Constitution), action that interferes with the "free exercise" of religion. It is eminently arguable that application of neutral, generally applicable laws of the sort the dissent refers to—such as zoning laws—would not constitute action taken "for," "in respect of," or "on account of" one's religion, or "discriminatory" action.

Assuming, however, that the affirmative protection of religion accorded by the early "free exercise" enactments sweeps as broadly as the dissent's theory would require, those enactments do not support the dissent's view, since they contain "provisos" that significantly qualify the affirmative protection they grant. According to the dissent, the "provisos" support *its* view because they would have been "superfluous" if "the Court was correct in *Smith* that generally applicable laws are enforceable regardless of religious conscience." I disagree. In fact, the most plausible reading of the "free exercise" enactments (if their affirmative provisions are read broadly, as the dissent's view requires) is a virtual restatement of *Smith*: Religious exercise shall be permitted *so long as it does not violate general laws governing conduct.* . . . This limitation upon the scope of religious exercise would have been in accord with the background political philosophy of the age (associated most prominently with John Locke), which regarded freedom as the right "to do only what was not lawfully prohibited," West, The Case Against a Right to Religion-Based Exemptions, 4 Notre Dame J. of Law, Ethics & Public Policy 591, 624 (1990). "Thus, the disturb-the-peace caveats apparently permitted government to deny religious freedom, not merely in the event of violence or force, but, more generally, upon the occurrence of illegal actions." And while, under this interpretation, these early "free exercise" enactments support the Court's judgment in *Smith*, I see no sensible interpretation that could cause them to support what I understand to be the position of JUSTICE O'CONNOR, or any of *Smith*'s other critics. No one in that camp, to my knowledge, contends that their favored "compelling state interest" test conforms to any possible interpretation of "breach of peace and order"—*i.e.*, that *only* violence or force, or any other category of action (more limited than "violation of law") which can possibly be conveyed by the phrase "peace and order," justifies state prohibition of religiously motivated conduct.

Apart from the early "free exercise" enactments of Colonies, States, and Territories, the dissent calls attention to those bodies', and the Continental Congress's, legislative accommodation of religious practices prior to ratification of the Bill of Rights. This accommodation—which took place both before and after enactment of the state constitutional protections of religious liberty—suggests (according to the dissent) that "the drafters and ratifiers of the First Amendment . . . assumed courts would apply the Free Exercise Clause similarly." But that legislatures sometimes (though not always) found it "appropriate," to accommodate religious practices does not establish that accommodation was understood to be constitutionally *mandated* by the Free Exercise Clause. As we explained in *Smith*, "To say that a nondiscriminatory religious-practice exemption is permitted, or even that it is desirable, is not to say that it is constitutionally required." . . .

The dissent's final source of claimed historical support consists of statements of certain of the Framers in the context of debates about proposed legislative enactments or debates over general principles (not in connection with the drafting of State or Federal Constitutions). Those statements are subject to the same objection as was the evidence about . . . legislative accommodation: There is no reason to think they were meant to describe what was constitutionally required (and judicially enforceable), as opposed to what was thought to be legislatively or even morally desirable. . . .

JUSTICE O'CONNOR, with whom JUSTICE BREYER joins except as to a portion of Part I, dissenting.

I dissent from the Court's disposition of this case. I agree with the Court that the issue before us is whether the Religious Freedom Restoration Act (RFRA) is a proper exercise of Congress' power to enforce § 5 of the Fourteenth Amendment. But as a yardstick for measuring the constitutionality of RFRA, the Court uses its holding in *Employment Div., Dept. of Human Resources of Ore.* v. *Smith* (1990), the decision that prompted Congress to enact RFRA as a means of more rigorously enforcing the Free

Exercise Clause. I remain of the view that *Smith* was wrongly decided, and I would use this case to reexamine the Court's holding there. Therefore, I would direct the parties to brief the question whether *Smith* represents the correct understanding of the Free Exercise Clause and set the case for reargument. If the Court were to correct the misinterpretation of the Free Exercise Clause set forth in *Smith*, it would simultaneously put our First Amendment jurisprudence back on course and allay the legitimate concerns of a majority in Congress who believed that *Smith* improperly restricted religious liberty. We would then be in a position to review RFRA in light of a proper interpretation of the Free Exercise Clause. . . .

I shall not restate what has been said in other opinions, which have demonstrated that *Smith* is gravely at odds with our earlier free exercise precedents. See *Church of Lukumi Babalu Aye, Inc.* v. *Hialeah* (1993) (SOUTER, J., concurring) (stating that it is "difficult to escape the conclusion that, whatever *Smith*'s virtues, they do not include a comfortable fit with settled law"); *Smith* (O'CONNOR, J., concurring). Rather, I examine here the early American tradition of religious free exercise to gain insight into the original understanding of the Free Exercise Clause—an inquiry the Court in *Smith* did not undertake. We have previously recognized the importance of interpreting the Religion Clauses in light of their history. *Lynch* v. *Donnelly*, (1984); *School Dist. of Abington Township* v. *Schempp*, (1963).

The historical evidence casts doubt on the Court's current interpretation of the Free Exercise Clause. The record instead reveals that its drafters and ratifiers more likely viewed the Free Exercise Clause as a guarantee that government may not unnecessarily hinder believers from freely practicing their religion, a position consistent with our pre-*Smith* jurisprudence. . . .

The principle of religious "free exercise" and the notion that religious liberty deserved legal protection were by no means new concepts in 1791, when the Bill of Rights was ratified. To the contrary, these principles were first articulated in this country in the colonies of Maryland, Rhode Island, Pennsylvania, Delaware, and Carolina, in the mid-1600's. These colonies, though established as sanctuaries for particular groups of religious dissenters, extended freedom of religion to groups—although often limited to Christian groups—beyond their own. Thus, they encountered early on the conflicts that may arise in a society made up of a plurality of faiths.

The term "free exercise" appeared in an American legal document as early as 1648, when Lord Baltimore extracted from the new Protestant governor of Maryland and his councilors a promise not to disturb Christians, particularly Roman Catholics, in the "free exercise" of their religion. Soon after, in 1649, the Maryland Assembly enacted the first free exercise clause by passing the Act Concerning Religion: "Noe person . . . professing to believe in Jesus Christ, shall from henceforth bee any waies troubled, Molested or discountenanced for or in respect of his or her religion nor in the free exercise thereof . . . nor any way [be] compelled to the believe or exercise of any other Religion against his or her consent, soe as they be not unfaithful to the Lord Proprietary, or molest or conspire against the civil Government." Act Concerning Religion of 1649.

Rhode Island's Charter of 1663 used the analogous term "liberty of conscience." It protected residents from being "in any ways molested, punished, disquieted, or called into question, for any differences in opinion, in matters of religion, and do not actually disturb the civil peace of our said colony." The Charter further provided that residents may "freely, and fully have and enjoy his and their own judgments, and conscience in matters of religious concernments . . .; they behaving themselves peaceably and quietly and not using this liberty to licentiousness and profaneness; nor to the civil injury, or outward disturbance of others." Charter of Rhode Island and Providence Plantations, 1663. Various agreements between prospective settlers and the proprietors of Carolina, New York, and New Jersey similarly guaranteed religious freedom, using language that paralleled that of the Rhode Island Charter of 1663. . . .

These documents suggest that, early in our country's history, several colonies acknowledged that freedom to pursue one's chosen religious beliefs was an essential liberty. Moreover, these colonies appeared to recognize that government should interfere in religious matters only when necessary to protect the civil peace or to prevent "licentiousness.". . .

The principles expounded in these early charters re-emerged over a century later in state constitutions that were adopted in the flurry of constitution-drafting that followed the American Revolution. By 1789, every State but Connecticut had incorporated some version of a free exercise clause into its constitution. . . .

The practice of the colonies and early States bears out the conclusion that, at the time the Bill of Rights was ratified, it was accepted that government should, when possible, accommodate religious practice. Unsurprisingly, of course, even in the American colonies inhabited by people of religious persuasions, religious conscience and civil law rarely conflicted. Most 17th and 18th century Americans belonged to denominations of Protestant Christianity whose religious practices were generally harmonious with colonial law. . . .

Nevertheless, tension between religious conscience and generally applicable laws, though rare, was not unknown in pre-Constitutional America. Most commonly, such conflicts arose from oath requirements, military conscription, and religious assessments. The ways in which these conflicts were resolved suggest that Americans in the colonies and early States thought that, if an individual's religious scruples prevented him from complying with a generally applicable law, the government should, if possible, excuse the person from the law's coverage. For example, Quakers and certain other Protestant sects refused on Biblical grounds to subscribe to oaths or "swear" allegiance to civil authority. Without accommodation, their beliefs would have prevented them from participating in civic activities involving oaths, including testifying in court. Colonial governments created alternatives to the oath requirement for these individuals. . . By 1789, virtually all of the States had enacted oath exemptions. . . .

The Religion Clauses of the Constitution represent a profound commitment to religious liberty. Our Nation's Founders conceived of a Republic receptive to voluntary religious expression, not of a secular society in which religious expression is tolerated only when it does not conflict with a generally applicable law. As the historical sources discussed above show, the Free Exercise Clause is properly understood as an affirmative guarantee of the right to participate in religious activities without impermissible governmental interference, even where a believer's conduct is in tension with a law of general application. Certainly, it is in no way anomalous to accord heightened protection to a right identified in the text of the First Amendment. . . .

Accordingly, I believe that it is essential for the Court to reconsider its holding in *Smith*—and to do so in this very case. I would therefore direct the parties to brief this issue and set the case for reargument.

I respectfully dissent from the Court's disposition of this case.

Source: Justia.com – US Supreme Court Center. http://supreme.justia.com/us/ 521/507/case.html

ARTICLES OF IMPEACHMENT OF PRESIDENT CLINTON (1998)

The third major attempt to impeach a U.S. president, which grew out of investigations surrounding failed land dealings known as the Whitewater Scandal that grew into an investigation into a sexual harassment lawsuit, filed by Paula Jones, a former Arkansas state employee. In his deposition Bill Clinton, under oath, denied having sexual relations with Monica Lewinsky. In the wake of the Monica Lewinsky scandal, President Clinton was charged with perjury and obstruction of justice. He was impeached by the House and acquitted by the Senate after a twenty-one-day trial. The impeachment highlighted party differences and was far more similar to the Andrew Johnson impeachment than to the impeachment charges brought against Richard Nixon.

Adopted by the Committee on the Judiciary of the House of Representatives.

Resolved, That William Jefferson Clinton, President of the United States, is impeached for high crimes and misdemeanors, and that the following articles of impeachment be exhibited . . . (Reported in House)

HRES 611 RH

House Calendar No. 281

105th CONGRESS

2d Session

H. RES. 611

[Report No. 105-830]

Impeaching William Jefferson Clinton, President of the United States, for high crimes and misdemeanors.

IN THE HOUSE OF REPRESENTATIVES

December 15, 1998

Mr. HYDE submitted the following resolution; which was referred to the House Calendar and ordered to be printed

RESOLUTION

Impeaching William Jefferson Clinton, President of the United States, for high crimes and misdemeanors.

> *Resolved*, That William Jefferson Clinton, President of the United States, is impeached for high crimes and misdemeanors, and that the following articles of impeachment be exhibited to the United States Senate:

Articles of impeachment exhibited by the House of Representatives of the United States of America in the name of itself and of the people of the United States of America, against William Jefferson Clinton, President of the United States of America, in maintenance and support of its impeachment against him for high crimes and misdemeanors.

Article I

In his conduct while President of the United States, William Jefferson Clinton, in violation of his constitutional oath faithfully to execute the office of President of the United States and, to the best of his ability, preserve, protect, and defend the Constitution of the United States, and in violation of his constitutional duty to take care that the laws be faithfully executed, has willfully corrupted and manipulated the judicial process of the United States for his personal gain and exoneration, impeding the administration of justice, in that:

On August 17, 1998, William Jefferson Clinton swore to tell the truth, the whole truth, and nothing but the truth before a Federal grand jury of the United States. Contrary to that oath, William Jefferson Clinton willfully provided perjurious, false and misleading testimony to the grand jury concerning one or more of the following: (1) the nature and details of his relationship with a subordinate Government employee; (2) prior perjurious, false and misleading testimony he gave in a Federal civil rights action brought against him; (3) prior false and misleading statements he allowed his attorney to make to a Federal judge in that civil rights action; and (4) his corrupt efforts to influence the testimony of witnesses and to impede the discovery of evidence in that civil rights action.

In doing this, William Jefferson Clinton has undermined the integrity of his office, has brought disrepute on the Presidency, has betrayed his trust as President, and has acted in a manner subversive of the rule of law and justice, to the manifest injury of the people of the United States.

Wherefore, William Jefferson Clinton, by such conduct, warrants impeachment and trial, and removal from office and disqualification to hold and enjoy any office of honor, trust, or profit under the United States.

Article II

In his conduct while President of the United States, William Jefferson Clinton, in violation of his constitutional oath faithfully to execute the office of President of the United States and, to the best of his ability, preserve, protect, and defend the Constitution of the United States, and in violation of his constitutional duty to take care that the laws be faithfully executed, has willfully corrupted and manipulated the judicial process of the United States for his personal gain and exoneration, impeding the administration of justice, in that:

(1) On December 23, 1997, William Jefferson Clinton, in sworn answers to written questions asked as part of a Federal civil rights action brought against him, willfully provided perjurious, false and misleading testimony in response to questions deemed relevant by a Federal judge concerning conduct and proposed conduct with subordinate employees.

(2) On January 17, 1998, William Jefferson Clinton swore under oath to tell the truth, the whole truth, and nothing but the truth in a deposition given as part of a Federal civil rights action brought against him. Contrary to that oath, William Jefferson Clinton willfully provided perjurious, false and misleading testimony in response to questions deemed relevant by a Federal judge concerning the nature and details of his relationship with a subordinate Government employee, his knowledge of that employee's involvement and participation in the civil rights action brought against him, and his corrupt efforts to influence the testimony of that employee.

In all of this, William Jefferson Clinton has undermined the integrity of his office, has brought disrepute on the Presidency, has betrayed his trust as President, and has acted in a manner subversive of the rule of law and justice, to the manifest injury of the people of the United States.

Wherefore, William Jefferson Clinton, by such conduct, warrants impeachment and trial, and removal from office and disqualification to hold and enjoy any office of honor, trust, or profit under the United States.

Article III

In his conduct while President of the United States, William Jefferson Clinton, in violation of his constitutional oath faithfully to execute the office of President of the United States and, to the best of his ability, preserve, protect, and defend the Constitution of the United States, and in violation of his constitutional duty to take care that the laws be faithfully executed, has prevented, obstructed, and impeded the administration of justice, and has to that end engaged personally, and through his subordinates and agents, in a course of conduct or scheme designed to delay, impede, cover up, and conceal the existence of evidence and testimony related to a Federal civil rights action brought against him in a duly instituted judicial proceeding.

The means used to implement this course of conduct or scheme included one or more of the following acts:

(1) On or about December 17, 1997, William Jefferson Clinton corruptly encouraged a witness in a Federal civil rights action brought against him to execute a sworn affidavit in that proceeding that he knew to be perjurious, false and misleading.

(2) On or about December 17, 1997, William Jefferson Clinton corruptly encouraged a witness in a Federal civil rights action brought against him to give perjurious, false and misleading testimony if and when called to testify personally in that proceeding.

(3) On or about December 28, 1997, William Jefferson Clinton corruptly engaged in, encouraged, or supported a scheme to conceal evidence that had been subpoenaed in a Federal civil rights action brought against him.

(4) Beginning on or about December 7, 1997, and continuing through and including January 14, 1998, William Jefferson Clinton intensified and succeeded in an effort to secure job assistance to a witness in a Federal civil rights action brought against him in order to corruptly prevent the truthful testimony of that witness in that proceeding at a time when the truthful testimony of that witness would have been harmful to him.

(5) On January 17, 1998, at his deposition in a Federal civil rights action brought against him, William Jefferson Clinton corruptly allowed his attorney to make false and misleading statements to a Federal judge characterizing an affidavit, in order to prevent questioning deemed relevant by the judge. Such false and misleading statements were subsequently acknowledged by his attorney in a communication to that judge.

(6) On or about January 18 and January 20-21, 1998, William Jefferson Clinton related a false and misleading account of events relevant to a Federal civil rights action brought against him to a potential witness in that proceeding, in order to corruptly influence the testimony of that witness.

(7) On or about January 21, 23 and 26, 1998, William Jefferson Clinton made false and misleading statements to potential witnesses in a Federal grand jury proceeding in order to corruptly influence the testimony of those witnesses. The false and misleading statements made by William Jefferson Clinton were repeated by the witnesses to the grand jury, causing the grand jury to receive false and misleading information.

In all of this, William Jefferson Clinton has undermined the integrity of his office, has brought disrepute on the Presidency, has betrayed his trust as President, and has acted in a manner subversive of the rule of law and justice, to the manifest injury of the people of the United States.

Wherefore, William Jefferson Clinton, by such conduct, warrants impeachment and trial, and removal from office and disqualification to hold and enjoy any office of honor, trust, or profit under the United States.

Article IV

Using the powers and influence of the office of President of the United States, William Jefferson Clinton, in violation of his constitutional oath faithfully to execute the office of President of the United States and, to the best of his ability, preserve, protect, and defend the Constitution of the United States, and in disregard of his constitutional duty to take care that the laws be faithfully executed, has engaged in conduct that resulted in misuse and abuse of his high office, impaired the due and proper administration of justice and the conduct of lawful inquiries, and contravened the authority of the legislative branch and the truth seeking purpose of a coordinate investigative proceeding, in that, as President, William Jefferson Clinton refused and failed to respond to certain written requests for admission and willfully made perjurious, false and misleading sworn statements in response to certain written requests for admission propounded to him as part of the impeachment inquiry authorized by the House of Representatives of the Congress of the United States. William Jefferson Clinton, in refusing and failing to respond and in making perjurious, false and misleading statements, assumed to himself functions and judgments necessary to the exercise of the sole power of impeachment vested by the Constitution in the House of Representatives and exhibited contempt for the inquiry.

In doing this, William Jefferson Clinton has undermined the integrity of his office, has brought disrepute on the Presidency, has betrayed his trust as President, and has acted in a manner subversive of the rule of law and justice, to the manifest injury of the people of the United States.

Wherefore, William Jefferson Clinton, by such conduct, warrants impeachment and trial, and removal from office and disqualification to hold and enjoy any office of honor, trust, or profit under the United States.

UNITED STATES V. MORRISON ET AL. (2000)

Lawsuit was brought under the Violence against Women Act. Alleging she was raped by three men who were students at Virginia Polytechnic Institute, Chrsity Brzonkala sued under the act, which provided a federal civil remedy for victims of gender-motivated violence. The Court struck down the law because, it argued, the Commerce Clause did not give Congress the authority to enact a law with such a remedy. Relying on Lopez, the Court saw the connection between gender-motivated violence and interstate commerce as far too tenuous. Congress could not regulate noneconomic, violent criminal conduct based solely on the combined effect that conduct might have on interstate commerce.

Chief Justice Rehnquist delivered the opinion of the Court.

In these cases we consider the constitutionality of 42 U. S. C. §13981, which provides a federal civil remedy for the victims of gender-motivated violence. The United States Court of Appeals for the Fourth Circuit, sitting en banc, struck down §13981 because it concluded that Congress lacked constitutional authority to enact the section's civil remedy. Believing that these cases are controlled by our decisions in *United States* v. *Lopez*, 514 U. S. 549 (1995), *United States* v. *Harris*, 106 U. S. 629 (1883), and the *Civil Rights Cases*, 109 U. S. 3 (1883), we affirm.

I

Petitioner Christy Brzonkala enrolled at Virginia Polytechnic Institute (Virginia Tech) in the fall of 1994. In September of that year, Brzonkala met respondents Antonio Morrison and James Crawford, who were both students at Virginia Tech and members of its varsity football team. Brzonkala alleges that, within 30 minutes of meeting Morrison and Crawford, they assaulted and repeatedly raped her. After the attack, Morrison allegedly told Brzonkala, "You better not have any . . . diseases." Complaint ¶ ;22. In the months following the rape, Morrison also allegedly announced in the dormitory's dining room that he "like[d] to get girls drunk and. . . ." *Id.*, ¶ ;31. The omitted portions, quoted verbatim in the briefs on file with this Court, consist of boasting, debased remarks about what Morrison would do to women, vulgar remarks that cannot fail to shock and offend.

Brzonkala alleges that this attack caused her to become severely emotionally disturbed and depressed. She sought assistance from a university psychiatrist, who prescribed antidepressant medication. Shortly after the rape Brzonkala stopped attending classes and withdrew from the university.

In early 1995, Brzonkala filed a complaint against respondents. . . .

Section 13981 was part of the Violence Against Women Act of 1994, §40302, 108 Stat. 1941–1942. It states that "[a]ll persons within the United States shall have the right to be free from crimes of violence motivated by gender." . . .

Every law enacted by Congress must be based on one or more of its powers enumerated in the Constitution. "The powers of the legislature are defined and limited; and that those limits may not be mistaken or forgotten, the constitution is written." *Marbury* v. *Madison*, 1 Cranch 137, 176 (1803) (Marshall, C. J.). Congress explicitly identified the sources of federal authority on which it relied in enacting §13981. It said that a "federal civil rights cause of action" is established "[p]ursuant to the affirmative power of Congress . . . under section 5 of the Fourteenth Amendment to the Constitution, as well as under section 8 of Article I of the Constitution." 42 U. S. C. §13981(a). We address Congress' authority to enact this remedy under each of these constitutional provisions in turn.

II

Due respect for the decisions of a coordinate branch of Government demands that we invalidate a congressional enactment only upon a plain showing that Congress has exceeded its constitutional bounds. See *United States* v. *Lopez*. . . .

As we discussed at length in *Lopez*, our interpretation of the Commerce Clause has changed as our Nation has developed. . . . We need not repeat that detailed review of the

Commerce Clause's history here; it suffices to say that, in the years since *NLRB* v. *Jones & Laughlin Steel Corp.* . . . Congress has had considerably greater latitude in regulating conduct and transactions under the Commerce Clause than our previous case law permitted. . . .

Lopez emphasized, however, that even under our modern, expansive interpretation of the Commerce Clause, Congress' regulatory authority is not without effective bounds. . . .

As we observed in *Lopez*, modern Commerce Clause jurisprudence has "identified three broad categories of activity that Congress may regulate under its commerce power." . . .

Petitioners . . . seek to sustain §13981 as a regulation of activity that substantially affects interstate commerce. Given §13981's focus on gender-motivated violence wherever it occurs (rather than violence directed at the instrumentalities of interstate commerce, interstate markets, or things or persons in interstate commerce). . . .

With [the principles enunciated in *Lopez*] underlying our Commerce Clause jurisprudence as reference points, the proper resolution of the present cases is clear. Gender-motivated crimes of violence are not, in any sense of the phrase, economic activity. While we need not adopt a categorical rule against aggregating the effects of any noneconomic activity in order to decide these cases, thus far in our Nation's history our cases have upheld Commerce Clause regulation of intrastate activity only where that activity is economic in nature. . . . Like the Gun-Free School Zones Act at issue in *Lopez*, §13981 contains no jurisdictional element establishing that the federal cause of action is in pursuance of Congress' power to regulate interstate commerce. Although *Lopez* makes clear that such a jurisdictional element would lend support to the argument that §13981 is sufficiently tied to interstate commerce, Congress elected to cast §13981's remedy over a wider, and more purely intrastate, body of violent crime.[5]

In contrast with the lack of congressional findings that we faced in *Lopez*, §13981 *is* supported by numerous findings regarding the serious impact that gender-motivated violence has on victims and their families. . . . But the existence of congressional findings is not sufficient, by itself, to sustain the constitutionality of Commerce Clause legislation. . . .

[But] in these cases, Congress' findings are substantially weakened by the fact that they rely so heavily on a method of reasoning that we have already rejected as unworkable if we are to maintain the Constitution's enumeration of powers. Congress found that gender-motivated violence affects interstate commerce "by deterring potential victims from traveling interstate, from engaging in employment in interstate business, and from transacting with business, and in places involved in interstate commerce; . . . by diminishing national productivity, increasing medical and other costs, and decreasing the supply of and the demand for interstate products." H. R. Conf. Rep. No. 103-711, at 385.

. . . Given these findings and petitioners' arguments, the concern that we expressed in *Lopez* that Congress might use the Commerce Clause to completely obliterate the Constitution's distinction between national and local authority seems well founded. See *Lopez, supra,* at 564. The reasoning that petitioners advance seeks to follow the but-for causal chain from the initial occurrence of violent crime (the suppression of which has always been the prime object of the States' police power) to every attenuated effect upon interstate commerce. If accepted, petitioners' reasoning would allow Congress to regulate any crime as long as the nationwide, aggregated impact of that crime has substantial effects on employment, production, transit, or consumption. Indeed, if Congress may regulate gender-motivated violence, it would be able to regulate murder or any other type of violence since gender-motivated violence, as a subset of all violent crime, is certain to have lesser economic impacts than the larger class of which it is a part. . . .

We accordingly reject the argument that Congress may regulate noneconomic, violent criminal conduct based solely on that conduct's aggregate effect on interstate commerce. The Constitution requires a distinction between what is truly national and what is truly local. . . . In recognizing this fact we preserve one of the few principles that has been consistent since the Clause was adopted. The regulation and punishment of intrastate violence that is not directed at the instrumentalities, channels, or goods involved in interstate commerce has always been the province of the States. See, *e.g., Cohens* v. *Virginia,* 6 Wheat. 264, 426, 428 (1821) (Marshall, C. J.). . . .

Because we conclude that the Commerce Clause does not provide Congress with authority to enact §13981, we address petitioners' alternative argument that the section's civil remedy should be upheld as an exercise of Congress' remedial power under §5 of the Fourteenth Amendment. As noted above, Congress expressly invoked the Fourteenth Amendment as a source of authority to enact §13981.

The principles governing an analysis of congressional legislation under §5 are well settled. Section 5 states that Congress may "'enforce,' by 'appropriate legislation' the constitutional guarantee that no State shall deprive any person of 'life, liberty or property, without due process of law,' nor deny any person 'equal protection of the laws.'" *City of Boerne* v. *Flores* (1997). Section 5 is "a positive grant of legislative power," . . . that includes authority to "prohibit conduct which is not itself unconstitutional and [to] intrud[e] into `legislative spheres of autonomy previously reserved to the States.'" *Flores* . . . [However] several limitations inherent in §5's text and constitutional context have been recognized since the Fourteenth Amendment was adopted.

Petitioners alternatively argue that, unlike the situation in the *Civil Rights Cases,* here there has been gender-based disparate treatment by state authorities, whereas in those cases there was no indication of such state action. There is abundant evidence, however, to show that the Congresses that enacted the Civil Rights Acts of 1871 and 1875 had a purpose similar to that of Congress in enacting §13981: There were state laws on the books bespeaking equality of treatment, but in the administration of these laws there was discrimination against newly freed slaves.

But even if that distinction were valid, we do not believe it would save §13981's civil remedy. For the remedy is simply not "corrective in its character, adapted to counteract and redress the operation of such prohibited [s]tate laws or proceedings of [s]tate officers." *Civil Rights Cases*, 109 U. S., at 18. Or, as we have phrased it in more recent cases, prophylactic legislation under §5 must have a "congruence and proportionality between the injury to be prevented or remedied and the means adopted to that end." . . . Section 13981 is not aimed at proscribing discrimination by officials which the Fourteenth Amendment might not itself proscribe; it is directed not at any State or state actor, but at individuals who have committed criminal acts motivated by gender bias.

Petitioner Brzonkala's complaint alleges that she was the victim of a brutal assault. But Congress' effort in §13981 to provide a federal civil remedy can be sustained neither under the Commerce Clause nor under §5 of the Fourteenth Amendment. If the allegations here are true, no civilized system of justice could fail to provide her a remedy for the conduct of respondent Morrison. But under our federal system that remedy must be provided by the Commonwealth of Virginia, and not by the United States. The judgment of the Court of Appeals is Affirmed. . . .

Justice Souter, with whom *Justice Stevens, Justice Ginsburg*, and *Justice Breyer* join, dissenting.

The Court says both that it leaves Commerce Clause precedent undisturbed and that the Civil Rights Remedy of the Violence Against Women Act of 1994, 42 U. S. C. §13981, exceeds Congress's power under that Clause. I find the claims irreconcilable and respectfully dissent. . . .

I

Our cases, which remain at least nominally undisturbed, stand for the following propositions. Congress has the power to legislate with regard to activity that, in the aggregate, has a substantial effect on interstate commerce. See *Wickard* v. *Filburn*, 317 U. S. 111, 124-128 (1942); *Hodel* v. *Virginia Surface Mining & Reclamation Assn.*, 452 U. S. 264, 277 (1981). The fact of such a substantial effect is not an issue for the courts in the first instance, *ibid.*, but for the Congress, whose institutional capacity for gathering evidence and taking testimony far exceeds ours. By passing legislation, Congress indicates its conclusion, whether explicitly or not, that facts support its exercise of the commerce power. The business of the courts is to review the congressional assessment, not for soundness but simply for the rationality of concluding that a jurisdictional basis exists in fact. See *ibid.* Any explicit findings that Congress chooses to make, though not dispositive of the question of rationality, may advance judicial review by identifying factual authority on which Congress relied. Applying those propositions in these cases can lead to only one conclusion. . . .

The Act would have passed muster at any time between *Wickard* in 1942 and *Lopez* in 1995, a period in which the law enjoyed a stable understanding that congressional power under the Commerce Clause, complemented by the authority of the Necessary and Proper Clause, Art. I. §8 cl. 18, extended to all activity that, when aggregated, has a substantial effect on interstate commerce. As already noted, this understanding was secure even against the turmoil at the passage of the Civil Rights Act of 1964, in the aftermath of which the Court not only reaffirmed the cumulative effects and rational basis features of the substantial effects test, see *Heart of Atlanta, supra,* at 258; *McClung, supra,* at 301–305, but declined to limit the commerce power through a formal distinction between legislation focused on "commerce" and statutes addressing "moral and social wrong[s]," *Heart of Atlanta, supra,* at 257.

The premise that the enumeration of powers implies that other powers are withheld is sound; the conclusion that some particular categories of subject matter are therefore presumptively beyond the reach of the commerce power is, however, a non sequitur. From the fact that Art. I, §8, cl. 3 grants an authority limited to regulating commerce, it follows only that Congress may claim no authority under that section to address any subject that does not affect commerce. It does not at all follow that an activity affecting commerce nonetheless falls outside the commerce power, depending on the specific character of the activity, or the authority of a State to regulate it along with Congress. My disagreement with the majority is not, however, confined to logic, for history has shown that categorical exclusions have proven as unworkable in practice as they are unsupportable in theory.

Obviously, it would not be inconsistent with the text of the Commerce Clause itself to declare "noncommercial" primary activity beyond or presumptively beyond the scope of the commerce power. That variant of categorical approach is not, however, the sole textually permissible way of defining the scope of the Commerce Clause, and any such neat limitation would at least be suspect in the light of the final sentence of Article I, §8, authorizing Congress to make "all Laws . . . necessary and proper" to give effect to its enumerated powers such as commerce. See *United States* v. *Darby,* 312 U. S. 100, 118 (1941) ("The power of Congress . . . extends to those activities intrastate which so affect interstate commerce or the exercise of the power of Congress over it as to make regulation of them appropriate means to the attainment of a legitimate end, the exercise of the granted power of Congress to regulate interstate commerce"). Accordingly, for significant periods of our history, the Court has defined the commerce power as plenary, unsusceptible to categorical exclusions, and this was the view expressed throughout the latter part of the 20th century in the substantial effects test. These two conceptions of the commerce power, plenary and categorically limited, are in fact old rivals, and today's revival of their competition summons up familiar history, a brief reprise of which may be helpful in posing what I take to be the key question going to the legitimacy of the majority's decision to breathe new life into the approach of categorical limitation.

Chief Justice Marshall's seminal opinion in *Gibbons* v. *Ogden, supra,* at 193–194, construed the commerce power from the start with "a breadth never yet exceeded," *Wickard* v. *Filburn,* 317 U. S., at 120. In particular, it is worth noting, the Court in *Wickard* did not regard its holding as exceeding the scope of Chief Justice Marshall's view of interstate commerce; *Wickard* applied an aggregate effects test to ostensibly domestic, noncommercial farming consistently with Chief Justice Marshall's indication that the commerce power may be understood by its exclusion of subjects, among others, "which do not affect other States," *Gibbons,* 9 Wheat., at 195. This plenary view of the power has either prevailed or been acknowledged by this Court at every stage of our jurisprudence. . . .

In the half century following the modern activation of the commerce power with passage of the Interstate Commerce Act in 1887, this Court from time to time created categorical enclaves beyond congressional reach by declaring such activities as "mining," "production," "manufacturing," and union membership to be outside the definition of "commerce" and by limiting application of the effects test to "direct" rather than "indirect" commercial consequences. . . . Since adherence to these formalistically contrived confines of commerce power in large measure provoked the judicial crisis of 1937, one might reasonably have doubted that Members of this Court would ever again toy with a return to the days before *NLRB* v. *Jones & Laughlin Steel Corp.,* 301 U. S. 1 (1937), which brought the earlier and nearly disastrous experiment to an end. And yet today's decision can only be seen as a step toward recapturing the prior mistakes. Its revival of a distinction between commercial and noncommercial conduct is at odds with *Wickard,* which repudiated that analysis, and the enquiry into commercial purpose, first intimated by the *Lopez* concurrence, see *Lopez, supra,* at 580 (opinion of *Kennedy,* J.), is cousin to the intent-based analysis employed in *Hammer* . . . but rejected for Commerce Clause purposes in *Heart of Atlanta* . . . and *Darby.*

Why is the majority tempted to reject the lesson so painfully learned in 1937? An answer emerges from contrasting *Wickard* with one of the predecessor cases it superseded. It was obvious in *Wickard* that growing wheat for consumption right on the farm was not "commerce" in the common vocabulary, but that did not matter constitutionally so long as the aggregated activity of domestic wheat growing affected commerce substantially. Just a few years before *Wickard,* however, it had certainly been no less obvious that "mining" practices could substantially affect commerce, even though *Carter Coal Co., supra,* had held mining regulation beyond the national commerce power. When we try to fathom the difference between the two cases, it is clear that they did not go in different directions because the *Carter Coal* Court could not understand a causal connection that the *Wickard* Court could grasp; the difference, rather, turned on the fact that the Court in *Carter Coal* had a reason for trying to maintain its categorical, formalistic distinction, while that reason had been abandoned by the time *Wickard* was decided. The reason was laissez-faire economics, the point of which was to keep government interference to a minimum. See *Lopez, supra,* at 605-606 (*Souter,* J., dissenting). The Court in *Carter Coal* was still trying to create a laissez-faire world out of the 20th-century economy, and formalistic commercial distinctions were thought to be useful instruments in achieving that object. The Court in *Wickard* knew it could not do any such thing and in the aftermath of the New Deal had long since stopped attempting the impossible. Without the animating economic theory, there was no point in contriving formalisms in a war with Chief Justice Marshall's conception of the commerce power.

If we now ask why the formalistic economic/noneconomic distinction might matter today, after its rejection in *Wickard,* the answer is not that the majority fails to see causal connections in an integrated economic world. The answer is that in the minds of the majority there is a new animating theory that makes categorical formalism seem useful again. Just as the old formalism had value in the service of an economic conception, the new one is useful in serving a conception of federalism. It is the instrument by which assertions of national power are to be limited in favor of preserving a supposedly discernible, proper sphere of state autonomy to legislate or refrain from legislating as the individual States see fit. The legitimacy of the Court's current emphasis on the noncommercial nature of regulated activity, then, does not turn on any logic serving the text of the Commerce Clause or on the realism of the majority's view of the national economy. The essential issue is rather the strength of the majority's claim to have a constitutional warrant for its current conception of a federal relationship enforceable by this Court through limits on otherwise plenary commerce power. This conception is the subject of the majority's second categorical discount applied today to the facts bearing on the substantial effects test.

Although Madison had emphasized the conception of a National Government of discrete powers (a conception that a number of the ratifying conventions thought was too indeterminate to protect civil liberties), Madison himself must have sensed the potential scope of some of the powers granted (such as the authority to regulate commerce), for he took care in The Federalist No. 46 to hedge his argument for limited power by explaining the importance of national politics in protecting the States' interests. The National Government "will partake sufficiently of the spirit [of the States], to be disinclined to invade the rights of the individual States, or the prerogatives of their governments." The Federalist No. 46, at 319.

Source: Justia.com – US Supreme Court Center. http://supreme.justia.com/us/529/598/case.html

CAMPBELL V. CLINTON (2000)

Another attempt by Congress to stymie the presidential use of the military and get the courts to enforce the War Power Resolution. This followed the decision of President Bill Clinton to use force in the former Yugoslavia in support of a NATO action to stop Serbian atrocities in Kosovo. Representative Tom Campbell had previously forced votes in the House under the War Powers Resolution to stop Clinton from bombing Serbia and Kosovo. When the sixty-day period mandated under the War Powers Reso-

lution ended, Campbell went to court. The court again found members of Congress had no standing. Campbell sought Supreme Court review but was turned down.

OPINION: SILBERMAN, *Circuit Judge:* A number of congressmen, led by Tom Campbell of California, filed suit claiming that the President violated the War Powers Resolution and the War Powers Clause of the Constitution by directing U.S. forces' participation in the recent NATO campaign in Yugoslavia. The district court dismissed for lack of standing. We agree with the district court and therefore affirm.

The government does not respond to appellants' claim on the merits. Instead the government challenges the jurisdiction of the federal courts to adjudicate this claim on three separate grounds: the case is moot; appellants lack standing, as the district court concluded; and the case is non-justiciable. Since we agree with the district court that the congressmen lack standing it is not necessary to decide whether there are other jurisdictional defects.

The question whether congressmen have standing in federal court to challenge the lawfulness of actions of the executive was answered, at least in large part, in the Supreme Court's recent decision in *Raines v. Byrd* (1997). *Raines* involved a constitutional challenge to the President's authority under the short-lived Line Item Veto Act. Individual congressmen claimed that under that Act a President could veto (unconstitutionally) only part of a law and thereby diminish the institutional power of Congress. Observing it had never held that congressmen have standing to assert an institutional injury as against the executive, the Court held that petitioners in the case lacked "legislative standing" to challenge the Act. . . .

It is uncontested that the Congress could terminate the [contested program] were a sufficient number in each House so inclined. Because the parties' dispute is therefore fully susceptible to political resolution, we would [under circuit precedent] dismiss the complaint to avoid "meddling in the internal affairs of the legislative branch." Applying *Raines*, we would reach the same conclusion.

There remains, however, a soft spot in the legal barrier against congressional legal challenges to executive action, and it is a soft spot that appellants sought to penetrate. . . .

In *Raines* the plaintiff congressmen had relied on *Coleman* to argue that they had standing because the presidential veto had undermined the "effectiveness of their votes." The Supreme Court noted that *Coleman* might be distinguished on grounds that the federal constitutional separation of powers concerns that underlay its decision in *Raines* (and which we emphasized in *Chenoweth*) were not present, or that if the Court in *Coleman* had not taken the case a question of federal law—the ratification *vel non* by the Kansas Legislature—would remain as decided by the Kansas Court. *But cf. Coleman,* 307 U.S. at 465-66 (opinion of Frankfurter, J.). But the Court thought it unnecessary to cabin *Coleman* on those grounds. *See Raines,* 521 U.S. at 824 n.8. Instead, the Court emphasized that the congressmen were not asserting that their votes had been "completely nullified":

They have not alleged that they voted for a specific bill, that there were sufficient votes to pass the bill, and that the bill was nonetheless deemed defeated. . . .

Nor can they allege that the Act will nullify their votes in the future in the same way that the votes of the *Coleman* legislators had been nullified. . . .

In addition, a majority of Senators and Congressmen can vote to repeal the Act, or to exempt a given appropriations bill. . . .

Here the plaintiff congressmen, by specifically defeating the War Powers Resolution authorization by a tie vote and by defeating a declaration of war, sought to fit within the *Coleman* exception to the *Raines* rule. . . .

The President here did not claim to be acting pursuant to the defeated declaration of war or a statutory authorization, but instead "pursuant to [his] constitutional authority to conduct U.S. foreign relations and as Commander-in-Chief and Chief Executive." . . . Legislators have standing whenever the government does something Congress voted against, still less that congressmen would have standing anytime a President allegedly acts in excess of statutory authority. As the government correctly observes, appellants' statutory argument, although cast in terms of the nullification of a recent vote, essentially is that the President violated the quarter-century old War Powers Resolution. Similarly, their constitutional argument is that the President has acted illegally—in excess of his authority—because he waged war in the constitutional sense without a congressional delegation. Neither claim is analogous to a *Coleman* nullification.

In this case, Congress certainly could have passed a law forbidding the use of U.S. forces in the Yugoslav campaign; indeed, there was a measure—albeit only a concurrent resolution—introduced to require the President to withdraw U.S. troops. Unfortunately, however, for those congressmen who, like appellants, desired an end to U.S. involvement in Yugoslavia, this measure was *defeated* by a 139 to 290 vote. Of course, Congress always retains appropriations authority and could have cut off funds for the American role in the conflict. Again there was an effort to do so but it failed; appropriations were authorized. And there always remains the possibility of impeachment should a President act in disregard of Congress' authority on these matters.

Appellants' constitutional claim stands on no firmer footing. Appellants argue that the War Powers Clause of the Constitution proscribes a President from using military force except as is necessary to repel a sudden attack. But they also argue that the WPR "implements" or channels congressional authority under the Constitution. It may well be then that since we have determined that appellants lack standing to enforce the WPR there is nothing left of their constitutional claim. Assuming, however, that appellants' constitutional claim should be considered separately, the same logic dictates they do not have standing to bring such a challenge. That is to say Congress has a broad range of legislative authority it can use to stop a President's war making. . . .

SILBERMAN, *Circuit Judge, concurring:*

Prior litigation under the WPR has turned on the threshold test whether U.S. forces are engaged in hostilities or are in imminent danger of hostilities. But the question posed by appellants—whether the President's refusal to discontinue American activities in Yugoslavia violates the WPR—necessarily depends on the statute having been triggered in the first place. It has been held that the statutory threshold standard is not precise enough and too obviously calls for a political judgment to be one suitable for judicial determinations. . . . I think that is correct. Appellants point to a House Report suggesting that hostilities for purposes of the WPR include all situations "where there is a reasonable expectation that American military personnel will be subject to hostile fire." That elaboration hardly helps. It could reasonably be thought that anytime American soldiers are confronted by armed or potentially armed forces of a non-ally there is a reasonable expectation that they will be subject to hostile fire. Certainly any competent military leader will assume that to be so.

Appellants argue that here there is no real problem of definition because this air war was so overwhelming and indisputable. It is asserted that the President implicitly conceded the applicability of the WPR by sending the report to Congress. In truth, the President only said the report was "consistent" with the WPR. In any event, I do not think it matters how clear it is in any particular case that "hostilities" were initiated if the statutory standard is one generally unsuited to judicial resolution. . . .

Appellants cannot point to any constitutional test for what is war. . . . Instead, appellants offer a rough definition of war provided in 1994 by an Assistant Attorney General to four Senators with respect to a planned intervention in Haiti, as well as a number of law review articles each containing its own definition of war. I do not think any of these sources, however, offers a coherent test for judges to apply to the question what constitutes war, a point only accentuated by the variances, for instance, between the numerous law review articles. For that reason, I disagree with Judge Tatel's assertion that we can decide appellants' constitutional claim because it is somehow obvious in this case that our country fought a war.

Judge Tatel points to numerous cases in which a court has determined that our nation was at war, but none of these cases involved the question whether the President had "declared war" in violation of the Constitution. . . . [The court noted a variety of instances going back to the late 1790s and the undeclared war with France.]

Even assuming a court could determine what "war" is, it is important to remember that the Constitution grants Congress the power to declare war, which is not necessarily the same as the power to determine whether U.S. forces will fight in a war. . . . There, petitioners challenged the authority of the President to impose a blockade on the secessionist States, an act of war, where Congress had not declared war against the Confederacy. The Court, while recognizing that the President "has no power to initiate or declare a war," observed that "war may exist without a declaration on either side." . . . In instances where war is declared against the United States by the actions of another country, the President "does not initiate the war, but is bound to accept the challenge without waiting for any special legislative authority." . . . Importantly, the Court made clear that it would not dispute the President on measures necessary to repel foreign aggression. The President alone must determine what degree of force the crisis demands.

I read the *Prize Cases* to stand for the proposition that the President has independent authority to repel aggressive acts by third parties even without specific congressional authorization, and courts may not review the level of force selected. . . . Therefore, I assume, *arguendo*, that appellants are correct and only Congress has authority to *initiate* "war." If the President may direct U.S. forces in response to third-party initiated war, then the question any plaintiff who challenges the constitutionality of a war must answer is, who started it? The question of who is responsible for a conflict is, as history reveals, rather difficult to answer, and we lack judicial standards for resolving it. . . .

Judge Tatel would substitute our judgment for the President's as to the point at which an intervention for reasons of national security is justified, after which point—when the crisis is no longer acute—the President must obtain a declaration of war. One should bear in mind that Kosovo's tensions antedate the creation of this republic.

In sum, there are no standards to determine either the statutory or constitutional questions raised in this case, and the question of whether the President has intruded on the war-declaring authority of Congress fits squarely within the political question doctrine. . . .

TATEL, Circuit Judge, *concurring:*

In my view, were this case brought by plaintiffs with standing, we could determine whether the President, in undertaking the air campaign in Yugoslavia, exceeded his authority under the Constitution or the War Powers Resolution.

To begin with, I do not agree that courts lack judicially discoverable and manageable standards for "determining the existence of a 'war.'" Whether the military activity in Yugoslavia amounted to "war" within the meaning of the Declare War Clause, U.S. CONST. art. I, § 8, cl. 11, is no more standardless than any other question regarding the constitutionality of government action. Precisely what police conduct violates the Fourth Amendment guarantee "against unreasonable searches and seizures?" When does government action amount to "an establishment of religion" prohibited by the First Amendment? When is an election district so bizarrely shaped as to violate the Fourteenth Amendment guarantee of "equal protection of the laws?" Because such constitutional terms are not selfdefining, standards for answering these questions have evolved, as legal standards always do, through years of judicial decisionmaking. Courts have proven no less capable of developing standards to resolve war powers challenges. . . .

The Government's final argument—that entertaining a war powers challenge risks the government speaking with "multifarious voices" on a delicate issue of foreign policy—fails for similar reasons. Because courts are the final arbiters of the constitutionality of the President's actions, "there is no possibility of 'multifarious pronouncements' on this question. *Chadha.* Any short-term confusion that judicial action might instill in the mind of an authoritarian enemy, or even an ally, is but a small price to pay for preserving the constitutional separation of powers and protecting the bedrock constitutional principle that "it is emphatically the province and duty of the judicial department to say what the law is." *Marbury v. Madison* (1803).

IRAQ WAR RESOLUTION (2002)

For what turned out to be dubious reasons, President Bush—although declaring he did not need congressional approval—sought and gained Congress's sanction to invade Iraq. Citing Iraq's ostensible links to Al Qaeda and the 9/11 tragedy and, most importantly, its supposed hidden weapons of mass destruction, the president asked for authority to send troops to that country if necessary. After some debate, Congress gave him the power to do so.

JOINT RESOLUTION
To authorize the use of United States Armed Forces against Iraq.

Whereas in 1990 in response to Iraq's war of aggression against and illegal occupation of Kuwait, the United States forged a coalition of nations to liberate Kuwait and its people in order to defend the national security of the United States and enforce United Nations Security Council resolutions relating to Iraq;

Whereas after the liberation of Kuwait in 1991, Iraq entered into a United Nations sponsored cease-fire agreement pursuant to which Iraq unequivocally agreed, among other things, to eliminate its nuclear, biological, and chemical weapons programs and the means to deliver and develop them, and to end its support for international terrorism;

Whereas the efforts of international weapons inspectors, United States intelligence agencies, and Iraqi defectors led to the discovery that Iraq had large stockpiles of chemical weapons and a large scale biological weapons program, and that Iraq had an advanced nuclear weapons development program that was much closer to producing a nuclear weapon than intelligence reporting had previously indicated;

Whereas Iraq, in direct and flagrant violation of the cease-fire, attempted to thwart the efforts of weapons inspectors to identify and destroy Iraq's weapons of mass destruction stockpiles and development capabilities, which finally resulted in the withdrawal of inspectors from Iraq on October 31, 1998;

Whereas in Public Law 105-235 (August 14, 1998), Congress concluded that Iraq's continuing weapons of mass destruction programs threatened vital United States interests and international peace and security, declared Iraq to be in "material and unacceptable breach of its international obligations" and urged the President "to take appropriate action, in accordance with the Constitution and relevant laws of the United States, to bring Iraq into compliance with its international obligations";

Whereas Iraq both poses a continuing threat to the national security of the United States and international peace and security in the Persian Gulf region and remains in material and unacceptable breach of its international obligations by, among other things, continuing to possess and develop a significant chemical and biological weapons capability, actively seeking a nuclear weapons capability, and supporting and harboring terrorist organizations;

Whereas Iraq persists in violating resolution of the United Nations Security Council by continuing to engage in brutal repression of its civilian population thereby threatening international peace and security in the region, by refusing to release, repatriate, or account for non-Iraqi citizens wrongfully detained by Iraq, including an American serviceman, and by failing to return property wrongfully seized by Iraq from Kuwait;

Whereas the current Iraqi regime has demonstrated its capability and willingness to use weapons of mass destruction against other nations and its own people;

Whereas the current Iraqi regime has demonstrated its continuing hostility toward, and willingness to attack, the United States, including by attempting in 1993 to assassinate former President Bush and by firing on many thousands of occasions on United States and Coalition Armed Forces engaged in enforcing the resolutions of the United Nations Security Council;

Whereas members of al Qaida, an organization bearing responsibility for attacks on the United States, its citizens, and interests, including the attacks that occurred on September 11, 2001, are known to be in Iraq;

Whereas Iraq continues to aid and harbor other international terrorist organizations, including organizations that threaten the lives and safety of United States citizens;

Whereas the attacks on the United States of September 11, 2001, underscored the gravity of the threat posed by the acquisition of weapons of mass destruction by international terrorist organizations;

Whereas Iraq's demonstrated capability and willingness to use weapons of mass destruction, the risk that the current Iraqi regime will either employ those weapons to launch a surprise attack against the United States or its Armed Forces or provide them to international terrorists who would do so, and the extreme magnitude of harm that would result to the United States and its citizens from such an attack, combine to justify action by the United States to defend itself;

Whereas United Nations Security Council Resolution 678 (1990) authorizes the use of all necessary means to enforce United Nations Security Council Resolution 660 (1990) and subsequent relevant resolutions and to compel Iraq to cease certain activities that threaten international peace and security, including the development of weapons of mass destruction and refusal or obstruction of United Nations weapons inspections in violation of United Nations Security Council Resolution 687 (1991), repression of its civilian population in violation of United Nations Security Council Resolution 688 (1991), and threatening its neighbors or United Nations operations in Iraq in violation of United Nations Security Council Resolution 949 (1994);

Whereas in the Authorization for Use of Military Force Against Iraq Resolution (Public Law 102-1), Congress has authorized the President "to use United States Armed

Forces pursuant to United Nations Security Council Resolution 678 (1990) in order to achieve implementation of Security Council Resolution 660, 661, 662, 664, 665, 666, 667, 669, 670, 674, and 677";

Whereas in December 1991, Congress expressed its sense that it "supports the use of all necessary means to achieve the goals of United Nations Security Council Resolution 687 as being consistent with the Authorization of Use of Military Force Against Iraq Resolution (Public Law 102-1)," that Iraq's repression of its civilian population violates United Nations Security Council Resolution 688 and "constitutes a continuing threat to the peace, security, and stability of the Persian Gulf region," and that Congress, "supports the use of all necessary means to achieve the goals of United Nations Security Council Resolution 688";

Whereas the Iraq Liberation Act of 1998 (Public Law 105-338) expressed the sense of Congress that it should be the policy of the United States to support efforts to remove from power the current Iraqi regime and promote the emergence of a democratic government to replace that regime;

Whereas on September 12, 2002, President Bush committed the United States to "work with the United Nations Security Council to meet our common challenge" posed by Iraq and to "work for the necessary resolutions," while also making clear that "the Security Council resolutions will be enforced, and the just demands of peace and security will be met, or action will be unavoidable";

Whereas the United States is determined to prosecute the war on terrorism and Iraq's ongoing support for international terrorist groups combined with its development of weapons of mass destruction in direct violation of its obligations under the 1991 ceasefire and other United Nations Security Council resolutions make clear that it is in the national security interests of the United States and in furtherance of the war on terrorism that all relevant United Nations Security Council resolutions be enforced, including through the use of force if necessary;

Whereas Congress has taken steps to pursue vigorously the war on terrorism through the provision of authorities and funding requested by the President to take the necessary actions against international terrorists and terrorist organizations, including those nations, organizations, or persons who planned, authorized, committed, or aided the terrorist attacks that occurred on September 11, 2001, or harbored such persons or organizations;

Whereas the President and Congress are determined to continue to take all appropriate actions against international terrorists and terrorist organizations, including those nations, organizations, or persons who planned, authorized, committed, or aided the terrorist attacks that occurred on September 11, 2001, or harbored such persons or organizations;

Whereas the President has authority under the Constitution to take action in order to deter and prevent acts of international terrorism against the United States, as Congress recognized in the joint resolution on Authorization for Use of Military Force (Public Law 107-40); and

Whereas it is in the national security interests of the United States to restore international peace and security to the Persian Gulf region:

Now, therefore, be it Resolved by the Senate and House of Representatives of the United States of America in Congress assembled,

SECTION 1. SHORT TITLE.
This joint resolution may be cited as the "Authorization for Use of Military Force Against Iraq Resolution of 2002".

SECTION 2. SUPPORT FOR UNITED STATES DIPLOMATIC EFFORTS.
The Congress of the United States supports the efforts by the President to—

(1) strictly enforce through the United Nations Security Council all relevant Security Council resolutions regarding Iraq and encourages him in those efforts; and

(2) obtain prompt and decisive action by the Security Council to ensure that Iraq abandons its strategy of delay, evasion and noncompliance and promptly and strictly complies with all relevant Security Council resolutions regarding Iraq.

SECTION 3. AUTHORIZATION FOR USE OF UNITED STATES ARMED FORCES.
(a) AUTHORIZATION- The President is authorized to use the Armed Forces of the United States as he determines to be necessary and appropriate in order to—

(1) defend the national security of the United States against the continuing threat posed by Iraq; and

(2) enforce all relevant United Nations Security Council resolutions regarding Iraq.

(b) PRESIDENTIAL DETERMINATION- In connection with the exercise of the authority granted in subsection (a) to use force the President shall, prior to such exercise or as soon thereafter as may be feasible, but no later than 48 hours after exercising such authority, make available to the Speaker of the House of Representatives and the President pro tempore of the Senate his determination that—

(1) reliance by the United States on further diplomatic or other peaceful means alone either (A) will not adequately protect the national security of the United States against the continuing threat posed by Iraq or (B) is not likely to lead to enforcement of all relevant United Nations Security Council resolutions regarding Iraq; and

(2) acting pursuant to this joint resolution is consistent with the United States and other countries continuing to take the necessary actions against international terrorist and terrorist organizations, including those nations, organizations, or persons who planned, authorized, committed or aided the terrorist attacks that occurred on September 11, 2001.

(c) War Powers Resolution Requirements-

(1) SPECIFIC STATUTORY AUTHORIZATION- Consistent with section 8(a)(1) of the War Powers Resolution, the Congress declares that this section is intended to constitute specific statutory authorization within the meaning of section 5(b) of the War Powers Resolution.

(2) APPLICABILITY OF OTHER REQUIREMENTS- Nothing in this joint resolution supersedes any requirement of the War Powers Resolution.

SECTION 4. REPORTS TO CONGRESS.

(a) REPORTS- The President shall, at least once every 60 days, submit to the Congress a report on matters relevant to this joint resolution, including actions taken pursuant to the exercise of authority granted in section 3 and the status of planning for efforts that are expected to be required after such actions are completed, including those actions described in section 7 of the Iraq Liberation Act of 1998 (Public Law 105-338).

(b) SINGLE CONSOLIDATED REPORT- To the extent that the submission of any report described in subsection (a) coincides with the submission of any other report on matters relevant to this joint resolution otherwise required to be submitted to Congress pursuant to the reporting requirements of the War Powers Resolution (Public Law 93-148), all such reports may be submitted as a single consolidated report to the Congress.

(c) RULE OF CONSTRUCTION- To the extent that the information required by section 3 of the Authorization for Use of Military Force Against Iraq Resolution (Public Law 102-1) is included in the report required by this section, such report shall be considered as meeting the requirements of section 3 of such resolution.

Source: http://www.whitehouse.gov/news/releases/2002/10/200210022.htm

ANNOTATED BIBLIOGRAPHY

The Almanac of the Unelected: Staff of the U.S. Congress. Lanham, MD: Bernan Press.

Published annually by various editors. Provides background information on the seven-hundred-plus staffers of the House and Senate.

Arnold, R. Douglas. *The Logic of Congressional Action.* New Haven, CT: Yale University Press, 1990.

Focuses on how representatives and senators relate to their constituents in deciding why and how to vote.

Asbell, Bernard. *The Senate Nobody Knows.* New York: Doubleday, 1978.

Although somewhat dated, a good look at the Senate through the eyes of Edmund S. Muskie over a one-year period.

Baker, Richard A. *The Senate of the United States: A Bicentennial History.* Malabar, FL: Krieger Publishing, 1988.

A history of the United States Senate littered with first-person recollections from the early period to the late 1980s.

Baker, Ross K. *House and Senate.* New York: Norton, 1989.

A comprehensive explanation of the difference between the two houses of Congress by comparing the two by interviewing members of both chambers and those involved in the legislative process more peripherally, such as journalists, lobbyists, and staff members.

Barone, Michael, and Grant Ujifsa, eds. *Almanac of American Politics.* Washington, DC: National Journal Group, 2008.

Good background source for all kinds of political minutiae at the local level. It provides biographical and historical information on congressmen and senators, including election results and breakdowns, makeup of various districts, voting patterns, etc.

Bickford, Charlene Bangs, and Kenneth R. Bowling. *Birth of the Nation: The First Federal Congress 1789–1791*. rev. ed. Lanham, MD: Rowman and Littlefield, 2002.

Brief but incisive work that emphasizes the importance of the First Congress. Using the constitutional developments prior to constitutional ratification as a background, the book focuses both on the specifics and the broader implications and meanings of events in the early years.

Binder, Sarah. *Minority Rights, Majority Rule: Partisanship and the Development of Congress*. Cambridge, UK: Cambridge University Press, 1997.

Explains one of the apparent key differences in how the House and Senate work by explaining why majorities tend to dominate the House while minorities can often set the agenda in the Senate.

Binder, Sarah A., and Steven S. Smith. *Politics or Principle: Filibustering in the United States Senate*. Washington, DC: Brookings Institution, 1997.

An attempt to debunk the mythology surrounding the filibuster in the U.S. Senate. The book suggests that very few of the perceptions of this procedural device are correct and applies that view to commentary on institutional change.

Biographical Directory of the United States Congress, 1774–2005. Washington, DC: U.S. Government Printing Office, Joint Committee on Printing, 2006.

Biography of every member of Congress from 1774 through the beginning of 2005. Frequently updated by online material.

Bond, R. Jon, and Richard Fleisher. *The President in the Legislative Arena*. Chicago: University of Chicago Press, 1992.

Takes a wider than common view of the executive branch and how it influences congressional action, going beyond merely the issue of whether legislation favored by the White House is passed or not. An emphasis is placed upon party ideology in Congress, as inherited by the president, rather than the president's own abilities to bargain with that branch.

Bowling, Kenneth R., and Donald R. Kennon, eds. *Inventing Congress: Origins and Establishment of the First Federal Congress*. Athens: Ohio University Press, 1999.

Series of essays that focuses on the First Congress and its historical and philosophical roots as well as its cultural development, evolution, etc. Product of two conferences sponsored by the United States Capitol Historical Society for studying the early years.

Bowling, Kenneth R., and Donald R. Kennon, eds. *Neither Separate nor Equal: Congress and the Executive Branch in the 1790's*. Athens: Ohio University Press, 2001.

Series of essays showing that the modern concept of three distinct branches of government was not apparent in the early years of the nation, either philosophically or practically.

Bowling, Kenneth R., and Donald R. Kennon, eds. *The House and Senate in the 1790's: Petitioning, Lobbying and Institutional Development*. Athens: Ohio University Press, 2002.

Collection of articles that touches on some of the issues surrounding lobbying and petitioning in the early days of Congress.

Bowling, Kenneth R., and Helen E. Veit, eds. *The Diary of William Maclay*. Vol. 9, *Documentary History of the First Federal Congress, 1789–1791*. Baltimore: Johns Hopkins University Press, 1989.

The only surviving diary of a senator in the First Congress. Because proceedings of the early years of the Senate were shrouded in secrecy—the chamber met in private—much information about what went on is lost. This diary fills in many gaps.

Brown, Sherrod. *Congress from the Inside: Observations from the Majority and the Minority*. 3rd ed. Kent, OH: Kent State University Press, 2004.

Insider view of the workings of Congress from a former insider. The latest edition includes the 2000 elections, the events of and reaction to September 11, and the war in Iraq. Explains how Congress works on a day-to-day basis regarding how members interact and make deals and the role of the chamber's power brokers.

Burgess, Susan R. *Contest for Constitutional Authority: The Abortion and War Power Debates*. Lawrence: University Press of Kansas, 1992.

Applying what she calls the "theory of departmental review" to congressional activity and legislation in the abortion debate and the fight over war powers, Burgess argues that no single branch has the final say on constitutional interpretation.

Campell, Colton C., and Paul Herrnson, eds. *War Stories from Capitol Hill.* **Upper Saddle River, NJ: Pearson Prentice Hall, 2004.**

Examines how representatives and senators balance the needs and desires of their constituents against their own consciences and political needs by looking at the workings of the legislature and the congressional process.

Canon, David T. *Actors, Athletes, and Astronauts: Political Amateurs in the United States Congress.* **Chicago: University of Chicago Press, 1990.**

This books aims to debunk what it perceives as a myth: that Congress is made up of career politicians. Instead, the author argues that as much as 25 percent of the legislature consists of amateurs, which calls for a rethinking of how Congress accomplishes what it does and why.

Caro, Robert A. *Lyndon Johnson: Master of the Senate.* **New York: Knopf, 2002.**

Detailed study of the life of one of the great leaders in the Senate. Gives insight not only into the character of Johnson himself, but also into how a masterful politician like him shepherded various bills through Congress, working with his colleagues.

Congress and the Nation. **10 vols. Washington DC: CQ Press, 2002. Vol. 1, 1945–1964; Vol. 2, 1965–1968; Vol. 3, 1969–1972; Vol. 4, 1973–1976; Vol. 5, 1977–1980; Vol. 6, 1981–1984; Vol. 7, 1985–1988; Vol. 8, 1989–1992; Vol. 9, 1993–1996; Volume 10, 1997–2001.**

Synopsis of important issues and the legislation that surrounds them.

Congressional Digest. **Washington, DC: Congressional Digest Corporation.**

Published monthly. Each *Digest* focuses on a single issue, highlighting opposing views.

Congressional Record. **Washington, DC: U.S. Government Printing Office.**

The official transcript of House and Senate proceedings. It is published daily when one or both houses of Congress are in session.

Congressional Research Service Reports.

Available through multiple sources on the internet. Provides a great amount of information about almost any aspect of government, and the Congress specifically. Also available through Penny Hill Press.

Congressional Roll Call. Washington, DC: CQ Press.

Published annually. A compilation of all House and Senate roll-call votes, with a short description of each vote.

Congressional Staff Directory. Washington DC: CQ Press.

Published three times a year in the spring, summer, and fall, giving brief background information about congressional members and staffers.

Cook, Timothy E. *Making Laws and Making News: Media Strategies in the House of Representatives.* Washington DC: Brookings Institution, 1989.

In explaining the connection and relationship between legislators and the media, this book shows how members of the House manipulate or use the media to push through their agendas by publicizing them as part of their legislative strategies to get bills passed.

Cox, Gary, and Matthew McCubbins. *Legislative Leviathan: Party Government in the House.* 2nd ed. Cambridge, UK: Cambridge University Press, 2007.

Focuses on the House of Representatives in the post–World War II era, emphasizing the roles of parties and committees and how they work to push their agendas through.

CQ Almanac. Washington, DC: CQ Press.

Published annually. A condensed view of the year's congressional activity, summarizing issues and voting.

CQ Weekly. Washington, DC: Congressional Quarterly.

Published weekly since 1945. Magazine that provides evenhanded articles on issues arising in Washington. Included are bill numbers, information on committee actions, floor votes, etc.

Currie, David P. *The Constitution in Congress: Descent into the Maelstrom, 1829–1861*. Chicago: University of Chicago Press, 1999.

Part of a series. This volume looks at constitutional development and Congress during the crucial period from the election of Andrew Jackson to the Civil War and discusses the emergence of some of the great statesmen of the day. As a legal historical analysis, much time is spent on various issues with major constitutional implications, from the nullification crisis to the beginning of the war.

Currie, David P. *The Constitution in Congress: The Federalist Period, 1789–1801*. Chicago: University of Chicago Press, 1999.

Part of a series. This volume looks at the federal government during its first twelve years and concludes that the key to understanding the Constitution is not the Supreme Court, but the interaction and initiatives of the legislative and executive branches.

Currie, David P. *The Constitution in Congress: The Jeffersonians, 1801–1829*. Chicago: University of Chicago Press, 2001.

Part of a series. Looks at the rise and fall of the Jeffersonian party in the first three decades of the nineteenth century. As with Currie's other volumes, the focus here is on how the various constitutional controversies of the day—in this case, the Louisiana Purchase, the War of 1812, the Burr Conspiracy, the Missouri Compromise—were battles between the president and the Congress rather than constitutional issues decided in the courts.

Currie, David P. *The Constitution in Congress: Democrats and Whigs, 1829–1861*. Chicago: University of Chicago Press, 2006.

Part of a series. This volume looks at antebellum America, focusing on the rise of the second and third party systems and the battle between Whigs and Democrats over Clay's American System, the Bank War, the exercise of presidential powers, and the growing crisis over the loci of power in the federal system.

Currie, James T. *The United States House of Representatives*. Malabar, FL: Krieger Publishing, 1988.

A history of the House of Representatives, interspersed with character studies, interesting stories, and documents.

Daschle, Tom. *Like No Other Time: The 107th Congress and the Two Years That Changed America Forever*. New York: Crown, 2003.

From an insider who was at the fulcrum of decision making as a leader of his party in the Senate at a pivotal time in American history. From the 2000 election through September 11 and the War on Terror and including various domestic events such as the Enron scandal, Daschle provides a unique viewpoint about what happened and why, as well as insight into what other leaders thought and did.

Davidson, Roger H., Susan Webb Hammond, and Raymond W. Smock, eds. *Masters of the House*. Boulder, CO: Westview Press, 1998.

Good study of various men who have dominated the House of Representatives from its beginning.

Davidson, Roger H., Walter J. Oleszek, and Frances E. Lee. *Congress and Its Members*. 10th ed. Washington, DC: CQ Press, 2005.

One of the definitive books on Congress. Explains what Congress is and how it works by breaking down its tasks, explaining the members' roles, and showing how it interacts with other branches of government and civil society.

Deering, Christopher J., and Steven S. Smith. *Committees in Congress*. 3rd ed. Washington, DC: CQ Press, 1997.

Intensive look at the committee system in both the Senate and House and how it has changed, or failed to.

Dirksen, Everett McKinley, and Frank MacKaman. *Education of a Senator*. Champaign: University of Illinois Press, 1998.

Memoir written by Senator Everett Dirksen, providing powerful insight into Congress from when he was first elected to the Senate in 1950 to his death in 1969.

Dodd, Lawrence, and Bruce Oppenheimer. *Congress Reconsidered*. 8th ed. Washington, DC: CQ Press, 2004.

Looks at the history of Congress and assesses the impact of a variety of variables, from who holds power to reforms of the institution.

Donald, David. *Charles Sumner and the Rights of Man*. New York: Knopf, 1970.

Although Sumner is perhaps most famous for the infamous incident with Preston Brooks, this book goes beyond that to study one of the seminal figures in congressional history, a senator who had a major impact on the period surrounding the Civil War.

Elving, Ronald D. *Conflict and Compromise: How Congress Makes the Law.* **New York: Simon and Schuster, 1995.**

By studying the history of the Family and Medical Leave Act of 1993, this volume shows how a bill can work its way through Congress, including the battles in committee and on the floor, to become a law.

English, Ross M. *The United States Congress.* **Manchester, UK: Manchester University Press, 2003.**

Basic overview of how Congress works, focusing on the period from the 1990s to the early twenty-first century and using the conflict between the Republican-controlled Congress and President Clinton to explain how Congress operates. Includes roles of members, the committee system, party functions, etc.

Evans, Diana. *Greasing the Wheels: Using Pork Barrel Projects to Build Majority Coalitions in Congress.* **New York: Cambridge University Press, 2004.**

Emphasizes the importance of congressional pork, and rather than viewing it as an inhibiting factor to good government, sees it as what makes the system work, often very effectively.

Fiorina, Morris P. *Divided Government.* **2nd ed. New York: Allyn and Bacon, 1996.**

Discusses divided government in American history, its causes, and the implications of such a government for public policy and government action.

Frey, Lou. *Inside the House: Former Members Reveal How Congress Really Works.* **Lanham, MD: University Press of America, 2001.**

Study of how the House operates by utilizing former members' experiences and observations. The book looks at all aspects of a House member's life, going beyond just the floor of Congress.

Gould, Lewis L. *The Most Exclusive Club: A History of the Modern United States Senate.* **Cambridge, MA: Basic Books, 2006.**

A history of the Senate in the twentieth century, it shows not only how the type of person who inhabits the chamber has changed, but how the Senate as a whole has shifted its focus and function. It is a fairly critical assessment of the body, as well as those who have served in it.

Greenberg, Ellen. *The House and Senate Explained: The People's Guide to Congress.* New York: Norton, 1996.

Introduction to how Congress works, from where certain people sit to common terms used in the conduct of business to the daily workings of the legislature.

Hall, Richard L. *Participation in Congress.* New Haven, CT: Yale University Press, 1996.

An in-depth look at sixty pieces of legislation that analyzes legislators' behavior at various stages of the legislative process to gain an understanding of the how and why of a piece of legislation and the effectiveness of individual members.

Hamilton, Lee. *How Congress Works and Why You Should Care.* Bloomington: Indiana University Press, 2004.

An insider's look at Congress. Attempts to provide an understanding of not only how a bill becomes a law but why, and is critical at times of the process and the institution.

Harris, Fred R. *Deadlock or Decision: The U.S. Senate and the Rise of National Politics.* New York: Oxford University Press, 1993.

Study of the evolution of the Senate through the twentieth century, looking at how it has evolved as an institution and is a product of its past mistakes and successes.

Harris, Fred R. *In Defense of Congress.* New York: St. Martin's Press, 1995.

An historical view of Congress at odds with some of the more traditional views that see the House and Senate as bodies disdained by the people and as more of a roadblock than an enabler in terms of passing legislation. As a former senator, the author provides both an insider's view and that of a critic.

Herrnson, Paul S. *Congressional Elections: Campaigning at Home and in Washington.* Washington, DC: CQ Press, 2003.

In-depth study of House and Senate races using breakdowns of election numbers and numerous interviews to analyze candidates' strategies.

Hibbing, John R., and Elizabeth Theiss-Morse. *Congress as Public Enemy: Public Attitudes toward American Political Institutions.* Cambridge, UK: Cambridge University Press, 1995.

Use of quantitative materials and focus groups to try to explain why Americans seemingly hate the very branch of government that is supposedly most representative of them.

Jacobson, Gary C. *Politics of Congressional Elections.* 6th ed. New York : Pearson Longman, 2004.

Focuses on congressional elections, and explains the elections in the context not only of Congress but of how they affect other parts of the American political system.

Johnson, Robert David. *Congress and the Cold War.* Cambridge, UK: Cambridge University Press, 2006.

Study of Cold War politics and the interaction between Congress and the presidency, and of how in the postwar period Congress has not been passive in the development of American foreign policy but, rather, an important player, through various mechanisms.

Jones, Charles O. *Separate But Equal: Congress and the Presidency.* 2nd ed. Chappaqua, NY: Chatham House, 1999.

First takes an overview of the presidency in the context of the idea of the separation of powers and then reviews the relationship between Congress and the president from Lyndon Johnson to Bill Clinton.

King, David C. *Turf Wars: How Congressional Committees Claim Jurisdiction.* Chicago: University of Chicago Press, 1997.

Argues that committee jurisdiction is fluid, not static, despite the view of many political scientists. The constantly changing jurisdictional boundaries stem from the efforts of representatives and senators to gain advantages in upcoming elections and the general nature of many bills.

Kingdon, John W. *Congressmen's Voting Decisions.* 3rd ed. Ann Arbor: University of Michigan Press, 1989.

Scrutinizes the manner in which members of the House make their decisions.

Koopman, Douglas L. *Hostile Takeover.* Lanham, MD: Rowman and Littlefield, 1996.

Looks at Congress between 1980 and 1995, studying the rise, fall, and rise again of the Republican Party, explaining how its eventual resurgence in the 1990s signaled a new range of political discourse.

Kravitz, Walter, ed. *American Congressional Dictionary.* 3rd ed. Washington, DC: CQ Press, 2001.

A-to-Z source on terms, mostly procedural, used in the House and Senate. Gives a detailed explanation of each term.

Krehbiel, Keith. *Pivotal Politics: A Theory of U.S. Lawmaking.* Chicago: University of Chicago Press, 1998.

Looks at divided government in America during the last quarter of the twentieth century and suggests it does not really influence the effectiveness or ineffectiveness of government, and downplays the importance of parties in the American political process.

Landsberg, Brian K. *Major Acts of Congress.* 3 vols. New York: Thomson-Gale, 2004.

Alphabetically lists and describes, in some detail, 262 selected congressional acts of historical significance in the evolution of American government.

Lehman, William. *Mr. Chairman.* Lanham, MD: Rowman and Littlefield, 2000.

An account by a former chairman of the House Appropriations Subcommittee on Transportation of life in Washington for a legislator in dealing with other members, the other branches, and the various lobbyists who crossed his path.

Lindsay, James. *Congress and the Politics of U.S. Defense Policy.* Baltimore: Johns Hopkins University Press, 1994.

Explanation of the role Congress played in developing and shaping U.S, foreign policy prior to the end of the Cold War.

Maltzman, Forrest. *Competing Principals: Committees, Parties, and the Organization of Congress.* Ann Arbor: University of Michigan Press, 1997.

While accepting the general notion of the importance of committees in directing legislation to the floor, Maltzman argues there is a more complicated process going on with members of Congress as concerned with their party, its platform, and outside forces. The result has been change in how committees operate.

Martin, Fenton S., and Robert U. Goehlert. *How to Research Congress.* Washington, DC: CQ Press. 1996.

Describes primary and secondary resources for researching Congress, including al-
manacs, bibliographical directories, encyclopedias, indexes, online services, journals,
and newspapers.

Mayhew, David R. *Congress and the Electoral Connection.* **2nd ed. New Haven, CT:
Yale University Press. 2004.**

Discusses reelection as the number one motivational factor in what drives legislators'
behavior and how they design public policy.

Oleszek, Walter J. *Congressional Procedures and the Policy Process.* **4th ed.
Washington, DC: CQ Press, 1995.**

Explanation of parliamentary procedure in Congress.

Palmer, Barbara, and Dennis Simon. *Breaking the Political Glass Ceiling: Women
and Congressional Elections (Women in American Politics).* **New York: Routledge,
2006.**

Exhaustive study of women in Congress, why and how they run or often do not run
for office. Suggests alternative reasons for the low number of women holding national
office.

Peters, Ronald M., Jr. *The American Speakership: The Office in Historical
Perspective.* **2nd ed. Baltimore: Johns Hopkins University Press, 1997.**

Peters focuses on the history of Congress through the office of the Speaker of the House,
tracing the evolution of the institution and looking at the various persons, especially
those in the latter half of the twentieth century, who ran the House.

Peterson, Merrill D. *The Great Triumvirate: Webster, Clay, and Calhoun.* **New York:
Oxford University Press, 1988.**

Looks at three of the most important members of Congress in the antebellum period—
John C. Calhoun, Henry Clay, and Daniel Webster—and the leadership role they played
as members of Congress in shaping American history to 1850 and, in fact, beyond.

Polsby, Nelson W. *How Congress Evolves.* **New York: Oxford University Press, 2004.**

Studies the changes in the House of Representatives in the latter half of the twentieth
century by focusing on the Democratic Party and its caucus. Explains how and why

Congress changed ideologically, becoming more liberal and then polarized. Also discusses the reforms that altered its internal decision-making process.

Poole, Keith T., and Howard Rosenthal. *Congress: A Political-Economic History of Roll Call Voting.* **New York: Oxford University Press, 2001.**

An impressive study of over sixteen million individual roll-call votes between 1789 and 2000 which concludes that legislators vote consistently according to an ideological position rather than a variety of other outside forces.

Price, David E. *The Congressional Experience.* **3rd ed. Boulder, CO: Westview Press, 2004.**

Insider book by former North Carolina representative David Price, who explains the inner workings of Congress and in the end presents a positive view of the legislature and how it often functions effectively, despite its at times anachronistic-seeming system, to solve problems faced by America.

Remini, Robert V. *Henry Clay: Statesman for the Union.* **New York: Norton, 1991.**

An incisive biography of one of the important people of the antebellum period. He helped shape compromises that both kept America from dissolution and helped put the pieces in place for eventual breakdown.

Remini, Robert V. *Daniel Webster: The Man and His Time.* **New York: Norton, 1997.**

Biography of one of the giants of American politics before the Civil War, shows how he played an important role in shaping American policy and deserves an important place in American history.

Remini. Robert V. *The House: The History of the House of Representatives.* **New York: Harper Collins, 2006.**

Written at the request of Congress, it explains how the House adapted to historical necessities, highlighting both the individuals who drove the institution and the events that helped shape its agenda. Its coverage runs from the first meeting in 1789 to the Republican revolution of the 1990s and beyond.

Rohde, David. *Parties and Leaders in the Postreform House.* **Chicago: University of Chicago Press, 1991.**

Looks at the reemergence of strong partisanship and parties in the House of Representatives in the wake of the congressional reforms of the 1970s.

Schick, Allen. *The Federal Budget: Politics, Policy and Process*. Washington, DC: Brookings Institution, 1995.

In explaining how the budget process has changed, this work shows the interaction, or at times the lack thereof, between the president and Congress, using contemporary examples.

Schickler, Eric. *Disjointed Pluralism: Institutional Innovation and the Development of the U.S. Congress*. Princeton, NJ: Princeton University Press, 2001.

Political science text that incorporates the idea of "disjointed pluralism" into the study of institutional change in Congress, looking at various interests and emphasizing the resiliency of Congress in dealing with that change. Schickler argues that multiple interests drive the changes in Congress.

Sharp, James Roger. *American Politics in the Early Republic*. New Haven, CT: Yale University Press, 1993.

Discussion of the first decade of the Republic and how Congress functioned during the rancorous days of the Federalist Era, up to the election of Jefferson as president. Explains how the realities of congressional politics of the day were often at odds with the assumption of civility as political parties arose and contentious agendas helped lay the seeds for later conflicts.

Sinclair, Barbara. *The Transformation of the U.S. Senate*. Baltimore: Johns Hopkins University Press, 1989.

Study of how the Senate as an institution has changed and what those changes mean for American government.

Sinclair, Barbara. *Legislators, Leaders and Lawmaking*. Baltimore: Johns Hopkins University Press, 1995.

Argues that the way the House functions changed in the wake of the reforms of the 1970s, and that a key element of the change is that the House majority party leadership is a more important factor in the legislative process. In particular, Democratic House leadership in the 1980s and 1990s is examined.

Sinclair, Barbara. *Unorthodox Lawmaking: The New Legislative Process in the U.S. Congress.* 3rd ed. Washington, DC: CQ Press, 2007.

Looks at the modern legislative process, that is, how a bill becomes a law and the various routes it takes to get there. Uses examples from the 1990s to highlight the process.

Smith, Norma, and Kathy Anderson. *Jeannette Rankin: America's Conscience.* Helena: Montana Historical Society Press, 2002.

Biography of the only person to vote against World War I and World War II. How she used her position, in Congress and out, to drive her agenda of conscience.

Smith, Steven S. *Call to Order: Floor Politics in the House and Senate.* Washington, DC: Brookings Institution, 1989.

Discussion of how changing times altered the role of politics on the floor of both houses of Congress. Reform, new rules, and new policy needs all served to change floor activity.

Smock, Raymond, ed. *Landmark Documents on the U.S. Congress.* Washington, DC: CQ Press, 1999.

Collection of primary documents covering various aspects of congressional history.

Stathis, Stephen W., ed. *Landmark Legislation, 1774–2002: Major U.S. Acts and Treaties.* Washington, DC: CQ Press, 2003.

Brief synopses of major congressional acts from the First Congress to the 107th.

Stern, Gary M., and Morton H. Halperin, eds. *The U.S. Constitution and the Power to Go to War: Historical and Current Perspectives.* Westport, CT: Greenwood Press, 1994.

Historical overview of the war powers over more than two hundred years. A series of essays that looks at a variety of issues from constitutional guidelines, the War Powers Resolution, the United Nations Charter, and the problems of covert operations and modern warfare.

Swift, Elaine K. *The Making of an American Senate: Reconstitutive Change in Congress, 1787–1841.* Ann Arbor: University of Michigan Press, 1996.

Explanation of how the Senate moved from being an elitist institution removed from the common man to the far more popular institution it is today. The key years for this change were the first six decades of its existence, as this work explains.

Tarr, David R., and Ann O'Connor. *Congress A to Z.* Washington, DC: Congressional Quarterly, 2003.

An alphabetical listing of a wide variety of topics pertaining to Congress.

Thurber, James A., ed. *Rivals for Power: Presidential-Congressional Relations.* 3rd ed. Lanham, MD: Rowman and Littlefield, 2003.

Series of essays that shows how the president and Congress work both together and at odds with each other. While the book focuses on the presidency, it does so in the context of Congress around a variety of topics including foreign policy, the budget process, and building coalitions in the Senate.

Tiefer, Charles. *Congressional Practice and Procedure: A Reference, Research, and Legislative Guide.* New York: Greenwood Press. 1989.

In-depth study of how Congress works from the moment a bill is introduced to how it works its way through the committee process. Provides good bibliographical information.

Van Tassel, Emily Field, and Paul Finkelman. *Impeachable Offenses: A Documentary History from 1787 to the Present.* Washington, DC: CQ Press. 1999.

Study of all impeachments including the Clinton impeachment, with extensive primary documents. Traces the process through both houses.

Weisberg, Herbert F. *Classics in Congressional Politics.* New York: Longman, 1999.

Series of essays that discusses institutional change; how members of Congress represent their constituents; elections; and, generally, how legislatures function.

Westerfield, Donald L. *War Powers: The President, the Congress and the Question of War.* Westport, CT: Praeger Publishers, 1996.

While somewhat dated because it does not include the twenty-first-century debates over the Iraq War, this is still a good discussion of why the War Powers Resolution is an anachronism in light of modern warfare capabilities. Studies the issue from the Founding Fathers to conflicts of the 1990s in the Persian Gulf and the Balkans.

Williams, T. Harry. *Huey Long.* **New York: Knopf, 1969.**

Seminal biography of one of the most influential politicians of the twentieth century. While his stay in Congress was short, its impact was great.

Zelizer, Julian E. *On Capitol Hill: The Struggle to Reform Congress and Its Consequences, 1948–2000.* **New York: Cambridge University Press, 2004.**

Studying reform on Capitol Hill, it traces the collapse of a Congress dominated by committees to the modern incarnation of the legislature, reflecting shifting party strengths, scandals, and intensely partisan elections.

Zelizer, Julian E., ed. *The American Congress: The Building of Democracy.* **Boston: Houghton Mifflin, 2004.**

A collection of forty essays about the history of Congress, ranging over a wide variety of topics, people, conflicts, and legislation.

INDEX

Note: italic page numbers indicate photos.

ABOUT THE AUTHOR

Gary P. Gershman, PhD, is assistant professor of history and legal studies in the Division of Humanities at Nova Southeastern University, Fort Lauderdale, Florida. He received a PhD from Duke University and JD from Villanova School of Law. Dr. Gershman specialized in constitutional law, electoral process and civil liberties, and among his many publications is *Death Penalty on Trial: A Handbook with Cases, Laws, and Documents* (ABC-CLIO, 2005)